# Prentice Hall Brief Review

# Global History and Geography

## Steven Goldberg / Judith Clark DuPré

**Order Information**

Send orders to:
PEARSON CUSTOMER SERVICE
P.O. BOX 2500
LEBANON, IN 46052-3009
or
CALL TOLL FREE 1-800-848-9500
(8:00 A.M.-6:00 P.M. EST)

• Orders can be placed via phone

Acknowledgements appear on page C-1, which constitutes an extension of this copyright page.

**Copyright © 2010 Pearson Education, Inc., or its affiliates.** All Rights Reserved. Printed in the United States of America. This publication is protected by copyright, and permission should be obtained from the publisher prior to any prohibited reproduction, storage in a retrieval system, or transmission in any form or by any means, electronic, mechanical, photocopying, recording, or likewise. The publisher hereby grants permission to reproduce pages xxxvii–lii, in part or in whole, for classroom use only, the number not to exceed the number of students in each class. Notice of copyright must appear on all copies. For information regarding permissions, write to Pearson Curriculum Group Rights & Permissions, One Lake Street, Upper Saddle River, New Jersey 07458.

Pearson Prentice Hall, and Pearson Prentice Hall are trademarks, in the U.S. and/or other countries, of Pearson Education, Inc., or its affiliates.

Regents Examinations and questions appear courtesy of the New York State Education Department/ New York Regents Exam.

13-digit ISBN  978-0-13-370424-2
10-digit ISBN     0-13-370424-6

3 4 5 6 7 8 9 10   V011   13 12 11 10

# Table of Contents

**New York Standards**

KEY Standard ⏜ Key Idea ⏜

**4.2**

## Unit 1 Ancient World: Civilizations and Religions (4000 B.C.–A.D. 500)    1

**Unit 1 Standards**

| | | | | |
|---|---|---|---|---|
| 1.1 | 2.1 | 3.1 | 4.1 | 5.1 |
| 1.2 | 2.2 | 3.2 | | |
| 1.3 | 2.3 | | | |
| 1.4 | 2.4 | | | |

## Unit 2 Expanding Zones of Exchange (500–1200)    35

**Unit 2 Standards**

| | | | | |
|---|---|---|---|---|
| 1.1 | 2.1 | 3.1 | 4.1 | 5.1 |
| 1.2 | 2.2 | | | |
| 1.3 | 2.3 | | | |

## Unit 3 Global Interactions (1200–1650)    71

**Unit 3 Standards**

| | | | |
|---|---|---|---|
| 2.1 | 3.1 | 4.1 | 5.1 |
| 2.2 | | | |
| 2.3 | | | |

# Table of Contents

**Unit 7 Standards**

| | | | | |
|---|---|---|---|---|
| 1.1 | 2.1 | 3.1 | 4.1 | 5.1 |
| 1.2 | 2.2 | | | |
| 1.3 | 2.3 | | | |
| 1.4 | 2.4 | | | |

**Unit 8 Standards**

| | | | | |
|---|---|---|---|---|
| 1.1 | 2.1 | 3.1 | 4.1 | 5.1 |
| 1.2 | 2.2 | | 4.2 | |
| | 2.3 | | | |
| | 2.4 | | | |

# About This Book

This book has been written to help you, the student, review your two-year global history and geography course. Its purposes are to:

- Help you focus on the key facts, themes, and concepts that you need to know to succeed on the Regents Examination in global history and geography.
- Allow you to become familiar with the format of the Regents Examination.
- Provide you with the test-taking skills you will need to apply your social studies knowledge to the Regents Examination.

## In This Book

In this book, the ninth- and tenth-grade global history and geography curriculum is presented chronologically. In other words, it is presented in time order, from earliest times to the present. Within this organization, there has been a careful attempt to group the material in meaningful eras, or periods of time in which certain types of activity were going on all over the world. For example, Unit 5 covers the period from 1750 through 1914. During this period of more than 160 years, revolutions were occurring all over the world, and nations formed and grew strong.

The book highlights the key themes and concepts that are woven throughout the global history and geography curriculum. Concentrating on themes and concepts will help you organize the global history and geography that you have studied. It will also start you thinking about history in ways that will help you excel on the Regents Examination.

## Four Overall Themes

Four overall themes—history; geography; economics; and civics, citizenship, and government—draw these units together. As you review and study, these themes will help you make connections between different times and places. In the side column, several types of help are available.

- **The Big Idea** notes at the beginning of each section organize the section content at a glance. This feature highlights key content in list form.
- **Preparing for the Regents** notes provide questions, explanations, and activities that will give you practice in applying your knowledge to Regents-type questions.
- **Key Themes and Concepts** notes summarize important content and link it to key themes and concepts.

Other sections of this book are also important.

- **Preparing for the Regents** provides instructions and hints for Regents success, using questions like those you will see on the test.
- **Questions for Regents Practice,** found at the end of each unit, will help you figure out your strengths and weaknesses as you practice taking the test.
- **Sample Regents Examinations** also appear at the back of the book.
- **Thematic Review** reviews key content within those themes that the Regents Examination may focus on.

The goal of this book is to help you attain success on the Regents Examination. It will focus your efforts in areas that will pay off on exam day. With this book, you will have the tools to master the material and present it effectively. Best of luck on exam day!

### Steven Goldberg

Steven Goldberg is the District Chairperson of Social Studies for the City School District of New Rochelle. He received his bachelor's degree in history from the University of Rochester, a master's degree in East Asian Studies from Yale University, and an administrative certificate from Teachers' College, Columbia University. He was a Fulbright Fellow to the Netherlands and studied at Sophia University in Tokyo. He is past president of both the New York State Council for the Social Studies and the New York State Social Studies Supervisory Association and has served on the executive board of the Westchester Council of the Social Studies and the National Council for the Social Studies. A consultant to the State Education Department, he has been on numerous Regents Examination committees, as well as the design team for Global History and Geography. In addition, he is a charter member of the Westchester Holocaust Education Center planning committee. He has traveled through Eastern and Western Europe, Japan, Mexico, and Israel.

### Judith Clark DuPré

Judith Clark DuPré is a retired social studies teacher from the Fairport School District and current College Supervisor for student teachers at the Ralph C. Wilson School of Education at St. John Fisher College. She received her bachelor's and master's degrees from the State University of New York, Brockport. She is past-president of the Rochester Area Council for the Social Studies, a member of the New York State Council for the Social Studies, and served on the Advisory Council of the International Studies Program at St. John Fisher College. She has been named to the Who's Who Among America's Teachers and has received the Rochester Area Outstanding High School Social Studies Teacher Award and the New York State Council Distinguished Educator Award. She was a Fulbright Fellow in China and has studied in Germany and Japan. As a consultant to the State Education Department, she has served on numerous Regents Examination Committees and contributed to several curriculum projects in Global Studies and Global History and Geography. She has traveled throughout Western and Eastern Europe, Russia, Southeast Asia, the Middle East, Africa, Australia, and South America.

## Standard 1:
## History of the United States and New York

Students will use a variety of intellectual skills to demonstrate their understanding of major ideas, eras, themes, developments, and turning points in the history of the United States and New York.

## Standard 2:
## World History

Students will use a variety of intellectual skills to demonstrate their understanding of major ideas, eras, themes, developments, and turning points in world history from a variety of perspectives.

## Standard 3:
## Geography

Students will use a variety of intellectual skills to demonstrate their understanding of the geography of the interdependent world in which we live—local, national, and global—including the distribution of people, places, and environments over Earth's surface.

## Standard 4:
## Economics

Students will use a variety of intellectual skills to demonstrate their understanding of how the United States and other societies develop economic systems and associated institutions to allocate scarce resources, how major decision-making units function in the United States and other national economies, and how an economy solves the scarcity problem through market and nonmarket economies.

## Standard 5:
## Civics, Citizenship, and Government

Students will use a variety of intellectual skills to demonstrate their understanding of the necessity for establishing governments; the governmental system of the United States and other nations; the U.S. Constitution; the basic civic values of American constitutional democracy; and the roles, rights, and responsibilities of citizenship, including avenues of participation.

# Key Themes and Concepts

Global history and geography can be best understood if it is organized by studying key themes and key concepts that recur in many times and places. Themes and concepts are mental images and classifications that help you to:

- understand important ideas.
- recognize global connections and linkages.
- see similarities and differences among events.
- determine the causes that lead up to events and the effects that result from events.

The Regents Examination uses a number of themes and concepts in constructing questions for the test. They are listed and explained below in four categories: history; geography; economics; and civics, citizenship, and government.

## History: Some Key Themes and Concepts

- **Belief Systems** means the established, orderly ways in which groups or individuals look at religious faith or philosophical tenets.
- **Change** is a basic alteration in things, events, and ideas.
- **Choice** means the right or power to select from a range of alternatives.
- **Conflict** is disagreement or opposition between ideas or groups, which may lead to an armed struggle.
- **Culture and Intellectual Life** means the patterns of human behavior that include ideas, beliefs, values, artifacts, and ways of making a living that any society transmits to succeeding generations to meet its fundamental needs. It also includes ways of thinking, studying, and reflecting on ideas and life.
- **Diversity** means understanding and respecting others and oneself, including any similarities or differences in language, gender, socioeconomic class, religion, and other human characteristics and traits.
- **Empathy** means the ability to understand others through identifying in oneself responses similar to the experiences, behaviors, and responses of others.
- **Identity** means awareness of one's own values, attitudes, and capabilities as an individual and as a member of various groups.
- **Imperialism** means the domination by one country of the political and/or economic life of another country or region.
- **Interdependence** means reliance upon others in mutually beneficial interactions and exchanges.
- **Movement of People and Goods** is the exchange of people, ideas, products, technologies, and institutions from one region or civilization to another, a process that has existed throughout history.
- **Nationalism** means a feeling of pride in and devotion to one's country or the desire of a people to control their own government, free from foreign interference or rule.
- **Urbanization** means the movement of people from rural to urban (city) areas.

## Geography: Some Key Themes and Concepts

The six essential elements of geography follow.

- **The World in Spatial Terms**—Geography studies the relationships among people, places, and environments by mapping information about them in a spatial context.
- **Places and Regions**—The identities and lives of individuals and peoples are rooted in particular places and in those human constructs called regions.
- **Physical Systems**—Physical processes, such as erosion and flooding, shape Earth's surface and interact with plant and animal life to create, sustain, and modify ecosystems.
- **Human Systems**—People are central to geography in that human activities help shape Earth's surface, human settlements and structures are part of Earth's surface, and humans compete for control of Earth's surface.
- **Environment and Society**—Environment means surroundings, including natural elements and elements created by humans. The physical environment is modified by human activities, largely as a consequence of the ways in which human societies value and use Earth's natural resources, and human activities are also influenced by Earth's physical features and processes.
- **The Uses of Geography**—Knowledge of geography enables people to develop an understanding of the relationships between people, places, and environments over time—that is, of Earth as it was, is, and might be.

## Economics: Some Key Themes and Concepts

- **Economic Systems** include traditional, command, market, and mixed systems. Each must answer the three basic economic questions: What goods and services are to be produced and in what quantities? How shall these goods and services be produced? For whom shall goods and services be produced?
- **Factors of Production** are human, natural, and capital resources that, when combined, can be converted to various goods and services (for example, land, labor, and capital are used to produce food).
- **Needs and Wants** means those goods and services that are essential, such as food, clothing, and shelter (needs), and those goods and services that people would like to have to improve the quality of their lives, such as education, security, health care, and entertainment (wants).
- **Scarcity** means the conflict between unlimited needs and wants and limited natural and human resources.
- **Science and Technology** means the tools and methods used by people to get what they need and want.

# Civics, Citizenship, and Government:
## Some Key Themes and Concepts

- **Citizenship** means membership in a community (neighborhood, school, region, state, nation, world) with its accompanying rights, responsibilities, and dispositions.

- **Civic Values** are those important principles that serve as the foundation for our democratic form of government. These values include justice; honesty; self-discipline; due process of law; equality; majority rule with respect for minority rights; and respect of self, others, and property.

- **Decision Making** means the process through which people monitor and influence public and civil life by working with others, clearly articulating ideals and interests, building coalition, seeking consensus, negotiating compromise, and managing conflict.

- **Government** means the formal institutions and processes of a politically organized society with authority to make, enforce, and interpret laws and other binding rules about matters of common interest and concern. Government also refers to the group of people—acting in formal political institutions at national, state, and local levels—who exercise decision-making power or enforce laws and regulations.

- **Human Rights** are those basic political, economic, and social rights to which all human beings are entitled, such as the right to life, liberty, security of person, and a standard of living adequate for the health and well-being of oneself and one's family. Human rights are inalienable and are expressed in various United Nations documents, including the United Nations Charter and the *Universal Declaration of Human Rights*.

- **Justice** means fair, equal, proportional, or appropriate treatment rendered to individuals in interpersonal, societal, or government interactions.

- **Nation-State** means a geographic/political organization that unites people through a common government.

- **Political Systems** include monarchies, dictatorships, and democracies and address certain basic questions of government, such as: What should a government have the power to do? What should a government not have the power to do? A political system also provides for ways in which parts of that system interrelate and combine to perform specific functions of government.

- **Power** is the ability of people to compel or influence the actions of others. Legitimate, or rightful, power is called authority.

# Preparing for the Regents

This section of the book provides you with strategies for success on the Regents Examination in Global History and Geography. Because you will need to pass the examination in order to graduate from high school, these strategies are important for you to learn and master. They will also help you to succeed in other types of academic work.

## Understanding Social Studies

To do well in your study of global history and geography and to pass the Regents Examination, you need to understand three related elements of social studies. On the Regents Examination, you will be asked to demonstrate your mastery of the *factual content* of the global history and geography course, the *concepts* that recur over time, and the *skills* you have mastered.

### Specific Factual Content
In a social studies course, you learn about specific historical events and figures. For example, you learn that the French Revolution occurred in 1789 and that Napoleon carried its ideals throughout much of Europe. This is part of the specific content of the global history and geography course you are taking.

### Concepts
In social studies courses, you also learn about themes and concepts such as *change and nationalism*. (See "Key Themes and Concepts," which begins on page 2 of this book.) You learn how the French Revolution brought change to France and other lands. You also examine the role that this revolution played in developing and spreading nationalism. In addition, you link developments in France to developments in other places and at different times. You may discuss the similarities and differences in other revolutions, or the types of factors that lead to revolutionary movements. Understanding these connections across place and time is as important as knowing facts about the events themselves.

### Skills
In a social studies course, you acquire skills. These skills help you to gather, organize, use, and present information. For example, you learn to interpret various types of documents. Historical documents include maps, graphs, and political cartoons. When you read a circle graph that illustrates class structure and land ownership in France, or when you interpret a political cartoon about Napoleon, you are using social studies skills.

## A Glossary of Skill Words

The following is a glossary of skill words that you will see often on the Regents Examination and in other social studies materials. Comprehending these words will help you do well on the Regents Examination.

**Analyze** to break an idea or concept into parts in order to determine their nature and relationships

**Assess** to determine the importance, significance, size, or value of

**Categorize** to place in a class or group; to classify

**Classify** to arrange in classes or to place in a group according to a system

**Compare** to state the similarities between two or more examples

**Contrast** to differentiate; to state the differences between two or more examples

**Define** to explain what something is or means

**Describe** to illustrate in words; to tell about

**Develop** to explain more clearly; to reveal bit by bit

**Differentiate** to state the difference or differences among two or more examples

**Discuss** to make observations using facts, reasoning, and argument; to present in some detail

**Evaluate** to examine and judge the significance, worth, or condition of; to determine the value of

**Explain** to make plain or understandable; to give reasons for

**Generalize** to reach a broad conclusion, avoiding specifics, or to base an overall law on particular examples

**Hypothesize** to present an explanation or an assumption that remains to be proved

**Identify** to establish the essential character of

**Illustrate** to make clear or obvious by using examples or comparisons

**Incorporate** to introduce into or include as a part of something

**Infer** to conclude or judge from evidence; to draw a conclusion through reasoning

**Investigate** to research; to inquire into and examine with care

**Organize** to arrange in a systematic way

**Recognize** to identify by appearance or characteristics

**Restate** to say again in a slightly different way

**Scrutinize** to investigate closely; to examine or inquire into critically

**Show** to point out; to set forth clearly a position or idea by stating it and giving data that support it

## Structure of the Regents Examination

You will have three hours to complete the Regents Examination. The test will include three types of questions.

### Multiple-Choice Questions

Together, the multiple-choice questions will account for 55 percent of the points to be earned. There are usually about 50 multiple-choice questions on the Regents Examination. Four possible choices will be provided for each question, only one of which is correct.

### Thematic Essay Question

There will be one question of this type on the test, and it will account for 15 percent of the points to be earned. You will be asked to write a thematic essay on a particular topic. Clear and definite directions will be provided to guide you in writing your essay.

### Document-Based Question

There will be one multisection document-based question, and it will account for 30 percent of the points to be earned. This question has two major parts. Part A requires that you look at several historical documents and answer one or more questions about each one. Part B requires that you write a clear essay, using evidence from these documents and your knowledge of global history and geography.

You will find examples of all of these types of questions at the end of every unit, in the sample tests, and in the part of the book you are now reading. By working with these examples, you will become familiar with the Regents Examination and build skills for approaching these types of questions. This work will help you get the highest score possible.

| Part I: Multiple Choice | 50 questions | 55% of Exam Grade |
|---|---|---|
| Part II: Thematic Essay | 1 question based on a specific theme | 15% of Exam Grade |
| Part III: Document-Based Question | Part A: Scaffolding (documents) Part B: Essay | 15% of Exam Grade 15% of Exam Grade |

## Strategies for the Regents Examination

The Regents Examination will cover material that you studied in your Global History and Geography course. Some subjects are more likely to appear on the test than others, however. This book will help you review these topics thoroughly.

This book will also teach you how to approach the topics in ways that will help you succeed on all parts of the Regents Examination. Several concepts are especially important.

### Understanding the Themes

The test will be built around major themes that recur throughout history. Many themes are listed and defined for you in the Key Themes and Concepts portion of this book. The most common Regents themes are reviewed with examples in the Thematic Review section of this book. As you prepare for the Regents Examination, keep in mind the themes that are most likely to appear on the test. Make sure that you understand these themes and can provide examples of each. Some of the most important themes are listed below.

Belief Systems

Change

Conflict

Culture and Intellectual Life

Diversity

Economic Systems

Geography and the Environment

Imperialism

Interdependence

Justice and Human Rights

Movement of People and Goods (Cultural Diffusion)

Nationalism

Political Systems

Science and Technology

Urbanization

## Making Connections Across Place and Time

You will do well on the test if you can make connections among events and developments in different parts of the world and in different time periods. As you study various regions and eras, try to see similarities and differences in events that took place. For example, revolutions occurred in many parts of the world in the 1700s and 1800s. How were these revolutions similar? How were they different? How did earlier revolutions have an impact on later ones? As you review global history and geography, look for patterns and generalizations that hold true across place and time.

## Understanding Causes and Impacts

The Regents Examination will also require that you understand the cause-and-effect links between events. As you review major events and turning points, make sure that you understand the factors and conditions that caused them. Then make sure that you can explain the impacts that these events had on later developments.

## Practice in Analyzing Documents

This review book provides you with many historical documents, including written documents, maps, tables, charts, graphs, and political cartoons. The multiple-choice and document-based parts of the test will require you to analyze many types of documents. You will be expected to take into account both the source of each document and the author's point of view.

## Developing Your Writing Skills

You will earn a higher score on the test if you practice and improve your ability to communicate through writing. Essay-writing skills are required for both the thematic essay and the document-based question. It is most important to write essays that demonstrate a logical plan of organization and include a strong introduction and conclusion.

# Multiple-Choice Questions

More than half of the points to be earned on the Regents Examination (55 percent) are earned by answering multiple-choice questions. You will therefore want to get the highest possible score in this section.

# Preparing for the Regents

## Strategies for Multiple-Choice Questions

Keep several points in mind when you are answering the multiple-choice questions on the Regents Examination.

1. Read the entire question carefully. Read all the choices before you make a decision.
2. Eliminate any choices that you are sure are not true, crossing them out in the test booklet.
3. Remember that in the Regents Examination, there is no penalty for guessing. (This is *not* true of all multiple-choice tests.) Therefore, you should make your best guess at an answer to *every* question.
4. See if there is a key phrase that signals what you should be looking for in the question. Not all questions have such phrases. However, you should be aware of certain signal words and phrases.

**Signals for Questions About Cause and Effect:** *one effect, one result, is most directly influenced by, have led directly to, have resulted in, a major cause of, are a direct result of*

**Signals for Questions That Require an Example:** *best illustrates, best reflects, are all examples of, best explains, is an example of*

**Signals for Questions That Ask for a Main Idea:** *main idea, primarily characterized by, formed the basis for*

**Signals for Questions That Ask About Similarities or Differences:** *are similar, one similarity, one difference between*

## Types of Multiple-Choice Questions

Although you will see many types of multiple-choice questions on the Regents Examination, all fall into one or more of the following general categories.

**Unit Content Questions** The test will include multiple-choice questions that cover material from each of the eight units in this book.

**Cross-Unit Questions** Questions that ask you to respond to historical situations or people discussed in several different units will also appear on the test. These questions often ask you to make a deduction that is *valid* (true) about the situations or people, find a *similarity* between them, or identify a *characteristic* that is common to all.

**Thematic Questions** Some questions will address general social studies themes such as nationalism, imperialism, political systems, or economic systems. These questions often ask you to provide *the best example of* something, explain *how it developed*, or describe *characteristics of* a particular concept or system. The themes that these questions may deal with are listed in the Key Themes and Concepts section of this book and highlighted in the Thematic Review.

**Questions Based on Documents** Some multiple-choice questions are based on documents. Types of documents that may appear include:

- A short passage
- A map
- A graph
- A table or chart
- A political cartoon

Such document-based questions often ask for the *main idea* of a passage or cartoon. Sometimes they ask you to identify an *accurate statement* or the statement *best supported by the data*. They may also ask you to choose the *valid conclusion* drawn from the document. These types of questions often require both skills in interpreting documents and factual knowledge of global history and geography.

## Sample Unit Content Questions

Each of the next two questions tests your knowledge of content from a specific unit of the Global History and Geography course.

1    A negative effect of the partitioning of India in 1947 was that
   (1) foreign rule was reestablished in India
   (2) Hinduism became the only religion practiced in India
   (3) the government policy of nonalignment further divided Indian society
   (4) civil unrest, territorial disputes, and religious conflict continued throughout the region

You know from the question that the answer must be an *effect* and that it must be *negative*. Choice 1 cannot be the answer, since British rule ended in 1947. Choice 2 is incorrect because Islam, Sikhism, and other religions besides Hinduism are practiced in India. Choice 3 cannot be correct, since nonalignment was a reaction to the Cold War, not to partition. Choice 4 is the correct answer because the creation of Pakistan and India increased tensions and conflicts between Hindus and Muslims in the region.

2    Which group had the greatest influence on early Russian culture?
   (1) Franks
   (2) Ottoman Turks
   (3) Byzantine empire
   (4) Roman Catholic Church

The important words in this question are *the greatest influence*. The Franks (Choice 1) were a Germanic tribe of the early Middle Ages. They had a strong effect on Western Europe but not on Russia. The Ottoman Turks (Choice 2) had an influence on Russia, but their influence occurred later. The Roman Catholic Church (Choice 4) had little influence because the Orthodox Christian Church was adopted by Russia. The Byzantine empire (Choice 3), however, is the correct answer because it had an enormous impact on early Russia.

## Sample Thematic Questions

Each of the next two multiple-choice questions deals with a specific theme or concept.

3    Which aspect of a nation's culture is most directly influenced by the physical geography of that nation?
   (1) form of government
   (2) population distribution
   (3) religious beliefs
   (4) social class system

The question involves physical geography and its influence on a nation. The key phrase in the question is *is most directly influenced*. If you understand physical geography, you know that it has a great influence on where people live. For example, people tend to live near sources of water. Large populations live where the geography easily allows settlement. The answer to this question would therefore be Choice 2. Geography sometimes influences forms of government (Choice 1), as in the Greek city-states, but it has a more direct influence on population distribution. It has even less influence on religious beliefs (Choice 3) and the social class system (Choice 4).

4   Which quotation best reflects a feeling of nationalism?
    (1)  "An eye for an eye and a tooth for a tooth."
    (2)  "A person's greatest social obligation is loyalty to the family."
    (3)  "For God, King, and Country."
    (4)  "Opposition to evil is as much a duty as is cooperation with good."

This question is about nationalism, a theme you need to understand to prepare for the Regents Examination. First, you must know what nationalism is: a feeling of pride in and devotion to one's country. Then you must decide which of the possible answers best expresses that idea. Choice 1 has to do with justice, not nationalism. Choice 2 has to do with social behavior and Choice 4 with moral behavior. Only Choice 3 expresses the idea of devotion to one's nation, so Choice 3 is the correct answer.

## Sample Cross-Unit Questions

Each of the next two questions deals with content from two or more units of the Global History and Geography course.

5   One similarity found in the leadership of Peter the Great of Russia, Kemal Atatürk of Turkey, and Jawaharlal Nehru of India is that each leader
    (1)  expanded his territory by invading Greece
    (2)  borrowed ideas and technology from Western Europe
    (3)  supported equal rights for women
    (4)  increased the power of religious groups in his nation

Each of these leaders appears in a different unit of this book. Note that this question asks for *one similarity*. This means that the answer must be true for all three leaders. Therefore, if you know that a choice is not true of even one leader, it cannot be the right answer. Choice 1 is not correct because none of the three leaders invaded Greece. Although each of these leaders supported some reforms or societal changes that involved women, none called for equal rights for women, so Choice 3 is incorrect. Peter the Great and Kemal Atatürk actually decreased the power of religious groups in their nations, so Choice 4 cannot be correct. All of these leaders did, however, borrow ideas and technology from the West, making Choice 2 the correct answer.

6   The societies of traditional China, feudal Japan, and czarist Russia were all characterized by
    (1)  a rigid class structure
    (2)  much interaction with other cultures
    (3)  great economic change
    (4)  rapidly changing social values

This question also asks you about content from several units of your Global History and Geography course. Familiarity with all three cultures would help you select Choice 1. None of the other choices is characteristic of *any* of the civilizations, so even if you were familiar only with czarist Russia, you would still be able to choose the correct answer (1).

## Sample Document-Based Questions

The remaining sample questions are based on historical documents.

Base your answer to question 7 on the map below and on your knowledge of social studies.

**African Kingdoms, 1000 B.C.–A.D. 1600**

7 Which conclusion regarding early African trade is supported by the information provided by this map?
(1) The kingdom of Zimbabwe grew rich from trade with Egypt.
(2) The kingdoms of West Africa traded with the city-states of East Africa.
(3) The Congo and Zambezi Rivers played an important role in Africa's early trade.
(4) The West African kingdoms had trading contacts with the cities of the Mediterranean.

The question asks which conclusion can be supported by information provided in the map. Only Choice 4 can be supported by information from the map. Trade routes are shown linking the West African kingdoms with the Mediterranean cities of Carthage and Tripoli. Even if any of the other selections are true, they *are not supported* by evidence in this map. The map provides no information about how rich Zimbabwe was, about trade with East African cities, or about the role of the Congo and Zambezi Rivers.

Base your answer to question 8 on the poem below and on your knowledge of social studies.

> May our country
> Taking what is good
> And rejecting what is bad
> Be not inferior
> to any other
> —Mutsuhito

8   According to this Japanese poem, Mutsuhito believed that Japan should modernize by
    (1) completely changing Japanese society
    (2) borrowing selectively from other societies
    (3) controlling other cultures that were superior
    (4) rejecting foreign influence

Here, you are asked to demonstrate understanding of Mutsuhito's poem. Choice 1 is not appropriate because the poem does not indicate whether Mutsuhito favored just a little change or massive change. Choice 3 is incorrect because the poem talks about borrowing from other cultures, not controlling them. Choice 4 is wrong because the poem advises rejection only of "what is bad." Choice 2 correctly summarizes the meaning of the poem.

Base your answer to questions 9 and 10 on the table below and on your knowledge of social studies.

### Statistics for Selected Nations of South Asia

| Nations | Bangladesh | Malaysia | Myanmar | Pakistan | Thailand |
|---|---|---|---|---|---|
| Population Density (per sq mi) | 2,294 | 164 | 181 | 440 | 303 |
| Per Capita Income (dollars) | 1,260 | 10,750 | 1,120 | 2,300 | 7,700 |
| Percentage of Labor Force in Agriculture | 65 | 21 | 67 | 47 | 43 |
| Literacy Rate (percentage | 38 | 83 | 83 | 38 | 94 |

9   Which nations have more than half of the labor force engaged in agriculture?
    (1) Bangladesh and Myanmar
    (2) Pakistan and Bangladesh
    (3) Thailand and Malaysia
    (4) Myanmar and Thailand

Question 9 asks you to examine one column of the table. Choices 2 and 3 are incorrect because none of those nations have more than 50 percent of the labor force engaged in agriculture. Choice 4 is incorrect because only Myanmar has the appropriate percentage. Choice 1 is correct, listing the two nations with more than half of the labor force in agriculture.

10  Which is a valid conclusion, based on the information in the table?
    (1) Bangladesh has the highest per capita income.
    (2) Myanmar has the smallest percentage of workers involved in farming.
    (3) Malaysia has the highest population density.
    (4) Thailand has the highest percentage of children enrolled in school.

For question 10, the correct answer is Choice 4. A high literacy rate (94 percent) indicates that a high percentage of children are learning to read in school. Choice 1 is not true: Bangladesh has nearly the lowest per capita income of the nations shown. Choice 2 is incorrect, since Myanmar has the highest percentage of workers involved in farming. Choice 3 is incorrect because Malaysia actually has the lowest population density, not the highest.

Base your answer to question 11 on the graph below and on your knowledge of social studies.

**Population Projections for Selected East and Southern African Nations**

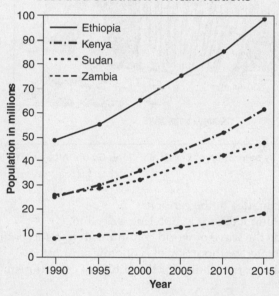

Source: *The World Bank*

11 Based on the information in the graph, which is a valid conclusion about the populations of East and Southern African nations?
   (1) The nation with the largest population in 1990 will have the lowest population in 2015.
   (2) Population will rise in all countries, but it will rise fastest in Ethiopia.
   (3) Populations will level off in all of these nations after the year 2005.
   (4) In 1995, the population of Zambia was approximately 28 million people.

You can rule out Choice 1 because the ranks of the nations changed very little if at all. You can eliminate Choice 3 because one glance at the lines shows all four populations continuing to rise more steeply after 1995. You can rule out Choice 4 by reading the graph and seeing that Zambia's population in 1995 was about 10 million. Choice 2, however, is a valid conclusion to draw from this graph.

Base your answer to question 12 on the cartoon below and on your knowledge of social studies.

THE OLD MAN AND THE SEA

By permission of Rex Babin, *Times Union*, Albany, NY.

12 What is the main idea of the cartoon?
(1) Cuba's fishing industry is suffering a decline.
(2) Castro rode the wave of world communism to a successful conclusion.
(3) Cuba is isolated without Soviet economic support.
(4) Castro bears responsibility for the failure of communism in Eastern Europe.

Questions on political cartoons require skill in interpreting such cartoons as well as knowledge of global history. When you look at a political cartoon, make sure that you can identify its elements. Many are symbolic. For example, the small boat marked *Cuba* represents the country of Cuba. The figure in it is a caricature of Fidel Castro, the president of Cuba. The carcass of the fish has a hammer and sickle, the national symbol of the former Soviet Union. The image communicates the idea that the Soviet Union is dead.

Choice 1 is incorrect because the cartoon is clearly about political issues, not about the Cuban fishing industry. You can rule out Choice 2 because the figure in the boat does not look happy. Also, you have read that Cuba has experienced difficulty since the fall of communism. Choice 4 is not correct because Castro is feeling the *effects* of change; he was not the *cause*. That leaves only Choice 2, which you know to be true: Cuba has had difficulties without Soviet support.

Base your answer to question 13 on the cartoon below and on your knowledge of social studies.

**13** Which conclusion is best supported by the cartoon?
(1) Imprisonment of political dissidents rarely ends opposition to the government.
(2) The United Nations supports punishment of acts of civil disobedience.
(3) Better media coverage would prevent the imprisonment of protesters.
(4) Mistreatment of political prisoners often results in their acceptance of government policies.

Again, you must first examine the cartoon and analyze its elements. The name *Mandela* and your knowledge of global history tell you that this cartoon shows the time when Nelson Mandela was in prison in South Africa. You notice that Mandela is of normal size when he enters prison in 1962 but has grown greatly by the time he emerges in 1990. His increased size represents his increased world stature during the time of his imprisonment. You can eliminate Choice 2 because it is untrue and because the United Nations is not featured in this cartoon. Choice 3 can be ruled out because media coverage is not shown by the cartoon. Choice 4 is also not supported by the cartoon, since there is no indication that Mandela accepted government policies. Instead, Mandela's changed size indicates that Choice 1 is the answer. Instead of stopping opposition by imprisoning Mandela, the South African government only succeeded in furthering his cause of opposition to apartheid.

## Thematic Essay Question

There will be one thematic essay question on the Regents Examination. It will count for 15 percent of the total points you may receive. This section of the exam requires you to understand, interpret, and explain a key social studies theme or concept. In your essay, you should be able to:

- State a main idea in a thesis statement.
- Develop it and add supporting details.
- Summarize it with an effective conclusion.

### Basic Characteristics

The directions for thematic essay questions always consist of three parts: a theme, a task, and suggestions.

**The Theme**  This part of the question identifies a broad social studies theme that will be the general topic of your essay. The theme is given more focus by a brief explanatory statement that follows the statement of the theme. (To review the most common themes tested in Regents Examinations, see the Thematic Review section at the end of this book.)

**The Task**  The second part of a thematic essay question is the task. The task section usually has three parts and presents the instructions you will need to write your essay. Generally, you will be asked to define or describe a theme or concept, to give a specific number of examples or results, and then to evaluate the theme or concept in some way. Typical forms of evaluation include describing causes or effects and evaluating positive or negative aspects.

**Suggestions**  The final part of a thematic essay question is the suggestions section. This part lists specific areas that you might choose to discuss in your essay. The suggestions might name people, nations, or civilizations, depending on the topic of the question. These are, of course, only suggestions, and you may choose to write about other examples that are relevant to the essay topic. Often, the suggestions will caution you not to choose the United States as your topic. If this warning is present, pay attention to it. You will not receive full credit for an answer that does not follow the directions.

### Strategy for the Thematic Essay Question

Keep the following strategies in mind as you approach a thematic essay question.

1. Read the entire question through first.
2. After you have read the question, begin jotting down any ideas you have.
3. After you have jotted down your initial ideas, begin to make a brief outline. Organization is important in writing a good essay. The outline does not need to be very detailed, but it should include enough information to help you remember all the points that you want to use in the essay. It should also help you to see whether your essay has a logical organization.
4. Use the suggestions to help you recall the importance of the theme in different places and times.
5. Develop your essay logically.
6. Do not merely list facts. Analyze and evaluate the information, and compare or contrast various aspects.
7. Make sure that you provide examples to support your ideas.

8. Make sure that you have completed each of the items listed in the task section.
9. Make sure that your essay has both a strong introduction and a strong conclusion. You cannot get full credit for your essay if either of these elements is missing or weak.

## Sample Thematic Essay Questions

The thematic essay questions included throughout this book will provide you with insight into the types of questions you will see on the actual Regents Examination. Below are two sample thematic essay questions. They follow the same format as those that will appear on the actual Regents Examination.

**Sample One**
*Directions*
Write a well-organized essay that includes an introduction, several paragraphs addressing the task below, and a conclusion.

**Theme: Geography**

> Geographic features can positively or negatively affect the development of a nation or region.

**Task:**

> Select *one* geographic feature from your study of global history.
>
> • Explain how this geographic feature has had an effect on the historical development of *two* nations or regions. Be sure to include specific historical examples in your essay.

You may use any geographic features from your study of global history. Some suggestions you might wish to consider include: river valley, mountain, desert, island, rain forest, and climate. Do not use the United States in your answer.

**Sample Two**
*Directions*
Write a well-organized essay that includes an introduction, several paragraphs addressing the task below, and a conclusion.

**Theme: Civilization**

> Throughout history, great civilizations have existed in various parts of the world. The cultural and intellectual achievements of these civilizations contributed to the advancement of humankind.

**Task:**

> • Define the term *civilization*.
> • Describe some examples of cultural or intellectual achievements made by past civilizations. Identify each example with the particular civilization that made the contribution.
> • Explain the lasting importance of each of these achievements or contributions to global history.

You may discuss any civilization from your study of global history, except the United States. Some civilizations you might wish to consider include ancient Egypt, classical Rome, the Gupta empire, classical China, or the Muslim golden age.

## Thematic Essay Scoring

Knowing how your essay will be scored will help you write it effectively. Essays are scored with point values from 0 to 5. An essay receiving a score of 5 answers the question in a complete, comprehensive manner. You would receive a score of 0 only if you failed to address the theme at all, wrote an essay that was completely illegible, or turned in a blank paper.

The scoring rubric that follows represents the generic criteria on which your essay will be scored.

## Generic Scoring Rubric

### Thematic Essay

**Score of 5:**
- Thoroughly develops all aspects of the task evenly and in depth
- Is more analytical than descriptive (analyzes, evaluates, and/or creates information)
- Richly supports the theme with many relevant facts, examples, and details
- Demonstrates a logical and clear plan of organization; includes an introduction and a conclusion that are beyond a restatement of the theme

**Score of 4:**
- Develops all aspects of the task but may do so somewhat unevenly
- Is both descriptive and analytical (applies, analyzes, evaluates, and/or creates information)
- Supports the theme with relevant facts, examples, and details
- Demonstrates a logical and clear plan of organization; includes an introduction and a conclusion that are beyond a restatement of the theme

**Score of 3:**
- Develops all aspects of the task with little depth or develops most aspects of the task in some depth
- Is more descriptive than analytical (applies, may analyze, and/or evaluate information)
- Includes some relevant facts, examples, and details; may include some minor inaccuracies
- Demonstrates a satisfactory plan of organization; includes an introduction and a conclusion that may be a restatement of the theme

**Score of 2:**
- Minimally develops all aspects of the task or develops some aspects of the task in some depth
- Is primarily descriptive; may include faulty, weak, or isolated application or analysis
- Includes few relevant facts, examples, and details; may include some inaccuracies
- Demonstrates a general plan of organization; may lack focus; may contain digressions; may not clearly identify which aspect of the task is being addressed; may lack an introduction and/or a conclusion

## Score of 1:
- Minimally develops some aspects of the task
- Is descriptive; may lack understanding, application, or analysis
- Includes few relevant facts, examples, or details; may include inaccuracies
- May demonstrate a weakness in organization; may lack focus; may contain digressions; may not clearly identify which aspect of the task is being addressed; may lack an introduction and/or a conclusion

## Score of 0:
- Fails to develop the task or may only refer to the theme in a general way; *OR* includes no relevant facts, examples, or details; *OR* includes only the theme, task, or suggestions as copied from the test booklet; *OR* is illegible; *OR* is a blank paper

# Document-Based Question

This type of question presents you with up to eight historical documents on a single subject. The documents may be letters, speeches, or other written records; maps; charts; political cartoons; graphs; or tables.

### Basic Characteristics

Questions based on historical documents have several characteristics. The documents provided give information or express viewpoints about a common theme. For space reasons, the samples you will see here and at the end of each unit will include only a few documents. Those on the test, however, may include up to eight documents.

A document-based question always has two parts. Part A requires short answers to specific questions about the documents. Part B requires you to write an essay. The themes for these essays are based on the same social studies themes and concepts as are used for thematic essays. Refer to the sample shown on the following pages as you read this information about document-based questions.

**General Directions** The question will begin with a set of directions. These directions will tell you what to do for each part of the question.

**Historical Context** Each question will contain a short statement that defines the historical context for the question. Read this statement carefully. It will help you understand the main topic to be discussed.

**Task** This statement defines the overall task that you will perform as you examine the documents provided.

**Part A: Short Answer** In this part of the question, you will be presented with the documents themselves. Documents that are quotations will be enclosed within boxes. The author of the quotation will be clearly identified. Documents may also be maps, charts, or political cartoons. Each document will be followed by one or possibly more questions. The questions will ask you to consider the viewpoint and source of the document. This is important because the author of a document may have a bias or a special motive that makes it difficult to accept his or her words as the whole truth. For example, a person who is trying to persuade soldiers to go into battle will not present the point of view of the opposing side very completely. Skills in interpreting the information in documents are very important.

**Part B: Essay** The essay portion of the question includes a set of general instructions and repeats the historical context. Pay very close attention to the instructions. Note that they call for a well-organized essay with both an introduction and a conclusion. They require you to use evidence from the documents to support your response. You should not, however, merely repeat the contents of the documents. Be sure also to include specific, related information from your knowledge of global history and geography. You must use additional relevant information that is not found in the documents. Otherwise you will not receive full credit for your essay. For the highest possible score, refer to all of the documents provided in the question, and include additional information from your knowledge of global history.

## Strategy for the Document-Based Question

**Answering Part A** Your first task is to answer each of the questions about the documents. Examine each passage carefully, and look closely at each image. Read the question or questions and then reexamine the documents. Keep in mind the historical context. Recognize the various viewpoints that are being expressed. Finally, write a clear answer to each question.

**Answering Part B** You can approach this part much as you would a thematic essay, except that you need to consider how to incorporate evidence from the documents provided as well as knowledge from your Global History and Geography course.

You will find it useful to make a brief outline as you did for the thematic essay, showing what you plan to use as a thesis statement, what your supporting facts will be, where you will use various documents for support, and what your conclusion will be.

Take a look at the scoring rubric that follows the sample document-based question. A rubric like this one will be used to score Part B of the document-based question.

To get a high score on the essay portion of the test, do the following:

- Complete all parts of the task thoroughly.
- Provide analysis and interpretation of all or most of the documents supplied in the question. Information from the documents must be included within the body of your essay.
- Include as much related outside information as you can. Relevant outside information is crucial to a high score. Support your essay with related facts, examples, and details.
- Write an essay that is organized clearly and logically. Outlining your essay will help you maintain a clear organization.
- After you have finished writing, check to be sure that you have included a strong introduction and a strong conclusion.

# Sample Document-Based Question

The following sample of a document-based question includes three documents. As already noted, a document-based question on the Regents Examination could show up to eight documents. Otherwise, the short-answer questions and essay question in this sample are similar to what you will see on the Regents Examination. For additional practice with questions based on documents, see the Questions for Regents Practice at the end of each unit as well as the sample tests.

**Historical Context:**

> Throughout history, leaders have had vastly differing viewpoints on whether violence or war is ever justified. Some leaders, for example, have felt that violence is justified for certain purposes. Others have believed that violence against others is never the right choice. These viewpoints have had powerful effects on historical events.

**Task:** Using information from the documents and your knowledge of global history, answer the questions that follow each document in Part A. Your answers to the questions will help you write the Part B essay, in which you will be asked to

> • Evaluate several viewpoints on whether violence or war is ever justified in order to achieve a desired goal

## Part A: Short-Answer

*Directions:* Analyze the documents and answer the question or questions that follow each document, using the space provided.

### Document #1

> *What difference does it make to the dead, the orphans and the homeless, whether the mad destruction is wrought under the name of totalitarianism or the holy name of democracy and liberty?*
>
> — **Mohandas Gandhi, 1948**

1 Does Gandhi think that violence may be justified if the cause is a good one? Explain your answer, referring to the quotation.

_____

_____

_____

_____

_____

_____

# Preparing for the Regents

## Document #2
## The Atomic Bomb

| PROBLEM |
| --- |
| Should U.S. President Truman use the atomic bomb against Japan? |

| Reasons FOR | Reasons AGAINST |
| --- | --- |
| • It would save American lives.<br>• It would bring a quick end to the war.<br>• It would show the power of the United States to any future enemies. | • It would cause massive destruction.<br>• Once used, it would more likely be used again.<br>• It would release deadly radioactivity. |

| Decision |
| --- |
| Truman orders atomic bomb dropped on Hiroshima and Nagasaki. |

| RESULTS |
| --- |
| • More than 110,000 die.<br>• Japan surrenders. |

2   List two reasons why President Truman decided to use atomic bombs against Japan.

_____

_____

_____

_____

_____

_____

3   Describe two reasons why some Americans disagreed with President Truman's decision.

_____

_____

_____

_____

_____

_____

**Document #3**

> *Brutality is respected. Brutality and physical strength. The plain man in the street respects nothing but brutal strength and ruthlessness—women, too, for that matter, women and children. The people need wholesome fear.*
>
> — **Adolf Hitler, 1936**

4  How did Adolf Hitler justify his inhumanity? Explain your answer, referring to the quotation.

_____

_____

_____

_____

_____

_____

**Document #4**

> *A government should not mobilize an army out of anger, military leaders should not provoke a war out of wrath. Act when it is beneficial, desist when it is not. Anger can revert to joy, wrath can revert to delight, but a nation destroyed cannot be restored to existence, and the dead cannot be restored to life.*
>
> — **Sun Tzu, *The Art of War*, c. 300** B.C.

5  Why did Sun Tzu say it is bad to start a war out of anger? Explain your answer, referring to the quotation.

_____

_____

_____

_____

_____

_____

**Document #5**

> *A revolution is not a dinner party, or writing an essay, or painting a picture or doing embroidery; it cannot be so refined, so leisurely and gentle, so kind, courteous, restrained, and generous. A revolution is an insurrection, an act of violence by which one class overthrows another.*
>
> **— Mao Zedong, leader of the Communist Revolution in China**

6 According to Mao, what means are necessary in order for a revolution to succeed? Explain your answer, referring to the quotation.

_____

_____

_____

_____

_____

_____

## Part B

## Essay

*Directions:* Write a well-organized essay that includes an introduction, several paragraphs, and a conclusion. Use evidence from *at least three* documents in your essay. Support your response with relevant facts, examples, and details. Include additional outside information.

**Historical Context:**

> Throughout history, leaders have had vastly differing viewpoints on whether violence or war is ever justified. Some leaders, for example, have felt that violence is justified for certain purposes. Others have believed that violence against others is never the right choice. These viewpoints have had powerful effects on historical events.

**Task:** Using information from the documents and your knowledge of global history and geography, write an essay in which you

> - Evaluate whether violence or war is ever justified in order to achieve a desired goal

**Guidelines:**

**In your essay, be sure to**
- Develop all aspects of the task
- Incorporate information from *at least three* documents
- Incorporate relevant outside information
- Support the theme with relevant facts, examples, and details
- Use a logical and clear plan of organization, including an introduction and a conclusion that are beyond a restatement of the theme

## Document-Based Question Scoring

Knowing how your document-based essay will be scored will help you write it effectively. Like thematic essays, document-based essays are scored with point values from 0 to 5. An essay receiving a score of 5 answers the question in a complete, comprehensive manner. You would receive a score of 0 only if you failed to address the theme at all, wrote an essay that was completely illegible, or turned in a blank paper.

The scoring rubric that follows represents the generic criteria on which your document-based essay will be scored.

## Generic Scoring Rubric

### Document-Based Question

**Score of 5:**
- Thoroughly develops all aspects of the task evenly and in depth
- Is more analytical than descriptive (analyzes, evaluates, and/or creates information)
- Incorporates relevant information from *at least* one more than half of the documents
- Incorporates substantial relevant outside information
- Richly supports the theme with many relevant facts, examples, and details
- Demonstrates a logical and clear plan of organization; includes an introduction and a conclusion that are beyond a restatement of the theme

**Score of 4:**
- Develops all aspects of the task but may do so somewhat unevenly
- Is both descriptive and analytical (applies, analyzes, evaluates, and/or creates information)
- Incorporates relevant information from *at least* half of the documents
- Incorporates relevant outside information
- Supports the theme with relevant facts, examples, and details
- Demonstrates a logical and clear plan of organization; includes an introduction and a conclusion that are beyond a restatement of the theme

**Score of 3:**
- Develops all aspects of the task with little depth *or* develops most aspects of the task in some depth
- Is more descriptive than analytical (applies, may analyze, and/or evaluate information)
- Incorporates some relevant information from some of the documents
- Incorporates limited relevant outside information
- Includes some relevant facts, examples, and details; may include some minor inaccuracies
- Demonstrates a satisfactory plan of organization; includes an introduction and a conclusion that may be a restatement of the theme

## Score of 2:

- Minimally develops all aspects of the task *or* develops some aspects of the task in some depth
- Is primarily descriptive; may include faulty, weak, or isolated application or analysis
- Incorporates limited relevant information from the documents *or* consists primarily of relevant information copied from the documents
- Presents little or no relevant outside information
- Includes few relevant facts, examples, and details; may include some inaccuracies
- Demonstrates a general plan of organization; may lack focus; may contain digressions; may not clearly identify which aspect of the task is being addressed; may lack an introduction and/or a conclusion

## Score of 1:

- Minimally develops some aspects of the task
- Is descriptive; may lack understanding, application, or analysis
- Makes vague, unclear references to the documents or consists primarily of relevant and irrelevant information copied from the documents
- Presents no relevant outside information
- Includes few relevant facts, examples, or details; may include inaccuracies
- May demonstrate a weakness in organization; may lack focus; may contain digressions; may not clearly identify which aspect of the task is being addressed; may lack an introduction and/or a conclusion

## Score of 0:

- Fails to develop the task or may only refer to the theme in a general way; *OR* includes no relevant facts, examples, or details; *OR* includes only the historical context and/or task as copied from the test booklet; *OR* includes only entire documents copied from the test booklet; *OR* is illegible; *OR* is a blank paper

## A Few Final Words

You have learned a number of strategies to help you prepare for the multiple-choice, thematic essay, and document-based questions on the Regents Examination in Global History and Geography. Try out these strategies on the practice tests included in the book and on the questions at the end of each unit. This practice will help you find out what works best for you and will allow you to become comfortable with the various types of questions found in the Regents Examination. As you practice more, you will also become confident of your ability to do well on the test.

Make sure you are well rested on the day of the examination. If you have devoted serious effort to your study of global history and geography, reviewed the material in this book, and used the many test items provided here for practice, you will be thoroughly prepared for the exam.

# Unit 1 Pre-Test

**Name** _____  **Date** _____

**Directions** Review the Preparing for the Regents section of this book. Then answer the following questions, drawn from actual Regents examinations. For each statement or question, choose the *number* of the word or expression that, of those given, best completes the statement or answers the question.

1. The Neolithic Revolution was characterized by the
   (1) change from nomadic herding to settled farming
   (2) growth of iron tool-making technology
   (3) migration of early peoples to the Americas
   (4) decline of large empires

2. Why did ancient civilizations develop in valleys of rivers such as the Nile, Indus, Tigris, and Euphrates?
   (1) The river valleys provided a source of fresh water and good farmland.
   (2) The rivers aided in the exploration of new territories.
   (3) The rivers provided power for industries.
   (4) The river valleys provided areas for recreation.

3. Hieroglyphic and cuneiform systems provided the basis for the development of
   (1) subsistence farming
   (2) painting and sculpture
   (3) oral traditions
   (4) recorded history

4. "If a son has struck his father, they shall cut off his hand. If a nobleman has destroyed the eye of a member of the aristocracy, they shall destroy his eye...."

   The idea expressed in this quotation is found in the
   (1) Ten Commandments
   (2) Twelve Tables
   (3) Justinian Code
   (4) Code of Hammurabi

5. Why did the ancient city-states of Athens and Sparta develop different political systems?
   (1) The Byzantine Empire dictated government policies.
   (2) Foreign travelers introduced new philosophies.
   (3) The mountainous topography resulted in the isolation of these city-states.
   (4) For over three centuries, civil wars raged in these city-states.

6. Which civilization first developed a civil service system, invented gunpowder, and manufactured porcelain?
   (1) Aztec        (3) Japanese
   (2) Chinese      (4) Roman

7. One similarity between Japanese Shintoism and African animism is the belief that
   (1) everything in nature has a spirit and should be respected
   (2) only one God exists in the universe
   (3) people's moral conduct determines their afterlife
   (4) religious statues should be erected to honor the gods

8. Which values are most closely associated with the fundamental principles of Buddhism?
   (1) competition and financial success
   (2) maintaining the caste system and providing education for all people
   (3) practicing nonviolence and giving up worldly desires
   (4) self-determination and democracy

**Name** _____  **Date** _____

9. In China, Confucianism emphasized the idea that
   (1) equality should exist between all members of society
   (2) salvation could be attained by prayer, meditation, and good deeds
   (3) individual goals should be placed ahead of the needs of the group
   (4) harmony could be achieved by the proper behavior of each member of a family or society

10. Christianity, Islam, and Judaism are similar in that they all ask their followers to
    (1) believe in reincarnation
    (2) strive for nirvana
    (3) follow a code of behavior
    (4) practice polytheism

11. One way in which the Han dynasty and the Roman Empire were similar is that both
    (1) governed large areas around the Mediterranean Sea
    (2) created democratic societies in which people elected their government officials
    (3) developed a social system in which great equality existed
    (4) promoted unity and communication by building a strong system of roads

12. Which statement explains a cause rather than an effect of the Bantu migration between 500 B.C. and A.D. 1500?
    (1) Techniques for herding and cultivating were spread to other peoples.
    (2) More than sixty million people now speak a Bantu language.
    (3) Trading cities developed along the coast of east Africa.
    (4) Population increases put pressure on agriculture.

13. The use of the Silk Road in Asia and caravan routes in northern Africa and southwestern Asia encouraged
    (1) self-sufficiency      (3) ethnocentrism
    (2) cultural isolation     (4) cultural diffusion

14. Culture is sometimes referred to as "a blueprint for living" because it
    (1) flourishes best in traditional societies
    (2) includes everything that contributes to a society's development
    (3) is determined by genetics
    (4) provides plans for exploration of new territory

# Unit 2 Pre-Test

**Name** _____   **Date** _____

**Directions** Review the Preparing for the Regents section of this book. Then answer the following questions, drawn from actual Regents examinations. For each statement or question, choose the *number* of the word or expression that, of those given, best completes the statement or answers the question.

1. Which factor most influenced a person's social position in early Indian societies?
   (1) education
   (2) birth
   (3) geographic location
   (4) individual achievement

2. One similarity between the Gupta Dynasty (A.D. 320–550) in India and the Tang Dynasty (A.D. 618–907) in China is that each dynasty
   (1) promoted equality for women
   (2) made advances in the arts, sciences, and mathematics
   (3) gained overseas colonies
   (4) developed a representative government

3. What is a major contribution of the Bzyantine Empire to global history?
   (1) preservation of Greek and Roman culture
   (2) construction of the pyramids
   (3) expansion of equal rights
   (4) invention of writing

4. Constantinople became the center of the Byzantine Empire because
   (1) the pope had made it the capital of the Christian world
   (2) it was a religious center for Muslims
   (3) its location made it the crossroads of Europe and Asia
   (4) it was geographically isolated from surrounding empires

5. The Justinian Code is considered a milestone because it
   (1) preserved many ancient Chinese legal decrees in writing
   (2) served as a model for European legal systems
   (3) became the first democratic constitution
   (4) united Muslim and Roman thought

6. An important contribution of the Byzantine Empire to Russia is the establishment in Russia of
   (1) Orthodox Christianity
   (2) representative democracy
   (3) a free-market economy
   (4) a jury system

7. The phrase "from southern Spain, across northern Africa, occupying the Arabian peninsula to Southeast Asia" once described the extent of the
   (1) Aztec Empire      (3) Gupta Empire
   (2) Pax Romana        (4) Muslim world

8. The Golden Age of Muslim culture was best known for its
   (1) attempts to colonize North America
   (2) frequent conflicts between Christians and Jews
   (3) advances in mathematics, science, and medicine
   (4) policies to reduce trade between the Middle East and China

9. The Age of Pericles in Athens, the Gupta Empire in India, and the Tang dynasty in China all experienced a golden age with
   (1) advancements in the principles of democratic governments
   (2) outstanding contributions in the arts and sciences
   (3) the end of foreign domination
   (4) the furthest expansion of their borders

10. During the feudal period in Europe, power and position in society were based on the
    (1) amount of money earned
    (2) level of education achieved
    (3) number of slaves owned
    (4) amount of land possessed

**Name** _____   **Date** _____

**Base your answer to question 11 on the quotations below and on your knowledge of social studies.**

"The pope is the only person whose feet are kissed by all princes. His title is unique in the world. He may depose [remove] emperors." – Pope Gregory VII (11th century)

"An emperor is subject to no one but to God and justice." —Frederick Barbarossa, Holy Roman Emperor (twelfth century)

**11.** The ideas expressed in these quotations show that during the Middle Ages in Europe
   (1) popes gave little attention to political matters
   (2) monarchs dominated the Church's leaders
   (3) popes and monarchs sometimes challenged the other's authority
   (4) monarchs and popes strengthened the role of the Church

**12.** The Roman Catholic Church during the Middle Ages in Europe can best be described as a church that
   (1) favored separation from secular governments
   (2) avoided involvement in social and educational matters
   (3) was a strong force that divided many people
   (4) was a stabilizing influence during a period of weak central governments

**13.** A major goal of the Christian Church during the Crusades (1096–1291) was to
   (1) establish Christianity in western Europe
   (2) capture the Holy Land from Islamic rulers
   (3) unite warring Arab peoples
   (4) strengthen English dominance in the Arab world

**14.** The Crusades indirectly contributed to the discovery of the New World by
   (1) forcing the religious conversion of the Muslim population
   (2) forcing the Turks to flee from Constantinople
   (3) stimulating European demand for goods from the East
   (4) increasing the power of the feudal lords

**15.** Many achievements of Islamic civilization reached European society by way of the
   (1) Crusades and eastern Mediterranean trading networks
   (2) merchant guilds and the Industrial revolution
   (3) Middle Passage and the Columbian Exchange
   (4) conquests of the Germanic tribes and trade along the Silk Road

# Unit 3 Pre-Test

**Name** _____  **Date** _____

**Directions** Review the Preparing for the Regents section of this book. Then answer the following questions, drawn from actual Regents examinations. For each statement or question, choose the *number* of the word or expression that, of those given, best completes the statement or answers the question.

1. Which geographic feature contributed most to the concept of cultural diffusion in Japan?
   (1) deposits of fertile soil
   (2) location near the mainland of Asia
   (3) vast mineral resources
   (4) numerous navigable rivers

2. The feudal system in both medieval Europe and early Japan were characterized by
   (1) a decentralized political system
   (2) religious diversity
   (3) an increased emphasis on education
   (4) the development of a wealthy middle class

3. Which factor contributed to the success of the vast empire created by the Mongols?
   (1) avoiding contacts with the West
   (2) paying monetary tribute to local rulers
   (3) employing superior military skills
   (4) converting conquered peoples to Confucianism

4. What was one influence of Mongol rule on the history of Russia?
   (1) Contact with kingdoms in western Europe greatly increased.
   (2) The Chinese writing system was introduced and adopted.
   (3) Most Russians converted from Orthodox Christianity to Islam.
   (4) Russian leaders adopted the idea of strong, centralized control of the empire.

5. Ibn Battuta and Marco Polo were similar in that both
   (1) ruled over vast empires that included diverse peoples
   (2) produced written records of their extensive travels
   (3) converted thousands of people to Christianity
   (4) fought to free their people from Mongol rule

6. • 1340s—Mongols, merchants, and other travelers carried disease along trade routes west of China,
   • 1346—The plague reached the Black Sea ports of Caffa and Tana.
   • 1347—Italian merchants fled plague-infected Black Sea ports.
   • 1348—The plague became an epidemic in most of western Europe.

   Which conclusion can be made based on these statements?
   (1) The plague primarily affected China.
   (2) The interaction of people spread the plague.
   (3) Port cities were relatively untouched by the plague.
   (4) The plague started in western Europe.

7. During the 1400s, the cities of Venice, Constantinople, and Canton achieved prominence because their
   (1) locations were favorable for trade
   (2) pleasant climates led to an increase in population
   (3) democratic governments attracted trade
   (4) military power led to industrialization

8. The introduction of banking, letters of credit, joint stock companies, and guilds contributed to the start of the
   (1) Renaissance
   (2) Agricultural Revolution
   (3) Enlightenment
   (4) Commercial Revolution

9. One way in which the writers of the Renaissance were influenced by the writers of ancient Greece was that the Renaissance writers
   (1) stressed the power of human reason
   (2) promoted the religious doctrines of the Roman Catholic Church
   (3) showed little interest in secular affairs
   (4) produced few new scientific ideas

**Name** _____   **Date** _____

10. What is meant by Machiavelli's belief that "the end justifies the means"?
    (1) Leaders may use any method to achieve what is best for the state.
    (2) The general public always acts in its own best interest.
    (3) Pleasing all of the people at any given time is possible.
    (4) Leaders must always act for the common good.

11. One major influence the Renaissance had on the Protestant Reformation was that the philosophers of the Renaissance
    (1) supported democratic forms of government
    (2) encouraged a questioning attitude
    (3) stressed the importance of life after death
    (4) denied the existence of God

12. Which action could be considered an effect of the Protestant Reformation?
    (1) posting of the Ninety-five Theses
    (2) decline in the power of the Roman Catholic Church
    (3) sale of indulgences
    (4) end of religious warfare

13. The Magna Carta can be described as a
    (1) journal about English feudal society
    (2) list of feudal rights that limited the power of the English monarchy
    (3) census of all tax-paying nobility in feudal England
    (4) statement of grievances of the middle class in England

14. The West African kingdoms of Ghana, Mali, and Songhai experienced economic prosperity because they all
    (1) controlled vast reserves of oil and gold
    (2) traded with many other nations
    (3) maintained highly structured feudal systems
    (4) solved tribal conflicts within their empires

15. One conclusion that can be reached from the evidence about Mansa Musa rule of Mali is that
    (1) Christianity was a dominant religion in Africa in ancient times
    (2) complex civilizations existed in West Africa, before the arrival of Europeans
    (3) trade was not necessary for a civilization to survive
    (4) the slave trade originated in West Africa

**Name** _____   **Date** _____

**Directions** Review the Preparing for the Regents section of this book. Then answer the following questions, drawn from actual Regents examinations. For each statement or question, choose the *number* of the word or expression that, of those given, best completes the statement or answers the question.

1. Inca terrace farming and Aztec floating gardens are examples of
   (1) the ability of civilizations to adapt to their region's physical geography
   (2) slash-and-burn farming techniques
   (3) Mesoamerican art forms symbolizing the importance of agriculture
   (4) colonial economic policies that harmed Latin American civilizations

2. One similarity of the Aztec, Maya, and Inca empires is that they
   (1) developed in fertile river valleys
   (2) maintained democratic political systems
   (3) coexisted peacefully with neighboring empires
   (4) created complex civilizations

3. The ethnocentric attitudes of various Chinese emperors can best be attributed to the
   (1) cultural isolation of China
   (2) failure of other nations to become interested in China
   (3) interest of Chinese scholars in other civilizations
   (4) great cultural diversity within China's borders

4. The fall of the Byzantine Empire to the Ottoman Turks (1453) prompted Spain and Portugal to
   (1) seek new trade routes to East Asia
   (2) extend religious tolerance to Muslim peoples
   (3) reform their political systems
   (4) expand the Catholic Inquisition into the Middle East

5. During the 1500s, technological advances in navigation, naval engineering, and mapmaking contributed directly to the start of the
   (1) Gupta Empire      (3) Age of Exploration
   (2) Mongol Empire     (4) medieval guilds

6. A major reason that the Spanish were able to conquer the peoples of the Americas was the
   (1) military technology of the Spanish conquerors
   (2) inability of the native peoples to adapt to Spanish culture
   (3) enforced slavery of the native peoples by the Spanish
   (4) unified resistance of native peoples to Spanish demands

7. Which statement about the *encomienda* system during the sixteenth and seventeenth centuries is accurate?
   (1) Aztec and Inca civilizations prospered.
   (2) Life expectancy among Native American populations increased.
   (3) Spanish influence declined in its colonies.
   (4) Many Native Americans were forced to labor on large estates.

8. In the 1600s, the interest of Europeans in Africa was based mainly on Europe's need to
   (1) market its surplus agricultural products
   (2) obtain workers for its colonies in the Americas
   (3) establish collective security arrangements
   (4) settle its surplus population on new lands

9. Which statement best explains the increase in the Atlantic slave trade in the 1700s?
   (1) Technological advances in shipping made the slave trade more profitable.
   (2) Converted African slaves worked with Spanish missionaries to conquer the native peoples.
   (3) Many Africans wished to settle in the Americas and paid their own passage.
   (4) As the Europeans developed their American colonies, their need for cheap labor increased.

**Name** _____     **Date** _____

10. Which statement describes an impact that the Columbian Exchange had on the lives of Europeans?

   (1) The transfer of new products and ideas encouraged economic growth.

   (2) New diseases were brought to Europe and resulted in massive deaths caused by a plague.

   (3) Native Americans immigrated to Europe and competed with Europeans for jobs.

   (4) Cross-cultural contacts between South America and Asia declined.

11. One principle in the theory of mercantilism is that colonies should be

   (1) granted independence as soon as possible

   (2) considered an economic burden for the colonial power

   (3) encouraged to develop their own industries

   (4) acquired as markets and sources of raw materials

12. The primary goal of most of Europe's absolute monarchs was to

   (1) support political freedom for the new middle classes

   (2) prevent contact with areas beyond Europe's borders

   (3) centralize their political control over their nations

   (4) maintain peaceful relations with neighboring nations

13. One similarity between the rule of Peter the Great of Russia and that of Akbar the Great of India was that both leaders

   (1) implemented strict religious codes of conduct within their nations

   (2) modernized and expanded their empires using ideas from other cultures

   (3) relied on peaceful resolutions of conflicts with neighboring peoples

   (4) introduced democratic ideas into their political systems

14. King Louis XIV of France, Peter the Great of Russia, and Suleiman the Magnificent of the Ottoman Empire were all considered absolute rulers because they

   (1) broke from the Roman Catholic Church

   (2) helped feudal lords build secure castles

   (3) instituted programs that provided more power to their parliaments

   (4) determined government policies without the consent of their people

15. The Magna Carta, the Petition of Right, and the English Bill of Rights were created to

   (1) limit the power of English monarchs

   (2) establish laws protecting the rights of Protestants

   (3) organize England's colonial empire

   (4) abolish the role of Parliament

# Unit 5 Pre-Test

**Name** _____ **Date** _____

**Directions** Review the Preparing for the Regents section of this book. Then answer the following questions, drawn from actual Regents examinations. For each statement or question, choose the *number* of the word or expression that, of those given, best completes the statement or answers the question.

1. Which statement best describes the effects of the works of Nicolaus Copernicus, Galileo Galilei, Sir Isaac Newton, and Rene Descartes?
   (1) The acceptance of traditional authority was strengthened.
   (2) The scientific method was used to solve problems.
   (3) Funding for education was increased by the English government.
   (4) Interest in Greek and Roman drama was renewed.

2. The Enlightenment philosophers believed that the power of government is derived from
   (1) divine right rulers
   (2) the middle class
   (3) a strong military
   (4) those who are governed

3. "Estates General Meet for First Time in 175 Years;" "National Assembly Issues Declarations of the Rights of Man;" "Reign of Terror Ends; Robespierre Dies"

   Which event in European history is most closely associated with these headlines?
   (1) Puritan Revolution
   (2) Hundred Years War
   (3) French Revolution
   (4) signing of the Magna Carta

4. Simón Bolívar, Josó de San Martín, and Toussaint l'Ouverture are important in Latin American history because they were
   (1) twentieth century caudillos
   (2) leaders of liberation movements
   (3) members of the Organization of American States (OAS)
   (4) winners of the Nobel Peace Prize

5. One of the main purposes of the Congress of Vienna (1814–1815) was to
   (1) promote the unification of Italy
   (2) preserve the German territories gained by Otto von Bismarck
   (3) restore the power of the Holy Roman Empire
   (4) establish a balance of power in Europe after the defeat of Napoleon

6. Which nineteenth century ideology led to the unification of Germany and of Italy and to the eventual breakup of Austria-Hungary and of the Ottoman Empire?
   (1) imperialism     (3) liberalism
   (2) nationalism     (4) socialism

7. The main cause of the mass starvation in Ireland during the nineteenth century was the
   (1) British blockade of Irish ports
   (2) failure of the potato crop
   (3) war between Protestants and Catholics in northern Ireland
   (4) environmental damage caused by coal mining

8. During the nineteenth century, industrialization in Great Britain differed from industrialization in Japan mainly because Great Britain
   (1) had greater deposits of natural resources
   (2) encountered government resistance to economic growth
   (3) used isolationism to increase its economic power
   (4) duplicated the factory systems used in China

9. Laissez-faire capitalism as attributed to Adam Smith called for
   (1) heavy taxation of manufacturers
   (2) strict government control of the economy
   (3) minimal government involvement in the economy
   (4) government investments in major industries

**Name** _____   **Date** _____

10. Karl Marx and Friedrich Engels encouraged workers to improve their lives by
    (1) electing union representatives
    (2) participating in local government
    (3) overthrowing the capitalist system
    (4) demanding pensions and disability insurance

11. The needs of the Industrial Revolution in nineteenth-century Europe greatly contributed to the
    (1) growth of overseas empires
    (2) beginning of the triangular trade
    (3) development of international peacekeeping organizations
    (4) promotion of political and economic equality in Asia and Africa

12. The theory of Social Darwinism was sometimes used to justify
    (1) the establishment of communist governments in Asia
    (2) Latin American revolutions in the early nineteenth century
    (3) the independence movement in India
    (4) European imperialism in the late nineteenth century

13. "Take up the White Man's Burden -
    Send forth the best ye breed -
    Go, bind your sons to exile
    To serve your captives' need. . . ."

    – Rudyard Kipling, The Five Nations (1903)

    The words of this poem have been used to support the practice of
    (1) imperialism      (3) cultural borrowing
    (2) isolationism     (4) self-determination

14. The Sepoy Rebellion in India and the Boxer Rebellion in China were similar in that both were
    (1) attempts to improve foreign trade
    (2) nonviolent resistance efforts
    (3) revolts against foreign influence
    (4) revolutions against traditional monarchs

15. During the Meiji Restoration, Japan's leaders focused on
    (1) isolating Japan from the influence of foreign ideas
    (2) existing peacefully with their Asian neighbors
    (3) increasing the Emperor's power by returning Japan to a feudal political system
    (4) modernizing Japan's economy to compete with Western nations

# Unit 6 Pre-Test

**Name** _____  **Date** _____

**Directions** Review the Preparing for the Regents section of this book. Then answer the following questions, drawn from actual Regents examinations. For each statement or question, choose the *number* of the word or expression that, of those given, best completes the statement or answers the question.

1. The Balkans were referred to as the "Powder Keg of Europe" in the period before World War I because of their
   (1) manufacturing ability
   (2) stockpiles of weapons
   (3) nationalistic rivalries
   (4) economic strength

2. Growing nationalism and militarism in Europe and the creation of secret alliances were
   (1) reasons for the rise of democracy
   (2) causes of World War I
   (3) requirements for economic development
   (4) reasons for the collapse of communism

3. The harsh terms included in the treaties ending World War I have been used to explain the
   (1) Fascist Revolution in Spain
   (2) Bolshevik Revolution in Russia
   (3) rise of Nazism in Germany
   (4) Armenian massacre in Turkey

4. In the 1920s and 1930s, Mustafa Kemal Atatürk changed the Turkish government by
   (1) introducing democratic reforms
   (2) increasing the power of the sultan
   (3) supporting absolutism
   (4) incorporating religious teachings into civil law

5. During the Russian Revolution of 1917, the slogan "peace, bread, and land" appealed to many Russian peasants because this slogan
   (1) called for continued Russian expansion in East Asia
   (2) supported an increase in the power of the Russian czar
   (3) addressed the needs and concerns of the peasants
   (4) promised to return all peasants to serfdom

6. What was the major goal of Joseph Stalin's five-year plans in the Soviet Union?
   (1) encouraging rapid industrialization
   (2) supporting capitalism
   (3) improving literacy rates
   (4) including peasants in the decision-making process

7. Which statement describes one major aspect of a command economy?
   (1) Supply and demand determines what is produced.
   (2) Most economic decisions are made by the government.
   (3) The means of production are controlled by labor unions.
   (4) The economy is mainly agricultural.

8. Which type of political system did V I. Lenin, Adolf Hitler, and Benito Mussolini establish in their countries?
   (1) constitutional monarchy
   (2) totalitarianism
   (3) representative democracy
   (4) theocracy

9. One characteristic of a totalitarian state is that
   (1) minority groups are granted many civil liberties
   (2) several political parties run the economic system
   (3) citizens are encouraged to criticize the government
   (4) the government controls and censors the media

**Name** _____   **Date** _____

10. Which global event caused the overall reduction of unemployment between 1914 and 1918?

    (1) the Great Depression

    (2) completion of the Panama Canal

    (3) World War I

    (4) World War II

11. What was a major reason for Adolf Hitler's rise to power?

    (1) provisions of the Treaty of Versailles

    (2) Germany's military support of Poland and France

    (3) strong German economy

    (4) refusal by the League of Nations to admit Germany as a member

12. In Europe during the 1930s, several national leaders, in order to preserve peace at any cost, agreed to the demands of an aggressor. This policy is referred to as

    (1) militarism          (3) reparation

    (2) nonalignment        (4) appeasement

13. What was a major reason for Japan's invasion of Manchuria in 1931?

    (1) The province of Manchuria was originally a Japanese territory.

    (2) The government of Japan admired Manchurian technical progress.

    (3) The people of Manchuria favored Japanese control.

    (4) Japan needed the natural resources available in Manchuria.

14. During World War II, which geographic features contributed most to the Soviet Union's defense against the German invasion?

    (1) deposits of many natural resources

    (2) size and climate

    (3) Atlantic ports and rivers

    (4) mountainous territory and desert areas

15. The Holocaust is an example of

    (1) conflict between political parties

    (2) violations of human rights

    (3) limited technological development

    (4) geography's influence on culture

# Unit 7 Pre-Test

**Name** _____  **Date** _____

**Directions** Review the Preparing for the Regents section of this book. Then answer the following questions, drawn from actual Regents examinations. For each statement or question, choose the *number* of the word or expression that, of those given, best completes the statement or answers the question.

1. The formation of the North Atlantic Treaty Organization (NATO), the division of Germany into East Germany and West Germany, and the Korean War were immediate reactions to
   - (1) Japanese military aggression in the 1930s
   - (2) the rise of German nationalism after World War I
   - (3) ethnic conflict and civil war in Africa in the 1950s
   - (4) communist expansion after World War II

2. One similarity between the Korean War and the Vietnam War is that both wars were
   - (1) resolved through the diplomatic efforts of the United Nations
   - (2) fought as a result of differing political ideologies during the Cold War
   - (3) fought without foreign influence or assistance
   - (4) caused by religious conflicts

3. Which statement best describes India's foreign policy between 1947 and 1990?
   - (1) It imitated Great Britain's policies.
   - (2) It usually reflected the policies of China.
   - (3) It rejected all assistance from communist dictatorships.
   - (4) It generally followed a policy of nonalignment.

4. One reason the Chinese Communists were able to gain control of China was primarily due to the support of the
   - (1) peasants
   - (2) landed elite
   - (3) foreigners
   - (4) warlords

5. Which development took place in China under Mao Zedong?
   - (1) The family became the dominant force in society.
   - (2) The Four Modernizations became the basis for economic reform.
   - (3) The people adopted the practice of ancestral worship.
   - (4) Communist teachings became required learning in all schools and universities.

6. Since the 1980s, Chinese leaders have tried to improve China's economy by implementing a policy of
   - (1) isolationism
   - (2) collectivization
   - (3) limited free enterprise
   - (4) representative government

7. What was one reason that India was divided into two nations in 1947?
   - (1) Indian leaders disagreed about India's role in the United Nations.
   - (2) Great Britain feared a unified India would be a military threat.
   - (3) The Soviet Union insisted that India should have a communist government.
   - (4) Differences between the Hindus and the Muslims created religious conflict.

8. One similarity in the actions of Ho Chi Minh and Jomo Kenyatta was that both leaders
   - (1) introduced Western ideas to their societies
   - (2) established democratic forms of government
   - (3) led nationalist movements
   - (4) supported separation of church and state

**Name** _____ **Date** _____

9. Which situation existed under the policy of apartheid in South Africa?

   (1) All people were guaranteed suffrage.
   (2) The black majority held the most political power.
   (3) Society was controlled by the white minority.
   (4) Social inequality was eliminated.

10. What was one factor that contributed to the downfall of apartheid in the Republic of South Africa?

    (1) The African National Congress was outlawed.
    (2) Afrikaners demanded that only they should have ruling power.
    (3) Many foreign countries boycotted South African products.
    (4) President de Klerk and Desmond Tutu were imprisoned.

11. A major source of the dispute between the Israelis and the Palestinians is that each side

    (1) wants to control oil resources in the area
    (2) has historic ties to the same land
    (3) believes in different interpretations of the same religion
    (4) has close military alliances with neighboring countries

12. Since the creation of the Organization of Petroleum Exporting Countries (OPEC), member nations have joined together to

    (1) determine the supply of oil on the world market
    (2) establish a policy of independence in trade
    (3) maintain a low price of oil per barrel
    (4) isolate themselves from the rest of the world

13. Mikhail Gorbachev instituted the policies of glasnost and perestroika to

    (1) reinforce the basic economic principles of communism
    (2) bring the Soviet Union into the European Economic Community
    (3) reform the Soviet Union politically and economically
    (4) gain acceptance for free political elections

14. One way in which Lech Walesa, Mikhail Gorbachev, and Nelson Mandela are similar is that each

    (1) led the people of his nation toward a more democratic government
    (2) fought for power for the black majority over the white minority
    (3) worked to end communism in his country
    (4) refused to participate in the United Nations

15. In Iran, both the Revolution of 1979 and the rise of Islamic fundamentalism have caused

    (1) an increase in women's rights
    (2) tension between traditionalism and modernization to continue
    (3) foreign control of natural resources to expand
    (4) the introduction of a communist form of government

**Name** _____  **Date** _____

**Directions** Review the Preparing for the Regents section of this book. Then answer the following questions, drawn from actual Regents examinations. For each statement or question, choose the *number* of the word or expression that, of those given, best completes the statement or answers the question.

**1.** What is a major reason for the differences in economic prosperity in various areas of the world today?

(1) an unequal distribution of resources
(2) the success of nationalist movements
(3) religious unity between nations
(4) membership in the United Nations

**2.** In many of the world's developing nations, improvements in life expectancy and health care have contributed to

(1) population pressures that limit economic development
(2) an increased number of epidemics
(3) a reduction in the need for land reform
(4) a steady rise in income for all citizens

**3.** As a society becomes more urbanized and industrialized, it tends to

(1) develop a more rigid class system
(2) modify traditional beliefs and customs
(3) resist cultural diffusion
(4) depend more on the extended family structure

**4.** The Green Revolution of the 1960s resulted in

(1) the destruction of large industrial enterprises
(2) an increase of food output in many developing nations
(3) a decrease in world agricultural output
(4) improvements in human genetic engineering

**5.** An example of economic interdependence is

(1) South Africans mining their gold and diamond resources
(2) the government of France issuing new currency
(3) Japan selling technological goods to buy Middle Eastern oil
(4) an Indian subsistence farmer waiting for the rains to water his crops

**6.** The main purpose of the European Union (EU) and the North American Free Trade Agreement (NAFTA) is to

(1) reduce the spread of nuclear weapons
(2) address the problem of international political corruption
(3) increase educational opportunities for underdeveloped nations
(4) stimulate economic growth for participating countries

**7.** Which issue continues to raise concern from the world community regarding the nations of India, Iraq, Pakistan, and North Korea?

(1) overpopulation
(2) ethnic cleansing
(3) desertification
(4) nuclear proliferation

**8.** Which environmental issue most concerns Central Africa, the Amazon River Basin, and the Malay Peninsula?

(1) nuclear contamination
(2) desertification
(3) overpopulation
(4) deforestation

**9.** • Chernobyl experiences nuclear disaster.
• Chlorofluorocarbons (CFCs) deplete the ozone layer.
• Rivers and seas are polluted throughout the world.

Which conclusion can best be drawn from these statements?

(1) Modern technology can have serious negative effects.
(2) Today's environment renews itself.
(3) Only developing nations have environmental problems.
(4) Most environmental problems originate in Europe.

**Name** _____    **Date** _____

10. The late twentieth century conflicts in Rwanda, Yugoslavia, and India were similar in that each was caused by the

    (1) deforestation conducted by multinational companies
    (2) collapse of communism
    (3) intervention of United Nations peacekeeping forces
    (4) rivalries between ethnic groups

11. Which statement best describes the impact of the computer on the global economy?

    (1) Countries can increase tariffs on imports.
    (2) Companies now market more products worldwide.
    (3) Wages have risen dramatically for most people in developing nations.
    (4) Prices of oil and other resources have declined worldwide.

12. The reason that the Organization of Petroleum Exporting Countries (OPEC) greatly influences the world today is that it

    (1) commands the loyalty of the worldwide Islamic community
    (2) develops and exports important technology
    (3) controls access to trade routes between the East and West
    (4) manages the oil supply that affects the global economy

# Ancient World:
## Civilizations and Religions (4000 B.C.–A.D. 500)

**Section 1:** Early Peoples and River Civilizations

**Section 2:** Classical Civilizations

**Section 3:** Rise and Fall of Great Empires

**Section 4:** Emergence and Spread of Belief Systems

## Unit Overview

Over the first thousands of years of human existence, people advanced in many different areas. A new era of human development began when humans discovered how to plant crops and domesticate animals. A more settled life and more dependable food sources allowed people to build civilizations with complex political, social, and religious structures. Civilizations began to interact with each other. They shared ideas and technology through such means as trade and conquest. Classical civilizations arose in Africa, Asia, and Europe. These civilizations made contributions to art, architecture, law, government, and other fields. Their achievements continue to affect society today. Ancient civilizations also made an impact on each other and on today's world through the development of powerful belief systems. These belief systems have spread throughout the world and affected cultural development and the course of history.

## Thematic Timeline Activity

Some of the many themes developed in Unit 1 are:

| | |
|---|---|
| change | movement of people and goods |
| geography | culture and intellectual life |
| urbanization | economic systems |
| political systems | belief systems |

Choose one of the themes listed above. As you review Unit 1, create a thematic timeline based on the theme you have chosen. Your timeline should stretch from 4000 B.C. to A.D. 500 and include major developments and key turning points having to do with your theme.

# Early Peoples and River Civilizations

## The Big Idea

The Agricultural Revolution led to the first civilizations. These early civilizations:

- relied on a traditional economy based on farming.
- were often located in river valleys.
- developed cities, systems of government, social structures, and belief systems.
- made contributions to later civilizations in technology, the arts, law, and other areas.
- exchanged ideas and developments with other cultures.

## Section Overview

Scientists believe that humans first appeared over two million years ago. The first humans were wandering hunters and gatherers. They made simple tools and weapons from stone, bone, and wood.

With the development of farming, ancient peoples gave up their nomadic lifestyles and established permanent settlements, which grew over time into civilizations. Early civilizations developed in river valleys. As populations grew, these peoples developed systems of government, social structures, and belief systems. Migration, trade, and warfare helped ideas move from one culture to another.

## Key Themes and Concepts

As you review this section, take special note of the following key themes and concepts:

**Environment** How did the earliest people adapt to their environment?

**Urbanization** How did the development of agriculture change the way early people lived?

**Political Systems** What types of government and social structure were created by early civilizations?

**Culture and Intellectual Life** What contributions did early people make to later civilizations?

**Movement of People and Goods** How did trade, warfare, and migration spread ideas among early civilizations?

## Key People and Terms

### Key People and Terms

Place each of the key people and terms into one of these four categories: people, culture, politics, economics.

As you review this section, be sure you understand the significance of these key people and terms:

| | | |
|---|---|---|
| nomads | polytheistic | empire |
| cultural diffusion | pharaoh | Code of Hammurabi |
| Neolithic | Fertile Crescent | Middle Kingdom |
| technology | ziggurats | dynasty |
| civilization | cuneiform | |

# Early Peoples

The first people lived more than two million years ago, in prehistoric times. Prehistory is the time before people invented writing.

## Hunters and Gatherers

The earliest people lived during the Old Stone Age, also called the Paleolithic age, which began more than two million years ago. Paleolithic people were **nomads,** or people who moved from place to place, hunting and gathering their food. Their simple social structure consisted of small groups of people who traveled together.

## Adapting to Their Environment

Stone Age people adapted to their environment. They made simple tools and weapons, such as digging sticks and spears, from stone, bone, or wood. During Paleolithic times, people developed language, which allowed them to communicate and cooperate during a hunt. Paleolithic people invented clothing made of animal skins. They used fire for warmth as well as for cooking food.

## Spiritual Beliefs

Paleolithic people developed some spiritual beliefs. Toward the end of the Old Stone Age, people began burying their dead with care, a practice suggesting that they believed in an afterlife. They buried tools and weapons with their dead.

## Migration

Evidence supports the theory that the earliest people lived in East Africa. Their descendants spread to every part of the world. During the Old Stone Age, people migrated north and east into Europe and Asia. After many years, some migrated over a land bridge into North America. Others migrated by boat to islands in the Pacific. Migration led to **cultural diffusion,** or the exchange of ideas, customs, and goods among cultures. Cultural diffusion also occurred through trade and warfare.

# The Neolithic Revolution

Environmental changes brought new climate patterns that contributed to the end of the Old Stone Age. Warmer weather allowed plants to grow where, previously, sheets of ice had dominated the landscape.

Around 10,000 B.C., people made two important discoveries. They learned to plant seeds to grow food, and they learned to domesticate animals. These discoveries meant that people no longer had to wander in search of food. They could live in permanent settlements. This change marked the beginning of the New Stone Age, or Neolithic period. Historians call these discoveries the Neolithic Revolution, or the Agricultural Revolution, because farming and domestic animals changed the way people lived.

## The Impact of Agriculture

After the Neolithic Revolution, more abundant food helped the population to increase. Humans' lives changed in many ways.

- **Permanent Settlements** People settled together in villages.
- **New Social Classes** When resources were scarce, groups went to war. Chiefs or headmen emerged. Some men gained prestige as warriors and had great power.
- **New Technology** People began to develop technology, or tools and skills they could use to meet their basic needs, such as calendars and plows. Other new technology included the wheel, metal weapons, and metal tools.

These changes paved the way for civilization to emerge.

## Note Taking

*Reading Skill:*
**Identify Main Ideas**
Make a concept web. Complete the circles with information about Paleolithic people. Add circles if necessary.

Paleolithic People

## Preparing for the Regents

- How did Paleolithic people acquire food from their natural environment?

## Key Themes and Concepts

**Movement of People and Goods**
Three important ways in which cultural diffusion occurs are through migration, trade, and warfare.

## Preparing for the Regents

The Neolithic Revolution was one of the great turning points of history. Farming and the domestication of animals changed the way people lived. A dependable source of food allowed villages to grow larger and develop into cities. People who lived in cities developed more complex forms of government and such concepts as division of labor and social classes.

# The Rise of Civilization

About 5,000 years ago, the first civilizations began to develop along river valleys. The rich, fertile farmlands of river valleys helped these civilizations to thrive. Most early civilizations were characterized by several basic features:

- Cities
- Central governments
- Traditional economy
- Organized religion
- Social classes
- Art and architecture
- Roads, bridges, and other public works
- System of writing
- Specialized jobs

## Cities and Central Government

Cities emerged as farmers cultivated land along river valleys and produced surplus food. Surplus food led to increased population. More systematic leadership than just a headman or council of elders was needed. Governments developed to make sure that enough food was produced and that the city was protected. Rulers also ordered that public works such as roads, bridges, and defensive walls be built.

## Traditional Economy

Traditional economies, based primarily on farming, grew up in early civilizations. Skilled craftsworkers made pottery, cloth, and other goods.

## Organized Religion

Ancient peoples were **polytheistic,** believing in many gods. Priests and worshipers tried to gain the favor of these gods through complex rituals. They hoped that the gods would ensure plentiful crops and protect their cities.

## Job Specialization and Social Classes

People began to specialize in certain jobs because no one person could master all the necessary skills to provide for himself or herself. People became ranked in classes according to their jobs. Priests and nobles were usually at the top of these societies, followed by warriors and merchants, with peasant farmers and slaves at the bottom.

Vocabulary Builder

ritual—(RICH oo ul) n. a ceremony that is always performed in the same way, in order to mark an important religious or social occasion

## Art and Architecture

Much early art and architecture consisted of temples and palaces, symbols of the power of rulers.

## System of Writing

Writing may have first developed in temples, where many types of records were kept. Early writing was picture writing, consisting of simple drawings. Over time the writing became more symbolic.

# Egypt

One of the earliest civilizations arose in Egypt about 5,000 years ago.

## Geographic Setting

Since most of Egypt is a desert, people settled along the Nile River. The Nile provided water for drinking and for irrigation of crops. Yearly floods soaked the land and left rich deposits of silt that kept the agricultural areas fertile. The river also served as a highway for travel.

Note Taking

Reading Skill:
Identify Supporting Details
Make a table. As you read, record information about Egypt.

| Egypt | |
|---|---|
| Concept | Main Idea |
| Geographic Setting | |
| Religion | |
| Government | |
| Social Structure | |

## Religion

Egyptians were polytheistic. The sun god Amon-Re was the chief god. Osiris was the god of the Nile. Osiris controlled the annual flood that made the land fertile. The Egyptians also believed in a host of other gods who served specific functions.

The cornerstone of the religious faith of the Egyptians was a belief in life after death. Egyptians prepared their dead for the afterlife through a preservation process called mummification.

## Government

The Egyptian ruler was called a **pharaoh.** Egyptians believed that the pharaoh was both a god and a king. In fact, when a pharaoh died, he was buried in a majestic pyramid. The pyramids took years to build and required enormous planning and organization. When the mummies of pharaohs were buried in pyramids, they were surrounded by possessions for use in the afterlife. After the death of a pharaoh, power usually passed to another member of the family. These ruling families were called dynasties.

## Social Structure

Egyptian society was divided into classes. The pharaoh held the highest position in society. Next were the priests, who served the gods and goddesses. Third were the nobles, who fought the pharaoh's wars, followed by the craftspeople and merchants. Near the bottom was the biggest group, the peasant farmers. Beneath the peasants were the slaves.

Women had a higher status in Egyptian society than in any other ancient civilization. A woman could own property, enter business deals, and obtain a divorce.

## Contributions

The Egyptians made many advances in science and art. The process of mummification helped them learn much about the human body, allowing them to diagnose many illnesses and perform surgery. Egyptians developed a calendar very similar to the one we use today. They also created a system of picture writing called hieroglyphics. Egyptian temples and monuments, as well as the pyramids, have survived thousands of years. Egyptian statues and paintings show daily life, ceremonies, and military victories.

# Mesopotamia

## Geographic Setting

To the north and east of Egypt, the **Fertile Crescent,** a crescent-shaped region of good farmland created by the Tigris and Euphrates Rivers, stretches from the Persian Gulf to the Mediterranean. The lack of natural barriers in the Fertile Crescent allowed frequent migrations and invasions, while the diversity of the people made it difficult to unite them into a single nation. In this area great civilizations arose, giving the Fertile Crescent the name "the cradle of civilization."

In the eastern end of the Fertile Crescent lies Mesopotamia. There early civilizations developed, along the banks of the Tigris and Euphrates Rivers. This river valley region was called Mesopotamia, from a Greek word meaning "land between the rivers." With few natural barriers, this area became a crossroads where people mingled and shared customs and ideas.

## Key Themes and Concepts

**Belief Systems**
Many early peoples had polytheistic belief systems. The gods were seen as closely tied to the forces of nature, and keeping them happy was essential to agriculture. Therefore, religious leaders became very important in early societies.

## Preparing for the Regents

The Egyptians formed a centralized government with the pharaoh as its focus. As in many ancient civilizations, the pharaohs claimed divine support for their rule and eventually claimed that they themselves were gods. This claim was an effective way to maintain power.

## Preparing for the Regents

- What geographical features of the Fertile Crescent helped civilization to grow and ideas to spread between cultures?

**The Ancient Middle East**
The Ancient Middle East is
a region that includes Egypt
and part of Asia. It is bordered
by Asia to the east, Europe
to the northwest, Africa to
the southwest, and the
Mediterranean Sea to the
west.

**Preparing for
the Regents**

Practice your map skills by
answering the following
questions about the map.

1. Which two rivers ran
through the Fertile
Crescent?

2. Which two river valley
civilizations are shown
on this map?

**Preparing for
the Regents**

The tools and other
technology that a
civilization develops
tells much about what is
important to that culture.
Early river valley civilizations
developed methods of flood
control and irrigation.

**Preparing for
the Regents**

- Compare Sumerian society
to Egyptian society. How
were they alike? How
were they different?

**Identify
Supporting
Details**

The Sumerians made many
contributions to the world.
List three.

## The Civilizations of the Fertile Crescent

**Sumerians** The first civilization in Mesopotamia was Sumer. City-states developed along the Tigris and Euphrates Rivers about 5,000 years ago. The Sumerians were polytheistic and built their cities around pyramid-like structures called **ziggurats.** A ziggurat had steps that people could climb to reach the shrine of that particular city's chief god or goddess. The Sumerians developed irrigation systems, dikes, and canals to provide protection from floods and water for crops. They grew wealthy from trade with places as far away as Egypt and India. Among the contributions the Sumerians made to the world were the first wheeled vehicles, a metal plow, and a 12-month calendar based on the cycles of the moon. Their number system was based on 60, which is the basis for our clocks' minutes and seconds. They also developed **cuneiform,** a wedge-shaped writing formed by pressing a pen-like instrument into clay.

**Babylonians** The Babylonians established an early **empire,** or groups of states or territories governed by one ruler. Babylon's most powerful ruler, Hammurabi, is best known for his set of laws called the **Code of Hammurabi.** This was the first major collection of laws in history. Although these laws favored higher classes over lower ones, they established standards of justice for all classes. Punishment was harsh, stressing the idea of "an eye for an eye, a tooth for a tooth."

# Indus River Valley

Like the civilizations that developed in Mesopotamia and the Nile Valley, Indian civilization evolved in a fertile river valley.

## Geographic Setting

The Indian subcontinent is a large, wedge-shaped peninsula that extends southward into the Indian Ocean. This peninsula is surrounded on the north and northwest by huge mountains, which often limited India's contacts with other cultures.

Winds called monsoons bring rain every summer. India depended on monsoons to grow their crops. When there was not enough rain, people could not grow crops. When there was too much, rivers rose to cause deadly floods.

## Indus Valley Cities

About 2500 B.C., at about the time when the pyramids were rising in Egypt, the first Indian civilization arose in the Indus River Valley. Archaeologists have found remains of impressive cities, but little is known about the civilization that produced them. However, it is clear that the Indus Valley civilization covered a large area and that its cities were well planned.

The two main cities of this civilization were Harappa and Mohenjo-Daro. Roads were laid out in a grid pattern, and each city was dominated by a structure built on a hill, probably a fortress or temple. Enormous granaries stored crops that were grown in outlying villages. Houses, which were made of bricks, had plumbing with baths and chutes that led to sewers.

Most Indus Valley people were farmers. They were the first to grow cotton and weave it into cloth. Merchants traveled far, trading even with the cities of Sumer.

## Aryan Invaders

Around 1750 B.C., for unknown reasons, Indus Valley civilization began to decline. Then, in about 1500 B.C., nomadic warriors called Aryans conquered the Indus Valley.

# China

## Geographic Setting

Chinese civilization grew up in the river valleys of the Huang He, or Yellow River, and the Yangzi. Geography—mountains, deserts, jungles, and an ocean—isolated Chinese culture more than it did many other early civilizations. Having little contact with other cultures, the early Chinese believed that their culture was the center of the Earth, so they called it the **Middle Kingdom.** Although China covers a huge area, until recent times most people lived only along the east coast or in the river valleys. Despite its isolation, China traded with other cultures. Chinese goods reached the Middle East and even beyond.

## Government

About 1650 B.C., a Chinese people called the Shang gained control of part of northern China. Although there was a king in Shang China, clans—groups of families—controlled most of the land. In this way Shang China was more similar to the small kingdoms of Aryan India or Sumer's city-states than to the centralized government of Egypt. The Shang set up the first **dynasty,** or ruling family, in China.

## Preparing for the Regents

Hammurabi used law to unite his empire. Later empires, including the Byzantine and Muslim empires, also used systems of law as unifying forces.

## Key Themes and Concepts

**Political Systems**
The well-planned cities of Harappa and Mohenjo-Daro suggest that these people must have had well-organized governments. Government officials probably planned these cities and made sure that there was a steady food supply.

## Purpose for Reading

**Purpose for Reading**
As you read the section about China, answer these questions.

1. Why did the Chinese call their culture the Middle Kingdom?

2. What were the main characteristics of the Shang government, society, and religion?

## Key Themes and Concepts

**Environment and Political Systems**
The Huang He flooded when heavy rains swelled the river. The need to control the river through public works may have contributed to the rise of a strong central government in China.

**Yin-Yang**

## Social Structure

Shang society resembled that of other ancient cultures. A class of noble warriors owned the land. Merchants and craftspeople earned a living in cities. Most people, however, were peasants and lived in farming villages.

## Religion

The Shang Chinese prayed to many gods and nature spirits. The Chinese looked to their dead ancestors to intercede with the gods to help the living, offering them sacrifices of food and other objects. The ancient Chinese also believed that the universe was held in a delicate balance between two forces, the yin and the yang. When these forces were in balance, peace and prosperity would result.

## Contributions

One of the most important achievements of China was written Chinese, which developed about 4,000 years ago. The ancient Chinese used a system of writing that included both pictographs (drawings of objects) and ideographs (drawings of thoughts and ideas). Because the Chinese writing system consisted of tens of thousands of characters, only the upper classes had the time to learn to read and write.

# Demographic Patterns and Migration

Demography is the study of human populations. Demographic patterns, or changes in populations over time, are often influenced by geographic features such as rivers. For example, ancient civilizations in Egypt, Mesopotamia, and India all developed in fertile river valleys. Rivers provided water for drinking and irrigation. Rivers also served as highways for the transport of people and goods.

## Bantu Migrations

As populations grew, some groups began to migrate in search of new lands to settle. The Bantu migrations are an example of this movement. The Bantu peoples originally lived in West Africa. Then, as the Sahara region began to dry out, these skilled farmers and herders migrated south and east in search of fertile land. Between 500 B.C. and A.D. 1500, Bantu settlers spread their knowledge of farming and ironworking, as well as their language, across the continent. Today, about a third of all Africans speak a language in the Bantu family.

# Summary

The earliest people were nomadic hunters and gatherers. When they learned how to grow food, they settled in villages. These changes led to the growth of civilizations. Early civilizations grew up in river valleys. Civilizations developed governments, economic systems, and social structures. Early civilizations also had complex systems of belief and made advances in technology, architecture, and legal systems. These advances were spread among early civilizations by migration, trade, and warfare.

# Classical Civilizations

## Section Overview

The classical civilizations of China, India, Greece, and Rome have had a strong impact on the world. Each of these civilizations was influenced by its particular geographic setting. Each had a strong, well-organized government and a prosperous economy that allowed it to thrive. Each civilization made important contributions in such areas as art, science, architecture, and law. The growth of global trade routes during this period allowed classical civilizations to share ideas and technology.

## Key Themes and Concepts

As you review this section, take special note of the following key themes and concepts:

**Geography** How did geographic conditions influence the development of classical civilizations?

**Government** What features of government allowed the classical civilizations of India, China, Greece, and Rome to remain strong?

**Culture and Intellectual Life** What contributions have the classical civilizations of India, China, Greece, and Rome made to later civilizations?

**Movement of People and Goods** How did trade routes link civilizations and lead to cultural diffusion?

## Key People and Terms

As you review this section, be sure you understand the significance of these key people and terms:

Mandate of Heaven
feudalism
Qin
Han dynasty
Maurya dynasty
bureaucracy
Asoka

polis
aristocracy
direct democracy
Hellenistic
republic
Senate
patricians

plebeians
Pax Romana
Laws of the
 Twelve Tables
aqueducts
Silk Road

## China (c. 1027 B.C.–A.D. 220)

### Geographic Setting

China was the most isolated of all ancient civilizations. China's culture developed separately from the civilizations of Egypt, the Middle East, and India. China was separated from these civilizations not only by long distances but by physical barriers. For example, high mountains existed to the west and southwest of China. Also, the Gobi Desert lay to the north and the Pacific Ocean to the east. After the Shang united the area around the Huang He and Yangzi rivers, civilization prospered there.

---

### The Big Idea

The classical civilizations of India, China, Greece, and Rome:

• had strong governments.

• developed ideas and technology that were important contributions to later civilizations.

• developed trade networks that enriched their economies and allowed them to exchange goods and technology.

### Key People and Terms

What do many of the key people and terms have in common? Explain.

### Vocabulary Builder

barrier—(BA ree ur) *n.* a physical object that keeps two areas, people, etc. apart

## Note Taking

*Reading Skill:*
**Recognize Sequence**
As you read Section 2, create a timeline of the classical civilizations. Write when the dynasties and rulers begin and end.

1027
Zhou Dynasty
begins

B.C.    A.D.

1100 B.C.    0    A.D. 500

## Zhou Dynasty (1027 B.C.–221 B.C.)

Between 1100 and 1000 B.C., the Zhou people overthrew the Shang and set up their own dynasty, which lasted nearly 800 years. The Zhou told the people that the gods had become angry at Shang cruelty and now had chosen the Zhou to rule. This right to rule was called the **Mandate of Heaven,** a divine approval to rule. From that time on, each new dynasty would claim the Mandate of Heaven. The Chinese later expanded this idea to explain the dynastic cycle, the rise and fall of dynasties.

### The Mandate of Heaven

## Preparing for the Regents

- Practice your chart reading skills by describing how a dynasty might lose the Mandate of Heaven.

**A Feudal Government** The Zhou kings granted control of large areas of land to their supporters. In a system called **feudalism,** local lords controlled their own regions but owed military service to the ruler. Over time, feudal lords came to hold the real power in China.

**Economy** The economy grew under the Zhou. After the Chinese began using iron to make tools, they could produce more food. Irrigation projects also increased crop yields. Trade expanded along new roads and canals built by feudal lords. The Chinese began for the first time to use money, which spurred the development of trade.

## Vocabulary Builder

yield—(yeeld) *n.* the amount of profits, crops, etc. that something produces

**Zhou Contributions** Under the Zhou, the Chinese made the first books. They also made progress in other areas. Astronomers studied planet movements and eclipses, developing an accurate calendar. The Chinese discovered how to make silk from the cocoons of the silkworm. Silk became a valuable Chinese export.

## The Qin Dynasty (221 B.C.–206 B.C.)

By 221 B.C., a leader of the Qin people proclaimed himself Shi Huangdi, meaning "First Emperor."

## Key Themes and Concepts

**Government**
Shi Huangdi was able to attain power because of divisions in the feudal Zhou government. He moved quickly to centralize his own government through political, economic, and cultural means.

**Centralized Government** After conquering the Zhou empire, Shi Huangdi centralized his power.

- He abolished the old feudal states and divided the country into military districts, each ruled by an appointed official.
- He standardized measurements.
- He created national coins.
- He promoted uniformity in Chinese writing.
- He repaired canals and roads.

**The Great Wall** Shi Huangdi's greatest achievement was the Great Wall. The wall was built to keep out invaders. Thousands of workers worked for years to build the wall.

## The Han Dynasty (206 B.C.–A.D. 220)

After Shi Huangdi's death in 210 B.C., the people revolted. A new dynasty, the Han, emerged. A peasant leader, Liu Bang, took control of China after Qin power collapsed. As emperor, he took the title Gao Zu. He reduced taxes and eased the harsh policies of the Qin. Gao Zu's policies allowed the dynasty he founded, the **Han dynasty,** to last for about 400 years.

**Government and Economy** The most famous Han emperor, Wudi, began his reign in 141 B.C. Wudi strengthened Chinese government by establishing a civil service system. Examinations based on the teachings of Confucius, not family influence, determined who would get government jobs. Wudi also strengthened the economy and improved canals and roads.

**Han Society** The civil service system had an impact on Han society and China for years to come. It established Confucian values in government and in daily life. Confucianism spelled out proper behavior for all parts of society. Men were thought to be superior to women. Because men were considered superior, women were excluded from taking civil service examinations and, thus, from holding positions in government. A few women, including religious recluses and noblewomen, did receive an education, however.

**Han Contributions** The Han period was a golden age in China.

- **Technology** The Chinese made technological advances such as learning how to make paper out of wood pulp. They also invented the wheelbarrow; the fishing reel; and the rudder, a device used to steer ships.

- **Science** In medicine the Han developed acupuncture, a technique in which needles are inserted under the skin to relieve pain or treat illness. The Chinese also experimented with herbal remedies and anesthesia. Furthermore, Han scholars wrote texts on chemistry, zoology, and botany.

- **Arts** Some craftsworkers created jade and ivory carvings. Other artisans worked in bronze, ceramics, and silk.

# India (c. 1500 B.C.–185 B.C.)

## Geographic Setting

The subcontinent of India juts out from the Asian continent. The Indian subcontinent includes three major geographic regions:

- The northern plain, fertile and well watered by the Indus and the Ganges
- The Deccan Plateau, dry and sparsely populated
- The coastal plains, flat land along the east and west coasts where farming, fishing, and trading can occur

This varied geography has made the subcontinent difficult to unite.

## Mauryan Empire (321 B.C.–185 B.C.)

Many competing kingdoms were spread across the northern plains. Into this battleground of rival kingdoms came Chandragupta Maurya. Chandragupta first gained power in the Ganges Valley, but with his army he soon conquered much of northern India. His descendants moved southward, dominating the Deccan Plateau. From about 321 B.C. to 185 B.C., the **Maurya dynasty** ruled over the first united Indian empire.

**Note Taking**

*Reading Skill:*
**Understand Effects**
Make a concept web. As you read, fill it in with the effects of the rule of the Han Dynasty in China. Add circles if necessary.

**Vocabulary Builder**

jut out—(jut owt) *v.* to stick out further than other things

**Preparing for the Regents**

- Practice your map skills by locating the Indus and Ganges Rivers and describing the invasion route used by the Aryans.

**Vocabulary Builder**

flourish—(FLUR ish) *v.* to develop well and be successful

**Key Themes and Concepts**

**Belief Systems**
One of the important contributions of the Mauryans was the spread of Buddhism into other parts of Asia.

**Well-Organized Government** The Maurya dynasty set up an efficient bureaucracy and a strong government with its capital at Pataliputra. A **bureaucracy** is a system of managing government through departments that are run by appointed officials. Officials collected taxes and oversaw the building of roads and harbors, which helped trade to flourish. Other officials managed government-owned factories and shipyards.

Maurya rule was harsh, however. Chandragupta was suspicious of his many enemies. A brutal secret police force reported on crime, corruption, and dissent within his empire.

**Asoka and Reform** Chandragupta's grandson Asoka ruled differently. Horrified by the brutality of a campaign to conquer the Deccan, Asoka rejected further conquest. He turned to Buddhism, hoping to rule by moral example rather than by violence. Asoka sent Buddhist missionaries across India. Despite his desire to promote Buddhism, he was tolerant of other beliefs.

Asoka's rule united his diverse people and brought peace and prosperity. After his death, however, the empire declined, and rival kingdoms once again competed for power.

**Maurya Contributions** The Maurya dynasty united much of India for the first time. Peace and prosperity resulted, and trade flourished. The capital at Pataliputra was one of the largest and richest cities of its time. The capital had schools and a library; learning was highly advanced. One of the most lasting contributions of the Maurya dynasty was the spreading of the Buddhist religion by means of missionary activity.

## Greece (c. 1750 B.C.–133 B.C.)

The ancient Greeks adapted ideas from many earlier cultures, such as those of Mesopotamia and Egypt. However, they also developed their own ideas about the role of the individual and how society is best governed.

### Geographic Setting

Greece, located in southeastern Europe, is made up of many mountains, isolated valleys, and small islands. This geography prevented the Greeks from building a large empire like that of Egypt or Mesopotamia. Instead the Greeks created many small city-states.

The Aegean and Mediterranean Seas were an important link to the rest of the world. The Greeks became skilled sea traders. They exchanged not only goods but ideas and technology as well. For example, the Greeks adapted the Phoenician alphabet for their own use.

### The Rise of City-States

As you know, Greece is divided by mountains into isolated valleys. In addition, hundreds of scattered islands exist off its coast. As a result, Greece did not form a large, unified empire, but existed as a collection of small city-states. A city-state was also known as a **polis.**

A polis typically was made up of two parts. There was a hilltop acropolis, which included marble temples. On the flatter ground below was the main city, within a wall. This area included the marketplace, theater, other public areas, and homes.

Between 750 B.C. and 500 B.C., the Greek city-states had several different types of government. At first, kings ruled the city-states. Over time, landowning nobles gained power, creating an **aristocracy,** a government ruled by the landholding elite.

The two most powerful city-states were Sparta and Athens. Though they shared Greek culture, they developed different ways of life.

### Militarism in Sparta

Sparta was a warrior society, and from an early age, boys trained for a lifetime in the military. At the age of seven, boys were moved into barracks, where they were toughened by a coarse diet, hard exercise, and rigid discipline. Girls were also trained to exercise rigorously and strengthen their bodies in order to give birth to healthy boys for the army. Although Sparta was an excellent military state, its power declined as a result of its rigid ways and its inability to change.

### Limited Democracy in Athens

A wise leader named Pericles ruled Athens from 460 B.C. to 429 B.C. Under Pericles, Athens had a **direct democracy,** in which a large number of the male citizens actually took part in the day-to-day running of the government. Women, however, did not participate, since Athenians believed that women were inferior to men and needed male guidance. Another group that did not participate in the Athenian democracy were enslaved people. Enslaved people had neither political rights nor any personal freedom. Even so, Athens gave a greater number of people a voice in government than did any other culture of its time.

### Key Themes and Concepts

**Movement of People and Goods**
All of the empires discussed in this section had trade ties with other cultures. Civilizations borrowed ideas and technology from trading partners and adapted them to their own use.

### Preparing for the Regents

- How did the geography of Greece affect both its economic activity and its political divisions?

### Recognize Cause

What was a cause of Sparta's decline in power?

### Preparing for the Regents

- How were the roles of women in the Athenian and Han societies similar?

- What impact did classical Greece have on the development of modern political systems?

Athens prospered during this time and became the cultural center of Greece. Great buildings were built; many thinkers, writers, and artists came to Athens.

## Athens and Sparta

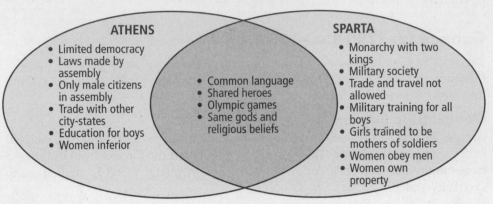

**ATHENS**
- Limited democracy
- Laws made by assembly
- Only male citizens in assembly
- Trade with other city-states
- Education for boys
- Women inferior

(Common)
- Common language
- Shared heroes
- Olympic games
- Same gods and religious beliefs

**SPARTA**
- Monarchy with two kings
- Military society
- Trade and travel not allowed
- Military training for all boys
- Girls trained to be mothers of soldiers
- Women obey men
- Women own property

**Preparing for the Regents**

- In what ways were the city-states of Sparta and Athens similar? In what ways were they different?

### Alexander the Great and the Hellenistic Age

Macedonia was a mountain kingdom north of Greece. In the 300s B.C., Philip of Macedonia conquered Greece, which had been weakened by years of civil war. His son, Alexander the Great, went on to build an empire that included the Nile Valley, Persia, and parts of India. Through his conquests Alexander spread Greek culture. A new Hellenistic culture arose that blended aspects of Greek, Persian, Egyptian, and Indian life. This culture gave more rights and opportunities to women, who even gained some political power. Although Alexander's empire fell apart soon after his death, Hellenistic culture had a lasting impact on the regions he had ruled.

### Greek and Hellenistic Contributions

Ancient Greek and Hellenistic culture left an enduring legacy. In addition to their ideas about government, Greeks made contributions in philosophy, literature, science, and the arts.

**Philosophy** Greek thinkers tried to use observation and reason to understand why things happened. The Greeks called these thinkers philosophers, a word that means "lovers of wisdom." Three of the most famous Greek philosophers were Socrates, Plato, and Aristotle.

**The Greek Philosophers**

| SOCRATES | PLATO | ARISTOTLE |
| --- | --- | --- |
| Developed Socratic method: learning about beliefs and ideas by asking questions | Believed government should control lives of people | Believed one strong and good leader should rule |
| Government put him to death | Divided society into three classes: workers, philosophers, and soldiers | Believed people learned through reason |

**The Greek Philosophers**

- **Socrates** (c. 469 B.C.–399 B.C.) was born in Athens. He was a stonemason and a teacher.

- **Plato** (c. 428 B.C.–347 B.C.) was a student of Socrates. He set up the Academy in Athens, the first known university in the Western world.

- **Aristotle** (384 B.C.–322 B.C.) was Plato's student and Alexander the Great's teacher.

**Vocabulary Builder**

epic—(EP ik) adj. an epic book, poem, or film that tells a long story about brave actions and exciting events

**Literature** The first Greek plays developed from religious festivals. Stories of the gods usually served as the basis for plays. Aeschylus, Sophocles, and Euripides wrote tragedies, plays that told stories of human conflict. Other Greek playwrights wrote comedies. In addition, the Greek poet Homer wrote epic poems that inspired many later writers. Greeks applied observation and logic to their writing of history. The Greek historian Herodotus is often called the Father of History because of his careful historical writing.

**Art and Architecture** The Greeks believed in beauty, balance, and order in the universe. Greek art and architecture reflected those ideas. Greek paintings and statues were lifelike, but they also showed the human body in its most perfect form. The most famous Greek building was the Parthenon. Architects today still use ancient Greek ideas, such as Greek column styles, in their buildings.

**Science** The astronomer Aristarchus discovered that the earth rotates on its axis and moves around the sun. Archimedes explored the principles of the lever and pulley. Hippocrates, a Greek physician, studied the causes of illness and looked for cures.

**Mathematics** Greek and Hellenistic thinkers made great strides in mathematics. Pythagoras developed a formula to measure the sides of a right triangle; Euclid wrote a book that became the basis for modern geometry.

**Key Themes and Concepts**

**Culture and Intellectual Life**
Greek art portrayed individuals in perfect form, a reflection of the Greek belief in beauty, balance, and order in the universe.

# Rome (c. 509 B.C.–A.D. 476)

## Geographic Setting

Rome is located near the center of Italy, a peninsula located in the Mediterranean. Unlike the geography of Greece, Italy's geography helped its people to unite. Low mountains presented fewer natural barriers. Fertile plains supported a growing population. In addition, the location of the Italian peninsula helped Romans to move easily through the lands of the Mediterranean.

**Key Themes and Concepts**

**Geography**
The location of Rome helped the Romans to carry on trade and build an empire around the Mediterranean Sea.

## The Roman Republic

The traditional date given for the founding of Rome is 509 B.C., when the Romans drove out the Etruscans who had ruled them. The Romans established a new form of government called a republic. In a **republic,** officials were chosen by the people. The most powerful governing body was the **Senate.** Senators were members of the landholding upper class, called **patricians.** These officials elected two consuls, who supervised the business of government and commanded the armies. The **plebeians**—farmers, merchants, artisans, and traders, who made up most of the population—had little power.

Under Roman law, the male head of the household had authority over his wife and family. During the late years of the republic and early years of the empire, however, women gained greater freedom. Roman women held prominent public roles and owned successful businesses.

**Preparing for the Regents**

• What impact did Rome have on the development of later political systems?

## The Roman Empire

By 270 B.C., Rome had conquered all of Italy. The Romans went on to conquer Carthage, Macedonia, Greece, and parts of Asia Minor. This expansion, however, led to a widening gap between rich and poor and also to increased corruption. Attempts at reform led to a series of civil wars. Out of this period of chaos, Julius Caesar came to power in 48 B.C. Caesar made new conquests as well as important reforms.

After Caesar was murdered, his grandnephew Octavian—later called Augustus— became ruler. Augustus ruled with absolute power, thus bringing the republic to an end. The age of the Roman empire had begun. The 200-year peace that began with Augustus is called the **Pax Romana,** or Roman peace. During this time, the Roman empire spread stability over a large area of the world, including parts of Europe, North Africa, and Southwest Asia.

**Recognize Effects**

**Geography**
List three effects of Pax Romana.

## Roman Contributions

Roman civilization spread to other lands. The Romans also absorbed the ideas of other cultures.

**Law** A system of laws was Rome's greatest achievement. It applied to all people and created a stable Roman empire. Many of its basic principles—including equality under the law, the right of the accused to face one's accusers and mount a defense, and the idea of being considered innocent until proven guilty—are the basis for systems of justice to this day.

In 450 B.C., the plebeians demanded written laws, saying that they could not know what the laws were if they were not written down. These **Laws of the Twelve Tables,** inscribed on twelve tablets, were displayed in the marketplace. Later, plebeians won the right to elect their own officials and serve in all kinds of government jobs.

**Art and Architecture** The Romans borrowed many Greek concepts in the arts and architecture. They used Greek-style statues in their homes and public buildings. Roman buildings were mighty and grand, however, instead of simple and elegant. Roman writers used the Latin language, which united the empire, to write great poetic, historical, and philosophical works.

**Engineering** The Romans were very practical. They built excellent roads, bridges, harbors, and **aqueducts**—bridge-like stone structures that carried water from the hills to the cities. The Romans also improved the arch and the dome.

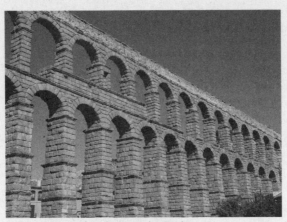

*A Roman aqueduct in Segovia, Spain*

## The Growth of Global Trade Routes

The classical civilizations engaged in trade with one another. These exchanges of goods, technology, and culture expanded from the time of the first Indian empire to the time of the Romans.

### Phoenician Trade

The Phoenicians were one of the earliest trading empires of the ancient Middle East. Phoenicia was made up of small city-states in the lands known today as Lebanon and Syria. Phoenicians made glass from sand, manufactured a purple dye from the sea snail, and created scrolls from Egyptian papyrus. Their ships carried valuable goods across the Mediterranean. As trade expanded, Phoenicia founded colonies throughout the region. The most important Phoenician contribution to history was the alphabet, developed to record business transactions. It is the basis of the alphabet we use today.

### India's Role in Trade

Even during early Indus Valley civilization, trade had gone on between the peoples of the Indian coast and Mesopotamian civilizations such as Sumer. During the 300s B.C., when Alexander expanded his territory into India, he opened a trade corridor between India and the Mediterranean. By 100 B.C., Indian goods such as

## Mediterranean Trade Routes

textiles, gems, and spices were in great demand. Some goods were sent overland into central Asia and China. Others went by ship to the Middle East, Egypt, East Africa, and Southeast Asia. Rome later became an eager market for Indian goods.

### China and the Silk Road
The Han dynasty opened a trade route called the **Silk Road** that eventually linked China with lands as far west as Mesopotamia. Silk and other Chinese goods moved west, while products such as muslin, glass, and new foods flowed into China.

The Silk Road eventually stretched for 4,000 miles. Few merchants traveled the entire distance. Most goods were traded at various markets along the way. In the west, groups such as the Persians controlled the Silk Road.

### Roman Trade
During the Pax Romana, trade flowed freely among the peoples of the Roman empire and other parts of the world. Egyptian farmers supplied grain; other Africans supplied ivory, gold, and even lions. Indians exported cotton and many spices to the Roman empire, and the Chinese supplied silk and other goods.

## Summary
Great civilizations arose in India, China, Greece, and Rome from the 300s B.C. through about A.D. 500. Strong, centralized governments allowed these civilizations to rise and remain strong. Their cultural contributions in the arts and architecture, science and engineering, and law have lasted to the present day. As global trade began to develop, these civilizations shared ideas and technology.

### Preparing for the Regents

• Practice your map skills by locating three grain-producing regions that were part of Mediterranean trade routes.

### Preparing for the Regents

List three contributions of each of the classical civilizations listed below.

India:

China:

Greece:

Rome:

# Rise and Fall of Great Empires

## Section Overview

The rise and fall of the Han dynasty and the Roman empire followed remarkably similar courses. Both empires gained power through conquest, strong central government, and profitable trade. Both eventually fell because of weak leadership, internal dissent, and aggressive invaders.

## Key Themes and Concepts

As you review this section, take special note of the following key themes and concepts:

**Political Systems** What factors contributed to the rise of both the Han dynasty and the Roman empire?

**Economic Systems** What was the importance of trade to the Han and Roman empires?

**Change** What factors contributed to the decline of both the Han and Roman empires?

## Key People and Terms

**Key People
and Terms**

Put each of the key people and terms into these two categories: Han dynasty or Roman empire.

As you review this section, be sure you understand the significance of these key people and terms:

| | | |
|---|---|---|
| **Wudi** | **Silk Road** | **Pax Romana** |
| **monopoly** | **Augustus** | |

## Factors Leading to Growth

Both the Han and the Roman empires reached their height between 200 B.C. and A.D. 200. Both empires began by throwing off oppressive rulers: the Qin in China and the Etruscans in Rome. Although many elements contributed to the growth of these two empires, the most important factors that sustained them were strong government and profitable trade.

### The Han Empire

**Key Themes
and Concepts**

**Political Systems**
Both the Han empire and the Roman empire instituted civil service systems. Working properly, such systems assured that officials were not just the most privileged or powerful people in the empire but instead were also skilled in government.

**Military Power** The most famous of the Han emperors, **Wudi,** conducted many military campaigns to secure and expand China's borders. Many of the battles he fought were attempts to drive nomadic peoples beyond the Great Wall.

**Government** Wudi worked to strengthen the Chinese government. He removed many harsh laws. Also, the civil service system helped him to choose wise officials. He set up an imperial university to train scholars in Confucian teachings.

**Economy and Trade** Initially, Wudi improved the economy internally by adding canals and roads to ease the movement of goods. He also had storage areas for grain set up throughout his empire. When grain was plentiful, the government would buy and store it. Then, when it became scarce, the government could sell it.

Another source of government revenue was income from the sale of iron and salt. Wudi created a government monopoly on these items. A **monopoly** is the complete control of a product or business by one person or group—in this case, the Han government. Sales of iron and salt allowed the government to have a source of income besides taxes. Wudi and later emperors also developed the **Silk Road,** a caravan route stretching from the Chinese capital to the Mediterranean Sea.

## The Roman Empire

**Military Power** The Romans were able to conquer partly because they had a strong, well-disciplined army. However, they also treated conquered peoples well, allowing them to keep their own governments and customs. In return, conquered lands were required to supply soldiers for the Roman army and pay taxes to Rome.

**Government** Emperor **Augustus,** who ruled the Roman empire from 31 B.C. to A.D. 14, stabilized the government. He, like the Han emperors, created a civil service system that ensured a supply of well-trained and well-educated government officials.

Both good and bad emperors followed Augustus. However, the 200-year period called the **Pax Romana,** or Roman peace, began with his reign. During this time, Roman rule brought order and prosperity to the empire. Roman legions maintained the road system and guarded the borders.

**Economy and Trade** Roman expansion allowed the empire to take over prosperous trade routes throughout the Mediterranean. The Mediterranean served as a natural highway for trade. In addition, the Romans built miles of fine roads that promoted trade and brought wealth into the empire. Grain from the Nile Valley, ivory and gold from Africa, spices and gems from India, and silk that came from China via the Silk Road flowed into the empire. Under Augustus the tax system was reformed, and new coins were issued to make trade easier.

### The Roman Empire, 44 B.C.

## Geographic Setting

The Han and Roman empires arose on opposite sides of the Eurasian landmass. Both, however, expanded their borders over time.

### Extent of the Han Empire

The Han empire was first located where the Qin had ruled: in eastern China. However, the empire expanded during Han times as Wudi secured and expanded China's borders. To the north, the Han moved into Manchuria and Korea. To the south, the empire moved into northern Vietnam. To the west, the Han gained territory in Tibet and central Asia.

### Vocabulary Builder

caravan—(KA ruh van) *n.* a group of people with animals or vehicles who travel together for safety, especially through a desert

### Key Themes and Concepts

**Economic Systems** Trade was encouraged in both the Han and Roman empires by extensive road systems.

*The Roman Empire*
*The Romans gained control of lands around the Mediterranean Sea through conquest and diplomacy.*

### Preparing for the Regents

• Name three lands that were part of the Roman empire in 44 B.C.

### Extent of the Roman Empire

Rome also expanded from its initial location in central Italy. The powerful Roman military first took over the Italian peninsula. By about 44 B.C., Roman power extended throughout the Mediterranean, from Spain to parts of Asia Minor. To the north, the Roman empire spread to what is now France as well as into parts of Great Britain.

## Causes of Decline

Both the Han and Roman empires grew weak as a result of internal problems and external pressures.

### The Han Empire

Expansion helped to strengthen the Han empire but also led to its decline.

- **Political Causes** Rulers that followed Wudi were unable to control powerful warlords in outlying areas.
- **Economic Causes** Some rulers did not maintain the systems of canals and roads, which were vital routes of commerce. As a result, the economy suffered. High taxes oppressed the peasants and thus led to a revolt.
- **Military Causes** In A.D. 220, warlords overthrew the last Han emperor, and the empire was split into several kingdoms. Invaders overran the Great Wall and set up their own kingdoms.

### The Roman Empire

Some of the same factors that led to the Han decline also led to the Roman decline. Overexpansion of the empire, high taxes, and foreign invasions all weakened the empire.

Roman emperor Diocletian divided the empire into two parts in a failed attempt to restore order. Although the decline of the Roman empire was a long, slow process, the year A.D. 476, when Germanic leader Odoacer ousted the emperor in Rome, is the date generally considered to mark its fall. The Eastern Roman empire survived, however, and became known as the Byzantine empire.

**The Fall of the Roman Empire**

| Military causes | Economic causes | Political causes | Social causes |
|---|---|---|---|
| • Visigoths and other Germanic peoples invaded the empire.<br>• Roman army lacked training and discipline.<br>• Romans were forced to hire foreign soldiers to defend borders. | • Heavy taxes were necessary to support the government.<br>• Farmers left land.<br>• Middle class disappeared.<br>• Romans used too much slave labor. | • Government became too strict.<br>• People stopped supporting government.<br>• Many officials were corrupt.<br>• Divided empire became weak. | • Population declined because of disease and war.<br>• People became selfish and lazy. |

## Summary

At opposite ends of the Eurasian landmass, two great empires thrived between 200 B.C. and A.D. 200. The Han empire in China and the Roman empire in the lands around the Mediterranean Sea shared many characteristics. Both grew through conquest and were supported for centuries by strong central governments. Far-flung trade thrived in both empires and led to prosperity. Eventually, however, internal weakness and external invasions brought about the decline of these two great empires.

# Emergence and Spread of Belief Systems

## Section Overview

Belief systems developed with the earliest humans, who saw the world as being full of spirits. With the rise of civilization, more complex belief systems developed. Hinduism and Buddhism emerged in India. In China, Confucianism and Taoism developed. In the Middle East, three great world religions—Judaism, Christianity, and Islam—grew. Each of these religions had its own beliefs and sacred texts, though all shared some concepts. Several of these religions spread and had an impact far beyond their places of origin.

## Key Themes and Concepts

As you review this section, take special note of the following key themes and concepts:

**Belief Systems** What are the characteristics of the major religions? How are they similar and different?

**Culture** How did major religions affect cultures?

**Movement of People and Goods** How did belief systems spread over large areas?

## Key People and Terms

As you review this section, be sure you understand the significance of these key people and terms:

| | | |
|---|---|---|
| animism | Buddha | hijra |
| brahman | nirvana | Qur'an |
| reincarnation | monotheistic | Sharia |
| karma | Torah | missionaries |
| dharma | Messiah | diaspora |
| Upanishads | Bible | |

## Major Belief Systems

Religious beliefs developed even in very early cultures. As civilizations arose in Africa, Europe, and Asia, more complex systems of belief developed.

### Animism

The belief that every living and nonliving thing in nature has a spirit is called **animism.** Animism was a feature of the belief systems of many early people. Stone Age paintings on the walls of caves probably express these early beliefs.

Religions of some early civilizations combined animism with reverence for ancestors. People in Shang China and in some traditional African societies, for example, believed that the spirits of deceased ancestors could affect life in a positive or negative way. The prayers of ancestors were thought to be an important way to influence the gods. Therefore, people would offer food and other necessities to their ancestors' spirits.

### The Big Idea

As civilizations developed and spread, so did belief systems and religions. These belief systems include:

- animism
- Hinduism
- Buddhism
- Confucianism
- Taoism
- Judaism
- Christianity
- Islam

### Key People and Terms

List the terms that relate to sacred texts. Write a sentence explaining the significance of each of these terms.

### Vocabulary Builder

reverence—(REV ur uns) *n.* great respect and admiration for someone or something

## Purpose for Reading

As you read the section on Hinduism, answer these questions.

1. What are the basic beliefs of Hinduism?

2. What system defines the social system of Hinduism? Explain.

## Key Themes and Concepts

**Belief Systems**
Define each of the following terms:

1. brahman

2. reincarnation

3. karma

4. dharma

# Hinduism

Hinduism is one of the oldest and most complex religions in the world. Unlike most major religions, Hinduism has no single founder. Hinduism developed and changed over 3,500 years, growing out of the diverse peoples who settled India. These groups include the original inhabitants of the Indus Valley as well as the nomadic Aryans who entered India in about 1500 B.C.

**Universal Spirit** Hindus believe in one unifying spirit, **brahman.** Because brahman is too complex for humans to understand, Hindus worship gods that give a more concrete form to brahman. The three most important Hindu gods are Brahma the Creator, Vishnu the Preserver, and Shiva the Destroyer. The goal of life is to achieve union with brahman.

**Reincarnation** Achieving union with brahman is said to occur as people free themselves from the selfish desires that separate them from the universal spirit. Most people cannot achieve this union in one lifetime. The concept of reincarnation, the rebirth of the soul in a new body, allows people to continue their journey toward union with brahman. People get closer to this union by being born into higher and higher levels of existence.

**Karma and Dharma** In each lifetime, a person can come closer to union with brahman by obeying the law of karma. Karma consists of all the deeds of a person's life that affect his or her existence in the next life. By living in a right way, a person will be reborn at a higher level. Evil deeds cause people to be reborn into a lower level. Good deeds involve following dharma, the moral and religious duties that are expected of an individual. A person's gender, class, age, and occupation all affect his or her dharma.

## The Caste System

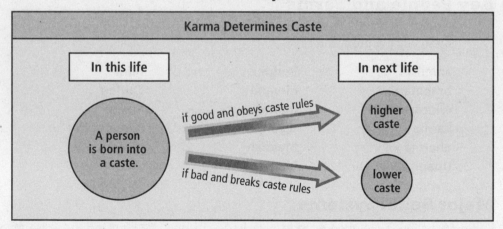

**Karma Determines Caste**

In this life — A person is born into a caste. — if good and obeys caste rules → higher caste — In next life

if bad and breaks caste rules → lower caste

## Analyzing Documents

Use the text on castes and the chart to answer the following questions:

• What judgment would Hindus make about the past life of an Untouchable?

• What judgment would Hindus make about the past life of a Brahmin?

**Castes** The caste system is an important part of Hinduism. Castes are social groups into which people are born and out of which they cannot move during a lifetime. However, a person may be born into a higher caste in the next life by acquiring good karma. The three basic caste groups during Aryan times were priests (Brahmins), warriors (Kshatriyas), and a group that included herders, farmers, artisans, and merchants (Vaisyas). Later, a separate group was created for non-Aryans. This group (Sudras) included farm workers and servants. The lowest-ranked people, called Untouchables, were at the bottom of the social system.

**Sacred Texts** Over several thousand years, Hindu teachings were developed and recorded in a number of sacred texts. These include the Vedas, collections of prayers and sacred verses, and the **Upanishads,** philosophical dialogues about Hindu beliefs.

## Buddhism

Buddhism also developed in India but later spread into other areas, such as China. Its founder, a prince named Siddhartha Gautama, was born a Hindu in the 500s B.C.

**The Enlightened One** Siddhartha Gautama left his wealthy home to search for the meaning of human suffering. While meditating under a sacred tree, he found the answer to his question, and he was thereafter referred to as the **Buddha,** or the Enlightened One.

**The Four Noble Truths** The central philosophy of Buddhism revolves around the Four Noble Truths.

1. All life is suffering.
2. Suffering is caused by desire for things that are illusions.
3. The way to eliminate suffering is to eliminate desire.
4. Following the Eightfold Path will help people overcome desire.

**The Eightfold Path** The Eightfold Path involves right views, right intentions, right speech, right conduct, right livelihood, right effort, right mindfulness, and right meditation. The ultimate goal is **nirvana,** union with the universe and release from the cycle of death and rebirth.

**Comparison With Hinduism** Buddhism accepts the Hindu concepts of karma, dharma, and reincarnation. However, Buddhism rejects the many Hindu gods as well as the rituals and priesthood of Hinduism. Buddhists do, however, accept the idea of religious communities that include monks and nuns. Buddhism also rejected the caste system.

**Sacred Texts** After the Buddha died, his teachings were collected into the *Tripitaka*, or "Three Baskets of Wisdom." This collection is made up of rules for Buddhist monks; sermons; and discussions of Buddhist beliefs. Later, other Buddhists added many more scriptures.

## Two Philosophies of China

The late Zhou dynasty was a troubled time in China. There were many wars, and economic and social changes disrupted everyday life. Beginning in the 500s B.C., several major Chinese philosophies developed. Two of the most important were Confucianism and Taoism. These philosophies shared the common purpose of restoring harmony.

**Confucianism** Confucius, born in 551 B.C., was China's most influential thinker. Confucius's teachings, collected in *The Analects*, taught people to accept their given places in society. These individual places were expressed through five key relationships.

Confucius believed that, except for friendships, none of these relationships was equal. Older people were superior to younger, for example, and men were superior to women. Every person had duties and responsibilities that depended on his or her position.

Other ideas of Confucius include the following:

- People are naturally good.
- Education should be the road to advancement in society.
- To ensure social order, the individual must find and accept his or her proper place in society.

### Recognize Effects

As you read the sections *Buddhism* and *Two Philosophies of China*, answer these questions.

1. What is the effect of following the Eightfold Path?

2. According to Confucius, what is the effect of following proper relationships in society?

### Preparing for the Regents

List two similarities and two differences between the Hindu and Buddhist religions.

Similarities:

1.

2.

Differences:

1.

2.

### Proper Relationships

Superior ruler, husband, father, elder brother

takes care of and sets good example for

owes loyalty and obedience to

Inferior subject, wife, son, younger brother

## Vocabulary Builder

mystic—(MIS tik) *n.* someone who follows the religious practice in which people try to get knowledge of truth and to become united with God through prayer and meditation

## Preparing for the Regents

• Make a chart comparing the basic ideas of Confucianism and Taoism.

**Taoism** Another influential Chinese philosophy was Taoism (often spelled *Daoism*). Taoism sought to help people to live in harmony with nature. Laozi, who founded Taoism, taught people to contemplate the Tao, or the "way" of the universe. Important virtues in Taoism are yielding and acceptance. Followers of Laozi rejected the world and human government and often withdrew to become hermits, mystics, or poets.

Taoists also believe in a balance between yin and yang. The yin stands for Earth, darkness, and female forces. The yang stands for Heaven, light, and male forces. The peace and well-being of the universe depend on harmony between yin and yang.

The beliefs of Taoism are collected in two works. Laozi is traditionally thought to be the author of the first, *The Way of Virtue*. A second text is the *Zhuang-zi*, written several centuries later. It contains fables, sayings, and dialogues.

## Judaism

The Hebrews were one of the nomadic groups who lived in the Fertile Crescent. According to Hebrew tradition, the Hebrews became enslaved in Egypt, and God helped them escape this slavery. By about 1000 B.C., the Hebrews had set up the kingdom of Israel with Jerusalem as its capital. They believed that God had promised them this land. Over time, Hebrew beliefs evolved into the religion we today call Judaism. Several beliefs are very important to Judaism.

**Belief in One God** Judaism is **monotheistic,** teaching a belief in one God. Most other religions of the time worshiped many gods and goddesses. The Hebrews believed that God was their special protector and was all-knowing, all-powerful, and present everywhere.

## Key Themes and Concepts

**Belief Systems**
Judaism influenced the development of two later monotheistic world religions: Islam and Christianity.

**Sacred Texts and Moral Teachings** According to the sacred scriptures of the Hebrews, the **Torah,** God made a covenant, or a binding agreement, to be the God of the Hebrews. Jews also believe that God gave them the Ten Commandments through Moses. These are laws that describe how people should behave toward God and each other. The Old Testament of the Bible includes the Torah, which is made up of five books. The Torah also sets out many other laws that establish the moral basis for Judaism.

Hebrew sacred scriptures also include the writings of spiritual leaders called prophets, who urged Hebrews to act according to God's teachings. The prophets preached a strong code of ethics, or moral standards of behavior. Judaic thought had a strong influence on two other world religions: Christianity and Islam.

**Judaism**

Prophets taught about moral standards and justice.

One true God is present everywhere.

God made a covenant with Abraham.

Judaism

The Torah is a sacred recording of laws and events in Jewish history.

God gave the Hebrews the Ten Commandments through Moses.

God chose the Hebrews as his people.

## Christianity

Christianity began in Palestine with the teachings of a Jew named Jesus in about A.D. 30. Beginning with a small group of followers, Christianity grew and spread to become the official religion of the Roman empire by A.D. 392.

**Life and Death of Jesus**   According to Christian tradition, Jesus' mother, Mary, had been told before his birth that he would be the Messiah. **Messiah** is the Jewish word, derived from Hebrew, for a savior sent by God. Jesus grew up worshiping God and following Jewish law. At about age 30, he began to travel through the countryside preaching and teaching new beliefs.

Many Jews and Romans worried that Jesus was dangerous. Around A.D. 29, the Romans arrested Jesus, tried him, and executed him by crucifixion. By this method a person was tied or nailed to a cross and left to die. After Jesus' death, many of his followers said that he had risen from the grave. His followers worked to spread his teachings. The Romans persecuted Christians, who set up an organized church. In A.D. 313, Roman Emperor Constantine ended the persecution of Christians. In A.D. 392, Christianity became the official religion of the Roman Empire.

**Teachings of Jesus**   The teachings of Jesus were rooted in Jewish tradition. For example, Jesus accepted the Ten Commandments that God had given to the Jews through Moses. At the same time, he preached new ideas. According to his followers, he was the son of God and the savior that the Jews had been expecting. His mission was to bring salvation and eternal life to anyone who would follow his teachings. Jesus taught mercy and sympathy for the poor and helpless. Jesus also preached brotherhood and the equality of people before God.

**Sacred Text**   The sacred text of Christianity is the Christian **Bible.** It has two parts. The Old Testament includes the Hebrew scriptures, books of law, history, prophetic writing, and poetry. The New Testament includes the Gospels (describing Jesus and his teachings) and other writings, mostly letters written by Christians that explain Christian doctrine.

### Christianity

- Faith in one God
- Salvation and eternal life go to those who follow Jesus
- Jesus was the son of God and the Messiah
- Jesus' teachings included mercy and sympathy for poor and helpless brotherhood and equality of people before God
- God gave the Hebrews the Ten Commandments through Moses
- The Bible includes the Old Testament from Judaism and the New Testament

**Christianity**

**Preparing for the Regents**

- Prepare a timeline that shows events in the growth of Christianity as well as several other global events of the same period.

**Compare and Contrast**

Look at the concept webs for Judaism and Christianity. Compare and contrast the information. Write two similarities and two differences.

**Key Themes and Concepts**

**Belief Systems**
Jews, Christians, and Muslims all believe in one God, and their holy writings share many themes and ethics. Despite these similarities, the three groups have often come into conflict, as they did during the Crusades in the 1000s. Even today, especially in the Middle East, these groups do not always coexist peacefully.

## Note Taking

*Reading Skill:*
**Recognize Sequence**
Keep track of the sequence of events described in this section about Islam. Use a chart like the one below. Add boxes as necessary.

## Vocabulary Builder

compassionate—(kum PASH un it) *adj.* feeling sympathy for people who are suffering; kind and generous

## Islam

In A.D. 622, a new religion called Islam arose in Arabia. Like Christians and Jews, people who follow Islam believe in one God.

**Life of Muhammad** In about 570, an Arab named Muhammad was born in Mecca. Muhammad became a caravan merchant, married, and had children. He was troubled, however, by the idol worship of the Arabs of the time. According to Muslim tradition, the angel Gabriel commanded Muhammad to spread the message of Islam.

Muhammad obeyed this command. Soon Meccan merchants sought to kill him. In 622, Muhammad and his followers left Mecca for Yathrib (later named Medina) on a journey known as the **hijra** (often spelled hegira). The hijra was a turning point for Islam. Muslim converts in Medina welcomed Muhammad, and the religion grew.

**Muslim Beliefs** The followers of Islam are called Muslims. All Muslims accept five basic duties, known as the Five Pillars. First, Muslims believe in one God, Allah, who is compassionate and all-powerful. Muhammad is God's greatest prophet. Second, Muslims are expected to pray five times daily. Third, Muslims are expected to give money to the poor. Fourth, Muslims are expected to fast from sunrise to sunset during the holy month of Ramadan. Fifth, Muslims are supposed to visit Mecca at least once in their lives.

**Sacred Text** The sacred scriptures of Islam are contained in the **Qur'an.** The Qur'an is the final authority on all matters and provides a guide to life for Muslims. Muslim scholars have also developed an immense body of laws, called the **Sharia,** that covers all aspects of life. Over time, this system of law acted as a means to unite Muslims of differing backgrounds.

### The Five Duties of Islam

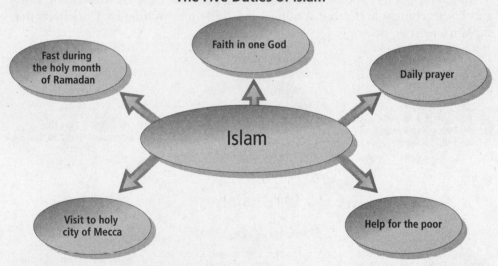

Fast during the holy month of Ramadan

Faith in one God

Daily prayer

Islam

Visit to holy city of Mecca

Help for the poor

## Key Themes and Concepts

**Movement of People and Goods**
Three ways in which religions spread were through missionary activity, military conquest, and trade.

## Expansion of World Religions

Some of the religions discussed here, such as Confucianism and Taoism, remained within a fairly limited geographical area. Hinduism spread throughout India and into Southeast Asia. Other religions spread more widely.

## Spread of Buddhism

Over the centuries, the Buddha's teachings won wide acceptance. The Mauryan ruler Asoka converted to Buddhism and sent messengers to spread Buddhist beliefs. Over time, traders and **missionaries,** or people dedicated to spreading a religion, spread Buddhism far beyond India to many parts of Asia, including China, Japan, Korea, and Southeast Asia. In India, where Buddhism started, it eventually declined.

## Spread of Judaism

Judaism spread in a unique way. The Romans expelled the Jews from Palestine in A.D. 135. This event became known as the **diaspora,** or scattering of people. Wherever Jews settled, they lived in close-knit communities and maintained their identity through the careful preservation of tradition.

## Spread of Christianity

Christianity first spread through the work of Christian missionaries such as Paul. Even though Roman rulers persecuted Christians, the religion continued to spread throughout the Roman empire. This occurred for many reasons. The poor and oppressed found comfort in Jesus' message of love and a better life after death. Also, Christian missionaries often added Greek concepts to their teaching of the religion, appealing to educated Romans as well as others. In 313, Emperor Constantine allowed freedom of worship throughout the Roman empire. Later, Emperor Theodosius made Christianity the official religion of the empire.

After the fall of the Western Roman empire, missionaries continued to spread Christianity throughout Europe. Trading networks also spread Christianity, especially as Europe began voyages of exploration and expansion in the 1400s. Europeans took Christianity with them when they established settlements in the Americas, Africa, and Asia.

## Spread of Islam

In the 150 years after the death of Muhammad, Islam spread over three continents. Skillful Arab fighters spread Islam through military conquest. Because the Arabs treated conquered peoples in a fair way, many people converted to Islam willingly. The teaching of Islam appealed to many because it emphasized honesty, generosity, and social justice.

Trade had always been considered an honorable occupation for Muslims. Muslims built vast trading empires. Merchants established trading networks with Africa, China, and India. In India, Muslim traders were an important means of spreading Islam. At the other end of the Eurasian landmass, Islam spread from North Africa into Spain.

## Summary

Many belief systems emerged over time in various parts of the world. In India, Hinduism and Buddhism developed. In China, Confucianism and Taoism were significant philosophies. In the Middle East, Judaism, Christianity, and Islam developed. All of these belief systems had important effects on the civilizations of their time as well as later on. Several belief systems spread widely through missionary effort, conquest, and trade.

**Identify Supporting Details**

Describe how each of these religions spread throughout the world:
- Buddhism:
- Judaism:
- Christianity:
- Islam:

**Key Themes and Concepts**

**Movement of People and Goods**
Although Christians were initially persecuted, Christianity spread throughout the Roman empire. Eventually, Christianity became the official religion of the empire.

**Preparing for the Regents**

Describe a major belief of each of the belief systems that follows.

Hinduism:

Buddhism:

Confucianism:

Taoism:

Judaism:

Christianity:

Islam:

# Questions for Regents Practice

**Multiple Choice**

*Directions:* Review the Test-Taking Strategies section of this book. Then answer the following questions, drawn from actual Regents examinations. For each statement or question, choose the *number* of the word or expression that, of those given, best completes the statement or answers the question.

1   One result of the Neolithic Revolution was
   (1) an increase in the number of nomadic tribes
   (2) a reliance on hunting and gathering for food
   (3) the establishment of villages and the rise of governments
   (4) a decrease in trade between cultural groups

2   The ancient civilizations of Mesopotamia and Egypt were similar in that both cultures
   (1) established trade routes to China
   (2) used the ziggurat form for their temples
   (3) developed along rivers
   (4) used a hieroglyphic writing system

3   "If a seignior [noble] has knocked out the tooth of a seignior of his own rank, they shall knock out his tooth. But if he has knocked out a commoner's tooth, he shall pay one-third mina of silver."

   —Code of Hammurabi

   Which idea of Babylonian society does this portion of the Hammurabi code of law reflect?
   (1) All men were equal under the law.
   (2) Fines were preferable to corporal punishment.
   (3) Divisions existed between social classes.
   (4) Violence was always punished with violence.

4   The early civilizations of the Nile River valley, Mesopotamia, and the Huang He were similar because they were
   (1) dependent on fertile land
   (2) monotheistic
   (3) industrialized societies
   (4) dependent on each other for trade

5   All citizens in ancient Athens had the right to attend the assembly, where they could meet in the open to discuss and cast votes. This situation is an example of
   (1) direct democracy
   (2) totalitarianism
   (3) parliamentary democracy
   (4) absolutism

6   A major contribution of the Roman empire to western society was the development of
   (1) gunpowder
   (2) the principles of feudalism
   (3) monotheism
   (4) an effective legal system

**7** A major impact of ancient Greece and Rome on western civilization was that

(1) the Greeks and Romans achieved a classless society, which was later copied in Western Europe

(2) Greek sculpture and Roman architecture were much admired and copied in Western Europe in later centuries

(3) Greece and Rome transmitted Islamic philosophy to the areas they conquered

(4) Greek and Latin are still widely spoken in universities throughout the West

**8** In traditional India, the caste system and the Hindu beliefs in karma and dharma most directly resulted in

(1) the establishment of a set of rules for each individual in society

(2) the rapid industrialization of the economy

(3) a strong emphasis on the acquisition of wealth

(4) a strong belief in the importance of education

**9** According to the teachings of Confucius, the key to the successful organization of society is that

(1) the ruler should be chosen democratically

(2) the evil in humans must be eliminated

(3) ancestor worship should be discontinued

(4) individuals should know and do what is expected of them

**10** The Qu'ran, Mecca, and the hijra (hegira) are most closely associated with the practice of

(1) Islam

(2) Judaism

(3) Christianity

(4) Buddhism

**11** One similarity between the Five Pillars of Islam and the Ten Commandments is that both

(1) support a belief in reincarnation

(2) promote learning as a means to salvation

(3) encourage the use of statues to symbolize God

(4) provide a guide to proper ethical and moral behavior

**12** One way in which the Eightfold Path and the Five Pillars of Islam are similar is that these rules

(1) represent codes of behavior

(2) restrict social mobility

(3) stress the spiritual being in all natural objects

(4) suggest a deep respect for nature and reincarnation

**13** Hammurabi's Code, the Ten Commandments, and the Twelve Tables were all significant to their societies because they established

(1) democratic governments

(2) official religions

(3) rules of behavior

(4) economic systems

**14** What was one effect of Alexander the Great's conquests?

(1) expansion of Hellenistic culture

(2) formation of the Christian church

(3) decreased importance of the Silk Roads

(4) increased support of the Mayan leaders

# Thematic Essay Question

In developing your answer, be sure to keep these general definitions in mind:

    (a) <u>describe</u> means "to illustrate something in words or tell about it"
    (b) <u>explain</u> means "to make plain or understandable; to give reasons for or causes of; to show the logical development or relationships of"

*Directions:*   Write a well-organized essay that includes an introduction, several paragraphs addressing the task below, and a conclusion.

**Theme:**   **Civilization**

> Throughout history, great civilizations have existed in various parts of the world. The cultural and intellectual achievements of these civilizations contributed to the advancement of humankind.

**Tasks:**

> - Define the term *civilization*
> - Describe some examples of cultural or intellectual achievements made by past civilizations
> - Identify each example with the particular civilization that made the contribution
> - Explain the lasting importance of each of these achievements or contributions to global history

  You may discuss any civilization from your study of global history, except the United States. Some civilizations you might wish to consider include ancient Egypt, classical Rome, the Gupta empire, classical China, or the Muslim golden age.

You are not limited to these suggestions.

**Guidelines:**

    **In your essay, be sure to**
- Develop all aspects of the task
- Support the theme with relevant facts, examples, and details
- Use a logical and clear plan of organization, including an introduction and a conclusion that are beyond a simple restatement of the theme

# Document-Based Question

This question is based on the accompanying documents. The question is designed to test your ability to work with historical documents. Some of these documents have been edited for the purposes of this question. As you analyze the documents, take into account the source of each document and any point of view that may be presented in the document.

**Historical Context:**

> Throughout global history, people have established different systems of government. They have been based on different views of how people should be ruled.

**Task:** Using the information from the documents and your knowledge of global history, answer the questions that follow each document in Part A. Your answers to the questions will help you write the Part B essay in which you will be asked to

> - Evaluate different perspectives on government
> - Discuss the best kind of government

In developing your answers, be sure to keep these general definitions in mind:

(a) <u>evaluate</u> means "to examine and judge the significance, worth, or condition of; to determine the value of"

(b) <u>discuss</u> means "to make observations about something using facts, reasoning, and argument; to present in some detail"

# Document-Based Question

## Part A: Short Answer

*Directions:*   Analyze the documents and answer the question or questions that follow each document, using the space provided.

### Document #1

### The Mandate of Heaven

1. According to this chart, how did Chinese rulers lose power?

_____

_____

2. How did Chinese rulers show that they had the Mandate of Heaven?

_____

_____

**Document #2**

*People become naturally spoiled by love, but are submissive to authority. . . . That being so, rewards should be rich and certain so that the people will be attracted to them; punishments should be severe and definite so that the people will fear them; and laws should be uniform and steadfast so that the people will be familiar with them.*

**—Hanfeizi, 200s B.C.**

3. According to this philosophy, what is the best way to make sure that people will respect and obey government?

_____

_____

**Document #3**

*We differ from other states in regarding the man who holds aloof from public life not as "quiet" but as useless; we decide or debate, carefully and in person, all matters of policy, holding, not that words and deeds go ill together, but that acts are foredoomed to failure when undertaken undiscussed.*

**—Speech of Pericles (431 B.C.) in Thucydides, History of the Peloponnesian War**

4. According to Pericles of Athens, what was the best way for a government to make decisions?

_____

_____

# Document-Based Question

## Part B

## Essay

*Directions:*    Write a well-organized essay that includes an introduction, several paragraphs, and a conclusion. Use evidence from *at least two* of the documents in your essay. Support your response with relevant facts, examples, and details. Include additional outside information.

### Historical Context:

Throughout global history, people have established different systems of government. They have been based on different views of how people should be ruled.

### Task:

Using the information from the documents and your knowledge of global history, write an essay in which you

- Evaluate different perspectives on government
- Discuss the best kind of government

### Guidelines:

**In your essay, be sure to**

- Develop all aspects of the task
- Incorporate information from *at least two* of the documents
- Incorporate relevant outside information
- Support the theme with relevant facts, examples, and details
- Use a logical and clear plan of organization, including an introduction and a conclusion that are beyond a restatement of the theme

# Expanding Zones of Exchange
## (500–1200)

## Unit Overview

During the period from about 500 to 1200, civilizations matured in various regions of the world. The Gupta dynasty united northern India. The Tang and Song dynasties each ruled a unified China. In southeastern Europe and the Middle East, the Byzantine empire carried on the traditions of Greece and Rome. The first Russian state was founded in Kiev. Islamic civilization flourished across several continents. In Europe, Christianity, feudalism, and the manor system dominated life.

As civilizations expanded, they often encountered one another. Sometimes the encounters were peaceful; at other times, violent. Always, however, encounters led to exchanges of people, goods, and ideas.

## Thematic Timeline Activity

Some of the many themes developed in Unit 2 are:

| | | |
|---|---|---|
| economic systems | diversity | interdependence |
| culture and intellectual life | power | political systems |
| movement of people and goods | belief systems | |

Choose one of the themes listed above. As you review Unit 2, create a thematic timeline based on the theme you have chosen. Your timeline should stretch from 500 to 1200 and include major developments and key turning points having to do with your theme.

# The Gupta Empire in India

## The Big Idea

During Gupta rule, the people of India:

• experienced peace and prosperity under a strong government.

• were influenced greatly by Hindu ideas.

• produced many achievements in the arts and sciences.

## Section Overview

The Gupta dynasty came to power in India in A.D. 320 and ruled until 550. The strong Gupta government, which gave power to local leaders, united much of the Indian subcontinent and ensured peace and prosperity. Hinduism had a very strong impact on Gupta society and cultural life. Gupta scientists and mathematicians made important discoveries and advances.

## Key Themes and Concepts

As you review this section, take special note of the following key themes and concepts:

**Political Systems** What were some key characteristics of Gupta rule?

**Belief Systems** How did Hinduism influence Gupta society and culture?

**Culture and Intellectual Life** What advances did people of the Gupta empire make in the arts and sciences?

### Key People and Terms

Place each of the key people and terms into these two categories: political system or culture/intellectual life.

## Key People and Terms

As you review this section, be sure you understand the significance of these key people and terms:

| | | | |
|---|---|---|---|
| Gupta dynasty | Untouchables | patriarchal | Arabic numerals |
| Pataliputra | joint families | decimal system | stupas |

### Note Taking

**Reading Skill:
Identify Effects**
Make a concept web. Fill in the impact of Hinduism on Gupta life. Add circles if necessary.

Impact of Hindusm on Gupta life

## Geographic Setting

About 500 years after the rule of the Maurya dynasty in India, the **Gupta dynasty** came to power. The Mauryas and the Guptas were the only early Indian civilizations to be able to unite the subcontinent under their rule. Both arose in the north and spread southward. Geography benefited the northern empires in various ways. Mountains helped protect these civilizations from foreign invaders. In addition, the Indus and Ganges Rivers flowed through the northern region, providing water and fertile soil. The Gupta period was one of peace and prosperity for India.

## The Influence of Hinduism

Hinduism had a strong impact on all areas of Gupta life. The Gupta dynasty adopted and actively promoted Hinduism. This set of beliefs affected the social life of Gupta villages through the caste system. Hinduism also had a strong effect on the flowering of cultural and intellectual achievements during the Gupta era.

## The Maurya and Gupta Empires

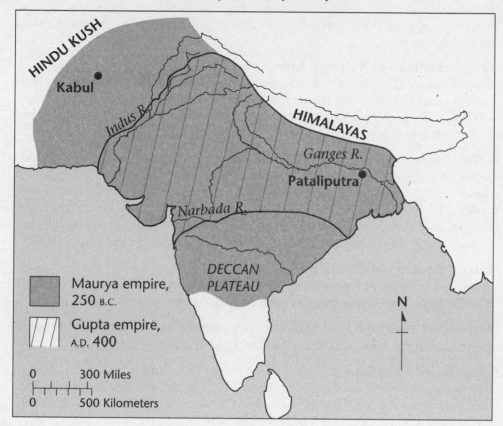

**The Maurya and Gupta Empires**
*The Maurya and Gupta emperors united much of India under one rule. These empires included parts of present-day India, Pakistan, Afghanistan, Bangladesh, and Nepal.*

### Preparing for the Regents

- What geographic features of India were beneficial to both the Maurya and Gupta empires? Explain.

## Gupta Government

### Central Government

Gupta emperors ruled over a spectacular court at **Pataliputra**, the former Mauryan capital on the Ganges River. An efficient central government allowed farming and trade to prosper and provided a stable background for advances in learning and the arts.

### Local Government

Although the Gupta rulers maintained a strong central government, they also gave great power to local leaders. These leaders were elected by merchants and artisans. In each village, a headman and council made decisions for the village. The most respected people of the village served on the council.

### Role of Women

In earlier times, women were allowed to serve on the councils. Over time, however, Hindu law placed greater restrictions on women, excluding them from participation.

## Hinduism and Gupta Society

Society came to be ordered by Hindu concepts during the Gupta period. Most Indian people lived in small villages, where Hindu ideas about caste and family regulated society.

### The Caste System

Caste had originated in early Aryan times, and by the time of Gupta rule, the system had expanded from four basic castes to include many more groupings.

### Key Themes and Concepts

**Political Systems**
Gupta emperors established a stable central government but also shared power with local leaders. The resulting peace and prosperity contributed to a golden age in India.

## Key Themes and Concepts

**Belief Systems**
Hindu beliefs governed village life, creating a stable society.

## Preparing for the Regents

- How did the Hindu caste system affect village and family life in Gupta India?

- Examine the role of women in Gupta life. How does it compare to the role of women in other civilizations and societies you have studied?

People believed that their karma, all the good and bad things they had done in life, determined their caste. People could not change their caste in one lifetime, but they could be born into a higher caste in the next life by fulfilling moral duties, or dharma.

### Organization of Village Life

The village was the center of Indian life during Gupta times. A cluster of homes built of earth and stone was surrounded by fields, where farmers grew their crops. Villages ran their own affairs and faced little interference from the central government as long as they paid their taxes.

Village life was governed by caste rules and traditions. These strong traditions created a stable society. People in the higher castes had the strictest rules, which were designed to keep them from being contaminated by people from lower castes. The **Untouchables** were outcasts who lived harsh lives. They were given the jobs that were considered "impure," such as cleaning the streets or digging graves. Untouchables had to live apart from the other members of Gupta society.

### Organization of Family Life

In villages, wealthier persons often lived in **joint families,** where parents, children, grandparents, uncles, and their children shared a common home.

**Patriarchal Structure** Indian families were patriarchal, with the father or oldest male heading the household. Heads of families had great authority.

**Children and Marriage** Indian children learned the family trade or worked in the fields and were taught what would be expected of them as adults. An important duty for parents was to arrange the marriage of their children. Hindu law required that people marry only within their own caste.

**Role of Women** Although the status of women varied throughout India, the role of women generally became more restricted over time because of the development of Hindu law. By the end of Gupta rule, upper-class women were largely restricted to their homes and had to cover themselves from head to foot when they went out. Lower-class women worked in the fields or did spinning and weaving.

## Scientific and Artistic Contributions

An environment of peace and prosperity allowed scientific and artistic achievements to flourish during the Gupta dynasty. Education took place at religious institutions. At Hindu and Buddhist centers, students learned subjects such as mathematics, medicine, physics, and languages.

### Mathematics

**Zero and the Decimal System** Indian mathematicians developed the concept of zero as well as the decimal system. The decimal system is the system we use, based on the number 10.

**Arabic Numerals** Gupta mathematicians developed the system of writing numerals that we use today. They are known as Arabic numerals because Arabs brought them from India to the Middle East and Europe.

### Medicine

Gupta physicians began to use herbs and other remedies to treat illnesses. Surgeons were able to set bones and repair facial injuries with plastic surgery. Furthermore, Gupta physicians vaccinated people against smallpox approximately 1,000 years before this practice began in Europe.

## Architecture

Architects built beautiful stone temples for Hindu worship. A typical shape was a square (symbolizing the Earth) within a circle (which stood for eternity). Hindu temples were filled with carvings of gods and goddesses, animals such as elephants and monkeys, and ordinary people.

Buddhist architects constructed **stupas,** large dome-shaped shrines that contained the remains of holy people. These Buddhist shrines were plain but included gateways with elaborate carvings that depicted the life of Buddha.

## Literature

Extraordinary works of literature were created during the Gupta dynasty. Fables and folk tales in the Sanskrit language were collected and recorded. These stories were carried west to Persia, Egypt, and Greece.

# End of Gupta Rule

After about 200 years, the Gupta empire declined because of weak rulers and foreign invasions. The invaders were the White Huns from central Asia, nomads who destroyed villages and disrupted trade in the Gupta empire.

# Summary

The Gupta dynasty reigned successfully through a strong central government that also gave great power to local leaders. Gupta rule helped India to enjoy peace and prosperity for 200 years. The rules and rituals of Hinduism governed daily life. The Gupta era became known for its significant contributions to science, medicine, mathematics, architecture, art, and literature.

## Key Themes and Concepts

**Culture and Intellectual Life**
Religion was a strong influence in Indian art and architecture. Gupta architects built beautiful temples for both the Buddhist and Hindu religions.

## Recognize Causes

What were the causes of the decline of the Gupta empire?

## Preparing for the Regents

Describe the achievements of the Gupta dynasty in each of the categories listed.

**Mathematics:**

**Medicine:**

**Architecture:**

**Literature:**

# Tang and Song Dynasties in China

## Section Overview

The Tang dynasty came to power in China in 618 and ruled until 907. This dynasty unified China and expanded the empire. The Song dynasty ruled China from 960 to 1279. Under the Tang and Song dynasties, government was efficient and society was well structured and stable. Farming and trade flourished. China produced great advances in literature, art, and architecture. During this period, Chinese culture spread to Japan.

## Key Themes and Concepts

As you review this section, take special note of the following key themes and concepts:

**Political Systems** How did the Tang dynasty unite China and keep it strong?

**Economic Systems** How did Tang and Song rulers help the economy to flourish?

**Culture and Intellectual Life** What were the Tang and Song dynasties' contributions to the arts and architecture?

**Movement of People and Goods** How did Tang and Song China influence Japanese culture?

## Key Terms

**Key Terms**

Place each of the key terms into these two categories: political system or art. Write a sentence for each term explaining your choice.

As you review this section, be sure you understand the significance of these key terms:

| | | |
|---|---|---|
| **Tang dynasty** | **gentry** | **pagoda** |
| **tributary states** | **calligraphy** | **porcelain** |
| **Song dynasty** | | |

## The Rise and Fall of Dynasties

After the Han dynasty declined in the A.D. 200s, China was divided for nearly 400 years. Then, in the 600s, a young general came to power. He took the name Tang Taizong and established the **Tang dynasty,** a powerful dynasty that ruled China from 618 to 907.

The Tang dynasty built a vast empire with its capital at Xian (Changan). Tang rulers forced Vietnam, Korea, and Tibet to become **tributary states.** These states remained independent, but their rulers had to acknowledge China's greater power and send tribute, or regular payment. Japan sent missions to China to conduct trade and study Chinese culture.

Government corruption, drought, and rebellions all contributed to the collapse of the Tang dynasty in 907. Then, in 960, a scholarly general named Zhao Kuangyin reunited China under the **Song dynasty.** China prospered under Song rule, but the dynasty was weakened by invaders. The Song dynasty was finally conquered by the Mongols in 1279.

## Government and Society

Confucianist beliefs guided both the nature of the government and the structure of the society. Confucian thought stressed social order based on duty, rank, and proper behavior.

### Skillful Government

Tang rulers revived the civil service system that had first been developed during the Han dynasty. People who wanted to hold office had to pass difficult examinations that emphasized Confucian philosophy. Rulers set up schools that prepared male students to take these exams. This system gave Tang and Song China a highly educated ruling class.

### Strict Social Order

China had a strict social structure under the Tang and Song dynasties. Chinese social structure consisted of three main classes: the gentry, the peasantry, and the merchants.

**Key Themes and Concepts**

**Government**
The Tang dynasty revived and improved the civil service system. As a result, both Tang and Song China had a highly educated ruling class.

**Vocabulary Builder**

revive—(rih VYV) v. to bring something back after it has not been used or has not existed for a period of time

**The Tang and Song Dynasties, 618–1215**

**Legend:**
- Tang dynasty
- Song dynasty, 1050
- Song dynasty, 1150
- Trade routes

**Preparing for the Regents**

• Use the map to explain how the extent of Song rule changed between 1050 and 1150.

*The Tang and Song Dynasties Dynasties ruled China for most of its history until 1912. Under the Tang and Song Dynasties, China experienced a prosperous economy and rich culture.*

**Preparing for the Regents**

Describe the role and status of each of the following groups in Tang and Song China.

Gentry:

Peasants:

Merchants:

Women:

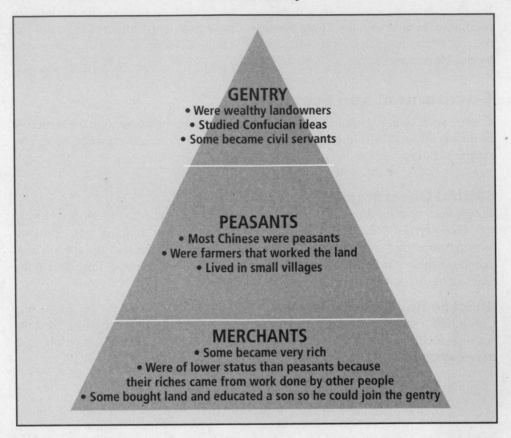

**Vocabulary Builder**

scholarship—(SKAHL ur ship) *n.* the knowledge, work, or methods involved in serious studying

**Key Themes and Concepts**

**Economic Systems**
Many aspects of Tang and Song rule benefited the economy. Land reform created more tax revenue. Improvements in farming increased productivity. The expansion of trade brought money into the empire from outside China. Better transportation improved economic efficiency.

**Gentry** The gentry were wealthy landowners who preferred scholarship over physical labor. Confucian thought was valued, and members of the gentry sometimes spent years studying it. The gentry had to pass a civil service examination to obtain honored positions in government.

**Peasants** Most Chinese were peasants. They worked the land and lived on what they produced. To supplement their income, they sometimes sold or traded handicrafts. Peasants lived in small villages that managed their own affairs.

**Merchants** Although some merchants acquired vast wealth, they held a lower social status than the peasants because their wealth came from the labor of others. As a result, some merchants bought land and educated their sons to enter the ranks of the gentry.

**Status of Women** Under the Tang and Song dynasties, many women held great authority. Within the home, women managed family finances, imposed discipline, and supervised servants. However, boys were still valued over girls. When a girl married, she was required to become a part of her husband's family and could never remarry.

## Economic Achievements
### Land Reform
During the Tang dynasty, a system of land reform redistributed land to peasants. Large landowners had less power, and peasants could contribute to government revenue by paying taxes.

## Expanded Trade

Foreign trade expanded under both the Tang and Song dynasties. Chinese merchants traded with India, Persia, and the Middle East. The Chinese became expert shipbuilders and emerged as a naval power. To improve trade, the government issued paper money—the world's first.

## Canals

Canals were built to encourage trade and improve transportation. The Grand Canal was the largest, linking the Huang He and the Yangzi. This canal allowed food from farms in southern China to be sent north.

# Literature and Arts

The arts were important during the Tang and Song dynasties. Chinese writers wrote short stories and poetry. Chinese landscape painting became popular during the Song period, and **calligraphy**—fine handwriting—flourished. Chinese architects created the **pagoda,** a temple with a roof that curved up at the corners. The Chinese became experts at making **porcelain,** a hard, shiny pottery.

# Chinese Influence on Japan

The Japanese first learned about Chinese culture through Korea. During the Tang dynasty, a Japanese prince sent nobles to China to study. Japanese nobles continued to bring Chinese ideas and technology back to Japan. By the 800s, as the Tang dynasty began to decline, the Japanese had begun to blend Chinese ideas with their own to create a unique culture.

**Draw Conclusions**

The Chinese influence over Japan changed from the 600s to the 1200s. Why?

### Japan Adapts Chinese Ideas

| 600s–700s | 800s | 900s–1200s |
|---|---|---|
| • Japanese study Chinese civilization.<br>• Emperor builds capital city modeled on Chinese capital.<br>• Japanese nobles adopt Chinese language, food, and style of dress.<br>• Japanese nobles adopt Chinese tea ceremony, music, dance, and gardens. | • Japanese stop traveling to China. | • Japanese keep some Chinese ways but build their own civilization.<br>• Japanese artists develop their own styles.<br>• Japanese change the Chinese system of writing. |

# Summary

Chinese civilization flourished under the Tang and Song. Efficient government was fueled by an educated ruling class, thanks to the revival of the civil service system. A fixed social structure added stability. Land reform, advances in farming, canals, and increased trade helped the empire economically. China made contributions in art, literature, and architecture. Chinese culture influenced other lands, including Japan.

**Preparing for the Regents**

List one achievement of the Tang or Song dynasty in each of the following categories.

**Government:**

**Economy:**

**Art:**

# The Byzantine Empire and Russia

## Section Overview

The Roman empire had been divided since the 200s. As the western half declined, the eastern half rose in importance. The emperor Constantine founded a capital on the site of Byzantium. Justinian, the greatest of the Byzantine emperors, ruled a vast empire with a centralized government and a codified set of laws. The Orthodox Christian Church became powerful as the official church of the Byzantine empire. The Byzantine empire blended Greek, Roman, and Christian influences and produced art and architecture that have lived on through the centuries. The empire also left a legacy in Russia. The Byzantines gave Russia a written language, and influenced Russian religion, government, art, and architecture.

## Key Themes and Concepts

As you review this section, take special note of the following key themes and concepts:

**Government** How did Justinian organize his government and code of law?

**Belief Systems** What was the significance of the Orthodox Christian Church in the Byzantine empire and Russia?

**Culture and Intellectual Life** How was the Byzantine empire able to preserve and spread Greek and Roman knowledge and culture?

**Movement of People and Goods** What influence did the Byzantine empire have on Russia and other areas of Eastern Europe?

## Key People and Terms

As you review this section, be sure you understand the significance of these key people and terms:

| | | |
|---|---|---|
| Justinian | icons | schism |
| autocrat | mosaics | Kiev |
| Justinian's Code | patriarch | czars |

## Geographic Setting

The Roman empire had been divided since the reign of Diocletian in the late A.D. 200s. As Germanic invaders weakened the western half, power shifted to the east. By 330, the emperor Constantine had built a splendid new capital in Constantinople, on the site of the Greek city of Byzantium. The Byzantine empire, as it came to be called, drew its name from this ancient city.

### Greatest Extent

At its height, the Byzantine empire covered an area from Rome through southeastern Europe and Asia Minor, down to Egypt and across North Africa. Even a portion of southern Spain was once part of the empire.

## Preserving and Spreading Culture

The city of Constantinople was on a peninsula overlooking the Bosporus, a strait connecting the Black Sea to the Mediterranean. The city possessed an outstanding harbor and was protected on three sides by water. From its central location Constantinople controlled key trade routes that linked Europe and Asia. Heir to Rome, the Byzantine empire blended Greek, Roman, and Christian influences and helped spread them to other regions of the world. In Russia, thriving trade with Constantinople helped Kiev become the center of the first Russian state.

### The Byzantine Empire

Map legend:
- Byzantine empire, 565
- Byzantine empire, about 1000

***The Byzantine Empire***
*The Byzantine Empire reached its greatest size by the year 565. By 1000, it had lost much of its territory to invading armies.*

**Preparing for the Regents**

- Practice your map skills by using the map to describe the extent of the Byzantine empire in 1000.

## Achievements of the Byzantine Empire

The Byzantine empire reached its peak under the emperor **Justinian,** who reigned from 527 to 565. Like other Byzantine rulers, Justinian was an **autocrat,** a single ruler with complete authority. Justinian hoped to recover the western Roman provinces that invading tribes had seized. During his reign, Byzantine armies did reconquer parts of North Africa, Italy, and southern Spain. These conquests were expensive, however, and they were temporary. The achievements of the Byzantine empire were in other areas.

### Justinian's Code of Law

Emperor Justinian is probably best known for his code of law. Soon after he became emperor, he set up a team of scholars to gather and organize the ancient laws of Rome. His collection became the "body of civil law," known today as Justinian's Code. His code included Roman laws, legal writings, and even a student handbook. Later emperors continued to update the code. By the 1100s, it had reached Western Europe, where it became the basis of law for both the Roman Catholic Church and medieval rulers. Even today, international law is influenced by Justinian's Code.

### Engineering and Architecture

The Byzantine empire extended Roman knowledge of engineering, especially in architecture. Justinian launched a building program designed to make Constantinople a dazzling city. The best known of his structures is the Church of Hagia Sophia, whose name means "Holy Wisdom." Byzantine architects blended Greek, Roman, Persian, and other Middle Eastern styles.

**Preparing for the Regents**

- How did Justinian go about reforming the law of the empire? What impact did Justinian's Code have on later legal systems?

**Preparing for the Regents**

Describe how the Byzantine empire preserved and transmitted Greek and Roman knowledge and culture in the categories named.

**Law:**

**Architecture:**

*Arabic calligraphy in Selimiye Mosque, Edirne, Turkey*

## Art

Byzantine artists made great contributions to religious art that influenced styles for many years. **Icons** were holy images of Jesus, the Virgin Mary, or saints of the Orthodox Christian Church. More than just paintings, they were supposed to create a sense that the sacred person was actually present. **Mosaics,** pictures or designs formed by inlaid pieces of stone or other materials, often showed biblical scenes. Beautiful mosaics adorned the interiors of churches, including the Hagia Sophia.

## The Orthodox Christian Church

The art and architecture of Constantinople reflected the importance of the Orthodox Christian Church in Byzantine life. By the time of Justinian, divisions had grown between the Church in Rome and the Byzantine Church. The Orthodox Christian Church, also called the Eastern Orthodox Church, was the Christian Church of the Byzantine empire.

**Imperial Authority Over the Church** The Byzantine emperor controlled the business of the Church and appointed the **patriarch,** the highest church official, in Constantinople. The emperor was considered Jesus' co-ruler on earth. Byzantine Christians did not believe that the pope in Rome had supreme authority over them.

**Differences With the West** Other divisions widened over time between the Church in the East and the Roman Catholic Church. Byzantine priests could marry, while Roman Catholic priests could not. Also, Greek (instead of Latin) was the language of the Byzantine Church. A major disagreement arose over the use of icons. Some people believed that the importance placed on them by the Orthodox Christian Church bordered on idolatry.

**Christian Schism** In 1054, there was finally a permanent split, or schism, between the Orthodox Christian Church in the East and the Roman Catholic Church in the West.

## Preservation of Greco-Roman Culture

The Byzantine empire remained a political and cultural force nearly 1,000 years after the fall of Rome. To Europe it was a symbol of the power and glory of Rome long after the Roman empire had faded. Justinian's Code preserved Roman law, and the accomplishments of Roman engineers were preserved and extended in Byzantine architecture.

Furthermore, Byzantine culture was strongly rooted in Greece. The Byzantine empire preserved Hellenistic (Greek) science, philosophy, arts, and literature. The empire even served to preserve some of the ancient texts of Greece, which were carried to the West as the Byzantine empire declined in the 1400s.

## Decline and Fall of the Empire

The Byzantine empire had reached its height under Justinian. In the centuries after his reign, the empire lost much land to invading armies. It was also weakened by internal court struggles and constant warfare. During the Fourth Crusade in

**Key Themes and Concepts**

**Political Systems**
In the Byzantine empire, the power of both the state and the Church was centered in the emperor.

**Key Themes and Concepts**

**Belief Systems**
The Roman and Byzantine Churches shared many common beliefs, yet their differences became too difficult to overcome. Many world religions have experienced schisms over time.

**Recognize Causes**

What were the causes of the decline of the Byzantine empire?

the early 1200s, western Christians took Constantinople and ruled it for 50 years. The final blow to the empire was the taking of Constantinople by the Ottoman empire in 1453.

## Russia and Eastern Europe

The first Russian state was established in the 800s. This early Russian state was centered in the city of **Kiev,** in present-day Ukraine. Kiev's location on the Dneiper River made the city easily accessible to Byzantine traders.

Around this time, states such as Poland, Hungary, and Serbia were established in Eastern Europe. Settlers arrived from Western Europe, Russia, and Asia, giving the region a wide variety of languages and cultural traditions. As in Russia, trade with the Byzantine empire helped bring Eastern Europe into the Byzantine sphere of influence. The Byzantines influenced both Russia and Eastern Europe in a variety of ways.

### Written Language

The Byzantines gave Russia a written language. Two Byzantine missionaries adapted the Greek alphabet in order to translate the Bible into Slavic languages as early as the 800s. This alphabet, called the Cyrillic alphabet after Cyril, one of the monks, is still used in Russia and other countries of Eastern Europe today.

### Orthodox Christianity

Byzantine missionaries carried Orthodox Christianity to Russia and other countries of Eastern Europe. The Orthodox Christian faith remains a powerful force through much of the region today. The close church-state relationship in the Byzantine empire also became a model for Russian government and religion. The Russian Orthodox Church became an important arm of state power.

### Autocratic Government

One Byzantine tradition that continued was that of autocratic rule, which became the norm in Russian government. Autocratic rulers in Russia were known as **czars** (also, tsars). *Czar* is the Russian word for *Caesar*.

### Art and Architecture

Russians adopted the religious art, music, and architecture of the Byzantine empire. Byzantine domes were transformed into the onion domes of Russian architecture.

## Summary

As the Roman empire in the West declined, the Byzantine empire grew in power. The lasting heritage of the Byzantine empire lay in its preservation of classical culture, its traditions of law and government, and its spreading of Christian beliefs. The Orthodox Christian Church, a powerful force in the empire, developed its own practices and traditions and split from the Roman Catholic Church. The Byzantine empire provided Russia and other Eastern European lands with a written language, art and architecture, and an autocratic style of government.

**Preparing for the Regents**

The fall of Constantinople was a turning point in global history. It marked a change in power in the region from the Christian Byzantine empire to the great Muslim trading empire of the Ottomans.

**Preparing for the Regents**

Describe how the Byzantine empire affected Russia in the areas listed.

**Language:**

**Religion:**

**Government:**

**Art and architecture:**

*St. Basil's Cathedral: a Russian Orthodox Church in Moscow, Russia*

# Islamic Civilization

The
**Big Idea**

The Muslim world:

• included lands and peoples from parts of three continents.

• preserved, blended, and spread the cultures of classical Greece, Rome, India, and other civilizations.

• enjoyed a prosperous golden age with advances in art, literature, mathematics, and science.

• spread new learning to Christian Europe.

## Section Overview

In the years after the death of Muhammad, Islam spread across parts of three continents. Muslim empires ruled over vast areas of land that included parts of Europe, Africa, and Asia. The Muslim world was influenced by many cultures, including those of ancient Greece, Rome, and India. During the 700s and 800s, Islam experienced a golden age. A diverse society, an economy based on flourishing trade, and achievements in the arts and sciences characterized this era. The achievements of Islam's golden age reached Europe through Muslim Spain and Italy as well as through the Crusades.

## Key Themes and Concepts

As you review this section, take special note of the following key themes and concepts:

**Diversity** What lands and peoples came under Muslim rule?

**Economic Systems** What was the importance of trade in the Muslim empires?

**Culture and Intellectual Life** What achievements did Muslim society produce in the arts and sciences?

**Interdependence** How did Islamic civilization interact with Christian Europe?

## Key People and Terms

**Key People and Terms**

What do many of the key people and terms have in common?

As you review this section, be sure you understand the significance of these key people and terms:

| | | |
|---|---|---|
| caliph | Shiite | Abbassid dynasty |
| Sharia | Umayyad dynasty | Averröes |
| Sunni | | |

## The Spread of Islam

Islam arose in the Arabian peninsula in the early 600s. In 632, Muhammad, the founder of Islam, died. Abu Bakr was elected the first **caliph,** or successor to Muhammad. The period when Muslims were ruled by caliphs, from Muhammad's death until the 900s, was called the caliphate. The Muslim world expanded during the caliphate.

### Diverse Lands and Peoples

In the years after Muhammad's death, Islam spread rapidly. Abu Bakr was successful in uniting Arabs in the Islam faith. His forces began an extraordinary military campaign that conquered parts of the Byzantine empire, the Persian empire, Egypt, and Spain. Their push into Europe was stopped only at Tours in 732. Over the following centuries, more and more people embraced Islam.

**Middle East** Arab armies took control of the Middle East in the early 600s. Syria and Palestine were quickly defeated by Arab forces. Persia and Egypt were conquered soon after.

**North Africa** Muslim armies carried Islam into North Africa in the mid- to late 600s. Muslim invaders initially fought African forces. Eventually, however, Muslims and North Africans joined forces to conquer Spain. Islam continued to spread to other parts of North and West Africa.

**Spain and Sicily** Muslim conquests included parts of southern and western Europe, especially Spain and the island of Sicily. Muslim Arabs and their North African allies attacked Spain in the early 700s. When Europe was weak, during the Middle Ages, the Muslims seized control of Sicily.

**India** In the early 700s, Muslim armies conquered the Indus Valley. For several hundred years, Islam did not spread beyond western India. In the 1000s and 1100s, however, Turkish converts to Islam conquered most of northern India. By the 1200s, the Turks had created a great Muslim empire on the subcontinent, with its capital at Delhi.

**Southeast Asia** After Muslims took control of northern India in the 1200s, Islam was carried into Southeast Asia. Islamic beliefs and civilization were spread mainly through trade. As Islam gradually spread to lands surrounding the Indian Ocean, thriving trade networks were established.

### Reasons for Muslim Success

One reason for the spread of Islam was that the Arabs were strong fighters. Their cavalry, mounted on camels and horses, overwhelmed their opponents. The Muslims were also successful partly because the Byzantine and Persian empires were weak from fighting wars against each other. Another important factor was that the Muslims were united by their belief in Islam. In addition, Muslim rulers often treated conquered peoples fairly. People in defeated empires welcomed Muslim rule after years of living under harsh rulers. Many converted to Islam.

## Islamic Law and Its Impact

As Islam spread, Islamic scholars developed a system of laws to help people interpret the Qur'an and apply it to everyday life. The **Sharia**—the Islamic system of law—regulated moral behavior, family life, business, government, and other areas of community life. The Sharia acted as a uniting force for Muslims. Unlike laws in the western world, the Sharia did not separate religious and worldly matters. It applied the Qur'an to all situations and aspects of life.

## Divisions Within Islam

Several decades after the death of Muhammad, divisions grew among Muslims about who should be Muhammad's successor. Followers split into two groups: **Sunni** and **Shiite.** Sunnis believed that the caliph should be chosen by Muslim leaders. Sunni Muslims did not view the caliph as a religious authority. Shiites believed that only the descendants of the prophet Muhammad should be his successors. They believed that the descendants of the prophet were divinely inspired.

The split between Sunni and Shiite Muslims continues to this day. Like the differing branches of Christianity, these branches of Islam share many basic beliefs, such as devotion to the same God and reverence for the same scriptures.

**Note Taking**

*Reading Skill:*
**Recognize Sequence**
Make a flow chart. Show the sequence of the spread of Islam. Add boxes as necessary.

early 600s
Middle East
Syria,
Palestine
Persia,
Egypt

**Vocabulary Builder**

<u>convert</u>—(KAHN vurt ) *n.* someone who has been persuaded to change their beliefs and accept a particular religion or opinion

**Key Themes and Concepts**

**Justice**
Islamic law was an important unifying element in the Muslim empires. Justinian had also unified his empire through a uniform code of law.

**Preparing for the Regents**

• Write a paragraph that describes several similarities and differences between the splits in the Christian Church and the division in Islam.

## Note Taking

*Reading Skill:*
**Summarize**
Make a table. Summarize the social patterns of Islam.

| Social Patterns of Islam | |
|---|---|
| Social Mobility | |
| Treatment of Conquered People | |
| Slavery | |
| Status of Women | |

## Preparing for the Regents

- What was the status of women under ancient Islamic law?

## Vocabulary Builder

seclude—(sih KLOOD) *v.* to remove or separate from social contact and activity

## Key Themes and Concepts

**Diversity**
The diversity of the Umayyad empire was one cause of its decline. The rich and the poor, Sunnis and Shiites, and Arabs and non-Arabs disagreed about important issues.

# Social Patterns

## Social Mobility

In some ways, Muslim society allowed more social mobility than did medieval European society. Under earlier dynasties, Arabs had considered themselves superior to non-Arabs, but this belief declined with later dynasties. It became possible to move up in the social order, especially through religious, scholarly, or military achievements.

## Treatment of Conquered Peoples

Islamic leaders imposed a special tax on non-Muslims, but they allowed people to practice their own faiths. Christians and Jews often served as doctors, officials, and translators in Muslim communities.

## Slavery

As in Greece and Rome, slavery was common in the Muslim world. Enslaved people from Spain, Greece, Africa, India, and central Asia were brought to Muslim cities. Most enslaved people worked as house servants, and some were skilled craftspeople. It was possible for enslaved people to buy their freedom. Also, if a slave converted to Islam, his or her children would be free.

## Status of Women

Islam teaches the spiritual equality of men and women. The Qur'an protected women of the time in ways that some societies did not. For example, it prohibited the killing of daughters and protected the rights of widows. Women had inheritance rights, could be educated, and had to consent to marriage freely. Nevertheless, in Muslim society, the roles and rights of women differed from those of men. For example, a daughter's inheritance was less than a son's.

As Islam spread, Muslims adopted some beliefs of non-Arab people. In Byzantium and Persia, for example, Arabs veiled women and secluded them in separate parts of their homes. Restrictions on women varied by region and class in Muslim civilization. Upper-class women were more likely to be restricted. In rural areas, women continued to participate in the economy.

# Muslim Empires

After the death of the fourth caliph in 661, many changes took place in the Muslim world. The **Umayyad dynasty** spread Islam to the Atlantic in the west and to the Indus Valley in the east. It was based in Damascus rather than Mecca. The expansion of Islam led to increased tensions between rich and poor, Sunnis and Shiites, and Arabs and non-Arabs. In 750, the **Abbassid dynasty** captured Damascus and moved the court to Baghdad, thus ending Arab domination of Islam. The Abbassid rulers enjoyed great wealth and power. Baghdad exceeded the size and wealth of Constantinople and ushered in a golden age for the Muslim world.

## Political Divisions

Around 850, Abbassid rule of Islamic civilization began to decline. Independent dynasties began to rule separate Muslim states. In the 900s, the Seljuk Turks adopted Islam and built their own empire. They took control of the Arab capital, Baghdad. Then, in the 1200s, the Mongols destroyed Baghdad. Even so, the Muslim religion continued to link people over three continents.

# Islam's Golden Age

At its height under the Abbassids, the Muslim world was composed of people from many cultures, including Arabs, Persians, Egyptians, and Europeans. Muslims absorbed and blended customs and traditions from many of the peoples they ruled. The glory of the empires was reflected in their emphasis on learning, achievements in the arts and sciences, and flourishing economies based on trade.

## The Golden Age of Muslim Civilization

| Art | Literature |
|---|---|
| • Used beautiful writing and patterns to decorate buildings and art<br>• Adapted Byzantine domes and arches<br>• Painted people and animals in nonreligious art | • Considered Qur'an most important piece of Arabic literature<br>• Chanted oral poetry<br>• Collected stories from other people |

**Muslim Civilization**

| Learning | Medicine |
|---|---|
| • Translated writings of Greek philosophers<br>• Developed algebra<br>• Observed Earth turning and measured its circumference | • Required doctors to pass difficult tests<br>• Set up hospitals with emergency rooms<br>• Studied diseases and wrote medical books |

## Preservation of Greco-Roman Culture

Muslim scholars translated the works of many of the Greek scholars. Muslim advances in mathematics, astronomy, and medicine were also based partly on their study of Greek and Indian knowledge.

## Education

The prophet Muhammad taught a respect for learning that continued to characterize Muslim culture throughout the ages. The Muslim empires included dazzling centers of learning such as Baghdad, Cairo, and Cordoba. The vast libraries and universities of these cities attracted a large and diverse number of well-paid and highly respected scholars.

## Art and Architecture

**Mosques and Palaces** Muslim architects were influenced by Byzantine domes and arches. The walls and ceilings of mosques and palaces were decorated with elaborate abstract and geometric patterns. Muslim religious leaders forbade artists to portray God or human figures in religious art.

**Calligraphy** Muslim artists were highly skilled in calligraphy, or artistic writing. Calligraphy decorated buildings and pieces of art. Often, Muslim calligraphers used verses from the Qur'an.

**Drawings and Paintings** In nonreligious art, some Muslim artists portrayed animal or human figures, although this was usually discouraged. Persian and Turkish artists adorned books with beautiful miniature paintings.

*Mevlana Mosque, Turkey*

## Key Themes and Concepts

**Culture and Intellectual Life** Education was an important part of Muslim culture. Cities such as Baghdad, Cairo, and Cordoba were powerful centers of learning.

## Key Themes and Concepts

**Belief Systems** Muslim religious art rarely depicted God or human figures because the Qur'an prohibited the worship of idols.

## Compare and Contrast

Describe the similarities and differences between the art of the Muslim civilization and the art of the Byzantine empire.

## Literature and Philosophy

**Poetry** A wide variety of themes dominated written Muslim poetry, from praise of important leaders to contemplation of the joys and sorrows of love. In addition, because the Qur'an was the most important piece of Muslim literature, many writers wrote poems based on this holy book.

**Tales** Muslim storytellers adapted stories from Greek, Indian, Jewish, and Egyptian culture, as well as others. The most famous collection of Muslim stories is *The Thousand and One Nights*, which includes fables, romances, and humorous anecdotes.

**Philosophy** Muslim scholars translated the philosophical works of Greek, Indian, and Chinese writers. In fact, the scholar Ibn Rushd, who was known in Europe as **Averröes,** strongly influenced medieval Christian scholars with his writings on Aristotle. The Jewish rabbi Maimonides influenced Christian scholars of the Middle Ages in much the same way.

## Mathematics and Science

**Algebra** Muslims studied Indian and Greek mathematics before making their own contributions. Muslims pioneered the study of algebra. Eventually, the works of some Muslim mathematicians were translated into Latin and studied in Europe.

**Astronomy** Greek and Indian astronomical discoveries resulted in Muslim development of astronomical tables. Muslim astronomers also observed the Earth's rotation and calculated the circumference of the Earth within a few thousand feet.

**Medicine** Muslim medicine was remarkably advanced. Doctors were required to pass difficult tests before they could practice. Hospitals were set up. Physicians studied various diseases and wrote books that became standard texts in Europe.

## Economic Achievements

The Muslim world developed a prosperous economy. Muslims had an extensive trade network and encouraged manufacturing. Agriculture also flourished.

**Trade** Merchants were honored in Muslim society. From 750 to 1350, Muslims established a large trade network across their empire. Traders not only exchanged goods but spread religious belief, culture, and technology as well.

Trading and a money economy allowed Muslims to take the lead in new business practices. They established partnerships, sold goods on credit, and formed banks to exchange different kinds of currency.

**Manufacturing** Guilds organized manufacturing in the Muslim world. Heads of guilds regulated prices, weights, and measurements, and they monitored product quality. Muslim craftworkers produced steel swords in Damascus, leather goods in Cordoba, and carpets in Persia.

**Agriculture** Muslim farmers grew crops such as sugarcane, cotton, medicinal herbs, fruits, and vegetables. These products were purchased and sold in many world markets.

### Key Themes and Concepts

**Culture and Intellectual Life**
Modern mathematics and science can trace many of their roots to the achievements of Islamic civilization.

### Preparing for the Regents

List two Islamic achievements in each of the following areas.

Mathematics:

Art:

Literature:

Medicine:

Economics:

### Vocabulary Builder

guild—(gild) *n.* an organization of people who do the same job or have the same interests

# Christian Europe Enriched by Islamic Civilization

The advances of the Muslim world gradually reached Christian Europe through Spain and Sicily. The Crusades also encouraged cultural diffusion.

### Muslim Spain

Spain became a magnificent Muslim cultural center. Muslim princes encouraged poetry, the arts, and learning. In Spain, the Muslims, who were called Moors, continued their policy of toleration, hiring Jewish officials and encouraging Christian students to study Greek thought.

### Muslim Sicily

During the early Middle Ages, Arabs gained control of Sicily and other Mediterranean islands. The island of Sicily was soon regained by Europeans, but a Muslim presence remained. Muslim officials provided effective government, and Arab merchants and farmers helped the economy to grow. Muslim culture graced the courts of the Christian kings.

### The Crusades

Crusaders came into contact with various Muslim peoples and cultures. Europeans were impressed with Muslim advancements in the arts and sciences as well as with their preservation of Greco-Roman culture. As a result, the advances of the Muslim world gradually influenced Christian Europe.

## Summary

The Muslim world was richly diverse. It spread across an extensive area in Europe, Africa, and Asia. Muslim empires had flourishing economies supported by a vast trade network. At its height, the Muslim world made great advances in fields such as literature, mathematics, astronomy, and medicine. In these areas, Muslims were greatly influenced by other cultures, including those of classical Greece and India. In time, Islamic civilization had a great impact on Christian Europe.

**Key Themes and Concepts**

**Interdependence**
It was through Muslim Spain and Sicily, as well as through the Crusades and the Muslim trading network, that the achievements of Islam's golden age reached European society.

**Key Themes and Concepts**

**Culture and Intellectual Life**
By adapting ideas from other cultures, Muslims were able to expand their knowledge and develop new ideas.

**Summarize**

Summarize how Christian Europe was enriched by Islamic civilization.

# Medieval Europe

## The Big Idea

During the Middle Ages in Europe:

- there was disorder for a time after the collapse of the Roman empire.

- wealthy landowners dominated society and provided people with protection.

- people relied on the Christian Church for spiritual and political guidance.

- achievements in art and architecture centered around Christianity.

## Section Overview

The Middle Ages, or **medieval** period, lasted from about 500 to the middle of the 1400s. The collapse of the Roman empire had left Western Europe with no unifying government. In response, political and social systems emerged, such as feudalism and manorialism, that were based on powerful local lords and their landholdings. A strict social hierarchy existed during the Middle Ages. The Christian Church emerged as a unifying force in Western Europe and had great influence over economic and social, as well as religious, life. Conditions gradually improved, allowing Europeans to build a new civilization based on Greco-Roman and Christian traditions.

## Key Themes and Concepts

As you review this section, take special note of the following key themes and concepts:

**Interdependence** What duties and responsibilities guided people's lives in medieval Europe?

**Political Systems** What roles did individual citizens play in the medieval feudal systems?

**Economic Systems** How did manorialism provide for people's basic economic needs?

**Belief Systems** What roles did the Church play in medieval society?

## Key People and Terms

### Key People and Terms

Which key people and terms relate to belief systems? Explain.

As you review this section, be sure you understand the significance of these key people and terms:

| | | |
|---|---|---|
| medieval | serfs | monasteries |
| Charlemagne | secular | anti-Semitism |
| chivalry | excommunicated | Gothic |
| manorialism | Pope Innocent III | |

## Geographic Setting

The geography of Europe had a powerful effect on the development of the area. Europe's location and resources helped determine the groups of people who settled there and the people who would try to control it.

### Location

Europe lay at the western end of the Eurasian landmass, which extends from present-day Portugal to China. Parts of Great Britain, Spain, France, Italy, Greece, and other areas of Eastern Europe had been within the Roman empire. Roman roads had allowed Roman and Christian customs to spread. As you have learned, Germanic tribes overran Europe from about 400 to 700, ending Roman rule.

## Resources

**Forests and Fertile Soil** Europe had many natural resources. Dense forests, with valuable timber, covered much of northern Europe, and the area's fertile soil was well suited for raising crops. In addition, minerals such as iron and coal lay untapped beneath the Earth's surface.

**Seas and Rivers** The oceans and seas that surrounded much of Europe were also important resources. People on the coasts fished the waters and used them as a means of trade and transportation. Large rivers in Europe also provided food and a means of travel.

# The Frankish Empire

The Germanic people who overran the Roman empire were warriors, farmers, and herders. Their culture differed greatly from that of the Romans they had conquered. Germanic tribes were governed by unwritten laws and customs and ruled by elected kings.

### The Rise of the Franks

From about 400 to 700, warrior tribes divided Europe and fought for control of various territories. During this time, the Franks emerged as the most powerful and successful of the tribes in Gaul, or present-day France. In the late 400s, Clovis, a brilliant and ruthless leader, became king of the Franks. Clovis is probably best known for his conversion to Christianity, which gained him a powerful ally in the Christian Church.

### Battle of Tours

As you have learned, Muslims had moved into Spain. They tried to advance into France. At the Battle of Tours in 732, the Franks defeated a Muslim army. Although Muslims continued to rule most of Spain, they advanced no farther in Western Europe.

### Charlemagne

During the 800s, Charlemagne, a Frankish king, built an empire that stretched across modern-day France, Germany, and part of Italy.

**Cooperation With the Church** In 800, Pope Leo III, the head of the Christian Church of the time, called for help against rebellious nobles in Rome. Charlemagne answered the pope's call and defeated the Roman nobles in battle. To show his gratitude, Pope Leo III, on Christmas Day 800, crowned Charlemagne "Holy Roman Emperor." The crowning of Charlemagne helped revive the ideal of a united Christian Church and empire.

After being named emperor, Charlemagne strengthened his rule and attempted to create a united Christian Europe. Working closely with the Roman Catholic Church, he helped spread Christianity to the far reaches of his empire.

**Government** Charlemagne appointed nobles to rule local areas. He gave them land, expecting them in return to help with the defense of the empire. As a way to control these rulers, Charlemagne regularly sent out officials called *missi dominici* to check on conditions throughout the empire.

**Learning** Charlemagne also encouraged learning. He set up a school to ensure the education of government officials. He also established libraries where scholars copied ancient texts, including the Bible and science and history texts written in Latin.

**Preparing for the Regents**

• How did Europeans use natural resources to provide for basic economic needs?

**Key Themes and Concepts**

**Change**
Clovis, king of the Franks, converted to Christianity. By doing this, he gained the support of the leaders of the Christian Church.

**Note Taking**

*Reading Skill:*
**Understand Effects**
Make a chart. Record the effects of Charlemagne's rule.

**Preparing for the Regents**

• Describe several ways in which Charlemagne sought to restore order to medieval Europe.

Charlemagne's Empire

*Charlemagne's Empire*
*Charlemagne was able to rule a large empire because of his strong personality, his powerful centralized government, and his effective military strategy.*

## Preparing for the Regents

Practice your map skills by answering the following questions.

1. Name two groups that were part of Charlemagne's empire.

2. Name two modern-day countries that include areas once ruled by Charlemagne.

**End of Charlemagne's Reign** When Charlemagne died in 814, his empire quickly fell apart as his heirs battled for control. In 843, Charlemagne's grandsons signed the Treaty of Verdun, which divided Charlemagne's empire into three separate kingdoms, one for each grandson.

Charlemagne had a lasting influence, however. His strong government was a model for future medieval rulers. He also helped spread Christianity to northern Europe.

# Feudalism and Manorialism

During the early part of the Middle Ages, kings were too weak to keep invaders out of their kingdoms. People began to leave towns and cities, banding together in the countryside for protection and survival.

### The Structure of Feudal Society

## Medieval Society

Everyone had a well-defined place in medieval society. People were born into their social positions, and there was little chance of moving beyond them. The nobility consisted of the kings and queens, greater lords, lesser lords, and knights. The elite class of nobles controlled the land and power. The lower class of peasants, who made up the bulk of the population, worked the land and served the nobles. The clergy was highly respected, due to the fact that the Christian Church dominated life during the Middle Ages.

## Feudalism

**Feudal Responsibilities** Feudalism was a loosely structured political system in which powerful lords (nobles) owned large sections of land. They divided their land into estates called fiefs, which were given to lesser lords called vassals. Vassals pledged their loyalty and military support to their lords in return for this land.

**Knighthood** Because people in medieval Europe were often at war, many nobles trained to become knights, or mounted warriors. They practiced strict discipline and learned how to ride well and handle weapons skillfully. In addition, knights were bound by a code of conduct known as **chivalry.** This code charged them to be brave, loyal, and true to their word. The code also required knights to protect women.

**Role of Noblewomen** Women played an active role in feudal society. A "lady" was in charge of her husband's estate while he was away serving his lord in battle. She was responsible for all household affairs including the raising of children. In preparation for their adult role, girls received training in household arts such as spinning, weaving, and the management of servants. Women had limited inheritance rights, however, since most possessions went to the eldest son.

## Manorialism

The basis for the medieval economy was **manorialism,** an economic system structured around a lord's manor, or estate. Manors often included one or more villages and the land surrounding them. Under the manorial system, each group in society had a place; each also had certain rights and responsibilities.

**Peasants and Lords** Most of the peasants who lived on the estate were **serfs.** Serfs were not enslaved, but they were bound to the land. They could not leave the estate without the lord's permission.

**Mutual Responsibilities** Serfs farmed the lord's land and did other work such as repairing roads and fences. In return for the service provided by peasants, the lord provided them with the use of several acres of land to farm. The lord was also supposed to protect them during times of war.

**Harsh Life for Peasants** For peasants, life on the manor was difficult and often harsh. Peasant men, women, and children worked long hours, and few peasants lived past the age of 35. In spite of such hardship, the lives of peasants were held together by the common thread of Christianity. Their celebrations—marriages, births, and holidays such as Christmas and Easter—were centered in the Christian Church.

## The Church in Medieval Life

During the Middle Ages, two distinct Christian churches emerged: the Orthodox Christian Church in the east and the Roman Catholic Church in the west. (The two branches split permanently in 1054.) The Roman Catholic Church became the main stabilizing force in Western Europe. The Church provided religious leadership as well as **secular,** or worldly, leadership. It also played a key role in reviving and preserving learning.

### Church Hierarchy

At the head of the Roman Catholic Church was the pope, whom followers believed to be the spiritual representative of Jesus on earth. Below the pope came archbishops, bishops, and local priests. For peasants and town dwellers, everyday life was closely tied to local priests and the village church.

### Spiritual Role of the Church

The main responsibility of the Church was to serve the spiritual needs of medieval society. Local priests instructed peasants and townspeople in the faith and provided comfort to them in troubled times. The Church taught that all men and women were sinners but that Christians could achieve salvation, or eternal life in heaven, through faith in Jesus, good works, and participation in sacraments, or sacred spiritual rituals. To escape the punishment of hell, they needed to take part in the sacraments of the Church.

**Preparing for the Regents**

Feudalism was based on personal agreements among individuals. This loose system of government differed greatly from the strong centralized government of Rome that existed before the Middle Ages.

**Preparing for the Regents**

• What was the most important economic resource in medieval Europe? Who controlled this resource? How did control of economic resources affect the power structure in medieval society?

**Key Themes and Concepts**

**Interdependence**
Feudalism and the manor system were both based on mutual responsibility. In feudalism, nobles owed duties to each other. In the manor system, nobles and peasants provided benefits to each other.

**Belief Systems**
Religion was an essential part of life for medieval people. The Roman Catholic Church spread the teachings of Jesus and administered the sacraments, including marriage and baptism.

## Preparing for the Regents

Identify four ways in which the Roman Catholic Church affected economic or political affairs during the Middle Ages.

1.

2.

3.

4.

## Vocabulary Builder

papal—(PAY pul) adj. relating to the pope

*The Medieval Church*
*Religion shaped the everyday lives of Christian Europeans. The Church controlled the spiritual lives of Christians. It was also a powerful political force because it had authority over all rulers, such as kings and emperors.*

## Secular Role of the Church

**Economic Power** The Church filled many secular, or worldly, roles during the Middle Ages. As the largest landholder in Europe, the Church had significant economic power. The Church also gained wealth through the tithe, a tax Christians were required to pay that equaled ten percent of their income.

**Political Power** The Church had its own set of laws, called canon law, and its own courts of justice. The Church claimed authority over secular rulers, but monarchs did not always recognize this authority. As a result, there were frequent power struggles between the pope in Rome and various kings and emperors.

Popes believed that they had authority over kings. Popes sometimes **excommunicated,** or excluded from the Catholic Church, secular rulers who challenged or threatened papal power. For example, **Pope Innocent III** excommunicated King John of England in the 1200s during a dispute about appointing an archbishop.

### The Medieval Church

**Everyday Life**
- Christians attended village churches.
- Some priests ran schools in village churches.
- All Christians paid taxes to Church.

**Power of Church**
- Pope led Roman Catholic Church.
- Church had its own laws and courts.
- Church excommunicated those who did not obey rules.

**Nuns and Monks**
- Some set up housing, hospitals, and schools for the sick and poor.
- Some became missionaries.
- Some preserved learning.

**Reform**
- Church became rich and powerful.
- Some clergy became corrupt.
- Reformers tried to make changes

## Monastic Orders

Some men and women became monks or nuns, leaving worldly society and devoting their lives to God. They entered **monasteries,** communities where Christian men or women focused on spiritual goals. Monks and nuns took vows of chastity, or purity, and of obedience to the abbot, or head of the religious order. They also took an oath of poverty. Monks and nuns fulfilled many social needs, such as tending to the sick, helping the poor, and educating children.

**Centers of Learning** In monasteries and convents (religious communities of women), monks and nuns also preserved ancient writings by copying ancient texts. Some monks and nuns taught Latin and Greek classics; others produced their own literary works.

**Missionary Work** Not all monks and nuns remained in monasteries. Some became missionaries, risking their lives to spread the message of Christianity. The Church sometimes honored its missionaries by declaring them saints. St. Patrick was a missionary who set up the Church in Ireland. St. Augustine was sent as a missionary to the Angles and Saxons in England.

## Women and the Church

The Church taught that women and men were equal in the sight of God. However, on earth, women were supposed to be subservient to men. There was some effort to protect women in medieval society. For example, the Church set a minimum age for women to marry. However, women were viewed in two opposing ways.

## Preparing for the Regents

- What role did monks and nuns play in preserving Greco-Roman culture?

## Preparing for the Regents

- Compare and contrast the roles of men and women in feudal society.

On one hand, the Church considered women weak, easily tempted into sin, and dependent on the guidance of men. On the other hand, women were seen as modest and pure in spirit, similar to Mary, the mother of Jesus.

## Jews in Medieval Europe

Numerous Jewish communities existed throughout Europe during the Middle Ages. While Jews in Muslim Spain and northern areas of Europe were generally tolerated, most Christians persecuted Jews. Not only did the Church bar Jews from owning land or practicing many occupations; many Christians blamed Jews for the death of Jesus. As a result, the foundations for **anti-Semitism,** or prejudice against Jews, were laid. Gradually, Christians began blaming Jews for all kinds of misfortunes, from famines to disease. In time, Jews migrated to Eastern Europe, where they set up communities that survived until modern times.

## Medieval Cultural Achievements

In early medieval times, life was very chaotic. People concentrated on protecting themselves from invasions and taking care of their own physical needs. Toward the end of the Middle Ages, however, European society became more stable and made cultural gains in the fields of literature, art, and architecture.

### Literature

Although the language of scholars was Latin, new stories and writings began to appear in the everyday languages of the people. Medieval literature included stories of knights and feudal lords as well as tales about the common people. Authors such as Dante and Chaucer wrote stories about warrior heroes and ordinary people who showed courage, humor, and morality.

### Architecture and Art

The architecture and art of the Middle Ages focused on glorifying God. Almost all of the artistic achievements of the time were a reflection of the power of the Church. With money from increased trade in the late Middle Ages, nobles and townspeople alike began contributing to great works of architecture and art.

**Roman Influences** Around the year 1000, towns began to build stone churches that reflected the influence of Rome. With thick supporting walls and towers and only small slits in the stone for windows, these structures were fortresslike and dimly lighted.

**The Gothic Tradition** The Gothic style of architecture first appeared in Europe in the early 1100s. These new buildings, unlike those in the Roman style, seemed to soar upward. The Gothic style was characterized by pointed arches and by flying buttresses, stone supports that stood outside the building. With this outside support, walls could be built higher, leaving space for huge stained-glass windows. These windows, along with sculptures and carvings inside the churches, often told biblical stories, serving to educate the illiterate people of medieval Europe.

## Summary

The Middle Ages was a troubled period in European history. After the Germanic invasions, society began to come together under the strict political organization supplied by feudalism and the economic system of manorialism. The Christian Church helped to unify Western Europe and touched every aspect of medieval life. Monasteries and convents became centers of learning; monks and nuns preserved ancient writings by copying ancient texts. As conditions improved and life became more stable, medieval Europe began to develop its own unique culture.

### Preparing for the Regents

- Describe the relationship between religion and art in both medieval Europe and Islamic civilization.

- What cultural contributions did medieval Europe make in literature? In architecture?

*Notre Dame Cathedral in Paris*

# The Crusades

The

# Big Idea

The Crusades:

- were driven by Christians' desire to force the Muslims from Palestine as well as to gain wealth and power.

- resulted in increased European trade with the Muslim world.

- temporarily increased the power of the Church and greatly strengthened feudal monarchs.

- introduced Europeans to the advances of Byzantine and Muslim civilizations.

## Section Overview

In the 1050s, Seljuk Turks, who were Muslims, invaded the Byzantine empire and conquered Palestine. The Christian Church called for a movement to drive the Muslims out of Palestine. For nearly 200 years, Christians fought a series of religious wars known as the **Crusades.** The wars failed to regain Palestine, and they left a legacy of ill will and distrust between Christians and Muslims. However, the Crusades had other effects as well. Trade increased, and the European economy expanded. Feudal monarchs gained more power, and Europeans learned of the existence of lands beyond their borders. Europeans also benefited from the learning and cultural achievements of Islam.

## Key Themes and Concepts

As you review this section, take special note of the following key themes and concepts:

**Imperialism** Why did Christians and Muslims engage in the Crusades?

**Change** What effect did the Crusades have on the economy of Europe?

**Power** How did the Crusades affect the power of the Church and feudal lords?

**Culture** How did the Crusades expand Europeans' view of the world?

## Key People and Terms

Choose one category for all of the key people and terms: political system, economic system, or belief system. Explain your choice.

## Key People and Terms

As you review this section, be sure you understand the significance of these key people and terms:

| | |
|---|---|
| Crusades | Holy Land |
| Urban II | Saladin |
| Council of Clermont | Richard the Lion-Hearted |

## Note Taking

*Reading Skill:*
**Recognize Sequence**
As you read, list the important dates for the Crusades. Record them in the order they occurred. Add boxes as needed.

| Crusades | |
|---|---|
| Date | Event |
| 1050 | Seljuk Turks invade Byzantine empire |
| 1095 | |
| | |

## Beginning of the Crusades

In the 1050s, the Seljuk Turks invaded the Byzantine empire. Over the next four decades, they overran most Byzantine lands in Asia Minor as well as Palestine. In 1095, the Byzantine emperor asked the pope, **Urban II,** for help. Pope Urban agreed. At the **Council of Clermont,** Urban encouraged French and German bishops to recover Palestine, or the **Holy Land,** as it was called by Christians. Christians referred to this area as the Holy Land because it was where Jesus had lived and taught. Muslims and Jews also considered the land holy. Christians who answered the pope's call were known as crusaders. Men and women from all over Western Europe left their homes to reclaim the Holy Land. Many never returned.

# Reasons for the Crusades

There were several other motives for the Crusades, some religious and some secular. These reasons included the following.

- Pope Urban believed that the Crusades would increase his power in Europe and possibly reunite the Eastern and Western churches.
- Christians believed that their sins would be forgiven if they participated in the Crusades.
- Nobles hoped to gain wealth and land by participating in the Crusades.
- Adventurers saw the Crusades as a chance for travel and excitement.
- Serfs hoped to escape feudal oppression by fighting in the Crusades.

**Preparing for the Regents**

- The Crusades were caused by a variety of factors. Describe several causes of the Crusades.

# An Initial Christian Victory

For 200 years, the fighting went on. Only the first of four Crusades, however, came close to achieving its goals. In 1099, Christians captured the city of Jerusalem. They followed the victory with a massacre of Muslim and Jewish inhabitants.

Crusaders divided their conquered lands into four small states called the crusader states. They divided these lands into feudal domains. Muslim leaders tried to regain these kingdoms, and this effort resulted in additional Crusades.

**Preparing for the Regents**

- During the Crusades, how do you think Muslims viewed Christians? How do you think Christians viewed Muslims?

# Saladin and Muslim Victory

## A Respected Muslim Leader

During the late 1100s, Saladin united the Muslim world. Both Muslims and Christians admired and respected Saladin. However, when Saladin marched toward Jerusalem, the Christians were determined to stop him.

## The Taking of Jerusalem

A Christian victory did not occur, however. The crusaders in Jerusalem surrendered. Saladin forbade his soldiers to kill, harm, or steal from the defeated crusaders.

**Richard the Lion-Hearted** became king of England in 1189. He was determined to retake Jerusalem from Saladin. During the Third Crusade, Richard won several victories. Richard's forces advanced to within a few miles of Jerusalem, but were unable to capture the city.

# The End of the Crusades

Later Crusades also resulted in failure for the Christians. The Fourth Crusade was supposed to regain Jerusalem, but the knights were diverted. After helping Venetian merchants defeat their Byzantine trade rivals, the knights looted Constantinople itself. What had started as a war of Christians against Muslims ended in a battle between rival Christian factions.

In Palestine, Muslims overran the crusader states. They captured Acre, the last city to fall, in 1291. This time the Muslims massacred Christian inhabitants after their victory.

**Vocabulary Builder**

loot—(loot) v. to steal things, especially from shops or homes that have been damaged in a war

# Impact of the Crusades

The crusaders failed to attain their main goal of retaking the Holy Land. Unfortunately, the Crusades left behind a legacy of religious hatred between

Christians and Muslims, since each group had committed terrible acts of violence against the other. Crusaders sometimes turned their hatred on Jews in Europe as they traveled to or from Palestine. At times crusaders destroyed entire Jewish communities.

The Crusades did, however, have some positive effects. Contact between Western Europeans and the Muslim world resulted in **cultural diffusion.** The European economy began to grow, and Europeans gained an expanded view of the world.

## Causes and Effects of The Crusades

*Use the Cause and Effect chart to answer the question: What were some of the benefits of the Crusades?*

| Causes | The Crusades | Effects |
| --- | --- | --- |
| • People wanted to free the Holy Land from Seljuk control.<br>• Many people wanted to get rich and gain new land.<br>• Some people wanted to see new places | | • Trade increased.<br>• People of different religions grew to hate each other.<br>• Popes became more powerful.<br>• Feudal kings became more powerful.<br>• Renting land helped to free serfs.<br>• Europeans became interested in traveling.<br>• People learned about other cultures. |

## Key Themes and Concepts

**Economic Systems**
The increase in trade that resulted from the Crusades had a significant impact on Europe. Desire for direct access to the riches of the East was one motive for the overseas explorations that began in the 1400s.

## Increased Trade

Trade with the Byzantine empire before the time of the Crusades had sparked the interest of Europeans in goods from the east. The amount of trade increased during the time of the Crusades. Crusaders returning to Europe brought with them interesting new fabrics, spices, and perfumes.

Merchants from the Italian city of Venice had built ships to transport crusaders. After the conflicts, these ships were available to carry products to and from Palestine. After the fall of the Christian states, Italian traders helped keep the trade routes to Palestine open. Sugar, cotton, and rice were just a few of the goods traded. The economies of both the East and the West benefited from this commerce.

## Encouragement of Learning

European interest in learning was stimulated as Europeans were introduced to Byzantine and Muslim culture. Europeans saw how the Byzantines and Muslims had preserved Greco-Roman learning and maintained great universities. Europeans were also exposed to advances these cultures had made in mathematics, science, literature, art, and geographical knowledge. Europeans gained a broader outlook and were introduced to many new ideas.

## Changes in the Church

The Crusades temporarily increased the power of the pope. Papal conflicts with feudal monarchs in Europe eventually lessened this power, however. In addition, the rift between the eastern and western churches was not healed. In fact, it was widened after the crusaders' attack on Constantinople.

## Changes in the Feudal System

The Crusades increased the power of monarchs, who had gained the right to increase taxes in order to support the fighting. Some feudal monarchs led crusaders into battle and thereby heightened their prestige.

At the same time, the institution of feudalism was weakening. Traditionally, lords had required grain or labor from their serfs. Now, needing money to finance the Crusades, they began to ask for payment of rent in money. Feudalism was weakened, and an economy based on money, not land, took hold.

# Summary

The Crusades began in the 1000s for a variety of reasons. For 200 years, Christians and Muslims fought one another and committed terrible massacres. However, both sides also had admirable leaders. The Crusades had several effects on Europe. Trade began to increase, and a money economy emerged. The Church temporarily gained power. Although feudal monarchs were strengthened, feudalism itself was weakened. Christian Europe was influenced by various aspects of Byzantine and Muslim civilization as a result of the Crusades.

**Vocabulary Builder**

rift—(rift) n. a situation in which two people or groups have had a serious disagreement and begun to dislike and not trust each other

**Preparing for the Regents**

List two ways the Crusades were a turning point for each of the following aspects of Europe.

The economy:

1.

2.

Learning:

1.

2.

Political power:

1.

2.

# Questions for Regents Practice

**Multiple Choice**

*Directions:* Review the Test-Taking Strategies section of this book. Then answer the following questions, drawn from actual Regents examinations. For each statement or question, choose the *number* of the word or expression that, of those given, best completes the statement or answers the question.

1   In traditional India, the caste system and the Hindu beliefs in karma and dharma most directly resulted in

   (1) the establishment of a set of rules for each individual in the society

   (2) the rapid industrialization of the economy

   (3) a strong emphasis on the acquisition of wealth

   (4) a strong belief in the importance of education

2   In traditional Chinese culture, which philosophy had the greatest influence on the development of social order and political organization?

   (1) Taoism

   (2) Shintoism

   (3) Confucianism

   (4) Marxism

3   After the fall of Rome, the eastern portion of the Roman empire became known as the

   (1) Persian empire

   (2) Byzantine empire

   (3) Mongol empire

   (4) Gupta empire

4   Which group had the greatest influence on early Russian culture?

   (1) Franks

   (2) Ottoman Turks

   (3) Byzantine empire

   (4) Roman Catholic Church

5   An important achievement of the Golden Age of Muslim culture was the

   (1) preservation of ancient Greek and Roman ideas

   (2) development of gunpowder

   (3) establishment of trade with South America

   (4) emergence of feudalism as a unifying force

6   Which factor helps explain the scientific and literary achievements of the Muslims during their golden age?

   (1) expansion of transatlantic trade

   (2) innovations introduced by the Europeans during the Renaissance

   (3) cultural diversity accepted by many Islamic governments

   (4) legal equality of all people in the Islamic empire

7   Which economic system existed in Europe during the early Middle Ages?

   (1) free market

   (2) socialism

   (3) manorialism

   (4) command

8   The growth of feudalism in Europe during the Middle Ages was primarily caused by the

   (1) rivalry between the colonial empires

   (2) suppression of internationalism

   (3) decline of the Roman Catholic Church

   (4) collapse of a strong central government

9  Which was a characteristic of feudalism?

   (1) Land was exchanged for military service and obligations.
   (2) Government was provided by a bureaucracy of civil servants.
   (3) Power rested in the hands of a strong central government.
   (4) Unified national court systems were developed.

10 "All things were under its domain. . . . Its power was such that no one could hope to escape its scrutiny."

   Which European institution during the Middle Ages is best described by this statement?

   (1) the guild
   (2) the knighthood
   (3) the Church
   (4) the nation-state

11 The art, music, and philosophy of the medieval period in Europe generally dealt with

   (1) human scientific achievements
   (2) religious themes
   (3) materialism
   (4) classical Greek and Roman subjects

12 Buildings such as the Gothic cathedrals in Western Europe and the Parthenon in ancient Greece reflect each society's

   (1) imperialist attitudes
   (2) cultural values
   (3) belief in democracy
   (4) rigid social structure

13 As the Middle Ages ended, the rise of a middle class in Western Europe can be attributed partly to the

   (1) economic policies of the Roman empire
   (2) increase in trade that resulted from the Crusades
   (3) strength of Christianity in medieval Europe
   (4) self-sufficiency of the manor system

14 One major result of the Crusades was

   (1) permanent occupation of the Holy Land by the Europeans
   (2) long-term decrease in European trade
   (3) conversion of most Muslims to Christianity
   (4) spread of Middle Eastern culture and technology to Europe

15 In Europe, the Crusades resulted in

   (1) a greater isolation of the region from the world
   (2) an increased demand for goods from the Middle East and Asia
   (3) the adoption of Islam as the official religion of many European nations
   (4) the strengthening of the feudal system

In developing your answer, be sure to keep these general definitions in mind:

   (a) <u>describe</u> means "to illustrate something in words or tell about it"
   (b) <u>explain</u> means "to make observations about something using facts, reasoning, and argument; to present in some detail"

*Directions:* Write a well-organized essay that includes an introduction, several paragraphs addressing the task below, and a conclusion.

**Theme:** **Culture and Intellectual Life**

> Throughout global history, political conditions in some civilizations have produced "golden ages."

**Task:**

> - Define the term *golden age*
> - Describe a golden age in a specific civilization you have studied. Give specific examples that show why the time is considered such a memorable one in that civilization's history
> - Explain the political, economic, and other conditions that help a golden age to occur

You may discuss any golden age you have studied. Some golden ages you may wish to consider include classical China, the Hellenistic Age, the Pax Romana, or the Muslim golden age. You are not limited to these suggestions.

You are *not* limited to these suggestions.
Do *not* use the United States in your response.

**Guidelines:**

**In your essay, be sure to**
- Develop all aspects of the task
- Support the theme with relevant facts, examples, and details
- Use a logical and clear plan of organization, including an introduction and a conclusion that are beyond a simple restatement of the theme

# Document-Based Question

This question is based on the accompanying documents. The question is designed to test your ability to work with historical documents. Some of these documents have been edited for the purposes of this question. As you analyze the documents, take into account the source of each document and any point of view that may be presented in the document.

**Historical Context:**

> Throughout global history, interactions between people of different belief systems have had a variety of results. Sometimes the interactions have been peaceful. At other times conflict has occurred.

**Task:** Using the information from the documents and your knowledge of global history, answer the questions that follow each document in Part A. Your answers to the questions will help you write the Part B essay in which you will be asked to

> - Evaluate the effects of interaction between people of different belief systems
> - Discuss both positive and negative effects

In developing your answers, be sure to keep these general definitions in mind:

(a) <u>evaluate</u> means "to examine and judge the significance, worth, or condition of; to determine the value of "

(b) <u>discuss</u> means "to make observations about something using facts, reasoning, and argument; to present in some detail"

# Document-Based Question

## Part A: Short Answer

*Directions:* Analyze the documents and answer the question or questions that follow each document, using the space provided.

### Document #1

> *Whoever honors his own [religion] and disparages another man's, whether from blind loyalty or with the intention of showing his own [religion] in a favorable light, does his own [religion] the greatest possible harm. Concord [peaceful harmony] is best, with each hearing and respecting the other's teachings. It is the wish of the [king] that members of all [religions] should be learned and should teach virtue.*
>
> **—Asoka, Edicts, about 270 B.C.**

1. Explain in your own words how Asoka felt people of one belief system should interact with followers of another belief system.

_____

_____

### Document #2

### The Spread of Islam

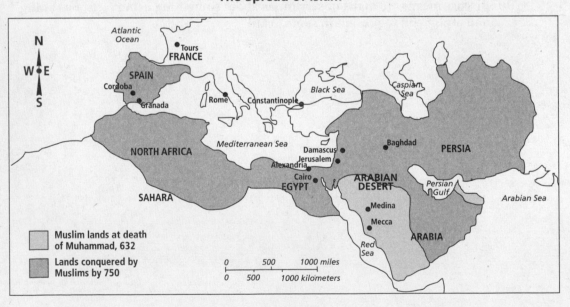

2. Over what areas did Muslim leaders exert control by A.D. 750?

_____

_____

**Document #3**

*For your brethren who live in the east are in urgent need of your help, and you must hasten to give them the aid which has often been promised them. For . . . the Turks and Arabs have attacked them. . . . They have occupied more and more of the lands of those Christians, . . . . If you permit them to continue . . . the faithful of God will be much more widely attacked by them. On this account I, or rather the Lord, beseech you as Christ's heralds to publish this everywhere and to persuade all people of whatever rank, foot-soldiers and knights, poor and rich, to carry aid promptly to those Christians and to destroy that vile race from the lands of our friends. . . . Christ commands it.*

—**Fulcher of Chartres, *Gesta Francorum Jerusalem Expugnantium*, 1095**
**[A contemporary account of Urban II's speech at the Council of Clermont]**

3. What does the speaker want Christians to do in response to his words?

_____

_____

# Document-Based Question

*Directions:* Write a well-organized essay that includes an introduction, several paragraphs, and a conclusion. Use evidence from *at least two* of the documents in your essay. Support your response with relevant facts, examples, and details. Include additional outside information.

**Historical Context:**

Throughout global history, interactions between people of different belief systems have had a variety of results. Sometimes the interactions have been peaceful. At other times conflict has occurred.

**Task:** Using the information from the documents and your knowledge of global history, write an essay in which you

> • Evaluate the effects of interaction between people of different belief systems
> • Discuss both positive and negative effects

**Guidelines:**

**In your essay, be sure to**

• Develop all aspects of the task
• Incorporate information from *at least two* of the documents
• Incorporate relevant outside information
• Support the theme with relevant facts, examples, and details
• Use a logical and clear plan of organization, including an introduction and a conclusion that are beyond a restatement of the theme

# Global Interactions
## (1200–1650)

## Unit Overview

In the years from 1200 through 1650, groups from various parts of the world came into contact with one another. In East Asia, cultural exchange occurred among China, Korea, and Japan. The Mongols established a vast empire that stretched from China westward into Europe. Over time, overland and sea trade routes linked more and more of the world and encouraged diffusion between the East and the West. In Europe, global interactions led to a new type of economy, based on money, and a new middle class. New ways of thinking emerged, in which old authority was questioned. Nations began to take shape as individual rulers gained power. In Africa, commerce contributed to the rise of powerful trading empires and the spread of Islam.

## Thematic Timeline Activity

Some of the many themes developed in Unit 3 are:

| | |
|---|---|
| interdependence | culture |
| movement of people and goods | change |
| nationalism | urbanization |
| economic systems | conflict |

Choose one of the themes listed above. As you review Unit 3, create a thematic timeline based on the theme you have chosen. Your timeline should stretch from 1200 to 1650 and include major developments and key turning points having to do with your theme.

# Early Japan and Feudalism

## The Big Idea

Early Japan:

- was strongly influenced by geography.

- borrowed selectively from Chinese culture.

- developed a feudal system.

- experienced stability and strong government during later feudal times.

## Section Overview

Even though Japan was always an island nation, it was not completely isolated. It was influenced by Korea and China. Japan was ruled by an emperor since about A.D. 500, but fights between rival warlords led to the development of feudalism in the 1100s. For several hundred years, military rulers controlled Japan. The dynasty that took power in 1603 brought stability and prosperity to Japan but imposed a rigid political and social order.

## Key Themes and Concepts

As you review this section, take special note of the following key themes and concepts:

**Geography** How did Japan's geographic setting contribute to its development?

**Movement of People and Goods** What influence did China and Korea have on Japan?

**Political Systems** How did the system of feudalism work in Japan?

**Economic Systems and Culture** In what ways did the economy and culture of Japan flourish during its later feudal age?

## Key Terms

**Place each of the key terms into one of these three categories: system of belief, political system, or cultural life.**

As you review this section, be sure you understand the significance of these key terms:

| | |
|---|---|
| Shinto | samurai |
| kami | bushido |
| Zen Buddhism | kabuki |
| shoguns | haiku |
| daimyo | |

## Preparing for the Regents

Describe two effects of geography on the development of Japanese culture.

1.

2.

## Geographic Setting

### Major Physical Features

Japan is made up of a chain of mountainous islands in the Pacific Ocean off the coast of mainland Asia. There are four main islands and more than 3,000 smaller islands. The Japanese islands are part of the Ring of Fire, a group of islands around the Pacific Ocean that are vulnerable to earthquakes and volcanoes. Underground earthquakes can cause deadly tidal waves to sweep over the islands, destroying everything in their path.

### Impact on Japanese Life

Because the islands of Japan are mountainous, the land is difficult to farm. Most of the population has always lived in narrow river valleys or along the coast. The rugged terrain has sometimes acted as a barrier to political unity.

The Japanese learned to use the sea both as a source of food and as a means of transportation from one island to another. The sea sometimes isolated Japan from other cultures, but it also acted as protection from invasion.

In addition, the experience of living in an unsettled natural environment that could bring volcanoes, earthquakes, and tidal waves taught the Japanese a deep respect for the forces of nature.

## Shintoism

The traditional Japanese religion is called **Shinto,** meaning "the way of the gods." Shinto is characterized by the worship of the **kami,** or spirits found in all living and nonliving things. Kami are thought to control the powerful forces of nature. Believers respect the kami and try to win their favor through prayer and offerings. The shared beliefs of the followers of Shinto eventually helped unite all of Japan. Shinto shrines still appear throughout Japan in places of unusual natural beauty or interest.

## Diffusion From Korea and China

Japanese culture features a unique blend of its own original traditions and ideas borrowed from the nearby civilizations of Korea and China. Korea often acted as a bridge between China and Japan.

Contact between Korea and Japan occurred as a result of both warfare and trade. Koreans introduced the Japanese to various aspects of Chinese culture.

Great interest in Chinese civilization was sparked among the Japanese. Around 600, a Japanese ruler sent nobles to study in China. For over a century, during the Tang dynasty, the Japanese upper classes imported cultural traditions and ideas directly from China. Between the 700s and the 1100s, the Japanese blended the best of China with their own traditions to produce a distinctly Japanese civilization.

### Chinese Influence on Writing
Around 500, the Koreans brought the Chinese system of writing to the Japanese. By the 800s, however, when Tang China began to decline, the Japanese adapted the Chinese system of writing to suit their own language and ideas.

### Buddhism
Koreans also brought Buddhism from China. The religion spread quickly, and it flourished alongside traditional Japanese religions. During feudal times, a Chinese sect called **Zen Buddhism** spread throughout Japan. Zen Buddhists value peace, simple living, nature, and beauty.

### Confucianism
The Japanese also were influenced by the Chinese philosophy of Confucianism, especially its ideas about proper behavior and social order. Although Buddhism took hold strongly in Japan, many Confucian ideas took root as well. These included ideas about family loyalty, honoring parents, and a respect for learning and the educated class.

### Customs and the Arts
Japanese courts adopted such Chinese customs as tea drinking and the tea ceremony. Chinese music and dancing, as well as Chinese garden design, became popular. In addition, the Japanese built their Buddhist monasteries to resemble Chinese monasteries.

### Key Themes and Concepts

**Belief Systems**
The Shinto belief system reflects the Japanese reverence for nature. Followers of Shintoism believe that all living and nonliving things possess divine spirits. This belief causes a strong respect for the natural world.

### Key Themes and Concepts

**Movement of People and Goods**
The Japanese people borrowed ideas selectively from their mainland neighbors, Korea and China. Korea acted as a bridge between China and Japan.

### Vocabulary Builder

sect—(sekt) *n.* a group of people with their own particular set of beliefs and practices, especially within or separated from a larger religious group

### Preparing for the Regents

List three ways in which China influenced Japan.

1.

2.

3.

## Feudal Society in Japan

**Emperor**
Highest rank in society but had no political power

**Shogun**
Actual ruler

**Daimyo**
Large landowners

**Samurai**
Warriors loyal to daimyo

**Peasants**
Three-fourths of population

**Artisans**

**Merchants**
Low status but gradually gained influence

# The Imperial Tradition

Early Japanese society was organized into clans with separate rulers and religious customs. Around A.D. 500, one clan, the Yamato, gained control over the largest island of Japan. They extended their rule and established themselves as the royal family of Japan, claiming to be direct descendants of the sun goddess. Between the 700s and 1100's, the emperor, who was revered as a god, presided over an elegant and sophisticated court. Although the Japanese emperor today no longer claims divinity, he still traces his roots to the Yamato clan.

# Feudal Japan

In the 1100s, the central authority of the Japanese emperor declined. Local warlords fought one another. While armies battled for power, a feudal system developed. Feudal society had distinct levels. All members of society had a defined place.

### Landowners and Warriors

Under the Japanese feudal system, the emperor still ruled in name, but powerful warrior nobles actually controlled the country. The Japanese warrior aristocracy consisted of the following groups.

**Shoguns** Under the feudal system, the real power lay in the hands of the shoguns, or top military commanders. Shoguns set up dynasties called shogunates.

**Daimyo** As in European feudalism, the shogun distributed land to vassal lords, called daimyo in Japan. The daimyo received land in exchange for a promise to support the shogun with their armies when needed.

**Samurai** The daimyo, in turn, granted land to lesser warriors called samurai, whose name means "those who serve." The samurai promised loyalty to the daimyo and lived by a strict code of conduct known as **bushido,** or "the way of the warrior." The samurai promised to be loyal, brave, and honorable. Honor was supremely important. A samurai who betrayed the code of bushido was expected to commit ritual suicide, an act called seppuku.

### Other Classes and Groups

**Peasants and Artisans** Peasants farmed the land, and artisans made weapons for the samurai. For their services, peasants and artisans were granted the protection of the samurai.

**Merchants** Despite the fact that they might possess more wealth than members of the upper classes, merchants were the lowest social class in medieval Japan. Over time, however, merchants gained more influence.

**Women** Early in the feudal period, women sometimes became warriors or ran estates. The status of women declined, however. Japanese feudal codes did not place women in high esteem. As time passed, inheritance was passed on to sons only.

# The Tokugawa Shogunate

In 1603, the Tokugawa shogunate came to power, bringing peace and stability to Japan for nearly 300 years.

## Centralized Feudal Government

The Tokugawa shoguns created a centralized feudal government. They halted the fighting among the powerful daimyo by at times forcing them to live at the capital of Edo (now Tokyo) instead of at their country estates. When the daimyo did leave the capital, their families were forced to stay under the shogun's careful watch.

## Economic Prosperity

The stability of the Tokugawa shogunate resulted in economic gains. New seeds, tools, and techniques allowed farmers to grow more food. The population grew, and towns were linked by roads. Trade increased. In the cities, a wealthy class of merchants emerged.

In addition, Tokugawa shoguns became extremely hostile toward foreigners. By 1638, they had barred all western merchants and prohibited Japanese from traveling abroad. During Japan's period of strict isolation, internal trade boomed. The economy prospered.

## Cultural Advances

During the Tokugawa shogunate, many Japanese learned Zen Buddhist practices, such as the tea ceremony and landscape gardening. At the same time, the Japanese made advances in the arts and theater. In **kabuki** theater, actors wore colorful costumes and acted out stories about families or events in history. In literature, Japanese poets created a Chinese-influenced form of poetry called **haiku**.

## Comparison With Europe

Japanese feudalism was similar to European feudalism. Both systems evolved in response to the basic desire for stability. In both Japan and Europe, emperors and kings were too weak to prevent invasions or halt internal wars. Feudalism provided a way for ruling classes to preserve law and order.

In the feudal systems of both Japan and Europe, everyone had a well-defined place in society. In both societies, power and wealth were concentrated in the hands of an elite land-owning class. As the class of respected warriors, Japanese samurai played a role similar to that of European knights. Peasants in both feudal systems worked the land and served the landowners in exchange for protection.

The position of women was different in Japan and Europe. In Japan, the status of women declined during feudal times. In Europe, the code of chivalry helped raise the status of women. Another difference was the role of religion. Leaders of the Catholic Church in Europe had more political power than Zen Buddhist monks in Japan.

# Summary

Japan was strongly influenced by geographic conditions. It borrowed cultural elements from China but adapted them to develop its own unique culture. A decline in the power of the emperor led to the development of feudalism in the 1100s. In the early 1600s, the Tokugawa shogunate emerged, bringing stability and a flowering of culture but also strict government and a social structure consisting of unequal classes. Landowners and warriors dominated Japanese society.

## Key Themes and Concepts

**Political Systems**
The Tokugawa shogunate brought stability to Japan by bringing the warring daimyo under central control.

## Note Taking

*Reading Skill:*
**Identify Supporting Details**
Make a table. List at least two details for each main idea.

| Tokugawa Shogunate | |
| --- | --- |
| Centralized Feudal Government | •<br>• |
| Economic Prosperity | •<br>• |
| Cultural Advances | •<br>• |

## Compare and Contrast

Compare and contrast Japanese feudalism and European feudalism.

List three similarities.

1.

2.

3.

List two differences.

1.

2.

## Preparing for the Regents

• How was the position of women different in feudal Japan and medieval Europe?

# The Mongols and Their Impact

The
# Big
# Idea

Mongol rule:

- covered a large area that included diverse lands and peoples.
- provided stability and prosperity.
- encouraged an exchange of goods and ideas between East and West.

## Section Overview

Around 1200, the Mongols swept out of the grasslands of central Asia to build the largest empire in the world. Under leaders such as Genghis Khan and Kublai Khan, fierce Mongol fighters conquered an area from China to Persia, entering even Europe. Often, Mongol rulers provided stability, peace, and prosperity. This stability encouraged cultural exchange between the East and the West. Mongol power declined gradually because of the size and diversity of the area they ruled, poor administration, and internal revolt.

## Key Themes and Concepts

As you review this section, take special note of the following key themes and concepts:

**Diversity** How did diversity both provide benefits and create problems for Mongol rulers?

**Culture** How did Mongol rule affect cultural development in the lands under their control?

**Interdependence** How did the exchange of goods and ideas throughout Eurasia increase with Mongol rule?

Key People
and Terms

What do most of the key people and terms have in common?

## Key People and Terms

As you review this section, be sure you understand the significance of these key people and terms:

| | | |
|---|---|---|
| Genghis Khan | Yuan dynasty | Pax Mongolia |
| Golden Horde | Mughal dynasty | Marco Polo |
| Kublai Khan | Akbar the Great | Ibn Battuta |

## Rise of the Mongols

The Mongols of central Asia were nomadic herders who roamed the grasslands with their horses and sheep. The Mongols were skillful riders and fierce fighters and raiders. Under their leader Genghis Khan, the Mongols built the largest empire in the world.

### Genghis Khan

Genghis Khan was born with the name Temujin in central Asia in the 1100s. After experiencing a difficult boyhood, Temujin became a courageous warrior and a skilled leader. As supreme ruler of the Mongol clans, he earned the title Genghis Khan, which meant "World Emperor."

With his organized and disciplined armies, Genghis Khan took most of Asia from Korea in the east to the Caspian Sea in the west. His armies advanced into Persia, India, and even northern China.

There were several reasons for these Mongol victories. The Mongols were skilled horsemen and bowmen. They also borrowed new military technology, such as cannons, from the Chinese and the Turks.

Key Themes
and Concepts

**Culture**
Mongol armies were made up of highly skilled horsemen. Armies were able to travel for days on horseback. The Mongols' expertise in horsemanship contributed greatly to their victories.

## Expansion to the West

**Eastern Europe**  During the time of Genghis Khan, the Mongols invaded Eastern Europe. They even came within reach of the Byzantine city of Constantinople. After the time of Genghis Khan, the Mongols attacked Russia, Hungary, and Poland.

One grandson of Genghis Khan, called Batu, led Mongol armies into Russia and other lands of Eastern Europe between 1236 and 1241. Known as the **Golden Horde** because of the color of their tents, this group conquered many Russian cities. They ruled from a capital on the Volga River for 240 years. Like other Mongols, the Golden Horde were fierce warriors but relatively tolerant rulers.

**The Middle East**  In the late 1300s, Timur, also called Tamerlane, gathered Mongol groups together and conquered areas of Persia, Mesopotamia, Russia, and India. Eventually a descendent of Tamerlane established the Mughal dynasty in India.

## A Mongol Dynasty in China

In 1279, **Kublai Khan,** another grandson of Genghis Khan, completed the job of conquering China by dominating the south. He ruled not only China but also Korea, Tibet, and parts of Vietnam.

Kublai Khan adopted a Chinese name for his dynasty, the **Yuan dynasty.** He did not want the Mongols to become absorbed into Chinese civilization, however. He gave the best government jobs to Mongol workers and allowed only Mongols to serve in the army, although Chinese officials still governed the provinces.

## Mughal India

Babur, a descendent of Tamerlane, established India's **Mughal dynasty,** which ruled from 1526 to 1857. Babur's grandson **Akbar the Great** was the greatest Mughal ruler. Although he was a Muslim, Akbar won the support of Hindus because of his tolerant policies.

# The Mongol Impact

Mongol power reached its greatest extent by about 1300. Mongol rule stretched throughout central Asia and China, into Russia and Europe, and into Southwest Asia and India.

## Destruction and Conquest

Fierce Mongol warriors spread terror and destruction throughout the regions they conquered. For example, Mongols devastated the thriving province of Sichuan in China. In Russia, the Golden Horde looted and burned Kiev and other Russian cities, killing countless inhabitants.

Despite brutality in war, most Mongol leaders ruled with tolerance. Genghis Khan respected academics, artists, and artisans. He listened to the ideas of scholars of many religions. His heirs continued both his conquests and his tolerant policies. Conquered peoples were often allowed to live as before, as long as they paid tribute to the Mongols.

## Lasting Effects on Russia

The Mongols ruled Russia for about 250 years. Mongol rule had a great long-term impact on Russia.

**Absolutist Government**  The absolute power of the Mongol rulers served as a model for later Russian rulers who also expected to rule without interference from groups such as nobles or the Church.

**Note Taking**

*Reading Skill:*
**Recognize Sequence**
As you read, list the important dates or periods for the rise of the Mongols. Record them in the order they occurred. Add boxes as needed.

| Rise of the Mongols | |
| --- | --- |
| Date | Event |
| 1100s | Genghis Khan was born |
| 1236–1241 | |

**Preparing for the Regents**

- Support this statement in a short paragraph: The Mongol empire in 1279 brought together many different groups and cultures.

**Key Themes and Concepts**

**Political Systems**
The Mongols were not oppressive rulers. They usually allowed people they conquered to live as they had before, as long as they paid to the Mongols the tribute they required.

**Preparing for the Regents**

Although Mongol rule brought varied peoples into contact, it cut off Russia from contact with Western Europe.

**Isolation** Mongol rule also cut Russia off from Western Europe. This isolation deprived Russia of many advances in the arts and sciences of the later Middle Ages and the Renaissance.

## Prosperity and Discontent in China

The Yuan dynasty ruled China for 150 years. They established peace and order in their kingdom. Great cities flourished in China under Kublai Khan. His capital of Khanbalik (now Beijing) was a large, well-planned city into which riches flowed. The city of Hangzhou was described as ten times the size of Venice, one of Italy's richest city-states.

However, only Mongols could serve in the military and hold the best government jobs. Chinese resentment resulted, and uprisings occurred.

**Preparing for the Regents**

• Using the map, describe the extent of Mongol rule.

### The Mongol Empire

*The Mongol Empire*
In 1294, the Mongol Empire was the largest in the world up to that time.

## Pax Mongolia and Global Trade

Political stability throughout much of Asia resulted from Mongol rule. This period of stability, known as the **Pax Mongolia,** allowed for an exchange of goods and ideas between the East and the West.

**The Silk Road and Trade** In the centuries before the rise of the Mongols, the Silk Road, the trade route that linked China to the Middle East, had become dangerous. Traders used it less. The Mongols, however, provided safe passage along the Silk Road; as a result, trade flourished. Products such as gunpowder and porcelain, as well as technology such as papermaking and the use of windmills, flowed west.

**Marco Polo and Ibn Battuta** Safer travel meant that people could explore other lands. Marco Polo, an Italian merchant, traveled to the court of Kublai Khan

**Key Themes and Concepts**

**Urbanization**
As China grew in importance as a center of trade and culture, European travelers such as Marco Polo wrote with awe of the cities of Kublai Khan.

in the late 1200s and remained for many years. His writings introduced Europeans to the beauty and riches of China.

Ibn Battuta, a scholar from Morocco, traveled at about the same time. He traveled first to Mecca and then through Asia Minor, Persia, India, Indonesia, and China. Later, he traveled to Spain. The record of his travels is of great interest to historians.

## Decline of Mongol Power

Mongol power declined for several reasons. Mongol lands were too large and diverse for one power to govern effectively. Although the Mongols were excellent fighters, they had little experience in government. They often depended on other people to do this job. Sometimes the people they chose were incompetent or corrupt.

The death of strong leaders also hurt Mongol power. After the death of Kublai Khan, for example, the Yuan dynasty broke apart. In both China and Russia, there had long been resentment of Mongol rule. In both countries a desire for independence from foreign rule provoked leaders to overthrow the Mongols and establish new dynasties.

## Summary

The Mongols conquered lands in Asia and Europe. Areas of Mongol rule included people of varied religions and nationalities, most of whom were allowed to continue their own ways of life. Mongol rule provided a period of stability and economic growth. Increased trade encouraged the movement of goods, ideas, and technology between the East and the West. As the pressures of such a diverse power grew, the Mongols declined.

**Key Themes and Concepts**

**Interdependence**
Marco Polo traveled from the West to the East and introduced Europeans to advanced Chinese culture. Ibn Battuta traveled from Africa throughout Southwest Asia and even to Spain. Both kept records of their travels. Their writings have been important to scholars all over the world.

**Vocabulary Builder**

resentment—(rih ZENT munt) n. a feeling of anger because something has happened that you think is unfair

**Preparing for the Regents**

List two causes of the decline of the Mongol empire.

1.

2.

# Global Trade and Interactions

## The Big Idea

Beginning around 1200, global trade and interactions increased as:

- the Ming dynasty prospered and China traded by both land and sea.
- goods from the East moved to Africa and Asia Minor and then to Europe.
- cities in Asia, Africa, and Europe grew.
- European coastal towns transported goods to the European interior.
- Portugal began to search for new routes to Asia.

**Key People and Terms**

What do four of the key people and terms have in common?

**Key Themes and Concepts**

**Urbanization** The prosperity of the Ming dynasty led to population growth and an increase in trade. In China, cities expanded.

## Section Overview

In the 1200s, global interactions increased. During the early Ming dynasty in China, trade thrived and cities grew. Goods continued to travel with Muslim traders by sea from China to Africa, where Venetian ships transported goods across the Mediterranean Sea to Europe. The population of Europe began to grow, leading to a revival of European trade and town life. Italian cities became flourishing centers of industry and trade. Also, the Hanseatic League gained control of trade in the Baltic and North Seas. In time, Portugal found a sea route to Asia, providing Europeans with easier access to the riches of the East. Trade and urbanization were slowed, however, by the coming of the bubonic plague in the 1300s. As a result, social, economic, and political upheaval occurred in Asia, Africa, and Europe.

## Key Themes and Concepts

As you review this section, take special note of the following key themes and concepts:

**Interdependence** What factors led to increased global trade from the 1200s to the 1500s?

**Movement of People and Goods** What were some of the major trade centers and trade routes from the 1200s to the 1500s?

**Urbanization** Why did cities grow in importance?

**Change** How did the plague affect the world socially, economically, and politically?

## Key People and Terms

As you review this section, be sure you understand the significance of these key people and terms:

| | | |
|---|---|---|
| Zheng He | Cairo | Hanseatic League |
| Canton | Venice | bubonic plague |
| Mogadishu | trade fairs | epidemic |

## Expansion of Chinese Trade

As you know, trade thrived in China under the Yuan dynasty in the 1200s. Goods traveled west along the Silk Road to Russia, Asia Minor, and lands beyond. Other goods, as well as travelers such as Marco Polo, traveled east.

The Ming dynasty took control of China in 1368, overthrowing the Mongols and driving them back behind the Great Wall. A time of economic prosperity and industrial growth followed. Population growth and expanded trade led to the growth of cities.

Ming rulers began a period of overseas expansion. In 1405, **Zheng He,** a Chinese admiral, set out with a fleet of ships. His goals were to promote Chinese trade and to collect tribute from less powerful lands.

The 1405 voyage was one of seven Zheng He would take between 1405 and 1433. During this time, he traveled through Southeast Asia, along the coast of India, around the Arabian Peninsula, and to the port cities of East Africa. He exchanged Chinese silks and porcelain for luxury items, including exotic animals for the imperial zoo. Along the way he convinced many people of the supremacy of Chinese culture.

The Chinese city of **Canton** became an important center for global trade. Canton, known today as Guangzhou, is located more than 90 miles inland from the South China Sea. In the 1500s, the Portuguese sent traders to Canton. In the 1600s, the Dutch and British followed. Europeans were allowed to trade with the Chinese in Canton, but only under strict limits.

## Major Trade Routes

Important trade routes enabled people and goods to move across Asia, Africa, and Europe.

### Across the Indian Ocean

Sea routes crossing the Indian Ocean and the Arabian Sea allowed easy trade between Asia and East Africa. Trading centers developed in eastern Africa. For example, **Mogadishu** and Great Zimbabwe thrived on trade across the Indian Ocean. European ships on their way to Asia often stopped at East African coastal cities.

### Overland Between the East and the West

A variety of overland trade routes linked Asia with the Middle East, North Africa, and Europe. Trade from China followed the Silk Road and entered Europe through Russia or Constantinople. Goods also traveled between Constantinople and India.

### Across the Mediterranean Sea

In the Middle East, Muslim traders brought goods to ports in Egypt, Syria, and Turkey. Major Egyptian ports included **Cairo** and Alexandria. In Egypt, goods could be transferred to Italian ships. Italian merchants carried the goods across the Mediterranean Sea to Europe.

## Resurgence of European Trade

Europeans were more and more interested in trade with the East. Improved methods of agriculture during the later Middle Ages allowed the European population to grow, leading to an increase in trade. The Crusades had also had an impact.

### Impact of the Crusades

As you have learned, one of the effects of the Crusades was increased European interest in the East. Returning crusaders brought back goods. Ships that had been used to carry crusaders back and forth to the Holy Land could now be used for trade. Even though the Muslims had captured the crusader states, trade continued between the Middle East and Europe through Italy.

### Italian City-States

By the late 1300s, northern Italian cities had become flourishing centers of industry and trade. Venice, Genoa, and Florence had grown rich and powerful. Venice in particular took advantage of its location to control the valuable spice trade with Asia. Eventually **Venice,** in partnership with Egypt, came to dominate trade with the East. The Venetians and their Muslim counterparts prospered.

### Key Themes and Concepts

**Interdependence**
The trade routes of this era linked Asia, Africa, and Europe. A growing economic interdependence characterized this period of history.

### Note Taking

*Reading Skill:*
**Identify Supporting Details**
Make a chart. List the major trade routes in each area.

| Major Trade Routes | |
| --- | --- |
| | Cities/Countries/Regions |
| Asia | |
| Africa | |
| Middle East | |
| Europe | |

## Preparing for the Regents

Discuss one reason for the growth of cities in each of the following areas.

China:

Italy:

Northern and Western Europe:

## Key Themes and Concepts

**Economic Systems**
Weak central governments during the earlier Middle Ages led merchants to band together for protection. The Hanseatic League, an organization made up of German towns and commercial groups, developed for this reason.

## Key Themes and Concepts

**Movement of People and Goods**
In the 1400s, Western Europeans were looking for ways to avoid the Muslim and Italian middlemen and obtain direct access to Asia's riches. This is why Portugal was looking for a new route to the East.

## Preparing for the Regents

Increases in trade transmitted not only goods and ideas but diseases as well. The Black Death spread across Eurasia and Africa along the trade routes.

After goods arrived in Venice, traders took them over the Alps and up the Rhine River to Flanders. From there, other traders took the goods throughout Europe, as far as England and to areas along the Baltic Sea.

## Trade Fairs and the Growth of Cities

Much trade within Europe went on at **trade fairs.** Trade fairs took place in towns where trade routes met, often on navigable rivers. These fairs contributed to the growth of European cities. Many traders came to settle in these areas, as did craftworkers and merchants. The population of towns increased. In time, some towns developed into large cities populated by thousands of people. The wealthiest cities were at either end of the trade routes: in Flanders in the north and in Italy in the south.

## The Hanseatic League

In northern Germany, groups of traders and merchants began to join together in the 1100s. Because central governments were still weak in Europe at this time, merchants sometimes banded together to protect their interests. By the mid-1300s, Lübeck, Hamburg, and many other northern German towns were members of the **Hanseatic League.** Eventually the league monopolized trade in the Baltic and North Seas. The league worked to make navigation safer by controlling piracy, building lighthouses, and training sailors.

## Portugal and the Spice Trade

Spices, such as pepper and cinnamon, were extremely valuable during the Middle Ages. Spices served many purposes. Not only were they used to preserve and flavor meats, but they were used in perfumes and medicines as well. The riches that spices could bring prompted many to risk their lives traveling to Asia to acquire them.

As the Ottoman empire expanded into Eastern Europe and the eastern Mediterranean, European trade routes were disrupted. As a result, Portugal, at the southwestern end of Europe, began to look for new routes. In the early 1400s, Portugal began to explore the coast of Africa. The goal was to find a direct sea route to the riches of the East. Before the end of the century, the Portugese found a route around the tip of Africa to the Indian Ocean. In the 1500s, the Portugese established posts in Africa, India, Japan, and China. Trade brought great wealth to Portugal.

# The Plague and Its Impact

The **bubonic plague,** also called the Black Death, was a highly contagious disease spread by the fleas that lived on rats. Shortly after being bitten by a flea, people developed swellings and black bruises on their skin. Within a few days, victims often died in agony. At the time, there was no cure for the plague, so many of those who became infected died.

## Outbreak in China

Although the bubonic plague had previously broken out in parts of Europe, Asia, and North Africa, it had died out on its own without affecting a large area. However, in the early 1300s, the plague appeared in Chinese cities. Rats, common in the cities of the time, carried the disease through the crowded urban centers.

## A Global Epidemic

The bubonic plague was a devastating **epidemic,** or outbreak that spreads quickly and affects a large number of people. The resurgence of trade that had been occurring since the 1100s had helped the plague to spread. Fleas from rats infested traders in the East, who then carried the plague to the Middle East. North Africa and Italy were hit next. By the mid-1300s, the plague had reached Spain and France. From there it swept across the rest of Europe.

## Effects of the Plague

The plague brought terror and devastation to all the regions it struck. Because of the number of deaths, the plague devastated economies around the world.

**Population Losses** In the early 1300s, when the plague first began to spread in China, about 35 million Chinese died. At its peak, the plague killed about 7,000 people a day in Cairo. Other regions of Africa and the Middle East suffered similar fates. By the time the worst of the plague was over, about one-third of the European population had died.

**Economic Decline** In killing so many people, the plague devastated economies around the world. In Europe, farm and industrial production declined. The people who were left were in a position to demand higher wages, and prices rose. When landowners and merchants took action to stop this wage increase, peasant revolts occurred.

Because it devastated the economies of Eurasia and North Africa, the plague also disrupted trade. Some cities and provinces that had grown rich through trade struggled to survive.

**Social and Political Change** Economic changes had social results, as the strictly defined levels of society that had been in place before began to break down. Feudalism declined as peasant revolts weakened the power of landowners over peasants. The decline of feudalism led to the growth of new political systems. In England and France especially, monarchs gained power and began to build more powerful nations.

**Confusion and Disorder** The plague threw society into disorder. Some people questioned their faith and the Church, turning to magic and witchcraft to try to save themselves. Others blamed local Jews, whom they said had poisoned the wells. As a result, thousands of Jews were murdered.

## Summary

Beginning in the 1200s, global trade and other interactions increased. China underwent a period of expanding overseas and overland trade. Trade between Asia, Africa, and Europe increased. The Crusades and a growing population helped European trade. Italian city-states transported goods across the Mediterranean Sea, becoming rich and powerful. Portugal found a direct sea route to the East. In the 1300s, however, the bubonic plague disrupted trade as well as social and political life in Europe, Asia, and parts of Africa.

**Preparing for the Regents**

Describe three ways in which the plague affected Europe, Asia, and North Africa during the 1300s.

1.

2.

3.

**Key Themes and Concepts**

**Change and Political Systems**
Many factors led to the decline of feudalism. One was that the social upheaval resulting from the plague led to the breakdown of Europe's strict social hierarchy.

# The Resurgence of Europe

The
## Big Idea

In Europe at the end of the Middle Ages:

- the commercial revolution brought new ways of doing business.

- the Renaissance introduced new ways of thinking and a flowering of culture.

- religious reformers challenged the authority of the Roman Catholic Church.

- monarchs increased their power and formed nation-states.

- limits were placed on the power of monarchs in England.

## Key People and Terms

Place each of the key people and terms into one of these four categories: system of thought or belief, culture, politics, or economics.

## Key Themes and Concepts

**Change**
Feudalism and the manor economy were based on land. Those who had land held wealth and power. A money economy gave a larger number of people the ability to gain wealth and to rise in society.

## Section Overview

From the 1300s through the 1700s, Europe underwent many changes. An increase in the importance of trade brought Europe not only an economy based on money but also a new middle class. The Renaissance brought new philosophies that emphasized the world and the individual. In art and literature, new styles and ideas emerged. Reformers challenged the power and authority of the Roman Catholic Church in a movement that divided the Church. Throughout this period, feudalism weakened. In England and France, nation-states were forming. In France, the monarchy gained power; in England, the monarch shared power with a representative body.

## Key Themes and Concepts

As you review this section, take special note of the following key themes and concepts:

**Economics** What factors led to the commercial revolution?

**Change** What were the causes and impacts of the Reformation and Counter-Reformation?

**Nationalism** How did the governments of France and England differ as they moved toward a stronger sense of nationhood?

## Key People and Terms

As you review this section, be sure you understand the significance of these key people and terms:

| | |
|---|---|
| guild | Martin Luther |
| apprentices | 95 Theses |
| capitalism | Protestant Reformation |
| commercial revolution | John Calvin |
| Renaissance | Ignatius Loyola |
| humanism | common law |
| Michelangelo | Magna Carta |
| Leonardo da Vinci | Parliament |

## The Commercial Revolution

With the expansion of trade and the growth of cities between about 1000 and 1300, new ways of doing business arose in Europe. Money grew in importance, and a new social class emerged.

### Towns and the Middle Class

A growing population and an increase in trade led to the growth of towns and cities. Urban centers based on trade gave new power to a rising new class—a middle class of merchants, traders, and artisans. They were called the "middle" class because they ranked between the older feudal classes of nobles and peasants.

## Importance of Guilds

Merchants and craftspeople formed guilds. A **guild** was a type of trade association. All of the people who worked in one craft, such as baking or weaving, would join together. Merchant guilds had great power. Typically, guilds did the following to protect the interests of their members:

- Made sure the quality of goods stayed high
- Provided social services for members, such as hospitals and aid to widows and children of members
- Regulated hours of work and prices of goods
- Ensured a supply of new artisans by training young people, called **apprentices,** in their crafts

## Rise of Capitalism

As feudalism was declining all over Europe, a new system called capitalism was emerging. **Capitalism** is based on trade and capital, the name for money used for investment. When the demand for a product is great, prices rise, and traders therefore profit. However, traders can lose everything when the demand falls. Early capitalists devised new business methods to create wealth. This and other changes are known as the **commercial revolution,** or business revolution.

## New Business Practices

The new middle class gathered together in various types of organizations. Business people were aided by banking and insurance services.

**Partnerships and Joint Stock Companies** Merchants sometimes joined together in partnerships. By pooling their capital, they could finance ventures that no single merchant could have afforded. In a partnership, a small group of merchants pooled their funds to finance a large-scale trading venture. A joint stock company allowed many merchants to pool their funds for business ventures. Joint stock companies invested in trading ventures around the world.

**Banking** Banking grew during this period. Individual merchants often did not have the capital they needed for an overseas trading venture. They borrowed from moneylenders, who developed systems of banking. Bankers also provided bills of exchange. These were needed because it was dangerous to travel over long distances with gold coins. Instead, a merchant deposited money with a banker in his hometown. The banker gave him a bill of exchange. The merchant could exchange this bill for cash in the city where he would be engaging in trade.

**Insurance** Insurance helped reduce business risks. For a small fee, a merchant's shipment was insured. If the merchant's goods were damaged or lost, the insurer paid the merchant most of the value of the shipment.

## Social Changes

The commercial revolution reshaped medieval society. For example, the use of money undermined serfdom and led to the decline of feudalism. Because feudal lords needed money to buy goods, peasants sold their farm products and began paying their lords with money rather than labor.

# The Renaissance and Humanism

The period from the 1300s to the 1500s was a time of great creativity and change in Europe. This period is called the Renaissance, which means "rebirth." It was a golden age in the arts, literature, and sciences.

## Note Taking

*Reading Skill:*
**Identify Effects**
Make a concept web. Fill in the circles with the effects of guilds. Add more circles if needed.

## Preparing for the Regents

- How does capitalism determine what goods and services are to be produced and in what quantities?

- Why were bankers important to the commercial revolution and the development of capitalism?

- What new business practices developed during the commercial revolution?

## Key Themes and Concepts

**Change**
The Renaissance represented a widespread change in worldview. Instead of concentrating on spiritual things, people began to focus more on the world in which they lived.

The Renaissance began in Italy in the mid-1300s and then spread northward. The cities of Italy were thriving centers of trade and manufacturing. Merchants in these cities had great wealth and were willing to use it to promote art and education.

**Preparing for the Regents**

Humanist thinkers used the Greeks and Romans as models. They also focused on individual achievement.

### New Ways of Thinking

During the Renaissance, Europeans developed a new way of thinking called **humanism.** During the Middle Ages, philosophers and writers had wondered about life after death. Renaissance humanists, on the other hand, were more curious about life in the present. Another feature of this new way of thinking was an emphasis on the achievements of the individual. Instead of religious issues, humanists examined worldly subjects that the ancient Greeks and Romans had studied. They hoped to use ancient learning to increase knowledge about their own times.

### Artistic Achievements

The Renaissance produced some of the greatest paintings, sculptures, and architecture in the history of the world. Renaissance architects rejected medieval forms of architecture. They returned to Greek and Roman styles for columns, arches, and domes. Artists were supported by merchants, popes, and princes.

**Preparing for the Regents**

Name three Renaissance artists, and describe an achievement of each.

1.

2.

3.

The art of the time reflected humanist concerns. Many paintings still had religious subjects, but others portrayed important contemporary figures. Renaissance art was very realistic. Renaissance artists learned the rules of perspective—the technique used to give art a three-dimensional effect. These artists also studied human anatomy and often worked from live models, so they could portray the body in amazingly accurate detail. Two of the most famous artists of the Renaissance were Michelangelo and Leonardo da Vinci.

**Artists of the Italian Renaissance**

*Artists of the Italian Renaissance*
*The Renaissance began in Italy in the mid-1300s. Over the next hundred years it spread to the rest of Europe. Rich merchants, princes, and popes took a great interest in the arts and gave financial support to artists.*

| Leonardo da Vinci | Michelangelo |
|---|---|
| • Painter, sculptor, inventor, architect, musician, engineer<br>• *Mona Lisa* (painting)<br>• Sketches and plans for flying machines and submarines | • Sculptor, engineer, poet, painter, architect<br>• *David* (statue)<br>• Dome of St. Peter's Church in Rome |
| **Raphael** | **Sofonisba Anguissola** |
| • Painter<br>• Student of Michelangelo and Leonardo da Vinci<br>• Paintings of the madonna, mother of Jesus | • Female artist<br>• *The Artist's Sisters Playing Cards* (painting)<br>• Painter for King Philip II of Spain |

**Michelangelo** Michelangelo was a sculptor, engineer, poet, painter, and architect. He is probably best known for his enormous mural on the ceiling of the Sistine Chapel in the Vatican. Michelangelo is also well known for his statue of the biblical character David.

**Leonardo da Vinci** The *Mona Lisa* is Leonardo da Vinci's most famous painting. Leonardo da Vinci was very much interested in human anatomy, and he dissected human corpses to see how muscles and bones worked. His sketches for flying machines and underwater boats were made centuries before the first airplane or submarine was actually built.

Leonardo da Vinci's sketch of a domed building.

**Northern Artists** In the late 1400s, German artist Albrecht Dürer studied the techniques of Italian masters in Italy. When he returned to his homeland, he helped to spread Italian Renaissance ideas. Dürer's paintings, engravings, and prints portray the religious upheaval of his age. Flemish painters Jan and Hubert van Eyck developed oil paint in the 1400s. In the 1500s, Pieter Bruegel painted lively, vibrant scenes of daily life. Peter Paul Rubens, another Flemish painter, blended the realism of Bruegel with the classical themes and artistic freedom of the Italian Renaissance in the 1600s.

## Literary Achievements

The humanist interest in this world was also expressed in the literature of the day. In the late Middle Ages, people had begun to write in the everyday language of ordinary people. Instead of scholarly Greek and Latin, they used vernacular languages such as Italian, French, English, and other languages.

**Dante** Dante Alighieri was an Italian writer who wrote in the years before the Renaissance took hold. Dante wrote about a journey through hell and heaven in his masterpiece *The Divine Comedy.* Because he wrote in the language of the Italian people, not in Latin, he is seen as a forerunner of the Renaissance.

**Cervantes** The work of Spanish writer Miguel de Cervantes shows the effects of the Renaissance as it moved westward. In the early 1600s, he wrote *Don Quixote.* Cervantes expressed Renaissance ideas by poking fun at the traditions of knighthood and chivalry. For example, Don Quixote, an old man who thinks he is a brave knight in battle with a giant, attacks a windmill.

**Shakespeare** William Shakespeare, writing in England around 1600, is another figure of the Renaissance. Shakespeare wrote extensively about human beings and the joys and sorrows of human life.

**Machiavelli** Niccolò Machiavelli wrote *The Prince* in the early 1500s. In this book he advises rulers on how to gain and maintain power. He tells rulers that they should use whatever methods are necessary to ensure their success. His work is seen today as a realistic picture of the politics of his time.

## Impact of the Printing Press

By 1300, papermaking and printing technology had reached Europe from China. The invention of movable type in the 1400s led to Johann Gutenberg's printing of the Bible on his press in Germany in 1456.

The printing press was important for the Renaissance and later intellectual development for the following reasons:

- **Books became more available.** Books became cheaper and easier to make.
- **Literacy increased.** Because books were more readily available, more people learned to read and write.
- **Ideas spread rapidly.** People also had access to new knowledge about such subjects as medicine and geography. Printed bibles increased the spread of religious ideas.

### Preparing for the Regents

- How did writing in the languages of ordinary people rather than Latin or Greek help Renaissance ideas to spread?

### Key Themes and Concepts

**Culture and Intellectual Life** Machiavelli, in writing about court and politics, expressed the interest of the Renaissance in worldly rather than only spiritual things.

### Preparing for the Regents

List three ways in which the printing press had an impact on European culture.

1.

2.

3.

## Note Taking

*Reading Skill:*
**Identify Main Idea and Supporting Details**
As you read Reformation and Counter-Reformation, complete an outline. Include the main ideas and supporting details. An outline has been started for you.

**Reformation and Counter-Reformation**
I. Causes of the Reformation
  A. Renaissance
    1.
    2.
  B.
  C.
II.

# Reformation and Counter-Reformation

In the 1500s, great changes occurred in European religious life: the Protestant Reformation and the Counter-Reformation.

## Causes of the Reformation

The movement that resulted in the Reformation did not have a simple cause. A number of factors led to its emergence.

- **The Renaissance** Humanism led people to question Church authority. They placed increasing faith in human reason.
- **Strong Monarchs** Strong national monarchs were emerging. Sometimes they increased their own power by supporting reformers against the Church.
- **Problems in the Church** As ordinary people examined the Church, some felt that its leaders were acting more like kings, fighting for power and wealth, than like representatives of God. Others objected to the Church charging increased fees for marriages and baptisms and selling indulgences, or pardons for sins.

## Protestant Reformers

**Martin Luther** By the 1500s, many Christians wanted to reform the Church. One such person was the German monk Martin Luther. Disgusted over the sale of indulgences, Martin Luther took action in 1517. He posted his famous **95 Theses,** which were 95 arguments against indulgences, on the door of a church in Wittenberg. This event sparked the **Protestant Reformation,** the period when Europeans broke away from the Catholic Church and formed new Christian churches.

Luther believed that people could reach heaven only through faith in God and that the pope could not grant a pardon for sins. He thought that the Bible was the only source of religious truth. Luther was excommunicated, or excluded from the Roman Catholic Church, for his radical views. The ideas of Luther, however, spread throughout northern Europe and Scandinavia, thanks in part to the printing press. Followers of Luther's beliefs were called Lutherans and—eventually—Protestants because they protested papal authority.

**John Calvin** John Calvin was another influential reformer. Born in France, Calvin was trained as a lawyer. Like Luther, Calvin believed that Christians could reach heaven only through faith in God. Calvin, however, had his own views on the power of God and the nature of human beings. He promoted the idea of predestination, the belief that God had determined before the beginning of time who would gain salvation. Calvin's followers lived strict, disciplined, and frugal lives. Calvinism spread to Germany, France, Scotland, and England.

Many other reformers also emerged. They included John Knox in Scotland and Huldrych Zwingli in Switzerland.

### Leaders of the Protestant Reformation

| Martin Luther | John Calvin |
|---|---|
| • did not believe in the sale of indulgences<br>• believed Christians reached heaven only through faith in God<br>• did not believe that priests had special powers<br>• had ideas that spread to northern Germany and Scandinavia<br>• had followers that later called themselves Protestants | • believed Christians reached heaven only through faith in God<br>• believed people are born sinners<br>• preached predestination<br>• had ideas that spread to Germany, France, Holland, England, and Scotland<br>• led a community in Switzerland |

# The Counter-Reformation

As the Protestant Reformation continued to spread, a reform movement was also taking place within the Roman Catholic Church. That movement is called the Counter-Reformation, or the Catholic Reformation. The purpose of the Counter-Reformation was to strengthen the Catholic Church as well as to keep Catholics from converting to Protestantism.

**The Council of Trent** Pope Paul III called the Council of Trent in 1545 to guide the reform movement. The council, which met on and off for 20 years, reaffirmed traditional Catholic beliefs and worked to end abuses in the Church. It also ended the sale of indulgences and created the Index—a list of banned books.

**Ignatius Loyola and the Jesuits** Another strong force in the Counter-Reformation was Ignatius Loyola. Loyola founded the Society of Jesus, also called the Jesuits. The Jesuits are a religious order that emphasizes spiritual and moral discipline as well as strict obedience to Catholic authority. Early Jesuits saw themselves as the defenders of the Catholic faith throughout the world. Many Jesuits became advisors to Catholic rulers. Jesuit missionaries spread Catholicism to Asia, Africa, and the Americas.

**The Inquisition** The Church used a court made up of Church officials to root out heresy by force. Trials were held, often using torture, to find people suspected of having beliefs that differed from official Church teachings.

## Key Themes and Concepts

**Belief Systems**
The Counter-Reformation was both an attempt to keep Catholics from leaving the Church and an effort to reform some aspects of the Church.

## Vocabulary Builder

banned—(band) *adj.* not officially allowed to meet, exist, or be used

heresy—(HEHR uh see) *n.* a belief that disagrees with the official principles of a particular religion

## The Protestant Reformation

**Long-Term Causes**
- Roman Catholic Church became more worldly
- Humanists urged return to simple religion
- Strong kings emerged and resented power of Church

**Short-Term Causes**
- Indulgences were sold in Germany
- Martin Luther wrote 95 Theses
- Luther translated the Bible into German
- Printing press helped spread ideas
- Reformers called for change

**The Protestant Reformation**

**Long-Term Effects**
- Loss of religious unity in Western Europe
- Religious wars broke out in Europe for more than 100 years
- Catholic Reformation took place
- Inquisition became stronger
- Many Jews forced into Eastern Europe

**Short-Term Effects**
- Peasants revolted
- Lutheran, Calvinist, Anglican, and other Protestant churches founded
- Holy Roman emperor weakened

# Effects of the Reformation

The Reformation had complex effects. Most obviously, it led to the formation of the Protestant churches. Other effects also occurred over time.

- **Religious and Political Divisions** The Reformation created a loss of religious unity in Western Europe. Political divisions resulted as well. Rulers often chose a religion for their nations. While some states remained Catholic, others became Protestant.

**Preparing for the Regents**

List and explain two causes and two impacts of the Reformation.

Causes

1.

2.

Impacts

1.

2.

- **Religious Conflicts** For more than 100 years after the Reformation, wars sparked in part by religion raged in Europe. In the 1500s, religious civil wars occurred in Germany and France, and Spanish Catholics battled English Protestants. The Thirty Years' War, involving many European states, occurred in the 1600s.

- **Anti-Semitism** The Reformation brought persecution to several groups, especially the Jews. Over time, restrictions placed on Jews by both Protestants and Catholics increased. For example, in some cities, Jews were forced to live in a separate neighborhood. Some Jews were expelled from their homes; others were murdered.

- **Witch Hunts** Religious fervor sometimes led people to accuse others of being witches, agents of the devil. Thousands of people, especially women, were put to death for this reason.

## Rise of Nation-States

During the late Middle Ages, kings, nobles, and the Church struggled for power. Feudalism was on the decline. Kings slowly began to increase their power. This shift occurred first in England and France, taking a somewhat different path in each country. These changes marked the beginning of feelings of nationalism—pride and devotion to one's country.

**Kings Increased Their Power**

**Kings in England**

- Decided who could build castles and where
- Forced vassals to obey them
- Established common law so that all people were treated the same
- Collected records of who owned land

- Added to their lands
- Set up organized government
- Collected taxes
- Created a royal treasury
- Set up royal courts and royal law

**Kings in France**

- Made throne hereditary
- Became allies with the Church
- Organized army
- Took French lands from English king

### Growth of Royal Power in France

When Hugh Capet became monarch in 987, feudal nobles did not perceive him as a threat to their power. However, Hugh and his heirs, known as the Capetians, slowly increased royal power. The Capetians made the throne hereditary. They also gained vast amounts of land by playing rival nobles against one another. They developed a system of tax collection as well.

The growth of royal power led in part to the Hundred Years' War, a conflict that occurred between England and France from the middle of the 1300s to the mid-1400s. When it looked as if the French would lose the war, a peasant woman named Joan of Arc managed to rally the French to victory. Killed by the English, she became an important focus of French national feeling.

Joan's efforts built up the power of the French monarchs. France's kings developed policies that weakened the power of the nobles and strengthened the power of the crown. The French representative body, the Estates General, did not limit the monarch's power during this period.

## Nationhood and Limited Monarchy in England

When the Anglo-Saxon King Edward died in 1066, his brother-in-law was chosen to rule. However, Duke William of Normandy claimed the English throne as well. A battle for the throne began. William invaded England and won the throne. As king, William the Conquerer exerted firm control.

**An English Legal System** William's successors strengthened English finance and law. Under Henry II, **common law,** or law that was the same for all people, was established. Henry broadened the system of royal justice by sending out traveling justices to enforce laws. Henry also developed an early jury system. When justices visited an area, a jury, or group of men sworn to speak the truth, was gathered by local officials. The jury determined which cases should be brought to trial.

**Magna Carta** English rulers clashed with nobles and the Church over efforts to extend royal power. In 1215, the nobility rebelled against King John and forced him to sign the Magna Carta, a charter that placed limits on the king's power. The Magna Carta stated, for example, that the monarch must obey the law and that the monarch could not raise taxes without first consulting his Great Council of lords and clergy.

**Parliament** During the 1200s, this council evolved into the representative assembly known as Parliament. In order to finance their wars, English monarchs repeatedly had to ask Parliament for funds, thus strengthening the power of Parliament.

**An English Church** The final break between the English monarchy and the Catholic Church occurred under Henry VIII in the 1500s. Angered that the pope refused to grant him an annulment of his marriage, Henry consulted Parliament and had a series of laws passed. Under these laws, Henry gained control of the English church. He created the Anglican Church, or Church of England. In 1558, Henry's daughter, Elizabeth I, became queen and firmly established England as a Protestant nation.

## Summary

A growing population and an increase in trade led to a commercial revolution in Europe and a rising middle class. At the same time, the Renaissance brought new ideas about the world and the place of people within it. Great works of art and literature emerged from this period. Inventions such as the printing press helped learning and new ideas to spread throughout Europe. There were also religious changes, as Protestant reformers challenged the authority of the Roman Catholic Church and founded new Christian churches. Throughout this period, feudalism weakened, while nations united under strong monarchs. In 1215, England instituted the Magna Carta, which placed limits on royal power. Under the Magna Carta, the English monarch shared power with Parliament, a representative body.

# African Civilizations

The
# Big
# Idea

Prior to 1600, people in Africa:

• formed diverse societies in different geographical areas.

• built trading empires in Ghana, Mali, Songhai, and Axum.

• became part of the global trade network through West African and East African trading states.

• were introduced to the religion of Islam.

• maintained traditions around village, family, and religious belief.

## Section Overview

Africa's varied climates and terrains contributed to the development of diverse societies on that continent. From about A.D. 800 to 1600, several civilizations rose and fell in Africa. West Africans built the powerful kingdoms of Mali and Songhai as they gained control over internal trade routes. In East Africa, the kingdom of Axum became a center of international trade. Africa played an important role in the global trading network. Trade with the people of Europe, the Middle East, and India encouraged an exchange of ideas between Africa and other lands. During this time, Islam became established in various parts of Africa. Still, traditional patterns of village, family, and religious life remained important through most of Africa.

## Key Themes and Concepts

As you review this section, take special note of the following key themes and concepts:

**Geography** How did the geography of Africa encourage the development of diverse civilizations?

**Power** What factors contributed to the rise and fall of powerful kingdoms in Africa?

**Movement of People and Goods** What links did Africa have with global trade routes?

**Culture** How did traditional art and literary forms reflect the beliefs of African peoples?

**Key People
and Terms**

Place each of the key people and terms into one of these categories: geography or power.

## Key People and Terms

As you review this section, be sure you understand the significance of these key people and terms:

| | | |
|---|---|---|
| savanna | Ghana | Songhai |
| desert | Mali | Axum |
| rain forests | Mansa Musa | Swahili |

**Key Themes
and Concepts**

**Geography**
The geographic diversity and geographic barriers of Africa led to the development of many different cultures on the continent.

## Africa's Varied Geography

As the second largest continent in the world, Africa accounts for one-fifth of the land surface on the Earth. Africa includes varied climates and terrains. Much of Africa is made up of **savanna,** or grassy plains. Despite hot weather and occasional droughts, this area generally has good soil and enough rain to support farming. It is therefore the most densely populated climate region. A large part of Africa, however, is made up of **desert,** or dry, barren land. The Sahara in North Africa is the world's largest desert, with extremely hot temperatures during the day and little vegetation. Africa also has a small belt of **rain forests** along the Equator and small areas of Mediterranean climate along the coast of North Africa and at the southern tip of the continent. In these areas, there is fertile farmland.

Africa has few good natural harbors. Because much of the interior is a high plateau, the rivers that flow down to the coast cascade through a series of rapids. Barriers such as these sometimes made travel difficult for Africans.

Despite geographic barriers, early Africans traveled within and beyond their continent. Much of this movement was linked to trade. Africa's gold, salt, iron, copper, and other minerals were important goods in early trade networks.

## Traditional Society and Culture

### Village Government

In most traditional African communities, power was shared among members of the community rather than exercised by a single leader. Within a village, decisions were often made by a process known as consensus. Village members gathered together for open discussions. Elders and other respected people presented their arguments before a general agreement was reached.

### Family Patterns

While the family was the basic unit of society in traditional Africa, patterns of family life varied in several ways. For example, the nuclear family was common in hunting and gathering societies. In a nuclear family, parents and children worked and lived together as a unit. In other communities, and more commonly, several generations lived in one household or near each other as an extended family.

Because traditional African social structures emphasized the group over the individual, extended families who descended from a common ancestor formed clans. Community values were greatly enhanced through identification with a particular clan.

### Religious Beliefs

Across Africa, religious beliefs were varied. Like many other ancient peoples, early Africans identified the forces of nature with divine spirits and worshiped many gods and goddesses. Many Africans believed that the spirits of their departed ancestors were present on Earth. They would call on these spirits for help in times of trouble. Some people in these long-ago African societies believed in one supreme being who was the creator and ruler of the universe.

## Rise and Fall of African Kingdoms

In Africa, towns soon became part of an important trade network. Gold and salt were the most important products that were traded. People needed salt in their diets to prevent dehydration, the dangerous loss of water from the body. There was plenty of salt in the Sahara, but there was little in the savanna. The people of the savanna traded the plentiful gold of their region to obtain salt from the Sahara.

Strong African rulers created powerful kingdoms by gaining control over the most profitable trade routes. Three trading kingdoms of West Africa were Ghana, Mali, and Songhai. The trading kingdom of Axum thrived in East Africa. Over time, Islam became an important social and religious force, particularly in North Africa and West Africa.

### Ghana

Around A.D. 800, the rulers of many farming villages united to create the kingdom of Ghana. Ghana had a powerful king who ruled over a splendid court in his capital of Kumbi Saleh. Income from the gold trade allowed him to maintain a

## Key Themes and Concepts

**Movement of People and Goods**
Throughout history, trade had a major impact on the societies of Africa. Trade brought new cultural influences to Africa, adding to its diversity.

## Note Taking

*Reading Skill:*
**Identify Main Ideas**
Make a table. As you read, write the main ideas about traditional society and culture in Africa.

| Government | Family | Religion |
|------------|--------|----------|
| • | • | • |
| • | • | • |

## Preparing for the Regents

- As you read, take note of what forces contributed to the rise and fall of the kingdoms of Ghana, Mali, Songhai, and Axum.

large army of foot soldiers and cavalry. This army helped the king to control and expand his kingdom.

Muslim merchants brought their religion and ideas when they settled in the kingdom of Ghana. The king had Muslim officials and thus was influenced by Muslim military technology and ideas about government. Ghana also absorbed Muslim cultural influences, such as Arabic writing and Muslim styles of architecture. Most of the people of Ghana, however, kept their traditional religious beliefs. Women in Ghana had a high status and played an active role in the economic life of the empire.

## Mali

Mali was also ruled by powerful kings, called mansas. Under **Mansa Musa,** the most powerful ruler, Mali extended its borders and dominated West Africa. Mansa Musa's large army kept order in the empire and protected it from attack. Although warriors were an elite class in Mali, most of its people were farmers and herders.

Mansa Musa ran an efficient government, appointing governors to rule particular areas. Mansa Musa converted to Islam, basing his system of justice on the Qur'an. He also made the city of Timbuktu a center of Muslim learning. The empire, however, declined in the 1400s, when the people could not agree on who should rule the kingdom.

### Key Themes and Concepts

**Belief Systems**
After Mansa Musa converted to Islam, he traveled to Mecca. In making this trip, he fulfilled one of the Five Pillars of Islam. His pilgrimage had a cultural impact on Mali, since Mansa Musa brought home Muslim scholars and artists and forged new trading ties.

*Kingdoms of West Africa*
*Trading centers developed over time throughout Africa. Powerful kingdoms took control of the prosperous cities and their trade.*

### Kingdoms of West Africa

| Ghana (800–1000) | Mali (1200–1450) | Songhai (1450–1600) |
|---|---|---|
| • Controlled trade in gold and salt across West Africa | • Conquered kingdom of Ghana | • Grew into largest West African state |
| • Women worked in business and government | • Mansa Musa became a great emperor | • Controlled important trade routes |
| • King had Muslim advisors | • Mali controlled gold trade routes | • Emperor set up Muslim dynasty |
| | • Timbuktu became a great trading city and center of learning | |

## Songhai

Like Ghana and Mali, the **Songhai** empire depended on a strong army to control trade routes. The emperor Sonni Ali built Songhai into the largest state that had ever existed in West Africa, bringing the wealthy city of Timbuktu under his control. Songhai established an efficient bureaucracy to govern the kingdom. Its people also expanded trade to Europe and Asia. Songhai prospered until the late 1500s, when civil war broke out. At that time, invaders from the north defeated the disunited forces of Songhai and caused the downfall of the kingdom.

## Axum

As in the kingdoms of West Africa, trade helped **Axum** become a powerful kingdom. Axum's location on the Red Sea helped Axumites command a thriving trade network linking Africa, India, and the Mediterranean world. Axum's population was descended from African farmers and from traders who had immigrated from Arabia. This merging of cultures introduced Jewish and Christian religious traditions to Axum. After being weakened by civil war and cut off from its harbors, Axum declined.

### Key Themes and Concepts

**Government**
The West African kingdoms were ruled by powerful emperors. They had strong armies to maintain order and protect the kingdoms from attack.

### Preparing for the Regents

• What influence did Islam have on the kingdoms of West Africa?

# Africa's Role in Global Trade

African states in both the eastern and western parts of the continent played a significant role in global trade. The Mediterranean and Red Seas linked Africa to the Middle East and Europe. In addition, the Indian Ocean linked East Africa to India and other Asian lands. Products from the African interior were transported overland to the coast and then out of Africa.

**African Kingdoms, 1000 B.C.–A.D. 1600**

*African Kingdoms*
*People of West Africa traded among themselves for many centuries. By about the 400s, this regional trade system had grown into an extensive trans-Saharan trade system connecting much of Africa. Over the centuries, different kingdoms controlled the routes.*

## Key Themes and Concepts

**Geography**
The bodies of water on Africa's east and west coasts were busy highways for trade with Europe and Asia. These contacts had an effect on Africa's history and culture.

## Hausa

In the 1300s, the Hausa people built city-states in what became present-day Nigeria. The products of Hausa cotton weavers and leatherworkers from the city-states traveled on caravans across the Sahara and sometimes were transported as far as Europe. By the 1500s, the Hausa dominated Saharan trade routes.

## Benin

In the rain forests on the Guinea coast, the Benin people traded ivory, pepper, and eventually enslaved people with their northern neighbors in the savanna. Benin traders also dealt with the Portuguese, who began arriving in growing numbers in the 1500s. The people of Benin learned how to cast bronze and brass. Benin bronze sculpture often portrays warriors and Benin rulers.

## East African City-States

Around 600, trading cities rose along the coast of East Africa as Arab and Persian merchants established trading communities. By 1000, East African port cities such

## Preparing for the Regents

Describe one positive and one negative effect of global trade on Africa.

**Positive:**

**Negative:**

as Mogadishu, Kilwa, and Sofala conducted a booming trade with India. Part of this commerce system included enslaved people, who were seized inland and then sold to Persian traders.

Trade led to a mixing of cultures in the city-states of East Africa. Over time, this blending of cultures resulted in the rise of a new language, **Swahili,** in which Arabic words were mixed with Bantu, an African language.

## Contributions

### The Arts

African art, most often created in ivory, wood, and bronze, was sometimes used for decorative purposes, such as jewelry. More often, however, art was closely tied to religion. Statues and masks, for example, were used in religious ceremonies and rituals.

African art also strengthened bonds within the community. Art linked people who created it with those who used it. Moreover, decorative patterns on an object often identified it as the work of a particular clan or as a possession of royalty.

### Literary Traditions

Africans used both oral and written literature to preserve their culture. Arabic was a common written language used by people in parts of Africa that were influenced by Islam. Today, Arabic documents offer insight into the laws, religions, and history of African societies.

Most often, histories and folk tales were passed down in oral form from generation to generation. Histories praised the heroism of famous ancestors or kings. Folk tales, on the other hand, blended fantasy and humor to teach important moral lessons.

### Education

In most African societies, it was the duty of the elders to teach boys and girls what their special roles would be in the community. The elders also passed down information about their clan's history and religious beliefs.

In the 1400s, Timbuktu in Mali had become a leading center of learning. Manuscripts were brought to Timbuktu to be sold at high prices. The university at Timbuktu, built by Mansa Musa, attracted students from all over the Muslim world.

### Commerce

The development of commerce by African kingdoms did much to establish trade routes that would endure for centuries. Commerce also introduced Africa to crops and animals from other lands. In addition, a rich mix of cultures developed. An unfortunate result of commerce, however, was the rise of trading enslaved people.

## Summary

Africa's geography encouraged the formation of separate kingdoms. After A.D. 800, powerful trading empires formed in western Africa. Through trade, Africans were introduced to Islam. During the same period, trading kingdoms on Africa's eastern coast were forming ties with India, the Middle East, and the Mediterranean. African societies were exposed to many new influences but retained the traditional importance of village, family, and religion.

### Preparing for the Regents

Traditional arts of Africa have had a lasting impact beyond Africa. Today many African Americans show pride in their heritage by displaying traditional African art in their homes. African music has influenced the development of jazz, rock, blues, and other styles of music.

### Vocabulary Builder

manuscript—(MAN yoo skript) *n.* a book or document written by hand

### Note Taking

*Reading Skill:*
**Identify Main Ideas and Details**
Make a concept web. Complete it with main ideas and details about the contributions of African societies. Add more circles if needed.

**Multiple Choice**

*Directions:* Review the Test-Taking Strategies section of this book. Then answer the following questions, drawn from actual Regents examinations. For each statement or question, choose the *number* of the word or expression that, of those given, best completes the statement or answers the question.

1 One similarity between the cultures of traditional China and traditional Japan was that
  (1) the educated class was held in high esteem
  (2) religion played a minor role in society
  (3) social mobility was encouraged
  (4) the people elected the political leaders

2 The code of bushido of the Japanese samurai is most similar to the
  (1) belief in reincarnation and karma of Hindus
  (2) practice of chivalry by European knights
  (3) teachings of Judaism
  (4) Enlightenment writers' theory of natural rights

3 When Russia was under Mongol domination, the effect on Russia was to
  (1) end feudalism
  (2) convert the Russian people to Hinduism
  (3) keep Russia isolated from Western Europe
  (4) reunite the Orthodox Christian Church with the Roman Catholic Church

4 Which was a major characteristic of the Renaissance?
  (1) conformity
  (2) humanism
  (3) mysticism
  (4) obedience

5 Which long-term effect did the Magna Carta and the establishment of Parliament have on England?
  (1) The system of mercantilism was strengthened.
  (2) The power of the monarchy was limited.
  (3) The new American form of government was adopted.
  (4) The influence of the middle class was reduced.

6 Which societal condition was basic to the development of Greek philosophy and Renaissance art?
  (1) rigid social classes
  (2) emphasis on individualism
  (3) religious uniformity
  (4) mass education

7 Which factor helped most to bring about the Protestant Reformation?
  (1) The Catholic clergy had lost faith in their religion.
  (2) Islam had attracted many converts in Western Europe.
  (3) Kings and princes in northern Europe resented the power of the Roman Catholic Church.
  (4) The exploration of the Americas led to the introduction of new religious ideas.

**8** Which was a major result of the Reformation?

(1) New Christian denominations emerged.

(2) Religious teachings were no longer allowed in the universities.

(3) The Crusades were organized.

(4) The power of the pope was strengthened.

Base your answers to questions 9 and 10 on the map below and on your knowledge of social studies.

**Trade Routes (13th – 15th centuries)**

9 One reason Italian city-states were able to dominate the trade pattern shown on the map was that they were

(1) centrally located on the Mediterranean Sea

(2) situated north of the Alps

(3) unified by the Hanseatic League

(4) located on the trade routes of the North Sea

10 The development of trade along the routes shown on the map led to the

(1) decline of the Greek city-states

(2) start of the Renaissance in Italy

(3) beginning of the Crusades to the Middle East

(4) first religious wars in Europe

11 African kingdoms such as Ghana, Songhai, and Axum flourished mainly because they

(1) controlled important trade routes

(2) developed self-sufficient economies

(3) became religious centers considered sacred by Africans

(4) received support from European colonial governments

12 Mansa Musa's journey to Mecca in the 1300s is evidence that

(1) the Crusades had a great influence on western Africa

(2) most African leaders were educated in the Middle East

(3) European culture was superior to the cultures of western Africa

(4) Islam had a major influence on the Mali empire

# Thematic Essay Question

In developing your answer, be sure to keep these general definitions in mind:

(a) <u>describe</u> means "to illustrate something in words or tell about it"

(b) <u>identify</u> means "to establish or indicate who or what someone (or something) is"

(c) <u>explain</u> means "to make plain or understandable; to give reasons for or causes of; to show the logical development or relationships of"

*Directions:*  Write a well-organized essay that includes an introduction, several paragraphs addressing the task below, and a conclusion.

**Theme:**  **Change**

> Throughout global history, events and changes have occurred that historians have considered turning points.

**Task:**

> - Describe what would make an event or a change a turning point in global history
> - Identify and describe two specific examples of turning points in global history
> - Explain why each of these events or changes is considered a turning point in global history. Provide specific examples of the impacts each had

You may discuss any major changes or turning points from any period of global history you have studied. Some periods you might want to consider are prehistoric times or Europe in the 1400s.

You are not limited to these suggestions.

Do not use the United States in your answer.

**Guidelines:**

**In your essay, be sure to**
- Develop all aspects of the task
- Support the theme with relevant facts, examples, and details
- Use a logical and clear plan of organization, including an introduction and a conclusion that are beyond a simple restatement of the theme

# Document-Based Question

This question is based on the accompanying documents. The question is designed to test your ability to work with historical documents. Some of these documents have been edited for the purposes of this question. As you analyze the documents, take into account the source of each document and any point of view that may be presented in the document.

**Historical Context:**

Throughout global history, cultures and civilizations have held different viewpoints on diversity in society. Diversity has been seen as both positive and negative.

**Task:**

Using the information from the documents and your knowledge of global history, answer the questions that follow each document in Part A. Your answers to the questions will help you write the Part B essay in which you will be asked to

---

- Evaluate the different viewpoints societies have held about diversity
- Discuss the positive and negative impacts that diversity may have on a society

---

In developing your answers, be sure to keep these general definitions in mind:

(a) <u>evaluate</u> means "to examine and judge the significance, worth, or condition of; to determine the value of"

(b) <u>discuss</u> means "to make observations about something using facts, reasoning, and argument; to present in some detail"

# Document-Based Question

## Part A: Short Answer

*Directions:*    Analyze the documents and answer the question or questions that follow each document, using the space provided.

**Document #1**

1. Use this map to support the statement that the Mongols ruled a diverse empire.

_____

_____

_____

## Document #2

*A nation is an association of those who are brought together by language, by given geographical conditions, or by the role assigned them by history, who acknowledge the same principles and who march together to the conquest of a single definite goal under the rule of a common body of law. . . . It is necessary that [a nation's] ideas be shown to other lands in their beauty and purity, free from any alien mixture.*

**—Giuseppe Mazzini, Italian nationalist leader, 1835**

2. Did Giuseppe Mazzini believe that diversity of ideas within a nation was positive or negative? Explain your answer.

_____

_____

_____

## Document #3

*To make our dream of a united, democratic, non-racial, non-sexist South Africa real is an immense challenge. Yet we look forward to the future with confidence and hope because we know that the people of South Africa — every racial group, every faith, every ethnic and language community in our country — are possessed of many talents, skills, and an infinite resourcefulness.*

**—Nelson Mandela, President of South Africa, 1994**

3. Does this document express a positive view of diversity? Explain your answer.

_____

_____

## Document #4

*India has not ever been an easy country to understand. Perhaps it is too deep, contradictory, and diverse.*
**—Indira Gandhi, Prime Minister of India, 1970s**

4. What problems caused by diversity does Indira Gandhi refer to in this quotation?

_____

_____

# Document-Based Question

## Part B

## Essay

*Directions:* Write a well-organized essay that includes an introduction, several paragraphs, and a conclusion. Use evidence from *at least three* of the documents in your essay. Support your response with relevant facts, examples, and details. Include additional outside information.

**Historical Context:**

Throughout global history, cultures and civilizations have held different viewpoints on diversity in society. Diversity has been seen as both positive and negative.

**Task:** Using the information from the documents and your knowledge of global history, write an essay in which you

- Evaluate the positive and negative impacts of diversity on a society
- Discuss whether you think diversity has a positive or negative influence today

**Guidelines:**

**In your essay, be sure to**
- Develop all aspects of the task
- Incorporate information from *at least three* of the documents
- Incorporate relevant outside information
- Support the theme with relevant facts, examples, and details
- Use a logical and clear plan of organization, including an introduction and a conclusion that are beyond a restatement of the theme

# The First Global Age
## (1450–1770)

Section 1: **Mesoamerican Civilizations**

Section 2: **The Ming Dynasty in China**

Section 3: **The Ottoman Empire**

Section 4: **Explorations, Encounters, and Imperialism**

Section 5: **Absolutism and the Puritan Revolution**

## Unit Overview

In the 1400s and 1500s, Europeans began exploring much of the world. These European explorers encountered rich and powerful civilizations in Africa, Asia, and the Americas. Thus began a period of increasing global interaction that continues to the present day. As interaction among civilizations increased, so did conquests and global exchanges. Around the world, these developments had significant impacts on the way people lived. One major result was that, by the 1600s and 1700s, Western European monarchs had increased their power within their own countries and around the world.

## Thematic Timeline Activity

Some of the many themes developed in Unit 4 are:

| | |
|---|---|
| economic systems | government |
| belief systems | change |
| places and regions | culture |
| movement of people and goods | political systems |

Choose one of the themes listed above. As you review Unit 4, create a thematic timeline based on the theme you have chosen. Your timeline should stretch from 1450 to 1770 and include major developments and key turning points having to do with your theme.

# Mesoamerican Civilizations

The
# Big
# Idea

The Mayas, Aztecs, and Incas:

- developed agriculture that could support large populations.

- placed great importance on religion.

- formed governments that ruled large empires.

- had advanced knowledge in areas such as agriculture, engineering, and architecture.

## Section Overview

Tens of thousands of years ago, Paleolithic hunters migrated to North America from Asia. People learned to cultivate plants and to domesticate animals. These changes led to an increase in population. In the Americas, complex societies developed. The Olmecs and, later, the Mayas and Aztecs ruled great empires in Mexico. In South America, the Incas conquered a vast area along the western coast. The people in these empires were skilled farmers, were devoted to their religions, and possessed advanced knowledge in many areas.

## Key Themes and Concepts

As you review this section, take special note of the following key themes and concepts:

**Economic Systems** Why was agriculture important to Meso-american civilizations?

**Belief Systems** What significance did religion have in the empires of the Americas?

**Government** What types of governments allowed Mesoamerican societies to rule large areas?

**Culture and Intellectual Life** What were the accomplishments and advances of the Mesoamerican empires?

## Key People and Terms

**Key People and Terms**

For each of the key people and terms, write a sentence explaining its significance.

As you review this section, be sure you understand the significance of these key people and terms:

| | |
|---|---|
| pre-Columbian | Incas |
| Mayas | terraces |
| Aztecs | quipus |

**Preparing for the Regents**

The Agricultural Revolution occurred throughout the world during Neolithic times.

## Geographic Setting

During the last ice age, large amounts of ocean water froze into thick ice sheets. A land bridge between Siberia and Alaska was created as the ocean levels dropped. Across this bridge, groups of Paleolithic hunters in Asia followed herds of bison and mammoths into North America. Over the following centuries, the nomadic hunter-gatherers in North America migrated eastward and southward. These first Americans settled in many different regions and had to adapt to a variety of climates and landforms, including woodlands, fertile plains, mountain ranges, and thick rain forests.

Slowly, between 8500 B.C. and 2000 B.C., important changes occurred. Groups of Americans learned to cultivate crops. They began to domesticate animals, perhaps in response to the disappearance of large mammals. Neolithic farmers in Mexico raised a variety of crops, including corn, beans, sweet potatoes, peppers, tomatoes, and squash. Farmers in South America domesticated llamas and other animals that were valued for their wool.

In the Americas, as in Africa and Eurasia, this agricultural revolution had a major impact on the population. Farmers settled into villages that sometimes developed into large religious centers, which could then grow into major cities. The first great American civilizations developed in Mesoamerica (also called Middle America), the region that includes Mexico and Central America.

**Ancient Cultures of Mexico**

**Ancient Cultures of Mexico**
*The descendants of the first Americans spread throughout the Americas. They established small settlements and large civilizations. Each society developed individual traits that set it apart. But they also shared some cultural elements, such as the architecture of the stepped pyramid.*

## Pre-Columbian Civilizations in the Americas

Civilizations that emerged in Mesoamerica are called pre-Columbian because they existed before the arrival of Christopher Columbus in 1492. The earliest of these major American civilizations was the Olmec Empire, which developed along the Gulf coast of Mexico and lasted from around 1400 B.C. to 500 B.C. The Olmecs built pyramid-shaped temples, invented a calendar and a system of writing, and were very religious. Through trade links, their influence extended over a large area, and characteristics of their civilization were common in later Mesoamerican civilizations.

## The Mayas

One major civilization influenced by the Olmecs was that of the Mayas, who flourished from about A.D. 300 to 900. During this period, the Mayas developed a complex agricultural society. They established large city-states in southern Mexico and throughout much of Central America.

**Preparing for the Regents**

- Compare the effects of the Agricultural Revolution that occurred in the Americas with the Agricultural Revolution in Eurasia. What were the similarities and differences?

## Farming and Trade

Farmers made up most of the Mayan population. Men usually cultivated the crops, which included maize (corn), beans, and squash. Women were in charge of turning these crops into food. Farmers paid taxes, in the form of food, to support the cities and their temples. The Mayas accumulated much wealth from a profitable trade system. Traders carried valuable honey, cocoa, and feathers across Central America along hard-packed dirt roads.

Mayan temple

## Religion

Because of the significance of religion to the Mayas, priests occupied an exalted place in the social hierarchy. These religious leaders held such importance because they alone could conduct the elaborate rituals that the Mayas believed would ensure bountiful harvests and victories in battle.

## Social Structure

Mayan civilization featured a distinct social hierarchy. Each Mayan city-state had its own ruling chief. Immediately below this chief were the nobles, who served as city officials and military leaders. Although those in the ruling class were usually men, women could occasionally obtain some degree of power. Most Mayas, however, were farmers.

## Contributions

**Architecture** In their cities, the Mayas built giant pyramid temples and large palaces. Elaborate paintings and carvings on the walls depicted events from Mayan history.

**Agriculture** Despite the tropical environment, the Mayas grew enough food to support large city populations. Farmers made this possible by clearing out the dense rain forests and then building raised fields that were capable of holding and draining rainwater.

**Learning and Science** Perhaps the most impressive achievement of the Mayas was their advanced learning. Mayas developed a hieroglyphic (picture) system of writing and recorded much of their knowledge in books made of bark. Mayan priests developed a very accurate 365-day calendar. They also used a numbering system and understood the concept of zero before Europeans did.

## Decline

Around A.D. 900, the Mayas abandoned their cities. Historians speculate that warfare or overpopulation may have caused agriculture to decline or that there were revolts by the lower classes. Remnants of this great culture remain, however. Today, millions of people in Guatemala and southern Mexico speak Mayan languages.

# The Aztecs

In the late 1200s, a nomadic group migrated from the north into the Valley of Mexico. They settled in the area, establishing their capital at Tenochtitlán. The Aztecs, who developed from this group, were fierce warriors. In the 1400s, the Aztecs used conquests and alliances to build a huge empire. Their capital grew to become a magnificent city with temples, palaces, gardens, and zoos.

## Aztec Expansion

The Aztecs founded Tenochtitlán in 1315. In the early 1400s, Aztec leaders began forming alliances with neighboring states. The Aztecs soon became the dominant power in what is now central Mexico. Then, through a series of military conquests over hundreds of smaller states, the Aztecs steadily expanded their empire. Each conquered state was given an Aztec governor. The Aztecs became wealthy from tribute, payment they took from conquered peoples. By the early 1500s, the Aztec empire covered most of Mexico and included about 30 million people.

## Social Structure

**Rulers, Nobles, and Priests** Unlike the Mayas, the Aztecs were ruled by a single emperor, who was chosen by a council of nobles and priests. Below this ruler was the noble class, from which officials, judges, and provincial governors were drawn.

**Warriors and Traders** The warriors came next in the Aztec class structure. A warrior might rise into the noble class through superior performance on the battlefield. Traders formed another group in Aztec society. They carried goods over long distances to exchange for exotic products from peoples who lived beyond the empire. Traders also scouted distant lands to help plan future conquests.

**Farmers and Slaves** Most of the people in the empire were farmers. Slaves made up the lowest class in the social structure. Members of this group were mainly criminals or enemy soldiers who had been captured. Despite their lowly status, they still had certain rights guaranteed by Aztec law. Some slaves even owned land and eventually bought their freedom.

## Religion

Religion was important to the Aztecs. As in Mayan society, priests gained significance because they led rituals that were believed to appease the gods, who would then prevent disasters. The Aztecs built a huge pyramid in the center of Tenochtitlán to honor their chief deity, the sun god.

To please their gods, Aztec priests offered many thousands of human sacrifices. Both the Olmecs and the Mayas had also practiced human sacrifice, but not on such a large scale. Aztec sacrificial victims were usually captured enemy soldiers.

## Contributions

**Learning and Science** Aztec priests devised an accurate calendar. They also established schools and recorded historical events. Aztec medical practices were advanced enough that practitioners could set broken bones and treat dental cavities.

### Preparing for the Regents

- Compare the achievements of the Mayas with those of one or more of the classical civilizations of Eurasia and Africa.

### Vocabulary Builder

alliance—(uh LY uns) n. an arrangement in which two or more countries, groups, etc. agree to work together to try to change or achieve something

### Key Themes and Concepts

**Power**
The Aztecs' ability to collect tribute from so many groups over such a large area illustrates their power in the region.

### Compare and Contrast

List two similarities and two differences between the Mayas and the Aztecs.

Similarities:

1.

2.

Differences:

1.

2.

### Preparing for the Regents

The development of a calendar was an important feature of nearly every early civilization. Calendars were useful in agriculture because they told early peoples when to plant and when to prepare for floods.

**Make Inferences**

What are some advantages of building a city on an island in a lake? What are some disadvantages?

**Preparing for the Regents**

• How was the Incan emperor similar to the pharaohs of ancient Egypt?

**Key Themes and Concepts**

**Government**
The Incan government used military power, local rulers, and an excellent road system to impose a more centralized control over the empire.

**Key Themes and Concepts**

**Culture and Intellectual Life**
Like many other groups throughout history, the Incas built upon the work of earlier civilizations to achieve even greater progress.

**Architecture and Engineering** The Aztec capital of Tenochtitlán was one of the great achievements of Mesoamerican civilization. Built on the site of present-day Mexico City, Tenochtitlán began as two small islands in Lake Texcoco. Engineers filled in parts of the lake and built wide stone causeways to connect Tenochtitlán to the mainland. Architects designed huge pyramid temples, an elaborate emperor's place, and busy outdoor markets. An estimated 200,000 people lived in Tenochtitlán in 1500, making it the largest and most densely populated settlement in Mesoamerica.

**Agriculture** As their population grew, the Aztecs found ingenious ways to create more farmland. They used a variety of fertilizers and converted swampy areas into productive farmland. They also built *chinampas*, artificial islands made of earth piled on reed mats that were anchored to the shallow bed of Lake Texcoco. On these "floating gardens" Aztec farmers raised corn, squash, and beans. The Aztecs' ability to produce an abundance of food was a major factor in the success of their empire.

## The Incas

In the 1400s, the Incas emerged from the Andes Mountains and conquered a large area that extended over 2,500 miles down the Pacific coast. The Incas ruled an empire made up of many separate conquered peoples.

### A Centralized Government

An emperor ruled the Incas. The first emperor was a warrior who led his armies through many successful campaigns of conquest. The emperor held absolute power and owned all of the people, land, herds, and mines. The emperor was also the chief religious leader and claimed divine status as the son of the sun.

The emperor headed a strong central government from the mountain capital at Cuzco. Nobles ran the provinces along with local chieftains from the conquered people of each area. Other officials collected taxes, enforced laws, and performed routine government business. The Incan government strictly controlled the lives of the millions of people within its empire. Everyone had to speak the same language, Quechua, and practice the Incan religion.

### An Empire Linked by Roads

The emperor could not have imposed this centralized rule over such a large area without a remarkable system of roads. Runners used these roads to carry news swiftly from far-off provinces to the emperor in the capital. This arrangement allowed him to keep a close watch on his empire. If necessary, Incan armies could move quickly over the roads to crush any rebellions that formed in distant corners of the empire.

### Religion

Incan religion affected all parts of daily life. The people worshiped many gods related to forces of nature as well as guardian spirits in the home. The chief Incan deity was the sun god. A powerful class of priests conducted rituals and led monthly religious festivals that featured sports and games.

### Contributions

**Engineering and Architecture** The Incan system of roads stands out as a major accomplishment of their civilization. It extended more than 12,000 miles, included hundreds of bridges, and even used tunnels and steps to pass through mountainous terrain.

The capital city of Cuzco was home to other Incan engineering feats. In the city center stood the giant Temple of the Sun, built with huge stone blocks and featuring inner walls lined with gold. The engineering of this temple was s advanced that the building was strong enough to withstand major earthquakes.

**Agriculture** Like the Aztecs, the Incas frequently borrowed and built upon id from other societies. Incan farmers used stone walls to improve upon terra built by earlier peoples. The improved terraces of the Aztecs held strips of in place on steep hillsides and prevented rain from washing away the The terraces made it possible to farm effectively in places where flat lan scarce.

**Communication** Incan government officials kept records by means of a system of knotted, colored strings called **quipus.** Historians believe that quipus may have been used to record dates and events as well as population and crop statistics.

**Science** The Incas had a calendar but were not as advanced in astronomy as the Mayas had been. One area in which the Incas excelled was medicine. They performed successful surgery to treat head wounds. The Incas also had knowledge about diseases and medicines; they used herbs as antiseptics.

UNIT 4
Section
2

### Achievements of Mesoamerican Civilizations

| Mayans | Aztecs | Incas |
|---|---|---|
| • Built giant pyramid temples | • Built city of Tenochtitlán by filling in part of a lake | • Built system of roads, bridges, and tunnels to connect empire |
| • Cleared rain forest and built raised fields for farming | • Drained swamps, built artificial islands and floating gardens for farming | • Built temple that withstood earthquakes |
| • Developed hieroglyphic writing | • Established schools | • Used terraces to farm sides of mountains |
| • Developed 365-day calendar | • Developed a calendar | • Kept records using knotted strings called quipus |
| • Used numbering system | • Treated broken bones and dental cavities | • Performed surgery and used herbs as antiseptics |

## Summary

Complex civilizations grew in the Americas from about 1400 B.C. to A.D. 1500. The Olmecs had the first major American civilization, followed by the Mayas and Aztecs in Mexico and Central America and by the Incas in South America. For all these civilizations, agriculture was a primary economic activity that allowed populations to grow. Religion unified the empires. The later Mesoamerican civilizations developed complex government systems and trade networks. Mesoamerican societies made advances in agriculture, medicine, mathematics, engineering, and other areas.

---

**Note Taking**

*Reading Skill:*
**Recognize Causes**
Make a chart. Show the causes of the success of the Incas. Add as many boxes as you need.

| Causes of the Success of the Incas |
|---|

---

**Preparing for the Regents**

List three ways in which the Incan and Roman empires were similar.

1.

2.

3.

# The Ming Dynasty in China

## Section Overview

In the mid-1300s, the Chinese overthrew foreign conquerors, the Mongols, and restored self-rule under the Ming dynasty. Ming China experienced an economic and cultural revival. In the early 1400s, China began voyages of exploration and came into contact with Europe. Later the empire turned inward, seeking to protect itself from outside influences. China did, however, greatly affect nearby Asian lands that fell into its zone of influence. Over time, Chinese culture exerted religious and cultural influence in Korea, Japan, and Southeast Asia.

## Key Themes and Concepts

As you review this section, take special note of the following key themes and concepts:

**Change** How did Chinese government, industry, and trade change after China overthrew its Mongol rulers and established a restored Chinese empire?

**Choice** Why did China choose to isolate itself from foreign trade after 1433?

**Culture** What impact did China have on other societies in Asia?

## Key People

As you review this section, be sure you understand the significance of these key people and terms:

| | |
|---|---|
| Ming dynasty | Zheng He |
| Middle Kingdom | Matteo Ricci |

## Restoration of Chinese Rule

In 1368, about 90 years after Mongol leader Kublai Khan had established Mongol rule in China, Chinese rule was restored under the **Ming dynasty.** Although the Mongols had improved trade and transportation, many Chinese resented foreign rule. In 1368, a peasant-led rebellion successfully overthrew Mongol rule, leading to the establishment of the Ming dynasty.

### The Big Idea

During the Ming Dynasty, the Chinese:

- restored Chinese rule and reaffirmed belief in Chinese superiority.

- achieved economic and cultural growth.

- after a brief period of exploration, sought to limit contact with most outsiders.

- continued to influence neighboring Asian countries culturally and intellectually.

### Key People and Terms

For each of the key people and terms, write a sentence explaining its significance.

### Key Themes and Concepts

**Change**
The Mongol Yuan dynasty, instituted by Kublai Khan, declined after his death. This decline, coupled with the fact that many Chinese hated their Mongol rulers, led to the uprisings that ended in the formation of the Ming dynasty.

## The Middle Kingdom

Under the Ming, China was once again ruled by the Chinese. Ming leaders sought to restore the country's greatness and its supremacy in the region. China traditionally thought of itself as the Middle Kingdom, the center of the earth and the source of civilization.

## Ming Government Reform

Ming rulers enacted reforms to improve the government. They brought back the civil service system. In this system, candidates had to pass a difficult exam. Confucian learning once again became important, because knowledge of Confucian classics was a key part of the exam. Ming leaders also established a board of censors to eliminate corruption in the bureaucracy.

## Looking Outward and Turning Inward

During the first several decades of the 1400s, the Chinese admiral **Zheng He** established trade links with many distant commerce centers and brought exotic animals back to China for the imperial zoo. After Zheng He's death in 1433, the Ming emperor banned the building of large oceangoing ships, and China, as a result, suddenly halted its voyages of exploration. The reasons for this abrupt change in policy were both economic and cultural. Zheng's voyages had not brought profits to the empire, and his fleets were costly to maintain. Also, Confucian scholars taught that China had the most advanced civilization in the world. Limiting contact with foreign influences therefore seemed the best way to preserve ancient traditions.

# Economic and Cultural Contributions

### Agriculture

Advances in agriculture, such as better fertilization methods, made it possible for farmers on China's eastern plains to produce enough food to support a large population. In the 1500s, corn and sweet potatoes were introduced from the Americas, further improving food production by Chinese farmers.

### Industry and Trade

The Chinese also made advances in industry during the Ming period. They utilized new technologies to increase manufacturing production. Industries such as the making of porcelain, tools, and paper thrived in Chinese cities. The Ming also repaired their neglected canal system to improve trade links across the country.

### Arts and Literature

The arts flowered during the Ming dynasty. Artists developed new styles of landscape painting and created beautiful porcelain jars and vases. Chinese silks were much admired by Europeans.

Confucian scholars produced classical poetry; other writers wrote popular fiction. Dramatic artists developed new art forms that combined drama, music, and dance.

**Vocabulary Builder**

censor—(SEN sur) n. a person who supervises the conduct and morals of others

**Preparing for the Regents**

• Why did China's attitude toward commercial contacts with foreign lands change after 1433?

**Recognize Effects**

What was the main effect of advances in agriculture in China?

**Preparing for the Regents**

• What contributions did the Ming dynasty make to China and to the world?

## Preparing for the Regents

- What attitudes did Europe and China hold regarding trade with one another?

## Key Themes and Concepts

**Culture**
China's ancient concept of itself as the Middle Kingdom, with a supreme culture, often motivated it to influence other cultures. It also made China unwilling, throughout much of its history, to be influenced by other cultures.

## Key Themes and Concepts

**Nationalism and Identity**
Because of its location on the Asian mainland, Korea was strongly influenced by China culturally and sometimes politically. Even so, Koreans developed their own culture and way of life.

# China and the West

## European Interest in China

When Portuguese and other European merchants reached East Asia in the 1500s, they were impressed by Chinese goods. European visitors to China wrote enthusiastically about the exquisite silks and porcelains they found there. Europeans were also fascinated with Chinese production of guns and gunpowder.

## Chinese Indifference

Ming leaders severely restricted foreign trade, believing European goods to be inferior. However, they allowed limited trade at the coastal outpost of Macao, near present-day Guangzhou. Imperial officials supervised this trade strictly.

Some European scholars, such as the Jesuit priest **Matteo Ricci,** did gain acceptance among the Ming. In the 1580s, the Chinese welcomed Ricci, who shared with them his knowledge of European arts and sciences. Although the Chinese were open to learning about European technology, they had little interest in the religious beliefs that Ricci and the Jesuits sought to promote.

# China's Impact Within Asia

Over time, Chinese civilization exerted a cultural influence over its neighbors in Asia. Korea, Japan, and Southeast Asia were affected by China's customs and values.

## Korea

Throughout history, China's civilization has influenced its smaller neighbor, Korea. At times, China even took political control of Korea. China affected Korea in many ways.

Korea continued to maintain its own culture, however. Sometimes, as with the Chinese civil service system, Korea made adaptations that fit its own traditions. After learning to make porcelain from the Chinese, Koreans developed a distinctive blue-green glaze called celadon. Korea also developed its own system of writing. The Korean language is unrelated to Chinese.

### China Influences Korea

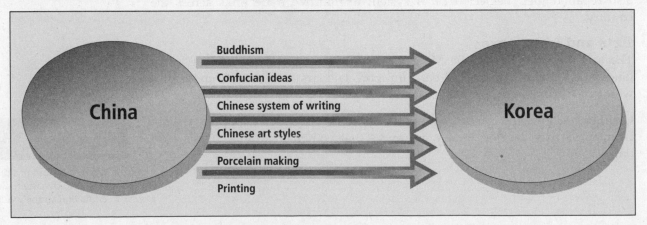

China → Korea:
Buddhism
Confucian ideas
Chinese system of writing
Chinese art styles
Porcelain making
Printing

## Japan

Korea served as a cultural bridge linking China with the Japanese islands. In the A.D. 500s, missionaries from Korea introduced Buddhism and other aspects of Chinese culture to Japan. In the centuries that followed, Japanese nobles studied in China, returning with Chinese ideas and technology. Later, however, the Japanese became less interested in China and began to blend Chinese ideas with their own.

Japanese paintings were often influenced by Chinese landscape techniques. Japanese artists developed their own styles, however, recreating historical events on magnificent scrolls. During Japan's feudal age, Japanese samurai increasingly adopted the beliefs of a Buddhist sect from China known in Japan as Zen. Zen Buddhism greatly influenced Japanese society, including its theater, literature, and art.

## Southeast Asia

The diverse cultural region of Southeast Asia consisted of a mainland area and scattered islands. It was greatly influenced by traders from China and India, who often passed through Southeast Asian ports. Buddhism, Hinduism, and Islam all entered the region.

Indian influences prevailed in much of Southeast Asia. In Vietnam, however, China exerted a greater influence. China had conquered Vietnam by the first century B.C., and it ruled the region for 1,000 years. Vietnam absorbed the Confucian civil service system and established a bureaucracy that resembled China's. Even so, Vietnam retained a strong cultural identity of its own.

# Summary

The Ming dynasty restored Chinese rule and remained in power for more than 250 years. During this period, China prospered economically and culturally. After 1433, however, the Chinese sought to limit contact with the outside world. Europeans established some trading posts in China, but the Chinese saw little value in products from the West. Chinese culture continued to exert a strong influence over Korea, Japan, and much of Southeast Asia, especially Vietnam.

**Analyzing Documents**

In what way did Korea influence Japan?

**Preparing for the Regents**

List two ways in which China influenced each of the following areas.

Korea:

1.

2.

Japan:

1.

2.

Southeast Asia:

1.

2.

# The Ottoman Empire

## Section Overview

In 1453, the Ottomans captured Constantinople and overthrew the Byzantine empire. Over the next 200 years, backed by military advances, the Ottomans built a large and powerful empire in Europe and the Middle East. During the reign of Suleiman, the Ottomans strengthened their government and military while spreading Islamic culture over a large area. Various religious beliefs, however, were tolerated within the empire. The Ottoman empire created impressive works of architecture, art, and literature. Ottoman expansion into Eastern Europe and the eastern Mediterranean disrupted European trade. As Europeans began to search for new trade routes in the 1400s, Ottoman domination was gradually weakened. This weakening, along with other factors, led to the decline of the empire.

## Key Themes and Concepts

As you review this section, take special note of the following key themes and concepts:

**Places and Regions** What lands came under control of the Ottoman empire?

**Belief Systems** How did the Ottoman empire extend Muslim influence and permit freedom of worship for people of other religions?

**Culture** What contributions did the Ottomans make to the arts and literature?

**Change** Why did Europeans seek new trade routes to East Asia?

## Key People and Terms

As you review this section, be sure you understand the significance of these key people and terms:

| | | |
|---|---|---|
| Constantinople | sultan | janissaries |
| Suleiman | millets | mosques |

## The Rise of the Ottoman Empire

By the 1400s, the once mighty Byzantine empire had been in decline for nearly two centuries. In the 1400s, it faced a growing threat from the Ottomans, a nomadic Turkish-speaking group that had migrated from central Asia into Asia Minor. In the previous century, the Ottomans had moved through Asia Minor and into the Balkans.

In 1453, Ottoman armies surrounded the Byzantine capital of **Constantinople.** During a two-month siege, Ottoman cannons pounded Constantinople's defensive walls, eventually allowing the attackers to break through and capture the city. The Ottomans changed the city's name to Istanbul and made this ancient Christian city the capital of their Muslim empire.

## Geographic Expansion

The Ottoman empire greatly expanded its territory in the century that followed the fall of Constantinople. With its well-armed forces and effective military strategies, the Ottoman empire grew quickly. After 1453, the empire made spectacular gains, conquering lands south to Mecca as well as along the Nile River in Egypt. The Ottomans also expanded further north into the Balkans and into Russia, capturing the Crimean peninsula. The Ottomans even laid siege to Vienna in 1529, causing great fear among Europeans. Ottoman forces failed to capture Vienna, however. Even so, by the 1500s, the Ottomans had built the largest, most powerful empire in the Middle East and Europe. At its peak, the Ottoman empire reached across three continents, from southeastern Europe through the Middle East and North Africa.

### Reasons for Ottoman Success

The success of the Ottomans was due in large part to new military technology. In addition to the cannons that smashed Constantinople's defenses, the Ottoman army equipped its foot soldiers with muskets. This strategy increased the soldiers' battlefield effectiveness and reduced the importance of mounted soldiers. The new military technology allowed Ottoman leaders to consolidate their rule within the empire as well as to conquer new lands.

## European Search for New Trade Routes

As the Ottoman empire expanded into Eastern Europe and the eastern Mediterranean, European trade routes were disrupted. For example, Ottoman control of the eastern Mediterranean interfered with Western Europe's trade with East Asia.

No longer able to depend on the old trade routes to Asia, Portuguese sailors sent explorers out over the oceans in search of new trade routes. They were followed later by other Europeans.

## Ottoman Achievements and Lasting Impact

### The Byzantine Heritage

The Ottoman empire absorbed many influences from the conquered Byzantine empire. As you know, the Byzantine heritage was itself a mingling of Greco-Roman and Middle Eastern influences. The Ottomans blended Byzantine culture with Muslim culture. Byzantine influences could be found in Ottoman government, social life, and architecture.

### Suleiman's Golden Age

**Suleiman,** called Suleiman the Magnificent by westerners, ruled the Ottoman empire from 1520 to 1566. Suleiman was a **sultan,** the name Turks gave to their rulers. An effective military leader who further modernized the army, Suleiman continued to add new territories to the empire.

The years of Suleiman's rule are considered the golden age of Ottoman history. A wise leader, Suleiman strengthened the government and improved the system of justice in his empire. As a Muslim, he based his law on the Sharia, the Islamic system of law. In fact, he was known to his subjects as Suleiman the Lawgiver. Although Suleiman held absolute power, he did consult with an advisor and a council in governing the empire. He also chose able officials to run the large bureaucracy he needed to supervise everyday matters of government.

**Preparing for the Regents**

- Describe the extent of Ottoman territory at the height of the empire.

**Key Themes and Concepts**

**Movement of People and Goods**
In the 1400s, Europeans wanted to get around the Muslim and Italian "middlemen" and gain direct access to Asian trade. Portugal, then Spain, and eventually other European nations sought a route to Asia that bypassed the Mediterranean.

**Preparing for the Regents**

Take note of how the Ottoman empire reflected the influence of many other cultures. Its architecture, for example, blended Greek, Roman, Persian, and Middle Eastern styles.

**Key Themes and Concepts**

**Culture**
Like other Muslim rulers, Suleiman based a system of laws on the Sharia. Developed by Quran scholars, the Sharia is the Islamic code of law. It covers moral issues, business dealings, government, and numerous other aspects of community and family life.

## A Diverse Society

The Ottomans ruled a vast area that included many diverse peoples with many religions. Nevertheless, the Ottomans held their empire together successfully for hundreds of years, thus making Islam the dominant cultural force throughout the region.

**Millets** Non-Muslims in the Ottoman Empire were organized into religious communities called millets. Each millet was allowed to maintain its own religious traditions and educate its people—as long as it obeyed Ottoman law.

**Janissaries** Ottoman leaders furthered Muslim influence by recruiting military and government officers from conquered groups. Some Christian families in the Balkans were required to turn their young sons over to the government. The boys were converted to Islam and trained for service. The best soldiers became janissaries, members of an elite force in the Ottoman army.

## Arts and Literature

Throughout the empire, Muslim architects built many palaces as well as Muslim houses of worship, or **mosques.** Muslim religious structures promoted the further spread of Muslim culture into the Christian areas of southeastern Europe.

Ottoman arts reflected Persian influences. Painters used Persian styles to create detailed miniatures and beautiful illuminated manuscripts. Ottoman writers and poets used Persian and Arab models to produce great works in the Turkish language.

# The Decline of the Ottoman Empire

Although the Ottoman empire survived into the twentieth century, it began to decline much earlier than that. The reasons for this decline came from both within and outside the empire.

## Internal Disorder

Problems developed within the Ottoman empire. Slowly, over time, nations were able to break free from foreign Ottoman rule. The empire also experienced government corruption and poor leadership in its later years.

## European Advances

The rising power of European nations was the major external reason for the Ottoman decline. In 1571, Spain and its Italian allies defeated an Ottoman fleet at Lepanto. Even while the Ottomans were adding to their empire in the 1400s and 1500s, they were increasingly being cut out of global trade.

By the 1700s, European commercial and military technology had surpassed that of the Ottomans. Also, industrially based European economies became stronger than the Ottoman economy, which was still based on agriculture. The commercial revolution in Europe, therefore, was a strong factor in Ottoman decline.

# Summary

During the 1400s and 1500s, the powerful Ottoman empire arose in Asia Minor. The empire expanded over time to cover a vast area, extending the influence of Islam. Ottoman architecture, literature, and other art forms flourished. The Ottoman empire dominated trade for many years, forcing European countries to begin seeking new routes to Asia. However, European advances in technology as well as internal disorder contributed to the fall of the empire.

# Explorations, Encounters, and Imperialism

## Section Overview

In the 1400s, seeking a greater share of the rich Asian spice trade, Europeans began to make oceanic voyages of exploration. Benefiting from new technology, the Portuguese and the Spanish were the first to establish global trade empires in the 1500s. The Dutch, English, and French soon joined them, competing for colonies in Asia, the Americas, and Africa during the 1600s and 1700s. These interactions had a great global impact as food, people, plants, animals, technology, and diseases passed from continent to continent.

## Key Themes and Concepts

As you review this section, take special note of the following key themes and concepts:

**Movement of People and Goods** How did global trade patterns change between the late 1400s and the 1700s?

**Science and Technology** What types of technology allowed Western Europeans to explore the oceans?

**Interdependence** What motives did Europeans have for establishing colonies between 1500 and 1700?

**Change** What major changes did the European expansion bring to peoples around the world?

## Key People and Terms

As you review this section, be sure you understand the significance of these key people and terms:

| | | |
|---|---|---|
| Reconquista | imperialism | triangular trade |
| cartographers | Ferdinand Magellan | Middle Passage |
| astrolabe | sepoys | encomienda |
| Vasco da Gama | conquistadors | Columbian Exchange |
| Christopher Columbus | plantations | mercantilism |

## The Eve of Exploration

As Europeans were looking for new routes to the riches of Asia, two nations in Western Europe, Portugal and Spain, took the lead. Both of these nations had the technology, resources, and political unity to support sea travel. Both of these nations had also struggled with Muslim rule in their countries and had created Christian kingdoms.

### Reconquista and Expulsions

The marriage of Ferdinand of Aragon to Isabella of Castile in 1469 brought together two powerful Spanish kingdoms. In 1492, Ferdinand and Isabella forced the Muslims from Granada, their last stronghold in Spain. This victory completed the Reconquista, a campaign begun by Christians in the 700s to recapture Spain

The
**Big
Idea**

Between the late 1400s and 1700s, Western Europeans:

• benefited from technology in mapmaking, navigation, shipbuilding, and weaponry.

• found new sea routes and dominated trade with Asia, Africa, and the Americas.

• competed with each other to establish profitable colonies.

• began global interactions that greatly affected people around the world.

**Key People and Terms**

Place each of the key people and terms into one of these categories: geography, economics, conflict.

**Preparing for the Regents**

• Why did Portugal and Spain pursue sea exploration?

from the Muslims. After achieving political unity in Spain, Isabella sought to establish religious unity. She launched a brutal crusade against the Moors (Muslims) and Jews who refused to convert to Christianity. Many people were killed, and about 150,000 were forced into exile.

### Reasons for European Exploration

Although Europeans had long traded in Asian countries, travel to the east had been disrupted by Ottoman control of the eastern Mediterranean, a situation that interfered with Western Europe's trade with Asia. By the 1400s, seeking to gain access to the Asian spices so highly valued on their continent, Europeans looked to reopen global trade links. Italian and Muslim merchants, however, controlled the routes between Asia and Europe. Muslim traders brought goods to the Mediterranean, and Italian traders carried the goods to the rest of Europe. Each time the goods changed hands, they became more expensive. To gain direct access to Asian trade, Portugal and Spain looked for new oceanic routes.

### Impact of Technology

Advances in technology greatly aided Europeans in their quest to explore the oceans.

**The Printing Press** In the mid-1400s, German printer Johann Gutenberg became the first person to use a printing press to print a book. Through the use of movable metal type, the printing press enabled people to make books quickly and cheaply. As a result, books became more readily available. Europeans were able to gain access to new ideas and information on a broad range of topics, including geography.

**Gunpowder** European explorers also benefited from advances in military technology. Since Arab traders had brought gunpowder to Europe in the 1200s, Europeans had been making advances in weaponry. By the late 1400s, the Portuguese were equipping their ships with sturdy cannons. Eventually, the use of cannons helped the Portuguese win control of the Indian Ocean trade network.

**Naval Technology** Mapmakers, or **cartographers,** created better maps and charts of the sea. Moreover, European sailors learned to use the magnetic compass to determine direction and the **astrolabe,** an instrument perfected by the Arabs, to figure out their latitude at sea. Europeans also built bigger and better ships. The Portuguese used caravels, ships whose sails, masts, and rudders allowed explorers to sail across or against the wind.

## Early Explorations and Encounters

### Around Africa to Asia

In 1415, Prince Henry, the son of the Portuguese king, carried out a plan to improve his country's navy. Known to later generations as Henry the Navigator, this prince gathered experts in science, mapmaking, and shipbuilding. Their work led to a fleet of ships that explored the coast of West Africa. In 1488, Bartholomeu Dias rounded the Cape of Good Hope at the southern tip of Africa.

About a decade later, **Vasco da Gama** followed Dias's route around Africa and traveled across the Indian Ocean to an Indian port. Although he lost half his ships, Da Gama returned home with Asian spices that he sold at a high profit. The Portuguese had established a successful all-water trade route to Asia and would soon expand their empire.

**Summarize**

In one sentence, summarize the reasons for European exploration.

**Preparing for the Regents**

• What technologies made European overseas expansion possible?

**Key Themes and Concepts**

Science and Technology
This instrument to the right, the astrolabe, was used to calculate the exact latitude of a ship.

**Note Taking**

*Reading Skill:*
**Recognize Sequence**
Make a table. List the important dates or general times for the early explorations and encounters. Record them in the order they occurred. Add boxes as needed.

| Early Explorations and Encounters | |
|---|---|
| Date | Event |
| | |
| | |
| | |

## Columbus Reaches the Americas

The success of the Portuguese inspired Ferdinand and Isabella of Spain to try to gain a share of the rich spice trade in the East. Furthermore, Isabella sought to spread Christianity.

In 1492, an ambitious Italian sailor from Genoa convinced the Spanish monarchs to finance his plan to reach Asia by sailing across the Atlantic Ocean. **Christopher Columbus** and his crew thus sailed west for India in three small ships, striking land after two months. Although he landed at an island in the Caribbean Sea, Columbus thought that he had reached islands off the coast of Asia. Later explorers realized that he had reached the Americas, a continent they had not known existed.

Spain and Portugal soon both claimed the islands that Columbus had explored in his voyages. In 1493, to settle the issue, Pope Alexander VI established the Line of Demarcation, which divided the non-European world into two zones. Spain could trade and explore west of the line; Portugal had the same rights east of the line. One year later, with the Treaty of Tordesillas, the two nations agreed to move the line.

## Europeans Compete for Colonies

The domination by one country of the political and/or economic life of another country is called **imperialism.** Europe's activities in Asia, Africa, and the Americas from the 1500s through the 1700s foreshadowed the major era of European imperialism in the 1800s.

### Imperialism in Africa

In the 1400s, the Portuguese explored the coasts of Africa, establishing a string of forts in the west and capturing several port cities in the east. The Portuguese, however, were unsuccessful in their attempts to push into the African interior. As a result, the Portuguese gained little profit from their victories.

In the mid-1600s, the Dutch arrived at the southwestern tip of Africa and established the Cape Town settlement. At Cape Town, Dutch sailors could repair their ships as they traveled to or from the East Indies. The Dutch farmers who settled in and around Cape Town were called Boers. The Boers ousted or enslaved many Africans, whom they considered their inferiors.

### Imperialism in Asia

Soon after European powers had established direct trading links with Asia, they sought to gain more permanent control there. First Portugal and then other nations set up colonies in Asia, creating competition in the region.

### European Trade in the East, 1700

*European Trade in the East, 1700 Merchants and traders established trading posts and ports throughout the Eastern Hemisphere. European ships carrying valuable goods criss-crossed the waters of Europe, Africa, and Asia.*

**Portugal** In the early 1500s, the Portuguese took control of the Indian trade network from the Muslims. The Portuguese seized the port of Malacca on the Malay Peninsula in the Indian Ocean, the most important Arab trading city. They also conquered cities on the east coast of Africa and destroyed Arab ships at sea. For most of the 1500s, Portugal controlled the spice trade between Europe and Asia.

Although the Portuguese were powerful at sea, they were not able to conquer much territory on land. Also, they caused much resentment with their intolerant policies. Portuguese missionaries and traders destroyed Hindu temples, massacred Muslims, and sank pilgrim ships. By the late 1500s, Portuguese power in the Indian Ocean was declining.

**Preparing for the Regents**

• Describe differences between Portuguese and Dutch trading activity in Asia.

**The Dutch** The first Europeans to challenge Portuguese domination of the Asian spice trade were the Dutch. In the late 1500s, Dutch fleets had established their own trade links with Asia. Soon their sea power surpassed that of the Portuguese. A group of wealthy Dutch merchants formed the Dutch East India Company in the early 1600s. In 1641, the Dutch seized Malacca from Portugal and began trading with China. The Dutch established closer ties with local leaders and stirred less resentment among Asians than had the Portuguese. Soon they dominated the Asian spice trade. Their trading empire did not begin to decline until the 1700s.

**Spain** Spain also founded colonies in Southeast Asia in the 1500s. Spain financed the voyage of Portuguese noble **Ferdinand Magellan** that completed the first circumnavigation of the world. To circumnavigate something is to go completely around it. During this voyage Magellan claimed the island chain that today is called the Philippines for Spain in 1521. (The islands were named for the Spanish king, Philip II.) This island group gave Spain a base from which to trade with China and spread Catholic teachings to East Asia.

**Identify Central Issues**

How did England gain control over India?

**England and France** In the 1700s, England and France became competing forces in the Asian trade network, concentrating on India. The Mughal dynasty in India had been rich and powerful in the 1600s, but weak rulers and civil wars early in the next century weakened the kingdom. The British and French East India Companies made alliances with local rulers, and each company organized its own army of **sepoys,** or Indian troops. In the 1750s, the British East India Company and its sepoys pushed the French out of their trading posts. The British East India Company forced the Mughal emperor to allow it to collect taxes in northeast India. Before long, the company was the real power in the region.

## Imperialism in the Americas
After Christopher Columbus landed in the West Indies, friendly relations existed between the Spanish and the Native Americans for a while. However, these friendly feelings did not last.

**Identify Causes**

List two reasons why Spanish conquistadors came to the Americas.

1.

2.

**Spanish Conquistadors** Many Spanish conquistadors, or conquerors, traveled to the Americas in the years following Columbus's voyages. Some of these adventurers came in search of gold; others wanted to convert the inhabitants of the land to Christianity.

One of the earliest conquistadors, Hernan Cortés, landed in Mexico in 1519. Two years later, having formed alliances with discontented peoples within the Aztec empire, Cortés had conquered the empire. In 1532, another conquistador, Francisco Pizarro, destroyed the Incan empire in Peru.

**Reasons for Spanish Success** The Spanish were able to conquer these empires so quickly for several reasons.

- The Spanish used armor, horses, and powerful weapons that the Native Americans had never seen before.
- The Spanish found allies among Native American groups who hated being ruled by the Aztecs or Incas.
- Diseases brought by Europeans killed millions of native people, causing them to believe that their own gods had deserted them.

**Battle for North America** Spain's profitable American empire attracted the attention of other European powers. Dutch, English, and French explorers had long searched North America for a Northwest Passage to Asia. By the 1600s, these nations had planted permanent colonies on the continent.

In the 1600s, the French settled Canada. Naming their colony New France, the French sent over fur trappers and missionaries and established forts and trading posts from Quebec to Louisiana.

In 1607, the English established their first permanent colony in North America at Jamestown. Throughout the 1600s, large numbers of English settlers followed. Some came for profit, others hoped to own land, and still others, such as the Puritans, came seeking religious freedom. The English monarch asserted control over his 13 American colonies, but they still had more self-government than the French or Spanish in North America.

Spain, France, England, and the Netherlands frequently clashed over territory and trade in North America. In the mid-1700s, the British defeated the French in the French and Indian War. The French then had to give up Canada, leaving much of North America to England.

# Triangular Trade and Slavery
## Causes of the Slave Trade

In the 1500s, Europeans came to view enslaved Africans as the most valuable African trade goods. At that time, Europeans began buying large numbers of Africans to satisfy the labor shortage on American **plantations,** or large estates. The slave trade eventually grew into a huge and profitable business. The trade that involved Europe, Africa, and the Americas was sometimes referred to as **"triangular trade"** because the sea routes among these three continents formed vast triangles.

## The Middle Passage

The voyage from Africa to the Americas on the slave ships was called the **Middle Passage**. Conditions were terrible on these ships. Hundreds of people were crammed onto a single ship. In fact, millions of Africans died on the way from disease, brutal mistreatment, or suicide. Those who survived were forced to work on plantations in the American colonies.

## Effects of the Slave Trade

By the 1800s, when the slave trade ended, an estimated 11 million Africans had been sent to the Americas. The slave trade caused local wars to develop in Africa. As a result, traditional African political structures were undermined. Through slavery, many African societies were deprived of the talents of strong, intelligent people. West Africa especially lost many young men and women. Some societies and small states disappeared forever. Other states formed, some of them dependent on the slave trade.

**Key Themes and Concepts**

**Science and Technology**
One of the reasons for the relatively swift Spanish conquest of the Americas was the military technology of European powers.

**Key Themes and Concepts**

**Government**
English monarchs allowed their colonists more self-government than the French or the Spanish did. English political traditions of representative government and limited monarchy took root in the English colonies.

**Note Taking**

*Reading Skill:*
**Identify Causes and Effects**
Make a flowchart. Show the causes and effects of the slave trade.

**Key Themes and Concepts**

**Human Rights**
Slavery involved a complete disregard for human rights. Enslaved persons lost their freedom and could be bought and sold. In the Middle Passage, enslaved people endured disease, overcrowding, and brutal mistreatment.

## Note Taking

*Reading Skill:*
**Identify Main Ideas and Details**
Make a concept web. Complete it with main ideas and details about the Spanish empire. Add more circles as needed.

## Key Themes and Concepts

**Change**
In the cultural blending described here, Europeans were influenced by Native American foods as well as African farming methods, music, cooking styles, and crops such as okra and palm oil.

## Vocabulary Builder

descent—(dee SENT) *n.* your family origins, especially your nationality or relationship to someone important who lived a long time ago

## Key Themes and Concepts

**Movement of People and Goods**
The introduction of American crops such as corn and potatoes to other continents contributed to population growth in Europe, Africa, and Asia in the 1700s.

# The Spanish Empire

During the 1500s, the Spanish empire in the Americas stretched from California to South America and brought great wealth to the nation. In return, the Spanish brought their government, religion, economy, and culture to the Americas.

- **Government** Spain maintained a strict control over its distant empire. The king ran the colonial government through his representatives, or viceroys, who ruled the provinces.

- **Religion** The Catholic Church was very important in the colonies. Church leaders helped run the government and worked to convert thousands of Native Americans to Christianity.

- **Encomienda System** Spanish law allowed its colonies to trade only with Spain. Growing sugar cane on large plantations became an important business activity in the colonial empire. Because plantations needed so many workers, the Spanish created the encomienda system. A conquistador, under this system, was granted land along with permission to demand labor or tribute from Native Americans in the area. After many of the overworked Native Americans died, the Spanish brought enslaved Africans to do the work.

- **Culture** Over time, the people in the colonies developed a new culture that combined European, Native American, and African traditions. These people spoke Spanish but also used Native American and African words. The art, architecture, and daily life in the empire were influenced by all three cultures.

- **Social Classes** A social structure developed that placed people in a hierarchy. The Spanish-born people at the top of the class structure were known as *peninsulares*. Creoles was the name given to those of European descent who were born in the colonies. *Mestizos* were people of mixed Native American and European descent, and *mulattoes* was the term for those of mixed African and European descent.

**Social Structure of the Spanish Colonies**

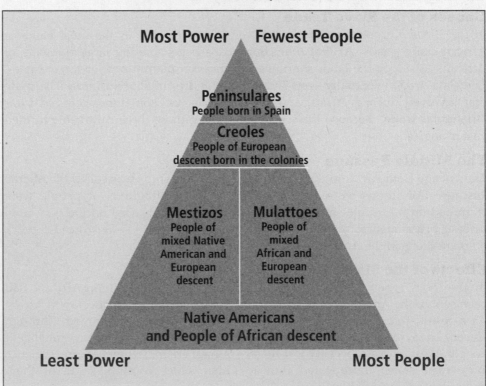

# The Columbian Exchange: Plants, Animals, People, and Diseases

A global exchange of people, plants, animals, ideas, and technology began during this time, leading to profound changes for people in Asia, the Americas, Africa, and Europe. Because it started with Columbus, it is called the Columbian Exchange.

Plants, including maize (corn) and potatoes, traveled to Europe, Africa, and Asia. Other plants, such as bananas and rice, traveled back to the Americas. From Africa and Asia, goats and chickens came to the Americas. Unfortunately, other exchanges occurred: diseases such as measles and typhus devastated populations in the Americas.

## European Capitalism and Mercantilism

Increased trade with the colonies encouraged European capitalism, the investment of money to make a profit. Joint stock companies grew in significance, since they allowed Europeans to gather the capital necessary to finance overseas voyages. Moreover, European nations adopted a new policy of mercantilism. This policy involved building up national wealth by exporting more goods than the nation imported. Colonies supplied the parent nation with raw materials and served as a market for its exports.

The expansion of capitalism and mercantilism affected the lives of many Europeans. Nobles became less powerful because their wealth was based in the land they owned. On the other hand, many merchants, whose wealth was based in trade, grew richer. A middle class developed on the continent during this period. The lives of peasants did not change significantly in the 1500s and 1600s.

**The Columbian Exchange**

From the Americas to Europe, Africa, and Asia

maize (corn)
potato
sweet potato
beans
peanut
squash
pumpkin
tomato
chili pepper
avocado
pineapple
cocoa
tobacco
quinine (a medicine)

wheat
sugar
banana
rice
grape (wine)
dandelion
horse
pig

cattle
goat
sheep
chicken
smallpox
measles
typhus

From Europe, Africa, and Asia to the Americas

**Preparing for the Regents**

• Describe two positive and two negative aspects of the Columbian exchange.

## Effects of European Imperialism

| Slave trade and disruption of African political, economic, and social life | New economic policies of mercantilism and expansion of capitalism led to increased standard of living for Europeans | Increased cultural diffusion of people, plants, animals, ideas, and technology throughout the world |
| --- | --- | --- |

## Summary

From 1500 to 1700, European nations set off on voyages of exploration, establishing empires and trade links around the world. Western European countries competed for colonies and trade in Asia, Africa, and the Americas. Slave trade between Africa and the Americas developed into a huge and profitable business. This European expansion had an enormous impact, resulting in many exchanges that altered the lives of people around the world.

**Preparing for the Regents**

• In what ways were the voyages of Columbus a major turning point in global history?

# Absolutism and the Puritan Revolution

## Section Overview

In the 1500s and 1600s, several rulers in Asia and Europe sought to centralize their political power. Claiming divine right, or authority from God, leaders such as Philip II in Spain and Louis XIV in France gained complete authority over their governments and their subjects. England resisted the establishment of absolutism. After a civil war, England's Parliament enacted a Bill of Rights that limited the English monarch's powers.

## Key Themes and Concepts

As you review this section, take special note of the following key themes and concepts:

**Government** How did monarchs in India, Spain, France, and Russia work to increase their political power in the 1500s and 1600s?

**Power** What ideas did absolute monarchs use to justify their power?

**Political Systems** In what ways was England's experience of absolutism different from that of other European countries?

**Choice** What choices did Parliament make in England to assure a check on absolutism?

## Key People and Terms

**Key People and Terms**

Place each of the key people and terms into one of these categories: religion or government/politics.

As you review this section, be sure you understand the significance of these key people and terms:

| | | |
|---|---|---|
| absolutism | Ivan the Terrible | Oliver Cromwell |
| Akbar the Great | Peter the Great | Glorious Revolution |
| Philip II | Puritans | English Bill of Rights |
| divine right | Thomas Hobbes | limited monarchy |
| Louis XIV | *The Leviathan* | |
| Jacques Bossuet | Puritan Revolution | |

## Global Absolutism

In the 1500s and 1600s, monarchs in Europe and Asia sought to centralize their power. This trend led to absolutism, in which autocratic rulers had complete authority over the government and the lives of the people in their nation.

### Absolutism in Mughal India

One place where absolutism appeared in the 1500s was India. In the last half of the 1500s, **Akbar the Great** ruled the powerful Mughal empire in India. Akbar strengthened the central government and made his empire larger and stronger than any in Europe at the time. He modernized the army, encouraged trade, and introduced land reforms. Akbar solidified his reign by recognizing India's diversity and promoting religious tolerance. Akbar's successors were not as strong. Mughal rulers in the late 1600s were much less tolerant, and Mughal power declined, allowing France and England to spread their influence in the region.

## Absolutism in Spain

In the 1500s, Spain became the most powerful nation in Europe. Wealth from its empire in the Americas helped Spain's power to grow.

**Charles V** From 1519 to 1556, Charles V, the grandson of Ferdinand and Isabella, was king of Spain as well as Holy Roman Emperor. Ruling such a large and diverse area in Europe took its toll on Charles, however. He faced military threats from the French, from German Protestant princes, and from the Ottoman empire under Suleiman. In 1556, an exhausted Charles gave up his titles and divided his empire. His brother Ferdinand became Holy Roman Emperor, and his son Philip ruled Spain, the Netherlands, and the vast Spanish overseas empire.

**Philip II** Ruling from 1556 to 1598, Philip II expanded his own power as well as the influence of the Catholic Church and the Spanish empire. Philip wanted to control all aspects of government, believing that he ruled by **divine right.** According to this way of thinking, the king is an agent of God, and his authority to rule comes directly from God. Philip was a hard-working ruler, and he did much to promote a golden age in Spain.

In the 1600s, however, Spanish power slowly declined as rulers spent too much money on wars overseas. The Spanish relied on gold and silver from their colonies and as a result neglected business at home. The middle class felt that they were being taxed too heavily and stopped supporting the government.

## Absolutism in France

By the late 1600s, France had replaced Spain as the most powerful European nation. Over time, French kings had increased royal power by increasing the influence of the government and reducing the power of the nobles. During the reign of King Louis XIII and his chief minister, Richelieu, the two groups who did not bow to royal authority—the nobles and the Protestant Huguenots—were subdued or defeated. Additionally, the French army became the strongest in Europe.

**The Sun King** Inheriting the throne in 1643 as a five-year-old child, **Louis XIV** ruled France for 72 years. He continued to strengthen the monarchy, taking the sun as the symbol of his power and commanding complete loyalty from his subjects. Louis's claim to absolute power was strengthened by a court preacher, Bishop **Jacques Bossuet.** Bossuet argued that as God's representative on Earth, the king was entitled to unquestioning obedience. During his reign, Louis:

- expanded the bureaucracy, appointing officials to collect taxes, recruit soldiers, and carry out his rule in the provinces.
- built the lavish, immense Palace of Versailles outside of Paris.
- organized a highly disciplined army, the strongest in Europe.
- persecuted the Protestant Huguenots, depriving the nation of many of its most hard-working and prosperous citizens.

**Louis's Legacy** Under Louis XIV, France was a wealthy, powerful state with great cultural influence. However, Louis's extravagant parties at Versailles and his costly wars left France in debt, and there was social unrest among the starving peasants. The French monarchy would not survive even a century after Louis XIV's death in 1715.

### Key Themes and Concepts

**Power**
Common features of absolute monarchies included strong armies, limited representative bodies, and high taxes.

### Preparing for the Regents

According to the concept of divine right, the king was above the law and could rule as he saw fit.

- Compare divine right to the ancient Chinese Mandate of Heaven, another form of the divine right concept.

### Key Themes and Concepts

**Power**
Armand Richelieu was a Roman Catholic cardinal. His role as advisor to the king—and virtual ruler of France—showed the power of the Catholic Church at that time.

### Preparing for the Regents

- Why did Louis XIV consider himself the "Sun King"? How is that name an example of his belief in absolutism?

## Note Taking

*Reading Skill:*
**Compare and Contrast**
Make a Venn diagram.
Show the similarities
and differences between
absolutism in Spain, in
France, and in Russia.

Absolutism

## Absolutism in Russia

During the 1400s, the city of Moscow became the center of power in Russia. The driving force behind Moscow's rising power was Ivan III, known as Ivan the Great. Ruling from 1462 to 1505, Ivan the Great built the framework for absolute rule in Russia. Following Ivan the Great, a long series of absolute rulers dominated Russia.

**Ivan the Terrible** Czar Ivan IV centralized royal power and introduced Russia to extreme absolute power. His harsh ruling style and fits of violence earned him the title "Ivan the Terrible." To enforce his will, Ivan organized a personal police force. Dressed in black robes, these agents of terror slaughtered rebellious nobles and destroyed towns suspected of disloyalty.

**Peter the Great** Peter the Great ruled Russia as czar from 1682 to 1725. Peter worked to centralize royal power and bring all Russians under his authority. He reduced the power of the nobility and gained control of the Russian Orthodox Church.

**Westernization Under Peter** Peter wanted to modernize Russia. He traveled to Western European cities to study western technology and brought back ideas on how to westernize Russia. For example, he copied European customs and dress, sent nobles to Europe to be educated, and developed mining and textiles. His capital at St. Petersburg served as his "Window on the West" to trade with Western Europe. However, Peter sometimes resorted to force and terror to achieve his goals.

*Statue of Peter the Great,
St. Petersburg*

**Peter's Strong Foreign Policy** Peter created the largest army in Europe in the late 1600s and used it to expand Russian territory and gain ports on the Baltic Sea. Russia also extended eastward, sending explorers across the Bering Strait into North America.

Peter failed at one of his goals, however: to gain a port that would not be closed due to freezing in winter. He fought the Ottoman Turks to gain a warm-water port on the Black Sea but did not succeed. However, Catherine the Great, another absolute ruler of Russia, would successfully acquire Black Sea ports in 1795.

# Reaction to Absolutism in England

While other nations turned to absolutism in the 1500s and 1600s, England moved in a different direction. England's Parliament managed to resist successfully the consolidation of royal power.

The royal Tudor family ruled England from 1485 to 1603. These monarchs, who included Henry VIII and Elizabeth I, generally worked well with Parliament. Even though the Tudors believed in divine right, they saw great value in maintaining good relations with Parliament.

In 1603, however, the English throne passed to the Stuarts. Lacking the diplomatic skills of the Tudors, the Stuarts with their absolutist tendencies came into conflict with Parliament.

## The Stuart Monarchs

The first Stuart king, James I, sought to increase his power, using divine right as his justification. Needing money for his wars and extravagant court life, he frequently clashed with Parliament over financial issues and foreign policy. Angering leaders in the House of Commons, James eventually dissolved

## Key Themes and Concepts

**Political Systems**
The tradition of sharing political power dates back to the Greek and Roman periods. In England, the Magna Carta of 1215 limited the ruler's power by protecting certain basic legal rights of English citizens and by forcing the monarch to consult an English council before raising taxes. To learn more about the Magna Carta, see Unit 3, Section 4.

Parliament and imposed his own taxes. The king also conflicted with **Puritans,** who were seeking to "purify" the church of England by eliminating Catholic practices.

The Stuart monarchs received support in their struggles with Parliament from the English thinker **Thomas Hobbes.** In *The Leviathan,* Hobbes wrote that people were by nature selfish and greedy and would fall into chaos unless ruled by a strong government that could suppress rebellion. Hobbes believed that an absolute monarchy—one that could command obedience—was needed to maintain order.

James's son Charles I inherited the throne in 1625. He continued his father's absolutist policies. Charles created problems during his reign by:

- putting his enemies in prison without trials.
- imposing very high taxes.
- angering the Puritans.
- dissolving Parliament.

Charles, however, had to summon Parliament back in 1640 to obtain funds to put down a Scottish rebellion. As a result, civil war broke out between Charles I and Parliament.

### The English Civil War

The English Civil War, sometimes called the **Puritan Revolution,** pitted Charles's supporters, the Cavaliers, against Parliament's forces, the Roundheads. The Roundheads, a group consisting of Puritans, country landowners, and town-based manufacturers, were led by the skilled military commander **Oliver Cromwell.** Cromwell's disciplined army won several battles against the Cavaliers and captured the king in 1647. Parliament put Charles I on trial and beheaded him in 1649.

Charles I was the first king ever to be tried and executed by his own subjects. This event shocked other European monarchies and signified that absolutism would not prevail in England.

### Cromwell and the Commonwealth

After Charles's execution, Parliament's House of Commons abolished the monarchy, the House of Lords, and the official Church of England. England became a republic, called the Commonwealth, with Oliver Cromwell as its leader. England's years as a republic were troubled, however. Supporters of Charles II, the uncrowned heir to the throne, attacked England from Ireland and Scotland. Cromwell led forces into Ireland to crush the uprising. In 1653, Cromwell took the title of Lord Protector and ruled through the army. By the time of his death in 1658, many people had become tired of Puritan rule.

### The Restoration

In 1660, Parliament invited Charles II, son of Charles I, to become king of England. This marked the restoration of the Stuart monarchy. In 1685, his brother, James II, inherited the throne. James quickly became unpopular because of his Catholicism and his absolutist policies.

### The Glorious Revolution

**Parliament Overthrows James II** Parliament, in 1688, fearing the return of Catholic dominance, took strong measures. Parliament asked James's daughter, Mary, and her Dutch husband, William, to take the English throne. William and

**Vocabulary Builder**

suppress—(suh PRES) *vt.* to stop people from opposing the government, especially by using force

**Key Themes and Concepts**

**Change**
The English Civil War was an important turning point in the history of constitutional government in England. The ideas of the Puritans also shaped the development of the colonies that became the United States in the 1700s.

**Note Taking**

*Reading Skill:*
**Identify Causes and Effects** Make a flowchart. Write the causes and effects of the English Civil War.

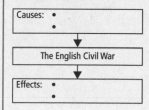

Causes: •
         •

↓

The English Civil War

↓

Effects: •
         •

Mary, both Protestants, arrived in England as James II fled to France, completing a bloodless transfer of power. This nonviolent overthrow is known as the **Glorious Revolution.**

### Vocabulary Builder

ensure—(en SHOOR) *v.* to make certain that something will happen properly

**English Bill of Rights** Before they could take power, William and Mary were forced to accept the English Bill of Rights, a set of acts passed by Parliament to ensure its superiority over the monarchy. This Bill of Rights:

- stated that the king must work regularly with Parliament.
- stated that the king must give the House of Commons financial control.
- abolished excessive fines and cruel or unusual punishment.
- affirmed habeas corpus, meaning that no person could be held in jail without first being charged with a crime.

With this Bill of Rights, England became a **limited monarchy,** a government in which a legislative body limits the monarch's powers.

**Toleration Act** The Toleration Act of 1689 granted Protestant dissenters, such as Puritans and Quakers, limited toleration. Catholics, however, were denied toleration.

### Key Themes and Concepts

**Political Systems**
Parliament imposed regulations that ensured its supremacy over the monarch with the English Bill of Rights.

### Revolution in England

| A.D. | 1600 | 1610 | 1620 | 1630 | 1640 | 1650 | 1660 | 1670 | 1680 | 1690 |
|------|------|------|------|------|------|------|------|------|------|------|

**1649** English execute Charles I.

**1688** During Glorious Revolution, William and Mary become king and queen.

**1603** Stuart dynasty takes power in England.

**1625** Charles I becomes king.

**1642–49** English Civil War takes place.

**1660** England restores the monarchy.

**1685** James II becomes king.

## Summary

Through the 1500s and 1600s, absolutism became dominant through much of Europe and parts of Asia. In India, Akbar the Great consolidated his power. In Spain, France, and Russia, absolutist monarchs claimed that they ruled by divine right and sought to extend their political power. While other nations accepted absolutism, England stood as a contrast to this trend. After the Puritan Revolution and the Glorious Revolution of the mid-1600s, the English Bill of Rights was passed, establishing England as a limited monarchy.

### Preparing for the Regents

- Outline the main points of the two competing political ideologies, absolutism and limited monarchy, described in this section.

**Multiple Choice**

*Directions:* Review the Test-Taking Strategies section of this book. Then answer the following questions, drawn from actual Regents examinations. For each statement or question, choose the *number* of the word or expression that, of those given, best completes the statement or answers the question.

1 One way in which the civilizations of the Sumerians, the Phoenicians, and the Mayas were similar is that all

(1) developed extensive writing systems

(2) emphasized equality in education

(3) established monotheistic religions

(4) encouraged democratic participation in government

2 An effect of a mountainous topography on Incan and Chinese civilizations was the development of

(1) industrialization

(2) a single-crop economy

(3) desalinization projects

(4) terrace farming

3 "The challenges of the Andes helped the Incas develop a thriving civilization." Based on this statement, what does the author believe?

(1) Language and religion are important to national unity.

(2) Cultural diversity flourishes in areas of agricultural prosperity.

(3) People can overcome the limitations of their environment.

(4) Natural resources are necessary for economic independence.

4 The Incas, the Romans, and the Mongols were similar in that all

(1) developed systems of writing

(2) extended control over neighboring peoples

(3) established industrial economies

(4) adopted democratic political systems

5 One factor that accounted for Chinese influence on traditional Japanese culture was the

(1) continuous warfare between the countries

(2) geographical location of the countries

(3) refusal of western nations to trade with Japan

(4) annexation of Japan into the Chinese empire

6 An observation that could be made about the Ottoman empire in the 1400s and 1500s is that the empire

(1) originated in Hungary

(2) had a strategic location between Europe and Asia

(3) was totally landlocked

(4) had control over most of Western Europe

7 Which was the characteristic of Western European nations that *most* enabled them to establish colonies in Asia and Africa?

(1) rigid social class structures

(2) self-sufficiency in natural resources

(3) frequent political revolutions

(4) advanced technology

8  One reason the Spanish conquistadors were able to conquer the Aztec and Inca empires rapidly is that

(1) these empires had no standing armies

(2) the Spanish had better weapons than the Aztecs and Incas did

(3) the Spanish greatly outnumbered the Aztecs and Incas

(4) the Aztecs and Incas joined together to fight the Spanish

9  In Latin America during the early period of Spanish colonialism, the deaths of large numbers of the native people led to

(1) a decline in Spanish immigration to the Americas

(2) the removal of most Spanish troops from the Americas

(3) the importation of slaves from Africa

(4) improved health care in the colonies

10  One major effect of the European slave trade on Africa was that the slave trade

(1) strengthened the traditional African economic systems

(2) led to a rapid decrease in tribal warfare

(3) hastened the decline of African kingdoms

(4) increased the number of trade routes across the Sahara

11  According to the theory of mercantilism, colonies should be

(1) acquired as markets and sources of raw materials

(2) considered an economic burden to the colonial power

(3) granted independence as soon as possible

(4) encouraged to develop their own industries

12  A major result of the European Age of Exploration was

(1) a long period of peace and prosperity for the nations of Western Europe

(2) extensive migration of people from the Western Hemisphere to Africa

(3) the fall of European national monarchies and the end of the power of the Catholic Church

(4) the end of regional isolation and the beginning of a period of European global domination

Base your answer to question 13 on the chart below and on your knowledge of world history.

### Social Structure of the Spanish Colonies

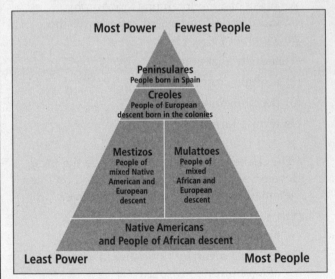

13  Based on the chart, which conclusion can be drawn about the social structure of the Spanish colonies?

(1) Power was evenly distributed among many people.

(2) Native Americans ruled over the Spanish.

(3) Native Spaniards dominated society.

(4) Creoles represented a majority of the population.

14 In English history, the Magna Carta (1215) and the Bill of Rights (1689) both reinforced the concept of

(1) a limited monarchy

(2) religious toleration

(3) a laissez-faire economy

(4) universal suffrage

15 During the Age of Absolutism (1600s and 1700s), European monarchies sought to

(1) increase human rights for their citizens

(2) centralize political power in their nations

(3) develop better relations with Muslim rulers

(4) encourage the growth of cooperative farms

# Thematic Essay Question

In developing your answer, be sure to keep this general definition in mind:

>  <u>discuss</u> means "to make observations about something using facts, reasoning, and argument; to present in some detail"

*Directions:*   Write a well-organized essay that includes an introduction, several paragraphs addressing the task below, and a conclusion.

**Theme:**   **Political Systems**

> Several empires and nations throughout global history have been ruled by strong leaders who have followed policies of absolutism.

**Task:**

> - Define the term *absolutism*, and identify the characteristics of absolutist rule
> - Select a nation or empire you have studied that was ruled according to the principles of absolutism. Identify the specific characteristics of absolutist government that existed in this nation or empire
> - Discuss the major positive and/or negative effects that absolutism had on this empire or nation.

You may discuss any nation or empire that you have studied. Some suggestions you may wish to consider are the Incan empire, the Byzantine empire, the Ming empire in China, the Ottoman empire of Suleiman the Great, Spain (Philip II); France (Louis XIV); or Russia (Peter the Great).

**You are *not* limited to these suggestions.**
**Do *not* use the United States in your answer.**

**Guidelines:**

**In your essay, be sure to**
- Develop all aspects of the task
- Support the theme with relevant facts, examples, and details
- Use a logical and clear plan of organization, including an introduction and a conclusion that are beyond a simple restatement of the theme

# Document-Based Question

This question is based on the accompanying documents. The question is designed to test your ability to work with historical documents. Some of these documents have been edited for the purposes of this question. As you analyze the documents, take into account the source of each document and any point of view that may be presented in the document.

**Historical Context:**

> Throughout history there has been widespread interaction among cultures. Sometimes the effects of this interaction have been positive, and at other times the effects have been negative.

**Task:** Using the information from the documents and your knowledge of global history, answer the questions that follow each document in Part A. Your answers to the questions will help you write the Part B essay in which you will be asked to

- Evaluate the major effects that exchanges between cultures have had on the groups involved
- Discuss both positive and negative effects

In developing your answers, be sure to keep these general definitions in mind:

(a) <u>evaluate</u> means "to examine and judge the significance, worth, or condition of; to determine the value of"

(b) <u>discuss</u> means "to make observations about something using facts, reasoning, and argument; to present in some detail"

# Document-Based Question

## Part A: Short Answer

*Directions:* Analyze the documents and answer the question or questions that follow each document, using the space provided.

### Document #1

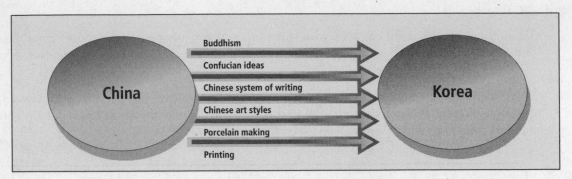

1. What were some of the effects of the interaction between China and Korea?

_____

_____

_____

### Document #2

*That which led the Spaniards to these terrible deeds was the desire for gold, to make themselves suddenly rich. . . . In a word their greed, their ambition gave occasion to their barbarism. For the Spaniards so little regarded the health of their souls that they allowed this great multitude to die without the least light of religion. The Indians never gave them the least cause to offer them violence until the excessive cruelties of the Spaniards, the torments and slaughters of their countrymen, moved them to take arms against the Spaniards.*
—**Bartolomé de Las Casas,** *Brief Report on the Destruction of the Indians,* **1542**

2. Summarize the point of view of this writer concerning the interaction between Spaniards and Native Americans in the 1500s.

_____

_____

_____

_____

## Document #3
### Atlantic Trade Routes, 1750

3. What negative effect did the Atlantic trade have on Africans? How did the Atlantic trade benefit Europeans?

_____

_____

# Document-Based Question

## Part B

## Essay

*Directions:*   Write a well-organized essay that includes an introduction, several paragraphs, and a conclusion. Use evidence from *at least two* of the documents in your essay. Support your response with relevant facts, examples, and details. Include additional outside information.

### Historical Context:

Throughout history there has been widespread interaction among cultures. Sometimes the effects of this interaction have been positive, and at other times the effects have been negative.

**Task:**   Using the information from the documents and your knowledge of global history, write an essay in which you

- Evaluate the major effects that exchanges between cultures have had on the groups involved.
- Examine both positive and negative effects.

### Guidelines:

**In your essay, be sure to**

- Develop all aspects of the task
- Incorporate information from *at least two* of the documents
- Incorporate relevant outside information
- Support the theme with relevant facts, examples, and details
- Use a logical and clear plan of organization, including an introduction and a conclusion that are beyond a restatement of the theme

# An Age of Revolutions (1750–1914)

## Unit Overview

The years between 1750 and 1914 were years of enormous change. The Scientific Revolution and the Enlightenment brought a completely new way of looking at the world. Monarchies were overthrown, and representative forms of government emerged. In some areas, people tried to return to previous ways. In other areas, however, feelings of nationalism arose that led to the growth of nations. During this same time, enormous changes were occurring in Europe and Japan. The Industrial Revolution brought changes in social structure and created new ways of living and working. Industrialization also spurred nations to build empires in Africa and Asia, creating an economy that spanned the globe.

## Thematic Timeline Activity

Some of the many themes developed in Unit 5 are:

| | | |
|---|---|---|
| change | political systems | science and technology |
| nationalism | conflict | culture and intellectual life |
| power | imperialism | |

Choose one of the themes listed above. As you review Unit 5, create a thematic timeline based on the theme you have chosen. Your timeline should stretch from 1750 to 1914 and include major developments and key turning points having to do with your theme.

# Scientific Revolution and Enlightenment

## The Big Idea

From the 1500s through the 1700s, Europeans:

• experienced the Scientific Revolution, which caused people to change their views about the universe.

• entered the Enlightenment, in which philosophers applied reason to society and government.

• developed ideas about basic human rights and proper government.

• began to consider democratic ideas and the concept of nationalism.

## Section Overview

In the 1500s and 1600s, the Scientific Revolution changed the way Europeans looked at the world. People began to make conclusions based on experimentation and observation instead of merely accepting traditional ideas. During the 1600s and 1700s, belief in the power of reason grew. Writers of the time sought to reform government and bring about a more just society. Despite opposition from government and church leaders, Enlightenment ideas spread. Some absolute rulers used their power to reform society. Over time, concepts of democracy and of nationhood developed from Enlightenment ideas and contributed to revolutions.

## Key Themes and Concepts

As you review this section, take special note of the following key themes and concepts:

**Science and Technology** How did the Scientific Revolution change the way Europeans looked at the world?

**Culture and Intellectual Life** How did the Scientific Revolution lead to the ideas of the Enlightenment?

**Government** What reforms did Enlightenment thinkers want to bring to government in the 1600s and 1700s?

**Change** What impact did the Enlightenment have on Europe?

### Key People and Terms

• What do many of the key people and terms have in common? Explain.

## Key People and Terms

As you review this section, be sure you understand the significance of these key people and terms:

| | |
|---|---|
| Scientific Revolution | natural laws |
| Nicolaus Copernicus | John Locke |
| heliocentric | natural rights |
| Galileo Galilei | Baron de Montesquieu |
| Isaac Newton | Voltaire |
| scientific method | Jean-Jacques Rousseau |
| René Descartes | enlightened despots |
| Enlightenment | Joseph II |

## New Ideas About the Universe

Throughout the Middle Ages, European scholars believed that Earth was the center of the universe. This idea was based on Greco-Roman theories and the teachings of the Church. However, European scientists began to think differently in the 1500s. Influenced by the critical spirit of the Renaissance, they questioned the old ideas about the world. This period of change was called the **Scientific Revolution**.

## Copernicus

In the mid-1500s, Polish scholar **Nicolaus Copernicus** challenged the belief that Earth was at the center of the universe. Using mathematical formulas, Copernicus suggested that the universe was **heliocentric,** or sun-centered. He said that the planets revolved around the sun. Most scholars rejected Copernicus's theory.

## Galileo

In the early 1600s, an Italian astronomer, **Galileo Galilei,** provided further evidence to support the heliocentric theory. He did this by observing the skies with a telescope he had constructed. Galileo's conclusions caused an uproar because they contradicted Church teachings about the world. Church leaders put Galileo on trial. Threatened with death, Galileo was forced to take back his ideas publicly.

## Newton

English scholar **Isaac Newton** built on the knowledge of Copernicus and Galileo. He used mathematics to prove the existence of a force that kept planets in their orbits around the sun. Newton called the force gravity, the same force that made objects fall toward Earth. Newton eventually theorized that nature follows uniform laws.

# New Ways of Thinking

## The Scientific Method

A new approach to science had emerged by the 1600s. It relied on experimentation and observation rather than on past authorities. This new way of thinking was called the **scientific method.**

**The Scientific Method**

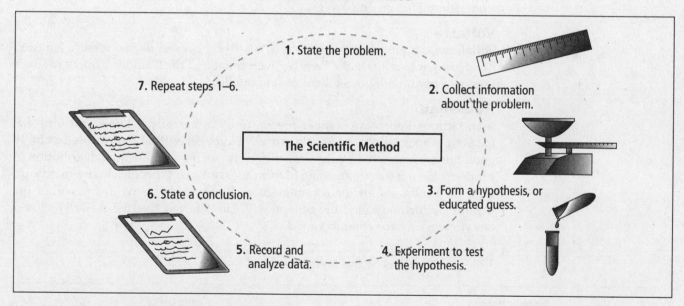

1. State the problem.
2. Collect information about the problem.
3. Form a hypothesis, or educated guess.
4. Experiment to test the hypothesis.
5. Record and analyze data.
6. State a conclusion.
7. Repeat steps 1–6.

The Scientific Method

## Descartes and Human Reasoning

Frenchman **René Descartes** challenged the idea that new knowledge should be made to fit existing traditional ideas. Descartes emphasized the power of human reason. He believed that reason, rather than tradition, should be the way to discover truth. The ideas of Descartes and other thinkers of the Scientific Revolution paved the way for other changes that would occur in Europe in the 1700s.

**Preparing for the Regents**

- How did the Scientific Revolution prepare the way for the Enlightenment?

- Thomas Hobbes was an Enlightenment thinker, even though his philosophy favored absolutism. Contrast Locke's theory of natural rights with the thinking of Thomas Hobbes and the theory of divine right.

## Key Themes and Concepts

**Government**
Locke's ideas about natural rights and the obligations of government later influenced both Thomas Jefferson's writing of the Declaration of Independence and the French revolutionaries.

# Science and the Enlightenment

During the Scientific Revolution, scientists used reason to explain why things happened in the physical universe. This success inspired great confidence in the power of reason. By the early 1700s, writers sought to use reason to discover **natural laws,** or laws that govern human behavior. By applying the scientific method of investigation and observation, scholars thought that they could solve the problems of society.

This way of thinking led to the Enlightenment, the period in the 1700s in which people rejected traditional ideas and supported a belief in human reason. The belief that logical thought can lead to truth is called rationalism. The Enlightenment introduced new ways of viewing authority, power, government, and law.

# Leading Thinkers of the Enlightenment

Four of the most influential Enlightenment philosophers were John Locke, Baron de Montesquieu, Voltaire, and Jean-Jacques Rousseau.

### Locke
**John Locke,** an English thinker of the late 1600s, believed that all people possess **natural rights.** These rights, he said, include the rights to life, liberty, and property. According to Locke, people form governments to protect their rights. If a government does not protect these rights, people have the right to overthrow it.

### Montesquieu
In the 1700s, French thinker **Baron de Montesquieu** wrote that the powers of government should be separated into three branches: legislative, executive, and judicial. This separation of powers would prevent tyranny by creating what is called a system of checks and balances. Each branch could keep the other two from gaining too much power.

### Voltaire
**Voltaire** was a French thinker of the 1700s who believed in free speech. He used his sharp wit to criticize the French government and the Catholic Church for their failure to permit religious toleration and intellectual freedom.

### Rousseau
**Jean-Jacques Rousseau,** another French philosopher of the 1700s, put forth his ideas in a book titled *The Social Contract.* He believed that people are naturally good but are corrupted by the evils of society, such as the unequal distribution of property. He felt that in agreeing to form a government, people choose to give up their own interests for the common good. Rousseau believed in the will of the majority, which he called the general will. He believed that the majority should always work for the common good.

## Thinkers of the Enlightenment

| Thomas Hobbes | John Locke |
|---|---|
| People are greedy and selfish. Only a powerful government can create a peaceful, orderly society. | People have natural rights. It is the job of government to protect these natural rights. If government does not protect these rights, the people have the right to overthrow it. |

| Baron de Montesquieu | Jean-Jacques Rousseau |
|---|---|
| The powers of government should be separated into three branches. Each branch will keep the other branches from becoming too powerful. | In a perfect society, people both make and obey the laws. What is good for everyone is more important than what is good for one person. |

# Impact of the Enlightenment

The ideas proposed by Enlightenment thinkers had a great impact throughout Europe in the 1700s. Greater numbers of people began to question established beliefs and customs. Enlightenment beliefs affected leaders and the development of nations.

## Government Censorship

As Enlightenment ideas gained in popularity, government and Church leaders worked to defend the established systems. They started a campaign of censorship to suppress Enlightenment ideas. Many writers, including Voltaire, were thrown into prison, and their books were banned and burned.

## Enlightened Despots

Some monarchs accepted Enlightenment ideas. They were known as **enlightened despots,** absolute rulers who used their power to reform society.

**Maria Theresa** Austrian ruler Maria Theresa implemented several reforms during her reign in the 1700s. She improved the tax system by forcing nobles and the clergy to pay taxes. This measure eased the tax burden on peasants. Maria Theresa also absorbed Enlightenment ideas on education and made primary education available to children in her kingdom.

**Joseph II** Maria Theresa's son, Joseph II, continued and expanded many of his mother's reforms. The most radical of the enlightened despots, Joseph modernized Austria's government, chose officials for their talents rather than because of their status, and implemented legal reforms. He also practiced religious toleration, ended censorship, and abolished serfdom. However, many of Joseph's reforms were later overturned.

**Catherine the Great** Catherine II, who became empress of Russia in 1762, read Enlightenment works and even corresponded with Voltaire and Montesquieu. As a result of her exposure to Enlightenment ideas, Catherine asked for the advice of nobles, free peasants, and townspeople. Never before had Russian citizens been allowed to advise the government. Catherine also built schools and hospitals, promoted the education of women, and extended religious tolerance. Unfortunately, many of Catherine's reforms were short-lived. Later in her reign, Catherine grew more repressive after a peasant uprising.

## Democracy and Nationalism

Enlightenment ideas inspired a sense of individualism, a belief in personal freedom, and a sense of the basic equality of human beings. These concepts, along with challenges to traditional authority, became important in the growth of democracy. Nationalism also grew. As people in a country drew together to fight for a democratic government, strong feelings of nationalism arose. In the late 1700s, Enlightenment ideas would contribute to an age of revolution.

# Summary

Beginning in the 1500s, the Scientific Revolution introduced a way of thinking based on observation and experimentation instead of acceptance of traditional authority. These changes inspired intellectuals to apply reason to the study not only of science but also of human society. The thinkers of the Enlightenment used this emphasis on reason to suggest reforms in government and society. Many Europeans, including several monarchs, were influenced by these ideas and sought to change the old order. These changes had an impact on all of Europe as democratic and nationalistic ideas grew and contributed to revolutions.

## Key Themes and Concepts

**Change**
The term *enlightened despot* almost seems like a contradiction. These rulers believed in absolute power but also saw the value of reforms in government.

**Nationalism**
In both the American and French Revolutions, Enlightenment ideas contributed to democratic movements as well as strong nationalistic feelings. To learn more about the American and French Revolutions, see Section 2 of this unit.

**Government**
Enlightenment thinkers sought to use reason to improve government and society. Although they were able to influence only a few leaders of their day, they created a whole new set of assumptions about the proper use of power, who had authority, and what made up a good and lawful government.

## Preparing for the Regents

• What policies did enlightened despots have in common?

# Political Revolutions

**Key People
and Terms**

- Place each of the key people and terms into these three categories: leader, government body, political document.

## Section Overview

In the late 1700s and early 1800s, revolutions shook Europe and the Americas. In North America in 1776, Great Britain's 13 colonies, inspired by Enlightenment ideals, declared their independence. They then fought the American Revolution to throw off British rule. In France, economic misery and social discontent led to a revolt against the absolute monarchy in 1789. Periods of chaos and reform were followed by the rise of Napoleon Bonaparte. Napoleon built an empire that was short-lived, but his military victories fanned French nationalistic feelings and spread the revolution's ideals. Inspired by the American and French Revolutions, revolutionaries in Latin America threw off Spanish rule.

## Key Themes and Concepts

As you review this section, take special note of the following key themes and concepts:

**Culture and Intellectual Life** What role did Enlightenment ideas play in the major revolutions of the late 1700s and early 1800s?

**Conflict** Why did the French people rebel against King Louis XIV?

**Change** What short-term and long-term effects did the revolutions of the late 1700s and early 1800s have on Europe and the Americas?

## Key People and Terms

As you review this section, be sure you understand the significance of these key people and terms:

| | |
|---|---|
| Declaration of Independence | Napoleon Bonaparte |
| Estates General | coup d'état |
| National Assembly | Napoleonic Code |
| Declaration of the Rights of Man and of the Citizen | Toussaint L'Ouverture |
| | Simón Bolívar |
| Maximilien Robespierre | José de San Martín |

## The American Revolution

By 1750, the British empire included 13 colonies along the eastern coast of North America. In 1776, the colonies declared their independence from Great Britain. Great Britain sent troops to crush the rebellion. However, with the aid of the French as well as the Dutch and Spanish, American forces defeated the British army and gained their independence. In their struggle, the colonists were inspired by Enlightenment ideals and by the traditions of British government. They established a new nation based on representative government and a guarantee of rights and freedoms.

## Influence of British Traditions

**Magna Carta and Parliament** The Magna Carta had limited the power of English monarchs. For example, it stated that the king could not raise new taxes without consulting the body that would later become Parliament. The American colonists interpreted this idea to mean that any taxation without representation was unjust. Because colonists had no representative in Great Britain's Parliament, they felt that Parliament had no right to tax them. They protested by using the slogan "No taxation without representation."

**English Bill of Rights** The English Bill of Rights inspired colonists to fight for the creation of their own bill of rights.

## Influence of the Enlightenment

The theories of thinkers such as Locke, Montesquieu, and Rousseau helped inspire the colonists' opposition to British policies after 1763.

**Paine's Common Sense** Influenced by Enlightenment ideas about a limited, representative government, Thomas Paine wrote in his pamphlet *Common Sense* that the colonists should no longer be the subjects of a distant monarch. Paine appealed to reason and natural law in his arguments for breaking away from Great Britain. His ideas were widely read in the colonies in 1776.

**The Declaration of Independence** Influenced by Locke and other Enlightenment thinkers, Thomas Jefferson drafted the Declaration of Independence. Jefferson wrote that governments rule only with the consent of the governed and that they should protect the unalienable rights of their citizens. The declaration also stated that people have a right to throw off governments that are unjust and that do not protect their citizens. After listing specific grievances against the British monarch, Jefferson wrote that the colonists were justified in forming their own government, independent of Great Britain.

**The Constitution** Like the Declaration of Independence, this document reflected the influence of Enlightenment ideas.

- **Social Contract** The Constitution of the United States set up a government by social contract. The government was established by the consent of the governed. The Constitution begins with these words: "We the People of the United States . . ."

- **Separation of Powers** Influenced by the ideas of Montesquieu, the Constitution created a republic in which power was to be divided between the federal government and the states. In addition, the writers of the Constitution established a government that divided powers among an executive, a legislative, and a judicial branch. Each branch could provide checks and balances on the other branches.

- **Protection of Rights** The Bill of Rights was added to the Constitution to protect the basic rights of American citizens, including freedom of speech and freedom of religion. The Constitution stated that it was the duty of the government to protect these rights.

## Impact of the American Revolution

The American Revolution had a great impact around the world.

- The American republic stood as a symbol of freedom to both Europe and Latin America.

- The United States Constitution created the most liberal government of its time. Other nations would copy the ideas in this document.

- The success of the American Revolution would soon inspire major global changes as other peoples challenged the power of absolute monarchs.

### Note Taking

***Reading Skill:***
**Identify Main Ideas**
As you read, fill in a table with main ideas about these political documents.

| Common Sense | Declaration of Independence | Constitution |
|---|---|---|
|  |  |  |
|  |  |  |
|  |  |  |

### Key Themes and Concepts

**Human Rights**
The Declaration of Independence reflects many of Locke's Enlightenment ideas. These ideas include people's natural rights to life and liberty, the role of the government in protecting those rights, and the right of people to overthrow unjust governments.

**Government and Change**
The United States Constitution contributed to change in other parts of the world. It was a model for many other nations that formed new governments in the years that followed.

### Preparing for the Regents

- Describe some Enlightenment ideas that inspired the American Revolution and influenced the founders of the United States of America.

- Why was the American Revolution an important turning point in global history?

## Stages of Political Revolutions

```
Emergence          Injustices of the
of a Strong   →    Old Regime
Leader                    ↓

Return of          Rule by
Moderates          Moderate
                   Reformers
    ↑                    ↓
        Rule by Radicals
    ←   Revolutionaries   ←
```

# The French Revolution

Soon after the American Revolution, a major revolution broke out in France. Starting in 1789, the French Revolution had a deep and lasting impact on France, Europe, and other areas of the world. The French Revolution followed a pattern common to many political revolutions. In this pattern, revolutions pass through different stages, caused by changes in leadership and shifts in power. Problems begin to appear in a country, and revolutionary groups form, hoping to correct the injustices. At the beginning of the revolution, moderate reformers come to power and as their compromise reforms fail, power passes to a more radical group of revolutionaries. The revolution grows more violent and extreme. A reaction to the violence follows, bringing moderates back to power. Often, at that point, there is a return to the old order as the people turn to a leader who promises order along with reform.

## Causes of the Revolution

Many injustices existed in prerevolutionary France. Political, social, economic, and intellectual factors combined to bring about the French Revolution.

**Absolute Monarchy** On the eve of revolution, France was an absolute monarchy. Under absolutism, most people in France were denied basic rights and any say in government.

**Social Inequality** Since the Middle Ages, everyone in France had belonged to one of three social classes called estates. The clergy were the First Estate; the titled nobility composed the Second Estate. These two classes held enormous wealth, did not have to pay taxes, and enjoyed other special rights and privileges. The Third Estate made up most of French society and included a bourgeoisie (middle class), poor city workers, and rural peasants, the largest group. The Third Estate, which resented its heavy tax burden and lack of rights, grew increasingly discontent.

## Key Themes and Concepts

**Economic Systems**
Much of the unrest in France was rooted in the unequal distribution of wealth as well as the unequal tax burden.

## Draw Conclusions

- How was daily life different for the Second Estate and the Third Estate in France in 1789?

## Preparing for the Regents

- Practice your graph skills by writing one or two sentences that state the main point of the graphs on this page.

### Population and Land Ownership in France, 1789

PERCENTAGE OF POPULATION, BY ESTATE

First Estate
Second Estate
Third Estate

98%
1.5%  0.5%

PERCENTAGE OF LAND OWNERSHIP, BY ESTATE

70%
10%  20%

**Economic Injustices** The situation in France became worse because of economic conditions in the late 1780s. The government, with its lavish court and expensive wars, spent more money than it earned. This debt added to the tax burden of the Third Estate. Bad harvests in 1789 caused food prices to rise. Peasants and city dwellers often did not have enough to eat and began to riot, demanding bread.

**Enlightenment** Through the 1600s and 1700s, Enlightenment thinkers were critical of France's absolute monarchy and called for democratic reforms. Enlightenment ideas led many French to question the traditional way of ordering society. It was not reasonable, they felt, for the First and Second Estates to have privileges at the expense of the Third Estate.

**English and American Examples** England's Glorious Revolution provided an example of how existing authority could be challenged. In addition, the French were inspired by the American colonies' successful fight for liberty and equality in the American Revolution.

## Stages of the Revolution

**The Revolution Begins** As conditions grew worse in France, demands for reform increased. In 1789, King Louis XVI finally called the **Estates General,** a body made up of representatives of all three estates, into session. After this, change came swiftly.

- **National Assembly** The Third Estate, the only elected group in the Estates General, declared itself the National Assembly. The National Assembly vowed to write a new constitution for France.

- **Seizure of the Bastille** Working-class people, already rioting over the price of bread, stormed a prison called the Bastille on July 14, 1789. Fighting broke out through city and countryside. In a period known as the Great Fear, peasants attacked nobles and destroyed their homes.

- **Moderates in Power** The king, frightened by the increasing turmoil, agreed to allow the National Assembly to begin reforms.

- **Declaration of the Rights of Man and of the Citizen** The National Assembly abolished the privileges of the First and Second Estates and adopted the Declaration of the Rights of Man and of the Citizen. Based partly on the Declaration of Independence, it contained many Enlightenment ideas.

- **A Limited Monarchy** By 1791, the Assembly had written a constitution. The Constitution of 1791 defined the role and purpose of a new government.
  - It set up a limited monarchy and a representative assembly.
  - It declared that people had natural rights and that it was the job of the government to protect those rights.
  - It put the Church under state control.

News about the French Revolution quickly spread across Europe. Many European rulers and nobles feared that revolutionary ideas would spread to their own countries. They threatened to intervene—with military force, if necessary—to save the French monarchy. In 1792, to fight tyranny and spread the revolution, France declared war on Austria, Prussia, Great Britain, and several other states.

**Preparing for the Regents**

- List three factors that led to the French Revolution.

  1.

  2.

  3.

**Preparing for the Regents**

- As you study the French Revolution, take note of the roles played by individual citizens. Members of the Third Estate formed the National Assembly. Working-class people stormed the Bastille, and peasants attacked the homes of nobles.

**Preparing for the Regents**

- What influences from the Enlightenment and the American Revolution can you see in the Declaration of the Rights of Man and the Citizen?

**The French Declaration of Rights**

**DECLARATION OF THE RIGHTS OF MAN AND OF THE CITIZEN**

- Written in 1789
- Uses American Declaration of Independence as model
- States that all men have natural rights
- Declares the job of government to protect the natural rights of the people
- Guarantees all male citizens equality under the law
- States that people are free to practice any religion they choose
- Promises to tax people according to how much they can afford

## Key Themes and Concepts

### Change
During the course of the revolution, the people in power changed, and ideas of those in power changed. At first, moderates were in power, and the constitution called for a limited monarchy. By 1793, the radicals were in control, and the king had been executed.

## Preparing for the Regents

- How did Napoleon gain popularity and rise to power?

**Radicals in Power** The war with the other European nations went badly for France. In 1792, radicals took control of the Assembly, ended the monarchy, and declared France a republic. Their slogan was "Liberty, Equality, Fraternity." In 1793, the king was executed for treason. This event was followed by a period in France called the Reign of Terror, led in part by **Maximilien Robespierre,** a radical revolutionary. During this time, tens of thousands of people were executed. Thousands more were put into prison. Within a year, however, the violence turned back on itself. Robespierre himself was executed, and the Reign of Terror ended.

**Moderates Return** Beginning in 1795, a five-man "Directory" supported by a legislature held power in France. This government was weak and inefficient. Rising bread prices brought the threat of riots. Into this chaotic situation stepped an ambitious military leader, Napoleon Bonaparte.

### Napoleon in Power

**His Rise to Power** When the revolution started, **Napoleon Bonaparte** was a low-level military officer with dreams of glory. Bonaparte rose in the ranks and won important victories against the British and Austrians. A popular general by 1799, Napoleon helped overthrow the weak Directory in a **coup d'état,** or revolt by military leaders to overthrow a government. He organized a new government and put himself in charge. Three years later, he took the title "Emperor of the French." Napoleon now had absolute power. The French people, hoping for stability, supported Napoleon at each step in his rise.

### Napoleon in Europe, 1812

***Napoleon's Empire*** *Napoleon's empire was at its largest in 1812. Most of the countries in Europe today have different names and borders.*

**His Achievements** Much of Napoleon's popularity came from his effective policies.

- **Economy** Napoleon controlled prices, supported new industry, and built roads and canals.
- **Education** Napoleon established a government-supervised public school system.
- **Napoleonic Code** The Napoleonic Code was a legal code that included many Enlightenment ideas, such as the legal equality of citizens and religious toleration.

**Napoleon's Empire** From 1804 to 1814, Napoleon ruled an empire. He conquered much of Europe. Napoleon often replaced the monarchs of defeated nations with his friends and relatives.

Of the European powers, only Great Britain and Russia remained beyond Napoleon's reach. Great Britain was shielded from French troops by a powerful navy and the English Channel.

**Napoleon's Fall** Napoleon's empire began to crumble for several reasons. First, most people in conquered states looked on Napoleon's armies as foreign oppressors. Inspired by nationalism, people across Europe revolted against French rule.

Another factor was Napoleon's invasion of Russia in 1812. As Napoleon's armies invaded from the west, the Russians retreated eastward. The "scorched earth" policy of the Russians, in which they burned crops and villages as they retreated, left the French troops hungry and cold. Most of Napoleon's army was lost during the long Russian winter.

The following year, an alliance of Russia, Great Britain, Austria, and Prussia defeated Napoleon, forcing him to step down in 1814. Napoleon returned to power in 1815, but the British and Prussians defeated him at the decisive Battle of Waterloo. This battle ended Napoleon's reign, and he lived the rest of his life in exile.

*British Prime Minister William Pitt and Napoleon carve a large plum pudding*

## Key Themes and Concepts

**Power**
Despite Napoleon's reforms, order and authority were still higher priorities for him than individual rights. The Napoleonic Code included many Enlightenment ideas, such as the equality of citizens under the law. However, it also undid some reforms of the revolution, such as rights that had been granted to women.

## Preparing for the Regents

- How did nationalism help Napoleon to build his empire? How did nationalism lead to Napoleon's defeat?

## Preparing for the Regents

- Practice interpreting political cartoons by answering these questions.

1. What does the large plum pudding represent? How do the slices represent Napoleon's quest for power?

2. Based on your knowledge of Napoleon's relationship with Great Britain, would this dinner be a cordial one? Explain.

## Effects of the French Revolution

The French Revolution and the reign of Napoleon transformed both France and Europe in many ways.

**Democratic Ideals** Napoleon's conquests spread the ideals of democracy throughout Europe. Groups struggled to achieve the goals of the French republic: "Liberty, Equality, Fraternity." People wanted liberty from absolute monarchs and unjust governments. They pursued equality by opposing social inequality and injustice. They expressed fraternity, or brotherhood, by working together for a common cause.

**Nationalism** Among the French, the revolution and the conquests of Napoleon inspired feelings of national pride. This pride and sense of national identity replaced earlier loyalty to local authority and the person of the monarch.

The conquests of Napoleon also increased nationalistic feeling across Europe and around the world. His conquests had a part in the eventual unification of both Italy and Germany. His weakening of Spain led to the Latin American independence movements.

# Latin American Independence Movements

In the late 1700s, Enlightenment and revolutionary ideas spread from Europe and the United States to Latin America. Educated Latin Americans read works by Enlightenment writers. They debated about political and social reform. Thomas Jefferson's Declaration of Independence and the Constitution were eagerly read. The success of the American Revolution showed that foreign rule could be thrown off. Latin Americans also were inspired by what the French Revolution had accomplished. Beginning in the 1790s, they struggled to gain independence as well as other rights and freedoms.

### Toussaint L'Ouverture

The French colony of Haiti was the first Latin American colony to revolt against European rule. In Haiti, French planters owned large sugar plantations. Here nearly half a million enslaved Africans lived and worked in terrible conditions. Moreover, the French gave few rights to free mulattoes (persons of mixed ancestry) living on the island.

In 1791, a self-educated former slave named **Toussaint L'Ouverture** led a revolt. Toussaint was familiar with the works of the Enlightenment thinkers and wanted to lead his people to liberty. Toussaint proved to be an effective military leader and gained control of much of the island. Haitian slaves won their freedom in 1798.

In 1802, Napoleon sent an army to Haiti to reestablish French dominance. Toussaint led a guerrilla war to gain Haitian independence. The French captured Toussaint, but yellow fever took a heavy toll on their forces. In 1804, Haitians declared their independence. Napoleon then abandoned the island. Haiti became a republic in 1820.

### Simón Bolívar

In South America in the early 1800s, an educated creole named **Simón Bolívar** led resistance movements against the Spanish. Bolívar had become an admirer of Enlightenment ideas and the French Revolution during a stay in Europe. He was also inspired by the American Revolution. He vowed to fight Spanish rule in South America. Called "the Liberator," Bolívar became one of the greatest Latin American nationalist leaders of this period.

**Struggle For Independence** In 1810, Bolívar started his long struggle against the Spanish. Over the next 12 years, he led a series of military campaigns that won independence for Venezuela, New Granada (present-day Colombia), Ecuador, Peru, and Bolivia. He then joined forces with **José de San Martín,** who had defeated the Spanish in Argentina and Chile in the 1810s.

**Difficulties Ahead** Despite his victories against the Spanish, Bolívar failed in his attempt to create a large, united Latin American state. Spain's former empire thus became divided into a number of separate independent states. These nations faced a long struggle to gain stability, achieve social equality, and eliminate poverty.

### Summarize

- Who were the key revolutionaries for independence in Latin America?

- What were their accomplishments?

### South America, 1790

### South America, 1828

## Summary

Enlightenment ideas about natural rights and rejection of absolutist authority inspired major revolutions in the late 1700s and early 1800s. Colonists in America declared independence from Great Britain in 1776 and created a government based on the ideas of Locke and Montesquieu. Influenced by the American Revolution, revolutionaries in France overturned the monarchy and created a new social order. Napoleon helped spread revolutionary ideals across Europe. Both the American and French Revolutions contributed to revolutions in Latin America in the early 1800s. Leaders such as Toussaint L'Ouverture and Simón Bolívar led popular movements to overthrow European rule.

### Key Themes and Concepts

**Change**
The revolutions of the late 1700s and early 1800s had several lasting effects. These included the creation of the United States, the spread of nationalism and democratic ideals, and the establishment of independent republics in Latin America.

# Reaction Against Revolutionary Ideals

## Section Overview

After the French Revolution, there was a reaction against revolutionary ideals. In 1815 at the Congress of Vienna, the leaders of the nations of Europe restored the old monarchies. In the following decades, conflicts between revolutionary ideals and the desire to maintain the old order would cause uprisings and repression. Although some reforms slowly took hold in Western Europe, absolutism remained strong in Russia. In Latin America, democratic reforms were slow to develop. In the early 1900s, however, Mexico experienced a political and social revolution accompanied by the growth of nationalistic feelings.

## Key Themes and Concepts

As you review this section, take special note of the following key themes and concepts:

**Power** How did leaders react to revolutionary ideals in Europe after the French Revolution and the reign of Napoleon?

**Political Systems** What barriers to reform existed in Russia and Latin America in the 1800s?

**Change** What reforms occurred in Mexico in the early 1800s?

**Key People and Terms**

- What do three of the key people and terms have in common? Explain.

## Key People and Terms

As you review this section, be sure you understand the significance of these key people and terms:

| | |
|---|---|
| Congress of Vienna | pogroms |
| Prince Clemens von Metternich | oligarchy |
| balance of power | caudillos |
| conservatism | cash crop economy |
| liberalism | Porfirio Díaz |
| nationalism | Emiliano Zapata |
| Russification | Francisco "Pancho" Villa |

**Key Themes and Concepts**

**Power**
The leaders at the Congress of Vienna wanted to keep France from dominating the continent. They also wanted to restore monarchs to power.

## The Congress of Vienna

After Napoleon's defeat, European diplomats met at the Congress of Vienna in 1815 to devise a peace settlement. The meeting was dominated by **Prince Clemens von Metternich** of Austria, who wanted to restore Europe to the way it was before the French Revolution. The decisions made at this meeting were designed to bring stability and order to Europe by repressing the feelings of nationalism and preventing liberal political change unleashed by the French Revolution and Napoleon.

**The Congress of Vienna**

| GOAL | ACTION |
|------|--------|
| To prevent France from going to war again | Strengthen countries around France<br>• Add Belgium and Luxembourg to Holland to create the kingdom of the Netherlands<br>• Give Prussia lands along the Rhine River<br>• Allow Austria to take control of Italy again |
| To return Europe to the way it was in 1792, before Napoleon | Give power back to the monarchs of Europe |
| To protect the new system and maintain peace | Create the Concert of Europe, an organization to maintain peace in Europe |

## Balance of Power and Restored Monarchs

Despite their sometimes different goals, the leaders at the Congress of Vienna accomplished a great deal. Much of what the leaders did at the Congress of Vienna occurred for two reasons. First, they wanted to establish a **balance of power,** or a distribution of military and economic power that prevents any one nation from becoming too strong. They also wanted to restore power to monarchs. The Congress of Vienna was the first of many reactions in Europe against the revolutionary ideals of the 1700s and 1800s. It was also a victory for conservatives. **Conservatism** was a set of beliefs held by those who wanted to preserve traditional ways. As conservatism clashed with the ideals of the French Revolution, revolutions would occur throughout Europe and Latin America.

## New Revolutions in Europe

The Vienna settlement helped to maintain peace among nations in Europe for almost 100 years. Revolutions did occur within nations, however. Revolutionaries were not happy with the results of the Congress of Vienna. They opposed the Congress's policy of trying to restore Europe to the way it had been before the French Revolution.

### Causes

Revolts occurred in many places across Europe from the time of the Congress through about 1850. There were two main causes of these revolutions.

- **Liberalism** People opposed the power of monarchs and sought democratic reforms.
- **Nationalism** People wanted independent nation-states that were free from foreign rule.

### Revolutions of 1830

In 1830, the French, alarmed by their monarch's attempt to restore absolutism, successfully revolted and created a constitutional monarchy. Attempts to gain independence in Greece and Belgium were successful while similar attempts in Italy, Germany, and Poland were defeated.

### Revolutions of 1848

Additional revolutions occurred in 1848, led by the events in France.

- **France** King Louis Philippe's government was denounced as corrupt, prompting another revolution in 1848. Louis Philippe stepped down, and a republic was established. Within months of the uprising, upper- and middle-class interests gained control of the government and violently put down a

**Vocabulary Builder**

clash—(klash) *v.* if two people or groups clash, they argue because they have very different beliefs and opinions

**Preparing for the Regents**

- Explain how the Congress of Vienna was a reaction against revolutionary ideals.

- Note that nationalism has its roots in the Enlightenment and the French Revolution.

- How do the events of 1848 reflect the long-term impact of the French Revolution?

**Key Themes and Concepts**

Interdependence
As had occurred in 1789, a revolution in 1830 in France affected the other nations of Europe.

## Revolutions in Europe, 1830 and 1848

**Revolutions in Europe** In 1830 and 1848, revolutions in Europe took place in many cities and countries. Most failed. However, Europe was changed by reforms that resulted from the revolts.

### Preparing for the Regents

• Use your map skills to tell which areas gained independence between 1830 and 1831.

workers' rebellion in Paris. The fighting left bitter feelings between the working class and the middle class.

• **Austrian Empire** When students revolted in Vienna in 1848, Metternich tried to suppress them. He resigned when workers rose up to support the students. As revolution quickly spread to other areas of the empire, the Austrian government agreed to certain reforms. However, the Austrian army soon regained control, and many revolutionaries were imprisoned, executed, or sent into exile.

• **Italy and Germany** Rebellions in Italy were successful just for short periods of time. In Germany, student protesters who were backed by peasants and workers demanded reforms. Although an assembly was formed, it was later dissolved as the revolutionaries turned on each other.

### Impact of the Revolutions

The revolutions that occurred in 1830 and 1848 frightened many of Europe's rulers. As a result, some agreed to reforms. For the most part, however, the revolts of 1830 and 1848 failed. There were several reasons for these failures.

• Most revolutionaries did not have widespread support.

• Sometimes the revolutionaries themselves were divided.

• Powerful government forces often crushed the revolts.

## Absolutism in Czarist Russia

### Impact of the French Revolution

While the countries of Western Europe were profoundly changed by the French Revolution, Russian czars strove to keep the ideals of the French Revolution—liberty, equality, and fraternity—from reaching their people. Unlike the countries of Western Europe, Russia changed very little throughout the 1800s.

### Political Conditions

Russian czars resisted reforms, fearing that change would weaken their control. Czars refused to introduce elements of democracy into their societies, although democratic ideals were gaining strength in Western European countries at that time.

### Social Conditions

**A Feudal Society** Russia had a rigid feudal social structure. Landowning nobles were powerful and resisted any change that would weaken their position. The middle class was too small to have any influence. Although serfdom had gradually disappeared in Western Europe by the 1700s, it had continued in Russia. Serfs were bound to the land, and the owner of the land had almost total power over the serfs who worked it.

**Freeing of the Serfs** Russia became involved in the Crimean War after trying to seize Ottoman lands along the Danube. Russia suffered a defeat in this war, making its leaders aware of the country's need to modernize and industrialize. Demands for reform, including freedom for the serfs, followed.

In 1861, during the reign of Alexander II, the serfs were freed. Freeing the serfs brought problems, however. Former serfs had to buy the land they had worked, and many were too poor to do so. Even those who could buy land often did not have enough to support their families. Discontent continued.

Many freed serfs moved off their land and into the cities, where they took jobs in industries. These freed serfs were sometimes part of the pressure for reform in Russia.

**Russification** Russia, as a vast empire, contained many ethnic minorities. The czars aimed to maintain tight control over these people as well as to encourage feelings of Russian unity. This policy of Russification was an attempt to make all groups think, act, and believe as Russians.

For example, Russian czar Alexander III persecuted non-Russians, including Poles, Ukrainians, and Armenians. He insisted on one language, Russian, and one church, the Russian Orthodox Church. Alexander also persecuted Jews, restricting the jobs they could have and even where they could live. These policies encouraged violent attacks on Jews, called **pogroms.** The authorities stood by and watched as the homes of Jews were burned and their businesses looted.

## Imperialism in Asia

In the 1700s, Russia had expanded to the Baltic Sea, to the Black Sea, and into Eastern Europe, occupying much of Poland. The Russians also expanded eastward across Siberia and beyond the Bering Strait, into Alaska. During the early 1800s, the Russians began their practice of exiling convicts to Siberia.

Czars in the 1800s added lands in central Asia. This territory gave Russia the largest and most diverse empire in Europe and Asia. The construction of the Trans-Siberian Railway, begun in the 1890s, extended Russian economic and political control over the region.

# Instability in Latin America

As you have learned, revolutionaries in Latin America had thrown off Spanish rule in the early 1800s. Life, however, did not improve for most people after they achieved independence. Revolts and civil wars broke out while poverty and prejudice continued. Many factors made it difficult for Latin American nations to benefit from the revolutions that had occurred.

## Geographic Barriers

The Latin American nations that gained independence in the 1800s covered a vast area, from Mexico to the southern tip of South America. This area included numerous geographic barriers, such as the Andes Mountains, that hindered attempts at creating a unified Latin America. Fights between various leaders and nationalistic feelings within different groups also kept Latin Americans from uniting.

## Social Injustice

Despite the establishment of Latin American republics with constitutions, democracy did not follow. One problem was that the colonial class structure remained largely intact. Creoles replaced peninsulares as the ruling class, and

**Key Themes and Concepts**

**Change**
Despite the problems faced by freed serfs, their emancipation in 1861 marked a major turning point in Russian history. A similar development occurred in the United States a few years later, when the enslaved African Americans were freed.

**Diversity**
Russian czars fought diversity in their nation. They tried to force minorities to abandon their own cultures and adopt Russian culture.

**Preparing for the Regents**

- How did conditions in Russia in the late 1800s contribute to the revolutions that occurred in the early 1900s?

**Key Themes and Concepts**

**Political Systems**
Three centuries of strong Spanish rule left most Latin Americans with little practical knowledge of how to establish a representative democracy.

land and wealth remained in their hands. This kind of system, in which ruling power belongs to a small, powerful elite, is known as an **oligarchy.** Mestizos, mulattoes, Indians, and Africans gained few rights and still faced racial prejudice. Most had to work as peasants on the large estates of the landowners.

### Military Rulers

Because of the strong rule that colonial empires had exerted in Latin America, people of these countries had little experience with self-government. Local military strongmen called **caudillos** put together their own armies and challenged central governments. Some caudillos were strong enough to gain control of governments. These dictators were repressive, usually ignoring existing constitutions. Their policies usually favored the upper class.

### Power of the Church

The Roman Catholic Church had acted as a stabilizing influence in Latin America. It also promoted education. But the Church had an interest in preserving the old order in Latin America. As in colonial days, the Church still owned large amounts of land. Liberals in Latin America hoped to end the Church's power over education and reduce its vast landholdings.

### Economic Problems

**Cash Crop Economies** Under colonial rule, Latin American economies had become dependent on trade with Spain and Portugal. Latin Americans relied on a cash crop economy. The colonies sent raw materials such as sugar, cotton, and coffee to Europe and had to import manufactured goods. Dependence on just one crop or even a few crops makes a nation's economy very unstable. If a drought or crop failure occurs, or if prices for the products fall, the economy can be devastated.

**Economic Imperialism** In the mid-1800s, some Latin American economies began to grow. Foreign investment allowed them to develop mining and agriculture. Foreigners also invested in transportation improvement, such as the development of ports and the building of railroads. Even so, there were few benefits for the majority of Latin Americans. The rigid class structure limited economic gains to the few at the top of the social structure. In general, only the upper classes and the foreign investors profited.

## The Mexican Revolution (1910–1930)

### Causes

General **Porfirio Díaz** ruled Mexico as a dictator in the late 1800s and early 1900s. Díaz brought economic advances to Mexico. Railroads were built and industry grew. However, the wealth went to a small upper class as well as to foreign investors. The rule of Díaz, who brutally suppressed opposition, left most Mexicans uneducated, landless, and poor. In 1910, the discontent boiled over into a revolution that forced Díaz from power.

### Key Figures

No one person led the revolution. Several local leaders gathered their own armies, destroying railroads and estates.

- **Emiliano Zapata,** an Indian, was one of the most famous leaders. He led a large peasant revolt in the south, calling for land reform.
- **Francisco "Pancho" Villa,** a rebel leader in the north, won the loyalty of a large number of peasants. When the United States supported the Mexican government against Villa, conflict erupted across the border between Villa and the United States government in 1916.

**Preparing for the Regents**

- In both Russia and Latin America, there were obstacles to reform. Which obstacles were shared by Russia and Latin America? Which obstacles were unique to Latin America?

- What economic problems can result from dependence on a cash crop economy?

**Preparing for the Regents**

- Compare the causes of the Mexican Revolution to those of the French Revolution.

- Venustiano Carranza was elected president of Mexico in 1917. He approved a new constitution that, with amendments, is still in force today.

## Effects of the Revolution

**The Constitution of 1917** The new constitution agreed to by Carranza in 1917 called for land reform, gave the government control of Church estates, and guaranteed more rights to workers and to women.

**Social Reforms** Reforms were eventually carried out in the 1920s, making Mexico the first Latin American nation to achieve social and economic reform for the majority of its people. For example, the government set up libraries and schools. Some Indian communities were given the opportunity to regain land that had been taken from them in the past.

**Economic Nationalism** Mexico, along with other countries of Latin America, experienced strong feelings of nationalism in the early 1900s. Much of the nationalistic spirit was aimed at ending economic dependence on industrial powers. Mexico became determined to develop its own economy. The Mexican government brought industries under government control or took over foreign-owned industries.

**Cultural Nationalism** In the 1920s and 1930s, nationalistic feeling caused writers in Mexico and other parts of Latin America to reject the influences of Europe. They began to take pride in Latin American culture, which displayed a mixture of Western European and Indian traditions. In Mexico, mural painting, which had been a common art form in the Aztec empire, was revived. Muralists such as Diego Rivera and José Clemente Orozco created works of great beauty. Many showed the struggles of the Mexican people for freedom.

# Summary

After the defeat of Napoleon, conservative leaders sought to suppress the ideals of the French Revolution and restore monarchy. In 1830 and 1848, uprisings against the old order occurred all across Europe. Although these revolts were mostly unsuccessful, the ideals behind them continued to have an impact on Europe. In Russia and in Latin America, numerous barriers to reform existed. In Mexico, however, reforms took place that benefited the majority of the population.

## Note Taking

*Reading Skill:*
**Identify Effects** Make a chart. As you read, record the effects of the Mexican Revolution. Include the main idea and at least one supporting detail.

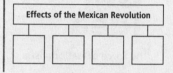

Effects of the Mexican Revolution

## Key Themes and Concepts

**Nationalism**
In Mexico, nationalism had economic and cultural aspects. Mexicans wanted to end their economic dependence on foreign powers. They also wanted to show their pride in Latin American culture.

## Preparing for the Regents

- Compare the reactions against revolutionary ideals in Europe, in Russia, and in Latin America in the 1800s.

# Global Nationalism

The force of nationalism:

- inspired revolutions in Europe and Latin America.

- led to a united Italy and a united Germany in the late 1800s.

- arose among Indians, Turks, and Jews.

- created conflict in the Balkans by the early 1900s.

## Section Overview

During the French Revolution, people in France expressed great pride in their nation. Nationalism later spread to other peoples, inspiring uprisings across Europe and in Latin America. In the 1860s, nationalism led to the unification of Italy. By 1871, Germany had also united. Outside Europe, nationalist movements took root in India, Turkey, and elsewhere. Among Jews, a movement arose to create a separate Jewish state in Palestine. As the 1800s drew to a close, nationalistic forces created tensions in the Balkans that set the stage for a world war.

## Key Themes and Concepts

As you review this section, take special note of the following key themes and concepts:

**Nationalism** How did nationalism cause revolutions?

**Nation-State** How did nationalism lead to the creation of nation-states in Italy and Germany?

**Change** How did nationalism affect Indians, Turks, and Jews?

**Diversity** How did nationalism cause conflict in the Balkans?

## Key People and Terms

**Key People and Terms**

- Place each of the key people and terms into these two categories: person or movement/political group.

As you review this section, be sure you understand the significance of these key people and terms:

| | |
|---|---|
| Giuseppe Mazzini | Zionism |
| Count Camillo Cavour | Indian National Congress |
| Giuseppe Garibaldi | Muslim League |
| Otto von Bismarck | Young Turks |
| kaiser | Pan-Slavism |

## Nationalism and Revolution

**Key Themes and Concepts**

**Nationalism**
Nationalism is a feeling of pride in and devotion to one's nation. It is a feeling that develops among people who may share a common language, history, set of traditions, or goal. Nationalism often causes people to join together to choose their own form of government, without outside interference.

As you have learned, nationalism is a feeling of strong devotion to one's country. This feeling often develops among people who share a common language and heritage. Nationalism played an important role in political revolutions of the 1800s.

Revolution and war in the 1790s created a strong sense of national unity in France. This feeling inspired French armies to battlefield success as they sought to spread the ideals of their revolution. Napoleon also inspired nationalism among the nations he conquered. However, nationalistic feelings encouraged conquered peoples to rise up against Napoleon. In the years following the French Revolution, nationalism led to upheaval in Europe and elsewhere.

*Unifies Germany and Italy*

*Breaks up Austrian and Ottoman empires*

## Unification Movements in Europe

Nationalistic feeling became an increasingly significant force for self-determination and unification in Europe.

### Italy

Ever since the Roman empire had fallen in the 400s, Italy had been divided into many small states. After Napoleon invaded Italy, he united some of the Italian states into the Kingdom of Italy. The Congress of Vienna, however, redivided Italy and put much of it under Austrian or Spanish control.

The three great leaders of Italian nationalism were Giuseppe Mazzini, Count Camillo Cavour, and Giuseppe Garibaldi.

- **Giuseppe Mazzini** formed the Young Italy national movement in 1831, but he was exiled for his views. His writings and speeches provided inspiration to the nationalist movement.
- **Count Camillo Cavour,** prime minister of the Italian state of Sardinia, shrewdly formed alliances with France and later with Prussia. He used diplomacy and war to drive Austrian power from Italy.
- **Giuseppe Garibaldi** was a soldier who led the forces that won control of southern Italy and helped it to unite with the north.

By 1861, Victor Emmanuel of Sardinia was crowned king of a united Italy. Rome and Venetia, at first not part of Italy, were included by 1870. With no tradition of unity, the new nation faced conflicts. The urban north quarreled with the rural south. Also, the Catholic Church resisted the new government. Despite economic growth, unrest grew in the late 1800s.

### Germany

Another national unification movement occurred in Germany. In the early 1800s, most German-speaking people lived in small states, to which they felt loyalty. During Napoleon's conquests, feelings of nationalism stirred in those Germans who wanted to be free of French rule. After Napoleon's defeat in 1815, some nationalists called for a united Germany. Metternich, however, blocked this idea at the Congress of Vienna.

**The Rise of Prussia** In the 1830s, Prussia set up a trade union among German states called the Zollverein. This agreement ended trade barriers between the states and was a step toward unity. More important, it established Prussia as a leader among the states.

### Key Themes and Concepts

**Nationalism**
In both Italy and Germany, the conquests of Napoleon inspired nationalism.

### Preparing for the Regents

- Explain one way in which each of the individuals listed here helped to unite Italy.

Mazzini:

Cavour:

Garibaldi:

### Compare and Contrast

- What are the similarities and differences between unification in Italy and unification in Germany?

In 1862, **Otto von Bismarck** was appointed chancellor of Prussia. Over the next decade, Bismarck, a strong and practical leader, guided German unification. Bismarck was not driven by a feeling of German nationalism, however. His loyalty was to the Prussian king. Unification was merely a means for him to make the Prussian king the ruler of a strong and united German state.

**"Blood and Iron"** Bismarck believed that the only way to unify Germany was through a policy he called "blood and iron." Bismarck had no faith in speeches and representative government. He believed that the only way to unite the German states was through war. In seven years, Bismarck led Prussia into three wars. Each war increased Prussia's prestige and moved the German states closer to unity.

- **Danish War** In 1864, Prussia allied with Austria to seize land from Denmark.
- **Austro-Prussian War** In 1866, Prussia turned against Austria to gain more land. Prussia overwhelmed Austria in just seven weeks. Several German states were united with Prussia in the North German Confederation.
- **Franco-Prussian War** In 1870, Bismarck used nationalism and the bitter memories of Napoleon's conquests to stir up support for a war against France. Prussia and its German allies easily defeated France. During the war, southern German states agreed to unite with Prussia.

In 1871, the German states united under the Prussian king, William I. As their ruler, William called himself the **kaiser,** a title that was derived from the name *Caesar* and meant "emperor."

## Zionism

The rise of nationalism in Europe had led to an intensification of anti-Semitism in the late 1800s. As citizens grew more patriotic about their own nations, they often grew more intolerant of those whom they saw as outsiders, including Jews. The pogroms that occurred in Eastern Europe and Russia are one example of this trend.

As anti-Semitism grew in Europe, some Jews moved to Palestine, the ancient Jewish homeland, buying land that they organized into farming communities. A Jewish journalist named Theodor Herzl became alarmed by the strong anti-Semitism he witnessed in France. In 1896, Herzl called for Jews to establish their own state. Herzl's writings helped to build Zionism, the movement devoted to building a Jewish state in Palestine. In 1897, he organized the first world congress of Zionists, which met in Switzerland. Herzl's dream of an independent Israel was realized a little more than 50 years later.

## Nationalism in Asia

National movements were also at work outside of Europe.

### India

Since the 1700s, the British had maintained control of the Indian subcontinent. Under British rule, nationalistic feelings began to stir among Indians, especially those who had been educated in the West. As Indian students learned about democracy and natural rights, they called increasingly for self-rule.

**Indian National Congress** In 1885, nationalist leaders in India formed the Indian National Congress, which became known as the Congress party. This group was made up mainly of Hindu professionals and business leaders. At first, the Congress party called merely for equal opportunity to serve in the government

**Preparing for the Regents**

- What role did Prussia and Bismarck play in German unification?

**Vocabulary Builder**

prestige—(prehs TEEZH) *n.* the respect and admiration that someone or something gets because of their success or important position

**Preparing for the Regents**

- The anti-Semitism that grew in Europe during the 1800s is an example of the negative effects of a group's nationalism on other peoples. Can you think of other examples of nationalism causing discrimination and violence against religious or ethnic minorities?

**Key Themes and Concepts**

Change
Western education introduced Indians to the ideals of democracy, nationalism, and basic human rights. This kind of thinking led eventually to self-rule for India. Western education brought change to other nations as well.

of India. They called for greater democracy and western-style modernization, looking ahead to self-rule.

**Muslim League** Initially, Muslims and Hindus cooperated in their campaign for self-rule. However, Muslims grew distrustful of the Indian National Congress because the organization was mostly Hindu. The increasing strength of Hindu nationalism alarmed Muslims. In 1906, Muslim leaders formed the Muslim League to protect their own rights and interests. They even talked about setting up a separate Muslim state. After World War I, calls for Indian self-rule increased, followed by demands for independence. This goal would finally be achieved in 1947.

## Turkey

In the 1800s, the multinational Ottoman empire faced challenges from the various ethnic groups in the empire.

**Young Turks** A group of liberals in the 1890s established a movement called the Young Turks. This group wanted to strengthen the Ottoman empire and end the threat of western imperialism. In 1908, they overthrew the sultan and took control of the government.

**The Armenian Massacre** The Young Turks supported Turkish nationalism. They abandoned traditional Ottoman tolerance of diverse cultures and religions. Muslim Turks turned against Christian Armenians who were living in the Ottoman empire. Accusing the Armenians of plotting with Russia against the Ottoman empire, the Turks unleashed a massacre that resulted in the death of over a million Armenians over the next 25 years.

### Nationalities in Eastern Europe Around 1870

*The Balkans* The peninsula in southeastern Europe is called the Balkans. In the late 1800s, this area was a center of conflict. The various peoples and empires competed for power.

## Preparing for the Regents

- How has nationalism been a force that divides as well as unifies? Give examples to support your answer.

- By the 1800s, the Ottoman empire was becoming weaker. How did European nations react to the decreasing power of the Ottomans?

- Choose one of the regions discussed in this section. Explain how nationalism remains a force in that region today.

## Note Taking

*Reading Skill:* Summarize
Make a chart. Summarize the main ideas about nationalism in the three areas listed in the chart.

| Nationalism | |
|---|---|
| Europe | •<br>• |
| Asia | •<br>• |
| Balkans | •<br>• |

# Nationalism and Conflict in the Balkans

Nationalism was a source of conflict in the Balkan peninsula of southeastern Europe. In the 1800s, the Ottoman empire still ruled much of the area, which was home to many groups. Among these were Serbs, Greeks, Bulgarians, and Romanians. During the 1800s, nationalist groups in the Balkans rebelled against foreign rule. From 1829 to 1908, Greece, Montenegro, Serbia, Romania, and Bulgaria all gained their independence.

The nations of Europe viewed the Ottoman empire as "the sick man of Europe." They hoped to gain land from the Ottoman empire. Russia, Austria-Hungary, Great Britain, and France all entered into alliances and wars that were designed to gain territory from the Ottoman empire.

Russia sponsored a nationalistic movement called **Pan-Slavism,** based on the idea that all Slavic peoples shared a common nationality. Serbia had a large Slavic population and was supported by Russia. Austria-Hungary, however, feared Serbian nationalism and angered Serbia by taking control in 1908 of two provinces that would have given Serbia access to the Adriatic Sea.

In the early years of 1900, crisis after crisis broke out on the Balkan peninsula. By 1914, the Balkans were the "powder keg of Europe." Tensions soon exploded into a full-scale global conflict: World War I.

# Summary

Starting in the late 1700s, nationalism became a major force that helped inspire uprisings across Europe and Latin America. In the mid-1800s, nationalism led to the creation of two strong, united nations: Italy and Germany. Nationalistic sentiments also spread among Indians, Turks, Jews, and other peoples. Nationalism did not always draw people together, however. In the early 1900s, nationalism created conflicts in southeastern Europe that drove the continent to the brink of war.

# Economic and Social Revolutions

## Section Overview

Starting around 1750, Europe experienced a series of major changes. They began with improvements in farming that led to an increase in population. These changes contributed to the Industrial Revolution. With the Industrial Revolution, social classes, people's roles, working conditions, and city life changed greatly. When the new conditions led to problems, differing thinkers wanted to solve them in different ways. Some groups emphasized the rights of individuals. Socialists and others stressed the needs of society as a whole. A period of reforms followed. By the early 1900s, the world had changed even more: Global migration occurred and movement toward a global economy accelerated.

## Key Themes and Concepts

As you review this section, take special note of the following key themes and concepts:

**Change** What changes occurred during the Agrarian Revolution?

**Science and Technology** What role did technology play in the Industrial Revolution?

**Economic Systems** What economic and social developments occurred as part of the Industrial Revolution?

**Political Systems** What parliamentary reforms came about as a result of the Industrial Revolution?

## Key People and Terms

As you review this section, be sure you understand the significance of these key people and terms:

| | | |
|---|---|---|
| Agrarian Revolution | Adam Smith | Robert Owen |
| enclosure | capitalism | socialism |
| Industrial Revolution | supply and demand | Karl Marx |
| factories | Thomas Malthus | suffrage |
| laissez faire | Social Darwinism | |

### The Big Idea

In the 1700s and 1800s in Europe:

- the Agrarian Revolution led to population growth.

- the Industrial Revolution eventually transformed economic systems and social conditions around the world.

- people proposed different ways to deal with the problems created by industrialization.

- economic life became more global, and mass migrations of people occurred.

### Key People and Terms

- Place each of the key people and terms into these three categories: science and technology, economic system, political system.

## The Agrarian Revolution

In 1750, most people still lived in small villages and made their own clothing and tools. In the century that followed, dramatic changes took place in the ways people lived and worked.

### Increased Food Production

The movement away from rural life began with the Agrarian Revolution, a change in methods of farming.

**Vocabulary
Builder**

dike—(dyk) *n*. a wall
or bank built to keep
back water and
prevent flooding

**Technology** The Dutch led the way by building dikes to protect their farmland from the sea and using fertilizer to improve the soil. The British discovered ways to produce more food. Jethro Tull invented the seed drill, which planted seeds in rows.

**Enclosure Movement** Landowners found a new purpose for enclosure, taking over and fencing off land that once had been shared by peasant farmers. The purpose of the enclosure movement was to replace the many small strip farms with larger fields. This practice made farming more efficient, improving agricultural production.

### Population Explosion

The Agrarian Revolution led to rapid population growth. With a better diet, women had healthier and stronger babies. In addition, improved medical care and sanitation helped people live longer. During the 1700s, Europe's population increased from 120 million to about 190 million.

## The Industrial Revolution

The Industrial Revolution was the period, beginning around 1750, in which the means of production of goods shifted from hand tools to complex machines and from human and animal power to steam power. During this period, technology developed rapidly and production increased. The Industrial Revolution brought great changes into people's lives.

### Causes of the Industrial Revolution

Industrialization began in Great Britain. Belgium, France, Germany, the United States, and Japan would all industrialize by the end of the 1800s. In time, the Industrial Revolution would spread throughout the world. It happened first in Great Britain for several reasons.

**Key Themes
and Concepts**

**Change**
As larger areas were
enclosed, farm yields
rose. Profits grew
because fewer people
were needed to work
the farms. Unemployed
farmers moved to cities.

**Preparing for
the Regents**

• How did the Agrarian
Revolution of the 1700s
contribute to the
Industrial Revolution?

**Preparing for
the Regents**

• Explain three reasons for
the start of the Industrial
Revolution.

1.

2.

3.

**The Industrial Revolution Begins in Great Britain**

| Geography | Population Growth and Change |
|---|---|
| Great Britain had plenty of iron ore and coal needed for industrialization. As an island, Great Britain had many natural harbors for trade and was protected from invasion. Rivers served both as a means of transportation and as sources of power for factories. | Growth in population due to the Agrarian Revolution led to more available workers. Because of the enclosure movement, fewer farm laborers were needed. People moved to the cities where they could work in factories. |
| **Capital for Investment** | **Energy and Technology** |
| The British overseas empire had made the economy strong. As a result, the middle class had the capital to invest in mines, railroads, and factories and the commercial and financial skills to manage investment. | Great Britain had experienced an energy revolution. In the 1700s, giant water wheels were used to power new machines. Soon coal was used to power steam engines, which would become an important power source for machines. |

## Factory System and Mass Production

The textile industry was the first to use the inventions of the Industrial Revolution. Before the Industrial Revolution, families spun cotton into thread and then wove cloth at home. By the 1700s, new machines were too large and expensive to be operated at home. Spinners and weavers began to work in long sheds that were owned by the manufacturers. These sheds, which brought workers and machines together in one place, became the first **factories.** At first, these factories were located near rapidly moving streams, which provided water power. Later, machines were powered by steam engines, fueled by coal. The factory system promoted mass production, meaning that goods were produced in huge quantities at lower cost.

## Effects of the Industrial Revolution

The Industrial Revolution brought about many economic and social changes.

**Laissez Faire Economics** Before the Industrial Revolution, European nations had followed a policy of mercantilism, which called for government regulations, such as tariffs, to achieve a favorable balance of trade. However, during the Enlightenment, a theory called laissez faire emerged, which argued that businesses should be allowed to operate free of government regulation. In 1776, **Adam Smith** wrote *The Wealth of Nations* which promoted laissez faire ideas. These ideas became the basis of the prevailing economic system during the Industrial Revolution. This system, known as **capitalism,** said that the economy should be governed by the natural forces of **supply and demand** and competition among businesses.

**Rise of Big Business** With new technology came the need for the investment of large amounts of money in businesses. To acquire this money, business owners sold stocks, or shares in their companies, to investors. Each stockholder therefore owned a part of the company. Stockholders allowed businesses to form corporations and expand into many areas.

**New Class Structure** In the Middle Ages, the two main classes in Europe had been nobles and peasants. During the 1600s, a middle class had emerged. The Industrial Revolution added more complexity.

- The upper class consisted of very rich industrial and business families. Members of these families often married into noble families.

- A growing upper middle class of business people and professionals—such as lawyers and doctors—emerged. Their standard of living was high. Below them a lower middle class of teachers, office workers, shopowners, and clerks existed.

- At the bottom of this social structure were factory workers and peasants. They benefited least from the Industrial Revolution. People in this class faced harsh living and working conditions in overcrowded cities.

**Urbanization** People moved from small villages to the towns and cities where factories were located. At first, conditions were very bad. Working-class people lived in crowded buildings. Without a sewage or sanitation system, garbage rotted in the streets. Disease spread.

**Working Conditions** Factory work hours were long. Men, women, and even children worked 12 to 16 hours a day. Mass production methods led to work that was boring. Many machines were dangerous.

### Preparing for the Regents

- As you study current events, keep in mind that the Industrial Revolution is still occurring in the developing nations of the world.

### Note Taking

*Reading Skill:*
**Identify Effects**
Make a chart. As you read, list the effects of the Industrial Revolution. Write details about each one. Add boxes as needed.

| The Industrial Revolution | |
| --- | --- |
| **Effects** | **Details** |
| Laissez-Faire Economics | • <br> • |
| | • <br> • |
| | • <br> • |

### Preparing for the Regents

- How did the Industrial Revolution lead to urbanization?

**Preparing for the Regents**

- How did the Industrial Revolution contribute to changing the roles of men and women?

**Changing Social Roles** The roles of men, women, and children changed in the new industrial society. Farming families had all worked the land together. Artisans had worked in their homes. Now the workplace became separated from the home.

The roles of middle-class men and women were redefined. Men worked in the public world of business and government. Women worked at home, where they were responsible for maintaining the dwelling and raising the children, including their moral instruction. Social class had an impact on family life. Middle-class children had a high standard of living and a better chance at education. Among the working class, on the other hand, children had to work long hours to help support their families. Working-class women also worked long hours, although they were paid less than men. Family life sometimes suffered as women worked 12 hours or more in a factory and then came home to care for their families.

**Improved Transportation** The growth of industry led to improvements in transportation.

- Roads and canals were built and improved.
- The steam locomotive was invented. Railroads grew.
- Steam engines powered ships at sea.

**Rising Standards of Living** Settlement patterns shifted over time. The rich lived in pleasant neighborhoods on the edges of the cities. The poor were crowded into slums in city centers, near factories. Over time, conditions in cities improved, however. In addition, people ate more varied diets and were healthier, thanks to advances in medicine.

## Competing Philosophies

The hardships and changes brought by the Industrial Revolution inspired many varying solutions. Several different ways of thinking competed against each other.

**Note Taking**

*Reading Skill:* **Identify Main Ideas and Supporting Details** As you read Competing Philosophies, complete an outline with the main ideas and supporting details. An outline has been started for you.

Competing Philosophies
I. Laissez-faire capitalism
  A. Adam Smith
    1. natural laws govern economic life
  B.
II.

### Laissez Faire Capitalism

Many economic thinkers supported Adam Smith's idea that natural laws governed economic life. **Thomas Malthus** published his *Essay on the Principle of Population* in 1798. He argued that because population tended to increase more rapidly than the food supply, the poor would continue to suffer. However, because he believed in laissez faire, he did not urge the government to step in to help the poor. He urged the poor to have fewer children.

### Social Darwinism

Other new ideas of the 1800s challenged long-held beliefs. In 1859, British naturalist Charles Darwin caused an uproar by saying that humans had evolved over millions of years. This theory of evolution, as it was called, stirred conflicts between religion and science.

Part of Darwin's theory involved the idea of natural selection. Using the ideas of Thomas Malthus, Darwin said that species naturally produced more offspring than the food supply could support. Members of each species had to compete to survive. Thus, natural forces selected the most able members, producing an improved species.

Later thinkers used Darwin's ideas to develop a theory known as **Social Darwinism.** According to Social Darwinism, successful businesspeople were successful because they were naturally more "fit" to succeed than others. War allowed stronger nations to weed out weaker ones. Social Darwinism played a part in racism, the belief that one race is superior to another. It also contributed to the rise in imperialism.

## Social Reformism

In contrast to laissez faire philosophy, which advised governments to leave business alone, other theorists believed government should intervene to improve people's lives. Many different types of social reformism arose. Socialists hoped to replace the capitalist economic system. Reform movements attempted to correct the abuses of child labor. Labor unions attempted to improve the dangerous working conditions in the factories.

## Socialism

**Socialism** concentrated less on the interests and rights of individuals and more on the interests of society. Industrial capitalism, the socialists claimed, had created a large gap between rich and poor. Under socialism, farms and businesses would belong to all the people, not to individuals. Different types of socialism emerged.

**Utopian Socialism** Early socialists, called Utopians, sought to create self-sufficient communities, where all property and work would be shared. Since all would have equal wealth, Utopians believed that fighting would end. In Scotland, **Robert Owen** set up a Utopian factory community.

**Marxist Socialism** German philosopher **Karl Marx** promoted a more radical theory, "scientific socialism." In 1848, Marx and German economist Friedrich Engels explained their ideas, listed here, in *The Communist Manifesto*.

- History was a class struggle between wealthy capitalists and the working class, or proletariat.
- In order to make profits, the capitalists took advantage of the proletariat.
- The proletariat would eventually rise up and overthrow the capitalist system, creating its own society.
- The proletariat society would take control of the means of production and establish a classless, communist society, in which wealth and power would be equally shared.

In the Soviet Union in the 1900s, Marx's ideas would lead to a communist dictatorship and a command economy, in which government officials made all economic decisions.

# Labor Unions and Reform Legislation

Throughout the 1800s, reform movements sought to address the negative impact of the Industrial Revolution. The actions of workers and reformers forced governments to examine and reform many of the worst abuses.

**Labor Unions** By the 1800s, workers in the same occupation began to join together to form organizations to press for reforms. These unions engaged in collective bargaining with their employers, negotiating for higher pay and better working conditions. Workers would strike, or refuse to work, if employers refused their demands. From 1799–1824, labor unions were illegal in Great Britain. Eventually, however, labor unions contributed to improved wages, hours, and conditions for workers.

**Preparing for the Regents**

- Create a chart listing and briefly explaining the competing philosophies that emerged during and after the Industrial Revolution.

**Vocabulary Builder**

abuse—(uh BYOOS) *n.* the use of something in a way that it should not be used

**Preparing for the Regents**

- Compare and contrast Utopian socialism with Marxist socialism.

**Note Taking**

*Reading Skill:*
**Identify Effects** Complete a concept web with the effects of labor unions. Add more circles if needed.

## British Reform Laws

*British Reform Laws* Throughout the 1800s, the British Parliament passed many important laws. These laws improved conditions for women, children, and the working class.

| DIRECTION OF REFORM | LAWS ENACTED |
|---|---|
| Toward greater human rights | 1884: Slavery is outlawed in all British colonies. |
| Toward more representative government | 1832: Reform Act of 1832 gave representation to new industrial towns.<br>1858: Law ended property qualifications for members of Parliament.<br>1911: Law restricted powers of House of Lords; elected House of Commons became supreme. |
| Toward universal **suffrage** (the right to vote) | 1829: Parliament gave Catholics the right to vote and to hold most public offices.<br>1867: Reform Act gave vote to many working-class working-class men.<br>1884: Law extended voting rights to most farmers and other men.<br>1918: Women won the right to vote. |
| Toward more rights for workers | 1825: Trade unions were legalized.<br>1840s to 1910s: Parliament passed laws<br>• limiting child labor.<br>• regulating work hours for women and children.<br>• regulating safety conditions in factories and mines.<br>• setting minimum wages.<br>• providing for accident and unemployment insurance. |
| Toward improved education | 1870: Education Act set up local elementary schools run by elected school boards.<br>1902: Law created a system of state-aided secondary schools. Industrial cities, such as London and Manchester, set up public universities. |

### Preparing for the Regents

1. Describe a reform law that helped women.

2. Describe a law that helped children.

**Reform Legislation** In the early 1830s, British lawmaker Michael Sadler persuaded Parliament to investigate the horrible conditions faced by child laborers in factories. **The Sadler Report** led to the Factories Regulations Act of 1833. This act prohibited children under the age of 9 from being employed in textile mills, and it limited the working hours of children under 18. This is just one of many types of reforms introduced in Great Britain in the 1800s. France and Germany enacted labor reforms as well.

## Education and the Arts

Artists, musicians, and writers also took new directions during the Industrial Revolution.

### Advances in Education

Governments had begun to set up public schools and require basic education for all children by the late 1800s. Schools not only taught subjects such as reading, writing, and mathematics but encouraged obedience to authority and punctuality as well.

### Romanticism

From about 1750 to 1850, a movement known as romanticism thrived. The romantics appealed to emotion rather than to reason. In this way romanticism

### Preparing for the Regents

• Discuss one important characteristic of each of these artistic movements.

Romanticism:

Realism:

was a rebellion against the ideas of the Enlightenment. It was also a reaction against the impersonal nature of industrial society.

### Realism

The mid-1800s brought an artistic movement known as realism to the West. Realists sought to show the world as it was. They often looked at the harsh side of life, showing poverty and cruel working conditions. Many writers, such as Charles Dickens, were critical of the abuses of industrial society and hoped to contribute to ending them.

## Global Impact of Industrialization

### Global Migrations

**A Wave of Migrations** Improvements in transportation, population growth, and social and political conditions led to a wave of global migrations from about 1845 through the early 1900s.

- Polish nationalists fled Poland for Western Europe and the United States after the Russian army crushed the revolt of 1830.
- Several thousand Germans moved to cities in the United States after the failed revolutions of 1848.
- Russian Jews, escaping pogroms, left Eastern Europe.
- Italian farmers, seeing economic opportunity, also traveled to the Americas.

**Mass Starvation in Ireland** Another migration occurred from Ireland. Under British rule, the majority of Irish farmland had been used to grow crops, such as wheat and oats, which were sent to England. The Irish themselves used the potato as their main food crop. This system supported the Irish population until 1845, when a disease destroyed the potato crop. Other crops were not affected. Still, the British continued to ship the other products out of Ireland. Four years later, one million Irish had died of starvation or disease. Millions of others moved to the United States and Canada.

### Movement Toward a Global Economy

By the mid-1800s, the Industrial Revolution had moved beyond Great Britain. New powers were emerging. As they became strong industrially, they competed for a share of the wealth in markets around the world. In addition, manufacturers traded with other countries for resources they needed. Steamships and railroads, and then automobiles and airplanes, made global trade easier and quicker. As markets expanded around the world and global trade increased, a new imperialism developed.

## Summary

In the mid-1700s, the Agrarian Revolution in Europe contributed to an increase in population. The Agrarian Revolution led to the Industrial Revolution, which began in Great Britain and then spread to other countries. Economic and social conditions around the world changed dramatically as a result of the Industrial Revolution. Many new ideas about how to deal with the problems of industrialization developed, and reforms were enacted. Eventually, industrialization led to mass migration and increased global trade.

**Preparing for the Regents**

- How did British policy contribute to starvation in Ireland and mass migration from Ireland?

**Note Taking**

*Reading Skill:*
**Recognize Sequence**
List the important events of the Economic and Social Revolutions. Record them in the order they occurred. Add boxes as needed.

| Date | Event |
|------|-------|
|      |       |
|      |       |
|      |       |

**Preparing for the Regents**

- Compare the ways in which the Neolithic Revolution, the Industrial Revolution, and the Computer Revolution changed human life.

# Japan and the Meiji Restoration

## Section Overview

In 1853, an American fleet sailed to Japan and ended over 200 years of isolation by opening Japan to trade. Soon afterward, Japan's ruling shogun was overthrown, and the Meiji Restoration began. During this period, Japan underwent a rapid period of modernization and industrialization. Changes took place within government, the economy, and social life. Within decades Japan became a modern industrial power and began to build an overseas empire.

## Key Themes and Concepts

As you review this section, take special note of the following key themes and concepts:

**Change** What political, social, and economic changes occurred in Japan in the late 1800s?

**Interdependence** How did Japan use western ideas to modernize and industrialize?

**Power** How did Japan become a global power by the early 1900s?

## Key People and Terms

As you review this section, be sure you understand the significance of these key people and terms:

| | |
|---|---|
| Matthew Perry | zaibatsu |
| Treaty of Kanagawa | Sino-Japanese War |
| Meiji Restoration | Russo-Japanese War |

## The Opening of Japan

In 1853, United States ships sailed into Edo (now Tokyo) Bay, ending more than 200 years of Japanese isolation. This contact led to changes that had a great impact on Japan.

### Tokugawa Isolation

European traders had first arrived in Japan in the 1500s. In the 1600s, the Tokugawa shoguns had gained control of Japan. They brought stability to Japan but also banned almost all contact with the outside world. Limited trade was allowed only with the Dutch at Nagasaki.

### Commodore Matthew Perry

In 1854, American warships commanded by Commodore **Matthew Perry** sailed to Japan. Perry presented a letter to the Japanese from the United States president, asking that Japan open its ports to trade. Europeans and Americans were not only offended by the Tokugawa isolation but resentful at not being able to use Japanese ports to resupply or repair their ships.

Impressed by the American show of strength, the shogun agreed to the Treaty of Kanagawa, ending his country's long period of isolation. It was the first of many treaties Japan would sign with foreign powers.

### The Treaty of Kanagawa

In the **Treaty of Kanagawa,** the shogun agreed to open two Japanese ports to American ships. The United States soon won other trading rights with Japan. In time, Great Britain, France, and Russia gained similar trading rights.

The Treaty of Kanagawa had a powerful impact on Japan.

- Some Japanese felt that the shogun had shown weakness in front of the foreigners by agreeing to the treaty.
- Some Japanese felt that Japan needed to modernize in order to compete with the industrialized West.
- A rebellion overthrew the shogun, restored the emperor to power, and launched Japan on the road to modernization and industrialization.

## Modernization and Industrialization

In 1867, daimyo and samurai led a rebellion that removed the Tokugawa shogun from power. In 1868, the emperor was established as the leader of Japan. The period from 1868 to 1912 is known as the **Meiji Restoration.** *Meiji* means "enlightened rule." During this time, the emperor and his advisors implemented a series of reforms that changed Japan forever.

### Borrowing From the West

The Meiji reformers were determined to strengthen Japan against the West. Members of the government traveled abroad to learn about western government, economics, technology, and customs. In addition, foreign experts were invited to Japan.

### Economic Development

The Meiji government used western methods and machinery to develop an industrial economy in Japan. The government built factories and then sold them to wealthy families. These families became powerful in banking and industry and were known as **zaibatsu.**

The government supported the economy by developing a banking system and a postal system. It also built railroads and improved ports. By the 1890s, the economy was flourishing. The population grew, and peasants migrated to the cities in search of jobs.

### Strong Central Government

Meiji reformers wanted to create a strong central government. They chose the government of Germany as their model. A constitution gave the emperor autocratic power and created a two-house legislature. Only one of the houses was elected, and suffrage was limited.

### Military Power

By the 1890s, Japan had a modern army and a strong navy. No longer were the samurai the only warriors—all men had to enter military service. When Japan and China fought over Korea in 1894, Japan won easily. Later, Japanese troops defeated Russian troops in Manchuria. This victory marked the first time in modern history that an Asian power defeated a European nation.

**Preparing for the Regents**

- What effects did the visit of Commodore Perry and the Treaty of Kanagawa have on Japan's development?

**Preparing for the Regents**

- Why did the Industrial Revolution occur earlier in Japan than in African and other Asian nations?

**Key Themes and Concepts**

Choice
- How did choosing a German model for government affect the development of Japan?

## Preparing for the Regents

- What changes were made in society during the Meiji Restoration? What group did not experience greater personal freedom?

- Practice your graph skills by answering the following questions.

1. During which five-year period did Japanese trade increase the most?

2. Why was Japanese trade increasing so much in the late 1800s?

*Japanese Exports and Imports*
*Meiji leaders made the economy a major priority. Imports and exports grew at an amazing speed.*

## Key Themes and Concepts

**Power**
Industrialization contributed to Japan's strong military. In turn, a strong military contributed to the nation's imperialistic success.

**Geography**
Japan, an island nation with few natural resources, had industrialized rapidly in the 1800s. How did geography affect Japan's decision to follow a policy of imperialism?

## Social Change

Meiji reforms established a system of public education and set up universities with western instructors to teach modern technology. Despite social reforms, however, class distinctions still existed. Also, Japanese women faced continuing inequality. Meiji reformers took away some political and legal rights that women had previously won.

### Japanese Exports and Imports

## Japan as a Global Power

Soon, like western powers, Japan used its industrial and military strength to begin a policy of imperialism. It sought colonies as sources of raw materials and as markets for finished products. Colonies were gained through war.

### Sino-Japanese War

In 1894, Japan's territorial ambitions in Korea led to war with China. The conflict, which lasted from 1894 to 1895, was called the **Sino-Japanese War.** Japan quickly won, gaining Formosa (later Taiwan) and treaty ports in China from the Chinese. Japan later made Korea a Japanese protectorate.

### Russo-Japanese War

From 1904 to 1905, Japan fought the **Russo-Japanese War** with Russia after the interests of the two nations conflicted in Korea. Japan's modern military defeated Russian troops and crushed Russia's navy. By 1910, Japan had complete control of Korea as well as parts of Manchuria.

### Dependence on a World Market

Japan's industrialization drew it increasingly into the global market. Its economy therefore became dependent on trade. An island empire with few natural resources, Japan relied on raw materials from outside the country. It needed foreign markets for its manufactured products. In the years ahead, Japan would continue to compete with other industrialized nations. It would also continue its policy of imperialism.

## Summary

In the mid-1800s, Japan ended its long policy of isolation. The Meiji government that took power in 1868 used western ideas to begin a program of modernization that quickly turned Japan into a major industrial power. In the 1890s and 1900s, Japan used its modern military to become a global imperial power.

# Imperialism

## Section Overview

From the mid-1800s through the first decades of the 1900s, western nations pursued an aggressive policy of expansion. European powers were motivated by economic, political, and social factors as well as by a strong sense of nationalism. During this time, Great Britain took control of India. In Africa, several European nations engaged in a scramble for colonies. Meanwhile, imperialistic nations forced unequal trade agreements on China. Imperialism had many immediate and long-term effects on the colonial nations and also had an impact on Europe and the rest of the world. Imperialism led to increased competition and conflict.

## Key Themes and Concepts

As you review this section, take special note of the following key themes and concepts:

**Imperialism** What factors led to the new imperialism of the 1800s?

**Power** How did imperialistic countries gain power over the peoples of Africa and Asia?

**Change** What were the effects of imperialism?

**Nationalism** How did imperialism lead to nationalistic feelings in China and other nations of Asia and Africa?

## Key People and Terms

As you review this section, be sure you understand the significance of these key people and terms:

| | | |
|---|---|---|
| imperialism | Opium War | Taiping Rebellion |
| "White Man's Burden" | Treaty of Nanjing | Boxer Rebellion |
| Sepoy Mutiny | spheres of influence | Sun Yixian |
| Boer War | | |

## The New Imperialism

**Imperialism** is the domination by one country of the political, economic, or cultural life of another country. Historians often divide imperialism into two periods.

- **The Old Imperialism** Between about 1500 and 1800, European nations established colonies in the Americas, India, and Southeast Asia and gained territory on the coasts of Africa and China. Still, European power in these regions of the world was limited.

- **The New Imperialism** Between 1870 and 1914, nationalism had produced strong, centrally governed nation-states. The Industrial Revolution had made economies stronger as well. During this time, Japan, the United States, and the industrialized nations of Europe became more aggressive in expanding into other lands. The new imperialism was focused mainly on Asia and Africa, where declining empires and local wars left many states vulnerable. In Africa, many states had been weakened by the legacy of the slave trade.

### The Big Idea

The imperialism that emerged in the mid-1800s had a lasting impact on the world.

- Powerful industrialized nations sought to gain power and economic might by building empires.

- Through economic and military power, Great Britain colonized and dominated India.

- European nations divided up the continent of Africa.

- Western powers and Japan established spheres of influence in China.

- Imperialism has had short-term and long-term effects on various regions of the world.

### Key People and Terms

- What do most of the key people and terms have in common? Explain.

### Key Themes and Concepts

**Imperialism**
The strong central governments and thriving economies of industrialized nations gave them the confidence to expand through imperialism.

## Causes of Imperialism

Several important factors combined to lead to the development of the new imperialism.

### Causes of the New Imperialism

| Economy | Politics and the Military | Society | Science and Invention |
|---|---|---|---|
| • Need for natural resources<br>• Need for new markets<br>• Place for growing populations to settle<br>• Place to invest profits | • Bases for trade and navy ships<br>• Power and security of global empire<br>• Spirit of nationalism | • Wish to spread Christianity<br>• Wish to share western civilization<br>• Belief that western ways are best | • New weapons<br>• New medicines<br>• Improved ships |

*The New Imperialism*
*From 1870 to 1914, European countries, the United States, and Japan gained control over much of the world.*

### Nationalism and Social Darwinism

A spirit of nationalism was one cause of the new imperialism. Because nationalism promotes the idea of national superiority, imperialists felt that they had a right to take control of countries they viewed as weaker. Social Darwinism also encouraged imperialism. This idea applied Darwin's theory of survival of the fittest to competition between nations. Social Darwinists argued that it was natural for stronger nations to dominate weaker ones.

### Military Motives

Military motives were linked to nationalism, since military power was a way to promote a nation's goals. Colonies were important as bases for resupply of ships. A nation with many colonies had power and security.

### Economic Motives

Imperialists needed raw materials to supply their factories. They needed foreign markets in which to sell their finished products. They needed places to invest their profits. Colonies could provide all these things.

### "White Man's Burden"

Rudyard Kipling's poem **"White Man's Burden"** offered a justification for imperialism. Kipling expressed the idea that white imperialists had a moral duty to educate people in nations they considered less developed. Missionaries spread western ideas, customs, and religions to people in Africa and Asia.

**Preparing for the Regents**

• How did the Industrial Revolution lead to imperialism?

## British in India

### British East India Company

The British East India Company had established trading rights in India in the early 1600s. By the mid-1800s, with the decline of the Mughal empire and the defeat of French rivals, this company controlled three fifths of India. The company employed Indian soldiers, called sepoys.

### The Sepoy Mutiny

In 1857, tensions rose. The British had angered the sepoys by demanding that soldiers follow rules that were against their religious beliefs. The **Sepoy Mutiny,** or the Sepoy Rebellion, called for Hindus and Muslims to unite against the British. The British, however, crushed the revolt.

The Sepoy Mutiny left bitter feelings. It also caused the British to change their policies. In 1858, Parliament ended the rule of the East India Company. The British government took direct command of India.

**The Effects of British Rule in India**

| GOOD EFFECTS |
| --- |
| • New roads and railroads link parts of India. |
| • Telegraph and postal systems unite people |
| • Irrigation systems improve farming. |
| • New laws mean justice for all classes. |
| • British schools offer education. |
| • Customs that threaten human rights are ended. |

| BAD EFFECTS |
| --- |
| • Indian resources go to Great Britain. |
| • British-made goods replace local goods. |
| • Farms grow cash crops rather than food crops; Indians go hungry. |
| • Top jobs go to the British. |
| • Indians are treated as inferiors. |
| • Great Britain tries to replace Indian culture with western ways. |

**Note Taking**

*Reading Skill:* **Identify Causes and Effects**
Make a flowchart to show the causes and effects of British rule in India.

# The Scramble for Africa

In the 1870s, King Leopold of Belgium sent a mission to the interior of Africa to establish trade agreements with leaders in the Congo River basin. The Belgian presence in the Congo set off a scramble among other European powers to establish their presence on the continent.

## The Berlin Conference

In 1884, to avoid conflict among themselves, European leaders met in Berlin, Germany, to set up rules for colonizing Africa. European powers divided Africa with little regard for the people who lived there. The new imperialism affected Africa strongly. In 1850, most of Africa had been free. Seventy years later, most of the continent was under European rule.

## Battle for Southern Africa

**The Zulu Empire** In the early 1800s in southern Africa, an African leader named Shaka organized Zulu warriors into a fighting force. He used his power against European slave traders and ivory hunters. Through conquest of other African groups, he united the Zulu nation.

**Arrival of Europeans** Dutch farmers, called Boers, had settled in southern Africa in the mid-1600s. They had built Cape Town as a supply station. In the 1700s, Dutch herders and ivory hunters began to move north. They fought African groups, such as the Zulus. In the early 1800s, the British acquired the Cape Colony from the Dutch.

**Zulu Resistance** Large numbers of Boers, resenting British rule, migrated north during the 1830s, coming into conflict with Zulus. Fighting between the Boers and the Zulus continued until late in the century.

The Zulus eventually came into conflict with the British as well. The Zulus experienced victory in 1879. Soon afterward, however, the superior weaponry of the British crushed the Zulu resistance. Others in Africa also resisted imperialism, including groups in Ethiopia and West Africa.

**The Boer War** Cecil Rhodes became prime minister of the Cape Colony in 1890. Under his leadership, Great Britain expanded its control of southern Africa.

In the late 1800s, Great Britain decided to annex the Boer republics. The Boers resisted and the Boer War began, lasting from 1899 to 1902. After heavy losses, the British won. In 1910, the Great British combined the Boer republics with the Cape Colony to form the Union of South Africa. The bitter struggles left a legacy of distrust and hatred.

**Draw Inferences**

The European leaders did not invite the African leaders to the Berlin Conference. Why not?

**Preparing for the Regents**

• How did the Zulus display a nationalistic response to imperialism?

**Vocabulary Builder**

annex—(uh NEKS) v. to take control of a country or area next to your own, especially by using force

**Anti-Slave Trade Legislation** Most European powers had abolished the slave trade before the scramble for African colonies began. For example, Denmark passed anti-slave trade legislation in 1803, followed by Great Britain in 1807, and France in 1818. Illegal slave trading, however, continued throughout the 1800s.

*The Scramble for Africa*
*During the late 1800s, European countries started to take over Africa. By 1914, they controlled nearly the entire continent.*

**Preparing for the Regents**

• Practice your map skills by identifying the colonial power that occupied each of the following areas: Algeria in 1830, Togo in 1884, and the Union of South Africa in 1910.

### The Scramble for Africa, 1880–1914

SPANISH MOROCCO 1912
MOROCCO 1912
TUNIS 1881
RIO DE ORO 1885
ALGERIA 1830
LIBYA 1912
EGYPT 1882
GAMBIA 1888
FRENCH WEST AFRICA 1874
ERITREA 1890
ANGLO-EGYPTIAN SUDAN 1889
FRENCH SOMALILAND 1884
BRITISH SOMALILAND 1884
PORTUGUESE GUINEA 1901
NIGERIA 1884
ETHIOPIA Independent
SIERRA LEONE 1808
LIBERIA Independent
GOLD COAST 1874
TOGO 1884
RIO MUNI 1901
CAMEROONS 1884
UGANDA 1895
ITALIAN SOMALILAND 1889
FRENCH EQUATORIAL AFRICA 1910
BELGIAN CONGO 1908
GERMAN EAST AFRICA 1885
BRITISH EAST AFRICA 1886
ANGOLA 1891
N. RHODESIA 1891
NYASALAND 1891
GERMAN SOUTH WEST AFRICA 1884
S. RHODESIA 1890
BECHU-ANALAND 1885
MOZAMBIQUE 1500
MADAGASCAR 1895
SWAZILAND 1907
UNION OF SOUTH AFRICA 1910
BASUTOLAND 1871

British
French
German
Italian
Other Europeans

Dates indicate year of colonization

# Imperialism in China

Since 1644, rulers of the Qing dynasty had refused to adopt western ways. As a result, the economic, political, and military strength of European imperialists was able to challenge China's Middle Kingdom.

## The Opium War and the Treaty of Nanjing

British merchants began to trade opium in China in the late 1700s. China tried to halt imports of the addictive drug. In 1839, to keep trade open, the British fought with China in a conflict called the **Opium War.** Great Britain's superior military and industrial strength led to a quick victory.

In 1842, Great Britain forced China to agree to the harsh terms of the **Treaty of Nanjing.** China had to pay for Great Britain's war costs, open ports to British trade, and give Great Britain the island of Hong Kong. China also had to grant British citizens extraterritoriality, the right to live under their own laws and be tried in their own courts. In the years that followed, other western powers forced China to

**Recognize Cause and Effect**

• What were the causes of the Opium War?

• What were the effects of the Opium War?

sign unequal treaties. The western powers carved out **spheres of influence,** areas in which an outside power claimed exclusive trade privileges.

## Chinese Reactions to Imperialism

Foreign imperialism led to further clashes between the imperialist powers and China—and among the Chinese themselves.

**The Taiping Rebellion** From 1850 to 1864, Chinese peasants, angry at their poverty and at corrupt Qing officials, rose up in revolt. The Taiping Rebellion resulted in millions of Chinese deaths and weakened China.

**The Boxer Rebellion** In 1900, a group known to westerners as the Boxers assaulted foreign communities across China in a conflict known as the Boxer Rebellion. Armies from Japan and the West, however, soon crushed the uprising and forced China to grant more concessions to foreign powers. After this defeat, greater numbers of Chinese called for western-style reforms.

**Sun Yixian and the Chinese Revolution** In the first decade of the 1900s, Chinese nationalism blossomed. Many reformers called for a new government. Sun Yixian, also called Sun Yat-sen, led the movement to replace the Qing dynasty. He had three goals:

- To end foreign domination
- To form a representative government
- To create economic security for the Chinese people

### Preparing for the Regents

- How did imperialism contribute to the rise of nationalistic feelings in China?

- Compare Japanese and Chinese responses to western industrial power and western imperialism.

### Vocabulary Builder

concession—(kun SESH un) *n.* something that you allow someone to have in order to end an argument or a disagreement

### Spheres of Influence in China Until 1914

### Preparing for the Regents

- Practice your map skills by describing Japan's sphere of influence in Asia in 1914. How do you think this influence benefited Japan?

*Spheres of Influence in China* The Western countries used diplomacy and war to gain power in China. They divided the country into special trade areas.

In 1911, workers, peasants, students, and warlords toppled the monarchy. Sun Yixian was named president of the Chinese Republic.

## Impact of Imperialism: Multiple Perspectives

The new imperialism had a major impact on the European nations and on their colonies.

### Effects on the Colonies

Imperialism had a number of short-term and long-term effects on the colonies themselves. Some were negative; others were positive.

**Short-Term Effects** Some effects were immediate.

• List three arguments that
were used by imperialist
powers to justify
imperialism.

1.

2.

3.

• List three motives people
of Africa and Asia had to
oppose imperialism.

1.

2.

3.

- Large numbers of Asians and Africans came under foreign rule.
- Local economies became dependent on industrialized powers.
- Some nations introduced changes to meet imperialist challenges.
- Individuals and groups resisted European domination.
- Western culture spread to new regions.
- Traditional political units were disrupted or destroyed.
- Famines occurred in lands where farmers grew export crops for imperialist nations in place of food for local use.

**Long-Term Effects** Other effects took longer to emerge.

- Western culture continued to influence much of the world.
- Transportation, education, and medical care were improved.
- Resistance to imperial rule evolved into nationalist movements.
- Many economies became dependent on single cash crops grown for export.

### Effects on Europe and the World

The West also changed because of imperialism.

- The West discovered new crops, foods, and other products.
- Westerners were introduced to new cultural influences.
- Competition for empires created and increased conflict between imperial powers. These conflicts sometimes led to war.
- The industrial nations controlled a new global economy.

## Summary

In the 1800s, industrialized powers greatly expanded their empires. Great Britain took control of India, and European nations occupied much of Africa. Imperial powers also forced China to grant trading concessions. This led to the growth of nationalism in China. Other effects of imperialism included the emergence of a global economy, the spread of western culture, and conflict between imperial powers.

**Key Themes
and Concepts**

**Nationalism**
Nationalist movements in
Asia and Africa often grew
out of resistance to imperial
rule.

**Multiple Choice**

*Directions:* Review the Test-Taking Strategies section of this book. Then answer the following questions, drawn from actual Regents examinations. For each statement or question, choose the *number* of the word or expression that, of those given, best completes the statement or answers the question.

1  John Locke and Jean-Jacques Rousseau would be most likely to support
   (1) a return to feudalism in Europe
   (2) a government ruled by a divine monarchy
   (3) a society ruled by the Catholic Church
   (4) the right of citizens to decide the best form of government

2  The writers and philosophers of the Enlightenment believed that government decisions should be based on:
   (1) fundamental religious beliefs
   (2) the concept of the divine right of kings
   (3) laws of nature and reason
   (4) traditional values

3  A primary cause of the French Revolution in 1789 was the
   (1) increasing dissatisfaction of the Third Estate
   (2) rise to power of Napoleon Bonaparte
   (3) actions of Prince Metternich
   (4) execution of Louis XVI

4  In a number of European countries in the 1800s, which situation occurred as a result of the influence of the French Revolution?
   (1) increase in religious conflict
   (2) rise of nationalistic movements
   (3) decentralization of governmental power
   (4) economic depression

5  During the early 1800s, which was a major influence on the struggles for political independence in Latin America?
   (1) poor conditions in urban centers in Latin America
   (2) the American and French Revolutions
   (3) the desire of the Roman Catholic Church in Latin America to escape European control
   (4) demands by Latin American workers to own their own factories

6  Nationalism is most likely to develop in an area that has
   (1) land suited to agriculture
   (2) adequate industry to supply consumer demands
   (3) a moderate climate with rivers for irrigation
   (4) common customs, language, and history

7  Which statement about nationalism is most accurate?
   (1) It becomes a unifying force among a people.
   (2) It encourages diversity within nation- states.
   (3) It prevents the rise of militarism.
   (4) It eliminates the ethnic identities of different groups.

8  Which term refers to the Jewish movement to establish a homeland in Palestine?
   (1) Zionism
   (2) Marxism
   (3) animism
   (4) secularism

**9** The theory of laissez faire capitalism advocates

(1) government control of the economy

(2) noninvolvement of the government in the economy

(3) government regulation of big business

(4) government sponsorship of labor unions

**10** An important result of the Industrial Revolution was the

(1) concentration of workers in urban areas

(2) increased desire of the wealthy class to share its power

(3) formation of powerful craft guilds

(4) control of agricultural production by governments

**11** The arrival of Commodore Matthew Perry in Japan in 1853 signaled the end of Japanese

(1) cultural contacts with the West

(2) policies of isolationism

(3) militarism in Southeast Asia

(4) trade relations with the United States

**12** In Japan, the period of the Meiji Restoration was primarily characterized by

(1) strict isolation

(2) feudal government

(3) religious revival

(4) reform and modernization

**13** Russia in the 1700s and Japan in the 1800s were similar in that both countries

(1) began the process of modernization after a long period of isolation

(2) developed democratic governments after years under absolute monarchies

(3) refused to accept western technological ideas

(4) adopted socialist economic systems after capitalism had failed

**14** "All great nations . . . have desired to set their mark upon barbarian lands, and those who fail to participate in this great rivalry will play a pitiable role in time to come."

This quotation supports the concept of

(1) socialism

(2) human rights

(3) revolution

(4) imperialism

**15** The Treaty of Tordesillas (1494), concerning Latin America, and the Berlin Conference (1884–1885), concerning Africa, were similar in that each agreement

(1) provided for self-government by native peoples

(2) declared that in these areas, monarchs rule by divine right

(3) divided an area into European-controlled segments

(4) suppressed revolts by native peoples against European imperialists

**16** The Boxer Rebellion of the early twentieth century was an attempt to

(1) eliminate poverty among Chinese peasants

(2) bring western-style democracy to China

(3) restore trade between China and European nations

(4) remove foreign influences from China

# Thematic Essay Question

In developing your answer, be sure to keep these general definitions in mind:

    (a) <u>describe</u> means "to illustrate something in words or tell about it"
    (b) <u>explain</u> means "to make plain or understandable; to give reasons for or causes of; to show the logical development or relationships of"

*Directions:*    Write a well-organized essay that includes an introduction, several paragraphs addressing the task below, and a conclusion.

**Theme:**    **Revolution**

> Throughout global history, there have been major political, economic, social, and cultural revolutions. These revolutions have had complex causes and left lasting impacts on people's lives.

**Task:**

> - Define the term *revolution*
> - Select a specific revolution that you have studied, and describe three of the factors that helped to bring about that particular revolution
> - Identify and explain at least one immediate effect and at least one long-term effect of this revolution on people's lives

   You may discuss any revolution from your study of global history, except the American Revolution. Some suggestions you may wish to consider are: the Commercial Revolution, the Reformation, the Enlightenment, the French Revolution, the Industrial Revolution, the Mexican Revolution, and the Russian Revolution. You are not limited to these suggestions.

**You are *not* limited to these suggestions.**
**Do not use the United States in your answer.**

**Guidelines:**

    **In your essay, be sure to**
    - Develop all aspects of the task
    - Support the theme with relevant facts, examples, and details
    - Use a logical and clear plan of organization, including an introduction and a conclusion that are beyond a simple restatement of the theme.

# Document-Based Question

This question is based on the accompanying documents. The question is designed to test your ability to work with historical documents. Some of these documents have been edited for the purposes of this question. As you analyze the documents, take into account the source of each document and any point of view that may be presented in the document.

Historical Context:

Throughout history, imperialism has been interpreted from multiple perspectives. Some have seen it as a beneficial influence, while others have seen it as a harmful influence.

Task: Using the information from the documents and your knowledge of global history, answer the questions that follow each document in Part A. Your answers to the questions will help you write the Part B essay in which you will be asked to

- Evaluate both the positive and the negative effects of imperialism

In developing your answers, be sure to keep this general definition in mind:

<u>evaluate</u> means "to examine and judge the significance, worth, or condition of; to determine the value of"

## Part A: Short Answer

*Directions:* Analyze the documents and answer the question or questions that follow each document, using the space provided.

### Document #1

*Modern progressive nations lying in the temperate zone seek to control "garden spots" in the tropics, [mainly in Africa, Latin America, and Asia]. Under [the progressive nations'] direction, these places can yield tropical produce. In return, the progressive nations bring to the people of those garden spots the foodstuffs and manufactures they need. [Progressive nations] develop the territory by building roads, canals, railways, and telegraphs. They can establish schools and newspapers for the colonies [and] give these people the benefit of the blessings of civilization which they have not the means of creating themselves.*

*– O.P. Austin, "Does Colonization Pay?" The Forum, 1900*

1. What nations does the author probably consider to be the "modern progressive nations"? Explain the reason for your answer.

_____

_____

### Document #2

*When the whites came to our country, we had the land and they had the Bible. Now we have the Bible and they have the land.*

**– African proverb**

2. Does this proverb express a positive or negative viewpoint toward the white missionaries? Explain.

_____

_____

### Document #3

#### "The Devilfish in Egyptian Waters"

3. What view of English imperialism is expressed in this cartoon? Explain.

_____

_____

**Document #4**

*To begin with, there are the exporters and manufacturers of certain goods used in the colonies. The makers of cotton and iron goods have been very much interested in imperialism. Their business interests demand that colonial markets should be opened and developed and that foreign competitors should be shut out. Such aims require political control and imperialism.*

*Finally, the most powerful of all business groups are the bankers. Banks make loans to colonies and backward countries for building railways and steamship lines. They also make loans to colonial plantation owners, importers, and exporters.*

**– Parker T. Moon, *Imperialism and World Politics*, 1926**

4. Based on this passage, explain two ways in which European businesspeople hoped to profit from imperialism.

_____

_____

## Part B
## Essay

*Directions:*    Write a well-organized essay that includes an introduction, several paragraphs, and a conclusion.  Use evidence from *at least **three*** of the documents in your essay. Support your response with relevant facts, examples, and details. Include additional outside information.

**Historical Context:**

Throughout history, imperialism has been interpreted from multiple perspectives. Some have seen it as a beneficial influence, while others have seen it as a harmful influence.

**Task:**    Using the information from the documents and your knowledge of global history, write an essay in which you

- Evaluate the positive and negative impacts of imperialism, developing a position either in favor of or against imperialism

**Guidelines:**

**In your essay, be sure to**
- Develop all aspects of the task
- Incorporate information from *at least* **three** documents
- Incorporate relevant outside information
- Support the theme with relevant facts, examples, and details
- Use a logical and clear plan of organization, including an introduction and a conclusion that are beyond a restatement of the theme

# Crises and Achievements
## (1900–1945)

## Unit Overview

Science and technology brought many benefits to society in the late 1800s and early 1900s. In most industrialized countries, life expectancy increased and standards of living rose. People became hopeful, for they had experienced peace for many years. However, the forces of nationalism, militarism, and imperialism were moving the world toward war. By the time World War I was over, people understood how science and technology could change their lives in negative ways. The war caused new social and economic problems. In Russia, a communist revolution produced a totalitarian state. Perhaps worst of all, the problems that had led to World War I remained unresolved. A second global conflict erupted in 1939, resulting in even greater destruction than the first.

## Thematic Timeline Activity

Some of the many themes developed in Unit 6 are:

| | | |
|---|---|---|
| change | nationalism | human rights |
| science and technology | political systems | economic systems |
| culture and intellectual life | power | |

Choose one of the themes listed above. As you review Unit 6, create a thematic timeline based on the theme you have chosen. Your timeline should stretch from 1900 to 1945 and include major developments and key turning points having to do with your theme.

# Scientific and Technological Achievements

## Section Overview

In the late 1800s and early 1900s, advances in science and technology led to dramatic changes in daily life. Medical discoveries and better sanitation allowed people to live longer, contributing to a population explosion. New inventions revolutionized energy production, communications, and transportation. Scientific discoveries led to new knowledge about the universe and the workings of the human mind.

## Key Themes and Concepts

As you review this section, take special note of the following key themes and concepts:

**Change** How did medical advances in the late 1800s affect life expectancy and population growth?

**Science and Technology** How did the scientific discoveries of the late 1800s and early 1900s change the way people lived?

**Culture and Intellectual Life** How did new theories affect the ways in which people thought about their world?

**Key People
and Terms**

What do all of the key people and terms have in common? Explain.

## Key People and Terms

As you review this section, be sure you understand the significance of these key people and terms:

| | | |
|---|---|---|
| Louis Pasteur | dynamo | radioactivity |
| germ theory | Thomas Edison | Albert Einstein |
| antibiotics | Marie Curie | Sigmund Freud |

## Advances in Medicine

A series of discoveries revolutionized the field of medicine at the turn of the twentieth century. These medical advances greatly improved health care and increased human life expectancy.

### The Germ Theory and Disease

Before the mid-1800s, the cause of disease was not clear, even to physicians. However, by the late 1800s, scientists were making great progress in this area.

**Louis Pasteur** In the 1600s, a Dutch scientist named Anton van Leeuwenhoek had discovered the existence of microbes, or germs, by using a microscope. He did not, however, recognize the role of these tiny organisms in causing disease.

In 1870, French scientist **Louis Pasteur** made two very important discoveries. He showed clearly the link between germs and disease. He also proved that killing certain germs stops the spread of certain diseases.

**Key Themes
and Concepts**

**Change**
The acceptance of the germ theory was a great step forward for medical science. Once microscopic organisms were recognized as a major cause of disease, scientists could move ahead in curing and preventing many deadly diseases.

**Robert Koch** In the 1880s, the German physician Robert Koch discovered the bacteria that caused tuberculosis. His discovery started the long process of developing a cure for this deadly disease. The work of Pasteur and Koch established the **germ theory** of disease, the idea that many diseases are caused by the action of microorganisms. After people learned about the germ theory, they washed more often and made other lifestyle changes to limit the spread of disease.

### Joseph Lister and Antiseptics

Before the mid-1800s, even a very minor surgical operation might be followed by infection and even death. An English surgeon named Joseph Lister became convinced that germs caused these infections. Lister insisted that doctors use antiseptics—substances that destroy or inhibit the growth of germs—on their hands, on their instruments, and on wounds. Lister's discoveries were a turning point in medicine, and they greatly reduced the number of deaths from infection in hospitals.

### Antibiotics

In 1928, another turning point in medicine occurred. English scientist Alexander Fleming discovered that a mold called *Penicillium* killed germs. This discovery paved the way for the development of a class of drugs called **antibiotics** that attacked or weakened the bacteria that cause many diseases. Antibiotics were not widely developed and used, however, until the 1940s.

## Improved Standard of Living

The advances of the late 1800s and early 1900s extended beyond the field of medicine. The standard of living of most Europeans began to rise.

### Better Wages and Working Conditions

In the early years of the Industrial Revolution, workers had found it difficult to improve their harsh job conditions. By the late 1800s, however, labor unions became legal in many countries of Europe. Unions, reformers, and working-class voters pushed for better working conditions and higher wages. Over time, wages improved. People ate more varied diets and lived in cleaner, safer homes. Reform laws regulated working conditions and provided social benefits to the elderly and the unemployed.

### Better Housing

Urban conditions were improving in the late 1800s and early 1900s. City governments paved their streets, making cities better places to live. Housing improved. Architects began to use steel to construct stronger, taller buildings.

### Improved Sanitation

Underground sewage systems, introduced first in London and Paris, made cities healthier places to live. With underground systems, waste no longer ran through the streets, spreading disease and polluting sources of drinking water. A supply of clean water was necessary to combat diseases such as tuberculosis and cholera. Death rates were dramatically cut after the introduction of the new sewer systems.

**Note Taking**

*Reading Skill:*
**Recognize Sequence**
As you read, list the dates or time periods of the important scientific and technological achievements. Record them in the order they occurred. Add boxes as needed.

| Date | Event |
| --- | --- |
| mid-1800s | Lister discovered that germs cause infections |
| 1870 | |

**Preparing for the Regents**

- How did reforms of the late 1800s and early 1900s affect the average quality of people's lives?

**Vocabulary Builder**

sewage—(SOO ij) *n.* the mixture of waste from the human body and used water that is carried away from houses by pipes under the ground

**Preparing for the Regents**

Describe an effect on daily life of each of these inventions.

Electricity:

Telephone:

Radio:

Automobile:

**Draw Conclusions**

How did the new inventions help business and industry?

## New Inventions

A tremendous number of new inventions appeared in the late 1800s and early 1900s. These inventions improved daily life in many ways.

**Use of Electricity** Early in the 1800s, Alessandro Volta and Michael Faraday had discovered how to produce small amounts of electricity. The later development of the **dynamo** enabled the generation of large amounts of electricity and made electricity a useful source of power. In 1879, an American inventor named **Thomas Edison** developed the first practical light bulb. Soon cities had electric street lights. By the 1890s, factories were powered by electricity. In homes, people used electricity to run appliances that made their lives more comfortable.

**The Telephone** In 1876, Alexander Graham Bell patented the telephone. His machine changed the human voice into electrical impulses, sent them through a wire, and then changed them back into sounds at the other end. The invention of the telephone transformed long-distance communication.

**The Radio** The telephone was an important means of communication, but it depended on wires. Guglielmo Marconi, in 1895, sent radio signals directly through the air. The first radios transmitted Morse code signals. The year 1906 marked the first voice broadcast over radio.

**The Automobile** Inventions also transformed transportation in the last half of the 1800s. In the 1870s, Nikolaus Otto developed a gasoline-powered internal combustion engine. In the 1880s, Gottlieb Daimler used Otto's engine to power the first automobile. By 1900, thousands of automobiles were on the roads of Europe and North America. Henry Ford's development of the assembly line for the mass production of automobiles made the United States a strong leader in the auto industry.

**The Airplane** The internal combustion engine also allowed humans to fly. In 1903, Orville and Wilbur Wright made the first powered flight.

### Technology of the Industrial Age

| INVENTOR OR DEVELOPER | NATION | INVENTION OR DEVELOPMENT | YEAR |
| --- | --- | --- | --- |
| Henry Bessemer | Great Britain | Process to turn iron ore into steel | 1856 |
| Alexander Graham Bell | United States | Telephone | 1876 |
| Thomas Edison | United States | Electric light bulb | 1879 |
| Gottlieb Daimler | Germany | Automobile | 1887 |
| Henry Ford | United States | Mass-produced automobile | 1903 |
| Orville & Wilbur Wright | United States | Airplane | 1903 |

## Population Explosion

In many ways, new technology made life healthier, safer, and easier. As a result, fewer children died, and the average life expectancy increased. In other words, people lived longer. Because of these changes, populations grew dramatically.

## Western Populations in the Late 1800s

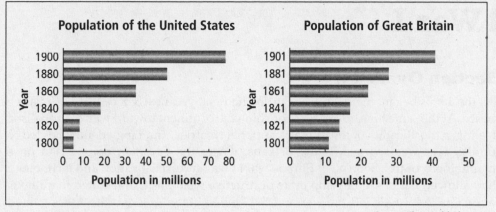

**Population of the United States**

Year
1900
1880
1860
1840
1820
1800

Population in millions
0 10 20 30 40 50 60 70 80

**Population of Great Britain**

Year
1901
1881
1861
1841
1821
1801

Population in millions
0 10 20 30 40 50

Source: *The World Almanac*

### Preparing for the Regents

Practice your graph skills by answering the following questions.

1. About how many people lived in Great Britain in 1801?

2. What was the approximate population of Great Britain in 1901?

3. What developments could explain the population growth shown in these two graphs?

## New Scientific Theories

While some scientists were developing knowledge and inventions that improved the quality of daily life, others were exploring the universe and the workings of the human mind.

### The Curies and Radioactivity

Just before the turn of the century, French scientist **Marie Curie** was experimenting with **radioactivity,** a powerful form of energy released by certain substances. Working with her husband, Pierre, Marie Curie discovered two new radioactive elements that the Curies called radium and polonium. The discoveries of these scientists had enormous effects on fields such as energy production, medicine, and military technology.

### Einstein and Relativity

In 1905, the German-born physicist **Albert Einstein** announced his theory of relativity. This theory revolutionized scientific thought. It proposed that space and time measurements are not absolute but are determined by many factors, some of which are not known. Einstein's work caused many people to question the common view of the universe as a machine that worked by easily understood laws.

### Freud and the Human Mind

During the same period, an Austrian physician named **Sigmund Freud** was questioning basic ideas about the human mind. He believed that a part of the mind, which he called the unconscious, drives much of human behavior. Freud felt that the tension between the drives of the unconscious mind and the demands of civilized society caused psychological and physical illness. Freud pioneered psychoanalysis, a new way of thinking about and treating mental illness.

## Summary

Scientific and technological advances brought many changes in the late 1800s and early 1900s. Improvements in medicine and sanitation led to a higher life expectancy, which caused an increase in population. People's lives were made easier by inventions such as electrical appliances, the telephone, and automobiles. In other areas of science, theories about the universe and the human mind shook ideas that had once been commonly accepted.

### Vocabulary Builder

element—(EL uh munt) *n.* a simple chemical substance such as carbon or oxygen that consists of atoms of only one kind

### Preparing for the Regents

The theories of both Einstein and Freud had an unsettling effect on many people of the time. The idea of a powerful unconscious mind or a universe without absolute laws disturbed many.

### Preparing for the Regents

• What benefits have resulted from the use of radioactive elements? What problems have resulted?

• Write a short paragraph about whether you think that science and technology bring more problems or more benefits into people's lives.

# World War I

## Section Overview

As the 1900s began, the people of Europe had enjoyed nearly a century of relative peace. At the same time, forces were pushing the continent toward war. Nationalistic feeling, a glorification of the military, imperial rivalries, and tangled alliances led to unrest. War was sparked in the Balkans, where the Ottoman empire had once maintained control. Soon all of Europe was at war. Industrialization and technology had allowed nations to develop more destructive weapons that resulted in millions of deaths. As Russia left the war and the United States entered, the Allies gained control and an armistice was signed. The costs of World War I were enormous.

## Key Themes and Concepts

As you review this section, take special note of the following key themes and concepts:

**Nationalism and Imperialism** What role did nationalism and imperialism play in causing World War I?

**Diversity** How did ethnic diversity in the Balkans contribute to starting the war?

**Science and Technology** What impact did innovations in science and technology have on World War I?

## Key People and Terms

**Key People and Terms**

What do three of the key people and terms have in common. Explain.

As you review this section, be sure you understand the significance of these key people and terms:

| | |
|---|---|
| militarism | total war |
| Bosnia | propaganda |
| Archduke Francis Ferdinand | neutral |
| Central Powers | armistice |
| Allied Powers | reparations |
| trench warfare | |

## Causes

Although the world seemed at peace in the early 1900s, powerful forces were pushing Europe toward war. These forces included nationalism, militarism, imperial rivalries, alliance systems, and the decline of the Ottoman empire.

## Nationalism

As you have learned, nationalism can bring people together. It can also, however, be a source of conflict. In Europe in the early 1900s, aggressive nationalism was a source of tension.

**Germany and France** Nationalism was strong in both Germany and France. Germany, now unified, was proud of its growing military and industrial strength. France, meanwhile, wanted to regain its position as a leading European power. It had lost the Franco-Prussian War in 1871. Besides having to pay money to Germany, France lost the provinces of Alsace and Lorraine. Many of the French people wanted revenge on Germany.

**Pan-Slavism** Russia had encouraged a form of nationalism in Eastern Europe called Pan-Slavism. The movement tried to draw together all Slavic peoples. Russia was the largest Slavic country, and it was ready to defend Serbia, a young Slavic nation in the Balkans. Throughout the Balkans, in fact, small Slavic populations looked to Russia for leadership in their desire for unity. The multinational empire of Austria-Hungary opposed Slavic national movements.

## Militarism

During the late 1800s, **militarism,** the glorification of military power, arose in many nations of Europe. This development led to fear and suspicion as nations became more willing to use military force to attain their national goals. There was an arms race, in which the great powers competed with each other to expand their armies and navies. One of the fiercest rivalries was between Great Britain and Germany.

## Imperialism and Economic Rivalry

Great Britain, France, Germany, and other nations competed for colonies and economic power. France and Germany competed especially for colonial gains in Africa. Great Britain and Germany competed industrially. Germany had industrialized rapidly, and the British felt threatened by this. Because of their mutual competition with Germany, Great Britain and France began to form close ties with each other.

## Alliance Systems

Increased tensions and suspicions led nations to form alliances. Nations agreed to defend each other in case of attack. By 1914, there were several alliances. The two most important were the Triple Alliance and the Triple Entente. The triple Alliance consisted of Germany, Austria-Hungary, and Italy. The Triple Entente consisted of Great Britain, France, and Russia.

## Decline of the Ottoman Empire

Other situations also set the stage for war. The Ottoman empire had become weak. British relations with the empire became strained after Great Britain signed an agreement with Russia. Germany, on the other hand, had taken an interest in establishing good relations with the Ottoman empire.

**The Armenian Massacres** Nationalistic feelings had caused periodic waves of violence against Armenians since the 1890s. New violence was a brutal result of the rivalry between Turkey, which ruled the Ottoman empire, and Russia. The Muslim Turks distrusted the Christian Armenians, believing that they supported Russia against the Ottoman empire. When Armenians protested oppressive Ottoman policies, the Turks unleashed a massacre on the Armenians. Additional massacres leading to the deaths of a million or more Armenians occurred over the next 25 years.

### Key Themes and Concepts

**Nationalism**
National rivalry between Germany and France contributed to tensions in Europe. Nationalist movements in the diverse Ottoman empire also created unrest, especially in the Balkan peninsula of southeastern Europe.

### Note Taking

*Reading Skill:*
**Identify Causes**
Complete a concept web with the causes of World War I. Add more circles if needed.

### Vocabulary Builder

rivalry—(RY vul ree) *n.* a situation in which two or more people, teams, or companies are competing for something, especially over a long period of time, and the feeling of competition between them

### Key Themes and Concepts

**Conflict**
European nations competed for territory in Africa and Asia. This competition led to added rivalries between European nations.

Vocabulary
Builder

powder keg—(POW dur keg)
n. a small container with
gunpowder or explosives

**The Balkan Powder Keg** The Ottoman empire's control over the Balkans had weakened over time. Serbia declared its independence in 1878, hoping to build a Slavic state in alliance with Russia. Serbia wanted control of **Bosnia** and Herzegovina, two provinces that would give landlocked Serbia an outlet to the Adriatic Sea. These provinces, however, were Ottoman provinces administered by Austria-Hungary. Austria opposed Serbian ambitions, fearing that the same kind of nationalism would spread to its own multinational empire. Also, Austria-Hungary feared Russian expansion.

Tensions grew, and in 1912, Serbia and its allies attacked the Ottoman empire. The great European powers were all interested in gaining lands from the crumbling empire. By 1914, the Balkans were known as the "powder keg of Europe." Any small spark was likely to lead to an explosion.

Preparing for
the Regents

Summarize how each of
the following **main** causes
contributed to World War I.

Militarism:

Alliance systems:

Imperialism:

Nationalism:

# The War Begins

### The Balkan Crisis

Not surprisingly, World War I began in the Balkans. Although many Serbs lived in Bosnia, it was still ruled by Austria-Hungary. Serb nationalists felt that Bosnia belonged to Serbia.

**Archduke Francis Ferdinand** was the heir to the Austrian throne. On June 28, 1914, the duke and his wife were traveling through Sarajevo, the capital of Bosnia. Gavrilo Princip, a member of a radical Slavic nationalist group that opposed Austrian rule, shot and killed the archduke and his wife.

Key Themes
and Concepts

Diversity
Serb nationalism led to the
assassination of Archduke
Francis Ferdinand. Slavic
groups in the Ottoman
empire hoped to unite
and throw off the rule of
Austria-Hungary.

### A Chain Reaction

After the assassination, the major nations of Europe responded. Each hostile action led to another hostile action.

**The Outbreak of War**

| |
|---|
| 1. Austria-Hungary blamed Serbia for the murders of the archduke and his wife and made harsh demands in Serbia. |
| 2. Serbia refused to comply with any of the demands. |
| 3. Austria-Hungary declared war on Serbia on July 28. |
| 4. Russia, a Slavic nation and a friend of Serbia, mobilized its forces in preparation for war. |
| 5. Germany, an ally of Austria-Hungary, declared war on Russia. |
| 6. Germany declared war on France, an ally of Russia. |
| 7. Germany invaded Belgium on August 3, 1914, so that German forces could enter France more easily. |
| 8. Great Britain declared war on Germany. |

Recognize Effects

How did Austria-Hungary
react to the murder of the
archduke?

## World War I: Who Was to Blame?

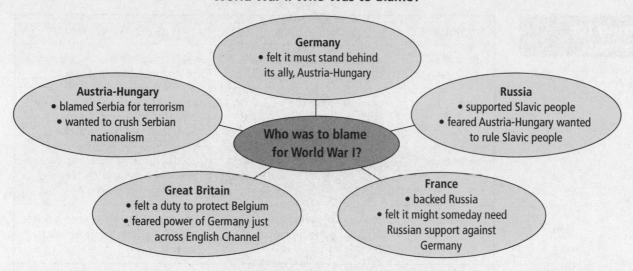

**Germany**
- felt it must stand behind its ally, Austria-Hungary

**Austria-Hungary**
- blamed Serbia for terrorism
- wanted to crush Serbian nationalism

**Russia**
- supported Slavic people
- feared Austria-Hungary wanted to rule Slavic people

**Who was to blame for World War I?**

**Great Britain**
- felt a duty to protect Belgium
- feared power of Germany just across English Channel

**France**
- backed Russia
- felt it might someday need Russian support against Germany

## Central Powers and Allied Powers

The two opposing sides in World War I were the Central Powers and the Allied Powers. The **Central Powers** were Germany, Austria-Hungary, and the Ottoman empire (later joined by Bulgaria). On the other side were the **Allied Powers:** Great Britain, France, and Russia. Italy at first remained neutral, but it eventually joined the Allies. Other nations, including the United States, also joined the Allies later.

There were three major fronts in Europe where fighting occurred. The Western Front extended across Belgium and northeastern France to the border of Switzerland. The Eastern Front ran from the Baltic Sea to the Black Sea. The Southern Front ran between Italy and Austria-Hungary. Fighting also took place in Africa and the Middle East.

## An Industrialized War

World War I was a war between groups of major industrial powers. New technology made this war an enormously destructive one. For example, Swedish chemist Alfred Nobel had invented dynamite in 1867. Used in mining and construction, it also became important in weaponry. Many of the other recent inventions of the time—the internal combustion engine, the airplane, and communications devices—were also put to military use.

### Trench Warfare

Heavy fighting took place along the Western Front, a 600-mile stretch from the English Channel to Switzerland. The Germans hoped to win an early victory there, but French and British troops stopped them. For four years, neither side could make any significant gains.

**Trench warfare** began, so called because the troops dug trenches along the front. Very little ground was gained by either side in this way, and many soldiers were killed.

### New Air and Sea Weapons

World War I was the first war to make full use of modern technology and machinery. Technology changed methods of warfare greatly.

**Preparing for the Regents**

- Study the graphic organizer and review the chain reaction of events that occurred in 1914. Which nation or group do you think was to blame for World War I? Explain.

**Preparing for the Regents**

List the members of the Central Powers and the Allied Powers.

**Central Powers:**

**Allied Powers:**

**Summarize**

What made World War I extremely destructive? Explain.

## Technology Changes Warfare

| Invention | Description | Use in World War I |
|---|---|---|
| Automatic machine gun | mounted gun that fires a rapid, continuous stream of bullets | made it possible for a few gunners to mow down waves of soldiers |
| Tank | armored vehicle that travels on a track and can cross many kinds of land | protected advancing troops as they broke through enemy defenses; Early tanks were slow and clumsy |
| Submarine | underwater ship that can launch torpedoes, or guided underwater bombs | used by Germany to destroy Allied ships; submarine attacks helped bring United States into war |
| Airplane | one- or two-seat propeller plane equipped with machine gun or bombs | at first, mainly used for observation; later, flying "aces" engaged in air combat |
| Poison gas; gas mask | gases that cause choking, blinding, or severe skin blisters; gas masks can protect soldiers from poison gas | lobbed into enemy trenches, killing or disabling troops; gas masks lessened the importance of poison gas |

## Civilian Life and Total War

The war was fought at home as well as on the battlefield. A war fought in this way is called a **total war.** In a total war, all of a nation's resources go into the war effort.

• Governments drafted men to fight in the war.

• Governments raised taxes and borrowed money to pay for the war.

• Governments rationed, or limited the supply of, goods at home so that the military could be provided for.

• Governments used the press to print **propaganda,** the spreading of ideas to promote a cause or to damage an opposing cause.

• Women at home took jobs that the soldiers had left behind. Some women joined the armed services. Other women went to the fronts as nurses.

## Major Turning Points of the War

Several events that took place during World War I are seen as major turning points. They include the withdrawal of Russia from the war and the entry of the United States into the war.

### Entry of the United States

**Key Themes and Concepts**

**Interdependence**
Why did the United States enter World War I? How was the entry of the United States a turning point?

Although the United States had allowed American ships to carry supplies to the Allies, the country had tried to remain **neutral** (not supporting either side) in the war. In 1917, however, Germany used unrestricted submarine warfare, meaning that it attacked any ships on the Atlantic, even if they were carrying American passengers. This policy brought the United States into the war in April 1917. The entry of the Americans helped the Allies win the war.

### Russian Withdrawal

In Russia, low morale contributed to a revolution in 1917. Early in 1918, Russia's new leader signed a treaty with Germany that took Russia out of the war.

## Costs of the War

On November 11, 1918, an **armistice,** or an agreement to end the fighting, was declared. The costs of World War I were enormous. It would take many years for people and nations to recover.

### Human Casualties

The costs of the war in terms of human lives were staggering.

- More than 8.5 million people had died.
- More than 17 million had been wounded.
- Famine threatened many regions.
- Disease was widespread in many regions.

### Economic Losses

All over the world, there were also economic and political losses.

- Factories, farms, and homes had been destroyed.
- Nations had huge war debts to repay.
- The Allies, bitter at the destruction, insisted that the Central Powers make **reparations,** payments for war damage they had caused.

**Percentage of Money Spent by Allies**

Key

☐ British Empire  ▨ Russia

▨ United States  ▥ France

## Summary

Nationalism, militarism, imperialism, and political rivalries led to World War I. In the Balkans, what began as a local incident blossomed into a global war. Industrialization and new technology made the weapons of World War I much more destructive than any that had been used before. The war caused great human and economic losses.

**Note Taking**

*Reading Skill:*
**Identify Causes and Effects**
Make a flowchart to summarize the causes and effects of World War I.

*Money Spent by Allies*
World War I cost an enormous amount of money. The Allies spent about 160 billion dollars.

**Preparing for the Regents**

- Based on the pie graph, which nation or groups of nations among the Allies spent the most money on World War I?

**Preparing for the Regents**

- In what way was World War I a turning point in global history?

# Revolution in Russia: Causes and Impacts

## Section Overview

Factors such as dissatisfaction with czarist rule, peasant unrest, and economic difficulties created long-term discontent in Russia. After a revolution in 1905, Czar Nicholas II agreed to reforms, but they failed to solve underlying problems. Hardships caused by World War I sparked a revolution that ended Nicholas's reign. Promises of peace, land, and bread allowed Vladimir Lenin and his Bolsheviks, later called Communists, to gain control of the country. After Lenin's death, Joseph Stalin created a communist dictatorship that controlled every aspect of people's lives. He brought the economy completely under government control. Stalin industrialized the country, focusing on heavy industry. Stalin also brought agriculture under state control, causing mass starvation in the process.

## Key Themes and Concepts

As you review this section, take special note of the following key themes and concepts:

**Change** Why did the Russian people demand change in 1917?

**Power** How did the Bolsheviks take control of the Russian government from the czar?

**Human Rights** What was life like in Stalin's totalitarian state?

**Economic System** How did Stalin's command economy affect the Soviet Union's industry and agriculture?

## Key People and Terms

### Key People and Terms

Place each of the key people and terms into these two categories: government or economy.

As you review this section, be sure you understand the significance of these key people and terms:

| | | |
|---|---|---|
| soviets | Joseph Stalin | five-year plans |
| Vladimir Lenin | Great Purge | collectives |
| Bolsheviks | totalitarian state | |
| New Economic Policy | command economy | |

## Long-Term Causes of Revolution

A variety of factors had been leading up to revolution in Russia for a long time. Through the 1800s and early 1900s, discontent grew as Russian czars resisted needed reforms.

### Czarist Rule

In the late 1800s, Alexander III and his son, Nicholas II, sought to industrialize the country and build Russia's economic strength. Although these czars wanted to import western industrialization, they hoped to block the ideals of the French Revolution. Still, Russian liberals called for a constitution and reforms that would eliminate corruption in government. Both Alexander and Nicholas used harsh tactics, such as the use of secret police, to suppress reform.

## Peasant Unrest

A rigid system of social classes still existed in Russia at the beginning of World War I. Landowning nobles, priests, and an autocratic czar dominated society. A small middle class was prevented from gaining power.

Peasants faced many difficulties. Most were too poor to buy the land they worked. Even those who owned land often did not have enough to feed their families. Even though industrialization had proceeded slowly, it had angered some peasants. Some opposed it because they feared the changes it brought and preferred the old ways.

## Problems of Urban Workers

Some peasants had moved to cities and found jobs in new industries. They worked long hours, and their pay was low. Most lived in slums that were nests of poverty and disease. It was among these workers that socialists spread ideas about revolution and reform.

## Diversity and Nationalism

Russia ruled a vast and diverse empire. It included many ethnic minorities. The czars maintained strict control over these groups. Under the policy of Russification, czars attempted to make all people in their empire think, act, and believe as Russians. However, ethnic minorities did not want their native cultures destroyed. Pockets of nationalism remained.

# Revolution of 1905

Russia's defeat in the Russo-Japanese War of 1904 triggered a crisis in Russia. On Sunday, January 22, 1905, peaceful marchers carrying a petition for reform were shot down by the czar's troops. "Bloody Sunday," as it was called, destroyed the people's faith and trust in the czar, and strikes and revolts exploded across the country.

In the face of this chaos, Nicholas made some changes. He agreed to reforms and promised to grant more rights, such as freedom of speech. He agreed to set up an elected national legislature, the Duma. However, the Duma had limited powers and did little to relieve peasant and worker discontent.

*The Russian Revolution of 1905*
*The "Bloody Sunday" killings were a turning point for the Russian people. It destroyed their faith and trust in the czar.*

### The Russian Revolution of 1905

**CAUSES**
- low spirits after defeat in 1904 war with Japan
- poverty and bad working conditions
- corrupt government
- persecution of minority groups
- "Bloody Sunday" killings

**Russian Revolution of 1905**

**RESULTS**
- The "October Manifesto"– Czar Nicholas II announces reforms and new freedoms.
- Nicholas II sets up the Duma, which must approve all laws.
- Nicholas II dissolves the first Duma when its leaders criticize the government.
- Pogroms continue.
- New voting laws limit powers of later Dumas.

## Key Themes and Concepts

**Economic Systems**
Russia had not industrialized fully enough to enjoy the benefits that industrialization can bring. Partial industrialization had not brought economic prosperity or a better standard of living to most people. The Russian middle class remained small and relatively powerless.

## Preparing for the Regents

Within each of the categories listed below, describe one specific condition that contributed to revolutionary feelings in Russia.

Czarist rule:

Peasant unrest:

Problems of urban workers:

Diversity and nationalism:

## Vocabulary Builder

trigger—(TRIG ur) *v.* to make something happen very quickly, especially a series of events

## Preparing for the Regents

- The 1904 war referred to in this chart is the Russo-Japanese War. How did the Russo-Japanese War contribute to revolution in Russia?

## Note Taking

*Reading Skill:*
**Recognize Sequence** Make a timeline. As you read Section 3, record the sequence of important events in Russia's history.

Russia loses Russo-Japanese War

1905

# World War I and the End of Czarist Rule

## A Nation in Chaos

As you have learned, Russia was one of the Allied Powers in World War I. With little industry, however, Russia was not ready to fight a modern war. Russian soldiers lacked adequate weapons and supplies, and Russia suffered a series of battlefield defeats. Food was scarce. Many soldiers lost confidence in Russia's military leadership and deserted.

## The March Revolution

In March 1917, military defeats and shortages of food, fuel, and housing in Russia sparked a revolt. In the capital city, St. Petersburg, rioters in the streets demanded bread. The czar's soldiers sympathized with the demonstrators and refused to fire on them. With no control over his troops and with the country nearing anarchy, Czar Nicholas II abdicated, or gave up his rule, in March 1917.

## Failure of the Provisional Government

After the removal of the czar, Duma officials set up a provisional, or temporary, government. Middle-class liberals in the government planned to write a constitution and promised democratic reforms. However, the provisional government continued the war against Germany, an unpopular decision that drained away men and resources. The new government implemented only moderate reforms that did little to end unrest among peasants and workers.

# The Bolshevik Revolution

The provisional government's slowness to bring about meaningful change led revolutionary socialists to plot further actions. They set up **soviets,** or councils of workers and soldiers, in Russian cities. At first, these soviets worked within the system set up by the government. Soon, however, they were taken over by a radical Socialist Party.

## Lenin Gains Support

Following the March Revolution, an exiled Russian revolutionary named **Vladimir Lenin** returned home. Lenin and Leon Trotsky headed a revolutionary Socialist Party, the **Bolsheviks.** Lenin and Trotsky followed the ideas of Karl Marx, but they adapted them to the Russian situation. For example, Marx had said that the urban workers would rise on their own to overthrow the capitalist system. Russia, however, did not have a large urban working class. Lenin therefore suggested that an elite group of reformers—the Bolsheviks—would guide the revolution in Russia.

Lenin gained the support of many people by making promises of "Peace, Land, and Bread." The Bolsheviks promised an end to Russia's involvement in the war. They promised land reform and an end to food shortages.

## Lenin Takes Over

The provisional government had lost the support of the people. In November 1917, the Bolsheviks led soldiers, sailors, and factory workers in an uprising that overthrew the government. The Bolsheviks, now called Communists, distributed land to the peasants and gave workers control of the factories and mines. The Communists, however, still faced a struggle to maintain control over Russia.

# Lenin Rules Russia

## Withdrawal From World War I

Lenin moved quickly to end Russian involvement in World War I. In March 1918, Russia signed the Treaty of Brest-Litovsk. The agreement was costly for Russia,

## Key Themes and Concepts

**Power**
Lenin and the Bolsheviks gained power by promising "Peace, Land, and Bread." The people were tired of Russia's involvement in the world war. Peasants wanted land reform. Everyone wanted shortages of food and other goods to end.

## Preparing for the Regents

The Communist revolution occurred in Russia, not in a fully industrialized nation as Marx had predicted. In industrialized countries, worker unrest had been eased by a higher standard of living. Also, representative governments in these countries allowed for some reforms. In Russia, however, rural poverty, limited industrialization, and autocratic rule led to revolution.

giving Germany a large amount of Russian territory. Lenin, however, believed that he needed to make peace with Germany at any price so that he could deal with his enemies at home.

## Russia's Civil War

From 1918 to 1921, Lenin's Red Army battled against forces loyal to the czar, called the Whites. Nationalist groups in the Russian empire also rose up against the Red Army at this time, winning independence for Estonia, Latvia, Lithuania, and Poland.

Both sides used brutal tactics during the war. To eliminate a potential rallying symbol for the Whites, Communists executed Czar Nicholas II and his entire family.

Great Britain, France, and the United States sent troops to help the Whites. This foreign intervention, however, stirred Russian nationalism. An inspired Red Army, under Trotsky's leadership, defeated its enemies by 1921.

**Тов. Ленин ОЧИЩАЕТ землю от нечисти.**

**Vladimir Lenin**
*Lenin (1870–1924) believed that only revolution could bring needed changes to Russia.*

**Preparing for the Regents**

• Lenin is the figure with the broom at the top of this poster. What is the point of the poster? Whom do the other figures represent?

## One-Party Government

Lenin's government had a constitution and an elected legislature. However, the Communist Party, not the people themselves, had the real power. The Communist Party was the only legal party, and only its members could run for office. The Party enforced its will through the military and a secret police force.

## New Economic Policy

During Russia's civil war, Bolshevik leaders had taken over banks, mines, factories, and railroads. This takeover had resulted in economic disaster. In 1921, Lenin adopted the **New Economic Policy.** Under this plan, also called the NEP, the government still controlled banks, large industry, and foreign trade. Some privately owned businesses were allowed, however. These helped the economy to recover.

## The Soviet Union

By 1922, Lenin and the Communists had gained control over much of the old Russian empire. The Communist government then created the Union of Soviet Socialist Republics, also called the Soviet Union. It was made up of diverse European and Asian peoples. Russia, the largest republic, controlled the other states in the Soviet Union.

# Stalin and Communist Dictatorship

Lenin died in 1924, ending the reign of Russia's first Communist leader. A new Soviet leader, **Joseph Stalin,** emerged. Stalin ruled through terror and brutality. In the 1930s, for example, out of fear that other Communist Party members were plotting against him, Stalin launched the **Great Purge.** During the Great Purge,

**Key Themes and Concepts**

**Political Systems**
How is communist government different from democratic government?

**Economic Systems**
The private ownership allowed by the New Economic Policy helped the Soviet economy to recover. Even in the early years, socialist economic policies met with limited success in the Soviet Union.

**Vocabulary Builder**

<u>diverse</u>—(duh VURS) *adj.* very different from each other

## Preparing for the Regents

Describe five specific ways in which Stalin failed to respect the human rights of Russians and minority national groups in the Soviet Union.

1.

2.

3.

4.

5.

## Summarize

Write a sentence explaining the term "Russification."

Stalin accused thousands of people of crimes against the government. Many of the accused were executed; others were exiled or sent to prison camps. For the next 20 years, he pursued ruthless policies that created a totalitarian state in the Soviet Union.

## Totalitarian Rule

Stalin turned the Soviet Union into a **totalitarian state.** In this form of government, a one-party dictatorship attempts to regulate every aspect of the lives of its citizens.

## Russification

Early in his rule, Stalin promoted individual local cultures. By the end of the 1920s, however, he had changed this policy. Stalin became a strong Russian nationalist. He began to create a Russian ruling elite throughout the Soviet Union. Like the czars before him, Stalin pursued a policy of Russification.

- He promoted Russian history, language, and culture, sometimes forbidding the cultural practices of native peoples.
- He appointed Russians to key posts in the government and secret police.
- He redrew the boundaries of many republics to ensure that non-Russians would not gain a majority.

## Life in a Totalitarian State

| Economics | Politics | Arts | Religion | Society |
|-----------|----------|------|----------|---------|
| • Growth of industry<br>• Growth of military<br>• Low standard of living<br>• Shortage of foods and consumer goods | • One-party dictatorship<br>• Total government control of citizens<br>• Total government control of industry and agriculture<br>• Use of propaganda to win government support | • Censorship of books, music, art<br>• Purpose of all art to praise communism<br>• Observation of artists, writers, and musicians by secret police | • Government war on religion<br>• Takeover of houses of worship<br>• Secret police control religious worship<br>• Communist ideals replace religious ideals | • Fear of secret police<br>• An upper class of Communist Party members<br>• Free education and health care<br>• Public transportation and recreation<br>• Jobs for women |

## Key Themes and Concepts

**Economic Systems**
In a command economy, the state controls all factories and businesses and makes all economic decisions. In a capitalist economy, businesses are privately owned and operated for a profit. The free market controls economic decisions.

**Power**
When peasants resisted Stalin's plan of collectivization, he ruthlessly eliminated them through starvation.

## A Command Economy

Stalin established a **command economy,** in which government officials made all basic economic decisions. Under Stalin, the government controlled all factories, businesses, and farms.

**Industrialization** One of Stalin's chief goals was to make the Soviet Union strong by turning it into a modern industrial power. In 1928, Stalin launched the first of a series of **five-year plans** to build industry and increase farm output. Emphasis was placed on heavy industry, while consumer goods were neglected. In the 1930s, Soviet production in oil, coal, steel, mining, and military goods increased. Across the nation, factories, hydroelectric power stations, and railroads were built.

Despite this progress, however, most Russians remained poor and endured a low standard of living. Soviet central planning created shortages in consumer goods. Also, to meet high production quotas, many factories mass-produced goods of low quality.

**Collectivization** Stalin forced peasants to give up their small farms and live on state-owned farms or on **collectives**, which were large farms owned and operated by peasants as a group. The collective owned all farm animals and equipment. The government controlled prices and farm supplies and set production quotas. Stalin's plan was for the collectives to grow enough grain for the workers in the cities and to produce surplus grain to sell abroad.

Many peasants resisted collectivization. They killed farm animals, destroyed tools, and burned crops. Stalin responded with a ruthless policy aimed at crushing all who opposed him. The government seized the land of those who resisted and sent the farmers to prison labor camps. There, many died from overwork or were executed.

**Forced Famine** The results of Stalin's policies were devastating. Some peasants continued to resist by growing just enough grain to feed themselves. The government then seized all the grain from some of those communities. Mass starvation resulted. In the Ukraine, where opposition to collectivization was especially strong, more than five million people died from starvation. Millions more died in other parts of the Soviet Union.

**Vocabulary Builder**

devastating—(DEV uh stayt ing) *adj.* badly damaging or destroying something

### First Leaders of the Soviet Union

**Lenin (Soviet leader 1917–1924)**
- *Chief goal: to create a classless society with production in the hands of the people*
- Allowed some private business; let some peasants hold land
- Standard of living rose for many workers and peasants

(shared)
- Spent time in Siberian exile before 1917 revolution
- Became Communist Party leader
- Used secret police to enforce Communist will
- Wanted to bring about a worldwide Communist revolution

**Stalin (Soviet leader 1924–1953)**
- *Chief goal: to make the Soviet Union into a modern industrial power with all production under government control*
- Created a command economy
- Brought all agriculture under government control; forced peasants to live on group farms
- Standard of living fell for most workers and peasants

**Preparing for the Regents**

Practice your chart-reading skills by answering the following questions.

1. What were two goals or practices that Lenin and Stalin held in common?

2. How did Stalin's chief goal differ from Lenin's?

## Summary

In the late 1800s and early 1900s, autocratic rule and poor economic conditions caused many Russians to demand political and social reforms. In 1917, this discontent led to a revolution that ended czarist rule in Russia. Bolshevik leader Vladimir Lenin gained power by promising better economic conditions and an end to Russian involvement in World War I. He then set up a Communist government. After Lenin's death, Joseph Stalin took over and established a totalitarian state, in which every aspect of life was controlled. Stalin's five-year plans boosted industry but did little to improve the life of the average worker. His collectivization of agriculture angered peasants, whose resistance resulted in mass starvation.

**Preparing for the Regents**

- To what extent was the Russian Revolution a turning point in global history?

# Between the Wars

## The Big Idea

After World War I:

- the Treaty of Versailles severely punished Germany.

- new nations formed and old empires collapsed.

- nationalist movements struggled to throw off foreign domination.

- women gained the right to vote in many countries.

- the global economy experienced a severe downturn.

- fascist powers took control in Italy and Germany.

- militarists took power in Japan.

## Section Overview

After World War I, global problems remained. The Treaty of Versailles punished Germany. The League of Nations had little power. Old empires had collapsed, and new nations had come into being. Nationalism continued to cause conflict. World War I had disillusioned many, altered society, and prompted new forms of expression. In Europe and the United States, women struggled to gain the right to vote. Then, in 1929, the global economy crashed, leading to a worldwide depression. During this time, fascism, a new kind of dictatorship, rose in Italy and Germany. In Japan, aggressive military leaders gained power.

## Key Themes and Concepts

As you review this section, take special note of the following key themes and concepts:

**Interdependence** How did the major powers try to resolve troublesome issues after World War I?

**Nationalism** What factors led to the nationalist movements of the 1920s and 1930s?

**Human Rights** What rights did women gain after World War I?

**Economic Systems** What were the causes and effects of the world economic crisis of the 1930s?

**Political Systems** What are the major characteristics of fascism?

## Key People and Terms

### Key People and Terms

Make a list of the people in the Key People and Terms. Also write each person's country.

As you review this section, be sure you understand the significance of these key people and terms:

| | | |
|---|---|---|
| Treaty of Versailles | Pan-Arabism | fascism |
| League of Nations | Mohandas Gandhi | Benito Mussolini |
| Kemal Atatürk | civil disobedience | Adolf Hitler |
| Reza Khan | Kuomintang | Third Reich |
| mandates | Great Depression | |

### Preparing for the Regents

The Treaty of Versailles did not resolve the issues that had led to World War I. Nationalism continued to be a cause of conflict. German discontent with the Treaty of Versailles would help lead to World War II.

## Treaty of Versailles

World War I had a lasting impact on international politics. In January 1919, the victorious Allies gathered at the palace of Versailles, outside Paris, to work out the terms of peace. United States President Woodrow Wilson and Prime Minister David Lloyd George of Great Britain joined French leader Georges Clemenceau. They were known as the "Big Three" of the meeting that would be called the Paris Peace Conference. These men had differing goals. Wilson stressed self-determination, by which people would choose their own government.

He also hoped to create a world organization that would guarantee peace in the future. Great Britain and France wanted to punish Germany and be sure that it would never again become a threat.

## Harsh Provisions for Germany

In the end, Great Britain's and France's ideas guided the **Treaty of Versailles.**

**Territorial Losses** Land was taken from Germany. Some of it was used to help create the new country of Poland. Alsace and Lorraine were returned to France. Germany also lost many of its overseas colonies.

**Military Restrictions** Germany's army and navy were limited. Germany had to remove its troops from the Rhineland, an industrial area along the French border.

**War Guilt** Germany had to accept full responsibility for the war and pay huge reparations, or large sums of money to help undo war damage. Accepting the blame and paying the reparations caused bitterness in Germany.

## The League of Nations

The Treaty of Versailles also formed the **League of Nations,** a group of more than 40 countries that hoped to settle problems through negotiation, not war. The countries that joined the League of Nations promised to take cooperative economic and military action against any aggressor state. Although the league had been Woodrow Wilson's concept, the United States never joined. Many Americans were afraid that participation in it would drag the United States into future European wars. In refusing to join, the United States weakened the League of Nations.

**Key Themes and Concepts**

Conflict
How did the League of Nations plan to deal with international conflict in the future?

**Preparing for the Regents**

Practice your map skills by listing five nations that were created as a result of World War I.

1.

2.

3.

4.

5.

*Europe After World War I*
*The peace treaties that ended World War I changed the map of Europe.*

## Europe After World War I

## Vocabulary
### Builder

carve out—(kahrv owt) v.
to divide land into smaller
parts and share it between
people

# Collapse of Empires

World War I caused the collapse of the Austro-Hungarian and Ottoman empires. New nations were carved out of their former territories.

## Breakup of Austria-Hungary

As a result of the war, the government in Austria-Hungary had collapsed. Several new nations were created out of the former empire. Austria and Hungary became independent nations. Czechoslovakia and Yugoslavia, two multinational states, were formed. Italy and Romania each gained land.

## Breakup of the Ottoman Empire

The Ottoman empire, one of the defeated Central Powers, collapsed in 1918. Most of the Arab lands of the Ottoman empire were placed under the control of Great Britain and France. In theory these countries were being prepared for self-determination. In practice, however, the Allies added to their own overseas empires by creating a system of territories administered by western powers. The remainder of the empire became the country of Turkey.

# Unfulfilled National Goals

Many nations were dissatisfied with the results of World War I. Various groups felt that their goals had not been achieved.

- Germany was horrified by the terms of the Treaty of Versailles.
- Italy had hoped to gain more land than it received. It had made a secret treaty with the Allies that was not fulfilled.
- Japan was angry because the Allies did not recognize its claims in China.
- China was angry that Japan had been given control over former German possessions in China.
- Russia was angry over the reestablishment of Poland and the creation of independent Estonia, Latvia, and Lithuania on lands that had been part of the Russian empire.

Nations and groups, however, waited and watched, hoping for a chance to change events in their favor.

# National Movements

The spirit of nationalism continued after World War I. Nations in the Middle East, Africa, and Asia struggled for self-determination. In many cases, nationalists were influenced by western ideas. Even so, they were determined to throw off western rule.

## Turkish Nationalism

**Kemal Atatürk** Mustafa Kemal was a general and a war hero in Turkey. After World War I, he led a Turkish nationalist movement. He overthrew the sultan, defeated western occupation forces, and declared Turkey a republic. Mustafa Kemal later called himself **Kemal Atatürk**. The name *Atatürk* meant "father of the Turks."

**Westernization and Modernization** Atatürk wanted to modernize and westernize Turkey. He believed that Turkey had to change to survive. In accomplishing his goals, he introduced great changes.

- Islamic law was replaced with a new law code, based on European models.
- The Muslim calendar was replaced with the western (Christian) one.

## Key Themes
### and Concepts

**Nationalism**
Mustafa Kemal wanted to unite Turks and throw off European domination. At the same time, he felt that Turkey must modernize and westernize to survive in the twentieth century.

## Preparing for the Regents

Some Turkish Muslims rejected westernization, believing that it was a betrayal of Islam. This conflict continues today. The government of Turkey remains secular, but some Islamic groups work strongly for a return to traditional ways.

- People were required to wear western dress.
- State schools were set up. Arabic script was replaced with the western (Latin) alphabet.
- Women no longer had to wear veils and were allowed to vote. They could work outside their homes.
- Turkey was industrialized. Atatürk built roads, railroads, and factories.

## Iranian Nationalism

Nationalists in Iran followed Turkey's lead. In Iran, the British and the Russians had carved out spheres of influence. In 1925, **Reza Khan,** an army officer, overthrew the ruler of Iran, called the shah. He set up his own dynasty and proclaimed himself shah. Reza Khan quickly tried to modernize and westernize Iran and make it fully independent. Factories, roads, and railroads were built. The army was strengthened. The western alphabet and western dress were adopted, and secular schools were set up. Islamic law was replaced by secular law, and women were encouraged to take part in public life. Reza Khan had the support of wealthy urban Iranians but not of Muslim religious leaders.

## Arab Nationalism

During World War I, many Arabs had helped the Allies. In return they had been promised independence. After the war, however, Great Britain and France divided up the Ottoman lands between themselves. They set up **mandates,** territories administered by European powers. France had mandates in Syria and Lebanon. Great Britain had mandates in Palestine and Iraq.

In the 1920s and 1930s, Arab nationalists sought to be free of foreign control. Arab nationalism gave rise to **Pan-Arabism.** This movement sought a unity of all Arab peoples based on their shared heritage.

## Zionism

Zionism, as you have learned, had arisen during the 1890s in Europe and the Middle East. Jewish people wanted to establish a Jewish state in Palestine. The situation was complex, however, since Arab peoples were already living there. The Allies had made conflicting promises during World War I. They had promised Arabs land that included Palestine. They had also pledged to set up a Jewish nation in the same region. As more Jews moved to Palestine to escape persecution in the 1930s, tensions grew.

## Indian Nationalism

Nearly 1 million Indians had served the Allied cause in Europe during World War I, and many had died. At home, however, Indians had few rights. During World War I, Great Britain had promised India greater self-government. After the war was over, Great Britain failed to fulfill these promises.

**The Amritsar Massacre** A turning point came in 1919. There were riots and attacks on British citizens in the city of Amritsar. In response, public meetings were banned. When a large group of Indians assembled on April 13, British troops fired on them without warning, killing about 400 people and wounding about 1,200 more. The incident convinced many Indians that British rule must be ended.

**Gandhi** In the 1920s and 1930s, a leader named **Mohandas Gandhi** headed the Indian nationalist movement. He taught that nonviolent resistance and **civil disobedience** (the refusal to obey unjust laws), rather than bloodshed, were the way to win rights. He used tactics such as boycotting, or refusing to buy, British goods and peaceful demonstrations such as the "Salt March." Gandhi embraced

### Vocabulary Builder

veil—(vayl) *n.* a thin piece of material that women wear to cover their faces at formal occasions or for religious reasons

### Key Themes and Concepts

**Change**
In Iran—unlike Turkey—modernization eventually led, in 1979, to an Islamic revolution in which the government turned from secularism.

### Preparing for the Regents

- What are the similarities among Pan-Slavism, Pan-Arabism, and Zionism? What are some differences?

**Mohandas Gandhi**
*Gandhi's philosophy reflected Western and Indian influences. His ideas inspired Indians of all religious and ethnic backgrounds.*

**Preparing for the Regents**

Write a brief statement about the historical importance of each of these figures.

Kemal Atatürk:

Reza Khan:

Mohandas Gandhi:

western ideas of democracy and nationalism. He rejected the caste system and urged equal rights for all, including women. India, however, did not achieve independence until 1947, one year before Gandhi's death.

### Chinese Nationalism

Chinese civilization was in great disorder during and after World War I. After Sun Yixian (also known as Sun Yat-sen), founder of the Chinese Republic, stepped down, rival warlords fought for power. The economy collapsed, and peasants faced great economic hardship. During this time, foreign powers—especially Japan—increased their influence in China.

**Rival Groups in China** After the death of Sun Yixian in 1925, an army officer named Jiang Jieshi (also known as Chiang Kai-shek) took over the **Kuomintang** Jiang's government, supported by middle class businessmen, did little to help the peasants. As a result the peasants were attracted to Mao Zedong and his Communist Party.

**Civil War** At first, the Nationalists and the Communists had worked together to unite China. Over time, however, Jiang Jieshi began to see the Communists as a threat. A civil war began between the Nationalists and the Communists that would last for 22 years.

## Literature and Arts: The Lost Generation

World War I had produced disquiet in social as well as political arenas. The war had shaken many people's long-held beliefs. Scientific discoveries—such as those of the Curies, Einstein, and Freud—had brought new understanding, but they had also cast doubt on the ideas of the past.

**Preparing for the Regents**

• How did World War I affect the literature and arts of the 1920s and 1930s?

The war itself had left scars on those who survived it. Writers, artists, and musicians throughout the 1920s and 1930s expressed a loss of hope, rejecting former rules and moral values. They became known as the "Lost Generation."

Writers such as Ernest Hemingway expressed a loss of faith in western civilization. Poet T. S. Eliot portrayed the modern world as spiritually empty and barren. Some painters stopped trying to reproduce the real world. In an attempt to express their feelings of loss of meaning, they experimented with color and distorted shapes.

## Women's Suffrage Movement

In the mid-1800s in western democracies, women had begun to demand greater rights. These included property rights and suffrage, or the right to vote. The first country in which women won the right to vote was New Zealand in 1893. In Great Britain, Parliament finally granted women over 30 the right to vote in 1918. By 1928, Great Britain had granted suffrage to all women over the age of 21. In the United States, President Wilson proposed the Nineteenth Amendment in 1918. This amendment gave American citizens over the age of 21 the right to vote, regardless of gender. Congress adopted the amendment two years later in 1920. Women also gained the right to vote in Canada, Finland, Germany, and Sweden in the early 1900s.

**Key Themes and Concepts**

**Justice and Human Rights** World War I brought great progress for women. Women kept the economy going at home by taking on jobs left vacant by men who became soldiers. Some joined the armed forces. This independence gave them a new sense of pride and confidence. After the war, women in various western democracies gained the right to vote.

# Worldwide Depression

After World War I, economic problems emerged in Europe. Soldiers, returning from the war, needed jobs. Nations had war debts to pay and cities to rebuild. In the decade following the war, the economies of many European countries began a shaky recovery. Middle-class families enjoyed a rising standard of living.

The United States, on the other hand, experienced an economic boom after the war. It became the world's leading economic power and made investments in Europe to promote recovery. These came to an end, however, with the crash of the American stock market in 1929. This event triggered the **Great Depression** of the 1930s, a time of global economic collapse.

## Causes of the Depression

Weaknesses in the economies of the United States and other nations around the world led to the Great Depression.

## Impact of the Depression

The collapse of the American economy had a ripple effect around the world. American investors pulled their money out of Europe, and placed high tariffs on imported goods. Nations that depended on American loans and investments or on exporting their goods to the United States, saw their economies collapse. Unemployment soared in many countries.

As the Great Depression continued, some people lost faith in democracy and capitalism. Extreme ideas of many types arose. Communists celebrated what they saw as the failure of capitalism. Strong leaders supported intense nationalism, militarism, and a return to authoritarian rule.

# The Rise of Fascism

Widespread economic despair paved the way for the rise of dictators. Strong leaders in Italy and Germany promised solutions.

**The Fascist State**

censorship and government control of news

strong military

extreme nationalism

use of violence and terror

FASCISM

state control of economy

blind loyalty to leader

rule by dictator

strict discipline

## Common Ideals of Fascism

**Fascism** is the rule of a people by dictatorial government that is nationalistic and imperialistic. Fascist governments are also anticommunist. Fascism emerged in both Italy and Germany after World War I.

## Key Themes and Concepts

**Economics and Interdependence**
Global economic interdependence was an important factor in the Great Depression. Because the United States economy was part of a network of trade and finance, the American stock market crash of 1929 had a worldwide effect.

## Note Taking

*Reading Skill:*
**Identify Causes and Effects**
Make a flowchart. Show the causes and the effects of the Great Depression.

| Causes | Event | Effects |
|--------|-------|---------|
| • • • | The Great Depression | • • • |

## Preparing for the Regents

• While reading the section on fascism, think of specific examples of how Hitler and Mussolini carried out some of the fascist policies shown on this chart.

## Key Themes and Concepts

**Political Systems**
Describe several ways in which fascism differs from democracy.

## Mussolini in Italy

Italy was troubled after World War I. Treaties had given away land that the Italians had expected to control. In addition, many war veterans could not find jobs. Trade was slow and taxes were high. Furthermore, workers went on strike.

**Benito Mussolini** took advantage of the unrest, gathering a following of war veterans and other unhappy Italians. He called his group the Fascist Party and pledged to solve the nation's problems and strengthen Italy. Mussolini promised to end unemployment and gain more land for Italy. He also vowed to outlaw rebellion among workers and stamp out all threats of communism.

In 1922, the Fascists used force and terror to gain control of Italy. They ended free elections, free speech, and the free press. They killed or jailed their enemies. Grasping desperately for order, Italians put the goals of the state above their individual rights.

## Hitler in Germany

**The Weimar Republic** After World War I, the kaiser stepped down. Germany was in chaos. The new democratic government, called the Weimar Republic, was blamed for agreeing to the harsh terms of the Versailles Treaty. Inflation created major economic problems. The troubles of the time led to the Nazi rise to power.

**Adolf Hitler** promised to provide jobs and rebuild German pride. He stated that the Germans were a superior race who were destined to build a new empire. In 1920, he headed the National Socialist German Workers, or Nazi, Party. His Party grew. In 1933, Hitler was appointed chancellor.

**Hitler as Dictator** Hitler's Germany, called the **Third Reich,** was a totalitarian state. He built a one-party government, ended civil rights, silenced his enemies with force, put businesses under government control, and employed many people in large public works programs. Germany's standard of living rose. Hitler rearmed Germany and rebuilt its military, which violated the Treaty of Versailles.

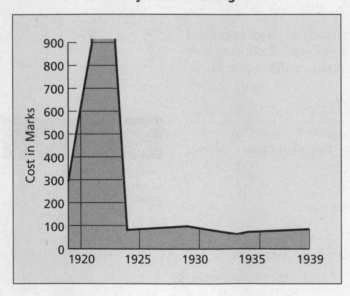

Germany: Cost of Living

*Adolph Hitler and the Nazis Adolph Hitler (1889–1945) and the Nazis wanted to create a new and powerful Germany. To achieve this goal, Hitler organized a brutal, totalitarian state.*

**NAZI RISE TO POWER**

**World War I**
• German war debts
• loss of German colonies
• wish for revenge

**Weak Government**
• doubts about Weimar Republic
• political quarrels
• wish to return to strong leader

**Economic Problems**
• inflation
• worldwide depression
• unemployment

**Leadership**
• use of terror and force
• idea of a super race
• shift of blame to minority groups

Hitler used the Jews as a scapegoat for Germany's problems. He instituted anti-Semitic policies. He used education and the arts as propaganda tools to push these policies. At first, Nazis organized boycotts of Jewish businesses, but by 1938 they were seizing the property and businesses of Jews and selling them to non-Jews. The Nuremburg Laws of 1935 took away the political rights and German citizenship of Jews. Few German citizens worried about Hitler's policies. Most were pleased at the growth of German pride and Germany's increased military and economic power.

### Totalitarianism in Nazi Germany

| Propaganda | Lack of Civil Liberties |
|---|---|
| The government controlled all sources of information–newspapers, radio, movies, and books. Schools taught Nazi ideas and children joined the Hitler Youth. Forbidden books were burned. | Only the Nazi Party was allowed and rival political parties were outlawed. The Gestapo (secret police) arrested and executed people without a trial. |
| **Anti-Semitism** | **Economic Controls** |
| Jews lost their property and citizenship. Their shops and synagogues were destroyed. They were forced to wear the yellow Star of David on their clothing. They were moved to ghettoes and concentration camps. | Agricultural and industrial production was controlled. Labor unions and strikes were outlawed. Germans were put to work building highways and weapons factories and drafted into the military. |

## Japan: Militarism and Expansion

Japan had moved toward greater democracy during the 1920s. However, there were underlying problems in Japanese society. The Great Depression that began in 1929 made these problems more apparent. Militarists and extreme nationalists gained power.

### Japanese Militarists of the 1930s

**CAUSES**

- unhappiness over loss of traditions
- loss of foreign markets due to Great Depression
- unemployment
- poverty among peasants
- feelings of nationalism
- demand for expansion of Japanese empire

**Rise of Militarists in Japan**

**EFFECTS**

- 1931 attack on Chinese province of Manchuria
- withdrawal from League of Nations
- anti-western feelings
- end of many democratic freedoms
- renewed practice of traditions
- increased honor for emperor
- renewed expansion and efforts to control China

## Summary

After World War I, conflict and turmoil continued. The Treaty of Versailles gave some nations self-determination, punished Germany severely, and created the League of Nations. New nations formed and old empires collapsed. Change occurred as nationalist groups struggled to overthrow foreign domination. Society and culture changed after the war, and people lost faith in old ideas. In 1929, the global economy plunged into a terrible depression. Fascism in Italy and Germany threatened the peace in Europe, while aggressive militarism by Japan caused tension in Asia.

### Vocabulary Builder

scapegoat—(SKAYP goht) *n.* someone who is blamed for something bad that happens, even if it is not their fault

**Preparing for the Regents**

- How did war and economic depression lead to the rise of fascism?

**Key Themes and Concepts**

**Power and Human Rights** Both Mussolini in Italy and Hitler in Germany improved the economies of their nations and brought order. The price of order, however, was loss of personal freedoms and human rights.

*Because of unrest in Japan in the 1930s, the government accepted military domination. It revived ancient warrior values.*

**Preparing for the Regents**

The militarists in Japan were determined to restore Japan to greatness, rid themselves of western influence, and gain foreign territories. Answer the following questions.

1. What economic problems led to the rise of militarism in Japan?

2. What were the political effects of the rise of militarism in Japan?

# World War II

## Section Overview

During the 1930s, Italy, Germany, and Japan sought to build new empires. At first, the democratic powers did not stop them. When German aggression became impossible to ignore, in 1939, World War II began. With advanced technology, the war covered a larger area and was more destructive than any before. Civilians became involved on a larger scale as well. At first, the Axis powers—Germany, Italy, and Japan—won major victories. After the entry of the United States and the Soviet Union into the war on the Allied side, however, the tide began to turn. The war finally ended in 1945. It had many lasting effects. There were enormous losses of life and property. The United Nations was formed to try to maintain peace. Europe became divided, with communist governments in Eastern Europe and democratic governments in Western Europe.

## Key Themes and Concepts

As you review this section, take special note of the following key themes and concepts:

**Power** What events led up to World War II?

**Science and Technology** How did new weapons technology affect the course of the war?

**Citizenship** How were the lives of individuals affected by the war?

**Change** What were the major turning points of the war that helped determine its outcome?

## Key People and Terms

As you review this section, be sure you understand the significance of these key people and terms:

| | | |
|---|---|---|
| appeasement | D-Day | concentration camps |
| Munich Conference | Hiroshima | Holocaust |
| Franklin Roosevelt | blitz | Bataan Death March |
| Pearl Harbor | Winston Churchill | United Nations |
| Stalingrad | genocide | |

## The Road to War

In the 1930s, Italy, Germany, and Japan aggressively sought to build new empires. The League of Nations was weak. Western countries were recovering from the Great Depression and did not want any more war. As a result, acts of aggression occurred and were allowed to go unchecked.

### Japan Invades China

The militaristic leaders of Japan wanted to build a Japanese empire. In 1931, Japan seized the Chinese territory of Manchuria. When the League of Nations condemned the action, Japan merely withdrew its membership from the League.

## The Big Idea

World War II:

- began when aggressive empire building by Germany, Italy, and Japan was opposed by Great Britain and France.
- was very destructive because of the technological power of new weaponry.
- was a total war that involved civilians as well as the military.
- created political and geographical divisions within Europe.
- affected global politics and culture for many years.

### Key People and Terms

What do three of the key people and terms have in common? Explain.

### Key Themes and Concepts

**Power**
Militarists had gained great power in Japan. Japan's successful aggression increased their political power.

This incident strengthened militarism in Japan. In 1937, the Japanese army invaded the Chinese mainland. They established a puppet government in the former Chinese Nationalist capital of Nanjing. Their invasion of this city was so brutal that it became known as the "rape of Nanjing." Japan continued to gain territory during the period of war with China.

## Italy Attacks Ethiopia

In 1935, the Italian army invaded the African country of Ethiopia. The Ethiopians resisted the attack, but their weapons were no match for the armored vehicles, aircraft, and poison gas of the Italians. The Ethiopian king appealed to the League of Nations. The league agreed to stop the sale of weapons and other war materials to Italy. However, the agreement was not honored by all nations.

## German Aggression in Europe

Hitler glorified war as a means of restoring German national pride. This philosophy led to a policy of expansion.

- Hitler rebuilt the German army, in violation of the Treaty of Versailles.
- In 1936, Hitler sent troops into the Rhineland. This was an area located on Germany's border with France. The Treaty of Versailles had required that Germany remove its troops from this border region.
- In 1938, Hitler made Austria part of the German empire. In the same year, he also forced Czechoslovakia to give Germany a border area called the Sudetenland, where many Germans lived.

## Appeasement

Western democracies adopted a policy of **appeasement.** Under this policy, nations gave in to aggressive demands to maintain peace. The western democracies responded weakly to German aggression. At the **Munich Conference** in 1938, western democracies agreed that Germany would seize control of the Sudetenland from Czechoslovakia.

### Military Aggression Leading to World War II

| 1935 Italy attacks Ethiopia | 1937 Japan invades China | 1939 Germany invades Poland / Germany takes Czechoslovakia |
|---|---|---|

| 1930 | 1932 | 1934 | 1936 | 1938 | 1940 |
|---|---|---|---|---|---|

| 1931 Japan invades Manchuria | 1936 Germany occupies Rhineland | 1938 Germany invades Austria / Germany seizes Sudetenland |
|---|---|---|

# World War II Begins

In the face of this weakness, Japan, Italy, and Germany formed the Rome-Berlin-Tokyo Axis. These nations agreed to fight Soviet communism and not to stop each other from making foreign conquests.

It began to be clear that appeasement had failed. Several events led to a declaration of war. In March 1939, Hitler took over the rest of Czechoslovakia. In August 1939, he made a pact with Joseph Stalin, the leader of the Soviet Union. In the

## Key Themes and Concepts

**Political Systems**
Leaders of Great Britain, France, and the United States knew that their citizens were reluctant to get involved in another costly war. This factor and others kept them from responding immediately to the aggression of Germany, Italy, and Japan.

## Preparing for the Regents

List five acts of aggression that led to World War II.

1.

2.

3.

4.

5.

Nazi-Soviet Pact, the two enemies agreed not to fight each other. In September 1939, Germany invaded Poland. Finally, Great Britain and France responded by declaring war on Germany. World War II had begun.

## The Axis Powers Advance

The war was fought between the Axis powers (Germany, Italy, and Japan) and the Allied powers (France and Great Britain). The Allies were later joined by the Soviet Union, China, and the United States. At first, Germany and its allies prevailed. Nazi forces conquered Poland in a swift, massive attack known as blitzkrieg, or lightning warfare. In April 1940, Hitler overran Norway, Denmark, the Netherlands, and Belgium. By June 1940, the Germans had entered Paris. Charles de Gaulle formed a French government in exile, calling on French forces to continue fighting Germany. These "Free French" worked from England to liberate their homeland.

*The Axis war machine extended across the world. It reached its height in Europe in 1942.*

### The World at War: World War II

## Turning Points of the War

The Axis powers won quick victories in the first several years of the war. Several events after 1940, however, are seen as turning points for the Allies.

### The Entry of the United States (1941)

Although the United States had declared its neutrality in the war, President **Franklin Roosevelt** met with England's prime minister, Winston Churchill, in August 1941, and they declared their common desire to end Nazi tyranny.

Roosevelt continued to supply arms to the Allies. To stop Japanese aggression, the United States banned the sale of war materials to Japan. Angered by the ban, Japan launched a surprise attack on American military bases at **Pearl Harbor,** Hawaii, on December 7, 1941. More than 2,400 people were killed, and many ships and planes were destroyed. In response, Franklin Roosevelt asked Congress to declare war on Japan. The entry of the United States into the war gave the Allies added strength.

### Battle of Stalingrad (1942–1943)

The Germans invaded the Soviet Union in 1941. After steadily advancing, they became stalled outside Moscow and Leningrad. Hitler turned south in 1942 to try to take **Stalingrad.** Russian troops and a freezing winter caused the German invaders to surrender in 1943. The Red Army drove the Germans out of the Soviet Union. Soon Soviet troops were advancing toward Germany.

### Invasion of Normandy (1944)

The Allies invaded France on June 6, 1944, also known as **D-Day**. Allied troops were ferried across the English Channel, landing on the beaches of Normandy. They broke through German defenses to advance toward Paris and freed France from German control. The Allies then moved from France into Germany.

## The War Ends

The war in Europe ended on May 7, 1945, with the Germans' surrender. Fighting in the Pacific would continue until the Japanese surrendered in August 1945.

### Yalta Conference

In February 1945, Roosevelt, Churchill, and Stalin met at a Soviet resort called Yalta. They knew then that the war was close to an end. The three leaders decided that at war's end, they would divide Germany temporarily. British, French, American, and Soviet forces would each control a zone of Germany. They agreed that Stalin would oversee the creation of new governments in Eastern Europe.

### Victory in the Pacific

Japan was greatly weakened, and the United States took the offensive after two Japanese fleets were severely damaged by Americans in 1942. Gradually, American forces recaptured Japanese-held islands south of Japan and advanced north. By 1944, the Americans had begun to bomb Japanese cities. The Japanese, however, refused to surrender.

### Hiroshima and Nagasaki

With no war in Europe, the Allies poured resources into the Pacific. By mid-1945, most of the Japanese navy and airforce had been destroyed. Japan's army was still strong, however. On August 6, 1945, an American plane dropped an atomic bomb on the Japanese city of **Hiroshima.** The bomb flattened 4 square miles of the city and killed 70,000 people. They dropped another bomb on Nagasaki, killing 40,000 people. Some militarists wanted to hold out, but on August 10, Japanese emperor Hirohito forced his government to surrender. Japan signed a peace treaty on September 2, 1945.

## Technology and World War II

Throughout the war, advanced technology led to more power, greater speed, and better communications. Technological innovation resulted in more widespread destruction than ever before.

**Preparing for the Regents**

Describe the significance of each of the following leaders.

Hitler:

Mussolini:

Stalin:

Churchill:

Roosevelt:

**Identify Effects**

Japan refused to surrender to the United States. What were the two main effects?

## Preparing for the Regents

- How did World War II affect civilian life? How did civilians contribute to the war effort?

# Civilian Life and Total War

Both the Allied powers and the Axis powers had engaged in total war. Cities became targets of bombing. In 1940, Germany began a **blitz,** or massive bombing, of London using warplanes. **Winston Churchill,** prime minister of Great Britain, rallied his people.

Democratic governments increased their power during the war. They ordered factories to produce war materials instead of civilian products. Prices and wages were fixed, and consumer goods were rationed.

Democratic governments sometimes limited the rights of individuals. In the United States and Canada, some people of Japanese descent were forced into internment camps. The British took similar action with those of German ancestry.

As men joined the war, women worked in the factories. They helped produce planes, ships, and ammunition. British and American women served in the armed forces by driving trucks and ambulances, decoding messages, and serving as nurses at field hospitals.

## Key Themes and Concepts

**Human Rights**
The Holocaust as well as other atrocities committed during World War II were extreme violations of human rights.

# The Holocaust

One of Hitler's goals was to create "living space" for Germans who he considered racially superior. He planned to destroy people he found inferior. Jews were the main target, but he also wanted to destroy or enslave others, including Slavs, Gypsies, and the mentally or physically disabled.

The attempt to destroy an entire ethnic or religious group is called **genocide.** Hitler committed genocide against the Jews. He began by limiting the rights and encouraging violence against Jews. On November 8, 1938, called Kristallnacht, organized violence began. Thousands of Jewish synagogues, businesses, cemeteries, schools, and homes were destroyed. The next day, 30,000 Jews were arrested for being Jewish and more restrictive laws on Jews and Jewish businesses began. Jews were forced to live in separate areas. Then, Hitler set up **concentration camps.** At death camps, like Auschwitz, Jews were starved, shot, or gassed to death. By 1945, more than six million Jews had died in what became known as the **Holocaust.**

# Other Wartime Atrocities

The Holocaust stands as the starkest example of wartime inhumanity. Several other incidents, however, also stand out as especially brutal aspects of World War II.

- The Japanese invasion of Nanjing in 1937 involved mass shootings and terrible brutality. As many as 250,000 Chinese were killed.
- In the Philippines, Japanese soldiers forced American and Filipino prisoners of war on a march up the Bataan peninsula. Along the way, prisoners were beaten, stabbed, and shot. This event became known as the **Bataan Death March.**
- In Poland, Soviet troops subjected thousands of Poles to imprisonment, torture, and execution.

# Impact of World War II

## Human Losses

World War II had killed as many as 75 million people. In European countries alone, about 38 million people died. The Soviets, however, had suffered the heaviest losses, with more than 22 million dead. The Holocaust had inflicted death and misery on millions of Jews and others in the Nazi concentration camps.

## Economic Losses

Throughout Europe and parts of Asia, cities were in ruins. Aerial bombardment had been very destructive. Coventry in England; Hamburg and Dresden in Germany; and Tokyo, Hiroshima, and Nagasaki in Japan were some of the hardest-hit cities. The European countryside was devastated as well. The economies of war-torn countries took many years to recover.

## War Crime Trials

At meetings during the war, Allied leaders had agreed to punish those responsible for "crimes against humanity." Trials were held in Nuremberg, Germany, from November 1945 through September 1946. Hitler was already dead, but 22 surviving Nazi leaders were tried at the Nuremberg trials. Some received the death penalty; others were imprisoned. Additional trials were held in Italy and Japan. The trials demonstrated that leaders could be held accountable for their actions during war.

## Occupied Nations

In order to prevent another world war and to promote democracy, western nations occupied West Germany and Japan. They built new governments with democratic constitutions, which protected individual rights and liberties.

However, Soviet forces occupied East Germany and most of Eastern Europe. They established communist governments in these nations, backed by the power of the Soviet Union. Thus, Europe was divided in two—between democracy in the West and communism in the East.

## The United Nations

World War II resulted in the formation of a new international body. In April 1945, representatives from nations around the world met in San Francisco to establish the **United Nations.** The purpose of the United Nations is to provide a place to discuss world problems and develop solutions. The two main bodies of the United Nations are:

- the General Assembly, which includes representatives from all member nations; each representative has one vote.
- the Security Council, with 15 member nations, 5 of which are permanent: the United States, Russia, France, Great Britain, and China.

# Summary

Germany, Italy, and Japan tried in the 1930s to build world empires. When Germany invaded Poland in 1939, World War II began, and the world faced the most devastating conflict in human history. During World War II, new weapons with massive power caused the loss of millions of lives. Civilians were greatly affected by the war, facing rationing, military attacks, and sometimes severe repression. The conflict continued until 1945. World War II resulted in millions of deaths, heavy economic losses, and brutality on a scale such as the world had not seen before. After 1945, the world became divided between communist and democratic forms of government.

**Compare and Contrast**

Compare and contrast the United Nations and the League of Nations.

# Questions for Regents Practice

**Multiple Choice**

*Directions:* Review the Test-Taking Strategies section of this book. Then answer the following questions, drawn from actual Regents examinations. For each statement or question, choose the *number* of the word or expression that, of those given, best completes the statement or answers the question.

Base your answer to question 1 on the graph below and on your knowledge of social studies.

**World Population 1800–1900**

1 What factors would best account for the rise in population shown on this graph after 1850?

(1) lack of public sewer systems

(2) the end of World War I

(3) medical advances and improved diets

(4) the decline of feudalism

2 A major cause of World War I was

(1) a decline in the policy of imperialism

(2) the existence of opposing alliances

(3) an increase in acts of aggression by England

(4) the spread of communism throughout Europe

3 In Eastern Europe after World War I, the greatest obstacle to national unity in many nation-states was the

(1) great ethnic diversity found in the region

(2) economic dependence of Eastern Europe on Japan

(3) acceptance of democratic traditions by most Eastern Europeans

(4) expansion of United States influence in the region

4 The Russian peasants supported the Bolsheviks in the 1917 revolutions mainly because the Bolsheviks promised to

(1) establish collective farms

(2) maintain the agricultural price-support system

(3) bring modern technology to Russian farms

(4) redistribute the land owned by the nobility

5 The French Revolution of 1789, the Chinese Revolution of 1911, and the Bolshevik Revolution of 1917 were similar in that these revolutions

(1) were led by ruthless dictators

(2) were motivated by a desire to overthrow a monarch

(3) led directly to the establishment of communism

(4) established a higher standard of living for the middle class

6 Which statement best describes the political situation that existed in the Soviet Union immediately after the death of Lenin in 1924?

(1) The nation adopted a constitutional monarchy.

(2) Trotsky and his followers assumed full control of the Communist Party.

(3) Popular elections were held to choose a new general secretary.

(4) A power struggle developed among Communist Party leaders.

7 "... The organizations of the revolutionaries must consist first, foremost, and mainly of people who make revolutionary activity their profession.... Such an organization must of necessity be not too extensive and as secret as possible...."

—V. I. Lenin, 1917

This quotation refers to Lenin's plan to

(1) defeat Germany in World War I
(2) establish representative democracy in Russia
(3) maintain Communist power in Western Europe
(4) overthrow the Russian government

8 Under Joseph Stalin, the Soviet Union emphasized centralized economic planning and five-year plans primarily to

(1) produce more consumer goods
(2) expand exports
(3) create an increased demand for high-quality imports
(4) develop heavy industry

9 A significant effect of Joseph Stalin's policy of collectivization on Soviet agriculture was

(1) a widespread food shortage
(2) an increase in the export of agricultural products
(3) a surplus of agricultural products
(4) the immediate creation of many small private farms

10 One similarity between Russia under the czars and the Soviet Union under Joseph Stalin is that in both types of government, these leaders

(1) tried to reduce their nation's influence in world affairs
(2) developed policies to limit industrial growth
(3) supported the creation of a national church
(4) established an authoritarian form of government

11 A study of the causes of the American, French, and Russian Revolutions indicates that revolutions usually occur because the

(1) society has become dependent on commerce and trade
(2) society has a lower standard of living than the societies around it
(3) existing government has been resistant to change
(4) lower classes have strong leaders

12 The harsh conditions imposed by the Treaty of Versailles after World War I helped lay the foundation for the

(1) rise of fascism in Germany
(2) uprisings during the French Revolution
(3) division of Korea along the 38th parallel
(4) Bolshevik Revolution in Russia

13 Mohandas Gandhi is best known for his

(1) use of passive resistance to achieve Indian independence
(2) desire to establish an Islamic nation
(3) opposition to Hindus holding public office
(4) encouragement of violence to end British rule

14 Which situation contributed to Adolf Hitler's rise to power in Germany after World War I?

(1) support of Hitler's radical policies by the Social Democrats in the Reichstag
(2) strong feelings of resentment and nationalism built up by economic and political crises
(3) refusal by the League of Nations to admit Germany as a member
(4) violence and terrorism promoted by Germany's former enemies

**15** Which was characteristic of France under Napoleon's rule and Germany under Hitler's rule?

(1) Democratic ideas and diversity were encouraged.

(2) Authoritarian control and a strong sense of nationalism prevailed.

(3) Peaceful relations with neighboring countries were fostered.

(4) Artistic and literary freedom flourished.

**16** Which policy best demonstrates appeasement?

(1) British policy toward Germany during the 1930s

(2) Japanese policy toward China in the 1930s

(3) Spanish policy toward Native Americans in the 1500s

(4) German policy toward the French during World War I

**17** Which series of events is arranged in the correct chronological order?

(1) The Treaty of Versailles is signed. Adolf Hitler becomes chancellor of Germany. German troops invade Poland.

(2) German troops invade Poland. The Treaty of Versailles is signed. Adolf Hitler becomes chancellor of Germany.

(3) Adolf Hitler becomes chancellor of Germany. The Treaty of Versailles is signed. German troops invade Poland.

(4) The Treaty of Versailles is signed. German troops invade Poland. Adolf Hitler becomes chancellor of Germany.

**18** The treatment of the Jews in Europe during World War II and of the Armenians in the Ottoman empire are examples of

(1) cultural diffusion

(2) fundamentalism

(3) modernization

(4) genocide

**19** Which was a major result of the Nuremberg trials?

(1) National leaders were held personally responsible for war crimes against humanity.

(2) The State of Israel was created as a home for victims of the war.

(3) Soldiers were required to pay for the property damages they caused during the war.

(4) Prisoners from all countries were immediately released from captivity.

# Thematic Essay Question

In developing your answer, be sure to keep these general definitions in mind:

    (a)  <u>describe</u> means "to illustrate something in words or tell about it"

    (b)  <u>explain</u> means "to make plain or understandable; to give reasons for or causes of; to show the logical development or relationships of"

*Directions:*    Write a well-organized essay that includes an introduction, several paragraphs addressing the task below, and a conclusion.

**Theme:**    **Nationalism**

> Throughout global history, nationalism has had positive and negative effects.

**Tasks:**

- Define the term *nationalism*
- Select one country or region you have studied
- Describe two specific examples of nationalism within that country or region
- Explain how each of the two examples had either a positive or negative impact on the future development of the country or region

You may use any nation or region from your study of global history, except the United States. Some suggestions you may wish to consider are: Latin America (1800s), Italy (1800s and 1900s), China (1900s), India (1900s), Kenya (post–World War II), and the Balkans (1900s).

**You are *not* limited to these suggestions.**
**Do *not* use the United States in your answer.**

**Guidelines:**

**In your essay, be sure to**
- Develop all aspects of the task
- Support the theme with relevant facts, examples, and details
- Use a logical and clear plan of organization, including an introduction and a conclusion that are beyond a simple restatement of the theme

# Document-Based Question

This question is based on the accompanying documents. The question is designed to test your ability to work with historical documents. Some of these documents have been edited for the purposes of this question. As you analyze the documents, take into account the source of each document and any point of view that may be presented in the document.

**Historical Context:**

> Throughout history, leaders have viewed power in many different ways. There have been a variety of viewpoints on the acquisition and use of power.

**Task:**   Using the information from the documents and your knowledge of global history, answer the questions that follow each document in Part A. Your answers to the questions will help you write the Part B essay in which you will be asked to

> - Discuss several viewpoints on the attainment and use of power
> - Evaluate positive and negative effects that the various viewpoints have had on people in different countries

In developing your answers, be sure to keep these general definitions in mind:

(a) <u>discuss</u> means "to make observations about something using facts, reasoning, and argument; to present in some detail"

(b) <u>evaluate</u> means "to examine and judge the significance, worth, or condition of; to determine the value of"

## Part A: Short Answer

*Directions:*     Analyze the documents and answer the question or questions that follow each document, using the space provided.

### Document #1

*Under the leadership of the working class and the Communist party, these classes [the working class, the peasantry, the petty bourgeoisie, and the national bourgeoisie] unite to create their own state . . . so as to enforce their . . . dictatorship over the henchmen of imperialism—the landlord class and bureaucratic capitalist class. . . . The people's government will suppress such persons.*

**– Mao Zedong, speech on the anniversary of the founding of the Communist party, 1949**

1  According to Mao Zedong, do all classes share power in a communist state? Explain.

_____

_____

2  Describe one goal that Mao thought a communist government should strive to achieve.

_____

_____

# Document-Based Question

**Document #2**
**The Fascist State**

3  According to this chart, what methods have fascist leaders used to acquire and maintain power?

_____

_____

**Document #3**

> *Passive resistance is a method of securing rights by personal suffering; it is the reverse of resistance by arms. When I refuse to do a thing that is repugnant to my conscience, I use soul-force.*
>
> **– Mohandas Gandhi,** *Hind Swaraj,* **1938**

4  What did Gandhi mean by the term *passive resistance*?

_____

_____

## Document #4

*The nation has placed its destiny in the hands and heads and hearts of its millions of free men and women; and its faith in freedom. . . . Freedom means the supremacy of human rights everywhere. Our support goes to those who struggle to gain those rights or keep them.*

**– Franklin D. Roosevelt, address to Congress in January 1941**

5 According to President Roosevelt, who or what is the ultimate source of power in the United States?

_____

_____

6 For what purpose did Roosevelt promise to use the power of the United States?

_____

_____

## Part B

### Essay

*Directions:*  Write a well-organized essay that includes an introduction, several paragraphs, and a conclusion.  Use evidence from *at least* **three** documents in your essay. Support your response with relevant facts, examples, and details. Include additional outside information.

### Historical Context:

Throughout history, leaders have viewed power in many different ways. There have been a variety of viewpoints on the acquisition and use of power.

### Task:

Using the information from the documents and your knowledge of global history, write an essay in which you

- Evaluate the differing views that leaders have had on the attainment and use of power
- Discuss how the views of at least two leaders have affected people of their own nations and people of other nations

### Guidelines:

**In your essay, be sure to**
- Develop all aspects of the task
- Incorporate information from *at least* **three** documents
- Incorporate relevant outside information
- Support the theme with relevant facts, examples, and details
- Use a logical and clear plan of organization, including an introduction and a conclusion that are beyond a restatement of the theme

# The Twentieth Century and Beyond (1945–the present)

## Unit Overview

After World War II, many nations participated in a struggle called the Cold War. On one side were communist states led by the Soviet Union and China. On the other side were noncommunist nations led by the United States. The Cold War finally ended in the 1980s with the collapse of the Soviet Union and the end of communism in Eastern Europe.

During the Cold War, imperialism ended and new nations were born. In the Middle East, there were many conflicts. Elsewhere, newly independent nations had to establish workable economic and political systems. In Latin America, there was political unrest.

## Thematic Timeline Activity

Some of the many themes developed in Unit 7 are:

| | | |
|---|---|---|
| change | economic systems | diversity |
| political systems | conflict | belief systems |
| human rights | nationalism | |

Choose one of the themes listed above. As you review Unit 7, create a thematic timeline based on the theme you have chosen. Your timeline should stretch from 1945 to the present and include major developments and key turning points having to do with your theme.

# Cold War Balance of Power

## The Big Idea

**After World War II:**

- West Germany and Japan developed democratic governments.

- the United States and the Soviet Union emerged as superpowers with differing political and economic systems.

- the Cold War developed, and the superpowers confronted one another throughout the world.

- the United Nations tried to maintain peace.

## Section Overview

After World War II, Japan and West Germany adopted constitutions that built democratic governments. Two major powers emerged from the war: the United States and the Soviet Union. Political and economic differences between the two led to a division of Europe that would last more than 40 years. The conflict between democracy and communism also spread around the globe, resulting in a buildup of arms as well as a race to explore space. The United Nations experienced both failure and success in its quest to maintain peace in the years after 1945.

## Key Themes and Concepts

As you review this section, take special note of the following key themes and concepts:

**Change** What impact did World War II have on the development of democracy in Germany and Japan?

**Political Systems** How did differing political systems help cause the Cold War between the United States and the Soviet Union?

**Conflict** How did the rivalry between the United States and the Soviet Union involve other nations around the world?

**Justice and Human Rights** What role does the United Nations play in the struggle for justice and human rights?

## Key People and Terms

**Key People and Terms**

Place each of the key people and terms into one of these two categories: political or military.

As you review this section, be sure you understand the significance of these key people and terms:

| | | |
|---|---|---|
| iron curtain | Truman Doctrine | surrogate |
| asylum | containment | Fidel Castro |
| superpowers | Marshall Plan | Cuban Missile Crisis |
| Cold War | NATO | nonaligned nations |
| satellites | Warsaw Pact | |

## A Divided Europe

**Preparing for the Regents**

- How were conditions in Europe after World War II similar to the conditions that existed after World War I? How were the two postwar periods different?

After World War II, with help from the United States and Great Britain, democracy and free enterprise were restored to the nations of Western Europe. Eastern Europe, however, was occupied by armies of the Soviet Union. Joseph Stalin, the leader of the Soviet Union, wanted to spread communism throughout the area. He hoped to create a buffer zone of friendly governments to prevent possible attacks from Germany and other western nations.

Although Stalin had promised free elections for Eastern Europe, he instead supported the establishment of procommunist governments throughout the region. Soon Europe was divided by an imaginary line known as the **iron curtain.** In the East were the Soviet-dominated communist countries. In the West were the western democracies, led by the United States.

# Germany and Japan Transformed

Both Germany and Japan had been physically and socially devastated by the war. The victorious Allied powers occupied the two countries.

Germany was divided into four zones of occupation. Great Britain, France, and the United States occupied the three zones in western Germany. The Soviet Union controlled eastern Germany. The United States alone occupied Japan.

## Democracy in West Germany

Germany's armed forces were disbanded, and the Nazi party was outlawed. Nazi war criminals were tried in the Nuremberg trials, and some were executed. In western Germany, the Allies helped set up political parties. Germans wrote a federal constitution. This constitution set up a democratic government and was approved in 1949. In that year, West Germany also regained self-government as the Federal Republic of Germany.

Germany's constitution included an article that guaranteed political asylum for people who were persecuted for political reasons. **Asylum** is protection from arrest or from the possibility of being returned to a dangerous political situation. For many years, Germany's asylum policy was the most liberal in Europe. Germany's recognition of its role in the persecution of Jews and other groups probably led to this constitutional guarantee. In the late 1990s, Germany began to restrict this right after large numbers of asylum seekers came to Germany for economic rather than political reasons.

**The Lessons of the Holocaust** Germany was deeply shaken by the experience of the Holocaust. Germans wanted to be sure that such a thing could not happen again. Today, Germany's relationship with the nation of Israel is very friendly. Germany and Israel have strong diplomatic, economic, and cultural ties. There has also been an attempt to financially compensate some of the victims of the Holocaust.

## Democracy in Japan

Like Germany, Japan was occupied after World War II by Allied troops, most of whom were American. Japan's armed forces were disbanded. Trials were held to punish people who had been responsible for wartime atrocities, and some of these people were executed. General Douglas MacArthur was the supreme commander of the American military government that ruled postwar Japan. The American government wanted to end militarism and ensure democratic government in Japan.

**Japan's New Constitution** In Germany, a German council had written the new constitution. Japan's constitution, on the other hand, was drafted by MacArthur and his advisors.

- It created a constitutional monarchy that limited the power of the emperor.
- It promised that Japan would not use war as a political weapon.
- It set up a democratic government. Representatives were elected to the Diet, the Japanese parliament.
- Women gained the right to vote.
- Basic rights, such as freedom of the press and of assembly, were guaranteed.

The Japanese government accepted this new constitution and signed a treaty that took away Japan's overseas empire. In 1952, the Allied occupation officially ended.

## Vocabulary Builder

disband—(dis BAND) v. to stop existing as an organization, or to make something do this

## Preparing for the Regents

- Why do you think Germany developed one of Europe's most liberal asylum laws?

## Key Themes and Concepts

**Change**
Describe two effects that Germany's experience in the Holocaust had on the nation's later development.

## Preparing for the Regents

- How were the political conditions in Germany and Japan similar after World War II? How were they different?

- How was the Japanese government after World War II different from the Japanese government that had existed before and during the war?

## Two Superpowers

After World War II, several powerful nations of the past were in decline. Germany was defeated and divided. France and Britain were economically drained and needed to concentrate on rebuilding. The United States and the Soviet Union emerged from World War II as the two world superpowers. The word *superpower* has been used to describe each of the rivals that came to dominate global politics in the period after World War II. Many other states in the world came under the domination or influence of these powers.

**Europe After World War II**

***Europe After World War II***
*In 1949, the U.S., Canada, and ten other countries formed the NATO military alliance. In 1955, the Soviet Union formed the Warsaw Pact military alliance with its seven satellites.*

### Preparing for the Regents

- Practice your map skills by listing the nations that were members of NATO and the nations that were members of the Warsaw Pact in 1955.

### Key Themes and Concepts

**Political and Economic Systems**
The Cold War was much more than just a military rivalry. It was a struggle between two very different political and economic systems.

### Preparing for the Regents

- What factors led to the breakup of the alliance between Britain, France, and the United States and the Soviet Union?

# The Cold War Begins

The United States and the Soviet Union had cooperated to win World War II. Soon, however, conflicts in ways of thinking and mutual distrust led to the Cold War—a continuing state of tension and hostility between the superpowers. This tension was a result of differences in political and economic thinking between the democratic, capitalistic United States and the communist Soviet Union. It was a "cold" war because armed battle between the superpowers did not occur.

The western powers feared the spread of communism. Stalin had forced pro-communist governments in Poland, Czechoslovakia, and elsewhere. These countries came to be known as **satellites** of the Soviet Union. When Stalin began to put pressure on Greece and Turkey, the United States took action.

### The Truman Doctrine

In March of 1947, President Harry S. Truman established a policy known as the **Truman Doctrine.** This was an economic and military program designed to help other nations resist Soviet aggression. It was based on the theory of **containment,** which involved limiting communism to areas already under Soviet control. The United States pledged to resist Soviet expansion anywhere in the world. Truman sent military and economic aid to Greece and Turkey so that they could resist the threat of communism.

## The Marshall Plan

The **Marshall Plan,** also proposed in 1947, was a massive economic aid package designed to strengthen democratic governments and lessen the appeal of communism. Billions of American dollars helped Western European countries recover from World War II. Although the United States also offered this aid to Eastern Europe, Stalin forbade these countries to accept it.

## Crisis in Germany

The division of Germany into four zones after World War II was supposed to be temporary. Soon Great Britain, France, and the United States had combined their democratically ruled zones. Tension grew between democratic western Germany and Soviet-controlled eastern Germany. Germany became a major focus of Cold War tension. The Allies were trying to rebuild the German economy, but Stalin feared a strong, united Germany. Berlin, the divided capital, was located in East Germany.

**The Berlin Airlift** In 1948, Stalin hoped to force the Allies out of Berlin by closing all land routes for bringing essential supplies to West Berlin. In response to the crisis, the western powers mounted a successful airlift. For almost a year, food and supplies were flown into West Berlin. Finally, the Soviets ended the blockade.

**A Divided Germany** This incident, however, led to the creation of the Federal Republic of Germany (West Germany) in 1949. Germany, like the rest of Europe, remained divided. In 1961, the East German government built a wall that separated East Berlin from West Berlin. East German soldiers shot anyone who tried to escape from East Germany.

## Opposing Military Alliances

**The NATO Alliance** After the Berlin airlift and the division of West Germany from East Germany, Western European countries formed a military alliance. It was called the North Atlantic Treaty Organization, or NATO. Members of NATO pledged to support each other if any member nation was ever attacked.

**The Warsaw Pact** In 1955, the Soviet Union formed the Warsaw Pact. It included the Soviet Union and seven of its satellites in Eastern Europe. This was also a defensive alliance, promising mutual military cooperation.

# The Cold War Heats Up

## Repression in Eastern Europe

The Soviet Union kept a tight grip on its Eastern European satellites. Tensions arose in both East Germany and Poland in the 1950s. In East Germany, a revolt was put down with Soviet tanks. In Poland, some reforms were made, yet the country remained under the domination of the Soviet Union. Though Stalin died in 1953, his successors continued his policy of repression.

**The Hungarian Revolt** In 1956, a revolution began in Hungary. It was led by Imre Nagy, who was a Hungarian nationalist and communist. Nagy ended one-party rule, got rid of Soviet troops, and withdrew Hungary from the Warsaw Pact. In response, the Soviet Union quickly sent in troops and tanks. Thousands of Hungarians died, and the revolt against Soviet domination was suppressed.

**The Invasion of Czechoslovakia** Another rebellion against Soviet domination occurred in Czechoslovakia in the spring of 1968, when Alexander Dubçek called for liberal reforms and the easing of communist controls. The government of Czechoslovakia eased censorship and began to plan for a new constitution. The

Soviet Union, however, sent troops to overturn the government and restore a communist dictatorship. Through these incidents, it became clear that the Soviet Union would use force whenever necessary to ensure the survival of communism and Soviet domination in Eastern Europe.

## Preparing for the Regents

- How did the Cold War lead to an arms race?

- What role did science and technology play in the Cold War?

## The Arms Race

Both the United States and the Soviet Union armed themselves, each preparing to withstand an attack from the other. The United States had developed the atomic bomb during World War II; Soviet scientists developed their own in 1949.

For 40 years, the two superpowers spent great amounts of money to develop more and more powerful weapons. The arms race raised the level of tension between the two superpowers. It also raised fears among many people that the superpowers might become involved in a conflict that would destroy the world.

## The Space Race

The superpowers also competed in space. In 1957, the Soviet Union launched *Sputnik*, a satellite, into orbit around the Earth. Congress soon established NASA, the National Aeronautics and Space Administration, to improve American space technology.

The race was on. In 1958, the United States launched its own first satellite. In 1961, the Soviets sent the first man into space. Then, in 1969, the United States was the first nation to put a man on the moon. Both the Soviet Union and the United States explored the military use of space with spy satellites. Many people were concerned about the high cost of space exploration and the extension of the Cold War into space.

# Conflicts Around the World

Although the United States and the Soviet Union did not engage in a war with each other, they did clash through **surrogate,** or representative, states. This meant that the United States and Soviet Union supported opposing forces in many nations throughout the world. These conflicts occurred in East Asia, the Middle East, Africa, and Latin America.

## The Cold War in East Asia

Cold War tensions grew into bitter wars in Korea in the 1950s and in Vietnam in the 1960s. In each case, the superpowers supported opposing sides with economic aid, advisors, and troops.

**Korean War (1950–1953)** After World War II, Korea, like Germany, was divided into two parts. North Korea was occupied by Soviet forces and South Korea was occupied by American forces. North Korean forces, seeking to unify the country under communist rule, invaded South Korea in 1950. United Nations forces, commanded by General Douglas MacArthur, drove the North Koreans back, invaded North Korea, and approached the Chinese border. Chinese soldiers then entered the war and pushed the UN forces back into the south. In 1953 an armistice was signed, leaving Korea divided at the 38th parallel with a demilitarized zone between the two countries.

**Vietnam War** In 1954, Vietnam was temporarily divided into a northern half, ruled by communist leader Ho Chi Minh, and a southern half, headed by non-communist Ngo Dinh Diem. Large numbers of American forces were eventually sent to Vietnam to prevent Ho Chi Minh from uniting Vietnam under northern rule. American forces, however, were not able to defeat the communist forces in Vietnam. In 1973, President Richard Nixon ordered a cease-fire and began to pull

## Key Themes and Concepts

**Power**
By supporting governments or rebel groups in other countries, the superpowers could exert their influence without engaging in a major armed combat.

## Note Taking

*Reading Skill:*
**Identify Main Ideas and Supporting Details**
As you read Conflicts Around the World, complete an outline with the main ideas and supporting details. An outline has been started for you.

Conflicts Around the World
I. East Asia
  A. Korean War (1950–1953)
    1.
    2.
  B.
II.

American forces out of Vietnam. In 1975, the North Vietnamese captured Saigon, reuniting Vietnam.

## The Cold War in the Middle East

**Arab States and Israel** In the 1950s, Gamal Abdel Nasser emerged as a leader in the Arab state of Egypt. He was determined to end western power in Egypt. In 1956, he nationalized the Suez Canal, ending British control. He received support from the Soviet Union and used Soviet money to build the Aswan High Dam. Under Nasser's leadership, Egypt took part in two wars against the Jewish state of Israel. While the Soviet Union supported Egypt, the United States supported Israel.

**Iran and Iraq** Rivalries over oil resources fueled Cold War tensions in the Middle East. The United States and the Soviet Union both became interested in Iran after vast oil fields were discovered there. An Iranian nationalist leader who had communist support tried to nationalize the oil industry in the early 1950s. The United States helped to keep him from power. The United States then supported the repressive anticommunist shah of Iran with weapons and advisors. An Islamic revolution in 1979 toppled the shah's regime.

The Soviet Union meanwhile supported Iraq, which had become a socialist dictatorship in the 1960s and also had oil reserves. The Soviet Union eventually also supported governments in Syria and Libya.

## The Cold War in Africa

**Congo** The Congo, a Belgian colony in Africa, became independent in 1960. The new premier asked for help in dealing with a revolt. The Soviet Union supported him against the rebels. Five years later, a strongly anticommunist dictator named Mobutu Sese Seko took control of the country, renaming it Zaire. Because of his anti-communist stance, he received the support of the West, allowing him to stay in power until the late 1990s.

**Angola** In southwestern Africa, the Portuguese colony of Angola gained independence in 1975, in the midst of a bloody civil war. After that, rival rebel groups continued their conflict with each other. One group, the MPLA, was supported by the Soviet Union and Cuba. The Soviet Union sent advisors and equipment; Cuba sent troops. The MPLA established a communist dictatorship in Angola. The United States tried to undermine this government, and South Africa supported the opposing group, UNITA. This confrontation continued until 1991.

## The Cold War in Latin America

**Cuba** Cuba had won independence from Spain in 1898. For 60 years, Cuba was strongly influenced by the United States. In 1952, Fulgencio Batista seized power. His government was repressive and corrupt. Among those who opposed Batista was a young lawyer named **Fidel Castro.** He organized a guerrilla army and fought against Batista. Once gaining victory in 1959, Castro established a communist dictatorship in Cuba.

Castro turned to the Soviet Union for support. Cuba became involved in the rivalry between the United States and the Soviet Union. In 1961, the United States backed a plot by Cuban exiles to invade Cuba at the Bay of Pigs. However, the invading forces were quickly crushed. In 1962, the United States imposed a trade embargo on Cuba.

Angered by American interference, Castro sought closer ties with the Soviet Union. Castro allowed the Soviets to build nuclear missile sites in Cuba, just

**Key Themes and Concepts**

**Needs and Wants**
The superpowers interfered in the governments of Iran and Iraq. One reason for their interest in these nations was the presence of oil reserves. Both super-powers needed oil to boost their economies.

**Identify Cause**
For what reason did the Cold War superpowers support opposite sides in Africa?

**Preparing for the Regents**

• Describe one way in which the Cold War influenced conflicts or events in each of the following regions.

Asia:

Middle East:

Africa:

Latin America:

## Note Taking

*Reading Skill:*
**Recognize Sequence**
List the important events of the Cold War in Cuba. Record them in the order they occurred. Add boxes as needed.

| Date | Event |
|------|-------|
| 1898 | |
| | |
| | |

90 miles off the coast of Florida. In 1962, U.S. President Kennedy demanded removal of the missiles from Cuba and ordered a naval blockade of Cuba. This incident, known as the **Cuban Missile Crisis,** ended when the Soviet leader, Nikita Khrushchev, agreed to remove the missiles in exchange for a pledge by Kennedy that the United States would not invade Cuba. The United States established a trade embargo with Cuba which was heavily supported by the Soviet Union until the collapse of communism. Cuba's economy has since suffered greatly from the loss of these trading partners.

### Causes and Impact of the Cuban Revolution

| Causes of the Cuban Revolution | Impact of the Cuban Revolution |
|--------------------------------|--------------------------------|
| **Political Conditions**<br>• Rule by a repressive dictatorship<br>• Corruption and bribery among government officials | **Political Changes**<br>• Creation of a communist dictatorship<br>• Denial of basic political rights and freedoms |
| **Economic Conditions**<br>• Control of Cuba's sugar plantations by the upper class<br>• Unequal distribution of wealth<br>• Foreign control of many businesses<br>• High unemployment despite prosperity | **Economic Changes**<br>• Establishment of collective farms, jointly operated under government supervision<br>• Government control of business and industry<br>• Seizure of foreign property with little or no compensation |

## The Nonaligned Nations

## Key Themes and Concepts

**Choice**
Nonaligned nations did not side with either the Soviets or the United States during the Cold War.

The nations that chose not to ally with either side in the Cold War were known as nonaligned nations. These nations remained neutral. India, Yugoslavia, and many African nations adopted a policy of nonalignment. Their goals were to make economic progress and to avoid involvement in the Cold War.

## The Role of the United Nations

During the course of the Cold War, the United Nations provided a forum for the superpowers to air their differences peacefully. While the Cold War was at its peak, however, countries tended to vote in blocs, either as allies of the United States or as allies of the Soviet Union. This practice limited the United Nations' effectiveness.

## Preparing for the Regents

• What role has the United Nations played in the Cold War and post–Cold War world?

After the end of the Cold War in 1991, the United Nations expanded several of its traditional roles. Today, it sends international peacekeeping forces to countries in conflict. The United Nations continues to provide many health services to less developed countries. It also supports the struggle for human rights throughout the world.

## Summary

## Preparing for the Regents

• Write a brief essay discussing why the Cold War took place and what impacts it has had on the world.

After World War II, with the help of the United States, democratic governments were established in Japan and West Germany. The United States and the Soviet Union emerged as two rival superpowers with differing political and economic systems. Their rivalry threatened peace around the world in a struggle called the Cold War that went on for more than 45 years. The two superpowers engaged in the buildup of arms, competition in space, and surrogate conflicts in other parts of the world. Despite difficulties, the United Nations remained a force for stability and peace.

# Economic Issues

## Section Overview

In the years after 1945, developing nations chose to develop either a market economy, a command economy, or a mixed economy. Countries in South Asia, Latin America, and Africa struggled to industrialize, improve agriculture, and curb population growth. In Western Europe and Japan, economies recovered and grew rapidly. West Germany and Japan became economic superpowers. The economies of the Pacific Rim, modeled on Japanese success, grew aggressively through trade and industrialization. After 1945, the economic interdependence of the world became clearer. When Middle Eastern oil suppliers limited oil in the 1970s, the economies of the West were hurt.

## Key Themes and Concepts

As you review this section, take special note of the following key themes and concepts:

**Economic Systems** What are capitalism and communism?

**Factors of Production** How have developing nations combined human, natural, and capital resources to promote economic development?

**Change** Why did Western Europe and Japan experience great economic growth after 1945?

**Needs and Wants** How has the need for petroleum affected international relations?

## Key People and Terms

As you review this section, be sure you understand the significance of these key people and terms:

| | | |
|---|---|---|
| developed nations | European Community | balance of trade |
| developing nations | European Union | Pacific Rim |
| mixed economy | euro | OPEC |
| Common Market | zaibatsu | |

## Market Economies and Command Economies

In the years after World War II, some nations were basing their economic development on the ideas of capitalism. Other countries were adopting command economies, such as that which existed under communism. The choices that countries made were often influenced by the Cold War. The United States and its allies supported market economies. The Soviet Union and its allies supported command economies.

> ### The
> # Big
> # Idea
>
> In the Cold War and post–Cold War eras:
>
> - countries developed market economies, command economies, or mixed economies.
>
> - developing nations struggled to strengthen their economies.
>
> - Western Europe and Japan experienced rapid economic recovery.
>
> - the nations of the world became increasingly interdependent.

> ### Key People
> #### and Terms
>
> - What do all of the key people and terms have in common? Explain.

## Comparison of Market Economies and Command Economies

|  | Market Economy | Command Economy |
|---|---|---|
| Ownership | All property, including the means of production, is privately owned. | The government owns the means of production, distribution, and exchange. |
| Economic decisions | Private businesses and individuals are free from public control so that they can make basic economic decisions, including what, where, how much, and at what prices goods will be produced. | Government officials make all basic economic decisions, such as what will be produced, when, and where. |
| Market controls | Prices are determined by supply and demand. Competition promotes high quality and low prices. | The government plans the economy. There is limited production of consumer goods and an emphasis on industrial growth. |

### Preparing for the Regents

- Compare and contrast market and command economies.

## The Economies of Developing Nations

After World War II, the United States, the Soviet Union, Japan, and the countries of Western Europe came to be called **developed nations.** They had modern agriculture and industries, advanced technology, and strong educational systems. Nations with limited resources and without modern industrial economies were called **developing nations.**

Economic obstacles include overpopulation, natural disasters, and indebtedness. After World War II, many developing nations began to build their economies. Some were just emerging from imperialism. Many had to decide which of the two major economic systems they would follow. Some nations took elements of both.

The issues faced by developing nations were unique to each nation. However, several goals were common:

- Building industry
- Improving agriculture
- Controlling population

### Key Themes and Concepts

**Economic Systems**
A mixed economy uses elements of both market and command economies. Developing nations, such as India and some nations of Africa, established mixed economies after 1945.

### Case Study: India

After India became independent in 1947, it developed a **mixed economy** that combined elements of market and command economies. Heavy industry was brought under government control, and the nation worked with a series of five-year plans. These plans set economic goals and managed resources. Dams were built to produce hydroelectric power. The government poured resources into heavy industries such as steel production. In addition, crop output was increased with new types of seeds, chemical fertilizers, and improved irrigation.

However, India also faced obstacles. India lacked oil and natural gas, slowing growth. Many government-run businesses were ineffective. Agricultural output was not enough to keep up with population growth. In the 1990s, pressure from lenders forced India to institute reforms. Some industries were privatized, and foreign investment was made easier.

### Case Study: Egypt

After Egypt became independent, Gamal Abdel Nasser installed a socialist government and economy. Nasser nationalized banks and businesses and instituted land reform. Peasant farmers were given land.

With the help of the Soviet Union, Egypt built the Aswan Dam. It controlled the flow of the Nile River and provided 2 million acres of additional farmland. However, it also increased the saltiness of the Nile and caused the soil of the Nile Delta to erode.

Nasser's successor, Anwar Sadat, encouraged foreign investment as well as free market practices. Sadat was assassinated in 1981. Sadat's successor, Hosni Mubarak, faced economic problems and a rising population. He also faced criticism from Islamic fundamentalists.

## Case Study: Latin America

After World War II, many Latin American nations experienced unrest. Complex difficulties have sometimes hindered development.

**Agricultural Reform** Many Latin American nations have had to grow more staple crops, such as corn and wheat, in order to feed their growing populations. Because overdependence on any single cash crop is risky, these nations have sought to diversify their agriculture. Some, however, still rely on cash crops. A few countries, believing that uneven distribution of land leads to poverty, have also tried to institute land reform in order to get more land into the hands of a greater number of people.

**Debt Crisis** Often, Latin American nations had to borrow money to build industries. When a worldwide recession hit, demand for goods fell. However, these nations still had to make high interest payments. Money went toward paying off loans rather than building industry.

**Free Market Reforms** Some Latin American governments used free market reforms as a way to recover from their economic crises. Government spending was reduced, and private owners were allowed to buy out state-owned industries. Slowly, economic progress was made.

**Population Explosion** Many Latin Americans see the need to control population. Some cultural and religious beliefs, however, work against population control. As a result, populations are still growing rapidly, creating a severe economic burden.

# Economic Recovery and Cooperation in Europe

After the end of World War II, the United States developed the Marshall Plan to encourage the economic development of Western Europe and to prevent the expansion of communism.

## West German Economic Miracle

Capital from the Marshall Plan and the leadership of a democratic government helped West Germany to recover. West Germans rebuilt their cities and factories and developed a strong industrial economy. High-quality German exports were in great demand around the world. The recovery in Germany was so dramatic that it was referred to as an "economic miracle." After East and West Germany were reunited in 1990, difficulties emerged as East Germans made the transition to a market economy.

## European Economic Unification

With aid from the Marshall Plan, other Western European countries also recovered quickly from World War II. The countries of Europe promoted their own prosperity through cooperation.

**European Coal and Steel Community** In 1952, France, West Germany, Belgium, Italy, the Netherlands, and Luxembourg set up the European Coal and Steel Community to regulate the coal and steel industries and spur economic growth.

## Vocabulary Builder

fundamentalist—(fun duh MENT uh list) *n.* someone who follows religious laws very strictly

## Preparing for the Regents

• Describe three economic problems that developing nations of Latin America face.

1.

2.

3.

## Preparing for the Regents

• Why do you think West Germany's economy achieved much greater success than East Germany's?

## Key Themes and Concepts

**Interdependence**
Many European countries prospered economically as a result of cooperation after World War II. Six Western European nations drew together in 1952 to form an economic community. Today, the European Union is made up of both Western and Eastern European nations.

**The Common Market** In 1957, these same six nations formed the **European Community** (EC), or Common Market. This organization expanded free trade by ending tariffs and allowing labor and capital to move freely across borders. Great Britain, Denmark, and Ireland later joined.

**European Union** In 1993, the EC expanded further and became the European Union. By 2008, the EU had 27 member states, including former communist countries such as Hungary and Poland. A new currency, the **euro,** was introduced in 1999. The EU aims to bolster Europe's trade position and its political and economic power in the world.

# Japan: An Economic Superpower

### Economic Reforms

As you have learned, the United States occupation of Japan after World War II helped to establish democracy in that nation. The United States also brought economic reforms to Japan. Japanese workers were given the right to form unions. Land reform divided up large estates among tenant farmers. The United States tried to break up the **zaibatsu,** the powerful family-owned business concerns that dominated Japanese economic life, but the reform effort achieved only limited success.

### Close Ties With the West

As the Cold War intensified, the United States and its allies viewed Japan less as a former enemy and more as a future ally. The outbreak of war in Korea in 1950 reinforced this view. Japan served as a staging area for operations in Korea. The American occupation of Japan ended in 1952. As Japanese industry prospered, the nation engaged in increased trade with the United States and other countries.

### How the Japanese Economy Succeeded

Japan rebounded rapidly from the economic devastation that followed World War II. Japan sent many manufactured items to other countries, building a favorable balance of trade. A country that has a favorable **balance of trade** exports more goods than it imports. Why was Japan so successful?

- Japan adapted the latest western technology to its own industries.
- Japan had a well-educated and highly skilled work force.
- Japanese savings gave banks capital to invest in industry.
- The government, prohibited from spending money on defense, poured funds into the economy.
- The government imposed high tariffs and strict regulations to limit foreign competition.

Recently, Japan's economy has not been so healthy. In the late 1980s, Japan was hit by an economic recession. Banks staggered under a mountain of bad debt, companies went bankrupt, and unemployment rose. Japan's government seemed powerless to end the recession.

# Economic Development of the Pacific Rim

Southeast Asia and East Asia are part of a region known as the Pacific Rim, a group of nations in Asia and the Americas that border the Pacific Ocean. The Pacific began to be an important highway for trade in the 1500s. In the latter half of the 1900s, activity in this area increased dramatically. Some people predict that the 2000s will be the "Pacific century." The size of the area's population makes it a huge market.

## Preparing for the Regents

- Answer the following questions.

1. How did the United States play a vital role in the economic recovery of Europe and Japan?

2. Why did the United States want Europe and Japan to enjoy economic recovery?

## Key Themes and Concepts

**Science and Technology** Among the many reasons for the rapid growth of the Japanese economy was the effectiveness with which Japan adapted western technology.

Four economies in the area have become known as the "Asian Tigers." Taiwan, Hong Kong, Singapore, and South Korea. The Asian Tigers are given this name because of their aggressive economic growth. These economies have followed the Japanese model. They experienced rapid industrialization that led to economic expansion and prosperity.

- **Taiwan** at first set up light industries, such as textile factories. In time, heavy industry developed and created a trade boom, the growth of industrial cities, and a higher standard of living.
- **Hong Kong** is a small island. Formerly a British colony, Hong Kong was returned to communist China in 1997 but was allowed to retain a capitalist economy. Hong Kong is a major financial center with many foreign banks and a busy stock market.
- **Singapore** is a city-state, located on a tiny island at the tip of the Malay Peninsula. Singapore includes one of the world's busiest harbors and is a center of trade.
- **South Korea** initially exported textiles and inexpensive goods. By the 1990s, South Korea was an economic powerhouse, exporting such higher-priced goods as automobiles.

## Oil, OPEC, and Economic Interdependence

Oil became the most important energy resource after World War II. Global economic interdependence is shown in the crises that have developed over oil. Much of the world's oil comes from the Middle East.

### The Formation of OPEC

In 1960, Iran, Iraq, Kuwait, Saudi Arabia, and Venezuela formed **OPEC**, whose initials stand for the Organization of Petroleum Exporting Countries. Other oil producers joined later and, in 2009, there were 12 members. OPEC's goal was to control the oil industry by setting production levels and prices.

### OPEC and Oil Crises

In 1973, OPEC nations halted exports of oil to certain countries. Egypt and Israel were at war, and Arab countries declared the embargo against the United States and other countries that supported Israel. Prices skyrocketed, affecting western economies by slowing growth. In the 1980s and 1990s, a surplus of oil allowed prices to fall.

## Summary

In the years after 1945, some countries developed market economies, while others developed command economies. Developing nations struggled to build their economies. Western Europe and Japan, with the help of the United States, achieved economic success. Through international trade, the Pacific Rim became important to the global economy. Interdependence characterized the world economy. Oil crises in the Middle East, for example, slowed western economic growth.

# Chinese Communist Revolution

## The
# Big
# Idea

Since 1949, a communist government has ruled China.

- Popular support and military power helped the Communists come to power.

- The programs of Mao Zedong hurt China economically and violated human rights.

- Deng Xiaoping brought economic reforms but not political reforms to China.

## Section Overview

The establishment of the People's Republic of China in 1949 began a new period in Chinese history. Communists had risen to power during the 1930s and 1940s by appealing to a large part of the population and by achieving military superiority. Under the communist dictatorship of Mao Zedong, however, programs such as the Great Leap Forward and the Cultural Revolution had negative economic results and restricted people's rights and freedoms. The next leader, Deng Xiaoping, made economic reforms but not political ones. The communist government continued to maintain strict control over people's lives.

## Key Themes and Concepts

As you review this section, take special note of the following key themes and concepts:

**Conflict** How did the Communists come to power in China by 1949?

**Human Rights** In what ways did the communist government improve the status of women in China? How has the Chinese government violated people's rights?

**Change** What changes did Mao Zedong bring to China after 1949?

**Economic Systems** How did Deng Xiaoping reform the economy, and what were the results?

## Key People
### and Terms

- What do three of the key people and terms have in common? Explain.

## Key People and Terms

As you review this section, be sure you understand the significance of these key people and terms:

| | | |
|---|---|---|
| **Mao Zedong** | **communes** | **Deng Xiaoping** |
| **Long March** | **Cultural Revolution** | **Tiananmen Square** |
| **Great Leap Forward** | **Red Guards** | |

## Key Themes
### and Concepts

**Geography**
China, the largest Asian country and the most populous nation in the world, is located in eastern Asia. Mountains, deserts, and jungles separate China from neighboring lands.

## Two Chinas

Today, China is the most populous nation in the world. There are two Chinas, however. The People's Republic of China is a communist state on the Asian mainland. It has a vast land area and many natural resources. Taiwan, also called the Republic of China, is a small island that today is one of the Asian Tigers. It has a noncommunist government. The People's Republic of China still considers Taiwan a part of China proper. Efforts to reunite the two Chinas have sometimes led to tension because Taiwan values its independence.

# Communist Rise to Power

As you recall, Jiang Jieshi (also called Chiang Kai-shek) had taken over the Guomindang, or Nationalist Party, after the death of Sun Yixian. In the mid-1920s, Jiang began to strike at the Communist Party, which he saw as a threat to his leadership.

**Mao Zedong** emerged as the leader of the Communists in the 1930s. Along with 100,000 of his followers, Mao fled the Guomindang forces in 1934 in a retreat known as the **Long March.** After traveling more than 6,000 miles, Mao set up a base in northern China with about 20,000 survivors of the march. In the years that followed, the Communists, the Guomindang, and Japanese invaders battled for control of China. After World War II, civil war continued. Finally, in 1949, Mao's Communists were victorious. Jiang and his followers fled to the island of Taiwan.

## Reasons for Communist Success

There were several reasons for the victory of Mao and the Communists over Jiang and the Guomindang.

- Mao won the support of the huge peasant population of China by promising to give land to peasants.
- Mao won the support of women by rejecting the inequalities of traditional Confucian society.
- Mao's army made good use of hit-and-run guerrilla warfare.
- Many people opposed the Nationalist government, which they saw as corrupt.
- Some people felt that the Nationalists had allowed foreigners to dominate China.

# Communism Under Mao Zedong

The Communists set up the People's Republic of China (PRC) in 1949. They wanted to transform China from an agricultural society into a modern industrial nation. Under communism, literacy increased, old landlord and business classes were eliminated, and rural Chinese were provided with health care. However, Mao set up a one-party dictatorship that denied people basic rights and freedoms.

## The Changing Role of Women

Traditionally, in China, women were treated as inferior to men. The only role for a woman recognized by the five Confucian relationships was that of wife. As a wife, a woman was considered inferior to her husband. The Nationalists did not change these policies greatly.

In Communist China, however, women gained some rights. Under the new Chinese constitution, women won equality under the law. They were now expected to work alongside men on farms and in factories.

Although Chinese women made progress, they did not have full equality with men. Only a few women had top jobs in government. Women were not always paid the same wages as men for doing the same work. Even so, the position of women improved under the Communists.

## The Great Leap Forward

In 1958, Mao launched a program called the **Great Leap Forward.** He called on the people to increase agricultural and industrial output. To make farms more productive, he created **communes,** groups of people who live and work together and hold property in common. Communes had production quotas, which were set amounts of agricultural or industrial output that they were to produce.

## Note Taking

*Reading Skill:*
**Recognize Sequence**
Keep track of important dates in Mao Zedong's rule in China. A table has been started for you. Add boxes as needed.

| Mao Zedong in China | |
| --- | --- |
| **Date** | **Event** |
| 1930s | |
| 1934 | |
| | |
| | |

## Preparing for the Regents

- Why were Mao and the Communists victorious over Jiang and the Nationalists in China's civil war?

## Key Themes and Concepts

**Change**
Describe three similarities between the Chinese Communist Revolution and other revolutions you have studied.

**Human Rights**
Chinese women gained some rights under communism. However, they never gained full equality. Very few women were able to acquire top government jobs, and most women did not get paid as much as men who did the same work.

**Political Systems**
Describe three similarities
between communism in
China and communism in
the Soviet Union.

1.

2.

3.

The Great Leap Forward failed. Commune-based industries turned out poorly made goods. At the same time, agricultural output declined. Bad weather added to the downturn, creating widespread famine.

### The Cultural Revolution

In 1966, Mao launched the **Cultural Revolution** to renew people's loyalty to communism and establish a more equitable society. Mao feared that revolutionary peasants and workers were being replaced by intellectuals in running the country. He shut down schools and universities throughout China and urged Chinese students to experience the revolution for themselves. Students formed groups of fighters called the **Red Guards.** They attacked professors, government officials, and factory managers, many of whom were exiled or executed.

#### Programs of Mao Zedong

*Programs of Mao Zedong*
*Mao Zedong built a*
*Communist totalitarian*
*state. His government and*
*programs tried to reshape*
*the economy and society.*

| Program | The Great Leap Forward | The Cultural Revolution |
|---|---|---|
| Goals | • Increase farm and factory output | • Renew communist loyalties |
| Methods | • Communes<br>• Production quotas | • Red Guards attack professors and other officials |
| Results | • Program fails<br>• Two years of hunger and low production | • Economy slows<br>• China closes to outside world<br>• People fear arrest<br>• Civil war threatened |

### United States Recognition

Vocabulary
Builder

<u>rage</u>—(rayj) *v.* if something
such as a battle, a
disagreement, or a storm
rages, it continues with
great violence or strong
emotions

The Cold War was raging in 1949. Consequently, the United States had refused to recognize the People's Republic of China. In the Korean War, Communist China and the United States took opposing sides. By the 1970s, however, this situation was changing. China won admission to the United Nations in 1971, and President Richard Nixon visited Mao Zedong in Beijing in 1972. In 1979, the United States officially recognized the People's Republic of China.

## Communism Under Deng Xiaoping

In 1976, Mao Zedong died. **Deng Xiaoping** took control. His leadership brought more economic freedom but little political change.

### Economic Reforms: The Four Modernizations

To make China a more modern country, Deng promoted foreign trade and more contact with western nations. He also introduced the Four Modernizations. These were concentrated in four areas.

- **Farming** methods were modernized and mechanized.
- **Industry** was upgraded and expanded.
- **Science and technology** were promoted and developed.
- **Defense** systems and military forces were improved.

**Limited Privatization** Deng got rid of Mao's unpopular communes. He allowed land to be leased to individual farmers. After delivering a certain amount of food to the government, farmers could grow anything they wished and sell it for profit. This system increased agricultural output. The government also allowed some private businesses to produce goods and offer services.

**Foreign Investment** Deng also welcomed foreign technology and capital. The government set up special enterprise zones where foreigners could own and operate businesses.

Preparing for
the Regents

• Describe two ways in
which Deng Xiaoping's
methods differed from
Mao Zedong's.

1.

2.

**Results of Reforms** Deng's policies had both positive and negative results. The economy grew, and some Chinese enjoyed a better standard of living. Foreign relations and trade improved. Crime and corruption grew, however, and the gap between rich and poor widened. Deng's economic changes caused some Chinese to demand greater political freedom.

## Tiananmen Square

The government was willing to grant economic reforms but not political ones. In May 1989, demonstrators in Beijing occupied **Tiananmen Square,** demanding more rights and freedoms. When they refused to disperse as ordered, the government sent in troops and tanks. Thousands of Chinese were killed or wounded. The incident showed how important it was for China's communist leaders to maintain control. Order was more important than political freedom. During the 1990s, efforts were made to force China to end human rights violations. However, these efforts had limited effects.

Source: Henry Payne reprinted by permission of United Feature Syndicate, Inc.

## Return of Hong Kong

In 1842, Great Britain had gained the island of Hong Kong, off the northern coast of China. During the years that Hong Kong was under British rule, it modernized and became wealthy.

In the 1980s, Britain and China decided that Hong Kong would return to Chinese rule in 1997. China agreed not to change Hong Kong's social or economic system for 50 years and to allow the island a degree of self-rule. The island was turned over to China on July 1, 1997.

## Summary

The Communists, under Mao Zedong, rose to power in China after World War II. Their appeal to peasants and to women, their superior army, and lack of support for the Nationalists led to victory for the Communists. The communist government severely restricted the rights and freedoms of most Chinese. Later leaders, such as Deng Xiaoping, allowed free market reforms but little political freedom. Violations of human rights in China have often made relations between China and the United States difficult.

**Vocabulary Builder**

disperse—(dis PURS) *v.* if a group of people disperse or are dispersed, they go away in different directions

**Preparing for the Regents**

• Why do you think the leaders of China were willing to accept western economic reforms but not western ideas about human rights and political freedom?

**Preparing for the Regents**

• Describe in your own words what this 1989 cartoon says about Chinese leadership and the wishes of the Chinese people.

**Key Themes and Concepts**

**Economic Systems**
• If Hong Kong is allowed to keep a free market economy, how might that affect the rest of China?

**Preparing for the Regents**

• Create a political cartoon that comments on a major development in China since the 1940s.

# Collapse of European Imperialism

## Key People and Terms

Place each of the key people and terms into these two categories: leader or conflict/cooperation.

## Section Overview

The period after World War II marked the final collapse of European imperialism. India gained independence in 1947 but struggled with ethnic and religious conflicts. In Africa, independence was achieved both through peaceful efforts and through bloody conflicts. In South Africa, years of racial separation ended, and black South Africans gained a voice in government. In Southeast Asia, the struggle for independence came to an end only after many years of civil and international war.

## Key Themes and Concepts

As you review this section, take special note of the following key themes and concepts:

**Imperialism** How did European imperialism collapse?

**Nationalism** How did nationalistic movements in Asia, Africa, and Southeast Asia result in independence?

**Political and Economic Systems** What kinds of political and economic systems developed in newly independent nations?

## Key People and Terms

As you review this section, be sure you understand the significance of these key people and terms:

| | |
|---|---|
| Mohandas Gandhi | African National Congress |
| Jawaharlal Nehru | Nelson Mandela |
| nonalignment | Desmond Tutu |
| Sikhism | F. W. de Klerk |
| Pan-Africanism | Ho Chi Minh |
| Kwame Nkrumah | Ngo Dinh Diem |
| Organization of African Unity | Khmer Rouge |
| Jomo Kenyatta | Pol Pot |
| tribalism | Aung San Suu Kyi |
| apartheid | |

## Indian Independence and Partition

Indian nationalists had been demanding independence since the 1800s. Indians were angered when, during World War II, the British put off granting them independence but expected them to support Great Britain in the war. **Mohandas Gandhi,** as you have read, played an important part in the independence movement with his policy of passive resistance. Over time, British control of India was weakened. Finally, in 1947, Britain granted independence to India. **Jawaharlal Nehru,** India's first prime minister, celebrated Independence Day with an impassioned speech, full of hope for India's future. Independence, however, brought some difficult problems.

## Muslim and Hindu Conflicts

In India, Hindus were the majority, and Muslims were the minority. The Muslim League had been demanding a Muslim state. Also, there had been fighting between Muslims and Hindus. In 1947, British officials drew borders that created Hindu India and Muslim Pakistan. Pakistan was made up of West Pakistan and East Pakistan, two widely separated areas that had high Muslim populations. East Pakistan later became the nation of Bangladesh.

The partition, or division, of India did not bring peace. Independence set off mass migrations of Muslims fleeing India and Hindus fleeing Pakistan. Millions were killed crossing the borders. Mohandas Gandhi tried to bring peace, but a Hindu fanatic assassinated him.

Although the worst violence began to lessen after Gandhi's death, conflicts continued to occur. In the years ahead, Indian and Pakistani forces would clash repeatedly over border disputes. Tensions between Hindus and Muslims still exist and continue to erupt into violence today.

## Indian Government and Foreign Policy

**A Democratic Nation** India is the world's largest democracy. It has a federal system of government, with powers divided between a strong central government and smaller local governments. For 40 years after independence, India was led by members of the Nehru family. Jawaharlal Nehru was the first prime minister.

Ethnic and religious conflicts have made democracy difficult for India. After Nehru's death, his daughter, **Indira Gandhi,** became prime minister in 1966. She was assassinated in 1984, and her son, Rajiv Gandhi, became prime minister. He too was assassinated, however, in 1991.

**Nonalignment** During the Cold War, India followed a policy of nonalignment. This policy, instituted by Jawaharlal Nehru, allowed India to accept help from both capitalist and socialist nations.

### Obstacles to Progress in India

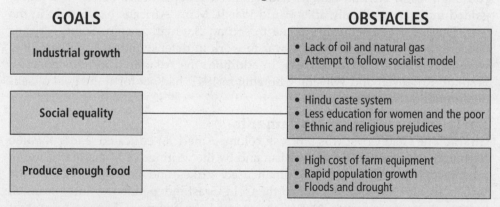

| GOALS | OBSTACLES |
|---|---|
| Industrial growth | • Lack of oil and natural gas<br>• Attempt to follow socialist model |
| Social equality | • Hindu caste system<br>• Less education for women and the poor<br>• Ethnic and religious prejudices |
| Produce enough food | • High cost of farm equipment<br>• Rapid population growth<br>• Floods and drought |

## Social Change in India

**The Caste System** The caste system, a system of social stratification, has been a part of Indian life for more than 2,000 years. In the 1900s, the system underwent change.

- Mohandas Gandhi campaigned to end the harsh treatment of the caste called Untouchables.
- The Indian constitution of 1950 banned discrimination against Untouchables.
- The government set aside jobs and places in universities for Untouchables.

### Key Themes and Concepts

**Nationalism**
In India, nationalism resulted in freedom from colonial rule. Religious conflict led to the creation of two nations: India and Pakistan.

### Note Taking

*Reading Skill:*
**Categorize**
Make a table. As you read, fill in the categories for India.

| India | |
|---|---|
| government | |
| foreign policy | |
| economy | |
| religion | |
| social system | |

### Key Themes and Concepts

**Economic Systems**
Nonalignment allowed developing nations to accept help from both communist and capitalist nations. India was a leader among nonaligned nations.

### Preparing for the Regents

- How is the caste system that exists in India today different from the caste system of the past?

In spite of improvements in the legal status of Untouchables, discrimination still exists. Although there are movements for caste reform, the system is still a part of Indian society. It has a stronger effect in rural villages than in urban areas.

**The Status of Women** The Indian constitution of 1950 also granted rights to women. It gave women the right to vote and recognized their right to divorce and inherit property. Indira Gandhi, a woman, became prime minister in 1966. As with the caste system, traditional restrictions on women are more persistent in rural areas.

## Sikh Separatism

**Sikhism** is a religion that began in India in the 1500s by blending elements of Islam and Hinduism. In the 1980s, there was an increased demand for self-rule by Sikhs in the state of Punjab. In the early 1980s, Sikh separatists occupied the Golden Temple in Amritsar to express their demands. Indira Gandhi, still prime minister at the time, sent troops. Many Sikhs died as a result. Not long after that, Gandhi herself was assassinated by two Sikhs who had served as her bodyguards. Continuing tension exists between Sikhs and Hindus.

## Dispute Over Kashmir

India and Pakistan have disputed control of the state of Kashmir since the partition of the Indian subcontinent in 1947. Although governed by the secular government of India, the population of Kashmir is predominantly Muslim. The two nations fought wars over Kashmir in 1947–1948 and in 1965 and maintain a fragile truce today. In recent years there have been a number of terrorist attacks by Islamic separatists, which raise the fear of war between these two nuclear powers.

# Independent Nations in Africa

A movement called Pan-Africanism had been nourishing nationalist movements in Africa since the 1920s. **Pan-Africanism** emphasized the unity of Africans and people of African descent all over the world.

Although a few African nations had achieved independence before 1945, most gained independence only after World War II. Many Africans had fought in the war. They resented returning home to second-class citizenship. Some Africans had migrated to cities during the war to work in defense industries. There they were exposed to nationalist ideas. In addition, the Atlantic Charter, signed by Franklin Roosevelt and Winston Churchill in 1941, had set forth the goal of self-determination for all nations.

## Early Independence Movements

**Ghana** The Gold Coast was a British colony. American-educated leader **Kwame Nkrumah,** inspired by Pan-Africanism and by the writings of Mohandas Gandhi, organized a political party. Nkrumah used strikes and boycotts to battle the British. In 1957, the British granted the Gold Coast independence, and Nkrumah became its prime minister. Nkrumah renamed the country Ghana, a name that linked the new nation to its African past. In 1963, Nkrumah created the **Organization of African Unity,** or OAU. This group promoted Pan-Africanism and the end of colonialism in Africa.

**Kenya** In the British colony of Kenya, the independence struggle was led by **Jomo Kenyatta.** He was a spokesman for the Kikuyu people, who had been driven off their land by European settlers. When some Kikuyu turned to violent means to gain liberation, the British jailed Kenyatta. Later, however, Kenyatta was released. In 1963, he became the first prime minister of an independent Kenya.

## Key Themes and Concepts

**Diversity**
India is a land of diverse peoples with differing religions and languages. The majority of the people is Hindu, but minorities hope to gain power; some even hope to create their own nations.

## Vocabulary Builder

truce—(troos) *n.* an agreement between enemies to stop fighting or arguing

## Preparing for the Regents

—List three ways in which World War II increased the desire for independence among Africans.

1.

2.

3.

## Preparing for the Regents

• Describe how nationalism led to independence in Ghana.

## Obstacles to Progress in Africa

Many of Africa's nations gained independence only after 1945, and more gained independence after 1959. The end of colonialism presented many challenges to the development of the countries of Africa.

Like other developing nations, African countries have focused on building industry and improving agriculture. Although industrial growth has sometimes been successful, many nations remain dependent on imports. Also, money borrowed to build industry created great debts. In some nations, such as Nigeria, people flocked to industrial centers. Food production fell, and rural poverty resulted. Cities could not keep up with population increases.

A continuing reliance on cash crops means that many African nations still need to import food to feed their growing populations. Cash crop economies also have other negative effects. For example, when oil prices fell, the economy of Nigeria—a nation rich in oil—nearly collapsed.

**Vocabulary Builder**

reliance—(rih LY uns) *n.* when someone or something is dependent on someone or something else

### Obstacles to Progress in Africa

**Population and Poverty**
- Population explosion
- Widespread hunger

**Economic Policies**
- Failed socialist and mixed economy problems
- Cash crops instead of food crops
- Lack of funding for rural development

**OBSTACLES**

**Political Problems**
- Power-hungry, greedy leaders
- Military takeovers
- Harsh dictators
- Ethnic and regional conflicts

**Land and Climate**
- Too much or too little rain
- Poor soil
- Tropical diseases
- Desert climate

**Economic Dependence**
- Need for foreign aid
- Need for imported equipment and goods
- High debts

**Preparing for the Regents**

- Practice your chart reading skills by listing and briefly explaining five obstacles to progress in Africa.

1.

2.

3.

4.

5.

Even so, Africa shows great potential.

- Many African nations have moved from a socialist model to a free market economy, experiencing growth as a result.
- Other nations have expanded mining and manufacturing and built factories to process agricultural products.
- Some nations have improved transportation and communication.

## Economic Links With Europe

Today, much of Africa suffers from trading patterns that were established during the age of imperialism. European nations had created colonial economies that depended on the export of raw materials and cash crops from Africa. Many African nations still rely on the export of just a few products. When the prices of these products fall, the nations' economies can be devastated. Many African countries also rely greatly on manufactured goods imported from Europe. As a result, these countries have trade deficits and rising debts.

Strong economic links have been maintained between many African nations and the colonial powers that once ruled them. Some former French colonies, for example, have adopted the French currency and many give preference to French products. This also occurs in countries that were once British colonies, especially those that are members of the Commonwealth, an association of former British colonies.

**Key Themes and Concepts**

**Imperialism**
The pattern of dependence fostered by imperialism made it difficult for most African nations to build strong economies and stable political systems.

## Preparing for the Regents

- How did the borders drawn by colonial powers eventually contribute to civil war in Africa?

# Ethnic Tensions and Nationalism

Most of the current national boundaries in Africa were established during the colonial period by Europeans. Unfortunately, the boundaries were made without consideration for the traditional territories of tribal and ethnic groups. As a result, some ethnic groups were separated into different nations. Other ethnic groups were united within nations. Today, therefore, loyalty to one's tribe is often stronger than loyalty to one's nation.

Nigeria is one of the many nations where **tribalism** has led to civil war. More than 200 ethnic groups live within the borders of Nigeria. At independence, several of the larger groups fought for power. Among these groups were the Muslim Hausa and Fulani peoples in the north and the Christian Ibo and Yoruba peoples in the south.

In 1966, a massacre of 20,000 Ibo took place. At the time, Hausa dominated the government. The next year, the Ibo declared their region independent, calling it Biafra. A war raged for several years. Nigeria imposed a blockade of Biafra that ended the war, but not before nearly a million people had been killed in the war or died of starvation.

## Preparing for the Regents

- Use your knowledge of global history and recent current events to compare the genocide that occurred in Rwanda with another historical example of genocide.

In Rwanda, ethnic conflict led to genocide. Before 1994, Rwanda was 85 percent Hutu and 14 percent Tutsi. In 1994, Hutu extremists, supported by government officials, launched a murderous campaign against the Tutsis. According to estimates, more than 500,000 people were killed in just a few months. The genocide was stopped when a Tutsi-led rebel army seized control of the government.

In 2002, 53 African countries formed a federation, the African Union (AU). Its goals include solving economic, social, political, and environmental problems in Africa. AU members deal with issues such as desertification, AIDS, and famine. Eventually the AU plans to create an economic bloc, such as the European Union.

The AU also works to control conflicts that spill refugees, violence, and economic destruction into neighboring countries. Such a conflict has been occurring in Darfur, a region of western Sudan, since 2003. Arabic militias have killed more than 200,000 villagers, with the quiet approval of the Sudanese government. More than two million villagers have become refugees. The UN is trying to get Sudan to agree to allow a UN peacekeeping force in the country.

## Vocabulary Builder

desertification—(dih zurt uh fih KAY shun) *n.* the process by which useful land, especially farm land, changes into desert

# End of Apartheid in South Africa

For nearly 350 years, Europeans ruled South Africa. Although South Africa won independence from Britain in 1910, its white citizens alone held political power. To control the nation's government and economy, whites in 1948 made official a system of **apartheid,** or separation of the races. Apartheid required black Africans and other nonwhites to live in certain zones, segregated public facilities and transportation, and forbade interracial marriage.

**The Anti-apartheid Movement** In 1912, a political party, later known as the **African National Congress** (ANC), was organized in South Africa. The ANC used violence as well as boycotts and nonviolent civil disobedience to oppose apartheid.

## Preparing for the Regents

- Describe the role of each of the following figures in the ending of apartheid.

Nelson Mandela:

Desmond Tutu:

F. W. de Klerk:

In 1960, the police killed 69 people and wounded 180 at a demonstration in Sharpeville. The South African government reacted by outlawing the ANC. In 1964, **Nelson Mandela,** an important ANC leader, was sentenced to life in prison. He became a powerful symbol of the struggle for freedom.

**Desmond Tutu,** a black Anglican bishop and civil rights leader, along with other activists convinced foreign nations and businesses to limit trade and investment in segregated South Africa. Over time, these nonviolent means of protest had a strong effect.

**F. W. de Klerk** became president of South Africa in 1989. Knowing reform was necessary, he legalized the ANC, repealed segregation laws, and released Mandela in 1990. In 1994, South Africa held an election in which people of all races could vote. Mandela was elected president. He was succeeded in 1999 by Thabo Mbeki.

### Truth and Reconciliation

The South African Truth and Reconciliation Commission (TRC) was set up by the new South African government to help deal with the violence and human rights abuses which occurred under apartheid. Its task was to discover and reveal past wrongdoing by the government, in the hope of resolving conflict left over from the past. Anyone who felt that he or she was a victim of its violence was invited to come forward and be heard. Perpetrators of violence could also give testimony and request amnesty from prosecution.

## Difficult Struggles in Southeast Asia

After World War II, growing nationalist feeling spread through Indochina and other parts of Southeast Asia. Southeast Asians fought against foreign imperialist powers to gain their freedom. They also fought among themselves in bloody civil wars.

**Southeast Asia**

**Note Taking**

*Reading Skill:* **Identify Causes and Effects**
Make a flowchart. Show the causes and effects of the formation of the TRC.

*Southeast Asia*
*Southeast Asia includes part of the Asian mainland and thousands of islands. By World War II, European countries and the United States had colonized much of the area.*

## Vietnam

Vietnam had been ruled by the French since the mid-1800s. During World War II, the Vietminh, an alliance of nationalist and communist groups, fought the occupying Japanese. After the war, the French hoped to regain Vietnam. Instead, **Ho Chi Minh,** leader of the Vietminh, declared Vietnam free. Defeated by the Vietminh, the French abandoned Vietnam. A 1954 conference in Geneva led to the division of Vietnam into a communist north and a non-commmunist south.

**The Vietnam War** Elections were supposed to be held in 1956 to unite Vietnam. However, the American-supported South Vietnamese government of **Ngo Dinh Diem** did not hold the elections because it feared that the Communists would win. Ho Chi Minh, now leader of communist North Vietnam, supported the Vietcong, a group of communist rebels who were trying to overthrow Diem. The United States sent troops to support Diem's government. The Vietnam War lasted from 1959 to 1975. By 1969, more than 500,000 Americans were serving in Vietnam. However, even with this help, the South Vietnamese could not defeat the communist forces. Growing antiwar sentiment in the United States forced President Nixon to withdraw American forces. In 1975, Saigon, the capital of the south, fell. The country was reunited under communist control.

## Cambodia

During the Vietnam War, Cambodia served as a supply route for the Vietcong and North Vietnamese forces. In 1969, American forces bombed and then invaded Cambodia to destroy that route. After the Americans left, Cambodian communist guerrillas, known as the **Khmer Rouge,** took control of the government. Under the leadership of **Pol Pot,** the Khmer Rouge began a reign of terror to remove all western influence from Cambodia. More than a million Cambodians were slaughtered in what has become known as the "Killing Fields." In 1979, Vietnamese forces invaded Cambodia and occupied the country. In the early 1990s, a settlement was negotiated to end the civil war. UN peacekeepers monitored elections, but some fighting continued.

## Myanmar

Myanmar, formerly called Burma, had been a British possession in the 1800s. In the mid-1900s, it gained independence, but it was plagued with ethnic tensions and ruled by a repressive military. Myanmar is a very poor country, and living standards have not improved in recent years.

Opposition to repression by the military rule grew through the 1980s. In 1990, the opposition party, led by **Aung San Suu Kyi,** won an electoral victory. However, the military rejected the election results and put Suu Kyi under house arrest. She was released in 1995, but rearrested and resentenced to house arrest in 2000 and 2003. Since then her sentence has been extended yearly.

## Summary

European imperialism collapsed throughout the world in the years after World War II. In India, independence was accompanied by conflicts among various ethnic and religious groups. In Africa, nations suffered from the legacy left by colonial rule. Tribal conflicts brought civil war to many nations. In South Africa, the repressive system of apartheid was finally ended. In Southeast Asia, it took years of war to drive out the French. Then another war erupted between communist North Vietnam and noncommunist South Vietnam. Despite United States intervention, the communist forces were victorious. In Cambodia, a civil war resulted in the death of approximately 1 million people.

### Key Themes and Concepts

**Conflict**
In Vietnam, a local independence movement became a major Cold War battleground.

### Note Taking

*Reading Skill:*
**Summarize**
Make a chart. Summarize the events connected to the struggles in Southeast Asia.

### Vocabulary Builder

plague—(playg) *v.* to cause pain, suffering, or trouble, especially for a long period of time

### Preparing for the Regents

- List three results of the collapse of European imperialism in the years after World War II.

1.

2.

3.

# Conflicts and Change in the Middle East

## Section Overview

Since 1945, the Middle East has been an area of tension and change. The state of Israel was created in 1948. After years of conflict between Israel and its Arab neighbors, the quest for peace began to achieve some success. In Lebanon, years of civil war ravaged the country. In Iran, an Islamic republic was born. Several international conflicts centered on Iraq, largely because of its dictator, Saddam Hussein. Throughout the Middle East, many Muslims have called for a return to a life based on Islamic law.

## Key Themes and Concepts

As you review this section, take special note of the following key themes and concepts:

**Diversity** How has the diversity of the Middle East affected its recent history?

**Conflict** What efforts have been made to end conflict between Israel and its Arab neighbors?

**Interdependence** Why did the Persian Gulf War involve many nations from around the world?

**Belief Systems** How is Islamic fundamentalism affecting life in the Middle East today?

## Key People and Terms

As you review this section, be sure you understand the significance of these key people and terms:

Palestine Liberation Organization (PLO)

Yasir Arafat

intifada

Camp David Accords

Yitzhak Rabin

King Hussein

Hamas

Ayatollah Khomeini

Islamic fundamentalism

Taliban

Saddam Hussein

Persian Gulf War

Kurds

## The Impact of Geography

The Middle East has been a crossroads for people of Africa, Asia, and Europe since ancient times. This fact has led to an enormous diversity of peoples, belief systems, and cultures. These differences have sometimes led to conflict.

The discovery of oil in the region brought power to some Middle Eastern nations. Oil is a vital part of the global economy. Oil resources, however, are not evenly distributed across the region. As a result, Middle Eastern countries have gone to war over control of oil-rich lands. Dependence on oil is one reason why countries around the world take an active interest in conflicts in the Middle East.

---

### The Big Idea

In the Middle East, since 1945:

- the creation of Israel has led to conflicts between Jews and Arabs.

- the search for peace between Jews and Arabs has met with some success.

- a revolution in Iran has led to an Islamic republic.

- Iraq has been involved in several international conflicts.

- many Muslims have urged a return to Islamic government and law.

### Key People and Terms

Place each of the key people and terms into these three categories: politics, conflict/cooperation, and belief system.

### Key Themes and Concepts

**Geography**
- What impact has geography had on the culture and history of the Middle East?

### Forces Shaping the Middle East

| Religious and Ethnic Differences | Natural Resources | Governments | Islamic Traditions |
|---|---|---|---|
| • Muslims, Christians, and Jews<br>• Different sects within religions<br>• More than 30 languages<br>• Religious, racial, and cultural prejudices<br>• Desire for a united Arab state | • Largest oil fields in the world<br>• Oil-rich nations gain wealth and political and economic power<br>• Limited water supply<br>• Arguments over dams and water rights | • Democracy in Israel and Turkey<br>• Rule by royal family in Jordan and Saudi Arabia<br>• Single-party dictators in Iraq and Syria | • Laws of Islam influence government, society, and personal life<br>• Antiwestern feelings<br>• 1990s revival of Islamic traditions |

## A Jewish State Among Arab Nations

Jews had begun migrating to Palestine in the late 1800s as part of the Zionist movement. During World War I, the British made conflicting promises to the Jews and Palestinians about creating a Jewish homeland in the area. After World War II and the Holocaust, there was increased support for a Jewish state in Palestine. However, both Jews and Palestinian Arabs claimed a right to the land of Palestine. Jews claimed that they were entitled to return to a land they had once ruled 3,000 years ago. The Palestinian Arabs claimed they were entitled to the land they took over circa 70 A.D., when the Jews were forced from their land by the Romans. Many violent clashes between these two groups have occurred since 1947.

### Creation of Israel

In 1947, the United Nations drew up a plan to divide Palestine, which was under British rule, into an Arab state and a Jewish state. Jews accepted the plan, but Arabs did not. In 1948, Great Britain withdrew, and Jews proclaimed the independent state of Israel, which was recognized by both the United States and the Soviet Union.

Israel developed rapidly. Between 1948 and the mid-1980s, nearly two million Jews migrated to Israel, some to escape persecution. The government built towns for settlers. A skilled workforce expanded the economy. American aid helped Israel as well.

### Palestinians and Arab-Israeli Wars

When the state of Israel was created, Arab nations vowed to drive the Jews out and restore Palestine as an Arab nation. Since 1948, there have been four full-scale wars and several smaller conflicts between Israel and the Arab states.

**War of Independence** The first Arab-Israeli war occurred in 1948 when six Arab states—Egypt, Iraq, Jordan, Lebanon, Syria, and Saudi Arabia—invaded Israel. Israel defeated the invaders and seized land which doubled its size. Over 700,000 Arabs became refugees, fleeing to neighboring countries. Most were placed in temporary refugee camps, which became permanent over time. The poverty and discrimination experienced by these Arab Palestinians fueled anger. Many dreamed of an Arab Palestinian state. Resistance took many forms.

**Palestine Liberation Organization (PLO)** In 1964, the Palestine Liberation Organization (PLO) was formed to push for self-rule for the Palestinians. Led by **Yasir Arafat,** the PLO used terrorist tactics and fought a guerilla war against Israelis at home and abroad.

**Further Wars** Another war was fought over the Suez Canal in 1956. In 1967, during the Six-Day War, Israel overran the Sinai Peninsula, the Golan Heights on the Syrian border, and East Jerusalem. In 1973, Egypt and Syria launched a war against Israel on the Jewish high holy day of Yom Kippur. The Israelis won all of these wars.

**Intifada** In 1987, young Palestinians, who had grown up in the Israeli occupied West Bank and Gaza, and who were frustrated with the lack of progress in gaining a Palestinian state, began widespread acts of civil disobedience called the intifada, or "uprising." Palestinians used boycotts, demonstrations, and attacks on Israeli soldiers by unarmed teenagers throwing rocks and bombs. The intifada continued into the 1990s. Crackdowns by the Israelis led to a wave of sympathy throughout the world for the Palestinians.

## Israel's Changing Borders

*Israel's Changing Borders*
*Modern Israel was established in 1948. Israel and its Arab neighbors fought three wars—in 1956, 1967, and 1973. In these wars, Israel defeated Arab forces and gained more land.*

### Preparing for the Regents

- Practice your map skills by answering the following questions.

1. What countries border Israel?

2. What areas were gained by Israel after the 1967 war?

## Attempts at Peace

Numerous attempts have been made to resolve the situation in Palestine. Limited progress has been made.

**Camp David Accords** In 1979, President Jimmy Carter invited President Anwar Sadat of Egypt and Prime Minister Menachem Begin of Israel to discuss terms of peace. The resulting treaty, the Camp David Accords, was based on the concept of "land for peace." Israel returned the Sinai Peninsula to Egypt in exchange for Egypt's recognition of Israel's right to exist. Sadat was later assassinated by a group of Muslim extremists angered by Egypt's peace with Israel.

**Oslo Peace Accords** In 1993, direct talks were held for the first time between Israel and the PLO. Arafat had renounced the use of terrorism which opened the door for Israeli Prime Minister **Yitzhak Rabin** to sign an agreement giving Palestinians in the Gaza Strip and West Bank limited self-rule. A year later, Jordan, led by **King Hussein,** also made a peace agreement with Israel. In 1995, Rabin was

### Vocabulary Builder

renounce—(rih NOWNS) v. to reject; to publicly say or show that you no longer believe in something, or will no longer behave in a particular way assassinated by right-wing Jewish extremists, opposed to making concessions to the Palestinians.

Israelis continued to build settlements in lands that Palestinians claimed while Palestinian riots and suicide bombers began increasing. In 2002, Israeli military forces invaded Palestinian-ruled areas that were centers of terrorist activities. They arrested or assassinated PLO and other Palestinian leaders. Many Palestinian civilians also died. The U.S., UN, EU, and Russia outlined a roadmap of peace. This plan would establish a Palestinian state, but the PLO had to make democratic reforms and end the use of terrorism. Peace prospects improved when Palestinian leader Yasir Arafat died in 2004.

### Continued Search for Peace

In 2005, cease-fire talks began, and Israel began withdrawing settlers and soldiers from Gaza and parts of the West Bank. In 2006, Palestinians elected **Hamas,** a party known for its social services and its hard-line policies towards Israel. Hamas uses terrorist methods, such as rockets and suicide bombings, against Israel. In 2008, Israel launched a devastating attack on Hamas and Gaza, dimming hopes for a peace settlement. However, the United States continues to work towards a peace settlement in the region.

## Civil War in Lebanon

North of Israel, Lebanon had gained independence after World War II. It was a thriving commercial center with a diverse population. Christians and Muslims lived there together peacefully. However, as Palestinian refugees entered Lebanon, especially after 1967, they created a Muslim majority. The PLO became powerful in Palestinian refugee camps.

A civil war between Christians and Muslims began in 1975. Israeli and Syrian forces participated in the conflict. By 1990, a degree of order had returned to Lebanon. In 2000, Israel withdrew its forces, and Syria followed reluctantly in 2005. In May 2005, Lebanon held its first legislative elections since the civil war. In 2006, Hezbollah, a radical Shi'a group, captured two Israeli soldiers, leading to a 34-day conflict with Israel.

### The Middle East and North Africa

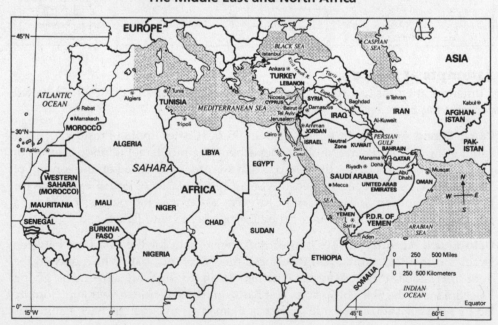

**Draw Conclusions**

- Why does the Arab-Israeli conflict continue today?

**Key Themes and Concepts**

**Diversity**
The diverse population of Lebanon, as well as outside political forces, led to civil war in Lebanon. Diversity has contributed to conflict throughout the Middle East.

*The Middle East and North Africa*
*The Middle East controls large oil resources and important waterways such as the Persian Gulf. Western nations have tried to prevent regional powers from interfering with the oil supply.*

**Preparing for the Regents**

- Which nations border the Persian Gulf?

# The Iranian Revolution

In 1953, Great Britain and the United States helped Muhammad Reza Pahlavi gain control of the Iranian government. He proclaimed himself the shah. He westernized and modernized the country; he also ruled as a dictator.

In the 1970s, opposition to the shah was led by the exiled **Ayatollah Khomeini.** *Ayatollah* is a title given to learned Shiite legal experts. With protests mounting, the shah fled Iran in 1979. Soon afterward, Khomeini returned, declaring Iran an Islamic republic. In 1989, Khomeini died, and more moderate leaders took control. Then, in 2005, elections put conservatives back in power. World concerns grew over Iran's nuclear program, which President Mahmoud Ahmadinejad has refused to curb.

## Impact of the Revolution

The Iranian revolution had effects in Iran and beyond.

- The new Iranian government was extremely hostile to the West, especially to the United States. Western books, music, and movies were banned.
- The government required strict adherence to Muslim religious tradition. There was no separation of religion and government.
- Many rights were taken away from women.
- Iranian militants seized the American embassy in Tehran and held a group of Americans hostage for more than a year.
- Iran encouraged Muslims in other countries to work to overthrow secular governments and establish Islamic republics.

# Islamic Fundamentalism

Beginning in the 1970s, increasing numbers of Muslims opposed westernization. They wanted to apply Islamic principles to the problems in their nations. This movement for reform, called Islamic fundamentalism by many westerners, has played a key role in the Middle East.

- **Libya** In 1969, Muammar al-Qaddafi established a government based on Islamic principles. He supported revolutionary organizations and activities in the Middle East and around the world. Qaddafi renounced terrorism in 1999.
- **Algeria** In 1992, the Algerian Islamic political party did well in elections. The ruling party feared that an Islamic revolution might occur. The military therefore seized power and took harsh measures against Islamic activists, resulting in the deaths of thousands of people. Since 2005, a newly elected government's offer of amnesty to terrorists who lay down their arms has not ended terrorist attacks by groups who want to return to strict Islamic rule.
- **Turkey** Throughout the 1900s, the government of Turkey based many of its policies on western models. In the 1990s, however, Islamic political parties gained increasing support and influence. They hoped to restore traditional Islamic government to Turkey.
- **Afghanistan** From 1979–1989, Afghanistan fought a Soviet invasion to prop up the Afghan Communist government. Following the Soviet withdrawal, the country was torn by civil war. An Islamic group, the **Taliban**, seized power in 1996 and set up an Islamic government. Following the terrorist attacks on the United States on September 11, 2001, an American-led force toppled the Taliban for sheltering **Osama bin Laden.** Despite gains toward building a stable central government, the Taliban still poses a threat to the stability of Afghanistan.

# Saddam Hussein and Iraq

Under the leadership of dictator **Saddam Hussein,** Iraq was involved in several conflicts in the Middle East.

### Iran-Iraq War

In 1980, Hussein's forces seized control of a disputed border area between Iraq and Iran. War broke out between the two nations. When both sides attacked oil tankers in the Persian Gulf, the United States Navy began to protect shipping lanes in the region. The war continued until 1988 and created extreme hardship in both nations.

### Persian Gulf War

In 1990, Iraq invaded Kuwait and seized its oil fields. The United States saw the Iraqi action as a threat to Saudi Arabia and to the flow of oil. The first response of the United States was to organize a trade embargo of Iraq. Peacekeeping troops from many western and Middle Eastern countries went to Saudi Arabia. When Iraq refused to withdraw from Kuwait, the 1991 **Persian Gulf War** began. The United States and its allies quickly won the war, and Kuwait was liberated. The United States continued to view Iraqi dictator Saddam Hussein as a very dangerous force. They hoped that the war would topple his dictatorship. He remained in power, however.

### Iraq War

In 2003, the United States and other nations invaded Iraq, claiming that Iraq's alleged possession of weapons of mass destruction posed an imminent threat to their security. They also cited Saddam Hussein's human rights abuses such as the use of torture and poison gas against the **Kurds,** an ethnic group living in northern Iraq. The invasion led to the quick defeat of the Iraqi military, and the eventual capture and execution of Saddam Hussein. However, it also led to an Iraqi insurgency, conflicts between Sunni and Shia Iraqi groups, and al-Qaeda operations in Iraq.

## Summary

The Middle East is an area of great diversity and economic importance. It is also an area of great conflict. The creation of the state of Israel in 1948 set off years of conflict between Arabs and Jews. A revolution occurred in Iran that created an Islamic republic. A growing influence in the area is that of Islamic fundamentalism, a movement to return to traditional Islamic ways. The aggressive actions of Iraqi leader Saddam Hussein led to a war that involved many countries of the world.

# Collapse of Communism and the Soviet Union

## Section Overview

Eastern Europe underwent great change in the 1980s and 1990s. The Soviet invasion of Afghanistan heightened Cold War tensions and added to Soviet economic problems. Mikhail Gorbachev came to power in the Soviet Union and took steps to reform the economy and allow more openness. His policies contributed to the collapse of communism in Eastern Europe and the breakup of the Soviet Union. By 1989, Germany was reunited. The former Soviet Union and its satellites experienced varying degrees of difficulty as they tried to establish new political and economic systems in their countries. New nations emerged in Eastern Europe, sometimes accompanied by violent ethnic conflict.

## Key Themes and Concepts

As you review this section, take special note of the following key themes and concepts:

**Change** What were the causes and impacts of the collapse of the Soviet Union?

**Diversity and Conflict** How has ethnic diversity contributed to conflict in Eastern Europe?

**Political and Economic Systems** What kinds of problems did Eastern European countries face in the transition to democracy and a market economy?

## Key People and Terms

As you review this section, be sure you understand the significance of these key people and terms:

| | |
|---|---|
| détente | Vladimir Putin |
| Mikhail Gorbachev | Lech Walesa |
| perestroika | Solidarity |
| glasnost | |

## The Big Idea

Between 1970 and 1990, the Soviet Union broke up, and communist control of Eastern Europe ended. During this period:

- the invasion of Afghanistan weakened the Soviet Union.
- Gorbachev's reforms led to the end of the Soviet Union.
- communist governments fell in Eastern Europe.
- ethnic divisions led to civil wars and the creation of new nations.

## Key People and Terms

For each of the key people and terms, write a sentence explaining its significance.

## Easing of Cold War Tensions

By the 1970s, the Cold War had been going on for more than 25 years. Both the United States and the Soviet Union realized that the tension could end in mutual destruction. Large amounts of money were spent by both powers on weapons. Under their leaders, Richard Nixon and Leonid Brezhnev, the United States and the Soviet Union promoted a period of **détente,** or lessening of tension. Détente involved:

- arms control talks and treaties.
- cultural exchanges.
- trade agreements.

## Soviet Invasion of Afghanistan

Détente came to a sudden end with the Soviet invasion of Afghanistan in 1979. The Soviet Union had invaded Afghanistan in order to keep a procommunist government in power there. This move convinced many in the West that the Soviet Union was still an aggressive force.

Relations between the two superpowers worsened. The United States increased defense spending to match the buildup of Soviet arms that had continued during the period of détente. In the Soviet Union, however, the war in Afghanistan was very unpopular.

### Preparing for the Regents

- Define the following two terms, and tell how they affected the Soviet Union.

Perestroika:

Glasnost:

Effect on the Soviet Union:

## Gorbachev in the Soviet Union

In 1985, **Mikhail Gorbachev** came to power in the Soviet Union. Gorbachev wanted to end Cold War tensions. He pulled troops out of Afghanistan. He also reformed the Soviet government and economy.

### Perestroika

Gorbachev restructured the failing state-run command economy in a process called **perestroika.** The goals were to stimulate economic growth and to make industry more efficient. Gorbachev also backed free market reforms. Perestroika had some negative effects, however. Inflation increased, and there were shortages of food and medicine.

### Glasnost

Gorbachev also called for **glasnost,** or openness. This policy ended censorship and encouraged people to discuss openly the problems in the Soviet Union. Gorbachev hoped to win support for his policies both among ordinary citizens and among members of the Communist Party.

*The Fall of the Soviet Union*
*The Cold War between the United States and the Soviet Union lasted almost 50 years. In the years around 1990, the struggle finally ended with the fall of the Soviet Union. After 69 years, the Soviet Union ceased to exist.*

**The Fall of the Soviet Union**

**CAUSES**
- Leadership of Mikhail Gorbachev
- Openness to democratic ideas (*glasnost*)
- Reshaping of economy and government (*perestroika*)
- Economic problems
- Freedom movement in Eastern Europe

**Fall of the Soviet Union**

**EFFECTS**
- Formation of the Commonwealth of Independent States
- Loss of role as world superpower
- End of the Cold War
- Economic hardships
- Conflicts between procommunist and prodemocratic groups
- Minority revolts and civil conflicts

### Preparing for the Regents

- Choose two of the causes shown in this chart and explain briefly how they led to the fall of the Soviet Union.

## Breakup of the Soviet Union

As Gorbachev eased political restrictions, people began to voice their nationalist sentiments. As you have learned, the Soviet Union was a multinational state. People in the non-Russian republics opposed Russian domination. In 1991, the Baltic republics of Estonia, Latvia, and Lithuania regained their independence. Soon, all the Soviet republics declared their independence. The Soviet Union ceased to exist.

In mid-1991, communist hardliners tried to overthrow Gorbachev and restore the previous order. Their attempt failed, but Gorbachev soon resigned. However, Gorbachev's reforms had helped to end communism throughout Eastern Europe. His policies also contributed to the breakup of the Soviet Union.

Source: Reprinted By Permission of Bob Englehart, The Hartford Courant

## Difficult Challenges for Russia

Boris Yeltsin became the Russian president. Yeltsin struggled to make the transition from communism to democracy. One of the most difficult challenges was converting the state-run command economy to a market economy. Industries and farms were privatized. Still, economic problems grew worse. Food shortages increased and unemployment rose.

Yeltsin retired in 1999. To succeed him, voters chose **Vladimir Putin.** For the first time in Russian history, power passed peacefully from one elected leader to another. Putin curbed the power of regional leaders and exerted control over the Duma, Russia's legislature. He also sought a new relationship with the West. In 2002, Russia signed a nuclear arms reduction agreement with the United States and began a new era of cooperation with NATO. Although Putin's policies have led to economic growth, there are growing concerns about his suppression of dissent and the future of democracy in Russia.

**Vocabulary Builder**

voice—(voys) v. to tell people your opinions or feelings about a particular subject

**Preparing for the Regents**

- Explain the meaning of the political cartoon on this page.

**Note Taking**

*Reading Skill:*
**Summarize**
Make a table. Summarize each leader's time in power.

| Soviet Union/Russian Leaders | |
|---|---|
| Gorbachev | |
| Yeltsin | |
| Putin | |

**Preparing for the Regents**

- Identify and explain three key events in the fall of communism in Eastern Europe.

# Eastern Europe Transformed

Throughout Eastern Europe, Gorbachev's reforms had sparked demands for democracy and national independence. Poland, East Germany, Romania, Bulgaria, and other countries of Eastern Europe broke away from Soviet control. Through much of the region, there were attempts to enact democratic reforms and make the transition from a command economy to a market economy.

## Lech Walesa and Solidarity in Poland

In the 1980s in Poland, economic hardships caused labor unrest. Led by **Lech Walesa,** workers organized **Solidarity,** an independent trade union. With millions of members, Solidarity called for political change.

At first, the Soviet Union pressured the Polish government to suppress Solidarity. The government outlawed the union and arrested Walesa and other leaders. However, communism's power was weakening. International pressure as well as internal pressure led to reform. In 1989, the first free elections in 50 years were held, and Solidarity candidates won. Lech Walesa became president. Poland joined NATO in 1999 and the European Union in 2004.

## East and West Germany United

Since World War II, Germany had been divided into a democratic western state and a communist eastern state. The Berlin Wall had been built in 1961 to keep East Germans from fleeing to the West.

**The Fall of the Berlin Wall** East Germans wanted to share the prosperity and freedom enjoyed by West Germans. By 1989, East German leaders could no longer count on support from the Soviet Union. A rising wave of protests forced the communist government from power. In November 1989, the Berlin Wall was torn down by joyous Germans.

## The Fall of Communism in Eastern Europe

*The Fall of Communism in Eastern Europe*
*Before 1990, the Soviet Union controlled Eastern Europe by force. As the Soviet Union weakened, Eastern Europeans demanded an end to Soviet domination.*

**Romania**
Freedom protests answered with violence, dictator arrested and executed: 1989

**Poland**
Free elections: 1989

**Hungary**
Breakup of Communist Party: 1989

**Freedom Sweeps Eastern Europe**

**East Germany**
Berlin Wall opened: 1989
Free elections: 1990

**Czechoslovakia**
Free elections: 1989

**Yugoslavia**
End of Communist Party control, promise of free elections: 1990

**Bulgaria**
Communist leader steps down: 1989

**Impact of Reunification** The people of Germany welcomed reunification of their country, but there were problems. West Germans had to pay higher taxes to finance the rebuilding of impoverished East Germany. Unemployment rose in East Germany during the transition to a market economy. Social unrest followed, with some right-wing extremists trying to revive Nazi ideology. Foreign workers, many of whom came from Turkey, were attacked. However, by the beginning of the twenty-first century, Germany had regained its position as the dominant economy in Europe.

## Ethnic Tensions Surface

Under communism, ethnic tensions in multinational states had been suppressed. With the fall of the Soviet Union, they resurfaced. Czechoslovakia split peacefully into two separate countries, the Czech Republic and Slovakia. Elsewhere, however, ethnic divisions often resulted in open warfare. In the early 1990s, for example, Armenia and neighboring Azerbaijan fought over a small area in Azerbaijan where many Armenians lived. Armenia eventually gained control of the area. In the Balkan peninsula, ethnic conflict ripped the multinational state of Yugoslavia. The Chechen people, whose Muslim culture is very different from that of the Russians, have fought for independence from Russia for over 150 years. In 1991, when the Soviet Union collapsed, Russia refused to recognize Chechnya as an independent nation. A bitter war began between the Russian army and Chechen separatists. Russian troops and air attacks destroyed sections of Chechnya, while Chechen terrorists conducted deadly attacks on civilians across Russia, including in Moscow theaters. Although Chechnya continues to declare its independence and carry out terrorist attacks, Moscow refuses to recognize the area as an independent nation.

## Summary

Cold War tensions eased in the 1970s, though they flared with the Soviet invasion of Afghanistan. During the 1980s, worker unrest in Poland led to the toppling of the communist government. During the same period, the reforms brought by Mikhail Gorbachev helped bring about the end of the Soviet Union and the collapse of communism throughout Eastern Europe. Germany reunited, and new nations were born. Sometimes these changes led to continuing ethnic conflict. Russia also experienced difficulty in its transition from a command economy to a market economy.

**Key Themes and Concepts**

**Economic Systems**
The reunification of Germany was a joyous moment for Germans, but restoring a market economy to East Germany created many problems.

**Recognize Cause and Effect**

- What are the causes of the Chechen fight for independence?

- What have been the effects?

**Preparing for the Regents**

- In what way was the collapse of communism and the Soviet Union a turning point in global history?

# Political and Economic Change in Latin America

## The Big Idea

Many changes have occurred in Latin America as:

- social and political factors have led to unrest.

- nations have struggled to establish democracy and improve their economies.

- drug trafficking has continued to have an impact on the region.

## Section Overview

Many of the nations of Latin America have experienced periods of unrest since 1945. In Argentina, a series of military regimes and repressive governments finally gave way to democracy in the last decades of the century. Guatemala endured a long civil war and has struggled to rebuild its society. Cuba underwent a revolution in 1959 that led to a communist dictatorship. In Nicaragua, years of strife between communists and counterrevolutionary groups gave way in the 1990s to a democratically elected government. Mexico has experienced more stability but has also had periods of revolt and unrest.

## Key Themes and Concepts

As you review this section, take special note of the following key themes and concepts:

**Conflict** What factors led to continuing conflict in Latin America?

**Change** What types of political changes occurred in Latin American nations after 1945?

**Political Systems** What role does democracy play in Latin America today?

## Key People and Terms

**Key People and Terms**

Place each of the key people and terms into these three categories: politics, economics, and cooperation.

As you review this section, be sure you understand the significance of these key people and terms:

Juan Perón

import substitution

dirty war

Mothers of the Plaza de Mayo

indigenous

Sandinistas

contras

Organization of American States

North American Free Trade Agreement

cartels

## Sources of Unrest

Latin America is a diverse region with a great variety of peoples and cultures. Geographic barriers have discouraged unity, yet the nations of Latin America share similar problems. After World War II, political and social upheavals threatened stability in Latin America. Many Latin American nations looked to authoritarian leaders to provide solutions.

## Argentina

By 1900, Argentina was the richest nation in Latin America. The Great Depression of the 1930s devastated the country, however. A military coup brought Juan Perón to power in 1946.

## Juan Perón

**Juan Perón** was a former army colonel. He appealed to Argentine nationalism by limiting foreign-owned businesses and by promoting **import substitution,** in which local manufacturers produce goods at home to replace imported products.

Perón gained popularity by boosting wages, strengthening labor unions, and beginning social welfare programs. Perón's government was repressive, however, and his economic policies led to huge debts. In 1955, he lost power in a military coup.

Juan Perón

### State Terrorism

Another military government took control in 1976. This government began a program of state terrorism against leftist guerrilla groups. In what came to be known as the **dirty war,** the military arrested, tortured, and killed thousands of people. As many as 20,000 people simply "disappeared."

Many of those who vanished were young people. Their mothers, organized as the **Mothers of the Plaza de Mayo,** marched silently every week in Buenos Aires for over thirty years, holding pictures of their missing children. Their protests demanding an accounting by the government of the whereabouts of their children won worldwide attention.

### Democracy Restored

In 1983, Argentina held elections. Voters returned a democratic government to power. The new government worked to control the military and restore human rights. However, economic problems persisted. In 2001, an economic crisis rocked the nation. The hardships led to widespread protests and continued instability.

## Guatemala

As you have learned, Cold War tensions caused the United States to view certain political movements in Latin America as threats. In Guatemala, the United States helped to overthrow Jacobo Arbenz in 1954, after his land reform program threatened United States business activities in Guatemala. Landowners and the military regained power.

A civil war soon began. The **indigenous** Indians, those who had lived there for years and who were in the majority, suffered. As many as 30,000 were killed in the fighting. Rebels finally laid down their arms in 1996, when a peace accord was reached. The accord brought hope for increased rights for all citizens of Guatemala, including its Indian population.

## Nicaragua

From 1936 to 1979, the Somoza family had governed Nicaragua. The Somozas were repressive but had close ties to the United States because of their anti-communist stance. In 1979, the **Sandinistas,** a group that included both reform-minded nationalists and communists, overthrew the Somoza government.

**Note Taking**

*Reading Skill:*
**Identify Main Ideas**
Make a table. As you read, fill in the main ideas for each Latin American country in Section 7.

| Change in Latin America | | |
|---|---|---|
| Country | Political Change | Economic Change |
| | | |
| | | |
| | | |
| | | |

**Preparing for the Regents**

- How did individual citizens make a difference in Argentina? What other examples of citizens making a difference can you think of in global history?

**Key Themes and Concepts**

**Power**
The United States has often intervened in the politics of Latin America. This intervention has caused resentment among many Latin Americans.

### The Sandinistas in Power

The Sandinistas set up a government under the leadership of Daniel Ortega. Many in the government were Socialists or Communists. The new government introduced some reforms and socialized policies. At the same time, it grew closer to Cuba and other communist nations.

### The Contras

In the 1980s, the Sandinistas faced armed opposition from the **contras,** a counterrevolutionary group. Fearing the spread of communism, the United States supported the contras in their fight against the Sandinistas. A civil war followed, leading to many deaths and weakening the Nicaraguan economy.

Other Central American countries helped both sides reach a compromise. In 1990, the Sandinistas handed over power to a freely elected president, Violeta Chamorro. Nicaragua still had to struggle to rebuild its economy, however.

**Identify Central Issues**

Why did the United States support the contras in Nicaragua in the 1980s?

## Mexico
### Politics in Mexico

After the Mexican Revolution, one party, the Institutional Revolutionary Party (PRI), dominated Mexican politics for 71 years. Between 1960 and 2000, there were periods of upheaval.

- In 1968, students in Mexico protested. The police and the military brutally suppressed the protests.
- In 1994, armed Indian Zapatista rebels in the southern state of Chiapas demanded social and economic reforms. Periodic outbreaks of violence occurred, but the group's goals were not achieved.
- Many groups called for election reforms. In 2000, the PRI lost Mexico's presidential election. Vicente Fox, from the National Action Party (PAN), was elected president. In 2006, Felipe Calderón of the National Action Party won the presidential election in a bitterly contested fight.
- In 2006, President Felipe Calderón began a nationwide military crackdown on Mexican drug cartels. The drug lords struck back with daily killings that threaten the stability of Mexico.

**Preparing for the Regents**

- Briefly explain causes of unrest in Latin America in each of the categories listed below.

**Gap between rich and poor:**

**Social classes:**

**Population and poverty:**

**Urban growth:**

**Causes of Unrest in Mexico**

| Gap Between Rich and Poor | Social Classes | Population and Poverty | Urban Growth |
|---|---|---|---|
| • Small group controls most of wealth<br>• Wealthy people against reforms | • Upper classes descended from Europeans<br>• Poor majority are mestizo, Native American, and African American | • Population explosion<br>• Not enough land to grow food | • Migration of peasants to cities<br>• Slums and urban shacks<br>• Not enough jobs |

**Unrest in Latin America**

## Economic Links With the United States

In the 1950s, the **Organization of American States,** or the OAS, was formed to strengthen democracy, promote human rights, and confront shared problems such as poverty, terrorism, illegal drugs, and corruption. Thirty-five nations in the Western Hemisphere, including Canada and the United States, belong to the organization. The OAS expelled communist Cuba in 1962.

In the 1990s, Mexico, the United States, and Canada signed the **North American Free Trade Agreement,** or NAFTA, a plan to allow free trade among the three nations. Many hoped that it would bring prosperity to Mexico by lowering trade barriers. Some business and investment did go to Mexico, but other manufacturers were hurt by competition from the United States.

Immigration provides another link between Mexico and the United States. Since the 1970s, millions of Mexicans have migrated to the United States, usually in search of better economic opportunities.

## Panama

In the late 1980s, United States officials suspected that the leader of Panama, Manuel Noriega, was helping criminal gangs called **cartels** smuggle drugs into the United States. United States troops invaded Panama in 1989 and arrested Noriega. Panama experienced greater stability in the 1990s.

### The Panama Canal

The Panama Canal was constructed by the United States in the early 1900s. By connecting the Atlantic and Pacific oceans, the canal shortens voyages between the two oceans by thousands of miles. The United States had controlled the canal since it first opened in 1914. Then, in 1977, the United States and Panama signed a treaty designed to gradually turn over control of the canal to Panama. Panama assumed complete control of the Panama Canal on January 1, 2000.

## The Role of Religion

The Catholic Church has played a major role in Latin American society since colonial times. Traditionally a conservative force, many church leaders became proponents of social reform during the late 1900s. Outspoken priests and nuns, for example, struggled against the oppressive military regimes that ruled many Latin American countries in the 1970s and 1980s. At the same time, evangelical Protestant groups have gained a growing following with the poor throughout Latin America.

## Summary

Many of the nations of Latin America have faced political unrest in the last decades of the twentieth century. Argentina suffered under military rule. Guatemala and Nicaragua experienced civil wars. Cuba was a Cold War battleground. Mexico also experienced unrest. Today, however, democracy is taking hold in the region. Still, some problems remain, including the presence and activity of international drug traffickers.

**Draw Conclusions**

- Why did the OAS expel Cuba in 1962?

**Key Themes and Concepts**

**Political Systems**
In Latin America and elsewhere around the world, drug trafficking causes political upheaval as well as social problems. Drug cartels put pressure on national governments and commit violent acts to gain their ends.

**Vocabulary Builder**

proponent—(pruh POH nunt) *n.* someone who supports something or persuades people to do something

**Vocabulary Builder**

evangelical—(ee van JEL ih kul) *adj.* evangelical Christians believe that they should persuade as many people as possible to become Christians

**Multiple Choice**

*Directions:* Review the Test-Taking Strategies section of this book. Then answer the following questions, drawn from actual Regents examinations. For each statement or question, choose the *number* of the word or expression that, of those given, best completes the statement or answers the question.

Base your answers to questions 1 and 2 on the graphs below and on your knowledge of social studies.

### Population and Food Production Growth

**Developed Countries**
Food production up 42%
Pop–ulation up 15%
1970    1985

**Developing Countries**
Population up 49%
Food production up 39%
1970    1985

**1** Which statement is *best* supported by the data in the graphs?

(1) Food production is rising in both developed and developing countries.

(2) Food production is rising at a faster rate in developing countries than in developed countries.

(3) Population is rising at a faster rate in developed countries than in developing countries.

(4) Population is rising at the same rate in both developing and developed countries.

**2** If the trends shown in the graphs continue, it is *most* likely that developing countries will

(1) be able to feed their populations and export food to developed countries

(2) narrow significantly the gap between their population growth and their food production

(3) have a lower birthrate than developed countries

(4) need to import food

**3** Which headline concerning the Soviet Union refers to a Cold War event?

(1) **"Yeltsin Assumes Power"**

(2) **"Trotsky Forms Red Army"**

(3) **"Germany Invades Soviet Union"**

(4) **"Warsaw Pact Formed"**

**4** "A group of planners makes all economic decisions. The group assigns natural, human, and capital resources to the production of those goods and services it wants. The group decides how to produce them and to whom to distribute them."

This description *best* applies to the

(1) manorial economy of feudal Europe

(2) mercantile economy of the 1700s in Europe

(3) command economy of the Soviet Union

(4) market economy of the United States

Source: Reprinted by permission of Bob Englehart,
The Hartford Courant

Base your answer to question 5 on the political cartoon above and on your knowledge of social studies.

**5** What is the cartoonist saying about the impact of democracy on the Soviet Union?

(1) Democracy covered up hidden problems in the Soviet Union.

(2) Democracy led to the development of the Soviet Union.

(3) Democracy had no impact on the Soviet Union.

(4) Democracy led to the breakup of the Soviet Union.

**6** The main reason the Chinese Communists gained control of mainland China in 1949 was that

(1) they were supported by many warlords and upper-class Chinese

(2) the United States had supported the Chinese Communist party during World War II

(3) Mao was a dynamic leader who had the support of the peasant class

(4) they had the support of the Nationalists and of Japan

**7** The Tiananmen Square massacre in China was a reaction to

(1) Deng Xiaoping's plan to revive the Cultural Revolution

(2) demands for greater individual rights and freedom of expression

(3) China's decision to seek western investors

(4) Britain's decision to return Hong Kong to China

**8** Which statement best explains why India was partitioned in 1947?

(1) The British feared a united India.

(2) One region wanted to remain under British control.

(3) Religious differences led to a political division.

(4) Communist supporters wanted a separate state.

9 From the perspective of the North Vietnamese, the war in Vietnam in the 1960s was a battle between

(1) fascism and liberalism

(2) nationalism and imperialism

(3) republicanism and totalitarianism

(4) theocracy and monarchy

10 One similarity shared by the Meiji emperors of Japan, Peter the Great of Russia, and Shah Reza Pahlavi of Iran was that they all supported policies that

(1) increased the power of the aristocracy

(2) introduced new religious beliefs

(3) kept their nations from industrial expansion

(4) westernized their nations

11 A nation governed by Islamic fundamentalists would be most likely to

(1) allow many different interpretations of the Quran

(2) adopt the values and culture of the West

(3) emphasize the traditional beliefs and values of the religion

(4) promote active participation of women in government

12 "Cuba today is a puppet still dancing after the puppet master's death."

In this 1993 newspaper quotation, which nation is referred to as the "puppet master"?

(1) Haiti

(2) Soviet Union

(3) Spain

(4) United States

13 One similarity between Lenin's New Economic Policy and Gorbachev's policy of perestroika is that both policies

(1) supported collectivization of farms in the Soviet Union

(2) allowed some aspects of capitalism in the Soviet economy

(3) increased citizen participation in the Soviet government

(4) strengthened governmental control over the Soviet republics

14 "Take sides. Neutrality helps the oppressor, never the victim. Silence encourages the tormentor, never the tormented."

—Elie Wiesel, Holocaust survivor

According to this quotation, which situation would have most concerned Elie Wiesel?

(1) formation of the United Nations

(2) the world's initial reaction to ethnic cleansing in Bosnia

(3) Arab reaction to the creation of Israel in 1948

(4) dismantling of the Berlin Wall

# Thematic Essay Question

In developing your answer, be sure to keep these general definitions in mind:

(a) <u>explain</u> means "to make plain or clear; render understandable or intelligible"
(b) <u>describe</u> means "to illustrate something in words or tell about it"
(c) <u>evaluate</u> means "to judge or determine the significance, worth, or quality of"

*Directions:*   Write a well-organized essay that includes an introduction, several paragraphs addressing the task below, and a conclusion.

**Theme:   Interdependence**

> Throughout global history, the world has been growing more and more interdependent. This process has accelerated in the twenty-first century.

**Task:**

- Explain what is meant by *global interdependence*.
- Describe two examples of interdependence.
- Evaluate the positive and negative effects of the examples of interdependence you have chosen on individuals and nations.

You may discuss any nations or regions and any example of interdependence from your study of global history and geography. Some suggestions you may wish to consider are economic interdependence, political interdependence, military interdependence, cultural interdependence, and technological interdependence.

**You are *not* limited to these suggestions.**
**Do not use the United States in your answer.**

**Guidelines:**

**In your essay, be sure to**
- Develop all aspects of the task
- Support the theme with relevant facts, examples, and details
- Use a logical and clear plan of organization, including an introduction and a conclusion that are beyond a simple restatement of the theme.

# Document-Based Question

This question is based on the accompanying documents. The question is designed to test your ability to work with historical documents. Some of the documents have been edited for the purposes of the question. As you analyze the documents, take into account the source of each document and any point of view that may be presented in the document.

**Historical Context:**

> After World War II, the world became divided by the Cold War. The Cold War policies of both superpowers affected nations around the world.

**Task:** Using the information from the documents and your knowledge of global history, answer the questions that follow each document in Part A. Your answers to the questions will help you write the Part B essay in which you will be asked to

> - Describe and evaluate the ways in which the Cold War affected nations around the world

**In developing your answers, be sure to keep this general definition in mind:**

> <u>discuss</u> means "to make observations about something using facts, reasoning, and argument; to present in some detail.

## Part A: Short Answer

*Directions:*    Analyze the documents and answer the question or questions that follow each document, using the space provided.

### Document #1

> *A shadow has fallen upon the scenes so lately lighted by the Allied victories. . . . From Stettin in the Baltic to Trieste in the Adriatic, an iron curtain has descended across the Continent. Warsaw, Berlin, Prague, Vienna, Budapest, Belgrade, Bucharest, and Sofia, all these famous cities and populations around them lie in what I must call the Soviet sphere and all are subject to a very high and, in many cases, increasing measure of control from Moscow.*
>
> **– Winston Churchill, from a speech given in Fulton, Missouri, 1946**

1. What image does Churchill use to talk about the division of Europe? Why is this image appropriate?

_____

_____

Document #2

**Europe After World War II**

2. Name two European countries that were allies of the Soviet Union during the Cold War.

_____

_____

3. Name two European countries that were allies of the United States during the Cold War.

_____

_____

## Document #3

*The divisive force is international communism. . . . It strives to break the ties that unite the free. And it strives to capture—to exploit [use selfishly] for its own greater power—all forces of change in the world, especially the needs of the hungry and hopes of the oppressed. . . . To counter the threat of those who seek to rule by force, we must pay the costs of our own needed military strength, and help to build the security of others.*

**– Dwight D. Eisenhower, Second Inaugural Address, January 21, 1957**

4. What did President Eisenhower promise to do in response to international communism? Why?

_____

_____

## Document #4

### United States Intervention in Latin America

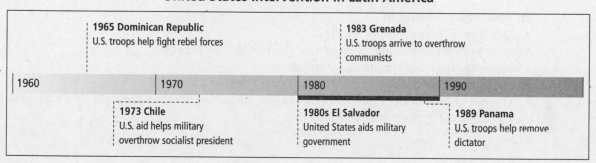

**1965 Dominican Republic**
U.S. troops help fight rebel forces

**1983 Grenada**
U.S. troops arrive to overthrow communists

1960    1970    1980    1990

**1973 Chile**
U.S. aid helps military overthrow socialist president

**1980s El Salvador**
United States aids military government

**1989 Panama**
U.S. troops help remove dictator

5. Explain how one event on this timeline was an effect of the Cold War.

_____

_____

# Document-Based Question

## Part B
## Essay

*Directions:* Write a well-organized essay that includes an introduction, several paragraphs, and a conclusion. Use evidence from *at least three* documents in your essay. Support your response with relevant facts, examples, and details. Include additional outside information.

**Historical Context:**

After World War II, the world became divided by the Cold War. The Cold War policies of both superpowers affected nations around the world.

**Task:** Using information from the documents and your knowledge of United States history, write an essay in which you:

- Describe and evaluate several effects of Cold War policies on nations around the world

**Guidelines:**

**In your essay, be sure to**
- Develop all aspects of the task
- Incorporate information from *at least three* of the documents
- Incorporate relevant outside information
- Support the theme with relevant facts, examples, and details
- Use a logical and clear plan of organization, including an introduction and a conclusion that are beyond a restatement of the theme

# The World Today: Connections and Interactions

## (1980–The Present)

Section 1: **Economic Trends**

Section 2: **Conflicts and Peace Efforts**

Section 3: **Social Patterns and Change**

Section 4: **Science and Technology**

Section 5: **The Environment**

## Unit Overview

The years since 1980 have been a time of great change. Developing nations face challenges as they strive to progress economically despite rising populations and huge debt. There have been many regional conflicts, and international terrorism remains a great threat to world order. The United Nations addresses many of these issues.

As many nations look to the future, they struggle with the tension between modernization and traditional values. Changes come at a quick pace. Advances in computer technology, space exploration, and medicine have changed the way people live. Still, many problems remain, especially in the global environment. Whatever may be the long-term solutions to these problems, they depend on nations working together toward common goals.

## Thematic Timeline Activity

Some of the many themes developed in Unit 8 are:

economic systems
interdependence
movement of people and goods
change

urbanization
science and technology
environment
power

Choose one of the themes listed above. As you review Unit 8, create a thematic timeline based on the theme you have chosen. Your timeline should stretch from 1980 to the present and include major developments and key turning points having to do with your theme.

# Economic Trends

## Section Overview

There is an economic division between the more prosperous countries of the global North and the developing countries of the global South. Developing countries face many obstacles, such as rapid population growth, debt, and unrest. In today's world, however, the global North and South are interdependent. Cooperation among nations can lead to improvements for all. However, problems in one area of the world may have powerful effects on the global economy.

## Key Themes and Concepts

As you review this section, take special note of the following key themes and concepts:

**Places and Regions**  What global economic divisions exist today?

**Economic Systems**  Why have some developing nations failed to achieve their goals?

**Interdependence**  How has economic interdependence affected the world?

## Key Terms

As you review this section, be sure you understand the significance of these key terms:

post-colonialism

trade deficit

refugees

globalization

World Trade Organization

International Monetary Fund

multinational corporations

Association of Southeast Asian Nations

North American Free Trade Association

## North and South: Differences in Development

There is an economic division between the relatively rich nations of the global North and the relatively poor nations of the global South.

### Wealthy Nations

The global North includes the nations of Western Europe and North America, along with Japan and Australia. These nations are highly industrialized and have high literacy rates and high standards of living.

### Poor Nations

The global South includes the developing countries of Asia, Africa, and Latin America. Many were once colonies. Much of the area remains poor and industrially undeveloped. Many developing nations are experiencing the problems of **post-colonialism.** Policies established during the age of imperialism continued after 1945. As a result, some nations have remained economically dependent on their former colonial rulers.

# Obstacles to Development

## Geography

Several factors have hindered progress in developing countries. Uncertain rainfall, lack of fertile land, and geographic barriers are problems faced by many nations. Some countries are small and have few resources.

Natural disasters such as earthquakes and hurricanes can be devastating to struggling economies. For example, in September 1998, Hurricane Mitch struck Central America. Flooding and mudslides led to deaths and left many survivors homeless. It will take years to rebuild damaged economies.

### Population Projections for Selected Eastern and Southern African Nations

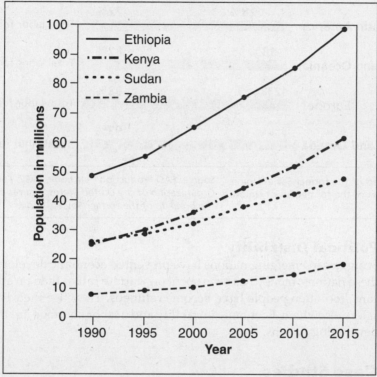

Source: The World Bank

## Population Growth

High birthrates and better medical care in many nations of the global South have led to overpopulation. Problems caused by overpopulation include inadequate food, housing, jobs, and medical care. Many developing nations have tried to reduce population growth. However, few countries other than China are willing to force people to limit family size.

## Past Economic Policies

After achieving independence, many new nations imposed socialist economic policies. Over time, socialism hindered economic growth. Beginning in the 1980s, some nations introduced market economies.

## Economic Dependence, Trade Deficits, and Debt

The global South is affected by post-colonialism. Much of the labor force is engaged in agriculture. The global South continues to depend on developed nations for manufactured goods and technology while exporting cash crops. These factors have led to trade deficits. A **trade deficit** is a situation in which a nation imports more than it exports.

### Cycle of Poverty

Economic struggles and the desire to develop quickly have led to heavy borrowing from foreign banks. In the 1980s, interest rates rose, and there was a global economic slowdown. Resources had to be spent on rising interest payments. This spending lowered productivity and increased debt.

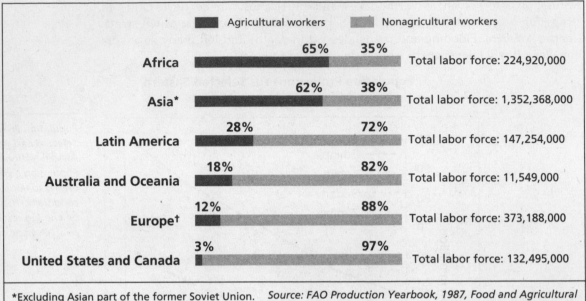

**Labor in Agriculture**

| | Agricultural workers | Nonagricultural workers |
| --- | --- | --- |
| **Africa** | 65% | 35% Total labor force: 224,920,000 |
| **Asia*** | 62% | 38% Total labor force: 1,352,368,000 |
| **Latin America** | 28% | 72% Total labor force: 147,254,000 |
| **Australia and Oceania** | 18% | 82% Total labor force: 11,549,000 |
| **Europe†** | 12% | 88% Total labor force: 373,188,000 |
| **United States and Canada** | 3% | 97% Total labor force: 132,495,000 |

*Excluding Asian part of the former Soviet Union.
†Including Asian part of the former Soviet Union.

*Source: FAO Production Yearbook, 1987, Food and Agricultural Organization of the United States. Figures are for 1987, prior to the breakup of the former Soviet Union.*

*Labor in Agriculture*
*For centuries, most people in Africa, Asia, and Latin America worked in agriculture. In recent decades, many countries have been diversifying their economies.*

**Preparing for the Regents**

• What evidence does this graph give of the economic division between the global North and the global South? How does having a large percentage of the population in agriculture affect a nation's economic progress?

## Political Instability

Struggles in emerging nations have prevented economic development. In many of these nations, money has been spent on warfare rather than on education or health care. Too often people have become **refugees.** They flee their homelands to seek safety elsewhere. Economic instability and a labor shortage are the results in some developing nations.

# Case Studies

### The Democratic Republic of the Congo

In the early 1960s, the Congo was torn by civil war as people from some 200 different ethnic groups competed for power. In 1965, army general Mobutu Sese Seko seized control. He renamed the country Zaire and established a brutal dictatorship. Under Mobutu's rule, Zaire's economy was ruined. Corrupt officials robbed the treasury. Roads were left to decay. Agriculture declined and mines closed.

In 1997, rebel forces removed Mobutu from power and renamed the country the Democratic Republic of the Congo. It continued its economic decline. Violence between rival militias was influenced by ethnic loyalties that crossed borders. A successful 2006 election did not end the violence, and fighting continued in eastern Congo between the various militia groups, the Congolese military force, and UN peacekeepers.

## Brazil

Military rulers controlled Brazil from the 1960s through the 1980s. Under their rule, Brazil experienced a boom. Foreign investment helped the nation develop heavy industry. The Amazon rain forest was exploited for economic profit. By building hydroelectric plants, Brazilians reduced their need for imported oil. However, while the middle and upper classes of Brazil enjoyed prosperity, many workers experienced extreme poverty. The government kept wages low to attract foreign investors and help businesses grow. As a result, working class people suffered.

In the 1990s, when democracy replaced military rule, Brazil faced serious economic troubles. Since 2000, its economy has stabilized due to new government policies, lower inflation, increasing exports, and lower rates of unemployment. New reforms have encouraged investment, economic growth, and judicial reform and strive to reduce the deforestation of the Amazon. However, Brazil remains an economically divided society.

# Economic Interdependence

## Globalization

Although people and countries in different parts of the world have been linked by trade for centuries, a global economy, the integration of national economies into the international economy, began to develop in the late 1800s. Advances in science and technology in the late twentieth century accelerated the pace of this **globalization.** Today, whatever happens in one part of the world has an effect on other areas.

**World Trade Organization** The World Trade Organization (WTO) was established in 1994 as a global organization to deal with the rules of trade between nations. Its nearly 150 members negotiate agreements, handle trade disputes, and provide assistance to developing countries. Many WTO meetings have been the scene of major protests by those who believe its policies favor rich nations and harm the environment.

**Dependence on Oil** Oil prices affect economies all over the world. When oil supplies are high, prices fall, and many economies benefit. However, when oil supplies are limited, prices rise, and many economies suffer. Inflation brought on by high oil prices has contributed to debt crises in developing nations. On the other hand, falling oil prices are damaging to economies that depend heavily on oil sales.

**Global Banking and Financial Markets** Many western banks make loans to developing nations to be used for modernization. As interest rates rose in the 1980s, however, and the world economy slowed, poor nations struggled to repay their loans. The **International Monetary Fund** (IMF) stepped in to work out agreements with debtor nations. Interest rates were lowered and payment schedules were renegotiated. In return, however, debtor nations had to adopt free market policies.

Financial markets are also linked. Changes in one part of the world affect others. When many Asian countries faced economic problems in the 1990s, stock markets in other parts of the world were shaken.

**Multinational Corporations** Businesses that operate in many countries are called multinational corporations. Many companies based in the global North have made investments in the global South. These enterprises bring new

### Key Themes and Concepts

**Environment and Society**
Brazil is a good example of the relationship that can occur between economic development and environmental protection. Developing the Amazon region helps Brazil economically. Some nations, however, feel that it has a negative global impact environmentally.

### Note Taking

*Reading Skill:*
**Understand Effects**
Make a table. As you read, list benefits and challenges of economic globalization. Add boxes as needed.

| Economic Globalization | |
|---|---|
| Benefits | Challenges |
| | |
| | |
| | |
| | |

### Vocabulary Builder

<u>debtor</u>—(DET ur) *n.*
a person, group, or organization that owes money

## Key Themes and Concepts

**Economic Systems**
How has economic decision making become more global as national economies around the world become increasingly interdependent?

## Draw Conclusions

Which countries benefit more from economic globalization—developed or developing countries? Explain.

## Preparing for the Regents

- Describe three policies that could help developing countries achieve greater economic prosperity.

technology. However, local industries may be damaged if they cannot compete with multinational corporations.

## Regional Cooperation

The economic success of the European Union led nations in other regions to create trade agreements with each other. They hoped that economic cooperation and free trade would spur economic development and reduce poverty in their nations.

**ASEAN** The **Association of Southeast Asian Nations** (ASEAN), formed in 1967, is made up of ten Southeast Asian countries. It coordinates policies among members in areas such as trade and agriculture and focuses on peace and stability in the region.

**NAFTA** In 1994, the **North American Free Trade Association** (NAFTA) was set up to eliminate tariffs and trade restrictions among Canada, the United States, and Mexico. There has been discussion about expanding the agreement to include other Latin American countries.

## International Drug Trade

Nations in Latin America, Africa, and Asia have been involved in the drug trade. The United States declared a "war on drugs" in the 1980s and pressured many countries to move against drug cartels. There has been some international cooperation to eliminate illegal drug trade. Sometimes the United States has linked this cooperation with trade or aid agreements.

## Summary

There is a great economic gulf between the global North and the global South. Developing countries struggle with obstacles that hinder their growth. These include population growth, trade deficits, debt, and instability. Meanwhile, global interdependence has resulted in greater cooperation among nations in banking and trade. While globalization has resulted in benefits to almost all nations, there is considerable debate that developed nations have benefited the most at the expense of poorer countries.

# Conflicts and Peace Efforts

## Section Overview

In the last several decades, some nations and organizations have continued to use violence to achieve political goals. In many areas of the world, ethnic and religious differences have sparked conflict. Even with the end of the Cold War superpower struggles, various areas of the world have become hot spots. In its peacekeeping role, the United Nations (UN) has intervened in many conflicts, with varying degrees of success. The UN also promotes human rights and helps with disaster relief throughout the world.

## Key Themes and Concepts

As you review this section, take special note of the following key themes and concepts:

**Power** For what purposes have various groups used terrorist tactics?

**Belief Systems** How have religious and ethnic differences contributed to instability and conflict?

**Interdependence** How does global interdependence cause local conflicts to have potentially global consequences?

**Conflict** How has the United Nations tried to promote world peace and security?

## Key People and Terms

As you review this section, be sure you understand the significance of these key people and terms:

| | |
|---|---|
| terrorism | Saddam Hussein |
| al Qaeda | Kurds |
| Irish Republican Army | Darfur |
| ethnic cleansing | Universal Declaration of |
| Slobodan Milosevic | Human Rights |
| Dalai Lama | |

## The Threat of Terrorism

### Nature of Terrorism

Terrorism is the deliberate use of unpredictable violence, especially against civilians, to gain revenge or achieve political goals. Terrorism is usually used by groups that do not have their own military power. Terrorists use tactics such as bombings, kidnappings, assassinations, and hijackings. In recent years, new fears about nuclear and chemical terrorism have developed. Terrorism spreads fear throughout the world. It may also lead to more violence if groups attempt to retaliate.

---

### The Big Idea

As conflicts continue in various parts of the world, so do efforts to restore and maintain peace.

- Terrorism is a threat to global peace.
- Religious and ethnic conflicts continue to cause unrest.
- Conflicts have occurred in a number of post–Cold War hot spots.
- The United Nations attempts to maintain peace and promote social and economic well-being.

### Key People and Terms

Place each of the key people and terms into one of these categories: belief system or conflict/cooperation.

### Key Themes and Concepts

**Conflict**
List three reasons why groups use terrorist tactics.

1.

2.

3.

Some recent uses of terrorism have been:

- in conflicts between extreme traditionalist groups and modern western societies (such as the 9/11 attacks by **al Qaeda** extremists).
- in disputes between nationalist groups over a homeland (as in Palestine and Israel).
- in domestic conflicts between insurgent groups and governments (as in Indonesia).

### Efforts to Stop Terrorism

The attacks on New York and Washington, D.C., on September 11, 2001, alarmed government leaders everywhere. The attacks showed how terrorism affects the security and stability of all nations. At the same time, leaders recognized that defeating terrorism will require a lengthy effort. Some nations not accustomed to cooperating are working together, while a few still harbor or support terrorists.

## Ethnic and Religious Tensions

Religious beliefs and ethnic loyalties have united groups and sometimes led to the growth of nations. These forces have also divided peoples and led to persecution and violence. In every conflict, each group involved has its own point of view.

### Northern Ireland

Ireland won its independence from Britain in 1922. Britain, however, kept control of the six northern counties, which had a mostly Protestant population. The south was mostly Roman Catholic.

In Northern Ireland, violence increased in the 1970s because of extremists in both the Protestant and Roman Catholic communities. Until 2005, the **Irish Republican Army** (IRA) used violence against the British and Protestant Irish. Their goal was to drive out the British and join with Ireland. Protestant groups retaliated. Despite many attempts at peace, the violence and divisions continued until 2005, when the IRA ended its call for violence. In 2007, a new power-sharing government took control from the British government.

### The Balkans and Ukraine

Yugoslavia was a multinational state created after World War I. Orthodox Christian Serbs, Roman Catholic Croats, Muslim Albanians, and other ethnic groups lived in Yugoslavia. Some areas were home to predominately one ethnic group, while several groups shared other regions.

By 1991, several of Yugoslavia's regions had declared independence. Some, like Slovenia, had only brief fighting. In more ethnically mixed areas, tensions flared. In Bosnia and Herzegovina, Serbs practiced **ethnic cleansing,** which is the act of removing or killing people of a certain ethnic group.

In 1992, **Slobodan Milosevic,** Serbian leader of the Yugoslavian government, encouraged or ordered brutal campaigns of ethnic cleansing against non-Serbians, such as the ethnic Albanians in Kosovo. In order to restore peace, NATO and the UN took military action in the region. In 2001, Milosevic was arrested and tried for war crimes and genocide by the UN's International Criminal Tribunal. He died in 2006 before its verdict. In 2003, Yugoslavia changed its name to Serbia and Montenegro. Montenegro gained its independence in 2006. Ethnic battles continued in Kosovo, which remained under Serbian control until it gained independence in 2008.

## Note Taking

*Reading Skill:*
**Identify Causes**
Make a chart. List the causes of each country/region's ethnic and religious tensions.

| Ethnic and Religious Tensions | |
|---|---|
| Country/Region | Causes |
| | |
| | |
| | |

## Key Themes and Concepts

**Belief Systems**
How have religious differences contributed to the conflict in Northern Ireland?

## Key Themes and Concepts

**Nationalism**
Authoritarian communist governments had kept nationalism in check in the years after World War II. After the collapse of communism, nationalism revived and resulted in civil wars.

In nearby Ukraine, a vicious campaign for president included the poisoning of the more pro-western candidate. A new election put this candidate into power, but disagreements between factions continued to divide the government.

**Ethnic Divisions in Yugoslavia Before 1990**

*Ethnic Divisions in Yugoslavia Before 1990*
*Before 1990, Yugoslavia was made up of six republics, similar to states in the United States. Each republic had a dominant ethnic group, but they also had ethnic minorities. Most people spoke the same language, Serbo-Croatian, but had different religions. Others spoke minority languages.*

**Preparing for the Regents**

• Practice your map skills by explaining how this map supports the idea that diversity has led to conflict in the Balkans.

## China and Tibet

In 1951, Tibet was invaded by the People's Republic of China. The Chinese promised that Tibet would be a highly autonomous area of China. China's military crackdown on Tibetan rebels in 1959 led to a full-scale resistance. Fearing capture, the **Dalai Lama,** the spiritual and political leader of Tibet, fled to India. China then began to collectivize the land and execute landlords as it began its efforts to impose Chinese culture on Tibet. Protests against the Chinese, initiated by Buddhist monks, flared up again in 2008. The Chinese government reacted strongly, imposing curfews and strictly limiting access to Tibetan areas. The Dalai Lama, in exile, claimed the Chinese were practicing cultural genocide and that Tibetan Buddhist culture was facing the threat of extinction.

## South Asia and Southeast Asia

Ethnic and religious conflicts continued on the Indian subcontinent.

• **Muslims, Hindus, and Sikhs** Both Muslims and Sikhs believe they are discriminated against by India's Hindu majority. Incidents of violence between these groups disturb India.

• **Indonesia** Indonesia's population is mostly Muslim, but in East Timor most people are Catholics. In 1999, when East Timor demanded independence, Indonesia's army responded with force, destroying much of the area's homes, roads, electric supply, and schools. Less than a month later, international peacekeepers arrived to allow East Timor to plan its independence. Despite its free elections in 2007, Timor-Leste remains Asia's poorest country. In 2002, Muslim extremists bombed civilains in other Indonesian areas. These extremists seem to be working with al Qaeda. Their goal is to create an Islamic government in Indonesia.

**Vocabulary Builder**

curfew—(KUR fyoo) *n.* a law that forces people to stay indoors after a particular time at night, or the time people must be indoors

## Vocabulary Builder

secessionist—(sih SESH un ist) *adj.* wanting one's country or state to be independent of another country

## Note Taking

*Reading Skill:*
**Recognize Sequence**
List the important events of the Iraq War. Record them in the order they occurred. Add boxes as needed.

| Iraq War | |
|---|---|
| Date | Event |
| | |
| | |
| | |
| | |

- **Sri Lanka** In 1976, the Tamil Tigers, a militant organization based in northern Sri Lanka began a violent secessionist campaign that sought to create an independent state for the Tamil minority in the north and east of Sri Lanka. Approximately 80,000 people died in the civil war that lasted until their defeat in 2009.

## International Hot Spots

Throughout the world, continuing international tensions have the potential to cause local and global violence.

### The Iraq War

At the end of the Persian Gulf War, the United Nations required that Iraq destroy its nuclear, biological, and chemical weapons as well as its missiles. The UN began a series of inspections to ensure compliance. In the late 1990s, Iraq's leader, **Saddam Hussein,** expelled the UN inspection team and refused to allow further inspections. In response, the United States and Britain staged air strikes against Iraq.

In 2001, the United States accused Iraq of supporting terrorists, such as al Qaeda, and of hiding weapons of mass destruction. UN inspectors searched for these weapons, but found none. In 2002, the UN denied President George W. Bush's request for military action against Iraq.

In March 2003, without UN support, the United States and its coalition forces invaded Iraq. A violent insurgency developed against the coalition troops, the new Iraqi government, and workers repairing war damage. Saddam Hussein was captured in December 2003. He was convicted of crimes against humanity and was hanged in December 2006.

In 2005, an Iraqi election took place amidst the violence. A new constitution was approved by voters and parliamentary elections were held. Major disagreements among Sunnis, Shiites and Kurds eventually led to the selection of a compromise candidate, Jawael al-Maliki, as prime minister and the formation of a new government in 2006.

## Preparing for the Regents

- What political, religious, and social forces led the cartoonist to depict the Iraqi election in this way?

Source: VIC HARVILLE/Stephens Media Group

Saddam Hussein was a Sunni Muslim and his brutal dictatorship favored Sunnis. However, the majority of Iraqis are Shiite Muslims. Clerics from both the Sunnis and the Shiites have devoted followings. Some of these religious leaders, al Qaeda fighters, and other Iraqis are using violence against Iraq's present government, its security forces, the western military, and each other. These groups disagree on Iraq's future government, culture, and degree of westernization. In 2007, the United States increased its military operations to end the internal violence. Although some progress was made, violence continued, but was often aimed at Iraqi civilians rather than the military. The election of President Barack Obama in 2008 led to a plan for a phased withdrawal of American troops from Iraq.

### The Kurds

Most Kurds are Sunni Muslims but are not Arabs. Millions of Kurds live in Turkey, Iraq, Iran, Armenia, and Syria. Kurds have experienced harsh treatment and repression, especially in Turkey and Iraq. Since 1920 they have tried to create an independent Kurdish state, with land from all these countries. In 2005, the Kurds became participants in the new Iraqi government. In early 2008, Kurdish Iraq was invaded by the Turkish military in an attempt to stop Kurdish rebel attacks in Turkey.

### North Korea

While South Korea moved closer to democracy and became more prosperous, North Korea was still ruled by a hard-line communist dictatorship and suffered severe economic hardships. Nevertheless, the North Korean government spent large sums of money on the military. Nations around the world grew more concerned about North Korea's nuclear capability, especially after North Korea tested nuclear explosive devices. The communist government's hope to unite the two Koreas under its rule adds more tension.

### India and Pakistan

The long-standing hostility between India, with its Hindu majority, and Pakistan, with its Muslim majority, continued into the new century. One hot spot was Kashmir, a region divided between Pakistan and India. In 2001 Islamic terrorists attacked India's parliament. This crisis escalated further, raising fears of a nuclear conflict since both India and Pakistan have tested nuclear weapons. Relations between the two countries improved and then disintegrated again. In 2007, Pakistan's political stability was shaken when exiled former Prime Minister Benazir Bhutto returned, only to be killed. It is suspected her death was planned by a Pakistani tribal leader with al Qaeda's help. The 2008 terrorist attacks on Mumbai by members of a Pakistan-based terrorist organization further damaged India's already strained relationship with Pakistan.

### Afghanistan

Soviet forces invaded Afghanistan in 1979 and supported a communist government there for ten years. During that time, more than three million Afghans fled their country, many to Pakistan. Afghan fighters resisted communist rule and finally forced the Soviets to withdraw. In the mid-1990s, the Taliban imposed an extreme form of Islam on Afghanistan. They also protected the terrorist group al Qaeda, which directed the 2001 attacks on the United States. In response, the United States launched an attack that drove the Taliban from power. The new Afghan government is supported by military from the United States and other countries, including Pakistan. But violence in both Afghanistan and Pakistan is partly attributed to a resurgence of the Taliban. The Taliban want to return to the strict religious laws and restricted life it created in Afghanistan before 2001. Afghanistan also must deal with a lack of modernization, land mines, thriving poppy fields which supply illegal opium, and foreign military intervention.

Key Themes
and Concepts

**Interdependence**
The United Nations is an international governing body. It is composed of more than 170 nations that cooperate to promote world peace and security.

# The United Nations

## Structure of the United Nations

The United Nations, or UN, was established in 1945. Its goals are to promote global peace and security as well as economic and social well-being. The UN has the power, through the votes of its more than 170 member nations, to take action against forces that threaten world peace.

The UN has five main bodies. The UN also has a number of specialized agencies. Some, such as the Food and Agriculture Organization (FAO) and the International Fund for Agricultural Development (IFAD), fight hunger through agricultural improvement. Others, such as the United Nations Children's Fund (UNICEF) and the World Health Organization (WHO), are concerned with health issues.

Preparing for
the Regents

Describe three different types of activities carried out by the United Nations.

1.

2.

3.

**The United Nations**

**Security Council**
Authorizes military and economic action to settle disputes; has 15 members; 5 are permanent

**Secretariat**
Responsible for administration of the UN; headed by Secretary General

**General Assembly**
Discusses issues and recommends actions; approves budget; has representatives from all member nations

**Economic and Social Council**
Promotes human rights and works for improved economic, social, and health conditions; 54 members elected by General Assembly

**International Court of Justice**
Rules on international legal disputes; made up of 15 judges elected by General Assembly and Security Council

## Peacekeeping Operations

The United Nations has taken action to maintain peace or restore order in places all over the world. The UN has had mixed success in keeping the peace. Although no worldwide conflicts have occurred, the sovereignty of individual nations often makes it difficult for the UN to enforce its wishes.

**Iraq** In August 1990, Iraqi troops invaded oil-rich Kuwait. The United Nations voted to impose economic sanctions on Iraq to force the troops to withdraw. When Iraq did not withdraw, the Security Council sent a multinational force which drove Iraq out of Kuwait.

**Note Taking**

*Reading Skill:*
**Identify Supporting Details**
Make a chart. Record the details of the United Nations Peacekeeping Operations in the three countries.

United Nations
Peacekeeping Operations

Iraq      Haiti      Sudan

**Haiti** From 1957 through 1986, Haiti was ruled by brutal dictators. In 1990, Haiti held free elections. However, Jean-Bertrand Aristide, the victor, was later ousted by a military coup. Several years later, UN forces helped restore Aristide to power and build a functioning democracy in Haiti.

**Sudan** Sudan has been torn by civil war for most of its 52 years. Its cultural diversity has been a factor in these wars. In 2003, pro-government Arabic militias began attacking black villagers and rebel groups in the Darfur region. All peace negotiations have failed. In 2007, forces from the African Union joined UN peacekeepers to try to end the violence. However, the Sudanese government is not cooperating. It has the support of China and Russia, who depend on Sudan's oil. The violence in **Darfur** was so great that the UN wanted to put several men on trial for their crimes there. Sudan's government refused to cooperate.

All those in favor that we stand up to the Serbs...

U.N. 1994 and 1995...

(adapted)

Copyright © 1994 by Jimmy Margulies, The Record, Hackensack, NJ

**Preparing for the Regents**

• How is the UN policy presented in this cartoon similar to the policy of appeasement practiced by the western democracies in the 1930s?

## Social and Economic Programs

The UN also promotes social and economic programs.

**Human Rights** In 1948, the United Nations adopted the **Universal Declaration of Human Rights.** This document states that human beings are born free and equal with dignity and rights. It goes on to list basic rights and freedoms that all people should have. Nevertheless, human rights are in peril in many parts of the world, including China and the Balkans.

**Disaster Relief** The United Nations has responded over the years to famine and other disasters. In the late 1960s, the UN helped save millions in Biafra from starvation during the Nigerian civil war. Other more recent examples of UN disaster relief include the following:

• In the early 1990s, UN forces brought food to Somalians who were caught up in a civil war.

• During the 1990s, the UN provided food to victims of conflict in Sri Lanka.

• The UN provided relief and recovery aid to Indonesia after the December 2004 tsunami and to Pakistan after the October 2005 earthquake.

## Summary

Terrorists use various tactics, such as bombings and kidnappings, to achieve their political goals. Terrorist activity creates a climate of fear and can lead to further violence. Ethnic and religious differences have sparked conflict in areas such as Northern Ireland and the Middle East. In many areas of the world, local conflicts threaten to become global struggles. The United Nations has intervened in various conflicts around the world to try to bring peace. It has also worked to promote human rights and bring relief to victims of famine and disaster.

**Key Themes and Concepts**

**Needs and Wants**
At its founding, the United Nations pledged to fight hunger, disease, and ignorance. Its programs to improve agriculture and promote health have accomplished these goals in many regions.

**Vocabulary Builder**

tsunami—(tsoo NAH mee) *n.* a very large wave, caused by extreme conditions such as an earthquake, that can cause a lot of damage when it reaches land

**Preparing for the Regents**

Identify two causes of conflict in the world today.

1.

2.

# Social Patterns and Change

## Section Overview

Near the end of the twentieth century, modernization and industrialization created tensions. In some countries, these events have brought new opportunities to women; in others they have not. Excessive population growth is a problem facing many nations around the world today. Rapid urbanization is also a widespread change. Another trend is migration—people move to seek economic opportunity or political freedom.

## Key Themes and Concepts

As you review this section, take special note of the following key themes and concepts:

**Change** What are the results of tension between tradition and modernization in societies today?

**Culture** What are the causes of overpopulation?

**Urbanization** What changes have resulted from the rapid urbanization that occurred in the late twentieth century?

**Movement of People and Goods** What patterns of migration have emerged in recent years?

## Key Terms

As you review this section, be sure you understand the significance of these key terms:

| | | |
|---|---|---|
| westernization | urbanization | chador |
| overpopulation | shantytowns | human trafficking |

### Key People and Terms

For each of the key terms, write a sentence explaining its significance.

## Modernization and Tradition

In most societies, there is strain between the forces of modernization and those of tradition. This is especially true in nonwestern societies. During the age of imperialism, modernization usually meant **westernization,** or adoption of western ways. Traditions were often weakened.

Many developing nations today hope to find a balance between modernization and tradition. They want to embrace modern technology but preserve traditions and religious beliefs. Two places where this struggle has been going on are Japan and the Middle East.

### Key Themes and Concepts

**Culture**
Nonwestern nations often want modern technology but do not want to lose completely their traditional culture and values.

### Japan

Japanese society has always been deeply traditional. The code of behavior that developed during feudal times gave each individual a very clear place in society. People had strictly defined duties toward each other. Families were patriarchal, or dominated by males. Individuals felt a strong sense of responsibility to their families or to a larger group. Personal desires mattered little.

In modern Japan, many of these values have survived. Tensions exist, however, in modern Japanese life.

**Role of the Individual** In the Japanese workplace, the sense of structure, duty, and individual sacrifice for the group remains strong. Japanese companies have always been based on teamwork. Although much was required of the worker, he or she had secure employment and was guaranteed advancement.

Recent economic difficulties, however, have weakened the Japanese economy and resulted in lost jobs. Devotion to the employer declined. At the same time, younger Japanese are less willing to sacrifice their personal lives for their jobs. Some people in Japan express concern about a weakening work ethic.

**Status of Women** Laws imposed after World War II ended some of the special legal privileges that were given to males in Japanese families. Women gained many rights, including the right to vote. In the 1970s, they entered the workplace in great numbers. However, traditional views of women keep them in lower positions than men in the workplace. Few women have moved into higher-level jobs in business or government.

## The Middle East

Traditionally, Muslim cultures of the Middle East placed great importance on kinship ties and patriarchial families. In some ways, women were subordinate to men. Women were expected to be modest and to remain secluded within their homes. Modernization and movement to cities have created tension regarding some of these traditions.

Today, there are great strains between the forces of westernization and tradition. Many Muslim countries have rejected western values—though not western technology. Some Muslims would like to abolish secular political systems and return to Islamic principles and the Sharia as a basis for government.

- **Saudi Arabia** The oil industry changed Saudi Arabia in many ways. Many people moved to cities, where the traditional extended family structure became weakened. There has been disagreement over the place of women in society. Some Saudi religious leaders today worry about the influence of western ideas, the education of women, and the effect of such modern technology as television.
- **Egypt** The most heavily populated of the Arab nations, Egypt has experienced a rapid shift in population from rural to urban areas. Social problems have resulted. In response, Muslim reformers in Egypt have called for a return to Islamic laws and customs. Islamic organizations have developed their own schools, medical services, and social services. At the same time, there is a call for a return to traditional practices based on the Quran and a rejection of westernization.
- **Gaza Strip** In 2005, Israeli settlers and military forces were withdrawn from the Gaza Strip. The Palestinian Authority's Al Fatah Party took control until Hamas, a Palestinian anti-Israeli terrorist group, created chaos and assumed control. They conducted rocket attacks on Israel from Gaza to which the Israeli military forces retaliated. Israel and Egypt closed Gaza's borders and economic sanctions destroyed the fragile Gaza economy.
- **Algeria** Once Algeria gained its independence from France, modernization followed, along with a strong desire to rid the country of French cultural influences. Many Algerians began to call for a return to traditional Islamic teachings. A period of intense unrest began in 1991. The army canceled an

## Identify Effects

What are two effects of recent economic difficulties in Japan?

## Vocabulary Builder

kinship—(KIN ship) *n.* a family relationship

## Preparing for the Regents

For each of the areas listed below, describe one way in which conservative, traditional people have responded to modernization.

**Saudi Arabia:**

**Egypt:**

**Gaza Strip:**

**Algeria:**

election when it looked as if a traditional Islamic group would win a strong majority. Violence between the government and Islamic extremists resulted in an estimated 80,000 deaths.

## Overpopulation

Overpopulation is an overabundance of people in a region or country that lacks sufficient resources to provide for them. In Asia, China and India face severe problems caused by overpopulation. Many nations in Africa and in Central and South America have very high birthrates, causing them to experience overpopulation problems as well.

### Cycle of Overpopulation

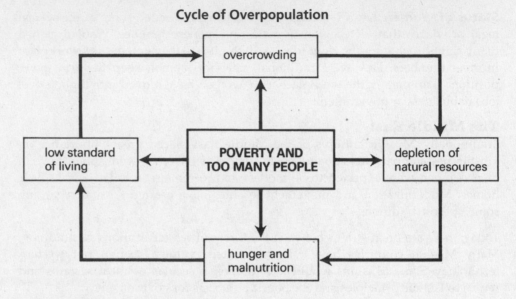

*Cycle of Overpopulation*
*Poverty is at the center of the cycle of overpopulation. Half of the world's population, or almost 3 billion people, live on less than $2 a day. About 1 billion people cannot read or write. Millions suffer from hunger and diseases.*

### Causes of Overpopulation

Reasons for overpopulation include the following:

- **Religious Beliefs** Some religions teach that it is essential to bring children into the world.
- **Cultural Factors** Some cultures promote the idea that it is necessary to have large families to carry on the family name and provide for parents in their old age.
- **Economic Factors** Some people feel that large numbers of children are necessary to help support the family economically.
- **Lack of Knowledge** Many people lack factual information about reproduction and birth control.

### Population Control Efforts

Several solutions to overpopulation have been proposed, foremost among which is family planning. The governments of some countries actively sponsor birth control programs. The Chinese government, for example, provides birth control information as well as financial incentives to couples who limit their offspring to one child. Throughout the world, however, family planning is difficult to achieve wherever cultural tradition or religious beliefs encourage large families.

## Urbanization

Urbanization, the movement of people to cities, is one of the most significant forces of social change, especially in the developing world.

## Reasons for Urbanization

In developing countries, many people have moved to the cities to find jobs and escape the poverty of rural areas. Cities also offer other attractions, such as better health care, educational opportunities, stores, and modern conveniences.

## Results of Urbanization

In the developing nations of Africa, South Asia, and Latin America, urbanization has had similar results.

**Cultural Change** In modern cities, people's traditional values and beliefs are often weakened. The caste system in India, for example, is less strong in urban areas than in rural areas. Women often have more opportunities for change in cities. Some people experience a feeling of being cut off from their earlier communities and customs.

**Poverty** Many people cannot afford to live in cities. They settle around the cities in **shantytowns,** areas of makeshift shacks that lack sewer systems, electricity, and other basic services. Crowded conditions often lead to water pollution and other environmental effects. Lagos in Nigeria, Mumbai and Kolkata in India, and Mexico City in Mexico are just some of the cities that have been unable to cope with waves of migration from rural areas.

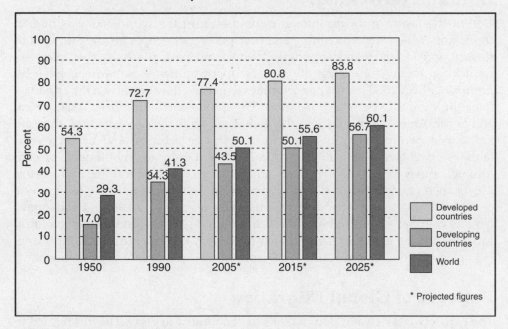

**Percent of Population That is Urban, 1950–2025**

## Solving Urban Problems

Developing nations are trying to solve the problems that have resulted from urbanization. Attempts are being made in several areas.

- Developing nations realize the importance of education. Many nations are striving to provide education for all, hoping to give their citizens a chance at better jobs and a better life.
- Religious individuals and groups have set up their own relief agencies. One example is the order founded by Mother Teresa in India, the Roman Catholic Missionaries of Charity.
- Developing nations are working to improve health care in crowded urban centers.

**Key Themes and Concepts**

**Change**
Industrialization and urbanization are powerful agents of social change in developing nations. Traditional ways are often weakened in large industrial cities.

**Preparing for the Regents**

Describe two problems that have resulted from urbanization in developing nations.

1.

2.

**Key Themes and Concepts**

**Decision Making**
What strategies are developing nations using to overcome the negative aspects of overpopulation and urbanization?

**Vocabulary Builder**

order—(AWR dur) *n.* a society of monks or nuns (people who live a holy life according to religious rules)

## Note Taking

*Reading Skill:*
**Identify Supporting Details**
Make a chart. List details about the status of women before and after 1900. What issues changed and where? What issues didn't change and where?

**Status of Women**

| Issue | What changed/ didn't change? | Where? |
|-------|------------------------------|--------|
|       |                              |        |
|       |                              |        |
|       |                              |        |

## Vocabulary Builder

lucrative—(LOOK ruh tiv) *adj.* a job or activity that is lucrative lets you earn a lot of money

## Key Themes and Concepts

**Movement of People**
Answer the following questions about global migration.

1. Give examples to show how ethnic tensions can cause migration.

2. Give examples to show how migration can cause ethnic tensions.

# Status of Women

Women's status changed greatly in the 1900s in the West. Women gained the right to vote and entered the workforce in large numbers. Some developing countries have also expanded the role of women, but others have limited it.

In the Middle East, the status of women varies greatly from country to country. Israel, for example, includes women in all facets of society. Israeli women are a part of the military forces. Golda Meir was prime minister. The status of women in Muslim countries varies widely. In Turkey, Syria, and Egypt, many urban women have given up some traditional practices, such as the wearing in public of the **chador,** a kind of robe that completely covers the body and most of the face. As you have read earlier in this section, women remain more traditional in other countries such as Saudi Arabia, Iran, and Afghanistan.

In most African nations, women won the right to vote when the countries gained independence. Their social status today often remains low, however. Many of the traditions of the past continue, including a subservient role for women. In rural areas, women traditionally work both at home and in the fields beside men. As men have migrated to the cities to find work in recent years, women have been left with more responsibilities.

# Human Trafficking

One of the fastest growing human rights issues in the world today is human trafficking, which is the recruiting and transporting of people for the purposes of slavery, forced labor, and servitude. Women are particularly at risk from sex trafficking. Criminals exploit the lack of opportunities these women have by promising them good jobs or opportunities to get an education. Then the criminals force the victims to become prostitutes. Thousands of children from Asia, Africa, and South America are sold into the global sex trade every year. Often they are kidnapped or orphaned, and sometimes they are actually sold by their own families. Parents may sell children to traffickers in order to pay off debts or gain income, or they may be deceived concerning the prospects of training and a better life for their children. In West Africa, some trafficked children have often lost one or both parents to the African AIDS crisis. Thousands of male (and sometimes female) children have also been forced to be child soldiers. Trafficking is a fairly lucrative industry. In some areas, such as Russia, Eastern Europe, Hong Kong, Japan, and Colombia, trafficking is controlled by large criminal organizations.

# Patterns of Global Migration

The gap between rich and poor nations has continued to grow. This rift has led to migration of people from poor regions to wealthier regions. Many immigrants have moved in search of better economic opportunities. Others have sought freedom from repressive governments.

- **Immigration to Germany** Until the late 1990s, Germany had a very liberal immigration policy. The German constitution guaranteed food, clothing, and shelter to refugees until their applications for citizenship were accepted or rejected. Many people entered Germany from Eastern Europe or the Middle East. Some were fleeing war-torn areas. Others were seeking jobs. Some Germans felt resentment, especially when the economy faced difficult times. Certain right-wing extremist groups attacked immigrants. The German constitution was amended in 1996 to restrict immigration.

- **Immigration to France** Within French society in the 1980s, more and more people took jobs in management and technology. A wave of immigrants from southeastern Europe and North Africa filled the need for agricultural and other manual labor. In the 1990s, immigrants made up between five and ten percent of the population of France. As in Germany, social and racial tensions emerged. When the economy took a downturn in the mid-1970s, the French government began to restrict immigration.

- **Immigration to the United States** In the 1980s and 1990s, immigration to the United States increased greatly. By 1997, one in every ten people in the United States had been born elsewhere. The majority of these immigrants were from Latin America and Asia. Some were illegal immigrants. The United States took action to halt illegal immigration, deny social benefits to illegal aliens, and return those who had entered the country illegally to their homelands.

## Summary

As nations in the developing world have modernized, tensions between modern and traditional ways of living and thinking have emerged. Women have gained new rights and roles in some nations, but they have been kept in traditional roles in others. Throughout the developing world, there has been population growth and movement to cities. Although urbanization has created more opportunities for some individuals, cities have often found it difficult to provide basic services for rising populations. Migrations have occurred as people have sought better economic opportunities and escaped political repression. These migrations have sometimes produced tension and violence.

### Note Taking

*Reading Skill:*
**Identify Effects**
Make a chart. Record the effects of immigration to the three countries.

### Preparing for the Regents

- To what extent are current migrations similar to earlier migrations? How are they different?

# Science and Technology

## Section Overview

In the last half of the twentieth century, science and technology have brought great changes. These changes are continuing today. The Green Revolution increased the food supply in developing countries. Computers and advances in telecommunications have brought an explosion of information and, with it, a greater need for education. Technology has allowed exploration of space. Medical breakthroughs have brought better health and longer life.

## Key Themes and Concepts

As you review this section, take special note of the following key themes and concepts:

**Science and Technology** How did science and technology change life in the last half of the twentieth century?

**Change** What social and economic changes are being produced by the Computer Revolution?

**Interdependence** In what ways is the world more interdependent than ever before?

## Key Terms

As you review this section, be sure you understand the significance of these key terms:

| | | |
|---|---|---|
| Green Revolution | Information | genetic engineering |
| Computer Revolution | Revolution | clone |
| Internet | literacy | AIDS |

## The Green Revolution

### Increasing the Food Supply

Throughout the 1900s, scientists applied technology in a number of ways to increase food production.

- **Irrigation** Farmers installed pumps to bring water from far below the surface of the earth and used other irrigation systems to distribute water.
- **Machinery** Farmers used machines, especially those powered by gasoline and diesel fuel, to increase yields from their land.
- **Fertilizer and Pesticides** Farmers enriched their soil with fertilizers and eliminated insect pests with pesticides.
- **New Varieties of Grains and Livestock** Scientists developed new, hardier grains and bred livestock that produced more meat or milk.

In the 1960s, farmers in developing countries applied some of these methods to increase their production of wheat and rice. Their efforts were so successful that the result was called the Green Revolution. In some countries, such as India and Indonesia, the Green Revolution doubled food output.

---

### The Big Idea

Science and technology have brought great change as:

- new agricultural methods increase the food supply.
- people are able to obtain, process, and transmit information more quickly than ever before.
- nations are exploring space.
- medical breakthroughs are improving the quality of life.

### Key People and Terms

Place each of the key terms into one of these categories: technology or medicine.

### Preparing for the Regents

- What were the benefits and limitations of the Green Revolution?

## Limits of the Green Revolution

The Green Revolution increased the food supply, but it did not solve the problems of world hunger and poverty. In some regions, population is still growing faster than food production. Also, technology has limitations. A region has to have enough water to start with to support new irrigation techniques. Also, irrigation systems, chemical fertilizers, and pesticides cost money that developing nations of the global South do not have. Poorer farmers usually cannot afford these innovations, and some have been forced off their land. Recently scientists have developed genetically modified food as another way to combat world hunger. Critics of this technology claim that malnutrition and hunger are often the result of politics that prevent food from reaching hungry people rather than lack of food. They say such foods are too expensive and that long-term effects of eating such foods are unknown.

### Key Themes and Concepts

**Science and Technology**
The benefits of technology are not enjoyed equally by the global North and the global South. Because technology is expensive, wealthier nations have an added advantage over poorer ones.

### New Technology: Benefits and Limits

| Technology | Benefits (+) | Limits (−) |
|---|---|---|
| **The Computer Revolution** | • Creates new jobs<br>• Links people, businesses, and nations<br>• Makes more information available | • Threatens some jobs<br>• Available only to those who can afford equipment<br>• Widens gap between the global North and the global South |
| **Medical breakthroughs** | • Prevents illnesses<br>• Wipes out diseases<br>• Increases life span | • Available only to nations and people who can afford them<br>• Presents new problems of quality of life and care of the aged |
| **Revolution in agriculture (The Green Revolution)** | • Increases food production<br>• Develops new food products | • May succeed only where rainfall is regular<br>• Requires costly chemicals<br>• High cost may force out small farmers |

### Summarize

Write a summary statement about the benefits and limits of new technology.

# The Information Age

## The Computer Revolution

Probably the most revolutionary development since the mid-1900s is the computer. The first computers were enormous machines that filled a large room and worked slowly. After the invention of the silicon chip, computers were miniaturized. Computers have allowed people to obtain, process, and distribute information very quickly. Businesses today depend on computers for their accounting, word processing, ordering, and many other systems. This great increase in the use of computers is often called the Computer Revolution.

## The Internet

By the 1990s, the Internet, a growing computer network, linked individuals, governments, and businesses all over the world. Many people make connections to the Internet through telephone or cable lines in their homes. With the Internet, people can communicate and do business more rapidly than ever before. At the same time, greater and greater amounts of information are available. The rapid spread of information, which began in the 1950s and increases with each passing year, is sometimes referred to as the **Information Revolution.**

### Preparing for the Regents

• How has the Internet increased global interdependence?

**Preparing for the Regents**

• Why is education so important to progress in today's world?

## Literacy and Education

The Information Revolution has had a great impact on education and the job market in the global North. In these nations, there has been a gradual decline in the number of jobs in industry and agriculture. New jobs are often based on information and communications services. Such jobs require more education and new types of learning, especially about technology.

Gains continue to be made throughout the world in **literacy,** the ability to read and write. Developing countries have recognized that economic and social progress depends in part on having a literate population. For this reason, most nations of the world provide—and, in fact, require—education through at least age 14.

# The Space Age

### Space Exploration

As you have learned, the space age began in the late 1950s with a space race between the United States and the Soviet Union. In the years after the breakup of the Soviet Union, the United States and Russia have cooperated on joint space ventures. Space shuttles circle Earth, and a permanent space station has been set up. Humans have walked on the moon; space probes have been sent to many planets.

### Satellites

A satellite is an object that is launched into orbit around the Earth, usually for observation or telecommunications purposes. Satellites can be used to:

• map and forecast weather.
• navigate in ships and aircraft.
• monitor changes in the natural environment.
• aid in rapid worldwide communications.

Satellites are used to transmit television and telephone signals globally. Signals are transmitted from one point on Earth to the satellite. The satellite transmits the signals to another point on Earth. This technology allows rapid reporting of events happening anywhere in the world.

# Medical Technology

Since 1945, medical science has achieved amazing successes. Throughout the world, people are living longer, infant mortality rates are lower, and people can enjoy a better quality of life.

### Important Advances

• **Antibiotics** Scientists have developed antibiotics to treat diseases.
• **Vaccines** Vaccines have wiped out diseases such as smallpox and prevented the spread of many other diseases.
• **Transplants** Surgeons developed and gradually improved procedures for the transplanting of organs to save lives.
• **Laser Surgery** Lasers, devices that make use of concentrated beams of light, have made surgery safer.

**Note Taking**

*Reading Skill:*
**Categorize**
Make a chart. List at least two advances in science and technology for each area.

| Advances in Science and Technology | |
| --- | --- |
| Food Production | • <br> • |
| Information Age | • <br> • |
| Space Age | • <br> • |
| Medicine | • <br> • |

## Difficult Challenges

- **Genetic Engineering** The process of genetic engineering, which involves changing the chemical codes carried by living things, holds promise for creating new drugs and curing disease. In 1997, the first **clone,** or exact genetic replica of an organism, was announced. Genetic engineering is controversial, however, because it has raised questions about how far science should go to change or create life.

- **New Epidemics** Challenges to medicine have arisen in recent decades. In the 1980s and 1990s, the disease called **AIDS** (acquired immunodeficiency syndrome) resulted in millions of deaths. Scientists searched for a cure for AIDS. Other epidemics include the pneumonic and bubonic plagues in southern India in 1994. Avian influenza (bird flu) was found to infect and kill humans. It spread from domestic and migratory birds to humans across Asia, Europe, and the Middle East. In 2009, the H1N1 virus raised fears of pandemic.

- **Drug-Resistant Microbes** The widespread use of antibiotics has allowed some types of microbes to become resistant to drugs. Certain diseases that the medical community thought were under control, such as tuberculosis, are becoming a threat again.

- **Destruction of Tropical Rain Forests** The world's tropical rain forests are the source of many medicinal plants. As these forests are being destroyed, scientists worry that valuable drugs in use today, as well as new ones that might have been discovered later, will be lost.

## Summary

Better food production, an explosion in information and communication, the exploration of space, and medical breakthroughs have changed the world. In many ways, science and technology have benefited people's lives. Many problems, however, remain to be solved.

# The Environment

## Section Overview

Many global environmental issues have arisen in the twentieth century. Pollution of water, land, and air threatens the health of all living things. Forests are being destroyed, species are disappearing, and deserts are growing. The safety of nuclear power plants and of nuclear waste disposal methods are additional environmental concerns.

## Key Themes and Concepts

As you review this section, take special note of the following key themes and concepts:

**Environment and Society** What environmental problems exist today?

**Interdependence** How do these issues affect people globally?

**Decision Making** How are nations working together to make decisions that will solve environmental problems?

## Key Terms

As you review this section, be sure you understand the significance of these key terms:

| | | |
|---|---|---|
| pollution | ozone layer | deforestation |
| acid rain | greenhouse effect | desertification |
| fossil fuels | | |

## Pollution

Pollution is the contamination of the environment, including air, water, and soil. Pollution is harmful to humans as well as to plants and other animal life. It takes many forms. Factories and automobiles release gases and soot into the air. These substances can cause respiratory disease. Water can become polluted by human wastes, fertilizers, pesticides, and toxic chemicals. These substances may lead to the development of cancers or even cause death. For this reason, many nations have set standards on both air and water quality. Pollution is resulting in several global problems.

### Acid Rain

Acid rain occurs when rain falls through air that is polluted by the burning of fossil fuels. **Fossil fuels** include coal, oil, and natural gas. Factories, automobiles, and other sources release these chemicals. Acid rain damages forests, lakes, and farmland. Because of winds, air pollution in one part of the world can cause acid rain in another. International agreements have been signed to reduce emissions of the substances that cause acid rain.

---

### The **Big Idea**

Today, the world faces many important environmental issues and concerns. These include:

- pollution.
- deforestation.
- endangered species.
- desertification.
- nuclear safety.

---

### Key People and Terms

What do four of the key terms have in common? Explain.

---

### Preparing for the Regents

Describe the possible causes and impacts of the following environmental problems.

Acid rain:

Depletion of the ozone layer:

Global warming:

---

## Depletion of the Ozone Layer

Some scientists are also concerned about depletion of the ozone layer, a layer of gases high in the atmosphere that protects the Earth from the dangerous ultraviolet rays of the sun. This layer is becoming thinner, perhaps because of the use of chlorofluorocarbons (CFCs) and other chemical pollutants. Depletion of the ozone layer could expose people to more solar radiation and result in increased skin cancer and eye disease. Ultraviolet rays might also damage crops and marine life. The United States and other developed countries have agreed to eliminate production and use of CFCs and other harmful substances. In 2002, a scientific organization found that these limitations were helping reduce harmful pollutants.

## Global Warming

Scientists are also concerned about a gradual rise in global temperatures. Many scientists believe that this phenomenon is caused by the **greenhouse effect,** in which warm air becomes trapped in the lower atmosphere. Possible causes of the rising temperatures that have been observed are the use of CFCs, the burning of fossil fuels, and the destruction of forests. Many scientists fear that this overall warming could affect agriculture and cause coastal flooding as polar icecaps melt. They also predict extinction of many plant and animal species. In 1997, a UN summit meeting on global warming set limits on types of emissions that are thought to contribute to the phenomenon. Many countries and some states in the United States have passed legislation requiring businesses to conform to these standards.

## Scarcity of Clean Water

Population growth, pollution, and climate change have increased the strain on natural resources such as clean water. Approximately one billion people worldwide lack access to clean water. In developing countries, the lack of clean water is linked to diseases such as malaria. In some places, such as Israel and Jordan, nations share lakes and rivers, and disputes over pollution or cutting off water supplies could lead to war. Industries have begun to develop clean water technologies. Organizations such as the United Nations have begun to focus on improving water quality and people's access to clean water.

# Deforestation

Deforestation is the destruction of forests, especially tropical rain forests. Deforestation is usually caused by development as nations harvest lumber or clear land to raise crops, graze cattle, or build homes. Some estimate that the world is losing more than 50 million acres of tropical forest each year. Brazil, India, and Indonesia are the nations where forests are disappearing at the highest rate.

## Effects of Deforestation

The effects of deforestation include changes in local weather patterns, a buildup of carbon dioxide in the atmosphere (which may lead to the greenhouse effect), soil erosion, and extinction of certain plants and animals.

## Global Solutions

One of the challenges in halting deforestation is that many of the world's great forests are in developing nations. These nations need the income they can receive from making use of forested land. Those who want to save the forests say that the economic needs of developing nations must be balanced against needs of the global population. Many nations gathered to debate these and other environmental problems at the UN-sponsored Earth Summit that was held in Rio de Janeiro, Brazil, in 1992.

**Vocabulary Builder**

depletion—(dih PLEE shun) n. the reduction of the amount of something that is present or available

**Identify Supporting Details**

What role has the UN played in solving the problems of:

• global warming?

• clean water?

• deforestation?

**Vocabulary Builder**

erosion—(ee ROH zhun) n. the process by which something is gradually reduced or destroyed

**Key Themes and Concepts**

**Needs and Wants**
The economic progress of some developing countries can conflict with the protection of the environment.

## Endangered Species
### Problems and Effects
A problem related to deforestation is the endangerment of various species of plants and animals. Various by-products of development—the clearing of land, the damming of waterways, and many types of pollution—all threaten to wipe out species of plants and animals.

If species are lost, the balance of the ecosystem of the world could be damaged severely. In addition, resources that people use for food and medicines may disappear.

### Global Solutions
Several international agreements have attempted to address the topic of endangered species. Some agreements, for example, have banned the shipment and sale of endangered animals. Some people have suggested that these species can best be protected through preserving their habitats. The 1992 Earth Summit addressed this issue. Other agreements have been made about specific animals, such as whales and tuna, which have been endangered by commercial fishing and other economic practices.

**Preparing for the Regents**

• Why are cooperative solutions needed for international problems such as drug trafficking, deforestation, and the preservation of endangered species?

*The Spreading Desert*
*Desertification is a major problem in Africa, especially in the Sahel region just south of the Sahara Desert. Here, there has been a large loss of farmland and pastures.*

**Preparing for the Regents**

Practice your map skills by answering these questions.

1. Where in Africa is the largest area of existing desert?

2. If desertification continues, what social conditions might result?

**The Spreading Desert**

Existing desert area
Probable desert area
Possible desert area

AFRICA

0    300    600    900    1200 Miles
0    400    800    1200 Kilometers

## Desertification
### Causes and Effects
Desertification is the changeover from arable land (land that can be farmed) into desert. Desertification is caused mostly by human activity, especially the following:

• **Overgrazing** by livestock such as sheep and cattle eliminates the grasses that hold the soil together to prevent erosion.

• **Cutting down forests** robs the land of another barrier to soil erosion.

As grass and trees are eliminated, the soil loses its nutrients. Without plant roots to hold the soil, wind erosion removes the fertile topsoil. The land is then unable to sustain plant life. The Sahara in Africa, for example, is expanding at the rate of about 50 miles per year. The expansion of deserts is one cause of famine.

### Controlling Desertification

Methods to control desertification include restricting livestock (to prevent overgrazing) and the planting of new trees to act as a barrier against erosion. These solutions are difficult to put into practice in developing countries, where farmers try to work as much land as possible. However, new farming methods, including improved irrigation, may help solve the problem.

## Nuclear Proliferation

The use of nuclear energy and the proliferation, or spread, of nuclear weapons both pose serious potential threats to the global environment.

### Accidents and Waste Disposal

In 1986, an accident at the Chernobyl nuclear power plant in the Soviet Union exposed people and crops to deadly radiation. Radiation was also blown across countries in Europe. This accident led to heightened concern about safe use of nuclear energy. Some nations stepped up their safeguards; others scaled back their nuclear power programs. Dangers are also posed by nuclear waste that is created by nuclear weapons production facilities.

Nuclear waste is radioactive and remains that way for many years. Exposure to high levels of radioactivity is very harmful to humans. Earlier methods of disposing of nuclear waste included dumping it at sea or burying it in deep wells. Both of these methods have been banned by the international community. Within nations and across the globe, solutions are being sought for the safe disposal of nuclear waste. Effective cleanup of nuclear waste is expensive, however. This expense makes other solutions more attractive for many nations.

### Nuclear Weapons

As the 1900s ended, the United States and Russia controlled over 90 percent of the world's nuclear weapons. China, Britain, France, India, and Pakistan were also publicly declared nuclear powers. It was widely accepted that Israel had a small, undeclared nuclear arsenal.

Several nations gave up their nuclear weapons in the 1990s. South Africa dismantled its nuclear weapons. The nuclear missiles stationed in the former Soviet republics of Belarus, Kazakhstan, and Ukraine were returned to Russia.

While tensions between the major nuclear powers have eased since the end of the Cold War, the threat of nuclear war still exists. There is concern that regional conflicts, such as the dispute between India and Pakistan, could escalate into a nuclear exchange. Both North Korea and Iran are actively developing nuclear programs. Another danger is that a terrorist group could obtain nuclear weapons. The world community monitors these situations and uses both diplomacy and sanctions to reduce these threats.

### Summary

Nations are working together to resolve the environmental issues that face the global community. These issues include air and water pollution, global warming, deforestation, desertification, and nuclear safety. Sometimes making decisions involves balancing the protection of the environment with the needs of individual nations. Only with global cooperation, however, will these problems be solved.

**Note Taking**

*Reading Skill:*
**Identify Supporting Details**
Make a flowchart. List the dangers of nuclear energy. Add boxes as you need them.

| Dangers of Nuclear Energy |
| --- |

↓

| |
| --- |

**Make Inferences**

Why might the United States and Russia not want to give up their nuclear weapons?

**Key Themes and Concepts**

**Interdependence**
How do environmental issues—both problems and solutions—demonstrate the interdependence of the modern world?

# Questions for Regents Practice

## Multiple Choice

*Directions:* Review the Test-Taking Strategies section of this book. Then answer the following questions, drawn from actual Regents examinations. For each statement or question, choose the *number* of the word or expression that, of those given, best completes the statement or answers the question.

Base your answer to question 1 on the graph below and on your knowledge of social studies.

Reserves of Oil (projected to 2030)

1  Which action will help slow the trend indicated by the graph?

(1) expanding Green Revolution technology

(2) increasing industrialization in developing countries

(3) using alternative energy sources

(4) lowering worldwide oil prices

2  Bombings, kidnappings, and hijackings are tactics most often used by

(1) imperialists

(2) terrorists

(3) nationalists

(4) absolutists

3  Economic development in Latin American nations has been hindered most by

(1) a scarcity of goods produced for trade and a lack of natural resources

(2) governments that are primarily concerned with preserving the environment

(3) problems of overpopulation, patterns of land distribution, and a lack of investment capital

(4) corporations that are not interested in the use of modern technology

4  Which is the major reason that the United Nations has often been unsuccessful in solving international disputes?

(1) The United Nations does not have sufficient funds to act.

(2) The disputing nations are usually not members of the United Nations.

(3) National sovereignty stands in the way of international cooperation.

(4) The United Nations charter does not provide a means to settle disputes.

5  Since 1990, people in Timor, Kosovo, and Kurdish Iraq have all protested their lack of

(1) membership in the European Union

(2) economic stability

(3) independent homelands

(4) representation in the Arab League

6  In many developing nations, rising levels of pollution and continued housing shortages are a direct result of

(1) increased urbanization

(2) a reliance on single-crop economies

(3) changing climatic conditions

(4) increasing nationalism

7 In Middle Eastern societies, women have increasingly been at the center of a conflict between the forces of modernization and the

(1) values of traditional Islamic culture

(2) pressure for a Palestinian homeland

(3) shortage of capital for industrial development

(4) need to reduce the birthrate

8 The major goal of the Green Revolution has been to

(1) decrease the use of modern farm machinery

(2) decrease population growth

(3) increase agricultural output

(4) increase the number of traditional farms

9 A valid statement about the technology in the 1900s is that technology has

(1) eliminated famine and disease throughout the world

(2) delayed economic progress in developing countries

(3) led to the adoption of free trade policies

(4) accelerated the pace of cultural diffusion

10 A study of the accident at the Chernobyl nuclear power plant in the Soviet Union and of the severe air pollution in Mexico City would lead to the conclusion that

(1) technology can cause problems throughout the world

(2) international trade is more profitable than domestic commerce

(3) modern science cannot solve most political problems

(4) agricultural nations have caused major world environmental problems

11 A major environmental problem affecting Latin America, sub-Saharan Africa, and Southeast Asia has been

(1) air pollution

(2) deforestation

(3) disposal of nuclear waste

(4) acid rain

# Thematic Essay Question

In developing your answer, be sure to keep these general definitions in mind:

    (a) <u>describe</u> means "to illustrate something in words or tell about it"
    (b) <u>evaluate</u> means "to judge or determine the significance, worth, or quality of"

*Directions:*    Write a well-organized essay that includes an introduction, several paragraphs addressing the task below, and a conclusion.

**Theme:**   **Science and Technology**

> Since 1945, technology has transformed human life. Advances have occurred in many different areas. These changes have had both positive and negative effects on human life.

**Task:**

> - Describe one scientific or technological advance made since 1945 that has had a significant impact on global history.
> - Give two examples of ways in which this advance has affected you or will have an effect on you in the future.
> - Evaluate the positive and negative effects of that scientific or technological advance on the lives of human beings.

You may discuss any scientific or technological advance that has come about since 1945. Some types of advances that you may wish to consider are discovery of nuclear power, the widespread use of the computer or of Internet technology, and medical advances.

**You are *not* limited to these suggestions.**

**Guidelines:**

**In your essay, be sure to**
- Develop all aspects of the task
- Support the theme with relevant facts, examples, and details
- Use a logical and clear plan of organization, including an introduction and a conclusion that are beyond a simple restatement of the theme.

# Document-Based Question

This question is based on the accompanying documents. The question is designed to test your ability to work with historical documents. Some of the documents have been edited for the purposes of this question. As you analyze the documents, take into account the source of each document and any point of view that may be presented in the document.

**Historical Context:**

People have held differing views about human rights throughout history and in different cultures. In the 1900s, however, there have been movements all over the world to ensure basic human rights for all people.

**Task:** Using the information from the documents and your knowledge of global history, answer the questions that follow each document in Part A. Your answers to the questions will help you write the Part B essay in which you will be asked to

- Describe and evaluate the progress of justice and human rights in the 1900s

In developing your answers, be sure to keep these general definitions in mind:

- (a) <u>describe</u> means "to tell or depict in written or spoken words; give an account of"
- (b) <u>evaluate</u> means "to examine and judge the significance, worth, or condition of; to determine the value of"

# Document-Based Question

*Directions:* Analyze the documents and answer the question or questions that follow each document, using the space provided.

### Document #1

Article 1  All human beings are born free and equal in dignity and rights. . . .
Article 2  Everyone is entitled to all the rights and freedoms . . . without distinction of any kind. . . .
Article 18  Everyone has the right to freedom of thought, conscience and religion. . . .
Article 19  Everyone has the right to freedom of opinion and expression. . . .
Article 25  Everyone has the right to a standard of living adequate for the health and well-being of himself and of his family, including food, clothing, housing and medical care. . . .

— **General Assembly of the United Nations, *The Universal Declaration of Human Rights*, adopted December 10, 1948**

1. Describe one economic right to which Document 1 says all people are entitled.

_____

_____

2. Which article or articles in Document 1 most closely support freedom of speech? Explain the reason for your choice.

_____

_____

### Document #2

*In many parts of the world the people are searching for a solution which would link the two basic values: peace and justice. The two are like bread and salt for mankind. Every nation and every community have the inalienable right to these values. No conflicts can be resolved without doing everything possible to follow that road...*

— **Lech Walesa, Nobel Peace Prize Lecture, 1983**

3. What point was Walesa trying to make by comparing peace and justice to bread and salt?

_____

_____

**Document #3**

4. Explain why some people in this cartoon have been waiting for hours, while others have been waiting for years.

_____

_____

_____

_____

_____

# Document-Based Question

## Part B
## Essay

*Directions:* Write a well-organized essay that includes an introduction, several paragraphs, and a conclusion. Use evidence from *at least two* documents in your essay. Support your response with relevant facts, examples, and details. Include additional outside information.

### Historical Context:

People have held differing views about human rights throughout history and in different cultures. In the 1900s, however, there have been movements all over the world to ensure basic human rights for all.

### Task:

Using information from the documents and your knowledge of global history and geography, write an essay in which you:

- Evaluate justice and human rights in the 1900s
- Describe advances in human rights as well as human rights violations
- Explain whether you think that the trend is toward greater human rights for all

### Guidelines:

**In your essay, be sure to**
- Develop all aspects of the task
- Incorporate information from *at least two* documents
- Incorporate relevant outside information
- Support the theme with relevant facts, examples, and details
- Use a logical and clear plan of organization, including an introduction and a conclusion that are beyond a restatement of the theme

The Regents Examination takes a thematic approach to history. This section of the book will help you to review the themes that are mostly likely to be tested on the thematic essay and document-based parts of the exam. It is important to remember that the themes used in this course span the entire two-year course. The events you choose to write about in the thematic essay may be taken from either ninth or tenth grade or both.

## Change

Change means basic alterations in things, events, and ideas. Throughout global history, major changes have had significant and lasting impacts on human development.

- **Neolithic Revolution** Some 11,000 years ago, people first developed farming methods and lived in permanent settlements. As a result, the first civilizations emerged.
- **Industrial Revolution** This change began in Europe in the 1700s and gradually spread throughout the world. Power-driven machinery in factories became the dominant means of production. The results of this change have included urbanization, a higher standard of living, and pollution of the environment.
- **Chinese Communist Revolution** In 1948, Mao Zedong established a Chinese Communist state. Since then, China has become a world economic power. Today, it works to control its growing population, as well as to adapt communism to modern needs.

Other examples of change are the Crusades, the spread of bubonic plague, the Renaissance, the Scientific Revolution, the Enlightenment, the Agrarian Revolution, the Reformation, African independence movements, and the emergence of Pacific Rim nations.

## Turning Points

Turning points are times when decisive changes occur. Turning points often have political, social, and cultural impacts.

- **Fall of Constantinople** This event, which occurred in 1453, marked the end of the Christian Byzantine empire and the emergence of the powerful Ottoman empire, a Muslim power that dominated the region for centuries.
- **Voyages of Columbus** The voyages of Columbus began the European race to colonize the Americas. A far-reaching exchange of people, plants, animals, and ideas occurred between Europe, the Americas, and Africa.
- **French Revolution** The French Revolution of 1789 had a powerful influence well beyond France, spreading democratic ideals and a spirit of nationalism throughout Europe and around the globe.
- **Collapse of Communism in the Soviet Union** The collapse of communism in the Soviet Union initiated years of change in Eastern Europe and brought an end to the Cold War.

Other examples of turning points include the signing of the Magna Carta, the American Revolution, independence movements in Latin America, and the Russian Revolution.

## Belief Systems

Belief systems are the established, orderly ways in which groups or individuals look at religious faith or philosophical tenets.

- **Hinduism** A religion more than 3,000 years old, Hinduism has had an enormous effect on India, Southeast Asia, and the rest of the world.
- **Buddhism** A religion founded in the 500s B.C. in India, Buddhism spread throughout Asia.
- **Judaism** The first great monotheistic religion, Judaism has had an important effect on several other world religions.
- **Christianity** Greatly influenced by Judaism, Christianity is a monotheistic religion centered on the teachings of Jesus Christ.
- **Islam** Also greatly influenced by Judaism, Islam is a monotheistic religion and has followers all over the world, especially in the Middle East, Africa, and Asia.

Other examples of belief systems are animism, Confucianism, Taoism, Shintoism, and Sikhism.

## Geography and the Environment

This theme has to do with relationships among people, places, and environments. Environment means the surroundings, including natural elements and elements created by humans.

- **Early River Civilizations** Early civilizations grew up around rivers. Rivers provided water for crops and for drinking, as well as a means of transportation.
- **Chinese Influence on Japan** Through the bridge of Korea, China had a strong influence on the culture of Japan.
- **Industrialization in Great Britain** Great Britain's natural resources, together with such geographical factors as rivers and natural harbors, allowed the Industrial Revolution to begin there.
- **Industrial Revolution: Impact on Environment** The Industrial Revolution had a lasting impact on the natural environment. For example, new sources of energy often created new types of pollution. Urbanization changed the landscape as cities and their suburbs grew.

Other examples of the impact of geography and the environment are the development of city-states in ancient Greece, the importance of the Middle East as a crossroads between three continents, and environmental problems such as desertification and the destruction of tropical forests.

## Economic Systems

Economic systems include traditional, command, market, and mixed systems. Each must answer the three basic economic questions: What goods and services are to be produced and in what quantities? How shall these goods and services be produced? For whom shall these goods and services be produced?

- **Traditional Economy** An economic system based on farming, often subsistence farming, is a traditional economy.

- **Manorialism** The economic system of Western Europe in medieval times was called manorialism. It was based on the manor, an estate that often included one or more villages and the surrounding lands.
- **Mercantilism** The economic policy in which nations sought to export more than they imported is known as mercantilism. Overseas empires were central to mercantilism, which led to imperialism.
- **Capitalism (Market Economy)** Capitalism is an economic system in which the means of production are privately owned and operated for profit. It developed as an economic system in the 1500s.
- **Marxist Socialism (Command Economy)** Marxist socialism is the economic system found in communist states such as the former Soviet Union and its satellites. It is characterized by ownership of property and operation of businesses by the state rather than by private individuals.

Other examples of topics connected with economic systems are laissez-faire economics, the commercial revolution, cash crop economies, and imperialism.

## Political Systems

Political systems, such as monarchies, dictatorships, and democracies, address certain basic questions of government such as: What should a government have the power to do? What should a government not have the power to do?

- **Monarchy** In monarchies, a king or queen exercises central power. Monarchies have been common since ancient times, and a few are still in existence today.
- **Feudalism** Feudalism was most prominent in medieval Europe and in Japan from about 1600 to the mid-1800s. It is a decentralized political system. In Europe, it declined with the growth of nation-states.
- **Democracy** Democracy, a system in which the people hold the ruling power—either directly or through elected representatives—had its roots in ancient Greece. It is a primary political system in the countries of the West today.
- **Totalitarianism** In a totalitarian system, a one-party dictatorship regulates every aspect of its citizens' lives. The Soviet Union under Stalin was a totalitarian state.

Other examples of political systems are the limited democracy of Athens, the militarism of Sparta and of Japan, absolutism, theocracy, communism, fascism, and apartheid.

## Culture and Intellectual Life

Culture includes the patterns of human behavior (encompassing ideas, beliefs, values, artifacts, and ways of making a living) that a society transmits to succeeding generations to meet its fundamental needs. Intellectual life involves ways of thinking, studying, and reflecting on aspects of life.

- **Roman Civilization** Rome left a great cultural and intellectual legacy to the western world, including a commitment to law and justice, the Latin language, and a body of great literature.
- **Gupta Golden Age** In India, from A.D. 320 through 550, lasting achievements in mathematics, medicine, arts, and architecture occurred, supported by the stable reign of the Gupta dynasty.

- **Islamic Golden Age** Between A.D. 750 and 1350, Islamic empires experienced a golden age. The roots of modern mathematics and science can be traced to this period.
- **African Civilizations** From the mid-1200s through the mid-1500s, Africa was the site of great activity in scholarship and art.
- **Renaissance Europe** The Renaissance in Europe, which began in the mid-1300s, was a time of great cultural and intellectual activity. Humanism—which recognized the importance of individual worth in a secular society—guided the Renaissance.

Other important eras of cultural and intellectual activity included early river civilizations, classical Chinese civilization, Mesoamerican civilizations, and the Enlightenment in Europe.

## Nationalism

Nationalism is a feeling of pride in and devotion to one's country or the desire of a people to control their own government. It is sometimes a divisive force and sometimes a force that unifies. In many cases, it is a source of conflict.

- **German and Italian Unification** In the mid-1800s, both Germany and Italy experienced unification. In each case, many small states joined into one nation.
- **India** Ideals of western democracy, as well as devotion to traditional Hindu and Muslim culture, sustained Indian nationalism through the first half of the 1900s, leading to independence in 1948.
- **Zionism** Since Roman times, Jews had dreamed of returning to Palestine. This dream grew into an international movement in the 1900s. By 1948, the nation of Israel had been created.
- **African Independence Movements** In 1945, just four European powers controlled nearly all of Africa. Less than 25 years later, a tide of nationalism had liberated many African peoples and set them on the road to self-determination.

Other historical situations in which nationalism had an impact are the development of the nation of Turkey, conflicts in the Balkans, the breakup of the Ottoman empire, Latin America in the 1800s and 1900s, Pan-Africanism, and Pan-Arabism.

## Imperialism

Imperialism is the domination by one country of the political and economic life of another country or region. Imperialism has had both positive and negative effects on colonies.

- **British in India** The British controlled India by the late 1700s. Although railroads and the British educational system benefited some Indians, local industries and Indian culture suffered, and Indians were treated as inferiors. India gained its independence in 1948.
- **European Powers in Africa** European nations carved up the continent of Africa in the late 1880s. Africa was a continent made up mainly of colonies until after 1945, when African peoples began to demand independence. The legacy of imperialism still affects Africa today.

- **Japan** An imperialist power from the Meiji period, Japan ruled Korea from 1910 to the end of World War II. It also controlled areas in China and Southeast Asia. Japanese imperialism was a cause of World War II.
- **Imperial Rivalry** Competition between imperial powers was one of the causes of World War I. Germany and France, especially, clashed over territory in Africa. Imperial rivalry was also a cause of many smaller wars.

Other civilizations that practiced imperialism include the Chinese Han dynasty, the Romans, the Byzantines, and the Mongols. The collapse of European imperialism still affects many regions of the world today.

# Diversity and Interdependence

Diversity involves understanding and respecting oneself and others, including differences in language, gender, socioeconomic class, religion, and other human characteristics and traits. It is closely related to interdependence, the reliance upon others in mutually beneficial interactions and exchanges. Sometimes the refusal to accept diversity leads to conflict.

- **Byzantine Empire** The Byzantine empire blended many diverse cultures. This diversity allowed it to preserve many differing traditions.
- **Balkans** This region of Eastern Europe has always been an area of great religious and ethnic diversity. Often this diversity has led to conflict.
- **Global Economy** In the 1900s, the world economy became more interdependent, a process that started during the age of imperialism. Today, the world's economy is truly global.
- **Environmental Issues** The global population shares the Earth, and what occurs in one part of the world often has an impact on many other areas. Increasingly, environmental decisions are reached by many nations working together for mutual benefit.

Other examples of diversity and interdependence include the links between the East and the West during the time of the Mongol empire, tensions that have arisen as a result of Islamic fundamentalism, and interactions among Muslims, Hindus, and Sikhs in India.

# Justice and Human Rights

Justice is fair, equal, proportional, or appropriate treatment given to individuals in interpersonal, societal, or government interactions. Human rights are those basic political, economic, and social rights to which all human beings are entitled. At times throughout history, justice and human rights have been violated.

- **Code of Hammurabi** Because the Code of Hammurabi was carved on a pillar in Babylon (around 1800 B.C.), all people could see what the laws were. This was the first major collection of laws in history.
- **English Bill of Rights** The English Bill of Rights was an important document because it limited the power of the monarchy and returned traditional rights to English citizens.
- **Irish Potato Famine** A blight that affected the main food crop for the Irish people in the mid-1800s created widespread famine when the British, who ruled

the island, continued to export crops that could have fed the Irish. At least a million Irish people died during the famine, also called the Great Hunger.

- **Tiananmen Square** When students in China demanded greater political freedom in the late 1980s, Chinese Communist authorities cracked down, wounding and killing many demonstrators.

Other examples of important developments in justice and human rights include the Laws of the Twelve Tables, Justinian's Code, the Sharia, and the Magna Carta. Violations of human rights include the Armenian massacres, the Holocaust, apartheid, the Khmer Rouge in Cambodia, and international terrorism.

## Movement of People and Goods

Cultural diffusion is the constant exchange of people, ideas, products, technology, and institutions from one region or civilization to another. Cultural diffusion has occurred throughout history.

- **Muslim Influence on Africa** Muslim traders spread Islam across Africa. Their contacts with diverse cultures allowed them to spread a great number of other ideas and technologies along with the religion of Islam.
- **Silk Road** This 4,000-mile trade route stretched from western China to the Mediterranean. For centuries, from the A.D. 100s onward, goods, ideas, and technology flowed along this route from East to West and back again.
- **Crusades** From the late 1000s through the late 1200s, Christian and Muslim armies battled for control of Palestine. A great deal of cultural diffusion occurred during and after the Crusades, as Europe increased its interest in goods and ideas from the Middle East.
- **Modern Communication** In today's world, computers, the Internet, and satellite communications allow ideas to be passed in moments over great distances.

Other examples of movement of peoples, goods, and ideas include the spread of belief systems (such as Buddhism and Confucianism to Japan), the Muslim influence on Europe, and patterns of global migration.

## Science and Technology

Science and technology means the tools and methods used by people to get what they need and want.

- **Neolithic Revolution** When people developed the knowledge and technology for farming and domesticating animals, permanent settlements grew.
- **Invention of the Printing Press** The printing press was a crucial breakthrough in technology, allowing ideas to spread.
- **Computer Revolution** Since the 1950s, our society has become increasingly dependent on computers and on digitized information.
- **Space Explorations** Humans have populated Earth and moved into the solar system. In recent years, space exploration has been a shared venture among major world powers.

Other examples of breakthroughs in science and technology are the improved standard of living that occurred in the 1800s, the Green Revolution, and advances in genetics.

# Conflict

Conflict has occurred throughout history, and its costs have sometimes been very high. The causes of conflict may be political, social, or economic.

- **Religious Conflicts** Conflicts between peoples of differing belief systems began in ancient times and still exist today in places as widespread as Northern Ireland, India, and the Middle East.
- **Political Revolutions** Violent revolutions occurred within nations from the late 1700s through the 1800s as groups sought democratic reform, national independence, or both.
- **World War I** Sparked by several complex causes, World War I was the first modern, fully industrialized war and the first truly global conflict.
- **The Cold War** After 1945, the United States and its allies were engaged in a global competition with the Soviet Union and its allies. Surrogate conflicts occurred as the two superpowers—the United States and the Soviet Union—exerted their influence throughout the world.

Other examples of conflict include the Crusades, World War II, the Russian Revolution, ethnic disputes in the Balkans and Africa, and Arab-Israeli conflict in the Middle East.

# Modern Global Connections and Interactions

Today's world is a web of connections and interactions. On every level, the people of the world meet, connect, interact, and sometimes collide. These interactions involve politics, economics, culture, or the environment.

- **Global Environmental Cooperation** Nations are becoming increasingly interdependent in their decisions about environmental issues, acknowledging that various peoples share one world.
- **Global Migrations** The last half of the 1900s was a time of great migration, especially from Africa, Asia, and Latin America to Europe and North America. Many people migrated to improve their economic conditions.
- **International Terrorism** Modern technology and transportation systems have allowed violent groups to express their frustration and anger globally through random acts of violence.
- **The United Nations** Created after World War II, the United Nations remains an organization through which nations can come together to seek peaceful solutions to global problems and conflicts.

Other examples of modern global connections and interactions include economic interdependence, nuclear proliferation, and the sharing of technology and ideas through the Internet.

# Glossary

**A**

**absolutism:** political system in which autocratic rulers have complete authority over the government and the lives of people in their nations

**acid rain:** toxic mixture that is produced when rain falls through polluted air

**African National Congress:** group formed by opponents to apartheid in South Africa that encouraged political activism by blacks

**Agrarian Revolution:** change in farming methods in the 1600s that improved the quality and quantity of farm products

**agribusiness:** large commercial farm owned by multinational corporation

**AIDS:** acquired immunodeficiency syndrome

**Allied Powers:** World War I alliance of Great Britain, France, and Russia, later joined by Italy, the United States, and others

**animism:** the belief that every living and nonliving thing in nature has a spirit

**antibiotic:** drug that attacks or weakens the bacteria that cause many diseases

**anti-Semitism:** prejudice against Jews

**apartheid:** South African government policy calling for separation of the races

**appeasement:** policy of giving in to an aggressor's demands in order to keep the peace

**apprentice:** young person who is learning a trade from a master

**aqueduct:** bridgelike stone structure that brings water from hills to cities, first used by ancient Romans

**Arabic numeral:** type of numeral first developed in India and used by many western countries today (1, 2, 3, etc.)

**aristocracy:** a government ruled by an upper class

**armistice:** agreement to end fighting

**Association of Southeast Asian Nations:** formed in 1967, group of nine Southeast Asian countries that coordinate policies among members in areas such as trade and agriculture

**astrolabe:** instrument used to determine latitude by measuring the position of the stars

**asylum:** protection from arrest or from being returned to a dangerous place from which one fled

**artifact:** an item made by humans that is used by archeologists to learn about past cultures

**autocrat:** a single ruler with complete authority

**B**

**balance of power:** distribution of political and economic power that prevents any one nation from becoming too strong

**balance of trade:** difference between how much a country imports and how much it exports

**Bataan Death March:** forced march of Allied prisoners by the Japanese during World War II

**Bible:** the sacred scriptures of Christianity

**blitz:** massive bombing

**Boer War:** war occurring from 1899 to 1902 between the British and the Boers, Dutch farmers; it began after the British tried to annex the Boer republics

**Bolshevik:** member of 1917 Russian revolutionary group

**bourgeoisie:** middle class in Marxism; it refers to Capitalists

**Boxer Rebellion:** event in 1900 in which a group known as Boxers assaulted foreign communities across China

**brahman:** single unifying spirit of Hindu belief

**bubonic plague:** a contagious disease that devastated the world in the 1300s

**bureaucracy:** system of managing government through departments run by appointed officials

**bushido:** code of conduct for samurai during feudal period in Japan

**C**

**caliph:** successor to Muhammad as political and religious leader of the Muslims

**calligraphy:** fine handwriting

**capitalism:** economic system in which the means of production are privately owned and operated for profit

**cartel:** an association of businesspeople; used to refer to the criminal gangs that produce and smuggle drugs internationally

**cartographer:** mapmaker

**cash crop economy:** economy based on the raising and selling of one crop or a small number of crops

**caudillo:** military dictator in Latin America

**Central Powers:** World War I alliance of Germany, Austria-Hungary, and the Ottoman empire (later joined by Bulgaria)

**chador:** cloak worn by some Muslim women

**chivalry:** the code of conduct followed by knights during the Middle Ages

**civil disobedience:** the refusal to obey unjust laws

**civilization:** community characterized by elements such as a system of writing, development of social classes, and cities

**clone:** exact genetic replica

**Cold War:** continuing state of tension and hostility between the United States and the Soviet Union after 1945 because of differences in political and economic philosophies

**collective:** large farm owned and operated by workers as a group

**Columbian exchange:** global exchange of people, plants, animals, ideas, and technology that began in the late 1400s

**command economy:** economy in which government officials make all basic economic decisions

**commercial revolution:** the business revolution that occurred in Europe after the Middle Ages

**common law:** uniform system of justice, developed in England, based on court decisions that became accepted legal principles

**Common Market:** See *European Community*

**commune:** community of people who live and work together and hold property in common

**Computer Revolution:** great increase in the use of computers

**concentration camp:** detention centers instituted by Adolf Hitler where Jews and others were starved, shot, or gassed to death

**Congress of Vienna:** conference held in 1815 among European diplomats that had the purpose of restoring order and stability to Europe

**conquistador:** name, meaning "conqueror," for certain explorers of the 1500s and 1600s

**conservatism:** set of beliefs held by those who want to preserve traditional ways

**Constitutional monarchy:** a government in which the power of the king is limited by law

**containment:** Cold War policy that involved limiting communism to areas already under Soviet control

**contras:** counterrevolutionary group in Nicaragua that opposed the Sandinistas

**Counter-Reformation:** actions taken by the Catholic Church in the 1600s to oppose Protestantism

**coup d'état:** a revolt by a small group intended to overthrow a government

**Crusades:** series of religious wars fought between Christians and Muslims from the late 1000s to the mid-1200s

**cultural diffusion:** the exchange of ideas, customs, goods, and technologies among cultures

**Cultural Revolution:** program launched in 1966 by Mao Zedong to renew loyalty to communism and purge China of nonrevolutionary tendencies

**cuneiform:** wedge-shaped writing formed by pressing a penlike instrument into clay

**czar:** term for autocratic ruler of Russia; Russian word for *Caesar*

**daimyo:** in feudal Japan, warrior lords who held a place below the shogun

**decimal system:** number system based on 10

**Declaration of Independence:** document drafted by Thomas Jefferson that declared American independence from Great Britain

**decolonization:** the process by which European colonies in Africa and Asia became independent states

**deforestation:** destruction of forests, especially tropical rain forests

***desaparecidos:*** word meaning "the disappeared ones," used to describe the thousands of people in Argentina who disappeared during the dirty war

**desert:** dry, barren land

**desertification:** the changeover of arable land into desert

**despot:** absolute ruler

**détente:** period in the 1970s during which there was an easing of tensions between the United States and the Soviet Union

**developed nation:** nation with established agriculture and industry, advanced technology, and a strong educational system

**developing nation:** nation with limited resources that faces obstacles in achieving modern industrial economies

**dharma:** in Hinduism, the moral and religious duties that are expected of an individual

**diaspora:** a scattering of people, as when the Jewish people were forced to leave their homeland in Palestine

**direct democracy:** system of government in which citizens participate directly rather than through elected representatives

**Dirty War:** period beginning in the late 1970s in Argentina during which the military arrested, tortured, and killed thousands of people

**divine right:** belief that a ruler's authority comes directly from God

**Domino Theory:** the belief that if one nation in Southeast Asia fell to Communism, the rest would soon follow

**dynasty:** ruling family

**empire:** group of states or territories governed by one ruler

**enclosure:** process of taking over and fencing off land once shared by peasant farmers

**encomienda:** system created by Spanish government in the Americas allowing colonists to demand labor or tribute from Native Americans

**English Bill of Rights:** a set of acts passed by Parliament to ensure its superiority over the monarchy and guarantee certain rights to citizens

**enlightened despot:** absolute ruler who used royal power to reform society

**Enlightenment:** the period in the 1700s in which people rejected traditional ideas and supported a belief in human reason

**epidemic:** an outbreak of disease that spreads quickly and affects a large number of people

**Estates General:** a French legislative body made up of clergy, nobles, and common people, such as businesspeople and peasants

**ethnic cleansing:** policy of forcibly removing or killing people of a certain ethnic group

**ethnocentrism:** the belief in the superiority of one's own race, culture, or nation

**euro:** European currency introduced in 1999

**European Community:** group of nations established in 1957 to expand free trade in Europe; also called *Common Market*

**European Union:** expansion of the European Community in the 1980s and 1990s; sometimes abbreviated EU

**excommunicate:** to exclude from the Roman Catholic Church as a penalty for refusing to obey Church laws

**factory:** place in which workers and machines are brought together to produce large quantities of goods

**fascism:** the rule of a people by a dictatorial government that is nationalistic and imperialistic

**feudalism:** system of government in which local lords control their own lands but owe military service and other support to a greater lord

**five-year plan:** one of a series of plans instituted by Joseph Stalin to build industry and increase farm output in the Soviet Union

**fossil fuels:** fuels such as coal, oil, and natural gas

**genetic engineering:** process of changing the chemical codes carried by living things to produce cures for disease, better drugs, and so on

**genocide:** attempt to destroy an entire ethnic or religious group

**gentry:** wealthy landowning class

**germ theory:** medical theory stating that many diseases are caused by microorganisms

**glasnost:** period of openness called for in the mid-1980s by Mikhail Gorbachev in the Soviet Union

**globalization:** the growing integration of economies and societies around the world

**Glorious Revolution:** in Great Britain, nonviolent overthrow of the government of James II that resulted in the reign of William and Mary

**Gothic:** style of European church architecture characterized by pointed arches and flying buttresses

**Great Depression:** global economic downturn that began in 1929

**Great Leap Forward:** program begun by Mao Zedong in China in 1958 to increase agricultural and industrial output

**Green Revolution:** development of new varieties of plants and improved agricultural techniques that resulted in greatly increased crop yields

**greenhouse effect:** process in which excess carbon dioxide in the atmosphere traps heat and causes rising global temperatures

**guild:** a type of trade association of merchants or artisans that was active in the Middle Ages

**Guomindang:** Chinese nationalist party formed by Sun Yixian

## H

**haiku:** form of Japanese poetry that expresses a feeling, thought, or idea in three lines

**Hanseatic League:** trade association of northern German towns in the mid-1300s

**heliocentric:** sun-centered

**Hellenistic:** type of culture, resulting from Alexander the Great's conquests, that blended eastern and western influences

**hijra:** Muhammad's flight from Mecca to Medina in 622; also spelled *hegira*

**heresy:** a religious belief that is opposed to the official teachings of a church

**Holocaust:** act of genocide by the Nazis during World War II in which more than six million Jews died

**Holy Land:** Palestine, a land holy to Jews, Christians, and Muslims

**humanism:** intellectual movement at the heart of the Renaissance that focused on worldly subjects rather than religious ones

## I

**icon:** holy image of Jesus, the Virgin Mary, or a saint of the Orthodox Christian Church

**imperialism:** domination by one country of the political, economic, or cultural life of another country or region

**Indian National Congress:** group formed by Hindu nationalist leaders in India in the late 1800s to gain greater democracy and eventual self-rule

**indigenous:** native to a country or region

**indulgence:** a pardon (forgiveness) for sins that was sold by the Catholic Church

**Industrial Revolution:** period in which production of goods shifted from using hand tools to using power-driven machines and from human and animal power to steam power

**Information Revolution:** the rapid spread of information that began in the 1950s and increases with each passing year

**International Monetary Fund:** in the 1980s, group that stepped in to work out agreements to help debtor nations repay their loans

**Internet:** vast computer network that ties together millions of computers

**Interpol:** the International Criminal Police Network

**intifada:** uprising mounted in 1987 by Palestinians in territory held by Israel

**iron curtain:** the imaginary line through Europe that divided the democracies of the West from the communist countries of the East

**Islamic fundamentalism:** movement by Muslim reformers who oppose westernization and want to apply Islamic principles to problems in their nations

## J

**janissaries:** members of an elite force in the army of the Ottoman empire

**jihad:** a Muslim holy war against the enemies of Islam

**Justinian's Code:** code of laws organized by the Byzantine emperor Justinian in the 500s

## K

**kabuki:** form of Japanese drama developed in the 1600s

**kaiser:** German word meaning "emperor," used for German kings of the late 1800s and early 1900s

**kami:** according to Japanese tradition, the spirits in all living and nonliving things

**karma:** in Hinduism, all the deeds of a person's life that affect existence in the next life

**Koran:** holy book of Islam

## L

**laissez faire:** policy allowing business to operate with little or no government interference

**Laws of the Twelve Tables:** laws of ancient Rome written on twelve tablets and displayed in the marketplace

**League of Nations:** group of more than 40 countries formed after World War I with the goal of settling problems through negotiation, not war

**liberalism:** way of thinking that supports personal freedom, democracy, and reform

**limited monarchy:** government in which a legislative body limits the monarch's powers

**literacy:** the ability to read and write

**Long March:** 1934 retreat by Mao Zedong and hisfollowers from the Guomindang

**Magna Carta:** a charter signed by the English king John in 1215 that placed limits on the king's power

**mandate:** after World War I, a territory that was administered by a foreign power

**Mandate of Heaven:** according to Chinese tradition, the divine right to rule

**manorialism:** an economic system structured around a lord's manor, or estate

**Marshall Plan:** American aid package for Europe proposed in 1947 to strengthen democratic governments and lessen the appeal of communism

**medieval:** the name for the period of the Middle Ages, from about 500 to the middle of the 1400s

**Meiji Restoration:** period from 1868 to 1912 in Japan in which Japan industrialized and modernized

**mercantilism:** economic policy by which a nation sought to export more than it imported in order to build its national wealth

**Messiah:** Jewish word for a savior sent by God

**mestizo:** a person of mixed parentage in Latin America

**Middle Kingdom:** traditional name for Chinese civilization, so-called because the Chinese believed China was the center of the Earth

**Middle Passage:** the voyage from Africa to the Americas on slave ships

**militarism:** the glorification of military power

**millet:** within the Ottoman empire, a religious community of non-Muslims

**missionary:** person dedicated to spreading a religion

**mixed economy:** economic system with both private and state-run enterprises

**monastery:** community where men or women focus on spiritual goals

**monopoly:** complete control of a product or business by one person or group

**monotheistic:** believing in one god

**mosaic:** picture or design formed by inlaid pieces of stone or other materials

**mosque:** Muslim house of worship

**multinational corporation:** a business that operates in many countries

**Munich Pact:** 1938 agreement between Great Britain, France, Italy and Germany that allowed Hitler to seize the Sudentenland

**Muslim League:** group formed by Muslims in India in the early 1900s to protect Muslim interests

**Napoleonic Code:** legal code of Napoleon that included many Enlightenment ideas

**National Assembly:** group formed mostly by the third estate in France in 1789 with the intention of writing a new constitution

**nationalism:** a feeling of pride in and devotion to one's country

**NATO:** acronym for the North Atlantic Treaty Organization, a pact between western nations who pledged to support each other if any member nation was attacked

**natural laws:** according to some philosophers, rules that govern human nature

**Neolithic:** the period of human culture characterized by the development of a system of settled agriculture; also called the New Stone Age

**neutral:** not supporting either side in a conflict

**New Economic Policy:** plan instituted by Lenin in 1921 that privatized some industries

**95 Theses:** list of 95 arguments against indulgences, posted by Martin Luther on the door of a church in Wittenberg, Germany, in 1517

**nirvana:** in Buddhism, union with the universe and release from the cycle of death and rebirth

**nomad:** person who moves from place to place in search of food

**nonalignment:** policy of not supporting either side in a conflict, such as the Cold War

**O**

**oligarchy:** government in which ruling power belongs to a few people

**OPEC:** acronym for the Organization of Petroleum Exporting Countries, a trade group that attempts to set world oil prices by controlling oil production

**Opium War:** conflict between Great Britain and China in 1839 over the opium trade

**Organization of African Unity (OAU):** group founded in 1963 by Kwame Nkrumah to promote Pan-Africanism and the end of colonialism in Africa

**overpopulation:** overabundance of people in a region or country that lacks sufficient resources to adequately provide for them

**ozone layer:** layer of gases high in the atmosphere that protects the Earth from the dangerous ultraviolet rays of the sun

### P

**Pacific Rim:** group of nations in Asia and the Americas that border the Pacific Ocean

**pagoda:** Buddhist temple with many levels and a roof that curves up at the corners

**Palestine Liberation Organization (PLO):** group formed in 1964 that represents many Palestinian nationalist groups

**Pan-Africanism:** movement emphasizing the unity of Africans and people of African descent all over the world

**Pan-Arabism:** movement emphasizing the unity of all peoples sharing a common Arab cultural heritage

**Pan-Slavism:** nationalistic movement that sought to unite Slavic peoples

**Parliament:** representative assembly of England

**patriarch:** the highest church official in the Orthodox Christian Church

**patriarchal:** family order in which the father or oldest male heads the household

**patrician:** member of the landholding upper class in ancient Rome

**Pax Mongolia:** period of stability through much of Asia created by Mongol rule from the late 1200s through the mid-1300s

**Pax Romana:** term meaning "Roman Peace" for a period covering about 200 years beginning with the reign of Augustus

**peninsulares:** European-born elite in Latin America

**perestroika:** restructuring of the government and the economy in the Soviet Union under Mikhail Gorbachev in the mid-1980s

**Persian Gulf War:** war in 1991 prompted by the Iraqi invasion of Kuwait in which a coalition of European and Arab powers drove Iraq out of Kuwait

**pharaoh:** ruler of ancient Egypt

**philosophe:** thinkers of the Enlightenment

**plantation:** large estate run by an owner or overseer

**plebeian:** member of the lower class in ancient Rome, which included farmers, merchants, artisans, and traders

**PLO:** (Palestine Liberation Organization) originally a terrorist group dedicated to the destruction of Israel;

later became an official organization representing Palestinians in negotiations with Israel

**pogrom:** violent attack on a Jewish community

**polis:** city-state in ancient Greece

**pollution:** contamination of the environment, including air, water, and soil

**polytheistic:** believing in many gods

**porcelain:** hard, shiny pottery

**post-colonialism:** term used to describe conditions shared by nations that were once colonies

**propaganda:** the spreading of ideas to promote a certain cause or to damage an opposing cause

**Protestant Reformation:** period when Europeans broke away from the Roman Catholic Church and formed new Christian churches

**purge:** the process of eliminating a nation of undesirable people

**Puritans:** group in England in the 1600s who sought to purify the church of England by eliminating Catholic practices

### Q

**quipus:** knotted strings used by Incan officials for keeping records

**Quran:** the sacred scriptures of Islam

### R

**radioactivity:** powerful form of energy released by certain substances

**Reconquista:** a campaign begun by Christians in the 700s to recapture Spain from the Muslims

**Red Guards:** groups of radical students formed in China during the Cultural Revolution

**refugee:** person who flees his or her homeland to seek safety elsewhere

**reincarnation:** in Hinduism, the rebirth of the soul in a new body

**Renaissance:** period of great creativity and change in Europe from the 1300s through the 1600s; the word means "rebirth"

**reparations:** payment for war damages

**republic:** system of government in which officials are chosen by the people

**Russification:** attempt by Russian rulers to make all groups under Russian rule think, act, and believe as Russians

**Russo-Japanese War:** war occurring from 1904 to 1905 between Japan and Russia; won by Japan

## S

**samurai:** member of the warrior class in Japanese feudal society

**Sandinistas:** group of revolutionaries that overthrew the Nicaraguan government in 1979

**satellite:** a smaller country that is economically or politically dependent on a more powerful country

**savanna:** grassy plain

**schism:** permanent split

**scientific method:** a method of discovering truth based on experimentation and observation rather than on past authorities

**Scientific Revolution:** period in the 1500s and 1600s in which scientific thinkers challenged traditional ideas and relied on observation and experimentation

**secondary source:** written information that is based on original or primary sources

**secular:** having to do with worldly rather than religious matters

**Senate:** the most powerful governing body of ancient Rome

**sepoy:** Indian soldier serving in the army set up by the British or French East India Companies

**Sepoy Mutiny:** rebellion fought by Hindu and Muslim sepoys against British rule in India in the mid-1800s

**serf:** in medieval Europe, peasant bound to the lord's land

**shantytown:** area of shacks that grows up around a city that is experiencing rapid growth

**Sharia:** the system of Islamic law

**Shiite:** one of the two main divisions of Islam

**Shinto:** traditional Japanese religion

**shogun:** in Japanese feudal society, top military commander

**Silk Road:** ancient trade route that linked China with lands to the west

**Sino-Japanese War:** war that lasted from 1894 to 1895 between Japan and China

**socialism:** system in which the people as a whole rather than private individuals own all property and operate all businesses

**Solidarity:** independent trade union formed in Poland in 1980

**soviet:** council of workers and soldiers set up by Russian revolutionaries in 1917

**sphere of influence:** area in which an outside power claims exclusive trade privileges

**stupa:** large dome-shaped Buddhist shrine

**suffrage:** the right to vote

**sultan:** Muslim ruler

**Sunni:** one of the two main divisions of Islam

**superpower:** name after 1945 for both the United States and the Soviet Union, the two nations that dominated global politics for more than four decades

**surrogate:** word for a representative state; used to describe smaller countries whose actions represented the interests of either the United States or the Soviet Union during the Cold War

**Swahili:** language that mixed Arabic words with Bantu, an African language

## T

**Taiping Rebellion:** peasant rebellion in China occurring between 1850 and 1864

**tariff:** a tax on imports

**technology:** tools and skills people use to meet their basic needs

**terrace:** a flat area of land on a steep hillside

**terrorism:** deliberate use of unpredictable violence, especially against civilians, to gain revenge or achieve political goals

**Torah:** the most sacred scriptures of Judaism

**totalitarian state:** form of government in which a one-party dictatorship attempts to regulate every aspect of the lives of citizens

**total war:** the channeling of all of a nation's resources into a war effort

**trade deficit:** a situation in which a nation imports more than it exports

**trade fair:** site of regular trading activity in medieval Europe

**trench warfare:** type of warfare in which troops dig trenches and fight from them

**tributary state:** independent state that must acknowledge the supremacy of another state and pay tribute to its ruler

**Truman Doctrine:** an economic and military program of the United States designed in 1947 to help other countries resist Soviet aggression

**United Nations:** international group formed in 1945 to provide a place to discuss world problems and develop solutions

**Universal Declaration of Human Rights:** document adopted in 1948 by the United Nations that sets out the basic human rights of all individuals

**Untouchables:** within the ancient Indian caste system, outcasts who lived harsh lives

**urbanization:** movement of people to cities

**utopian:** a plan for creating a perfect social order

**Warsaw Pact:** defensive alliance among the Soviet Union and its satellites promising mutual military cooperation

**westernization:** process of adopting western ways

**Young Turks:** movement established by Turks in the late 1800s to reform the Ottoman Empire

**zaibatsu:** Japanese families that became powerful in banking and industry

**Zen Buddhism:** sect of Buddhism that spread throughout Japan

**Zionism:** movement dedicated to building a Jewish state in Palestine

# Index

# Acknowledgements

## Staff Credits:

The people who make up the *Global History and Geography Brief Review team*—representing design, editorial, marketing, and production services—are listed below. Bold type denotes the core team members.

**Jane Breen**, **Jennifer McQueeney Creane**, Kerry Dunn, **Thomas Ferreira**, Rebecca Hall, **Linda D. Johnson**, Julie Orr, Rachel Youdelman

## Additional Credits:

The Quarasan Group, Inc.: Chicago, IL

English Language Learning Consultant: Anita Raducanu

Lapiz Digital Services: Chennai, India
Lapiz, Inc.: Boston, MA

## Text and Image Credits

Note: Every effort has been made to locate the copyright owners of materials reprinted in this book. Omissions brought to our attention will be corrected in subsequent printings. All otherwise uncredited photos copyright © 2010 Pearson Education.

**Cover** Styve Reineck/Shutterstock **Page 1,** Temple of Castor and Pollux, Rome, Courtesy of Gretchen Medeiros; **16** Emei/Shutterstock; **35** Carcassonne, France, Courtesy of Gretchen Medeiros; **46** Sufi/Shutterstock; **71** Library of Congress Prints and Photographs Division [LC-USZ62-5476]; **87,** *Sketch for a Church Dome* (ca. 1500), Leonardo da Vinci. Ink on paper. Private collection; **108** Laura Gilpin/Library of Congress Prints and Photographs Division [LC-USZ62-55139]; **139** *The French Revolution: Burning the Royal Carriages at the Chateau d'Eu* (1848), Currier and Ives. Hand-colored lithograph. Library of Congress, Prints and Photographs Division [LC-USZC2-2370]; **149** British Cartoon Prints Collection/Library of Congress Prints and Photographs Division [LC-USZC4-8791]; **183** *The Devilfish in Egyptian Waters* (1882), American cartoon/The Granger Collection, New York; **185** *U.S. Army Pilot in Front of Airplane* (1918). Photographic print. Library of Congress Prints and Photographs Division [LC-USZ62-99040]; **199** Viktor Nikolayevich Deni/The Granger Collection, New York; **225** U.S. Air Force; **241** Henry Payne/United Feature Syndicate, Inc. Reprinted by permission; **257** Bob Englehart/The Hartford Courant. Reprinted by permission; **261** Library of Congress Prints and Photographs Division [LC-USZ62-13849]; **265** Bob Englehart/The Hartford Courant. Reprinted by permission; **282** Vic Harville/Stephens Media Group; **285** Copyright © 1994 Jimmy Margulies/*The Record*, Hackensack N.J.; **305** John Trever/Albuquerque Journal.

**Regents Exams: June 2009 4** Octopus Publishing Company; **7** N and N Publishing Company; **8** Chan Lowe; **14** McGraw-Hill Companies; **15** Courtesy of Library of Congress. **January 2009 7** State of Missouri Historical Society; **12** Public Domain. **August 2008 3** Courtesy of Library of Congress; **6** Courtesy of Library of Congress; **7** Linda Godfrey **9** Mike Thompson/ Detroit Free Press; **15** From Skolnik, Fred. Encyclopedia Judaica 22 Volume Set , 2E. 2006 Gale, a part of Cengage Learning , Inc. Reproduced with permission; **20** The Guardian News & Media Ltd. "History's Greatest Migration" from *The Guardian, September 5, 1947.* Copyright © The Guardian News & Media Ltd. Used by permission. **June 2008 3** McGraw-Hill Companies; **7** Getty Images; **14** Steve Greenberg; **20** Jeff Danziger; **21** Scientific American, Inc. "Thwarting Nuclear Terrorism" from Scientific American Magazine, February 2006 by Alexander Glaser & Frank N. von Hippel. Copyright © 2006 by Scientific American, Inc. All rights reserved. Used by permission. **January 2008 4** Octopus Publishing Group; **5** Jarret Publishing; **8** Aracdio Esquivel **9** Zapiro; **10** Brian Gable/ The Globe and Mail; **13** Mary Evans Picture Library; **20** Courtesy of Dr. Katie Hill. **August 2007 3** Illustration from WORLD HISTORY: PEOPLE AND NATIONS by Antole G. Mazour and John M. Peoples, copyright 1993 by Holt, Rinehart and Winston, Inc. and reprinted by permission of Houghton Mifflin Harcourt Publishing Company; **4** McGraw-Hill Companies; **6** Pearson **8** The Herb Block Foundation; **9 T** McGraw-Hill Companies; **9 B** Clay Bennett/ Christian Science Monitor; **10** Dana Summers/ The Orlando Sentinel; **21** By permission of Michael Ramirez and Creators Syndicate, Inc.

This section contains an actual Regents Examination in Global History and Geography that was given in New York State in June 2009.

Circle your answers to Part 1. Write your responses to the short-answer questions in the spaces provided. Write your thematic essay and document-based essay on separate sheets of paper. Be sure to refer to the test-taking strategies in the front of this book as you prepare to answer the test questions.

## Part I

## Answer all questions in this part.

*Directions* (1–50): For each statement or question, write on the separate answer sheet the *number* of the word or expression that, of those given, best completes the statement or answers the question.

1 One reason that many historians study geography is to

(1) help predict changes in government
(2) show connections between people and places
(3) tell when events took place
(4) explore the value systems of early people

2 **"Greek Statues Unearthed in Pompeii"**

**"Chinese Porcelain Found at Zimbabwe Dig"**

**"Mixtec Textiles Found Near Aztec Ruins"**

Which concept is illustrated by these headlines?

(1) colonialism      (3) ethnocentrism
(2) isolationism      (4) cultural diffusion

3 What was a result of the Neolithic Revolution?

(1) Civilizations developed.
(2) Humans first learned to use fire.
(3) Life expectancy declined.
(4) People began hunting and gathering for food.

4 ..."One theory is that there were waves of migration, one moving through the east of Africa and another making its way through the centre of the continent. In Zambia, there is evidence of at least three routes of migration – from the great lakes, from the Congo forest and from Angola." ...

Source: BBC, The Story of Africa: Early History

This passage about the early history of Africa describes migrations associated with which group of people?

(1) Phoenicians      (3) Moors
(2) Bantu      (4) Babylonians

5 Which belief system is considered monotheistic?

(1) Jainism      (3) Judaism
(2) Daoism      (4) Shinto

6 How did the geography of the Italian peninsula influence the development of the Roman Empire?

(1) The unnavigable rivers in the northern part of the peninsula protected the Romans from their neighbors.
(2) The harsh climate prevented agricultural production on the Italian peninsula.
(3) The lengthy, rugged seacoast encouraged frequent invasions of the Italian peninsula.
(4) The location of the peninsula contributed to Roman control of the Mediterranean region.

7 • Hinduism was the dominant religion.
   • Murals were painted on the Ajanta cave walls.
   • The concept of zero and the decimal system were introduced.

Which empire is described by these statements?

(1) Gupta      (3) Persian
(2) Maurya      (4) British

8 The early Russian civilization adopted the Eastern Orthodox religion, the Cyrillic alphabet, and different styles of art and architecture through contact with

(1) traders from China
(2) conquering Mongol invaders
(3) Vikings from northern Europe
(4) missionaries from the Byzantine Empire

9 Technological achievements made during the Tang and Song dynasties were important because they

(1) were used to defeat Kublai Khan
(2) contributed to economic growth and cultural advancement
(3) increased contact with the Americas
(4) led to social equality between men and women

12 What was a major characteristic of the Renaissance in Europe?

(1) Secular achievements were emphasized.

(2) Suffrage was granted to men and women.

(3) Most literature was written in Arabic.

(4) Most ancient Greek and Roman ideas were rejected.

13 What was one result of the travels of Marco Polo?

(1) Africa remained isolated.

(2) Ottoman power decreased.

(3) Colonies were established in Japan.

(4) Interest in Asian cultures increased.

Base your answer to question 15 on the graphic organizer below and on your knowledge of social studies.

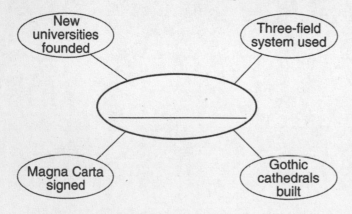

15 Which title best completes this graphic organizer?

(1) Improvements Under the Tokugawa
(2) Achievements of Medieval Europe
(3) Developments in Ancient Ghana
(4) Changes Resulting From the Counter Reformation

16 Which advancement in technology revolutionized the way ideas were spread throughout western Europe in the 15th century?

(1) development of the astrolabe
(2) introduction of the telegraph
(3) improvements to the printing press
(4) creation of the telescope

17 Which phrase best completes the partial outline below?

> I. Achievements of the Incas
>   A. _____
>   B. Kept records using quipus
>   C. Built stone structures without using mortar

(1) Cast bronze statues
(2) Created a system of terrace farming
(3) Invented a foot stirrup
(4) Developed chariots

18 Prices in Spain rose as colonies supplied large amounts of gold and silver. This suggests that Spanish imports of gold and silver led to

(1) food shortages
(3) inflation
(2) unemployment
(4) self-sufficiency

19 Which form of political leadership is most closely associated with Ivan the Terrible, Suleiman the Magnificent, and Philip II of Spain?

(1) democratic
(3) communist
(2) absolutist
(4) theocratic

20 According to John Locke, the purpose of government is to

(1) protect the natural rights of individuals
(2) serve the monarch
(3) create overseas settlements
(4) stimulate the economy

21 Which characteristic is associated with an economy based on the principles of laissez-faire?

(1) prices based on supply and demand
(2) production quotas established by the central government
(3) distribution of goods determined by the customs of a traditional society
(4) some goods exchanged for other goods of equal value

22 One way in which Toussaint L'Ouverture, Simón Bolívar, and José de San Martín are similar is that they

(1) supported the Reconquista
(2) led independence movements
(3) fought for Native American suffrage
(4) defended the encomienda system

23 The Sepoy Rebellion is considered an important event in Indian history because it was one cause of the

(1) independence movement in India
(2) secession of Bangladesh from Pakistan
(3) establishment of French colonies in India
(4) creation of the Mughal Empire by Muslims

24 The term *empire* is best defined as

(1) a political unit that has a common religious faith
(2) a government ruled by the consent of the people
(3) an extensive territory under the rule of a single authority
(4) a country that requires conquered peoples to assimilate

25 The Triple Alliance and the Triple Entente contributed to the start of World War I by

(1) failing to include Germany and France as members
(2) threatening countries in the Western Hemisphere
(3) allowing Japanese aggression in Korea
(4) increasing tensions between European countries

Base your answer to question 26 on the statement below and on your knowledge of social studies.

The breakup of the Austro-Hungarian Empire led to the creation of several new states and the expansion of others. These new states soon established trade restrictions and began collecting tariffs when goods crossed their borders.

26 Which conclusion is most valid concerning the breakup of the Austro-Hungarian Empire?

(1) International cooperation led to the settlement of border disputes.
(2) Transition from a command to a free-market economy was difficult.
(3) Political independence led to trade barriers.
(4) Tariffs resulted in increased trade.

Base your answer to question 27 on the map below and on your knowledge of social studies.

## European Colonization in 1913

Source: Les Rowntree et al., *Diversity Amid Globalization*, Prentice Hall (adapted)

27 Many of the political divisions shown on this map were directly related to the

(1) Meiji Restoration     (3) Berlin Conference

(2) Opium Wars     (4) Boer War

---

28 The 1930s depression in Germany contributed to the rise of the Nazi Party because

  (1) economic hardships increased political instability

  (2) five-year plans of the communists failed

  (3) the Reichstag nationalized private property

  (4) the Weimar Republic imposed totalitarianism

29 Mohandas Gandhi's protests during India's independence movement were often successful because of his application of

  (1) an appeasement policy

  (2) civil disobedience

  (3) traditional caste beliefs

  (4) divide-and-conquer principles

Base your answer to question 30 on the cartoon below and on your knowledge of social studies.

Source: Kime, O'Donnell and Osborne, *World Studies: Global Issues and Assessments,* N & N Publishing

30 In the view of this cartoonist, Russia under Lenin's rule was characterized by

(1) a continuation of traditional life
(2) the introduction of capitalism
(3) support for a constitutional monarchy
(4) rejection of the czarist system

31 The primary purpose of the United Nations is to

(1) control world grain prices
(2) promote democratic governments
(3) resolve conflicts between nations peacefully
(4) unite all nations militarily through alliances

32 World War II was a turning point for many European colonies in Africa and Asia because the war led to

(1) the occupation of most European colonies by United Nations troops
(2) increased efforts by these colonies to gain independence
(3) the expansion of European imperialism
(4) decreased friction between the Europeans and their colonies

33 The purpose of the Marshall Plan after World War II was to

(1) promote the spread of militarism
(2) force the losing nations to help areas destroyed in the war
(3) rebuild national economies to stabilize governments
(4) strengthen the alliances that had won the war

34 The Organization of Petroleum Exporting Countries (OPEC) is best known for its efforts to

(1) develop workable alternatives to fossil fuels
(2) bring Western oil technology to the Middle East
(3) stop the export of oil to non-Arab nations
(4) establish production quotas to control the price of oil

35 One way in which the Korean War and the Vietnam War are similar is that both

(1) resulted in unification of two formerly independent nations
(2) reflected the success of the Western policy of containment
(3) attempted to remove French imperialists from power
(4) developed from Cold War tensions

36 One similarity in the results of the revolutions led by Fidel Castro in Cuba and by the Sandinistas in Nicaragua is that both

(1) restored a monarchy
(2) destroyed a theocracy
(3) followed Marxist principles
(4) protected freedom of the press

Base your answer to question 37 on the cartoon below and on your knowledge of social studies.

Source: Chan Lowe, *The South Florida Sun Sentinel*

37 What does this 2005 cartoon imply?

(1) The instability in the Middle East has been ongoing.
(2) The peace process in the Middle East is gaining ground.
(3) The Middle East has greatly changed over thirty years.
(4) The media shapes society's perception of the Middle East.

38 One way in which the Great Leap Forward and the Four Modernizations are similar is that each was an attempt to

(1) increase farm and factory output
(2) develop a democratic government
(3) strengthen economic ties with communist neighbors
(4) reduce the gap between rich and poor

39 The term *Green Revolution* refers to

(1) an overthrow of the government by radical parties
(2) increased agricultural production based on technological advancements
(3) a drastic change in the environment based on global warming
(4) decreased food production caused by terrorism

40 Which statement about the economy of Japan today is most accurate?

(1) Abundant arable land has led to prosperity.
(2) Possession of nuclear weaponry has assured a strong economy.
(3) Economic development has occurred without political freedom.
(4) A lack of natural resources has not limited economic growth.

41 Many achievements made during the Golden Ages of both Islam and the West African Kingdoms reached European societies by way of

(1) trade networks in the Mediterranean Sea region
(2) trade expeditions between China and Africa
(3) the voyages of Ferdinand Magellan
(4) the travels of Commodore Matthew Perry

42 In European and Japanese feudal societies, social status was usually determined by

(1) marriage
(2) birth
(3) individual abilities
(4) education and training

43 The policy of establishing colonies to gain wealth by controlling colonial trade is called

(1) socialism          (3) mercantilism
(2) fascism            (4) communism

44 Which document established the principle of limited monarchy in England?

(1) Twelve Tables      (3) Act of Supremacy
(2) Magna Carta        (4) Balfour Declaration

Base your answers to questions 45 and 46 on the map below and on your knowledge of social studies.

Source: *Learning from Maps,* Prentice Hall (adapted)

45 Which letter identifies the peninsula that is home to Mecca, the religious center of Islam?

(1) *A*                    (3) *C*
(2) *B*                    (4) *D*

46 Which letter identifies the peninsula that was the site of the Vietnam conflict and the atrocities of Pol Pot?

(1) *A*                    (3) *C*
(2) *B*                    (4) *D*

47 For years, the Sahara was an obstacle for Europeans while Africans used the desert as a highway. Which conclusion is supported by this statement?

(1) Trade between Africa and Europe decreased.
(2) African empires generally avoided contact with Europeans.
(3) Desertification reduced the amount of arable land available to Africans and Europeans.
(4) Initially, Europeans lacked the knowledge and skills needed to travel in the desert.

48 The Boxer Rebellion and the work of Sun Yixian (Sun Yat-sen) are most closely associated with the

(1) Long March
(2) Golden Age of China
(3) Cultural Revolution
(4) rise of nationalism in China

49 The term *iron curtain* refers to the

(1) scars left on the land by the trenches of World War I
(2) no-fly zone in northern Iraq after the Persian Gulf War
(3) border established between India and Pakistan after World War II
(4) western boundary of Soviet domination in Europe during the Cold War

50 Poles in 1918 and Jews prior to 1948 are examples of

(1) peoples without their own state
(2) colonized peoples in the British Empire
(3) groups that joined the North Atlantic Treaty Organization (NATO)
(4) groups represented on the United Nations Security Council

**Answers to the essay questions are to be written in the separate essay booklet.**

**In developing your answer to Part II, be sure to keep these general definitions in mind:**

(a) <u>explain</u> means "to make plain or understandable; to give reasons for or causes of; to show the logical development or relationships of"

(b) <u>describe</u> means "to illustrate something in words or tell about it"

(c) <u>discuss</u> means "to make observations about something using facts, reasoning, and argument; to present in some detail"

## Part II

### THEMATIC ESSAY QUESTION

*Directions:* Write a well-organized essay that includes an introduction, several paragraphs addressing the task below, and a conclusion.

**Theme: Human Rights**

> Throughout history, there have been many examples where groups of people have been denied their human rights. Individuals, groups, and governments have attempted to end many of these human rights violations although they have not always been successful.

**Task:**

> Select *two* different examples from history where human rights have been denied to groups of people and for *each*
>
> * Explain the historical circumstances that led to the denial of human rights
> * Describe how the human rights of that group were denied
> * Discuss an action taken by an individual, a group, or a government that attempted to end the human rights violations

You may use any example of human rights violations from your study of global history. Some suggestions you might wish to consider include the indigenous people in Latin America during the Encounter, Jews in Russia during the pogroms, the Armenians under the Ottomans, blacks under apartheid in South Africa, Chinese students in Tiananmen Square, Bosnian Muslims in the former Yugoslavia, and women under the Taliban in Afghanistan.

**You are *not* limited to these suggestions.**

**Do *not* use examples of human rights violations that occurred in the United States in your answer.**

**Guidelines:**

**In your essay, be sure to**

* Develop all aspects of the task
* Support the theme with relevant facts, examples, and details
* Use a logical and clear plan of organization, including an introduction and a conclusion that are beyond a restatement of the theme

NAME _____ SCHOOL _____

## Part III

## DOCUMENT-BASED QUESTION

This question is based on the accompanying documents. The question is designed to test your ability to work with historical documents. Some of these documents have been edited for the purposes of this question. As you analyze the documents, take into account the source of each document and any point of view that may be presented in the document.

**Historical Context:**

> While economic and social changes have occurred throughout history, certain time periods have seen great changes. These time periods include the **Middle Ages,** the **Industrial Revolution in England,** and the **Age of Globalization.**

**Task:** Using the information from the documents and your knowledge of global history, answer the questions that follow each document in Part A. Your answers to the questions will help you write the Part B essay in which you will be asked to

> Choose *two* time periods mentioned in the historical context and for *each*
> - Describe the economic *and/or* social changes that occurred during that time period
> - Discuss an impact of a change on society or on a specific group of people

In developing your answers to Part III, be sure to keep these general definitions in mind:

(a) <u>describe</u> means "to illustrate something in words or tell about it"

(b) <u>discuss</u> means "to make observations about something using facts, reasoning, and argument; to present in some detail"

# Part A
# Short-Answer Questions

*Directions:* Analyze the documents and answer the short-answer questions that follow each document in the space provided.

## Document 1

> The manorial system, widespread in the West from Charlemagne's time onward, was not at first favorable to the development of agriculture and commerce. Manors tended to be self-sufficient; the economy was closed. People lived in their small world, in constant fear of the strange world beyond, from which came only evil. The best they could hope for was to endure; and they endured.
>
> In the eleventh and following centuries things took a turn for the better. Life became more stable; population increased; new lands were brought under cultivation and old lands rendered [made] more productive. New agricultural techniques were introduced. The power of legumes [nitrogen-fixing plants] to nourish and revive exhausted soils was recognized, and the science of manuring developed—marl [lime-rich mud] and ashes being employed in combination with animal manures. The quality of herds was improved by selection and crossbreeding. Flowing water was put to work, operating gristmills and providing power for forges. Windmills whirled on plains and uplands, and men even attempted, with some success, to construct tidal mills. . . .

Source: Morris Bishop, *The Middle Ages*, Houghton Mifflin

1 According to Morris Bishop, what are *two* changes that occurred during the medieval period? [2]

(1) _____

_____

Score ☐

(2) _____

_____

Score ☐

## Document 2

> . . . Then, just as the Crusaders had been inspired at least in part by commercial motives, those 200 years of constant coming and going between East and West obviously gave trade a tremendous boost. Merchants, studying the itineraries [routes] of the cross-bearers [crusaders] who paved the way, discovered the most direct routes between eastern Mediterranean ports and the heart of Europe. Venice was a particularly active port of entry for goods imported from the Middle East and India. From there the goods traveled a well established route through the Brenner Pass, up the Rhine to Brussels and then north to the Baltic Sea. Many a town which lies along this course owes its existence to a brisk demand for exotic wares from the East by medieval Europeans. . . .

Source: "Legacy of the Crusades," *Aramco World*

2 According to this excerpt from "Legacy of the Crusades," what is *one* economic change brought about by the Crusades during the medieval period? [1]

_____

_____

Score ☐

## Document 3

> . . . In a word, Europe was turning from a developing into a developed region. The growth of industry meant the growth of cities, which in the eleventh and twelfth centuries began to abandon their old roles of military headquarters and administrative centers as they filled with the life of commerce and industry. Some, like Genoa, once Roman villages, mushroomed, while others, like Venice, appeared out of nowhere. Still others, calling themselves simply "New City" (Villanova, Villeneuve, Neustadt), were founded by progressive rulers. Instead of growing haphazardly, they were built on a plan, typically a grid pattern with a central square, church, and market buildings. Beginning in tenth-century Italy, businessmen and craftsmen in many cities established what they called "communes," declaring themselves free men who owed allegiance only to a sovereign who collected taxes but otherwise left them alone. Astute lords granted charters exempting city dwellers from feudal obligations—"so that my friends and subjects, the inhabitants of my town of Binarville, stay more willing there," sensibly explained one lord. Under the rubric "Free air makes free men," even serfs were declared emancipated if they maintained themselves in a city for a year and a day. . . .

Source: Frances & Joseph Gies, *Cathedral, Forge, and Water Wheel: Technology and Invention in the Middle Ages*, Harper Perennial (adapted)

3 According to Frances and Joseph Gies, what was *one* impact of the growth of European cities on medieval European societies? [1]

_____

_____

Score ☐

**Document 4a**

Permission to use this third-party content has not been granted to Pearson. View content at nysedregents.org.

**Document 4b**

### Use of Inventions in the Factory System

Merchant buys raw wool from sheep raiser and sells to factory ➡️ Carding machines comb the raw wool and Samuel Crompton's spinning machine, called the mule, is powered by water and spins thread ➡️

Source: Drawn by T. Allom

Edmund Cartwright's automatic power loom weaves thread into cloth

⬅️ Ink rollers are used to add designs to fabric

Fabric is shipped to markets ⬅️

4b Based on this chart, how is cloth produced in the factory system? [1]

_____

_____

Score ☐

## Document 5

### Industrial Revolution

. . . The first phase of the industrial revolution made traditional society obsolete [no longer useful] because it was incompatible with the basic requirements of an industrial economy. Among these requirements was the commercialization of agriculture. Land had to be treated as a commodity that could be bought and sold in order to produce enough food to feed a growing urban population and to make some rural labor redundant [excessive] so that people would move to the cities to work in the new factories. Traditional societies varied widely across the globe but everywhere they were based on the land and nowhere was land simply a commodity. It was, instead, the basis of a complicated network of obligations and privileges, a social structure binding owner to field worker, lord to peasant. It was these traditional institutions, these social worlds, that the industrial revolution threatened and that it ultimately swept away. . . .

Source: Michael Mandelbaum, *The Ideas that Conquered the World*, Public Affairs

5 According to Michael Mandelbaum, what is *one* change that resulted from the Industrial Revolution? [1]

_____

_____

Score ☐

**Document 6a**

> . . . I have frequently visited many of the Cotton Factories in this neighbourhood, with friends who came from a distance; on coming out, it has always been a general reflection, that the children were very great sufferers, and seemed sickly and unhealthy; being obliged to work such long hours under such unfavourable circumstances. As I dedicate an hour or two every morning to giving advice to the poor, I have a great many opportunities of witnessing the bad effects of such confinement on the health of children; frequently the parents say their children were stout and healthy, until they were sent out, and confined so close and long in the Factory; but now they had become delicate and sickly. . . .

Source: Robert Agnew, M.D., "Observations on the State of the Children in Cotton Mills," Manchester, March 23, 1818

6a According to Dr. Agnew, what is **one** impact the Industrial Revolution had on children?  [1]

_____

_____

Score ☐

**Document 6b**

In this excerpt, Friedrich Engel's discussion with a middle-class gentleman shows the attitude of the middle class about the living conditions of the factory workers.

> . . . One day I walked with one of these middle-class gentlemen into Manchester. I spoke to him about the disgraceful unhealthy slums and drew his attention to the disgusting condition of that part of the town in which the factory workers lived. I declared that I had never seen so badly built a town in my life. He listened patiently and at the corner of the street at which we parted company he remarked: "And yet there is a great deal of money made here. Good morning, Sir.". . .

Source: Friedrich Engels, *The Condition of the Working Class in England*, Stanford University Press (adapted)

6b According to Friedrich Engels, what is **one** result of the Industrial Revolution on the living conditions of factory workers?  [1]

_____

_____

Score ☐

## Document 7

... Welcome to the mixed-up world of "globalization"—a growing worldwide marketplace where business transactions routinely span the planet and national borders are growing fuzzier and fuzzier. It wasn't always this way. Chances are, your parents wore American-made clothes, ate American-made food, and drove American-made cars. But a boom in world trade has changed all that. And what you buy may be the least of it.

The expansion of world trade has unleashed a multitude of dramatic changes. Whole countries have seen their fortunes soar as foreign investment has poured in, creating factories and providing jobs for millions of people. Other countries have been left behind. In the process, billions of lives are affected, for better and worse. . . .

Source: Herbert Buchsbaum, "Living in a Global Economy," *Scholastic Update,*
March 7, 1997

7 According to Herbert Buchsbaum, what is *one* economic change that has occurred as a result of globalization? [1]

_____

_____

Score ☐

**Document 8**

### Your Complaints Circle Globe

... When an American calls a toll-free number in the United States to report a broken appliance or complain about the wrong sweater ordered from a catalog, the call is often routed through fast fiber-optic cables to a center in India. ...

International call centers based in India will generate $8 billion in revenue by 2008, says NASSCOM, a technology industry trade group in India. Growth is accelerating as globalization and government deregulation expand telecommunications in India and lower its cost.

"The potential is unlimited," says Prakash Gurbaxani, founder and chief executive of 24/7 Customer.com, a customer service center in Bangalore whose American clients include Web sites AltaVista and Shutterfly.com. Anticipating more business, the company's supermarket-sized call center is filled with dark-screened PCs and dwarfs its 300 employees. ...

Source: Associated Press, *Syracuse Herald American*, June 24, 2001

8 Based on this newspaper article, what is *one* impact that globalization is having on India? [1]

_____

_____

Score ☐

## Document 9

... TODAY, GLOBALIZATION IS being challenged around the world. There is discontent with globalization, and rightfully so. Globalization can be a force for good: the globalization of ideas about democracy and of civil society have changed the way people think, while global political movements have led to debt relief and the treaty on land mines. Globalization has helped hundreds of millions of people attain higher standards of living, beyond what they, or most economists, thought imaginable but a short while ago. The globalization of the economy has benefited countries that took advantage of it by seeking new markets for their exports and by welcoming foreign investment. Even so, the countries that have benefited the most have been those that took charge of their own destiny and recognized the role government can play in development rather than relying on the notion of a self-regulated market that would fix its own problems.

But for millions of people globalization has not worked. Many have actually been made worse off, as they have seen their jobs destroyed and their lives become more insecure. They have felt increasingly powerless against forces beyond their control. They have seen their democracies undermined, their cultures eroded.

If globalization continues to be conducted in the way that it has been in the past, if we continue to fail to learn from our mistakes, globalization will not only not succeed in promoting development but will continue to create poverty and instability. Without reform, the backlash that has already started will mount and discontent with globalization will grow. . . .

Source: Joseph E. Stiglitz, *Globalization and Its Discontents*, W. W. Norton & Co., 2003

9a According to Joseph E. Stiglitz, what is **one** *positive* effect of globalization?  [1]

_____

_____

Score ☐

b According to Joseph E. Stiglitz, what is **one** *negative* effect of globalization?  [1]

_____

_____

Score ☐

# Part B
# Essay

*Directions:* Write a well-organized essay that includes an introduction, several paragraphs, and a conclusion. Use evidence from *at least four* documents in your essay. Support your response with relevant facts, examples, and details. Include additional outside information.

**Historical Context:**

> While economic and social changes have occurred throughout history, certain time periods have seen great changes. These time periods include the **Middle Ages,** the **Industrial Revolution in England,** and the **Age of Globalization.**

**Task:** Using the information from the documents and your knowledge of global history, write an essay in which you

> Choose *two* time periods mentioned in the historical context and for *each*
> - Describe the economic *and/or* social changes that occurred during that time period
> - Discuss an impact of a change on society or on a specific group of people

**Guidelines:**

**In your essay, be sure to**
- Develop all aspects of the task
- Incorporate information from *at least four* documents
- Incorporate relevant outside information
- Support the theme with relevant facts, examples, and details
- Use a logical and clear plan of organization, including an introduction and a conclusion that are beyond a restatement of the theme

This section contains an actual Regents Examination in Global History and Geography that was given in New York State in January 2009.

Circle your answers to Part 1. Write your responses to the short-answer questions in the spaces provided. Write your thematic essay and document-based essay on separate sheets of paper. Be sure to refer to the test-taking strategies in the front of this book as you prepare to answer the test questions.

## Part I

### Answer all questions in this part.

*Directions* (1–50): For each statement or question, write on the separate answer sheet the *number* of the word or expression that, of those given, best completes the statement or answers the question.

1 Which topic is central to the study of economics?

(1) tracking the development and spread of diseases
(2) understanding the causes of ethnic rivalries
(3) examining the distribution and use of limited resources
(4) studying the growth and role of political parties

2 Which feature would most likely appear on a physical map?

(1) population densities
(2) land usage patterns
(3) climatic patterns
(4) mountain ranges

3 Where does the archaeological evidence gathered by Louis and Mary Leakey suggest the earliest humans developed?

(1) Great Rift Valley
(2) Amazon rain forest
(3) Himalaya Mountains
(4) Philippine archipelago

4 A direct result of the Neolithic Revolution is that people

(1) began living in permanent settlements
(2) developed a nomadic way of life
(3) depended on hunting and gathering
(4) used crop rotation to increase agricultural output

5 Subsistence farming can best be defined as

(1) harvesting a surplus of crops to be sold for profit
(2) producing just enough food for a family's survival
(3) domesticating animals to transport goods
(4) irrigating crops to increase production

6 Which practice is most closely associated with a person of the Islamic faith?

(1) refraining from eating meat on Fridays
(2) praying five times a day
(3) following the Eightfold Path
(4) worshipping many gods

7 The Gupta Empire was best known for its

(1) advances in mathematics and medicine
(2) efforts to resist European imperialism
(3) development of the barter system
(4) construction of Angkor Wat

8 A major contribution of the Byzantine Empire was the

(1) invention of the wheel and gunpowder
(2) participation of citizens in government
(3) diffusion of Hindu beliefs
(4) preservation of Greek science and Roman engineering

9 Which political system is best described in the outline below?

I. _____
   A. Decentralized government
   B. Based on loyalty and service
   C. Code of chivalry
   D. Military elite

(1) Oligarchy          (3) Feudalism
(2) Absolutism         (4) Democracy

10 What was one direct result of the Crusades?

(1) Trade increased between Europe and the Middle East.
(2) Islamic kingdoms expanded into Europe.
(3) Arabs and Christians divided the city of Jerusalem between them.
(4) Alexander the Great became a powerful leader in Eurasia.

11 Which statement about government during the Tokugawa period in Japan is most accurate?

(1) The power of the emperor was absolute and supreme.

(2) The real power was held by foreign countries.

(3) Actual power was held by the shogun.

(4) Political power was in the hands of the merchant class.

12 One way in which the Silk Roads and the West African trade routes are similar is that along both routes

(1) the main items exchanged were ivory and tobacco

(2) concrete was used to improve the surface of the roads

(3) a single currency was used to make transactions easier

(4) ideas were exchanged as merchants interacted with each other

13 The use of the geographic terms *Near East* and *Far East* reflects

(1) the distance of nations from Mecca

(2) a European view of the world

(3) a Japanese perspective of Asia

(4) the location of Southwest Asia in relation to North Africa

14 • The introduction of gunpowder helped bring an end to feudalism.

• The printing press played an important role in causing the Reformation.

These statements best reflect the idea that

(1) environmental changes can affect human society

(2) contact with other societies can lead to conflict and war

(3) economic change can be slow and almost unnoticed

(4) technological advances can lead to major change

15 Martin Luther was primarily dissatisfied with the Roman Catholic Church because he

(1) thought the church lacked structure

(2) disagreed with the sale of indulgences

(3) blamed the church for not curing people who had the plague

(4) believed that kings should have more power to appoint clergy

16 • Dominated the eastern Mediterranean Sea (1500s)

• Conquered Egypt and Syria (1517)

• Laid siege to Vienna (1529)

Which empire is most closely associated with these events?

(1) Ottoman Empire　　(3) Persian Empire

(2) Spanish Empire　　(4) Russian Empire

17 A major agricultural advancement of the Incas was the

(1) domestication of cattle

(2) use of a steel plow

(3) terracing of mountains for farming

(4) development of floating gardens

18 What was a significant effect of the Columbian exchange?

(1) The Aztec conquered a vast empire.

(2) Potatoes were introduced into the diet of some Europeans.

(3) Prince Henry the Navigator established a school for sailors.

(4) China closed its borders to foreigners.

19 What was a direct result of the trans-Atlantic slave trade on African cultures?

(1) Many African communities faced economic disaster.

(2) European industrial factories were established throughout Africa.

(3) Animism was no longer practiced in Africa.

(4) Africans across the continent hired Europeans to train their military.

20 According to the European policy of mercantilism, colonies should

(1) benefit the mother country
(2) trade openly with various countries
(3) be left alone to manage their own affairs
(4) attempt to gain independence as soon as possible

21 Louis XIV and Peter the Great would most likely agree with the expression

(1) "government should leave businesses alone"
(2) "countries should settle differences without war"
(3) "do not question government authority"
(4) "all men are created with natural rights"

22 What was one effect of the French Revolution?

(1) Differences between ethnic groups were eliminated.
(2) Communism became popular.
(3) Militarism was discouraged.
(4) Nationalistic feelings were stimulated.

23 In *The Communist Manifesto*, Karl Marx and Friedrich Engels expressed the idea that

(1) religion should be the most important factor in society
(2) power should be determined by a person's wealth
(3) profits from work should belong to the workers
(4) supply and demand should control prices

24 Adam Smith would most likely agree with which statement?

(1) Revolution is the only solution to economic problems.
(2) Five-year plans are necessary in order to industrialize.
(3) All nations would benefit from an agricultural economy.
(4) Government should follow a laissez-faire policy.

25 Which region was most affected by decisions made at the Berlin Conference of 1884?

(1) Latin America
(2) South Asia
(3) East Asia
(4) Africa

Base your answer to question 26 on the 19th-century song lyrics below and on your knowledge of social studies.

. . . What has poor Ireland done, mother, —
  What has poor Ireland done,

That the world looks on, and sees us starve,
  Perishing one by one?

Do the men of England care not, mother, —
  The great men and the high, —

For the suffering sons of Erin's isle,
  Whether they live or die? . . .

— A. M. Edmond,
*"Give Me Three Grains of Corn, Mother"*

26 Which event is most closely associated with the conditions described in these lyrics?

(1) civil war
(2) famine
(3) Glorious Revolution
(4) independence from Great Britain

27 One way in which the Sepoy Rebellion in India and the Boxer Rebellion in China are similar is that both attempted to

(1) remove foreign influences
(2) restore democracy
(3) modernize their economy
(4) end religious conflict

28 The Opium Wars of the mid-19th century marked the beginning of the

(1) rivalry between China and Taiwan
(2) domination of China by foreign powers
(3) decline of European influence in East Asia
(4) global effort to combat drug use

29 The primary reason France and Japan were interested in controlling parts of Indochina in the 20th century was to

(1) dominate the Indian Ocean
(2) obtain valuable natural resources
(3) stop the spread of communism
(4) prevent Spanish colonization

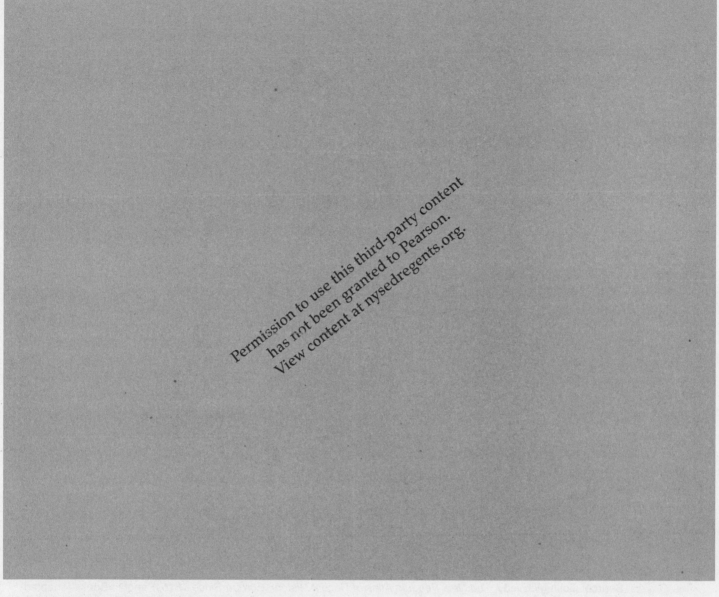

Permission to use this third-party content has not been granted to Pearson. View content at nysedregents.org.

31 Which leader is most closely associated with the rise of fascism in Italy prior to World War II?

(1) Ho Chi Minh  (3) Mao Zedong
(2) Winston Churchill  (4) Benito Mussolini

32 The South African government's policy of racial separation between 1948 and 1994 was called

(1) Pan-Africanism  (3) apartheid
(2) democratization  (4) suffrage

33 The Iranian Revolution of 1979 resulted in the establishment of

(1) a secular Western-style democracy
(2) a constitutional monarchy
(3) a military dictatorship
(4) an Islamic state

34 Mikhail Gorbachev contributed to the fall of communism in the Soviet Union and Eastern Europe by

(1) introducing the policies of perestroika and glasnost
(2) violating nuclear arms agreements
(3) invading Afghanistan
(4) signing the Camp David Accords

35 Which group of countries earns much of their revenue from the sale of oil?

(1) China, Korea, Jordan
(2) Turkey, Brazil, Lebanon
(3) Argentina, Malaysia, Chile
(4) Saudi Arabia, Nigeria, Venezuela

Base your answers to questions 36 and 37 on the map below and on your knowledge of social studies.

Source: Colin McEvedy, *The New Penguin Atlas of Recent History: Europe Since 1815,* Penguin Books (adapted)

36 In 1968, the areas labeled Estonian SSR, Belorussian SSR, and Moldavian SSR referred to

(1) republics that were part of the Soviet Union
(2) members of the Central Powers
(3) independent nations of Eastern Europe
(4) members of the Organization of Petroleum Exporting Countries (OPEC)

37 In 1968, the area east of the bold black boundary included members of the

(1) Triple Alliance
(2) Warsaw Pact
(3) European Union (EU)
(4) North Atlantic Treaty Organization (NATO)

Base your answer to question 38 on the cartoon below and on your knowledge of social studies.

**The Meeting Will Now Come To Order**

Source: D. R. Fitzpatrick, *St. Louis Post-Dispatch* (adapted)

38 The main idea of this 1949 cartoon is that the United Nations would

(1) work to solve pollution problems
(2) meet only when world crises erupted
(3) bridge the gap between world powers
(4) prevent the Cold War

39 Which statement about the Green Revolution is most accurate?

(1) It reduced the amount of chemical pollutants in the environment.
(2) It increased food output in many developing countries.
(3) It decreased dependence on fossil fuels.
(4) It attempted to end colonial rule.

40 Which problem in the savanna regions of Africa is caused by population pressures and overuse of the land?

(1) rain forest destruction
(2) desertification
(3) air pollution
(4) flooding

41 One way in which Pax Romana and Pax Mongolia are similar is that both were characterized by

(1) political stability
(2) unifying religious institutions
(3) representative forms of government
(4) social equality for men and women

42 The Twelve Tables were the written laws of

(1) ancient Babylonia
(2) the Mauryan Empire
(3) the British Empire
(4) ancient Rome

43 Which period in European history is most closely associated with the emergence of trade fairs, the founding of guilds, and the creation of the Hanseatic League?

(1) Age of Pericles
(2) Commercial Revolution
(3) Age of Reason
(4) Glorious Revolution

44 One way in which the English *Magna Carta* (1215), the French *Declaration of the Rights of Man and the Citizen* (1789), and the Japanese Constitution (1947) are similar is that all these documents

(1) limited the power of the monarch
(2) provided for universal suffrage
(3) created a theocracy
(4) equalized taxes

45 One way in which Emperor Meiji and Atatürk are similar is that they both promoted

(1) isolation and nationalism
(2) capitalism and democracy
(3) revolution and absolutism
(4) reform and modernization

46 Urbanization in developing nations today is similar to urbanization in 19th-century England because in both cases

(1) many people moved to rural areas
(2) governments developed policies of forced migration
(3) ties to extended families increased
(4) many farm workers went to cities to look for jobs

Base your answer to question 47 on the graphic organizer below and on your knowledge of social studies.

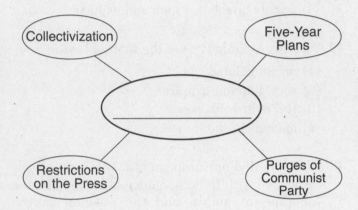

47 Which title best completes this graphic organizer?

(1) Saddam Hussein and the Persian Gulf War
(2) Sun Yixian (Sun Yat-sen) and the Defeat of the Manchu Dynasty
(3) Joseph Stalin and the Rise of a Totalitarian State
(4) Jawaharlal Nehru and the Modern Industrial State of India

48 Before September 1939, the European response to Hitler's actions included

(1) following a policy of appeasement
(2) blockading the coast of Germany
(3) forcing Germany to sign the Versailles Treaty
(4) creating alliances under the United Nations Charter

49 **"Czar Abdicates! Provisional Government Formed"**
**"Peasants Promised 'Peace, Land, and Bread'"**
**"Reds and Whites Fight Bloody Civil War"**

Which revolution is the focus of these headlines?

(1) Mexican          (3) Chinese
(2) Russian          (4) Cuban

Base your answer to question 50 on the passage below and on your knowledge of social studies.

. . . The only way to go was up. And, on June 26, 1948, planes from all over the world were employed to begin an airlift to fly needed food and supplies to the Berliners. The Soviets attempted to frighten away the Allied planes. One Soviet plane, trying to tighten the blockade, fired on a British plane as it attempted to land in Berlin. Both planes crashed, killing all aboard. But the airlift continued. . . .

Source: Doris M. Epler, *The Berlin Wall*, The Millbrook Press

50 The events described in this passage occurred soon after

(1) World War I          (3) the Korean War
(2) World War II         (4) the Six-Day War

**Answers to the essay questions are to be written in the separate essay booklet.**

**In developing your answer to Part II, be sure to keep these general definitions in mind:**

(a) <u>explain</u> means "to make plain or understandable; to give reasons for or causes of; to show the logical development or relationships of"

(b) <u>discuss</u> means "to make observations about something using facts, reasoning, and argument; to present in some detail"

**Part II**

**THEMATIC ESSAY QUESTION**

*Directions:* Write a well-organized essay that includes an introduction, several paragraphs addressing the task below, and a conclusion.

**Theme: Geography**

> Geographic factors have affected the development of nations and regions. These factors have also promoted or hindered cultural diffusion.

**Task:**

> Select *two* different geographic factors and for *each*
> - Explain how the geographic factor affected the development of a specific nation/region
> - Discuss how that geographic factor promoted *or* hindered cultural diffusion

You may use any geographic factor from your study of global history. Some suggestions you might wish to consider include deserts, rivers, mountains, plains, islands, irregular coastlines, straits, climate, and location.

**You are *not* limited to these suggestions.**

**Do *not* write about geographic factors in the United States in your response.**

**Guidelines:**

**In your essay, be sure to**
- Develop all aspects of the task
- Support the theme with relevant facts, examples, and details
- Use a logical and clear plan of organization, including an introduction and a conclusion that are beyond a restatement of the theme

NAME _____ SCHOOL _____

## Part III

### DOCUMENT-BASED QUESTION

   This question is based on the accompanying documents.  The question is designed to test your ability to work with historical documents.  Some of these documents have been edited for the purposes of this question.  As you analyze the documents, take into account the source of each document and any point of view that may be presented in the document.

**Historical Context:**

   Throughout history, individuals have made major contributions to the world.  Their achievements have had an impact on global history. Three of these individuals are **Leonardo da Vinci**, **Toussaint L'Ouverture**, and **Mohandas Gandhi**.

**Task:** Using the information from the documents and your knowledge of global history, answer the questions that follow each document in Part A.  Your answers to the questions will help you write the Part B essay in which you will be asked to

> Select *two* individuals mentioned in the historical context and for *each*
> - Describe the historical period during which the individual lived
> - Describe a major achievement of this individual
> - Discuss the impact of this achievement on global history

In developing your answers to Part III, be sure to keep these general definitions in mind:

   (a) <u>describe</u> means "to illustrate something in words or tell about it"
   (b) <u>discuss</u> means "to make observations about something using facts, reasoning, and argument; to present in some detail"

# Part A
# Short-Answer Questions

*Directions:* Analyze the documents and answer the short-answer questions that follow each document in the space provided.

**Document 1**

> . . . In the Middle Ages to praise man was to praise God, for man was a creation of God. But Renaissance writers praised man himself as a creator. They played down the sinfulness he was born with and emphasized his ability to think and act for himself, to produce works of art, to guide the destiny of others. They freed man from his pegged place in the medieval hierarchy, halfway between matter and spirit, and allowed him to roam at will, through all the levels of being, sometimes identifying himself with the brutes, sometimes with the angels. He was seen as the ruler of nature—the lord, although not the Lord, of creation.
>
> This new vision of man sprang from a heightened awareness of self. Medieval men had been preoccupied with searching their souls, but Renaissance men were much more intrigued with exploring, and indeed parading, their own personalities. Petrarch is a perfect example. Although his serious interests centered on his work in discovering and editing ancient texts, Petrarch was also interested in himself. In his letters, designed for posterity [future generations] as well as his friends, he left a record of his reactions to love affairs and friendship, to mountains and the flowers in his garden. They are an intellectual and emotional self-portrait, the first since antiquity [ancient times]. . . .

Source: John R. Hale, *Great Ages of Man: A History of the World's Cultures: Renaissance,* Time-Life, 1965

1 In what way did man's view of the world change between the European medieval period and the Renaissance according to John R. Hale? [1]

_____

_____

Score ☐

### Document 2

Leonardo da Vinci studied the anatomy of the human body while he was apprenticed to Andrea del Verrocchio. To learn about the body, he dissected and studied human corpses. Da Vinci was interested in the structure and the function of the various parts of the human body. His drawings reflect what he learned as he studied.

Note: Leonardo da Vinci recorded information in his notebooks by writing backward. →

Source: David Reuteler's website, "The Drawings of Leonardo Da Vinci"

2 According to this document, state **one** of Leonardo da Vinci's contributions to science.   [1]

_____

_____

Score

**Document 3**

> . . . It was as an artist that Leonardo attempted the fusion of anatomy with medical science through [the scientist] della Torre. This attempt was itself a great peak reached from those first modest beginnings of anatomy in the botegas [works] of Pollaiuolo and Verrocchio. The renaissance of anatomy could never have occurred without those long, distasteful hours of adventurous dissection and patient drawing. Without this artistic surge for knowledge the medical professors of anatomy, droning [speaking] their prosings [thoughts] from a tainted Galenic text [medical book written by Galen], could never have found a way of recording Galenic anatomical errors, let alone their corrections. . . .

Source: Kenneth D. Keele, "Leonardo daVinci's Influence on Renaissance Anatomy,"
*Medical History*, October 1964

3 What are *two* impacts of Leonardo da Vinci's work according to Kenneth Keele? [2]

(1) _____

_____  Score [ ]

(2) _____

_____  Score [ ]

## Document 4

> ### Revolt on the Island of Saint-Domingue
> ### (present-day Haiti), 1791
>
> . . . The seeds of independence were first sown among free black soldiers sent by the white French governors to fight against the British in the American War of Independence, where they were exposed to anti-colonial ideas. Later, the French Revolution's notions of liberty, equality, and brotherhood inspired an independence movement among the minority white settlers and a highly fragmented socioeconomic mix of free blacks. When the white population defied an order from France to enfranchise [give rights to] free blacks, it triggered a violent revolt that involved changing alliances among free blacks and the large slave population. After promulgating [announcing] a constitution in 1801 and overcoming a military force sent by Napoleon (First Consul, 1799–1804; Emperor, 1804–1814/1815), Haiti successfully declared its independence. Its success, along with that of the American War of Independence, inspired a number of anti-colonial struggles throughout Latin America. . . .

Source: New York Public Library, *Russia Engages the World*, online exhibition (adapted)

4*a* Based on this document, identify **one** situation that led to Haiti's declaration of independence from France.  [1]

_____

_____

Score ☐

*b* Identify **one** impact the Haitian revolt had on global history as stated in this document.  [1]

_____

_____

Score ☐

## Document 5

Toussaint L'Ouverture used this letter to rally the blacks in San Domingo (Haiti).

> August 29, 1793
>
> Brothers and friends.
>
> I am Toussaint L'Ouverture, my name is perhaps known to you. I have undertaken vengeance. I want Liberty and Equality to reign in San Domingo. I work to bring them into existence. Unite yourselves to us, brothers, and fight with us for the same cause, etc. . . .

Source: C. L. R. James, Lettres de Toussaint L'Ouverture, *The Black Jacobins,* The Dial Press (adapted)

5 According to this letter, what did Toussaint L'Ouverture want to achieve in San Domingo?  [1]

_____

_____

Score ☐

**Document 6**

C. L. R. James has stated that the success of the Haitian Revolution was almost entirely the result of the leadership of Toussaint L'Ouverture.

> . . . The work of Toussaint, Dessalines, Christophe, and Pétion endures in Hayti [Haiti], but what they did went far, far beyond the boundaries of the island. The Haytian revolution has had a profound influence on the history of the nineteenth century. . . .
>
> So far the negative aspect. There were others more positive. Hayti gave the impulse to and subsidised [supported] the first national revolutions in Spanish America. When the Spanish American colonies saw that such a small and weak community could win and keep its freedom, they took courage to fight for their own emancipation from European imperialism. In dark days, Bolivar the Liberator, ill and in distress, was welcomed by Pétion, nursed to health and given courage to lead the struggling nationalities against Spain. He failed and returned to Hayti. He was once again befriended. Pétion supplied him with arms, munitions, men, money, and printing material, and thus fortified he left Hayti to begin the campaign which ended in the emancipation of the Five States. Pétion asked nothing in return but the freedom of the slaves. . . .

Source: C. L. R. James, *The Black Jacobins*, The Dial Press

6 What were *two* ways that the work of Toussaint L'Ouverture and his successors influenced global history according to C. L. R. James? [2]

(1) _____

_____

Score [   ]

(2) _____

_____

Score [   ]

**Document 7**

This is an excerpt from a pledge put forth by the Indian National Congress (INC) on January 26, 1930. It encouraged members of the INC and Indian nationalists to strive for complete independence.

> . . . We believe that it is the inalienable right of the Indian people, as of any other people, to have freedom and to enjoy the fruits of their toil and have the necessities of life, so that they may have full opportunities of growth. . . .
>
> India has been ruined economically. The revenue derived from our people is out of all proportion to our income. Our average income is seven pice (less than two pence) per day, and of the heavy taxes we pay 20 per cent. are raised from the land revenue derived from the peasantry and 3 per cent. from the salt tax, which falls most heavily on the poor.
>
> Village industries, such as hand-spinning, have been destroyed, leaving the peasantry idle for at least four months in the year, and dulling their intellect for want of handicrafts, and nothing has been substituted, as in other countries, for the crafts thus destroyed.
>
> Customs and currency have been so manipulated as to heap further burdens on the peasantry. British manufactured goods constitute the bulk of our imports. Customs duties betray clear partiality for British manufactures, and revenue from them is used not to lessen the burden on the masses but for sustaining a highly extravagant administration. Still more arbitrary has been the manipulation of the exchange ratio which has resulted in millions being drained away from the country. . . .

Source: Jawaharlal Nehru, *Jawaharlal Nehru: An Autobiography,* John Lane the Bodley Head, 1939

7 State **two** ways the British ruined the economy of India based on the excerpt of this pledge used by Nehru. [2]

(1) _____

_____

Score ☐

(2) _____

_____

Score ☐

## Document 8

This passage was written by Mohandas Gandhi to help explain how India can become free.

> . . . EDITOR: Passive resistance is a method of securing rights by personal suffering; it is the reverse of resistance by arms. When I refuse to do a thing that is repugnant [offensive] to my conscience, I use soul-force. For instance, the Government of the day has passed a law which is applicable to me. I do not like it. If by using violence I force the Government to repeal the law, I am employing what may be termed body-force. If I do not obey the law and accept the penalty for its breach, I use soul-force. It involves sacrifice of self.
>
> Everybody admits that sacrifice of self is infinitely superior to sacrifice of others. Moreover, if this kind of force is used in a cause that is unjust, only the person using it suffers. He does not make others suffer for his mistakes. Men have before now done many things which were subsequently found to have been wrong. No man can claim that he is absolutely in the right or that a particular thing is wrong because he thinks so, but it is wrong for him so long as that is his deliberate judgment. It is therefore meet [proper] that he should not do that which he knows to be wrong, and suffer the consequence whatever it may be. This is the key to the use of soul-force. . . .

Source: M. K. Gandhi, *Hind Swaraj or Indian Home Rule,* Navajivan Publishing House, 1946

8 What contribution did Mohandas Gandhi make to the Indian independence movement according to this document?    [1]

_____

_____

Score ☐

**Document 9**

. . . Campaigns to reform discriminatory laws through nonviolent action—such as the civil rights movements in the United States—are one example of how human rights have been advanced through the use of nonviolent action. More significant, however, has been the remarkable upsurge [rise] in nonviolent insurrections [uprisings] against authoritarian regimes. Many of the individual revolts have received major media attention—such as those in China, the Philippines and Eastern Europe—and certain political consequences of these largely prodemocracy movements have been analyzed. However, there has been little recognition of the significance of the increasing utilization of nonviolent methods to affect change in nations where guerrilla warfare from below or gradualistic reform from above were once seen as the only alternatives. Despite the diffusion of nonviolence as a conscious strategy through movements around the world in recent decades, little is understood about how or why nonviolence works as a technique for securing social change. "Nonviolence" is not even a category in the mainstream academic lexicon [vocabulary]. . . .

Source: Stephen Zunes, "Nonviolent Action and Human Rights," *Political Science and Politics,*
American Political Science Association, June 2000

9 What impact did the use of nonviolent action have on global history according to Stephen Zunes? [1]

_____

_____

Score ☐

# Part B
# Essay

*Directions:* Write a well-organized essay that includes an introduction, several paragraphs, and a conclusion. Use evidence from *at least four* documents in your essay. Support your response with relevant facts, examples, and details. Include additional outside information.

**Historical Context:**

> Throughout history, individuals have made major contributions to the world. Their achievements have had an impact on global history. Three of these individuals are **Leonardo da Vinci**, **Toussaint L'Ouverture**, and **Mohandas Gandhi**.

**Task:** Using the information from the documents and your knowledge of global history, write an essay in which you

> Select *two* individuals mentioned in the historical context and for *each*
> - Describe the historical period during which the individual lived
> - Describe a major achievement of this individual
> - Discuss the impact of this achievement on global history

**Guidelines:**

**In your essay, be sure to**
- Develop all aspects of the task
- Incorporate information from *at least four* documents
- Incorporate relevant outside information
- Support the theme with relevant facts, examples, and details
- Use a logical and clear plan of organization, including an introduction and a conclusion that are beyond a restatement of the theme

This section contains an actual Regents Examination in Global History and Geography that was given in New York State in August 2008.

Circle your answers to Part 1. Write your responses to the short-answer questions in the spaces provided. Write your thematic essay and document-based essay on separate sheets of paper. Be sure to refer to the test-taking strategies in the front of this book as you prepare to answer the test questions.

# Part I

## Answer all questions in this part.

*Directions* (1–50): For each statement or question, write on the separate answer sheet the *number* of the word or expression that, of those given, best completes the statement or answers the question.

1 Ethnocentrism is best defined as
  (1) the belief that one's culture is superior to all others
  (2) military preparation for a civil war
  (3) love and devotion to one's country
  (4) a belief in one god

2 • The east is bordered by the Yellow Sea.
  • The population is concentrated along the coast and in the river valleys.
  • Mountains, plateaus, and deserts dominate the western region.

  To which country do all of these geographic statements apply?
  (1) England          (3) Nicaragua
  (2) China            (4) Philippines

3 Which social scientist primarily studies how people change resources into goods and services?
  (1) archaeologist    (3) economist
  (2) sociologist      (4) psychologist

4 The Neolithic Revolution is considered a turning point in history because it
  (1) influenced climatic changes
  (2) included the domestication of plants and animals
  (3) encouraged a nomadic lifestyle
  (4) caused a decline in population

5 The primary reason the Bantu-speaking people of West Africa migrated southward and eastward between 500 B.C. and A.D. 1500 was to
  (1) flee warfare
  (2) seek religious freedom
  (3) establish a colonial empire
  (4) find land for farming and grazing

6 Which action is most closely associated with polytheism?
  (1) praying in a synagogue
  (2) accepting the Eightfold Path
  (3) worshipping many gods
  (4) reading the Koran

Base your answer to question 7 on the graphic organizer below and on your knowledge of social studies.

7 Which item best completes this graphic organizer?
  (1) Development of the Wheel
  (2) Preservation of Greek and Roman Culture
  (3) Creation of the Compass
  (4) Utilization of Cuneiform

8 In western Europe, feudalism developed after the
  (1) Roman Empire collapsed
  (2) Renaissance began
  (3) city of Constantinople fell
  (4) Mongols invaded

9 Letting some farmland remain unplanted as a means of increasing food production is most closely associated with

(1) modern irrigation methods
(2) the three-field system
(3) the enclosure movement
(4) slash-and-burn agriculture

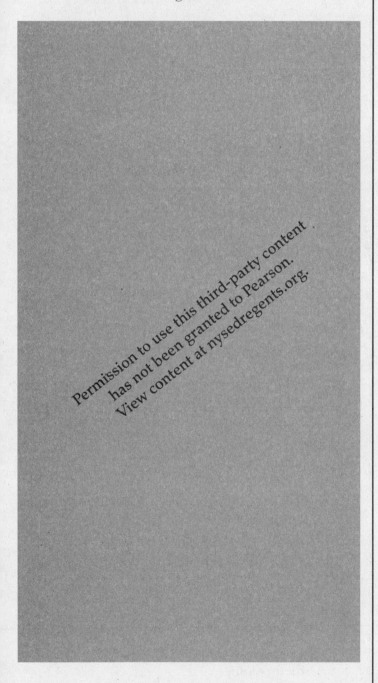

Permission to use this third-party content has not been granted to Pearson. View content at nysedregents.org.

Base your answer to question 11 on the Japanese print below and on your knowledge of social studies.

Source: *Hiroshige*, Prestel Postcard Book, 1997

11 Based on this print, which statement reflects an important theme in Japanese art and culture?

(1) Nature is a powerful force.
(2) Beauty is found in technological innovations.
(3) Realistic portrayals create a harmonious effect.
(4) Traditional activities should be expressed in simple forms.

12 What was an impact of Korea's geographic location on the history of East Asia?

(1) isolating Russia from Japan
(2) protecting China from Mongol invaders
(3) preventing Europeans from colonizing East Asia
(4) serving as a cultural bridge between China and Japan

13 Which situation was a result of Pax Mongolia?

(1) Trade increased between Europe and Asia.
(2) China became isolated from its neighbors.
(3) Warfare between Japan and Vietnam escalated.
(4) Europeans conquered the Aztecs and Incas.

14 • Sir Francis Drake circumnavigated the globe.
   • England defeated the Spanish Armada.
   • William Shakespeare wrote his play *Richard III*.

These events occurred during the reign of

(1) Charlemagne
(2) Elizabeth I
(3) Peter the Great
(4) Suleiman the Magnificent

15 Which geographic feature of Spain and Portugal most enhanced their ability to engage in exploration?

(1) peninsular location
(2) mountainous region
(3) extensive river system
(4) fertile plain

16 The journeys of Vasco da Gama, Bartholomeu Dias, and Christopher Columbus became possible in the late 1400s because of the

(1) support of exploration by the English government
(2) trade connections established by Ibn Battuta
(3) effects of the Atlantic slave trade
(4) development of new navigational instruments and technology

17 Which statement demonstrates a major characteristic of mercantilism in colonial Latin America?

(1) Colonies developed local industries to compete with Spain.
(2) Spanish colonies traded freely with English colonies.
(3) Spain instituted democratic governments in its colonies.
(4) Colonies were a source of raw materials for Spain.

18 The encomienda system in colonial Latin America led to the

(1) use of forced labor
(2) establishment of trade unions
(3) increase in landownership by Native Americans
(4) weakening of the power of peninsulares

19 Which heading best completes the partial outline below?

I. _____
   A. Writings of Thomas Hobbes
   B. Divine right theory
   C. Centralization of political power
   D. Reign of Louis XIV

(1) Beginning of Global Trade
(2) Growth of Democracy in Europe
(3) Rise of Absolutism
(4) Age of Exploration

20 One way in which Montesquieu, Voltaire, and Rousseau are similar is that they were

(1) philosophers during the Age of Enlightenment
(2) chief ministers during the French Revolution
(3) leaders of the Italian unification movement
(4) supporters of the Counter Reformation

21 Increased agricultural production in England in the late 1700s contributed directly to

(1) the development of a worldwide communications network
(2) the introduction of manorialism
(3) a decrease in the power of the monarch
(4) an increase in life expectancy

22 Which statement about railroad systems in the 19th and early 20th centuries is accurate?

(1) Imperialists rejected the use of railroads in their colonies.
(2) European governments opposed the development of railroads.
(3) Railroads helped promote the factory system and urbanization.
(4) Railroads made transportation of goods less efficient.

Base your answer to question 23 on the passage below and on your knowledge of social studies.

. . . The need of a constantly expanding market for its products chases the bourgeoisie over the whole surface of the globe. It must nestle everywhere, settle everywhere, establish connections everywhere. . . .

— Karl Marx and Friedrich Engels

23 Which historical event do Marx and Engels believe created the situation described in this passage?

(1) Cold War
(2) World War I
(3) Russian Revolution
(4) Industrial Revolution

24 What was the main reason for the extensive Irish emigration to North America in the 1840s?

(1) mass starvation     (3) civil war
(2) military draft       (4) smallpox outbreak

25 What was a principal reason for the success of European colonialism in Asia in the late 1800s?

(1) Asians respected Europeans as representatives of an advanced civilization.
(2) Europe was able to dominate military and commercial relations with Asia.
(3) Europeans respected Asian laws and customs.
(4) Many Asians adopted European religious practices.

26 Which action in Japanese history occurred during the Meiji Restoration?

(1) Japan modernized its economy.
(2) Mongols invaded the islands of Japan.
(3) The Japanese government adopted an isolationist policy.
(4) Buddhism became the official religion of Japan.

27 The annexation of Korea and Japan's invasion of Manchuria were attempts by Japan to

(1) spread Shinto beliefs
(2) protect human rights
(3) acquire natural resources
(4) establish theocratic governments

Base your answers to questions 28 and 29 on the telegram below and on your knowledge of social studies.

Nicholas II
*Telegram to Wilhelm II*
*July 29, 1914, 1:00 A.M.*

Am glad you are back. In this most serious moment, I appeal to you to help me. An ignoble [despised] war has been declared upon a weak country [Serbia]. The indignation [resentment] in Russia, shared fully by me, is enormous. I foresee that very soon I shall be overwhelmed by the pressure upon me, and be forced to take extreme measures which will lead to war. To try and avoid such a calamity [disaster] as a European war, I beg you in the name of our old friendship to do what you can to stop your allies from going too far.

— Nicky

28 Which conclusion is best supported by this telegram?

(1) Russia started to mobilize for war against Serbia.
(2) Nicholas II condemned the efforts of Wilhelm II.
(3) Russia supported the use of extreme measures.
(4) Nicholas II hoped diplomacy would prevent war.

29 Which war is most closely associated with the telegram Nicholas II sent to Wilhelm II?

(1) the Franco-Prussian War
(2) the Russo-Japanese War
(3) World War I
(4) World War II

Base your answers to questions 30 and 31 on the cartoon below and on your knowledge of social studies.

**"THIS WILL MAKE YOU FORGET THE PEACE TERMS."**

Source: Rollin Kirby, *The New York World,* March 28, 1919
(adapted)

30 This cartoonist is referring to the way Germany was affected in 1919 by

(1) the Congress of Vienna
(2) its defeat of Napoleon
(3) the Treaty of Versailles
(4) its defeat in World War II

31 This 1919 cartoon suggests that Germany may come under the influence of

(1) moderates     (3) radicals
(2) conservatives     (4) isolationists

32 Mohandas Gandhi's protests in India were a response to Great Britain's

(1) support of Zionism
(2) practice of humanitarianism
(3) introduction of socialism
(4) policy of colonialism

Base your answers to questions 33 and 34 on the table below and on your knowledge of social studies.

**Collective Farms of the USSR (Soviet Union) 1929–1940**

| Year | No. of collective farms in 1,000s |
|------|-----------------------------------|
| 1929 | 57.0 |
| 1930 | 85.9 |
| 1931 | 211.1 |
| 1932 | 211.1 |
| 1933 | 224.6 |
| 1934 | 233.3 |
| 1935 | 245.4 |
| 1936 | 242.2 |
| 1937 | 243.7 |
| 1938 | 242.4 |
| 1939 | 241.1 |
| 1940 | 236.3 |

— Paul Halsall, *Internet Modern History Sourcebook,*
(adapted)

33 Between which two years did the number of collective farms increase the most?

(1) 1929 and 1930     (3) 1934 and 1935
(2) 1930 and 1931     (4) 1939 and 1940

34 Which Soviet policy is most closely associated with the information in this table?

(1) Lenin's New Economic Policy
(2) Stalin's five-year plans
(3) Brezhnev's policy of détente
(4) Gorbachev's policy of glasnost

35 One similarity between Adolf Hitler and Benito Mussolini is that both

(1) led fascist states
(2) supported communism
(3) rejected militarism
(4) remained in power after World War II

Base your answer to question 36 on the cartoon below and on your knowledge of social studies.

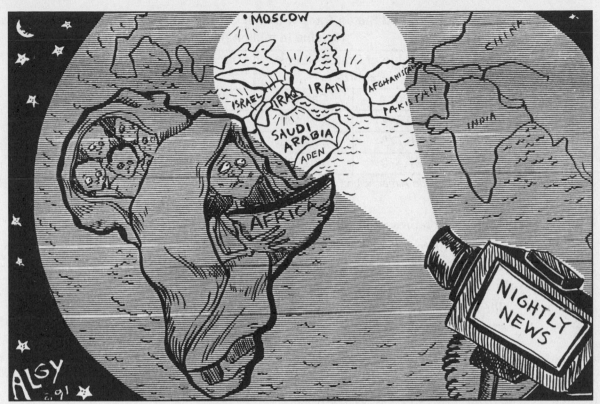

Source: Linda Godfrey, *Walworth County Week*

36 What does this cartoon suggest about news coverage of world events?

(1) Social concerns are often overemphasized.
(2) Africa's issues are often overshadowed by events in other regions.
(3) Too much time is devoted to European affairs.
(4) Africa's problems can be solved if global powers cooperate.

37 What has the end of communism in the Soviet Union caused many countries in Eastern Europe to do?

(1) shift to a command economy
(2) maintain a communist form of government
(3) pursue free-market economic policies
(4) join the Warsaw Pact

38 Which type of warfare did Mao Zedong, Fidel Castro, and Ho Chi Minh all engage in as leaders of revolutionary movements in their respective nations?

(1) guerilla
(2) trench
(3) unrestricted submarine
(4) biological

Base your answer to question 39 on the speakers' statements below and on your knowledge of social studies.

*Speaker A:* Medical facilities and public transportation are readily available in New Delhi.

*Speaker B:* Homelessness and crime continue to increase in New Delhi.

*Speaker C:* New Delhi offers many employment opportunities.

39 One way in which these speakers are similar is that all are expressing their opinions about

(1) rural poverty          (3) urban issues
(2) interdependence     (4) nationalism

Base your answer to question 40 on the chart below and on your knowledge of social studies.

**United States Trade with Mexico and Canada**
**($ value in millions)**

| Year | $ Value of United States Exports to | | $ Value of United States Imports from | |
|------|--------|--------|--------|--------|
|      | Mexico | Canada | Mexico | Canada |
| 1994 | 50,844 | 114,439 | 49,494 | 128,406 |
| 1998 | 78,773 | 156,603 | 94,629 | 173,256 |
| 2002 | 97,470 | 160,923 | 134,616 | 209,088 |

Source: *The World Almanac and Book of Facts,* World Almanac Books, 2004 (adapted)

40 The economic trend represented in this chart is most likely an effect of the creation of the

(1) Organization of American States (OAS)
(2) North Atlantic Treaty Organization (NATO)
(3) North American Free Trade Agreement (NAFTA)
(4) Organization of Petroleum Exporting Countries (OPEC)

41 Which statement about the Balkan Peninsula since 1995 is most accurate?

(1) Bosnia-Herzegovina and Croatia are now both controlled by Yugoslavia.
(2) Ethnic tensions and conflict continue to be a problem in much of the region.
(3) Slobodan Milosevic of Serbia became the first democratically elected leader of the region.
(4) The Balkan Peninsula has become one of the most prosperous regions in Europe.

42 Which revolution led to the concept of banking, the creation of guilds, and the development of capitalism in Europe?

(1) Commercial       (3) Scientific
(2) Agricultural     (4) Industrial

43 The introduction of Buddhism into Japan and of Christianity into Africa are examples of

(1) modernization       (3) cultural diffusion
(2) ethnic conflict     (4) isolation

44 A goal of both the Boxer Rebellion in China and the Mau Mau movement in Kenya was to

(1) promote laissez-faire capitalism
(2) end foreign control
(3) develop modern industries
(4) create a totalitarian state

Base your answers to questions 45 and 46 on the statement below and on your knowledge of social studies.

"Therefore those preachers of indulgences are in error, who say that by the pope's indulgences a man is freed from every penalty, and saved;"

45 Which period in European history is most closely associated with this statement?

(1) Roman Empire
(2) Crusades
(3) Protestant Reformation
(4) Enlightenment

46 This statement reflects a controversy over the proper

(1) roles of women      (3) types of education
(2) forms of prayer     (4) means of salvation

47 Simón Bolívar, José de San Martin, and Toussaint l'Ouverture are best known as

(1) scientists who supported the heliocentric theory
(2) leaders of Latin American independence movements
(3) early Spanish explorers of the New World
(4) communist leaders of the 19th century

Base your answer to question 48 on the cartoon below and on your knowledge of social studies.

Source: Mike Thompson, *Detroit Free Press* for *USA Today*, May 28, 2002

48 What is the main idea of this 2002 cartoon?

(1) The technology of the Cold War now threatens peace in Asia.
(2) The risk of nuclear conflict has been eliminated.
(3) Nuclear power presents a possible solution to energy shortages in southern Asia.
(4) Mediation has lessened tensions between India and Pakistan.

49 A. Kemal Atatürk rises to power in Turkey.
   B. Pericles rules during the Golden Age of Athens.
   C. Ayatollah Khomeini seizes power in Iran.
   D. Robespierre comes to power during the French Revolution.

What is the correct sequence of these events?
(1) $C \to B \to A \to D$     (3) $A \to C \to B \to D$
(2) $B \to C \to D \to A$     (4) $B \to D \to A \to C$

50 The Communist Revolution in China differed from the 19th-century Marxist ideals because this revolution was primarily supported by the

(1) warlords     (3) factory owners
(2) peasants     (4) gentry

Answers to the essay questions are to be written in the separate essay booklet.

In developing your answer to Part II, be sure to keep these general definitions in mind:

(a) <u>explain</u> means "to make plain or understandable; to give reasons for or causes of; to show the logical development or relationship of"

(b) <u>discuss</u> means "to make observations about something using facts, reasoning, and argument; to present in some detail"

## Part II

## THEMATIC ESSAY QUESTION

*Directions:* Write a well-organized essay that includes an introduction, several paragraphs addressing the task below, and a conclusion.

### Theme: Geography (How Humans Change Their Environment)

Throughout global history, human societies in various nations and regions have changed their physical environments to meet their needs. Societies have built structures, removed vegetation and resources, and modified the land to meet their needs. These changes have often had different results.

**Task:**

Select *two* different nations/regions and for *each*
- Explain why the society modified their environment
- Explain how the people of that specific nation/region modified their physical environment
- Discuss the effect this modification had on that nation/region

You may use any nation or region from your study of global history. Some suggestions you might wish to consider include Middle East (modified the land), Africa (modified the land), Japan (modified the land), Great Britain (removed resources), South Africa (removed resources), Brazil (removed vegetation), China (built a structure), and East Germany (built structures).

**You are *not* limited to these suggestions.**

**Do *not* select the United States or a region of the United States as an example in your answer.**

**Guidelines:**

**In your essay, be sure to**
- Develop all aspects of the task
- Support the theme with relevant facts, examples, and details
- Use a logical and clear plan of organization, including an introduction and a conclusion that are beyond a restatement of the theme

NAME _____ SCHOOL _____

## Part III

## DOCUMENT-BASED QUESTION

This question is based on the accompanying documents. The question is designed to test your ability to work with historical documents. Some of these documents have been edited for the purposes of this question. As you analyze the documents, take into account the source of each document and any point of view that may be presented in the document.

**Historical Context:**

Throughout history, migrations of people have affected countries and regions. These migrations have been both voluntary and involuntary and include *Africans to the Americas, Jews to Palestine and Israel,* and *Hindus/Muslims between India and Pakistan.*

**Task:** Using the information from the documents and your knowledge of global history, answer the questions that follow each document in Part A. Your answers to the questions will help you write the Part B essay in which you will be asked to

---

Select *two* migrations mentioned in the historical context and for *each*

- Describe the historical circumstances surrounding the voluntary or involuntary migration
- Discuss an impact the migration had on the country or region from which the group left *and/or* an impact the migration had on the new destination

---

**You may *not* use the migration of Hindus and Muslims
between India and Pakistan as two separate migrations.**

In developing your answers to Part III, be sure to keep these general definitions in mind:

(a) <u>describe</u> means "to illustrate something in words or tell about it"

(b) <u>discuss</u> means "to make observations about something using facts, reasoning, and argument; to present in some detail"

## Part A
## Short-Answer Questions

*Directions:* Analyze the documents and answer the short-answer questions that follow each document in the space provided.

**Document 1**

---

### The Big Business of Slave Trading

. . . When in 1517 Bishop Bartolomeo de Las Casas advocated [supported] the encouragement of immigration to the New World by permitting Spaniards to import African slaves, the trading of humans in the New World formally began. Las Casas was so determined to relieve Indians of the onerous [difficult] burden of slavery that he recommended the enslavement of Africans. (Later, he so deeply regretted having taken this position that he vigorously renounced it.) The ban against the use of Africans was removed, and Charles II issued licenses to several Flemish traders to take Africans to the Spanish colonies. Monopoly of the trade went to the highest bidders. Sometimes it was held by Dutch traders, at other times by Portuguese, French, or English. As West Indian plantations grew in size and importance, the slave trade became a huge, profitable undertaking employing thousands of persons and involving a capital outlay of millions of dollars. By 1540 the annual importation of African slaves into the West Indies was estimated at 10,000. . . .

Source: Franklin and Moss, *From Slavery to Freedom: A History of African Americans*, Alfred A. Knopf

---

1 According to Franklin and Moss, what was **one** reason enslaved Africans were imported to the "New World" by Europeans?  [1]

_____

_____

Score ☐

**Document 2**

. . . Large-scale sugar plantations, established first in Brazil and, after 1645, in the Caribbean islands, were enormously profitable. Plantations in Cuba gave more than a 30 percent return on capital investment; those in Barbados returned 40 to 50 percent. These islands became societies whose economies relied heavily on the labor of African captives. In 1789, one-third of the population of Cuba was comprised of Africans. Between 1730 and 1834, up to 90 percent of the populations of Jamaica, Antigua, and Grenada were Africans. In Brazil in 1800, half the population was African. . . .

Source: Willie F. Page, *Encyclopedia of African History and Culture,* Volume III, Facts on File

2 According to Willie F. Page, what was *one* impact of the arrival of Africans on Brazil and on the Caribbean Islands? [1]

_____

_____

Score ☐

## Document 3

> ... **Long-Term Effects.** The trade in African slaves brought about the largest forced movement of people in history. It established the basis for black populations in the Caribbean and in North and South America. At the same time, it disrupted social and political life in Africa and opened the door for European colonization of the continent. ...
>
> The shift in European demand from gold, foodstuffs, and such products to slaves changed the relations among African groups and states. The prices Africans received for slaves made it more profitable for them to take captives from their neighbors than to establish networks for producing and selling other goods. In this way the slave trade encouraged strong states to raid weaker states for slaves. As a result, many African societies were torn by organized slave wars and general banditry. Successful slave-raiding and trading societies formed new states that were dominated by military groups and constantly at war with their neighbors. ...

Source: John Middleton, ed., *Africa: An Encyclopedia for Students,* Volume 4, Thomson Learning

3 Based on this excerpt from *Africa: An Encyclopedia for Students*, state **two** effects of the slave trade on Africa.  [2]

(1) _____

_____

Score ☐

(2) _____

_____

Score ☐

**Document 4a**

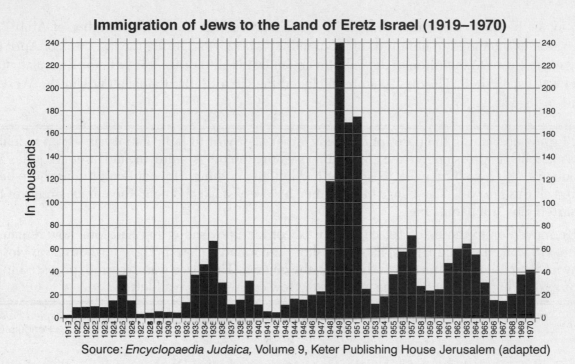

### Immigration of Jews to the Land of Eretz Israel (1919–1970)

Source: *Encyclopaedia Judaica,* Volume 9, Keter Publishing House Jerusalem (adapted)

**Document 4b**

**1938**
Kristallnacht occurs
in Germany

**1947**
Palestine is
partitioned

**1950**
Law of the Return
is passed

1920    1930    1940    1950    1960    1970

**1920**
Britain accepts
mandate for Palestine

**1933**
Hitler rises to
power

**1941**
Final Solution
implemented

**1948**
Israel declares
Statehood

**1956**
Crisis occurs over
Suez Canal

**1967**
Six Day War
erupts

4 Based on these documents, identify ***two*** specific reasons large numbers of Jewish immigrants moved to the Palestinian/Israeli region between 1920 and 1970. [2]

(1) _____

_____    Score ☐

(2) _____

_____    Score ☐

## Document 5a

Arab Palestinians began to leave their homes in cities in December 1947. The number of Arab Palestinians leaving their homes increased to hundreds of thousands by May 1948. During the last week of April in 1948, as the fighting came closer to their home, the Palestinian family in this passage left Jaffa for Ramallah. On May 14, 1948, Israel was established. This new country included the city of Jaffa. Ramallah was in the West Bank that became part of Jordan.

> . . . I grew up hearing the description of my father's last visit to Jaffa, and it has left an indelible [permanent] impression on me. My father's entire holdings were in and around Jaffa, the products of his own hard work. His father had left him nothing. How difficult it must have been to bid all this farewell. The image of my father, his every step echoing in the empty streets of the deserted city, still haunts me. . . .
>
> He moved on to the marketplace, empty except for a few shops that had somehow remained open. He walked passed Hinn's, his barbershop, and found it closed. The courthouse was closed, as were the clinics, the nurseries, the cafés, the cinema. The place was deserted, prepared to be captured. What have we done, he wondered. How could we have all left? . . .

Source: Raja Shehadeh, *Strangers in the House: Coming of Age in Occupied Palestine,*
Penguin Books

5a Based on this account by Raja Shehadeh, what was **one** impact on the city of Jaffa when the Palestinians left? [1]

_____

_____

Score ☐

## Document 5b

This excerpt describes the early days of the State of Israel in 1949 when many people, including the Jews from displaced camps in Europe, were migrating into and out of the region.

> . . . At any rate, the return of the Arabs to their homes became increasingly difficult with the rise of another cataclysmic event—the mass influx of the Jews from all over the world. They had been coming, even in the midst of hostilities, at the rate of a thousand a day, in larger numbers than had been expected, and in much larger numbers than the country was ready to accommodate. The squeamishness of the Custodians of Abandoned (Arab) Property had to give way to the onrush of this deluge [flood of people] and the early comers and some of the old-timers helped themselves to whatever was left of the former Arab houses. . . .

Source: M. Z. Frank, Introduction to "From the Four Corners of the Earth," *Sound the Great Trumpet,* Whittier Books

5b According to M. Z. Frank, what was *one* effect of the Jewish migration on Israel? [1]

_____

_____

Score ☐

## Document 6

Richard Willstätter, a German Jewish chemist, won a Nobel Prize in 1915. In 1938, during Nazi rule, he managed to flee Germany. Many others fled before 1938 and some fled after.

> . . . Willstätter's story demonstrates that the exodus of German Jews was one of the most astonishing migrations in history. It included not only Nobel Prize winners but thousands of other scientists, artists, academics, engineers, and professional men and women in every category. And since this was an entire population and not the usual young person in search of a fortune, it was made up of whole families, middle-aged couples, and even the elderly, like Betty Scholem, who settled in a small town in Australia, tending a sweetshop with one of her sons. Driven out of their country, they took their talent and skills and culture with them and made the rest of the world richer for it. . . .

Source: Ruth Gay, *The Jews of Germany*, Yale University Press

6 According to Ruth Gay, what was *one* way Germany was hurt by the migration of German Jews?  [1]

_____

_____

Score ☐

**Document 7**

> **Partition**
>
> . . . Gandhi's beliefs were based, in part, on ancient Hindu ideals. This may have added to the hatred and suspicion that had always existed between Hindus and Muslims. The Muslims were afraid that they would have no power in the new India. Although the Hindu leaders, including Gandhi, tried to reassure the Muslims, no agreement could be reached. The country was finally divided into two parts—the independent Muslim state of Pakistan and a predominately Hindu state—the Democratic Republic of India. . . .

Source: Jean Bothwell, *The First Book of India,* Franklin Watts

7 According to Jean Bothwell, what was **one** cause of the migration of Muslims and Hindus?   [1]

_____

_____

Score ☐

**Document 8**

---

### History's Greatest Migration
#### 4,000,000 People Cross the Punjab to Seek New Homes

The mass migration and exchange of populations in the Punjab—Moslems moving west into Pakistan and Hindus and Sikhs trekking east into India—have now reached a scale unprecedented in history. Accurate statistics are impossible to obtain, but it is reasonable to estimate that no fewer than four million people are now on the move both ways.

What this means in terms of human misery and hardship can be neither imagined nor described. Within the past few weeks the conditions over a wide area of Northern India, including the whole of the Indus Valley and part of the Gangetic Plain, have deteriorated steadily. It is no exaggeration to say that throughout the North-west Frontier Provinces, in the West Punjab, the East Punjab, and the Western part of the United Provinces the minority communities live in a state of insecurity often amounting to panic.

Farther afield in the eastern parts of the United Provinces and to a less extent in Bihar and Bengal, much tension and friction prevail but there has hitherto been little movement of population. . . .

---

Source: *Guardian*, Thursday, September 25, 1947

8 Based on this article in the *Guardian*, state **two** ways the region of South Asia was affected by the mass migration of people in 1947. [2]

(1) _____

_____

Score ☐

(2) _____

_____

Score ☐

**Document 9**

. . . And there were many [examples where untouchables were invisible during the partition]. In January 1948, two social workers, Sushila Nayyar and Anis Kidwai, went to visit Tihar village on the outskirts of Delhi. They had heard that a rich Hindu from Pakistan had left behind huge properties when he had moved, and had therefore, like many people, effected an exchange of property with a rich Muslim in Tihar to whom the land belonged. Each took the other's property. But neither was obliged to carry on with the other's business. The Hindu, therefore, threw out all previously employed workers from his newly acquired piece of property. Most of these were Muslims, but about a third were Harijans [untouchables]. The Muslims made their way to one or the other of the two Muslim camps that had been set up in the city. But for the Harijans, displaced in a war that was basically centred around Hindu and Muslim identities, there was nowhere to go. No camps to help them tide over the difficult time. No recourse to government— all too preoccupied at the moment with looking after the interests of Muslims and Hindus, no help from political leaders whose priorities were different at the time. . . .

Source: Urvashi Butalia, *The Other Side of Silence,* Duke University Press, 2000

9 According to Urvashi Butalia, what was *one* impact the migration of Muslims and Hindus had on South Asia? [1]

_____

_____

Score

# Part B
## Essay

*Directions:* Write a well-organized essay that includes an introduction, several paragraphs, and a conclusion. Use evidence from *at least **four*** documents in your essay. Support your response with relevant facts, examples, and details. Include additional outside information.

**Historical Context:**

Throughout history, migrations of people have affected countries and regions. These migrations have been both voluntary and involuntary and include ***Africans to the Americas, Jews to Palestine and Israel,*** and ***Hindus/Muslims between India and Pakistan.***

**Task:** Using the information from the documents and your knowledge of global history, write an essay in which you

Select ***two*** migrations mentioned in the historical context and for ***each***
- Describe the historical circumstances surrounding the voluntary or involuntary migration
- Discuss an impact the migration had on the country or region from which the group left *and/or* an impact the migration had on the new destination

**You may *not* use the migration of Hindus and Muslims
between India and Pakistan as two separate migrations.**

**Guidelines:**

**In your essay, be sure to**
- Develop all aspects of the task
- Incorporate information from *at least **four*** documents
- Incorporate relevant outside information
- Support the theme with relevant facts, examples, and details
- Use a logical and clear plan of organization, including an introduction and a conclusion that are beyond a restatement of the theme

This section contains an actual Regents Examination in Global History and Geography that was given in New York State in June 2008.

Circle your answers to Part 1. Write your responses to the short-answer questions in the spaces provided. Write your thematic essay and document-based essay on separate sheets of paper. Be sure to refer to the test-taking strategies in the front of this book as you prepare to answer the test questions.

## Part I

### Answer all questions in this part.

*Directions* (1–50): For each statement or question, write on the separate answer sheet the *number* of the word or expression that, of those given, best completes the statement or answers the question.

Base your answer to question 1 on the announcement below and on your knowledge of social studies.

# Discovery
### OF
# Ancient Relics.

A Full, True, and Interesting Account of that Remarkable and Important Discovery made yesterday in taking down the old houses in the Castle-hill, when there was found a box containing several Ancient Coins, a Massy Gold Ring, an old fashioned Dirk, and a Wonderful Prophecy made in the year 1550, respecting great events which are to happen this present year.

Source: Broadside published in Edinburgh, Scotland, 1831 (adapted)

1 Which term best describes the items mentioned in this announcement?

(1) icons          (3) artifacts
(2) fossils        (4) replicas

2 One way in which South Korea, Saudi Arabia, and India are geographically similar is that each is located on

(1) an island      (3) an isthmus
(2) an archipelago (4) a peninsula

3 Which statement represents a characteristic of democracy?

(1) Religious leaders control government policy.
(2) Citizens are the source of power in government.
(3) The government limits the thoughts and actions of the people.
(4) The laws of the government are made by influential military officers.

4 The Bantu cleared the land, then fertilized it with ashes. When the land could no longer support their families, the Bantu moved further south. By 1110 B.C., the Bantu had spread their rich culture throughout central and southern Africa.

Which agricultural technique is described in this passage?

(1) irrigation        (3) slash-and-burn
(2) terrace farming   (4) crop rotation

5 Which ancient civilization is associated with the Twelve Tables, an extensive road system, and the poets Horace and Virgil?

(1) Babylonian   (3) Phoenician
(2) Greek        (4) Roman

6 The term *feudalism* is best defined as a

(1) holy war between Christians and Muslims
(2) process in which goods are traded for other goods
(3) division of political power between three separate branches
(4) system in which land is exchanged for military service and loyalty

7 Which title best completes the partial outline below?

I. _____

   A. Incorporation of European and Arabic ideas in architecture
   B. Preservation of Greco-Roman ideas
   C. Spread of Orthodox Christianity into Russia
   D. Development of Justinian Code

(1) Age of Discovery   (3) Persian Empire
(2) Byzantine Empire   (4) Crusades

Base your answer to question 8 on the illustration below and on your knowledge of social studies.

Source: Barry K. Beyer et al., *The World Around Us: Eastern Hemisphere,* MacMillan Publishing (adapted)

8 Based on the information in this illustration, which statement about the society of ancient Egypt is accurate?

(1) The women had equal status to the men.
(2) The social structure was hierarchical.
(3) Social mobility was unrestricted.
(4) Soldiers outnumbered farmers.

9 Which statement about the Mongol Empire is accurate?

(1) The Mongols developed a highly technological society that emphasized formal education.
(2) European monarchies became a model for the early Mongol governments.
(3) Pax Mongolia led to regional stability, increasing trade on the Silk Road.
(4) The Mongols adopted Roman Catholicism as the official religion of the empire.

10 Which period in European history is most closely associated with Leonardo da Vinci, Michaelangelo, William Shakespeare, and Nicolaus Copernicus?

(1) Early Middle Ages  (3) Age of Absolutism
(2) Renaissance  (4) Enlightenment

11 What was one of the primary reasons for the spread of the bubonic plague?

(1) increase in trade
(2) colonization of the Americas
(3) development of the manorial system
(4) economic decline

12 Which situation is considered a cause of the other three?

(1) Religious unity declines throughout Europe.
(2) The Catholic Counter-Reformation begins.
(3) The power of the Roman Catholic Church decreases.
(4) Martin Luther posts the Ninety-five Theses.

Base your answer to question 13 on the table below and on your knowledge of social studies.

**Population of the Largest Medieval Cities in 1250 and 1450**

| The 10 largest cities in 1250 | | The 10 largest cities in 1450 | |
|---|---|---|---|
| 1 Hangchow | 320,000 | 1 Peking | 600,000 |
| 2 Cairo | 300,000 | 2 Vijayanagar | 455,000 |
| 3 Fez | 200,000 | 3 Cairo | 380,000 |
| 4 Kamakura | 200,000 | 4 Hangchow | 250,000 |
| 5 Pagan | 180,000 | 5 Tabriz | 200,000 |
| 6 Paris | 160,000 | 6 Canton | 175,000 |
| 7 Peking | 140,000 | 7 Granada | 165,000 |
| 8 Canton | 140,000 | 8 Nanking | 150,000 |
| 9 Nanking | 130,000 | 9 Paris | 150,000 |
| 10 Marrakesh | 125,000 | 10 Kyoto | 150,000 |

Source: Tertius Chandler, *Four Thousand Years of Urban Growth*, St. David's University Press (adapted)

13 Which statement can best be supported by the information in this table?

(1) The population of Paris increased between 1250 and 1450.

(2) The populations of Cairo and Nanking were higher in 1250 than in 1450.

(3) The population of most large cities exceeded one million people in 1450.

(4) The population of Peking increased more than the population of Canton between 1250 and 1450.

---

Base your answer to question 14 on the passage below and on your knowledge of social studies.

It would be wrong to call the Ottoman Empire a purely Islamic state. It was not. It was a state that claimed some kind of an attachment, some kind of allegiance to Islam, but combined it with other forms of heritage from the Byzantine tradition or from the Turkic tradition that did not really correspond to Islam. So they always had this very, very pragmatic approach to Islam.

— Professor Edhem Eldem, Bogazici University, NPR News, *All Things Considered*, August 18, 2004

14 This author is suggesting that during the Ottoman Empire

(1) religion was mingled with historic traditions

(2) most people belonged to minority religions

(3) rulers tried to separate politics from religion

(4) rulers operated under a strict set of laws

15 • Foreign rulers were overthrown.
   • Admiral Zheng He established trade links.
   • Civil service exams were reinstated.

These events in history occurred during the rule of the

(1) Mughal dynasty in India

(2) Abbasid dynasty in the Middle East

(3) Ming dynasty in China

(4) Tokugawa shogunate in Japan

16 What was the primary economic policy used by the Spanish with their Latin American colonies?

(1) embargoes          (3) boycotts

(2) tariffs             (4) mercantilism

17 In *Two Treatises of Government*, John Locke wrote that the purpose of government was to

(1) keep kings in power

(2) regulate the economy

(3) expand territory

(4) protect natural rights

Base your answer to question 18 on the map below and on your knowledge of social studies.

Source: Peter N. Stearns et al., *World Civilizations: The Global Experience*, Pearson (adapted)

18 Which generalization is best supported by the information on this map?

(1) No trade occurred between East Africa and the Persian Gulf region.

(2) The monsoon winds influenced trade between East Africa and India.

(3) Trading states developed primarily in the interior of East Africa.

(4) Trade encouraged the spread of Islam from East Africa to Arabia.

Base your answer to question 19 on the summaries of the "New Laws" quoted below and on your knowledge of social studies.

. . . Art. 31. All Indians held in encomienda by the viceroys, by their lieutenants, royal officers, prelates, monasteries, hospitals, religious houses, mints, the treasury, etc., are to be transferred forthwith to the Crown. . . .

Art. 38. Lawsuits involving Indians are no longer to be tried in the Indies, or by the Council of the Indies, but must be pleaded before the King himself. . . .

— New Laws issued by Emperor Charles V, 1542–1543

19 One purpose of these laws was to

(1) reduce local authority and increase central control

(2) increase religious authority and limit secular influences

(3) guarantee citizenship to Indians while supporting traditional practices

(4) promote economic development while expanding political rights for Indians

20 One major effect of Napoleon's rule of France was that it led to

(1) an increase in the power of the Roman Catholic Church

(2) massive emigration to the Americas

(3) trade agreements with Great Britain

(4) a restoration of political stability

21 Which idea is most closely associated with laissez-faire economics?

(1) communes

(2) trade unionism

(3) subsistence agriculture

(4) free trade

22 In the 19th century, a major reason for Irish migration to North America was to

(1) gain universal suffrage

(2) avoid malaria outbreaks

(3) flee widespread famine

(4) escape a civil war

23 A major goal of both the Sepoy Mutiny in India and the Boxer Rebellion in China was to

(1) rid their countries of foreigners
(2) expand their respective territories
(3) receive international military support
(4) restore an absolute monarch to the throne

24 Early exploration of Africa by Europeans was hindered by the

(1) lack of natural resources in Africa
(2) alliances between African kingdoms
(3) isolationist policies of European monarchs
(4) many different physical features of Africa

25 Which action taken by the Meiji government encouraged industrialization in 19th-century Japan?

(1) building a modern transportation system
(2) limiting the number of ports open to foreign trade
(3) forcing families to settle on collective farms
(4) establishing a system of trade guilds

26 One goal of the League of Nations was to

(1) promote peaceful relations worldwide
(2) stimulate the economy of Europe
(3) bring World War I to an end
(4) encourage a strong alliance system

27 • Five-year plans
• Collectivization of agriculture
• Great Purge

Which individual is associated with all these policies?

(1) Adolf Hitler          (3) Deng Xiaoping
(2) Joseph Stalin         (4) Jawaharlal Nehru

28 Japan's invasion of Manchuria, Italy's attack on Ethiopia, and Germany's blitzkrieg in Poland are examples of

(1) military aggression   (3) containment
(2) appeasement           (4) the domino theory

29 Which statement about the worldwide Depression of the 1930s is a fact rather than an opinion?

(1) Political leaders should have prevented the Depression.
(2) Germany was hurt more by the Treaty of Versailles than by the Depression.
(3) The economic upheaval of the Depression had major political effects.
(4) World War I was the only reason for the Depression.

30 Which group was accused of violating human rights in the city of Nanjing during World War II?

(1) Americans             (3) Japanese
(2) Chinese               (4) Germans

31 One way in which the Hitler Youth of Germany and the Red Guard of China are similar is that both organizations

(1) required unquestioning loyalty to the leader
(2) helped increase religious tolerance
(3) hindered imperialistic goals
(4) led pro-democracy movements

32 • French intent to recolonize Indo-China after World War II
• United States desire to prevent the spread of communism
• United States support for the French in Southeast Asia

These ideas are most closely associated with the

(1) causes of the conflict in Vietnam
(2) reasons for the Nationalist settlement of Taiwan
(3) factors that led to the Korean War
(4) results of the Marshall Plan

33 Which country is most closely associated with the terms *pass laws*, *homelands*, and *white minority rule*?

(1) El Salvador           (3) Iran
(2) South Africa          (4) Israel

Base your answer to question 34 on the photograph below and on your knowledge of social studies.

**Mahatma Gandhi demonstrating cotton-spinning on his own *charka* in Mirzapur, 1925.**

Source: Stanley Wolpert, *Gandhi's Passion: The Life and Legacy of Mahatma Gandhi*, Oxford University Press

34 During the Indian independence movement, the activity shown in this photograph inspired the Indian people to

(1) stop buying British goods

(2) reject Muslim rule

(3) join the Indian army

(4) expand British textile manufacturing

Base your answers to questions 35 and 36 on the passage below and on your knowledge of social studies.

. . . (1) Internally, arouse the masses of the people. That is, unite the working class, the peasantry, the urban petty bourgeoisie and the national bourgeoisie, form a domestic united front under the leadership of the working class, and advance from this to the establishment of a state which is a people's democratic dictatorship under the leadership of the working class and based on the alliance of workers and peasants.

(2) Externally, unite in a common struggle with those nations of the world which treat us as equals and unite with the peoples of all countries. That is, ally ourselves with the Soviet Union, with the People's Democracies and with the proletariat and the broad masses of the people in all other countries, and form an international united front. . . .

Source: Mao Tse-Tung [Mao Zedong], *Selected Works*, Volume Five, 1945–1949, New York International Publishers

35 In this passage, Mao Zedong is suggesting that China

(1) create a government under the leadership of industrialists

(2) give up its independence and become a part of the Soviet Union

(3) rely on the United Nations for economic aid

(4) join with the Soviet Union as a partner in communism

36 In this passage, Mao Zedong is using the ideas of

(1) Thomas Malthus

(2) Adam Smith

(3) Karl Marx

(4) Jiang Jieshi (Chiang Kai-Shek)

Base your answer to question 37 on the time line below and on your knowledge of social studies.

**1978** Camp David Accords are signed

**1987** PLO begins the first Intifada

**2004** Israel destroys suspected weapons workshop in Gaza

**1973** Egypt attacks Israel on Yom Kippur

**1982** Israel invades Lebanon

**1993** Rabin agrees to withdraw from Palestinian territory

37 Which conclusion can be drawn from this time line?

(1) Israel withdrew from the Camp David Accords.

(2) The Palestinian army is superior to the Israeli army.

(3) Long-lasting peace in the Middle East has been difficult to achieve.

(4) Neighboring countries have not been involved in the Arab-Israeli conflict.

38 The destruction of the Berlin Wall and the breakup of the Soviet Union signify the

(1) end of the Cold War

(2) collapse of the Taliban

(3) strength of the Warsaw Pact

(4) power of the European Union

39 In the 20th century, urbanization affected the developing nations of Africa, Asia, and Latin America by

(1) reducing literacy rates

(2) weakening traditional values

(3) strengthening caste systems

(4) increasing the isolation of women

40 Which statement about the impact of the AIDS epidemic in both Africa and Southeast Asia is most accurate?

(1) Life expectancy in both regions is declining.

(2) The availability of low-cost drugs has cured most of those infected.

(3) The introduction of awareness programs has eliminated the threat of the disease.

(4) Newborn babies and young children have not been affected by the disease.

41 In August 1990, Iraq invaded Kuwait. The United Nations response led to the Persian Gulf War of 1991. This response is an example of

(1) détente          (3) totalitarianism

(2) empire building    (4) collective security

42 One similarity between the Roman Empire and the Ottoman Empire is that both

(1) reached their height of power at the same time

(2) developed parliamentary governments

(3) ensured equality for women

(4) declined because of corruption in government

43 Which statement regarding the impact of geography on Japan is most accurate?

(1) Large plains served as invasion routes for conquerors.

(2) Arid deserts and mountains caused isolation from Asia.

(3) Lack of natural resources led to a policy of imperialism.

(4) Close proximity to Africa encouraged extensive trade with Egypt.

45 The Age of Exploration led directly to the

(1) establishment of European colonies
(2) start of the Puritan Revolution
(3) invention of the magnetic compass
(4) failure of the Congress of Vienna

46 Which revolution was caused by the factors shown in this partial outline?

I. _____

   A. Bankruptcy of the treasury
   B. Tax burden on the Third Estate
   C. Inflation
   D. Abuses of the Old Regime

(1) Russian     (3) French
(2) Mexican    (4) Cuban

47 One way in which José de San Martín, Camillo Cavour, and Jomo Kenyatta are similar is that each leader

(1) made significant scientific discoveries
(2) led nationalist movements
(3) fought against British imperialism
(4) became a communist revolutionary

48 One way in which Vladimir Lenin's New Economic Policy and Mikhail Gorbachev's policy of perestroika are similar is that both

(1) allowed elements of capitalism within a communist economic system
(2) strengthened their country's military defenses
(3) supported censorship of news and of personal correspondence
(4) increased tensions during the Cold War

49 Which set of events in 19th- and 20th-century Chinese history is in the correct chronological order?

(1) Great Leap Forward → Opium Wars → Long March → Four Modernizations

(2) Four Modernizations → Long March → Opium Wars → Great Leap Forward

(3) Opium Wars → Long March → Great Leap Forward → Four Modernizations

(4) Long March → Four Modernizations → Great Leap Forward → Opium Wars

50 A study of Spain during the late 1400s, the Balkan States during the early 1900s, Rwanda during the 1990s, and Central Asia today shows that

(1) civil disobedience is an effective way to bring about change

(2) people have been encouraged to question tradition

(3) colonial rule has a lasting legacy

(4) ethnic conflicts have been a recurring issue in history

Answers to the essay questions are to be written in the separate essay booklet.

In developing your answer to Part II, be sure to keep these general definitions in mind:

(a) <u>explain</u> means "to make plain or understandable; to give reasons for or causes of; to show the logical development or relationships of"

(b) <u>discuss</u> means "to make observations about something using facts, reasoning, and argument; to present in some detail"

## Part II

## THEMATIC ESSAY QUESTION

*Directions:* Write a well-organized essay that includes an introduction, several paragraphs addressing the task below, and a conclusion.

**Theme: Belief Systems**

> The world has many different belief systems. Each is distinctive, but all greatly influenced the lives of their followers and the society in which the belief system was practiced.

**Task:**

> Choose *two* major belief systems and for *each*
> - Explain key beliefs *and/or* practices
> - Discuss an influence the belief system had on the lives of its followers or the society in which it was practiced

You may use any example from your study of global history. Some suggestions you might wish to consider include animism, Buddhism, Christianity, Confucianism, Daoism, Islam, Judaism, legalism, and Shinto.

**You are *not* limited to these suggestions.**

**Do *not* use the United States as the focus of your answer.**

**Guidelines:**

**In your essay, be sure to**
- Develop all aspects of the task
- Support the theme with relevant facts, examples, and details
- Use a logical and clear plan of organization, including an introduction and a conclusion that are beyond a restatement of the theme

NAME _____   SCHOOL _____

In developing your answers to Part III, be sure to keep these general definitions in mind:

    (a) <u>describe</u> means "to illustrate something in words or tell about it"

    (b) <u>discuss</u> means "to make observations about something using facts, reasoning, and argument; to present in some detail"

## Part III

## DOCUMENT-BASED QUESTION

    This question is based on the accompanying documents. The question is designed to test your ability to work with historical documents. Some of these documents have been edited for the purposes of this question. As you analyze the documents, take into account the source of each document and any point of view that may be presented in the document.

**Historical Context:**

> *Genocide, threats to the environment,* and *weapons of mass destruction* are problems that the world has had to face. Various attempts have been made by the international community and its members to address and resolve these problems.

**Task:** Using the information from the documents and your knowledge of global history, answer the questions that follow each document in Part A. Your answers to the questions will help you write the Part B essay in which you will be asked to

> Select *two* problems mentioned in the historical context and for *each*
> - Describe the problem
> - Discuss attempts made to address *and/or* resolve the problem

## Part A
## Short-Answer Questions

*Directions:* Analyze the documents and answer the short-answer questions that follow each document in the space provided.

**Document 1**

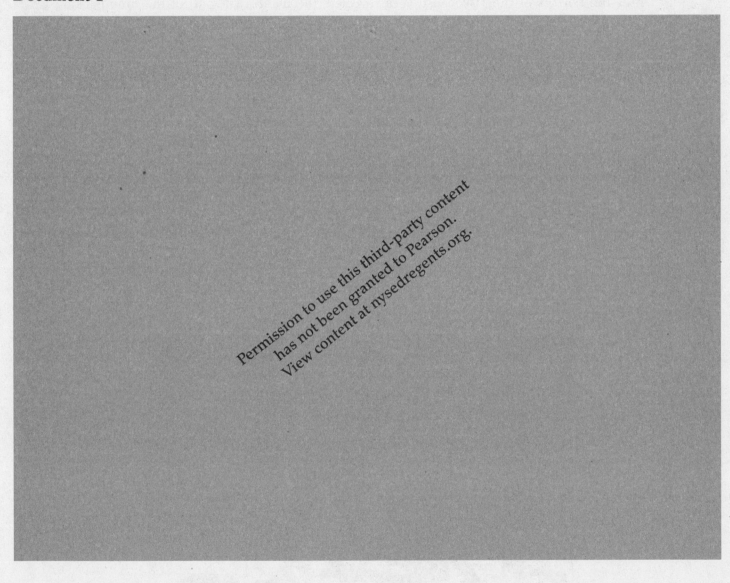

Permission to use this third-party content has not been granted to Pearson. View content at nysedregents.org.

_____

_____

Score ☐

## Document 2a

> ... In 1948, the fledgling UN General Assembly adopted an international Convention on the Prevention and Punishment of the Crime of Genocide, which came into force in 1951. That convention defines genocide as "acts committed with intent to destroy, in whole or in part, a national ethnic, racial or religious group," including inflicting conditions calculated to lead to a group's destruction. . . .
>
> After the horrors of the Holocaust were revealed, the mantra [slogan] of the time became "never again." But it would take four decades, with the creation of the International Criminal Tribunal for the former Yugoslavia in 1994, before the international community would finally come together to prosecute the crime of genocide again.
>
> Why did it take so long, despite atrocities and mass killings in Cambodia, East Timor, and elsewhere? . . .

Source: Irina Lagunina, "World: What Constitutes Genocide Under International Law, and How Are Prosecutions Evolving?," Radio Free Europe/Radio Liberty, 9/10/2004

2a According to Irina Lagunina, what was **one** criticism of the international community's response to genocide? [1]

_____

_____

Score ☐

## Document 2b

Source: Steve Greenberg, *Seattle Post-Intelligencer,* March 29, 1999 (adapted)

2b Based on this 1999 cartoon, identify **two** specific groups that have been victims of genocide. [1]

(1) _____

(2) _____

Score ☐

**Document 3**

... Undeniably, there have been terrible human rights failures—in Cambodia, Bosnia, Rwanda. There, and elsewhere, national constitutions and international norms failed to deter; international institutions and powerful governments failed to respond promptly and adequately. (The expectation that they would fail to respond no doubt contributed to their failure to deter.) But international human rights may be credited with whatever responses there have been, however inadequate, however delayed; and international human rights inspired all subsequent and continuing efforts to address the terrible violations. The major powers have sometimes declared gross violations of human rights to be "threats to international peace and security" and made them the responsibility of the UN Security Council, leading to international sanctions (and even to military intervention, as in Kosovo in 1999). International tribunals are sitting to bring gross violators to trial; a permanent international criminal tribunal to adjudicate [judge] crimes of genocide, war crimes, and crimes against humanity is being created. Various governments have moved to support international human rights and made their bilateral and multilateral influence an established force in international relations. . . .

Source: Louis Henkin, "Human Rights: Ideology and Aspiration, Reality and Prospect," *Realizing Human Rights,* St. Martin's Press, 2000

3 Based on this document, state *one* attempt made to address the problem of genocide. [1]

_____

_____

Score [ ]

## Document 4

> At the dawn of the twenty-first century, the Earth's physical and biological systems are under unprecedented strain. The human population reached 6.3 billion in 2003 and is projected to increase to about 9 billion in the next half century. The United Nations estimates that one-third of the world's people live in countries with moderate to high shortages of fresh water and that this percentage could double by 2025. Many of the world's largest cities are increasingly choked by pollution. As carbon dioxide and other greenhouse gases build in the atmosphere, the average surface temperature of the Earth has reached the highest level ever measured on an annual basis. The biological diversity of the planet is also under heavy stress. Scientists believe that a mass extinction of plants and animals is under way and predict that a quarter of all species could be pushed to extinction by 2050 as a consequence of global warming alone. Without question, the human impact on the biosphere will be one of the most critical issues of the century. . . .

Source: Norman J. Vig, "Introduction: Governing the International Environment,"
*The Global Environment: Institutions, Law, and Policy,* CQ Press, 2005 (adapted)

4 According to Norman J. Vig, what are *two* environmental problems that pose a threat to the world? [2]

(1) _____

_____

Score ☐

(2) _____

_____

Score ☐

## Document 5

Desertification is a major environmental problem. Nearly one-quarter of the Earth's land is threatened by this problem. China is one of those areas.

Source: China National Committee for the Implementation of the U.N. Convention to Combat Desertification (adapted)

Whipped by the wind, sand from Sky Desert swept through this village [Longbaoshan] last month like sheets of stinging rain, clattering against dried corn husks and piling up in small dunes against buildings.

Longbaoshan, a farming community about 40 miles northwest of Beijing, stands on the front line of China's losing war against the country's advancing deserts. Driven by overgrazing, overpopulation, drought and poor land management, they are slowly consuming vast areas of the country in a looming ecological disaster.

Official figures tell a frightening story.

Between 1994 and 1999, desertified land grew by 20,280 square miles. Desert blankets more than a quarter of China's territory. Shifting sands threaten herders and farmers in a nation with one-fifth of the world's population and one-fifteenth of its arable land. Scientists warn of calamity if the government fails to stop the sands.

"Pastures, farmland, railroads and other means of transportation will be buried under sand," said Dong Guangrong, a research fellow in environmental engineering at the Chinese Academy of Sciences. "People will be forced to move.". . .

In March, the worst sandstorm in a decade blinded the capital, painting the sky yellow and engulfing 40-story buildings as visibility dropped to less than a football field. Beijingers gritted their teeth as a seasonal storm known as the Yellow Dragon dumped 30,000 tons of sand on the city. People on the street covered their mouths with surgical masks or their faces with scarves in a futile attempt to keep the sand out. . . .

Officials here are trying to stop the sands by building green buffers. A project intended to protect Beijing in advance of the 2008 summer Olympic Games involves reclaiming desertified land in 75 counties. . . .

Source: Frank Langfitt, "Desertification," *The Post-Standard*, May 13, 2002 (adapted)

5a Based on this document, state *one* problem desertification poses in China.  [1]

_____

_____

Score ☐

b Based on this document, state *one* attempt the Chinese officials have made to address the problem of desertification.  [1]

_____

_____

Score ☐

**Document 6**

### Selected Efforts to Preserve the Environment

| 1972 | Stockholm—United Nations Conference on Human Environment—beginning of organized international effort to safeguard the environment |
|---|---|
| 1973 | The Convention on International Trade in Endangered Species of Wild Fauna and Flora (CITES)—restricts trade in 5,000 animal and 25,000 plant species |
| 1987 | Montreal Protocol—binding agreement on protection of the ozone layer |
| 1992 | Rio de Janeiro "Earth Summit"—produced treaties on climate change and biodiversity |
| 1994 | The World Conservation Union (IUCN)—published a revised Red List of endangered and threatened species, creating a world standard for gauging threats to biodiversity |
| 1997 | Kyoto Protocol—negotiated an agreement on obligations to reduce greenhouse gases in the atmosphere |
| 2004 | European Union—issued its first-ever pollution register containing data on industrial emissions and representing a "landmark event" in public provision of environmental information |
| 2006 | United Nations General Assembly—declared the International Year of Deserts which led to the United Nations Convention to Combat Desertification |

Source: "Environmental Milestones," World Watch Institute (adapted)

6 Based on this document, identify *two* ways the international community has attempted to address environmental problems.  [2]

(1) _____

_____

Score ☐

(2) _____

_____

Score ☐

**Document 7**

## The Twentieth Century's Deadly Yield

### Weapons of mass destruction generally refer to biological, chemical, and nuclear weapons.

**1991**
UN orders Iraq to destroy all weapons and related technology, then begins inspections.

U.S.S.R. dissolves; U.S. starts nonproliferation aid program in former U.S.S.R.

**1950s–1960s**
U.S. identifies dozens of viral and bacterial agents that can be weaponized. Testing done on animals and humans.

**1925**
Geneva Protocol bans the use of chemical and biological weapons in war.

**1945**
U.S. drops first atomic bombs on Hiroshima and Nagasaki.

**1972**
U.S., U.S.S.R., and more than 100 other nations sign Biological Weapons Convention. U.S. continues defensive research; Soviets violate pact.

**1998**
India tests nuclear weapons. Pakistan tests its first nuclear weapon.

| 1910 | 1930 | 1950 | 1970 | 1990 |

**1899**
Two dozen countries sign Hague Convention, pledging not to use toxic gases or other poisons as weapons.

**1949**
U.S.S.R. tests its first nuclear weapon.

**1962**
Cuban missile crisis brings world to brink of nuclear war.

**1974**
India tests its first nuclear weapon.

**1993**
Chemical Weapons Convention opens for signature.

**1983–88**
Chemical weapons used extensively in Iran-Iraq war; thousands die.

Source: "Weapons of Mass Destruction," *National Geographic*, November 2002 (adapted)

7a Using the information on this time line, identify **one** way a weapon of mass destruction was used. [1]

_____

_____

Score ▢

b Using the information on this time line, identify **one** attempt made to address a problem related to weapons of mass destruction. [1]

_____

_____

Score ▢

## Document 8

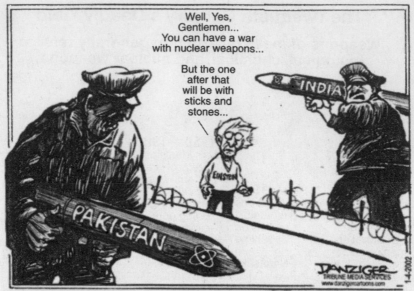

Source: Jeff Danziger, Tribune Media Services, January 4, 2002 (adapted)

8 Based on this cartoon, state **one** reason nuclear weapons pose a threat to the world community. [1]

_____

_____

Score ☐

## Document 9

Civilian uranium is found at nonmilitary sites. It is used to conduct scientific and industrial research or to produce radioisotopes for medical purposes. This uranium can also be used to make highly enriched uranium (HEU), which is used in nuclear weapons.

### Overview/Securing Civilian Uranium 235

- Terrorists who acquired less than 100 kilograms of highly enriched uranium (HEU) could build and detonate a rudimentary but effective atomic bomb relatively easily. HEU is also attractive for states that seek to develop nuclear weapons secretly, without having to test them.
- Unfortunately, large quantities of HEU are stored in nuclear research facilities worldwide—especially in Russia, often under minimal security.
- The U.S. and its allies have established programs to bolster security measures, convert reactors to use low-enriched uranium (which is useless for weapons) and retrieve HEU from research-reactor sites around the world. Dangerous gaps remain, however.
- High-level governmental attention plus a comparatively small additional monetary investment could go a long way toward solving the problem for good.

Source: Glaser and von Hippel, "Thwarting Nuclear Terrorism," *Scientific American,* February 2006

9 Based on this article by Glaser and von Hippel, state an attempt being made by the United States and its allies to improve the security of highly enriched uranium (HEU). [1]

_____

_____

Score ____

# Part B
# Essay

*Directions*: Write a well-organized essay that includes an introduction, several paragraphs, and a conclusion. Use evidence from *at least four* documents in your essay. Support your response with relevant facts, examples, and details. Include additional outside information.

## Historical Context:

*Genocide, threats to the environment,* and *weapons of mass destruction* are problems that the world has had to face. Various attempts have been made by the international community and its members to address and resolve these problems.

**Task:** Using the information from the documents and your knowledge of global history, write an essay in which you

Select *two* problems mentioned in the historical context and for *each*
- Describe the problem
- Discuss attempts made to address *and/or* resolve the problem

## Guidelines:

**In your essay, be sure to**
- Develop all aspects of the task
- Incorporate information from *at least four* documents
- Incorporate relevant outside information
- Support the theme with relevant facts, examples, and details
- Use a logical and clear plan of organization, including an introduction and a conclusion that are beyond a restatement of the theme

This section contains an actual Regents Examination in Global History and Geography that was given in New York State in January 2008.

Circle your answers to Part 1. Write your responses to the short-answer questions in the spaces provided. Write your thematic essay and document-based essay on separate sheets of paper. Be sure to refer to the test-taking strategies in the front of this book as you prepare to answer the test questions.

## Part I

### Answer all questions in this part.

*Directions* (1–50): For each statement or question, write on the separate answer sheet the *number* of the word or expression that, of those given, best completes the statement or answers the question.

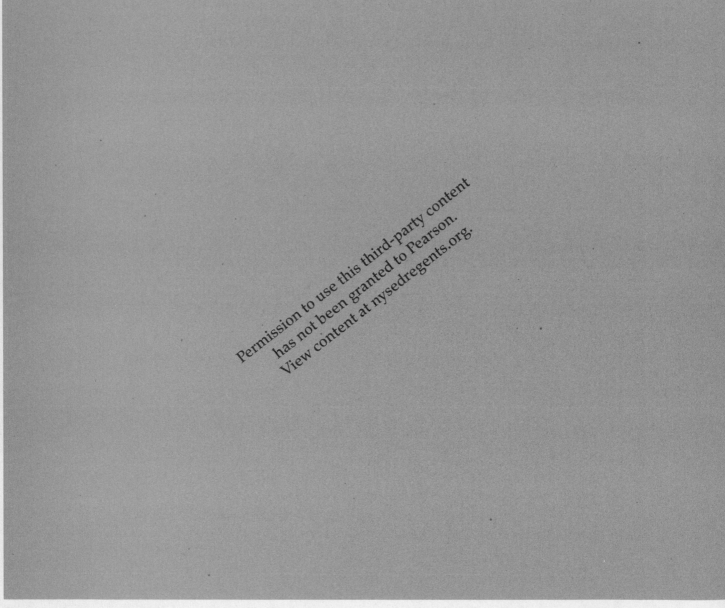

2 Slash-and-burn techniques are typically practiced by

(1) people who live along rivers that deposit rich soil during floods

(2) subsistence farmers who plant an area until the soil loses its fertility

(3) farmers who rely on chemical fertilization and pesticides

(4) nomads who use pastures for their livestock

3 Which feature would most likely be included in an economic system based on traditional agriculture and self-sufficiency?

(1) banks    (3) gold standard

(2) barter    (4) tariffs

4 Which geographic factor had a major influence on the development of both Egyptian and Babylonian civilizations?

(1) river valleys
(2) cool temperatures
(3) locations near a strait
(4) mountains

5 Which description accurately identifies Socrates, Plato, and Aristotle?

(1) rulers of the Roman Republic
(2) artists of the Italian Renaissance
(3) religious leaders of the Protestant Reformation
(4) philosophers of ancient Greece

Base your answer to question 6 on the passage below and on your knowledge of social studies.

. . . The actual journey to Mecca [Makkah] began on the fifth of *Dhu al-Hijjah*, 1393 (the 29th of December, 1973, according to the Gregorian calendar), at Beirut International Airport, but it was not until the afternoon of the seventh that I donned [put on] the *Ihram* [robe] and drove along on the road from Jiddah to Mecca. The road was crowded with cars, buses and trucks all packed with pilgrims chanting the Hajj refrain, the *Talbiyah*: . . .

— Michael E. Jansen, *An American Girl on the Hajj*

6 This passage describes the experience of a follower of

(1) Christianity　　(3) Hinduism
(2) Islam　　　　　(4) Judaism

7 In China, the development of civil service examinations and a belief in filial piety reflect the influence of

(1) Shinto　　　　(3) Confucianism
(2) Jainism　　　 (4) Buddhism

8 One way in which the Code of Hammurabi, the Twelve Tables, and the Justinian Code are similar is that each

(1) legalized monotheistic beliefs
(2) established legal standards
(3) provided records of economic activity
(4) supported republican governments

9 Which heading best fits the partial outline below?

I. _____

　A. People become more aware of the outside world.
　B. Merchant and craft guilds help commercial centers grow into cities.
　C. Trade routes develop to supply the growing demand for new products.
　D. Monarchs centralize control and increase their power.

(1) Seljuk Turks Dominate Europe
(2) Democracy Ends in Eastern Europe
(3) Feudalism Declines in Western Europe
(4) Religion Becomes Powerful Force in Europe

10 One way in which the African kingdoms of Ghana and Mali are similar is that they

(1) established their wealth through trade
(2) improved their military strength with the use of gunpowder
(3) opened trade routes to the Americas
(4) adopted Christianity as their major religion

11 One way in which the travels of Marco Polo and Ibn Battuta are similar is that they resulted in

(1) an increased interest in different cultures
(2) the development of slavery
(3) a reduction in trade
(4) the discovery of East Asia

12 • Classical Greco-Roman ideas were revived.
　• Wealthy patrons supported the arts and education.
　• Humanism spread throughout western Europe.

Which period in European history is most closely associated with these statements?

(1) Early Middle Ages　　(3) Renaissance
(2) Industrial Revolution　(4) Hellenistic Period

Base your answer to question 13 on the map below and on your knowledge of social studies.

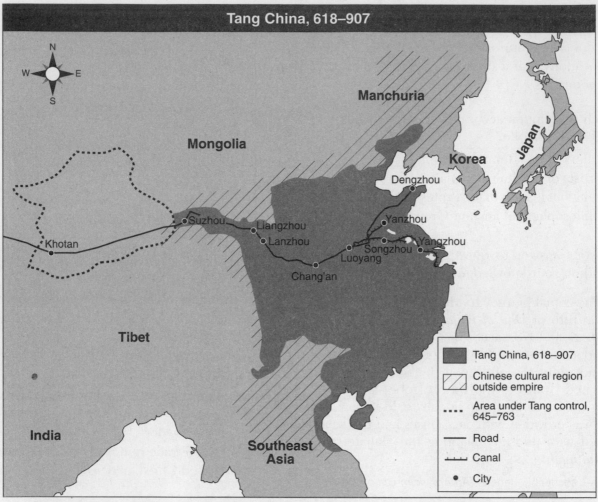

Source: Patrick K. O'Brien, general editor, *Oxford Atlas of World History*, Oxford University Press (adapted)

13 Which statement about the Tang dynasty is best supported by the information on this map?

(1) It experienced conflict in coastal areas.

(2) Its boundaries extended to India.

(3) It gained territory in Tibet and Korea.

(4) It exchanged goods using overland routes.

14 One similarity between Martin Luther and Henry VIII is that they

(1) argued against the establishment of a theocratic state

(2) protested against the ideas of the Enlightenment

(3) died during the Reign of Terror

(4) challenged the teachings of the Catholic Church

15 • Literacy rates rise.
   • Shakespeare's sonnets circulated.
   • Secular ideas spread.

Which innovation led directly to these developments?

(1) printing press    (3) paper currency

(2) astrolabe         (4) caravel

Base your answer to question 16 on the drawing below and on your knowledge of social studies.

**A Typical Medieval Manor**

Source: James Killoran et al., *The Key to Understanding Global Studies*, 5th edition, Jarrett Publishing Company (adapted)

16 What inference can be drawn from the location of the church in this drawing?

(1) The mill was managed by the church.
(2) Religion played a significant role in the lives of the residents.
(3) The church controlled trade within the manor.
(4) The church played a limited role in education.

17 Which geographic feature had the greatest influence on the development of the Inca Empire?

(1) deserts          (3) river valleys
(2) irregular coastline     (4) mountains

18 What was one reason the Spanish conquistadors were able to conquer the Aztec Empire?

(1) The Spanish soldiers made effective use of their military technology against the Aztecs.
(2) Aztec religious beliefs promoted nonviolence.
(3) Spain joined the Incas in their fight against the Aztecs.
(4) The Spanish cavalry outnumbered the Aztec warriors.

19 Which statement describes an impact of the Columbian exchange on the lives of Europeans?

(1) The combination of new products and ideas promoted economic growth.
(2) Native Americans immigrated to Europe and competed with Europeans for jobs.
(3) Millions of Europeans were killed by new American diseases.
(4) Introduction of the Native American religions resulted in the decline of the Roman Catholic Church.

20 A common goal of Philip II of Spain and Louis XIV of France was to

(1) spread Calvinism
(2) promote political revolutions
(3) maintain absolute power
(4) isolate their nations

Base your answer to question 21 on the speakers' statements below and on your knowledge of social studies.

*Speaker A:* My king has brought together the best mapmakers and scientists to study navigation. The expeditions he has sponsored will increase Portugal's trade with the East and make us wealthy.

*Speaker B:* My people lost their land and were forced to work in the mines and fields. They received little economic benefit.

*Speaker C:* My queen has chartered joint-stock companies to control trade with our colonies.

*Speaker D:* My people were enslaved and have endured unspeakable hardships. Many died during the Middle Passage.

21 Which two speakers would most likely support mercantilism?

(1) A and B        (3) B and D
(2) A and C        (4) C and D

22 • Parliament offered the throne to King William and Queen Mary.
   • Catholic King James II fled England for France.
   • Parliament agreed to joint rule with the monarch.

These events are most closely associated with the

(1) Crusades
(2) French Revolution
(3) Glorious Revolution
(4) Reconquista

23 At the Congress of Vienna (1815), the governments of Europe reacted to the French Revolution and the rule of Napoleon by attempting to

(1) restore old regimes to power
(2) spread the idea of democracy
(3) encourage nationalist movements
(4) promote the European free-trade zone

24 One political objective of both Otto von Bismarck and Giuseppe Garibaldi was to

(1) overthrow divine right monarchies
(2) unify their nations
(3) establish communist systems
(4) form an alliance with Great Britain

25 Karl Marx predicted that laissez-faire capitalism would result in

(1) a return to manorialism
(2) a revolution led by the proletariat
(3) fewer government regulations
(4) an equal distribution of wealth and income

26 The Portuguese control of Macao and the British control of Hong Kong in China are examples of

(1) collectivization        (3) self-determination
(2) imperialism             (4) containment

27 Commodore Matthew Perry's visits to Japan in 1853 and 1854 resulted in the

(1) colonization of Japan by the United States
(2) transfer of spheres of influence to China
(3) introduction of Christianity to Japanese society
(4) opening of trade and diplomatic relations with Japan

28 The term *militarism* can best be defined as

(1) loyalty to a nation or ethnic group
(2) buildup of armaments in preparation for war
(3) avoidance of military involvement in civil wars
(4) control of territories for economic and political gain

29 A primary reason for Japan's involvement in the Sino-Japanese War and the Russo-Japanese War was to

(1) acquire natural resources in Manchuria and Korea

(2) control trade and markets in Southeast Asia

(3) end Japan's policy of isolationism

(4) remove foreign invaders from Japanese soil

Base your answer to question 30 on the passage below and on your knowledge of social studies.

. . . His Majesty's Government view with favour the establishment in Palestine of a national home for the Jewish people, and will use their best endeavours to facilitate the achievement of this object, it being clearly understood that nothing shall be done which may prejudice the civil and religious rights of existing non-Jewish communities in Palestine, or the rights and political status enjoyed by Jews in any other country. . . .

30 This 1917 passage is taken from a document known as the

(1) Truman Doctrine

(2) Marshall Plan

(3) Fourteen Points

(4) Balfour Declaration

31 Which slogan is associated with the Bolshevik (Russian) Revolution?

(1) "An Eye for an Eye"

(2) "Peace, Land, and Bread"

(3) "Liberty, Equality, Fraternity"

(4) "Take up the White Man's Burden"

32 Which action is most closely associated with Atatürk (Mustafa Kemal)?

(1) beginning the Zionist movement

(2) starting the Palestine Liberation Organization

(3) using Western practices to modernize Turkey

(4) enforcing Islamic law

33 Which aspect of the economy was emphasized in Joseph Stalin's five-year plans?

(1) heavy industry

(2) consumer goods

(3) famine relief

(4) private landownership

34 Mohandas Gandhi is most closely associated with the

(1) support of violence and terrorism to end British rule

(2) desire to strengthen the caste system

(3) use of civil disobedience to gain political freedom

(4) establishment of a national religion in India

35 ". . . Seventy thousand people were killed instantly, and many more would die — 60,000 by November and another 70,000 by 1950. Most of them would be victims of a new method of killing — radiation. . . ."

— Ronald Takai

The situation described in this passage was the direct result of which World War II event?

(1) blitz of London

(2) attack on Pearl Harbor

(3) D-Day invasion of Normandy

(4) bombing of Hiroshima

36 Between 1945 and 1947, the differences between the Hindus and the Muslims in India led to the

(1) Sepoy Mutiny

(2) Salt March

(3) policy of nonalignment

(4) partitioning of the subcontinent

37 What was a major reason for the formation of the North Atlantic Treaty Organization (NATO) in 1949?

(1) to control European trade

(2) to resist Soviet aggression

(3) to support the blockade of Berlin

(4) to strengthen communist governments

38 In Egypt, Gamal Abdel Nasser's seizure of the Suez Canal continued his policy of

(1) attracting investments from Western banks
(2) supporting the rights of British workers
(3) eliminating criticism of political opponents
(4) establishing national control of vital resources

Base your answer to question 39 on the cartoon below and on your knowledge of social studies.

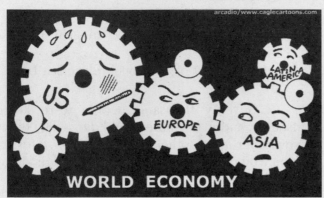

Source: Arcadio Esquivel, Costa Rica, *La Nacion*; Panama, *La Prensa*

39 Which concept is illustrated in this cartoon?

(1) nonalignment        (3) nationalism
(2) interdependence      (4) socialism

40 The histories of Latvia, Estonia, Lithuania, and Finland have been greatly affected by their

(1) proximity to Russia
(2) abundant oil reserves
(3) aggressive foreign policies
(4) alliances with Israel

41 In 1989, the government of China responded to the challenge of protests in Tiananmen Square by

(1) halting trade with the West
(2) allowing democratic elections
(3) sending in tanks and troops to end the demonstrations
(4) calling for a special session of the United Nations Security Council

42 Which heading best completes the partial outline below?

I. _____

  A. Korea remains divided at the 38th parallel.
  B. East and West Berlin are split by a wall.
  C. Strategic arms limitation talks begin.

(1) Emerging Nations of the World
(2) Results of the Cold War
(3) Economic Benefits of World War II
(4) Ethnic Conflicts in the World

43 Which action occurred in the Soviet Union under Mikhail Gorbachev?

(1) Peasants were forced onto collective farms.
(2) Citizens experienced more personal freedoms under glasnost.
(3) The United States and the Soviet Union ended diplomatic relations.
(4) The Soviet government increased its control over the Orthodox Church.

44 Which statement is a fact rather than an opinion?

(1) The growing economy of Brazil threatens the economic power of the United States.
(2) Free trade will lower the standard of living for workers in developed nations.
(3) The European Union (EU) has issued a common currency called the euro.
(4) Developing nations will never be able to compete with developed nations.

Base your answer to question 45 on the cartoon below and on your knowledge of social studies.

Source: Jonathan Shapiro (Zapiro), *Sowetan,* 1994

45 What is the main idea of this cartoon?

(1) Nelson Mandela has completed South Africa's reconstruction.

(2) Although black South Africans have overcome many obstacles to achieve freedom, many struggles lie ahead.

(3) The mountains of South Africa have hindered black South African participation in national elections.

(4) The reconstruction of South Africa can only be achieved through violence, treason, and defiance.

46 A study of the fall of the Roman Empire (476) and of the collapse of the Soviet Union (1991) shows that powerful empires can

(1) lose strength when mercenaries enforce reforms

(2) be threatened only when directly attacked by outsiders

(3) conquer more than one continent and remain stable

(4) be weakened by both internal and external pressures

47 A comparison of the feudal system in Europe and the encomienda system in Latin America shows that both systems

(1) awarded land to the elite

(2) promoted religious tolerance

(3) relied on global trade for goods

(4) used a parliamentary system of government

Base your answer to question 48 on the cartoon below and on your knowledge of social studies.

**Russian Economy**

Source: Brian Gable, *The Globe and Mail*, Toronto, Canada (adapted)

48 The main idea of this 1990s cartoon is that Russia is

(1) deciding between a capitalist or a communist system
(2) attempting to restore military power
(3) expressing concern about how the rest of the world views its government
(4) maintaining a balance between a civilian and a military government

49 • Location — included lands surrounding the eastern Mediterranean Sea

• People — Turks, Arabs, Greeks, Muslims, Christians, and Jews

• Nickname during the 19th and early 20th centuries — "Sick Man of Europe"

Which empire is described by these characteristics?

(1) Gupta          (3) Roman
(2) Mongol         (4) Ottoman

50 Which sequence of Russian events is in the correct chronological order?

A. Catherine the Great westernizes Russia.
B. Ivan III defeats the Mongols.
C. Khrushchev places missiles in Cuba.
D. Czar Nicholas II abdicates the throne.

(1) $A \rightarrow B \rightarrow C \rightarrow D$          (3) $B \rightarrow C \rightarrow A \rightarrow D$
(2) $B \rightarrow A \rightarrow D \rightarrow C$          (4) $D \rightarrow A \rightarrow C \rightarrow B$

**Answers to the essay questions are to be written in the separate essay booklet.**

**In developing your answer to Part II, be sure to keep these general definitions in mind:**

(a) <u>describe</u> means "to illustrate something in words or tell about it"

(b) <u>discuss</u> means "to make observations about something using facts, reasoning, and argument; to present in some detail"

## Part II

## THEMATIC ESSAY QUESTION

*Directions:* Write a well-organized essay that includes an introduction, several paragraphs addressing the task below, and a conclusion.

**Theme: Change**

> Not all revolutions are political. Nonpolitical revolutions have brought important intellectual, economic, and/or social changes to societies.

**Task:**

> Identify *two* nonpolitical revolutions that brought important intellectual, economic, and/or social changes to societies and for *each*
> - Describe *one* change brought about by this nonpolitical revolution
> - Discuss an impact this nonpolitical revolution had on a specific society or societies

You may use any nonpolitical revolution that brought important intellectual, economic, and/or social changes from your study of global history. Some suggestions you might wish to consider include the Neolithic Revolution (10,000–6,000 B.C.), the Commercial Revolution (11th–18th centuries), the Scientific Revolution (16th–18th centuries), the Enlightenment (17th–18th centuries), the Agricultural Revolution (18th–19th centuries), the Industrial Revolution in Europe (18th–19th centuries), and the Green Revolution (late 20th century).

**You are *not* limited to these suggestions. However, do *not* choose a *political* revolution as one of your two revolutions.**

**Guidelines:**

**In your essay, be sure to**
- Develop all aspects of the task
- Support the theme with relevant facts, examples, and details
- Use a logical and clear plan of organization, including an introduction and a conclusion that are beyond a restatement of the theme

NAME _____ SCHOOL _____

In developing your answer to Part III, be sure to keep these general definitions in mind:

(a) <u>describe</u> means "to illustrate something in words or tell about it"

(b) <u>discuss</u> means "to make observations about something using facts, reasoning, and argument; to present in some detail"

### Part III

### DOCUMENT-BASED QUESTION

This question is based on the accompanying documents. The question is designed to test your ability to work with historical documents. Some of these documents have been edited for the purposes of this question. As you analyze the documents, take into account the source of each document and any point of view that may be presented in the document.

**Historical Context:**

> Throughout history, governments have sometimes attempted to control the thoughts and actions of their people. Three such governments include **Russia under the rule of Peter the Great, Germany under the rule of Adolf Hitler,** and **China under the rule of Mao Zedong.** The efforts of these governments greatly affected their societies.

**Task:** Using the information from the documents and your knowledge of global history, answer the questions that follow each document in Part A. Your answers to the questions will help you write the Part B essay in which you will be asked to

---

Choose **two** governments mentioned in the historical context and for **each**

- Describe the efforts of the government to control the thoughts **and/or** actions of its people
- Discuss an impact of this government's efforts on its society

---

## Part A
## Short-Answer Questions

*Directions:* Analyze the documents and answer the short-answer questions that follow each document in the space provided.

**Document 1a**

### Peter the Great

Source: Chris Hinton, *What is Evidence?* John Murray, Ltd.

**Document 1b**

. . . A year later, in January 1700, Peter transformed persuasion into decree [law]. With rolling drums in the streets and squares, it was proclaimed that all boyars [Russian nobles], government officials and men of property, both in Moscow and in the provinces, were to abandon their long robes and provide themselves with Hungarian or German-style caftans. The following year, a new decree commanded men to wear a waistcoat, breeches, gaiters, boots and a hat in the French or German style, and women to put on petticoats, skirts, bonnets and Western shoes. Later decrees prohibited the wearing of high Russian boots and long Russian knives. Models of the new approved costumes were hung at Moscow's gates and in public places in the city for people to observe and copy. All who arrived at the gates in traditional dress except peasants were permitted to enter only after paying a fine. Subsequently, Peter instructed the guards at the city gates to force to their knees all visitors arriving in long, traditional coats and then to cut off the coats at the point where the lowered garment touched the ground. "Many hundreds of coats were cut accordingly," says Perry, "and being done with good humor it occasioned mirth [humor] among the people and soon broke the custom of wearing long coats, especially in places near Moscow and those towns wherever the Tsar came.". . .

Source: Robert K. Massie, *Peter the Great: His Life and World,* Alfred A. Knopf

1 Based on these documents, state *two* ways Peter the Great tried to control the actions of his people. [2]

(1) _____

_____

Score ☐

(2) _____

_____

Score ☐

## Document 2

> . . . Peter's military reform would have remained an isolated incident in Russian military history had it not left a distinct and deep impression on the social and intellectual composition of all Russian society, and even influenced future political developments. The military reform itself made necessary other innovations, first to maintain the reorganised and expensive military forces, and then to ensure their permanency. The new recruiting methods, by spreading military obligations to classes hitherto [up to this time] exempt, and thus affecting all social classes, gave the new army a more varied composition, and completely altered existing social relationships. From the time that noblemens' serfs and servants joined the new army as ordinary recruits instead of only as menials or valets [servants], the position of the nobility, which had been preponderant [dominant] in the old army, was completely changed. . . .

Source: Vasili Klyuchevsky, translated by Liliana Archibald, *Peter the Great,* St. Martin's Press

2a According to Vasili Klyuchevsky, what was **one** way Peter the Great attempted to control the Russian people? [1]

_____

_____

Score ☐

b According to Vasili Klyuchevsky, what was **one** effect Peter the Great's reform had on the Russian nobles? [1]

_____

_____

Score ☐

**Document 3**

---

**Emergence of "Dual Russia"**

The Petrine [Peter's] Reform is often seen as the main cause and the starting point of the irrevocable [unalterable] split of Russian society into two parts. Peter's reforms transformed the upper levels of Russian society while the masses remained largely unaffected by them. Peter had forced the nobility to acquire technical knowledge of Western Europe and to adopt European styles of dress and manners. An increasingly Europeanized education of the upper classes brought with it a familiarity with the philosophies and theories of the Enlightenment. Soon many Russian nobles even preferred to speak the languages of Western Europe (particularly French and German) to Russian. By the nineteenth century their world was European in dress, manners, food, education, attitudes, and language, and was completely alien to the way of life of the Russian popular masses. . . .

---

Source: Alexander Chubarov, *The Fragile Empire: A History of Imperial Russia*, Continuum

3 According to Alexander Chubarov, what was **one** long-term effect Peter the Great's reform had on the upper classes of Russian society?  [1]

_____

_____    Score ☐

**Document 4a**

> . . . On the night of May 10, 1933, thousands of Nazi students, along with many professors, stormed universities, libraries, and bookstores in thirty cities throughout Germany. They removed hundreds of thousands of books and cast them onto bonfires. In Berlin alone, more than twenty thousand books were burned. The book burnings were part of a calculated effort to "purify" German culture. Since April 12, the Nazi German Student Association had been purging libraries, working from lists of books deemed "un-German." The authors of some of the books were Jews, but most were not. . . .

Source: Michael Berenbaum, *The World Must Know: The History of the Holocaust as Told in the United States Holocaust Memorial Museum*, Little, Brown and Co.

4a According to Michael Berenbaum, what was **one** way the Nazi Party attempted to control the thoughts of the German people? [1]

_____

_____

Score ☐

**Document 4b**

> . . . The Hitler Youth movement was formed for the express purpose of creating loyal subjects to the state. By 1935, over three million boys and girls aged 10 and older were enrolled. "We were born to die for Germany" was one of their popular slogans. In addition to a strenuous physical fitness program, they received training in the use of weapons and heard lectures on Nazi ideology.

Source: Chartock and Spencer eds., *Can It Happen Again?*, Black Dog & Leventhal

4b According to the editors of *Can It Happen Again?*, what was **one** method used by the Nazi Party to influence the thinking of the young people of Germany? [1]

_____

_____

Score ☐

## Document 5

In this excerpt Horst Krüger, a German author and prisoner of war, describes his reaction to reading a newspaper account of Hitler's death. He is reflecting on the state of the press while Hitler was in power.

> . . . When I first began to read the newspapers, he was already in power. I knew nothing but a subservient [obedient], bellicose [hostile], boastful press. I always felt it was a proven fact that Hitler had also conquered and occupied the German language, and my parents had always told me, "What you read in the papers isn't true, but you musn't say so. Outside, you must always act as if you believe everything." The German language and lies had become one and the same thing to me. Home was the only place where you could speak the truth. What you read in the papers was always a lie, but you weren't allowed to say so. And now I was holding a newspaper that was in German and that did not lie. How was it possible? How could language and truth coincide? How did it happen that you could believe something you saw in print? It was the first free German paper of my life. . . .

Source: Horst Krüger, *A Crack in The Wall: Growing Up Under Hitler,* Ruth Hein, tr., Fromm International Publishing Corporation

5 According to Horst Krüger, what was **one** impact of the Nazi government on German society? [1]

_____

_____

Score ☐

## Document 6

This is an excerpt from the opening statement of Chief Prosecutor Robert H. Jackson at the trial of the major war criminals before the International Military Tribunal given on November 21, 1945.

> . . . Germany became one vast torture chamber. Cries of its victims were heard round the world and brought shudders to civilized people everywhere. I am one who received during this war most atrocity tales with suspicion and scepticism [doubt]. But the proof here will be so overwhelming that I venture to predict not one word I have spoken will be denied. These defendants will only deny personal responsibility or knowledge.
>
> Under the clutch of the most intricate web of espionage and intrigue that any modern state has endured, and persecution and torture of a kind that has not been visited upon the world in many centuries, the elements of the German population which were both decent and courageous were annihilated [reduced to nothing]. Those which were decent but weak were intimidated. Open resistance, which had never been more than feeble and irresolute, disappeared. But resistance, I am happy to say, always remained, although it was manifest in only such events as the abortive effort to assassinate Hitler on July 20, 1944. With resistance driven underground, the Nazi had the German State in his own hands.
>
> But the Nazis not only silenced discordant voices. They created positive controls as effective as their negative ones. Propaganda organs, on a scale never before known, stimulated the Party and Party formations with a permanent enthusiasm and abandon such as we, democratic people, can work up only for a few days before a general election. They inculcated [impressed upon] and practiced the Führerprinzip [leadership principle] which centralized control of the Party and of the Party-controlled State over the lives and thought of the German people, who are accustomed to look upon the German State, by whomever controlled, with a mysticism [a power to believe] that is incomprehensible to my people [the United States public]. . . .

Source: *Trial of the Major War Criminals Before the International Military Tribunal,*
Nuremberg, 14 November 1945–1 October 1946

6 According to Chief Prosecutor Jackson, what was **one** effect the Nazi government's actions had on the people of Germany? [1]

_____

_____

Score ☐

**Document 7**

This is an account of Nien Cheng's experiences during the Cultural Revolution. This excerpt describes what was happening the day she was sent to the Detention House.

> . . . The streets of Shanghai, normally deserted at nine o'clock in the evening, were a sea of humanity. Under the clear autumn sky in the cool breeze of September, people were out in thousands to watch the intensified activities of the Red Guards. On temporary platforms erected everywhere, the young Revolutionaries were calling upon the people in shrill and fiery rhetoric to join in the Revolution, and conducting small-scale struggle meetings against men and women they seized at random on the street and accused of failing to carry Mao's Little Red Book of quotations or simply wearing the sort of clothes the Red Guards disapproved of. Outside private houses and apartment buildings, smoke rose over the garden walls, permeating the air as the Red Guards continued to burn books indiscriminately. . . .

Source: Nien Cheng, *Life and Death in Shanghai*, Penguin Books

7 According to Nien Cheng, what were **two** actions taken by the Red Guards in an attempt to control the thoughts of the people during Mao's rule in China? [2]

(1) _____

_____

Score ☐

(2) _____

_____

Score ☐

**Document 8**

**In Following the Revolutionary Road, Strive for an Even Greater Victory**

Mao as the Reddest Red Sun in people's hearts, floating above Tiananmen Square. At the front of the huge, Little Red Book-waving crowd are the figures of a worker, peasant, and soldier, while representatives from other occupations stand just behind. The Book was compiled from Mao's Selected Works by Lin Biao in the early 1960s to be used for propaganda work in the People's Liberation Army. After the Cultural Revolution began, it became an integral part of the ritual of Mao worship. By 1970, this kind of orchestrated adulation [staged praise] and the power of Lin Biao were both at their zenith [height].

Source: *Picturing Power: Posters from the Chinese Cultural Revolution Exhibit,* Indiana University

8 According to this document, what was ***one*** way that Mao's government attempted to influence the people of China? [1]

_____

_____

Score ☐

**Document 9**

. . . Between 1966 and 1976, a whole generation of teenagers failed to receive a real education; other Chinese came to call them "the lost generation." At least twenty thousand people lost their lives because of the Cultural Revolution.

. . . Because of the Cultural Revolution, many Chinese young people grew up with no knowledge of traditional Chinese customs and beliefs. Needing to fill that gap, some of them began looking to the West — especially to the Western ideals of democracy, freedom, capitalism, and individualism. . . .

Source: *Great Events: The Twentieth Century 1960–1968,* Salem Press

9 Based on this excerpt from *Great Events*, state **one** impact the Cultural Revolution had on Chinese society. [1]

_____

_____

Score ☐

# Part B
# Essay

*Directions:* Write a well-organized essay that includes an introduction, several paragraphs, and a conclusion. Use evidence from *at least **four*** documents in your essay. Support your response with relevant facts, examples, and details. Include additional outside information.

### Historical Context:

Throughout history, governments have sometimes attempted to control the thoughts and actions of their people. Three such governments include **Russia under the rule of Peter the Great, Germany under the rule of Adolf Hitler,** and **China under the rule of Mao Zedong.** The efforts of these governments greatly affected their societies.

**Task:** Using the information from the documents and your knowledge of global history, write an essay in which you

> Choose *two* governments mentioned in the historical context and for *each*
>
> - Describe the efforts of the government to control the thoughts *and/or* actions of its people
> - Discuss an impact of this government's efforts on its society

### Guidelines:

**In your essay, be sure to**

- Develop all aspects of the task
- Incorporate information from *at least **four*** documents
- Incorporate relevant outside information
- Support the theme with relevant facts, examples, and details
- Use a logical and clear plan of organization, including an introduction and a conclusion that are beyond a restatement of the theme

# Regents Examination – August 2007

This section contains an actual Regents Examination in Global History and Geography that was given in New York State in August 2007.

Circle your answers to Part 1. Write your responses to the short-answer questions in the spaces provided. Write your thematic essay and document-based essay on separate sheets of paper. Be sure to refer to the test-taking strategies in the front of this book as you prepare to answer the test questions.

## Part I

### Answer all questions in this part.

*Directions* (1–50): For each statement or question, write on the separate answer sheet the *number* of the word or expression that, of those given, best completes the statement or answers the question.

1 Which source of information is considered a primary source?

(1) travel diary of Ibn Battuta
(2) modern novel about the Golden Age of Islam
(3) textbook on the history of North Africa
(4) dictionary of English words adapted from Arabic

2 Which continent's economic and political development has been influenced by the Andes Mountains and the Amazon River?

(1) Asia (3) Europe
(2) Africa (4) South America

3 • Planting wheat and barley
• Domesticating animals
• Establishing permanent homes and villages

At the beginning of the Neolithic Revolution, the most direct impact of these developments was on

(1) religion and government
(2) transportation and trade
(3) diet and shelter
(4) climate and topography

4 • Kushites adapted Egyptian art and architecture.
• Greeks adopted Phoenician characters for an alphabet.
• Arabs used the Indian mathematical concept of zero.

These actions are examples of

(1) filial piety (3) scientific research
(2) cultural diffusion (4) ethnocentrism

5 Which belief system is most closely associated with the terms *Eightfold Path*, *Four Noble Truths*, and *nirvana*?

(1) Buddhism (3) Judaism
(2) Christianity (4) Shinto

6 ..."If a man has knocked out the teeth of a man of the same rank, his own teeth shall be knocked out. If he has knocked out the teeth of a plebeian (commoner), he shall pay one-third of a mina of silver."...

— Code of Hammurabi

Which statement is supported by this excerpt from Hammurabi's code of laws?

(1) All men are equal under the law.
(2) Fines are preferable to physical punishment.
(3) Law sometimes distinguishes between social classes.
(4) Violence must always be punished with violence.

7 Confucianism had a strong impact on the development of China mainly because this philosophy

(1) established a basic structure for military rule
(2) provided a basis for social order
(3) contained the framework for a communist government
(4) stressed the importance of the individual

8 The terms *masters*, *apprentices*, and *journeymen* are most closely associated with the

(1) encomienda system of Latin America
(2) guild system of Europe in the Middle Ages
(3) civil service system of China during the Tang dynasty
(4) caste system of India

Base your answers to questions 9 and 10 on the map below and on your knowledge of social studies.

Source: Mazour and Peoples, *World History: People and Nations*, Harcourt Brace Jovanovich (adapted)

9 Which statement is best supported by the information on this map?

(1) The Roman Empire extended over three continents.

(2) Rivers kept invaders out of the Roman Empire.

(3) Alexandria served as the eastern capital of the Roman Empire.

(4) Carthage was eventually destroyed by the Romans.

10 Based on the information provided by this map, which body of water was most likely the center of Roman trade?

(1) Red Sea      (3) Atlantic Ocean

(2) Black Sea      (4) Mediterranean Sea

Base your answer to question 11 on the map below and on your knowledge of social studies.

### Trade about A.D. 1000

Source: Farah and Karls, *World History,
The Human Experience*,
Glencoe/McGraw-Hill (adapted)

11 Based on the information provided by this map, which statement about Constantinople is accurate?

(1) Africans traded more goods in Constantinople than in any other area.
(2) Constantinople was a city located on the Mediterranean Sea.
(3) Gold was the primary commodity that China sent to Constantinople.
(4) Constantinople was an important trading center.

12 One major characteristic of the Renaissance period is that the

(1) Catholic Church no longer had any influence in Europe
(2) manor became the center of economic activity
(3) classical cultures of Greece and Rome were revived and imitated
(4) major language of the people became Latin

13 ". . . Therefore those preachers of indulgences are in error, who say that by the pope's indulgences a man is freed from every penalty, and saved; . . ."

— Martin Luther

Which period in European history is most directly related to this statement?

(1) Age of Exploration
(2) Scientific Revolution
(3) Crusades
(4) Protestant Reformation

14 The economies of the western African civilizations of Ghana, Mali, and Songhai relied on

(1) industrial growth
(2) shipbuilding
(3) textile production
(4) trans-Saharan trade routes

15 A major reason for Zheng He's voyages during the 15th century was to

(1) promote trade and collect tribute
(2) establish colonies in Africa and India
(3) seal off China's borders from foreign influence
(4) prove the world was round

16 What was one effect of the Columbian exchange?

(1) rapid decline in European population
(2) economic instability in China and Japan
(3) introduction of new foods to both Europe and the Americas
(4) spread of Hinduism into Latin America

17 From the 15th to the 18th centuries, absolute monarchs of Europe and Asia sought to

(1) increase the power of the Catholic Church
(2) centralize their political power
(3) redistribute land to the peasants
(4) strengthen feudalism

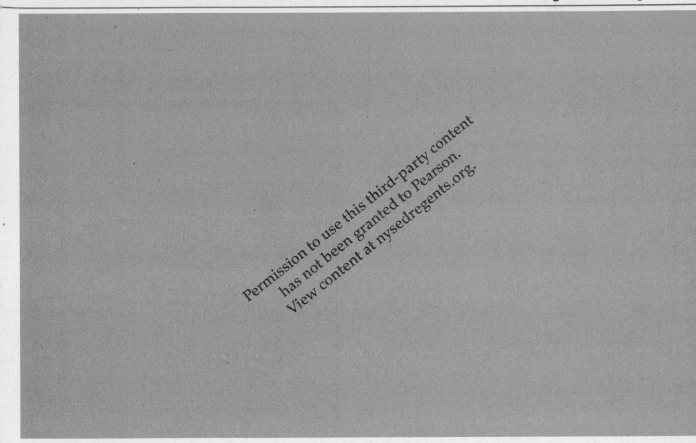

19 Which person is credited with saying "L'état, c'est moi" (I am the state)?

(1) Louis XIV     (3) Karl Marx

(2) John Locke     (4) Queen Isabella

20 Seventeenth-century scholars Galileo Galilei and René Descartes faced serious challenges to their scientific theories because their ideas

(1) were based on the Bible

(2) contradicted traditional medieval European beliefs

(3) relied only on teachings from non-Christian cultures

(4) were not supported by scientific investigations

21 Which statement expresses an idea of the Enlightenment?

(1) The king is sacred and answers only to God.

(2) History is a continuous struggle between social classes.

(3) Those who are the most fit will survive and succeed.

(4) All individuals have natural rights.

22 The breakdown of traditions, increased levels of pollution, and the expansion of slums are negative aspects of

(1) militarism     (3) pogroms

(2) collectivization     (4) urbanization

23 Which heading best completes this partial outline?

I. _____

  A. Rivalries between powerful countries over colonies

  B. Breakup of large empires

  C. Demand for self-determination by ethnic groups

(1) Reasons For Communist Revolutions

(2) Effects of Nationalism

(3) Methods of Propaganda

(4) Formation of Democratic Governments

Base your answer to question 24 on the passage below and on your knowledge of social studies.

. . . The factory owners did not have the power to compel anybody to take a factory job. They could only hire people who were ready to work for the wages offered to them. Low as these wage rates were, they were nonetheless much more than these paupers could earn in any other field open to them. It is a distortion of facts to say that the factories carried off the housewives from the nurseries and the kitchens and the children from their play. These women had nothing to cook with and [nothing] to feed their children. These children were destitute [poor] and starving. Their only refuge was the factory. It saved them, in the strict sense of the term, from death by starvation. . . .

— Ludwig von Mises, *Human Action, A Treatise on Economics*, Yale University Press

24 Which statement summarizes the theme of this passage?

(1) Factory owners created increased hardships.
(2) Factory owners preferred to use child laborers.
(3) The factory system allowed people to earn money.
(4) The factory system created new social classes.

25 What was one impact of industrialization on Japan during the Meiji Restoration?

(1) Japan became more isolated from world affairs.
(2) Demand for natural resources increased.
(3) Japan became a colonial possession of China.
(4) Traditional practices of Bushido were reintroduced.

Base your answer to question 26 on the map below and on your knowledge of social studies.

Source: Robert Feeney et al., *Brief Review in Global Studies*, Prentice Hall (adapted)

26 This map illustrates the concept of

(1) ethnocentrism    (3) containment
(2) socialism         (4) imperialism

27 Which region was described as "the powder keg of Europe" prior to World War I?

(1) Iberian Peninsula    (3) Balkan Peninsula
(2) British Isles        (4) Scandinavia

Base your answer to question 28 on the passage below and on your knowledge of social studies.

. . . In order to obtain Arab support in the War, the British Government promised the Sherif of Mecca in 1915 that, in the event of an Allied victory, the greater part of the Arab provinces of the Turkish Empire would become independent. The Arabs understood that Palestine would be included in the sphere of independence.

In order to obtain the support of World Jewry, the British Government in 1917 issued the Balfour Declaration. The Jews understood that, if the experiment of establishing a Jewish National Home succeeded and a sufficient number of Jews went to Palestine, the National Home might develop in course of time into a Jewish State. . . .

— Summary of the Report of the
Palestine Royal Commission, 1937

28 Which conclusion is best supported by this passage?

(1) The British made no promises to either the Arabs or the Jews.
(2) The Arab-Israeli conflict can be traced in part to British promises.
(3) The United Nations did not try to prevent conflict in the Middle East.
(4) Only the Jews were promised an independent state in Palestine.

29 • Led the Russians in a second revolution (1917)
• Promised "Peace, Land, and Bread"
• Established the New Economic Policy (NEP)

Which leader is being described by these statements?

(1) Czar Nicholas II    (3) Vladimir I. Lenin
(2) Nikita Khrushchev    (4) Mikhail Gorbachev

Base your answer to question 30 on the passage below and on your knowledge of social studies.

. . . A weary, exhausted, nerve-racked group of men it was indeed that, about noon November 1, assembled in a gully north of Sommerance [France] to rest and dig in for the night. The artillery was still firing furiously, but the enemy's barrage [bombardment] had ceased very suddenly about 10:00 a.m. and now only occasional shells from long-range rifles would explode in the vicinity. The weather was gloomy and the moist air chilled one to the bones. Yet it was with that meticulous [methodical] care that is characteristic of worn-out men, that we prepared our foxholes, carrying boards and iron sheeting from abandoned machine-gunners' dugouts in order to make our "houses" as comfortable as possible, even though only for one night. . . .

Source: William L. Langer, *Gas and Flame in World War I*, Knopf/Borzoi

30 Which means of warfare is described in this passage?

(1) guerilla    (3) biological
(2) nuclear    (4) trench

31 A major goal of Joseph Stalin's five-year plans was to

(1) encourage communist revolutions in the colonies of the European powers
(2) transform the Soviet Union into an industrial power
(3) expand the Soviet Union's borders to include warm-water ports
(4) reduce the amount of foreign aid coming from the Western Hemisphere

Base your answer to question 32 on the chart below and on your knowledge of social studies.

## NAZI RISE TO POWER

**World War I**
- German war debts
- Loss of German colonies
- Wish for revenge

**Weak Government**
- Doubts about Weimar Republic
- Quarrels among political groups
- Wish to return to strong leader like the Kaiser

**Economic Problems**
- Inflation
- Worldwide depression
- Unemployment

Source: *Guide to the Essentials of World History,* Prentice Hall (adapted)

32 Based on the information in this chart, which situation gave rise to Nazi power in Germany?

(1) global prosperity and trade
(2) success of the Weimar Republic
(3) political and economic instability
(4) expansion of Germany's colonial empire

Base your answer to question 33 on the passage below and on your knowledge of social studies.

. . . "We may anticipate a state of affairs in which two Great Powers will each be in a position to put an end to the civilization and life of the other, though not without risking its own. We may be likened to two scorpions in a bottle, each capable of killing the other, but only at the risk of his own life.". . .

— J. Robert Oppenheimer, July 1953

33 This statement expresses concern about the

(1) threats to the environment by developed and developing economies
(2) differences between command and market economies
(3) economic costs of World War II
(4) dangers of the Cold War

Base your answer to question 34 on the cartoon below and on your knowledge of social studies.

### Sending Forth Another Dove

Source: Herblock, May 13, 1941 (adapted)

34 The main idea of this 1941 cartoon is that Japan, Italy, and Germany

(1) had formed an alliance for peace
(2) were determined to defeat communism
(3) had supported a peaceful international solution
(4) were committed to aggression

35 At the end of World War II, the British decided to partition the Indian subcontinent into the nations of India and Pakistan. What was a primary reason for this division?

(1) India had adopted a policy of nonalignment.
(2) Religious differences had led to conflicts between Hindus and Muslims.
(3) Most of India's valuable resources were located in the south.
(4) British India's Muslim minority controlled most of India's banking industry.

Base your answer to question 36 on the graph below and on your knowledge of social studies.

**World Petroleum Reserves**

Source: John T. Rourke, *International Politics on the World Stage*, McGraw-Hill, 2003 (adapted)

36 Which conclusion is best supported by the information provided on this graph?

(1) The United States has adequate petroleum reserves to meet future needs.
(2) Nations lacking major petroleum reserves cannot industrialize.
(3) Overproduction of petroleum products has caused inflation in the Middle East.
(4) Most of the world's largest petroleum reserves are located in the Middle East.

Base your answer to question 37 on the cartoon below and on your knowledge of social studies.

Source: Clay Bennett, *Christian Science Monitor*, 2002

37 What does this cartoon suggest about the introduction of the EURO in Europe?

(1) Additional countries were created.
(2) Isolation among nations increased.
(3) Communist economic policies were adopted.
(4) Economic barriers between nations decreased.

38 The Four Modernizations of Deng Xiaoping in the 1970s and 1980s resulted in

(1) an emphasis on the Five Relationships
(2) a return to Maoist revolutionary principles
(3) a move toward increased capitalism
(4) the end of the communist system of government

39 One way in which Ho Chi Minh, Fidel Castro, and Kim Jong Il are similar is that each

(1) set up democratic governments
(2) used Marxist political principles
(3) overthrew a ruling monarch
(4) promoted Confucian principles

40 In the late 20th century, the Green Revolution had the greatest impact on

(1) grain production in India
(2) political freedom in Russia
(3) economic reforms in Cuba
(4) traditional customs in Japan

Base your answer to question 41 on the illustration below and on your knowledge of social studies.

## A European View

41 Which policy is portrayed in this illustration?

(1) nonalignment

(2) laissez-faire capitalism

(3) perestroika

(4) mercantilism

---

Base your answer to question 42 on the cartoon below and on your knowledge of social studies.

Source: Dana Summers, *The Orlando Sentinel* (adapted)

42 What is the main idea of this cartoon?

(1) The original causes of apartheid have not been eliminated.

(2) Apartheid improved race relations in South Africa.

(3) Peace can be achieved by nonviolence.

(4) Hate is caused by poverty.

43 Ethnic cleansing in Bosnia, the killing fields of Cambodia (Kampuchea), and the dirty war in Argentina are all examples of

(1) nationalist revolts

(2) human rights violations

(3) international terrorism

(4) religious conflicts

44 Studying the architectural features of the Parthenon, Notre Dame Cathedral, and the Taj Mahal provides information about the

(1) beliefs and values of a given culture

(2) climatic changes in an area

(3) 19th-century use of technology

(4) influence of Chinese design

45 Which geographic factor had the most influence on the development of Inca society and Japanese society?

(1) frequent monsoons

(2) large deserts

(3) mountainous topography

(4) tropical climate

Base your answer to question 46 on the diagram below and on your knowledge of social studies.

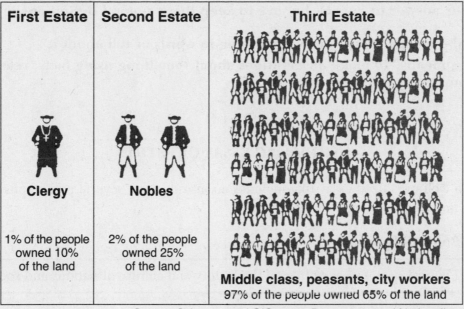

Source: Schwartz and O'Connor, *Democracy and Nationalism,*
Globe Book Company (adapted)

46  Which revolution resulted from the division of society shown in this diagram?

(1) Puritan (1642)

(3) Mexican (1910)

(2) French (1789)

(4) Russian (1917)

47  The golden ages of the Roman, Byzantine, and Ottoman Empires can be attributed in part to

(1) cultural isolation
(2) stable governments
(3) command economies
(4) distinct social classes

48  One way in which Simón Bolívar, Jomo Kenyatta, and Mohandas Gandhi are similar is that each

(1) led a nationalist movement
(2) used nonviolent tactics
(3) supported imperialism
(4) opposed communism

49  Which factor most hindered the efforts of both Napoleon and Hitler to conquer Russia?

(1) climate
(2) fortifications
(3) advanced technology
(4) lack of ports

50  One way in which the Sepoy Mutiny in India, the Zulu resistance in southern Africa, and the Boxer Rebellion in China are similar is that each resulted from

(1) government policies of ethnic cleansing
(2) attempts by democratic forces to overthrow the monarchy
(3) native reaction to foreign interference in the region
(4) government denial of access to fertile farmland

Answers to the essay questions are to be written in the separate essay booklet.

In developing your answer to Part II, be sure to keep these general definitions in mind:

(a) <u>describe</u> means "to illustrate something in words or tell about it"

(b) <u>discuss</u> means "to make observations about something using facts, reasoning, and argument; to present in some detail"

## Part II

## THEMATIC ESSAY QUESTION

*Directions:* Write a well-organized essay that includes an introduction, several paragraphs addressing the task below, and a conclusion.

**Theme: Political Systems**

> Political systems have affected the history and culture of nations and societies.

**Task:**

> Choose *two* different political systems and for *each*
> • Describe the characteristics of the political system
> • Discuss how the political system has affected the history *or* culture of a specific nation or society

You may use any political systems from your study of global history. Some suggestions you might wish to consider include absolute monarchy, constitutional monarchy, parliamentary democracy, direct democracy, theocracy, communism, and fascism.

**You are *not* limited to these suggestions.**

**Do *not* use the United States as an example of a nation or society.**

**Guidelines:**

**In your essay, be sure to**
• Develop all aspects of the task
• Support the theme with relevant facts, examples, and details
• Use a logical and clear plan of organization, including an introduction and a conclusion that are beyond a restatement of the theme

NAME _____    SCHOOL _____

In developing your answers to Part III, be sure to keep this general definition in mind:

> <u>discuss</u> means "to make observations about something using facts, reasoning, and argument; to present in some detail"

## Part III

## DOCUMENT-BASED QUESTION

This question is based on the accompanying documents. It is designed to test your ability to work with historical documents. Some of these documents have been edited for the purposes of this question. As you analyze the documents, take into account both the source of each document and any point of view that may be presented in the document.

**Historical Context:**

> Throughout history, natural resources such as water, coal, oil, and diamonds have both helped and hindered the development of nations and regions.

**Task:** Using information from the documents and your knowledge of global history, answer the questions that follow each document in Part A. Your answers to the questions will help you write the Part B essay, in which you will be asked to

---

- Discuss how natural resources have helped **and/or** hindered the development of specific nations **or** regions

---

**Do *not* use the United States as the specific nation or region.**

## Part A
## Short-Answer Questions

*Directions:* Analyze the documents and answer the short-answer questions that follow each document in the space provided.

**Document 1**

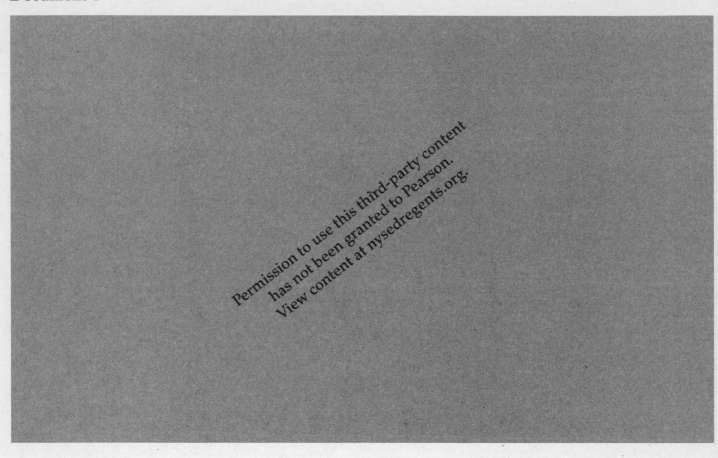

_____

_____

Score ☐

**Document 2a**

> ### "Farmers in India Await the Rains, and Despair"
> REWARI, India—When the monsoon rains that sweep across India every year failed to arrive in late June, the farmers here began to worry.  Now, as they scan the empty blue skies for signs of clouds, their worry is turning to despair.
>
> Broad swaths [wide areas] of India are seeing the country's worst drought in 15 years.  Here in the northern state of Haryana, the level of rainfall until July 24 was 70% below average; for the country as a whole, it was 24% below normal.  Since July 24, there has been little relief for the hardest-hit areas.
>
> Under these parched [very dry] conditions, economists say, India's growth could wilt, since agriculture accounts for a quarter of gross domestic product [GDP] and sustains [supports] two-thirds of the nation's billion-strong population. Before the drought, economists were expecting agricultural expansion of around 2% and GDP growth of 4.5% to 6% in the current fiscal year, which began April 1.  Now they are predicting that agricultural production will remain stagnant or even turn negative, shaving something like half a percentage point off overall economic growth. . . .

Source: Joanna Slater, *The Wall Street Journal*, August 6, 2002

2a Based on this excerpt by Joanna Slater, state **one** negative impact the lack of rain has had on the economy in India.   [1]

_____

_____

Score ☐

## Document 2b

> ### "Indian Monsoon Drenches the Land; Marketers Drench the Consumer"
>
> BOMBAY, India—One year after a crippling drought, plentiful rains are sweeping across India—and delivering a flood of good news for its economy.
>
> Agriculture's contribution to India's gross domestic product [GDP], its total output of goods and services, has declined over the past decade as the service and industrial sectors have grown. Nevertheless, the showers are a relief for farmers, who depend on the monsoon to irrigate their crops. They are also a boon [benefit] to sales of everything from tractors to shampoo; a good harvest puts more money in the pockets of rural consumers, improving the fortunes of companies ranging from Anglo-Dutch Unilever to Honda Motor Co. of Japan to South Korea's Samsung Electronics Co.
>
> Agriculture still sustains two-thirds of India's billion-strong population and contributes a quarter of its GDP, which economists predict will expand by as much as 6.5% in the fiscal year ending next March, partly because of the abundant rains and the resurgent [recovered] farm sector. . . .

Source: Joanna Slater, *The Wall Street Journal*, July 24, 2003

2b Based on this excerpt by Joanna Slater, state **one** positive impact that abundant levels of rain have had on the economy in India. [1]

_____

_____

Score ☐

**Document 3**

### Great Britain, 1750–1850

**Legend:**
- Chief industrial textile area in 1850
- Other industrial areas in 1850
- Chief pre-industrial textile areas 1750
- △△△ Major coal fields
- • Cities

Source: Holt and O'Connor, *Exploring World History Workbook*, Globe Book Company (adapted)

3 Based on this map, state **one** way that coal affected the development of Great Britain between 1750 and 1850. [1]

_____

_____

Score ☐

**Document 4**

> . . . The lives of factory workers in Manchester, and in the other new industrial cities rising up around Britain, were shaped by the burning of coal just as the coal miners' lives were shaped by the digging of it. Coal made the iron that built the machines the workers operated as well as the factories they worked in, and then it provided the power that made the machines and factories run. Coal gas provided the lights the workers toiled [worked] under, letting their work day start before dawn and end after dusk. When they left the factory doors, they would walk through a city made of coal-fired bricks, now stained black with the same coal soot that was soiling their skin and clothes. Looking up, they would see a sky darkened by coal smoke; looking down, a ground blackened by coal dust. When they went home, they would eat food cooked over a coal fire and often tainted with a coal flavor, and with each breath, they would inhale some of the densest coal smoke on the planet. In short, their world was constructed, animated, illuminated, colored, scented, flavored, and generally saturated by coal and the fruits [results] of its combustion. . . .

Source: Barbara Freese, *Coal: A Human History*, Perseus Publishing

4 According to Barbara Freese, what are **two** effects that coal had on factory workers in the industrial cities of Great Britain during the Industrial Revolution? [2]

(1)_____

_____

Score ☐

(2)_____

_____

Score ☐

## Document 5

Kuwait became a major supplier of oil during the late 1940s and the 1950s. Kuwait made a deal with foreign oil companies in return for payments. This money changed the way many people earned a living in Kuwait and led to a change in Kuwait's economic infrastructure.

> . . .The government's efforts to modernize the City of Kuwait resulted in a construction boom, particularly in the period 1952 to 1965. Foreign planning consultants, architects, engineers, construction firms, and labor planned and created a city with the best material and technologies the industrial world could supply. In contrast to the land acquisition program, however, government outlays in this period to create social overhead capital did generate considerable economic activity. In addition to a great many public buildings, commercial centers, apartment blocks, and suburban community projects built in the period, the following were also constructed:
>
> 1. 176 government schools and 32 private schools.
>
> 2. 8 hospitals, 2 sanatoria [treatment centers], 37 dispensaries and health centers, 148 school dispensaries and 9 centers for preventive medicine.
>
> 3. 1,100 kilometers of paved roads.
>
> 4. A number of electric power stations and an expansive network for distribution and street lighting laid; between 1956 and 1965, installed capacity increased from 30,000 kwh to 370,000 kwh. . . .

Source: Jacqueline S. Ismael, "The Economic Transformation of Kuwait," *The Politics of Middle Eastern Oil*, Middle East Institute

5 According to Jacqueline S. Ismael, what are *two* ways Kuwait used its oil resources to improve the city of Kuwait? [2]

(1)_____

_____

Score ☐

(2)_____

_____

Score ☐

**Document 6**

**"I can't see a reason to go to war with Iraq...."**

Source: Michael Ramirez, *Los Angeles Times,* January, 2003 (adapted)

6 Based on Michael Ramirez's cartoon, in what way did Iraqi oil contracts influence the French government in 2003? [1]

_____

_____

Score ☐

**Document 7**

. . . When De Beers discovered diamonds in Botswana in 1969, the government had been independent for three years, and the men running it were traditional chiefs who owned cattle. They came from a desert culture where people have to scrimp and save to survive the long, dry season.

During three decades, Botswana's leaders have carefully guided what became the world's fastest-growing economy. They invested in roads, schools and clinics. In stark contrast to the rulers of Angola and Congo, they created an African nation devoted to improving the lives of its people. In 1965, only about half of primary school-aged children attended school. Today, 90 percent of that group is enrolled. Life expectancy, which was less than 50 at independence, is now near 70.*

Phones work in Botswana, potholes get repaired, garbage gets picked up, and a lively press pokes fun at the government without fear. At $3,600 per year, the gross national product per capita is seven times higher than the average for sub-Saharan Africa. The standard of living is higher than in South Africa, Turkey or Thailand.

"Diamonds are not devils," said Terry Lynn Karl, professor of political science at Stanford and author of "The Paradox of Plenty," (University of California Press, 1997), a book about the poisonous mix of natural resources, big money and thieving elites in developing countries. "What matters is that there be a tradition of good government and compromise in place prior to the exploitation of these resources.". . .

* Correction: The United Nations says that because of AIDS, the figure has fallen sharply and is 41, no longer close to 70.

Source: Blaine Harden, "Africa's Gems: Warfare's Best Friend," *New York Times*, April 6, 2000
Correction published April 17, 2000

7 According to Blaine Harden, what are *two* ways the sale of diamonds affected Botswana? [2]

(1)_____

_____

Score ☐

(2)_____

_____

Score ☐

## Document 8

In 1980, diamonds were discovered at Gope in the Central Kalahari Game Reserve (CKGR). Since 1997, the government of Botswana has been removing the Bushmen from this area. Many wish to return to their traditional homelands.

> . . . In a recent court case concerning the Bushmen's right to return to their ancestral lands, Tombale assured the court that the evictions had nothing to do with diamonds. This was strange, because the bushmen's lawyers had never mentioned diamonds. They were just defending the Gana and Gwi Bushmen's right to live on lands they had occupied for thousands of years.
>
> And yet when Margaret Nasha said in February 2002 that the relocation of the Gana and Gwi was not unprecedented she cited an example of people being relocated 'to give way for projects of national interest' in Jwaneng. They were, in fact, relocated to make way for a diamond mine.
>
> As Botswana's foreign minister Mompati Merafhe has explained: 'Many Bushmen have been removed because of economic interests. In Orapa, my area, a great chunk of people were removed because of the mine. Botswana is where it is today because of this facilitation. These people are no exception.'. . .
>
> Meanwhile, back in the Kalahari the Botswana government has been parcelling up the CKGR into diamond concessions and sharing them out between De Beers, the Australian-based company BHP Billiton and the Canadian outfit Motapa Diamond Inc. And by November last year virtually the entire game reserve, bar [except for] a small bite-sized chunk in the northwest, had been dished out.
>
> So either the government has pulled off a fat scam by selling dud concessions to three unsuspecting multinationals — or it's lying. . . .

Source: "Why are the Bushmen being evicted?" *The Ecologist*, September 2003

8 Based on this excerpt from *The Ecologist*, state **one** impact the 1980 discovery of more diamonds has had on the people of Botswana. [1]

_____

Score [ ]

# Part B
# Essay

*Directions:* Write a well-organized essay that includes an introduction, several paragraphs, and a conclusion. Use evidence from at least *five* documents in your essay. Support your response with relevant facts, examples, and details. Include additional outside information.

**Historical Context:**

> Throughout history, natural resources such as water, coal, oil, and diamonds have both helped and hindered the development of nations and regions.

**Task:** Using the information from the documents and your knowledge of global history, write an essay in which you

> • Discuss how natural resources have helped *and/or* hindered the development of specific nations *or* regions

**Do *not* use the United States as the specific nation or region.**

**Guidelines:**

**In your essay, be sure to**
- Develop all aspects of the task
- Incorporate information from *at least five* documents
- Incorporate relevant outside information
- Support the theme with relevant facts, examples, and details
- Use a logical and clear plan of organization, including an introduction and conclusion that are beyond a restatement of the theme